Echoes of a Distant Clarion

Memoirs and Occasional Papers
Association for Diplomatic Studies and Training

In 2003, the Association for Diplomatic Studies and Training (ADST) created the Memoirs and Occasional Papers Series to preserve firsthand accounts and other informed observations on foreign affairs for scholars, journalists, and the general public. Sponsoring publication of the series is one of numerous ways in which ADST, a nonprofit organization founded in 1986, seeks to promote understanding of American diplomacy and those who conduct it. Together with the Foreign Affairs Oral History program and ADST's support for the training of foreign affairs personnel at the State Department's Foreign Service Institute, these efforts constitute the Association's fundamental purposes.

J. Chapman Chester
FROM FOGGY BOTTOM TO CAPITOL HILL
Exploits of a G.I., Diplomat, and Congressional Aide

Robert E. Gribbin
IN THE AFTERMATH OF GENOCIDE
The U.S. Role in Rwanda

James R. Huntley
AN ARCHITECT OF DEMOCRACY
Building a Mosaic of Peace

Armin Meyer
QUIET DIPLOMACY
From Cairo to Tokyo in the Twilight of Imperialism

William Morgan and Charles Stuart Kennedy, eds.
AMERICAN DIPLOMATS
The Foreign Service at Work

James M. Potts
FRENCH COVERT ACTION
IN THE AMERICAN REVOLUTION

Echoes of a Distant Clarion

Recollections of a Diplomat and Soldier

John G. Kormann

Memoirs and Occasional Papers
Association for Diplomatic Studies and Training

NEW ACADEMIA PUBLISHING VELLUM Books

Washington, DC

Library of Congress Control Number: 2007928838
ISBN 978-0-9794488-2-9 paperback (alk. paper)
ISBN 978-09794488-3-6 hardcover (alk. paper)

NEW ACADEMIA PUBLISHING   VELLUM Books
P.O. Box 27420, Washington DC, 20038-7420
info@newacademia.com
www.newacademia.com

To Roger Hewes Wells, PhD, my father-in-law. Without his persistent urging this account would never have been written.

Sound, sound the clarion, fill the fife!
To all the sensual world proclaim,
  One crowded hour of glorious life
Is worth an age without a name.
              –Sir Walter Scott, Old Mortality

"...as life is action and passion, it is required
of a man that he share the passion and action
of his time, at the peril of being judged not
to have lived."
              –Chief Justice Oliver Wendell Holmes, Jr.
              Memorial Day Address, 1884

Contents

x   Contents

Preface

I intend in these pages to present an encompassing account of my life. The usual memoir focuses on the career of the officer in question with only a short discussion of his early life and experiences. Generally there are only minor references to the family and the overall settings conditioning that person's work. However, from beginning to end I endeavor to include the parents and siblings who provided my family with support as we ventured into far-flung places around the world. Above all it was my desire to give proper recognition to my wife, Elsa Wells Kormann, whose selfless contribution to our government, not only as a diplomatic spouse but also as researcher and assistant, was prodigious.

More than the usual time is spent on my boyhood in New York City during the Depression years and on youthful adventures in the days before World War II, because these aspects to some extent shaped what was to come later. My military experiences as an enlisted soldier and paratrooper in combat ingrained an attitude in me toward fellow soldiers that carried through many years of service. Sections of the book relate to my duty as a military intelligence agent in the German Rhineland during World War II and later in Berlin. These offer the reader insight into incidents in which I was personally involved and which to my knowledge have never been revealed despite the passage of many years.

A television producer who interviewed me for a series of programs on "Germans and Democracy" said he was interested in doing so because my exposure to his subject had spanned more than half a century. He noted my participation in efforts to apprehend Nazi war criminals, counter Soviet espionage and subversive activities in Berlin, "democratize" the Germans as part of the American occupation forces, and, years later, strengthen German-American relations as a diplomat.

Assignments in the Department of State afforded me an opportunity to be a further player in the Cold War. I was also posted to places overseas where significant events transpired: the Philippines with the arrival of the Marcoses; Libya with the Arab- Israeli War of 1967 and the emergence of al Quadhafi; and Egypt with Sadat and the Kissinger "shuttle diplomacy." Some of the more intriguing experiences in the book came as a result of assignments outside the normal scope of a Foreign Service officer's duties. Concurrent service as an Army Reserve officer in the intelligence, special operations, and civil affairs fields also provided me with an exposure to activities in the defense arena particularly helpful in following crises in the Middle East. Throughout my career, military service was useful to me as a diplomat.

A word should be provided as to why I chose *Echoes of a Distant Clarion* as the book's title. Firemen used the high-pitched clarion in earlier years to trumpet alarm. While gathering thoughts for this narrative, memory echoed most vividly those times when danger was present.

In the final pages of this book, I conclude: "Over several decades our family has survived the vicissitudes of Foreign Service life on four continents intact and remains close-knit." Sadly, however, in the years of my retirement and shortly after completing these pages, my elder son, Wells Bradford Kormann, succumbed at age fifty-one to melanoma. As a youth, he appears many times in the following pages. After an outstanding career in the army and the Department of Defense, he became the chief engineer and division director for the National Library Service, where he was instrumental in developing the Talking Books and other materials for the blind and physically handicapped. He died honored for his distinguished service to his country and fellow human beings. Our family was blessed to have shared his years with him.

Looking back, there may have been advantages to growing up during the Depression and the challenging times before World War II. It was a period when high schools as such came into prominence. Young people, who normally might have gone into the work force after completing an elementary education were kept in school so as not to join the unemployed competing for scarce jobs. It was a time when only 5 percent of high school graduates went to college, and they, mostly white male. Despite the difficulties, those years prepared many a young man for World War II: the war was their crucible, and for those veterans who returned from that conflict there were numerous educational and employment opportunities. All this was to my benefit. However, I had no idea when I first sought a position with the Department of State what the future had in store. I consider myself fortunate to have been able to be both a Foreign Service officer and an Army Reserve officer in a long and exciting career. It is hoped that the reader will gain a sense of what an adventure it was.

J.G. K.
Chevy Chase, Maryland

Acknowledgments

I would like to thank the Association for Diplomatic Studies and Training (ADST) and its president, Ambassador Kenneth L. Brown, for assistance in the publication of this book. It is a privilege to be included in its Memoirs and Occasional Papers series. I am particularly grateful to Publishing Director and Series Editor Margery Boichel Thompson for all her efforts on my behalf.

I also extend my appreciation to my granddaughter, Christina Louise Lowe, for her proofreading, as well as to ADST Senior Fellow Stephen H. Grant and ADST interns Matthew Petit, Isabelle Chiaradia, and Katie Frink, for their skillful work on the final manuscript, and to ADST intern Daniel J. Mallinson, for artfully enhancing the photographs.

Echoes of a Distant Clarion

1
Boyhood Years

The story is told that cowbells were rung on upper Fifth Avenue in New York City the night I was born in Dr. Leff's Hospital at close to midnight on July 30, 1924.[1] My parents, John Matthew and Elsie Behr Kormann, had hoped for a son and after eight pregnancies finally succeeded. Their family already consisted of three daughters, Eleanor (1908), Elsie (1911), and Johanna (1912). A fourth daughter, Alma (1918), died shortly after birth. The Kormann saga is a typical American tale, one of a handsome twenty-six-year-old Austrian meeting a pretty twenty-year-old German girl on board the North German Lloyd ocean liner *Oldenburg* in 1906 en route to the United States. Together they shared the magic moment when the Statue of Liberty came into view.

It was Elsie Behr's second trip to the United States. She was vivacious and adventuresome and, at age sixteen in 1901, left home to stay with an aunt in New York. She persuaded her father, the owner of a cigar factory in Achim, a town on the outskirts of Bremen, that she wished to become a nurse and wanted to study in America. However, soon after her arrival she was caught up in the housework of her aunt's family. That was not at all to her liking, but hoping that things would change, she stayed for more than a year before requesting her father to bring her home. Upon arriving in Achim, she told her family about her trip and her stay in New York. When she elaborated about her adventures at sea—of going over in steerage far down in the ship among the masses of immigrants, of the sickness, and of her ability to function as a nurse—her father became indignant. He asked why she had been in steerage when he had paid for a proper cabin. He was incensed that he had been cheated and promptly contacted the steamship authorities, demanding an explanation and a refund, which he received.

My grandfather, Gottlieb Behr, was a well-known person of substance in the Bremen area. Besides a cigar factory, he owned twelve rental cottages, in addition to his home and real estate investments. He was an officer of the state-run insurance system, a member of the school board, a trustee of the Lutheran Church, and prominent in Socialist Party circles. My mother used to recount that the Kaiser sent a representative from Berlin to attend my grandfather's funeral in 1912. He and his wife, Elise Uphoff Behr, had twelve children, six of whom were subsequently to immigrate individually to the United States, marry, and establish businesses of their own. Their eldest son, Johann (John), was the first to leave, in 1893 at age sixteen, after an argument with his father. Within a few years and with hard work, he started his own grocery business in Brooklyn. His son, also named John, would later become chairman of the board of the Swingline Corporation, a Fortune 500 Company.

In 1901 Maria Elise (Elsie), my mother, was the next to depart. On both the 1901 and 1906 crossings, my mother was processed through Ellis Island, but my father was not. Records of the ship's manifest indicate that he was on a business trip, carrying $125 in currency, a large sum in those days, and would be staying at the Geneva Club at 205 West 98th Street, a prestigious address. He listed his last place of residence as Vienna. His manner and dress would later prompt my Behr uncles to label him the "big shot."

Johann Mattheus (John Matthew) Kormann, my father, was born in Graz, Austria, in 1879. His father was the owner of a wholesale meat distributing business. His mother, the daughter of one of the richest men in the city, was a local beauty, but spoiled and ungenerous. Young Johann and his sister were packed off to live with an aunt, because their mother was temperamentally unsuited to care for them. After completing his formal education, Johann was employed by the manager of an elite hotel in Vienna, where he mastered the basic skills of hotel management. By his early twenties, he was working for the Ritz Carlton Company, traveling on business for them to Constantinople, Port Said, Alexandria, Corfu, and other places in the Mediterranean basin.

My parents were married in a civil ceremony in 1906 in New York City, a few months after their arrival. At the outset, my father was affiliated with the St. Regis Hotel, but within a year he purchased a confectionery business on upper Fifth Avenue. He provided the financing and the business technique, but it was my mother, as time went on, who became the backbone of the business, managing the staff and much of the daily operations. Beginning with bonbons, they expanded into making ice cream, and finally into the restaurant business as well. As a boy, I remember their concern about their competitors, Louis Sherry and Schrafft's. They imported a large state-of-the-art ice cream manufacturing machine from Switzerland and by the end of World War I were solidly established. A framed common share stock certificate for ten shares of "Kormann's Confectionery,

Inc." signed by my father as president of the firm and by my mother as secretary, hangs in my office as a reminder of those days.

They purchased an apartment building next to their business, a twenty-five-room summer house at the shore in Far Rockaway on Long Island, and substantial property in Florida.[2] The family made regular visits to relatives in their 1924 Cadillac touring car. Among the fixtures in the latter were small flower vases fastened to the walls near the rear windows. I can still see them in my mind's eye, a symbol of a bygone gracious age.

During this period, my parents traveled to Europe several times and helped bring over three of my mother's brothers and a sister by providing a base for them to stay. Dietrich (Uncle Dick) Behr came, remained a relatively short time, and moved on to California. Hermann worked with the family for a while, tried his hand at the grocery business, and subsequently purchased a farm and gasoline station in upstate New York. He retired a wealthy man in the 1960s, when his properties were purchased for the New York State Thruway.[3] Friedrich (Uncle Fritz) had an engineering background, worked for others for a while, and eventually purchased a grocery business on Long Island. His son, Frederick Behr Jr., inherited his father's technical bent and attended the Massachusetts Institute of Technology. He later became a professor of engineering at the University of California. Zelli (Aunt Cilly) married a German war veteran, who had been badly wounded in 1917 and later immigrated to the United States. They went into the delicatessen business in Brooklyn.

This extended family provided me with a wonderful source of togetherness, and many of my childhood memories are filled with visits to relatives and the activities of my cousins. Uncle Dick remained unknown to me. He had been somewhat of a black sheep and the family had essentially lost touch with him. Only my mother maintained an infrequent correspondence with Dick over the years. She was surprised in the late 1950s to receive an invitation from his lawyers to fly out to his funeral at the expense of his estate. She was even more taken back upon arriving in Los Angeles to learn that he was a prominent man, the owner of a vast moving business that serviced Hollywood. His funeral was an elaborate affair attended by dignitaries and movie stars. He had never married, was well known and liked in the community, and was a generous contributor to local charities. My mother, thereafter, took great delight in tweaking the rest of the family for what they had missed by not keeping up with Uncle Dick. Why, he might even have introduced them to movie stars Clark Gable and Gloria Swanson!

In addition to family members they brought over, there were others who worked in my parents' business or household to repay their passage. These people were instrumental in shaping my future, for they provided a succession of nannies who assisted my busy mother in raising me. They enabled me to converse equally in German and in English. I delighted in the German fairy tales they read to me and soon was reading them myself. I was immersed in the wonders that knowledge of a foreign language can bring. I attribute being commissioned an officer in the field at the close of World War II in part to my ability to speak German. It later played a role in my appointment as a U.S. resident officer with the Department of State in Germany and, subsequently, launched me into a career in diplomacy. On the other hand, I can also recall the day my mother took me to kindergarten, where I soon learned it was not a multilingual world. One of the teachers reproved me for something and I responded in German. I had been so used to being instructed in German by our girls that I automatically lapsed into it when someone addressed me authoritatively. I never did it again because she severely chastised me.

My elementary school, P.S. 170, was typical of the city's public schools at the time.[4] Classes were large, about forty pupils, but unlike today, discipline was strict. The clothes closet served two purposes: you either hung your coat there or you were marched into it by the teacher, who whacked your behind with a ruler, yardstick, or pointer. There were no locker rooms, but it seems to me that every classroom had a clothes closet! I received my share of discipline. On one occasion, the teacher was provoked enough to send me home with a note for my parents. I was foolish not to give it to them, only to have my mother discover it in a shirt pocket. The roof fell in! My mother, who was the real disciplinarian in the family, took her belt to me and the sting of that thin piece of leather has never been forgotten.

The teachers did their best to make instruction interesting, assigning projects related to the seasons of the year or to individual holidays. We made drawings and construction paper cut-outs of turkeys, pumpkins, and pilgrims for Thanksgiving; Santa Clauses, Christmas trees, and holly for Christmas; and hatchets and cherry trees for Washington's Birthday. It was grand. In fourth grade, one of our teachers heightened class interest by playing a game after each spelling test. The children who passed with a good grade would leave the room. Several of the other children would then write a number on the blackboard. The teacher would select one number and show it to the class. The children outside would then return and each pick one of the numbers on the board; the one with the number selected by the teacher would win a prize.

On two occasions in a row, I won the prize, which made the teacher quite suspicious. The next time I was able to play, the teacher had the pupils write down a number, then erase it and write a new number on the board. I remember returning to the room and circling number 65. I knew the instant I put the chalk to the blackboard that it would again be the winning number. Throughout my life there have been moments like that for which I have never been able to account.

As children, my sisters and I were expected to make ourselves useful in the family business and at home, which also set a good example for the staff. Some of it was fun, but most of it was not. Making bonbons and wrapping candy boxes were skills soon learned. Then there was the making of ice cream sodas, malted milks, ice cream frappes, banana splits, and ice cream sandwiches, all of which was fun at first, but after a few busy hours serving scores of customers, it lost its charm. To this day, I think I can still compete with the best soda jerks!

Consequently I never lacked friends, who were always eager to sample my wares—on the house, of course. In those days a French ice cream soda with the works (whipped cream and cherry) cost a dime, an ice cream cone with two scoops cost a nickel, and a malted milk with an egg beaten in a dime. In the restaurant, the Blue Plate Special dinner, which varied on any given day, might consist of two lamb or pork chops, two vegetables, salad, and bread and butter and cost 25 cents. It even included coffee.

By the time I came of age, my sisters, who were considerably older, were well out of these activities and engaged in their own professions. They might as well have been there, however, as I was constantly chided about how helpful they had been when they were young and what a slacker I was.

I remember some of the friends I had as a young boy. One in particular, Paul Tolksdorf, was the son of the man my father hired to serve as superintendent of our apartment building. He was a year older than I, but we were great pals. The Tolksdorfs lived in the building and I loved to visit with them. Paul's mother baked the most wonderful, rich, brown bread, which had a crisp crust. She would serve it to "her boys" with unsalted butter spread on it, sprinkled with sugar. We would have done anything for a slice of that bread hot out of the oven. In 1936, Mr. Tolksdorf, who had an engineering background, decided to return to Germany with his family. He had heard all manner of good things about how prosperous Hitler's Germany was becoming and how the trains ran on time. What a fateful decision that was to be. I never heard from Paul again. Late in 1945, while I was with the army in Berlin, I received a letter from my mother enclosing a small card. It had a black border and at the top, in the center, a black Maltese cross. Below it was the picture of a young man wearing a German sailor hat. The inscription on the card said, "Radio Operator Paul Tolksdorf, lost in the U-boat Service at sea, will forever be enshrined in the memory of the Fatherland."

Significant in my development was my relationship with young men who worked for my father. Charlie Taubinger and his pal, George Altdorf, were with us during the worst years of the Depression, 1931–36. Big and tough, born of German immigrant parents from the coal-mining areas around Allentown and Scranton, Pennsylvania, they came to New York City looking for any kind of work they could find and found a home with us. Typically, they would spend long hours working with the ice cream machines in the basement or at other tasks, and then be given an hour or two off in the evening before returning to clean the restaurant's kitchen. During these respites, weather permitting, with me in tow, they would go off to Central Park, two blocks away to play ball. Football was what they loved most. Often we would play in the dark, with the lights of a distant street lamp providing the only illumination. I soon learned to run back punts kicked high into the night sky. It was difficult to see the football, much less catch it. When I did catch the ball or pick it up, I would run for my life for the goal behind them. They were merciless in tackling me, or what was worse, in making me tackle them!

When I got hurt it was "stiff upper lip" all the way. I soon learned that size was only one factor, and that if you tackled hard around the shins or ankles, you could bring a person down regardless of his size. Seeing the great concern over having the proper equipment and safety today, I marvel that I did not break every bone in my body. I did get banged up quite a bit, somewhat to my mother's dismay. Her cure was to take a piece of raw steak from the restaurant's freezer and place it on my latest bruise. She was far from today's doting parent, however, and took my injuries in stride as a part of a boy's growing up process. Much truth lies in the statement: "It is all in what you get used to!" When I became older, my parents moved to another neighborhood near fashionable Riverside Drive. There I played organized football and my training with Charlie stood me in good stead. I found that reckless abandon as a runner and hard-hitting as a tackler made me feared by those with whom I played.

Charlie used to tell me stories about his home and about the bus rides he would take when he had an opportunity to visit his family. By today's standards, Allentown is a couple of hours from New York, but to me then it seemed like a journey to the other side of the earth. The buses he took always had exciting names like the "Golden Eagle" or "Red Arrow" or "Greyhound" and they invariably roared along at breakneck speed. I was beside myself with excitement when he invited me to go home with him on one occasion. I begged my parents to allow me to go. It was an eye-opener for me.

The Taubingers lived in a small, wood-frame cottage alongside a railroad track. Mr. Taubinger worked as a part-time fireman on a locomotive. Charlie and I, at one point, walked up and down the track picking up pieces of coal that had fallen or been tossed off passing trains.

The coal fueled the kitchen stove and served to warm the rest of the house. The Taubingers were a poor but loving family and did their best to make me feel at home. I returned to New York a much wiser nine-year-old, appreciative of all the advantages my parents were bestowing on me. It made me realize that other people had to struggle for their existence.

Although my memories of the "golden years," before the stock market crash of 1929, are vague, I do remember receiving a magnificent rocking horse for my third birthday, which we celebrated at our summer home at Far Rockaway. The rocking horse was the closest thing one can imagine to a full-sized, stuffed pony from a taxidermy shop. Our summer home on Long Island played a special role in my early years. It was a virtual palace, with a circular driveway centered around a water fountain and a lovely statue. A large, clapboard structure in the style of a Victorian beach hotel, it featured a wrap-around screened porch, with another screened porch off bedrooms on the second floor. It had a basement and was three stories high, topped by a large fenced widow's walk. From there, one could watch the ocean a quarter of a mile away. The summers of my first twelve years were spent at Far Rockaway, blessedly, since New York City in July and August was without today's air-conditioning and sweltering.

The drives to and from Far Rockaway in those days were always something of an adventure. It was a distance of only 20–25 miles, but with tie-ups due to breakdowns on the bridges, incessant flat tires, and mechanical problems, the drive in my father's Cadillac seemed interminable. Other times, we would take the Long Island Railroad from Pennsylvania Station in the city to Wave Crest, the nearest station to our house which was called Wave Crest Lodge.

Weather permitting, the days were spent at the beach. The shore at that location faces the open Atlantic, with no outer islands or barriers. On a rough day, the breakers could be mountainous. I can still feel the force of them, as I would often be knocked off my feet, ground into the sandy bottom, and washed ashore. We built castles in the sand and watched the tide come in and dissolve them. A favorite game consisted of toy wooden motorboats chasing one another through the shallows; it was always the "rum-runners against the Coast Guard," a clear sign that we were kids growing up in the prohibition era. The large waves and powerful currents of the Atlantic at the Far Rockaway shore helped make me a strong swimmer at an early age. By my midteens, I had already passed several lifesaving and water safety programs, enabling me subsequently to function as a lifeguard. With this training, I was able later in life to rescue a number of persons under a variety of circumstances during my time in the army and the Foreign Service.

As the Depression deepened, my family endeavored, with only limited success, to make our summer home pay for itself by turning it into a small hotel. It took the joy out of the place, particularly for my sisters, who were made to assist in its operation. I was still too young to be of much use other than to run errands. By 1936–38, it was obvious that Wave Crest Lodge was too expensive to maintain, and it was sold to pay the steep taxes. The neighborhood was still quite fashionable, containing the homes of a number of Wall Street millionaires. The house across the road, so the family tale goes, belonged to a wealthy banker, who committed suicide as a result of the stock market crash.

In 1942, I went back to see our place and was shocked to see it empty, in terrible disrepair, and badly damaged by vandals. A visit to the area in 1985 was even more disheartening. In less than half a century, the entire region had changed from a quasi-rural beach community to city streets and high rises, not much different from the Bronx or Brooklyn. No recognizable trace remained of the places I had wandered as a boy.

My family was wealthy in the 1920s, as were many of our friends. Sadly, I watched the area where my parents had their business go downhill from 1935 on. The Fifth Avenue neighborhood around 110th Street gradually changed from upper middle class in the twenties to transitional in the middle thirties to Spanish Harlem today. Up until 1941, Mayor Fiorello LaGuardia lived in an apartment house two blocks from my parents' establishment—a building we moved into a year later. By that time we no longer owned an apartment house and Dad drove a Studebaker rather than a Cadillac.

Nonetheless, in the late thirties and early forties New York was full of exciting things for a young person: one could travel many miles from Westchester County and the Bronx in the north to Brooklyn and Coney Island in the south for a nickel. The picturesque double-decker buses of the Fifth Avenue Coach Company ran the ten-mile length of Manhattan, were considered upper class, and cost a dime. They started out going along Fifth Avenue and then, near the family business on 110th Street, angled across town to Riverside Drive and up along the Hudson River.

New York was a magical place where a boy had the wonders of the world at his grasp. Three major museums and a planetarium lay within relative walking distance of our apartment building at 1324 Fifth Avenue. The Museum of the City of New York was located less than half a mile down the Avenue. It contained marvelous exhibits and ship models, which I particularly liked. A mile farther was the world-renowned Metropolitan Museum of Art, with its vast assemblage of paintings and cultural objects. Three long blocks across Central Park from there, one visited the great Museum of Natural History and the Hayden Planetarium. And in those days, unlike today, everything was free!

Furthermore, along Fifth Avenue in the same general area were the mansions of the great nineteenth century millionaires, housing brilliant collections open to the public. On top of this, we had the Central Park Zoo as well as the outdoor park pavilions featuring famous orchestras, musicians, and stars of the opera and stage. I can remember many happy afternoons trekking to the museums, at first while young with my older sisters, and later with my friends. On the way, we would buy ice shaved snow cones in the summer, hot chestnuts and large warm soft pretzels in the winter, or Cracker Jack in any season.

The city brought a boy into contact with many children from his or other neighborhoods. Living on the edge was a part of life. Not infrequently, toughs from Little Italy to the east, the Irish from Columbus and Amsterdam Avenues to the west, or blacks from Harlem to the north, would appear. Later, the influx of Puerto Ricans would add to the mix. A boy learned to fight and to take care of himself. If he was fortunate, he was taught survival skills by an older brother or a friend who had received instruction from an expert of sorts.

Boxing, wrestling, and Ju Jitsu were things to know, and Charles Atlas, weight lifting, and Dynamic Tension were the rage. I spent half the day going around with my muscles in tension. Even so, I never went from the "90 pound weakling" to Atlas's "250 pound Mr. America." I did, however, develop large muscles and strength sufficient to tear a two-inch-thick Manhattan telephone book in half with my bare hands— a feat I was once later requested to perform on the stage. Unfortunately, this muscle building also resulted in my never being able to buy a suit off the rack, since I required a large jacket but pants for small waist sizes.

My parents placed considerable value on participation in the arts. As a result, my three sisters learned to play musical instruments with considerable proficiency. Eleanor mastered the piano, as did Johanna, while Elsie was talented with the violin. A great joy for my parents, particularly my father, was to have the girls play for their guests after dinner on Sunday afternoons. It was a special treat to be invited to the Kormanns'; my mother was an excellent cook and my father a connoisseur of fine wines, besides being the owner of a restaurant.

A frequent guest was Miss Rehberg, a small, elderly, handicapped woman, who was a missionary. She made a point of being uncomfortable with the red, white, and dessert wines being served to all the other guests, since she believed in total abstinence. My mother's mischievous solution to the problem was to lace the fresh fruit salad, which she invariably offered, with sauterne wine, giving it a very refreshing taste. All of us who were in on this secret could hardly contain ourselves as we watched Miss Rehberg spoon the last drop of juice from her salad bowl and then take on a jolly composure for the rest of the dinner. On other occasions, however, her doleful influence on my mother precluded me from ever breaking the Sabbath by going to the movies. For a while, I was not even allowed to play ball on Sunday afternoons.

Aside from entertaining us on Sunday afternoons, the girls also often participated in musical activities in church. Elsie was a first violinist with the West End Presbyterian Church Orchestra, an organization that was well known in local music circles. For years, as an adjunct to her public school teaching, Johanna taught piano in the evenings at home. When my time came to learn a musical instrument, I was started on the violin. I found it to be squeaky, scratchy, and disagreeable, so Johanna went to work with me on the piano. Compared to her other pupils, who were mostly adults paying for their lessons and seriously interested, I must have been a trial. She finally gave up in despair. It is one of the great regrets of my life that my parents did not come down on me hard at this point, making me stop the nonsense and insisting that I learn to play some instrument.

My father, who had a fine singing voice, which I to some degree inherited, might have stipulated that I take lessons in that field. At a minimum, I would have become reasonably adept in reading music, the lack of which I found later to be a great loss. Although the New York public schools required some music class work, I never absorbed much more than "music appreciation." Even so, there is enough of a blur of musical scales and notes in my memory, as well as a considerable knowledge of the great classical works and composers, to tell me that it would not have taken much to immerse me truly in music. This, plus the later wide-ranging exposure I had to some of the finest young talent in the country as a student at the High School of Music and Art, made it all the more a pity.[5]

I was, or at least I thought so at the time, a sly youngster. Concocting a scheme to extricate myself from musical drudgery, I told my parents that as a substitute for having to learn a musical instrument, I would become an artist and at an early age, I developed a liking for drawing and working in crafts. Instead of music, I proposed at about the age of ten, that I be allowed to become proficient at art. My mother, who loved drawing as a child, readily agreed. My father, with his Viennese background, was more reluctant in accepting my proposal. My parents stated that this was serious business and that I was to produce at least one worthy piece of art work a week. However, having talked my way out of musical studies, I must have sensed that I did myself a wrong, for hour after hour during my school homework I would listen to WQXR, the classical music station.

I also found myself singing a lot, trying to imitate the male voices I heard on the radio.

The years that followed saw a number of amusing incidents related to my singing. One took place at this period in my childhood. At the time, we were living on West 112ᵗʰ Street,[6] just a short distance from the Cathedral of St. John the Divine. I became friends with a young Irish boy, John Sheahan, who lived on the other side of Amsterdam Avenue. We both were about twelve and played football and street games together. He had learned to play a "squawk box," a little concertina, which had a few note buttons on the side. He was adept at playing simple melodies, particularly the traditional Irish tunes. I got a kick out of listening to him play and sing and soon found myself joining in. Going to the movies at the time cost ten cents, and neither of us had any money. Allowances were virtually unknown. Though later I was to earn money selling the *Saturday Evening Post* magazine and shining shoes, at that stage we were broke.

We came upon the idea of making money by playing the concertina and singing for handouts in the Irish taverns along Amsterdam and Columbus Avenues, of which there was one in practically every block. As I look back upon it now, it was almost a scene out of Charles Dickens. Here were two apple-cheeked young boys, dressed, as was the custom in the mid-thirties, in knickers, knee-length stockings, and tweed caps, entering those dimly lit "speakeasies." These establishments usually contained a long wooden bar, behind which were mirrors and numerous bottles of spirits. More often than not, there was sawdust on the floor. Working men sat or stood at the bar or were seated at small tables along the opposite wall. The place was filled with the unmistakable sounds of Irish accents.

At our entrance, the bartender would almost immediately react by saying, "No kids allowed in here!" for fear of losing his ABC license (Alcoholic Beverage Commission Permit). My partner then in his little Irish brogue would respond, "Oh please sir, we have only come to play and sing some Irish tunes for the gentlemen." It had to be one tough bartender who could withstand that supplication, or the ire of those rough patrons, who came to the defense of the little fellows. I cannot remember how we broke the ice. I think John opened with "Did Your Mother Come from Ireland?"

Our audience was enthusiastic as we sang "When Irish Eyes Are Smiling" and "The Rose of Tralee." By the time we sang "Mother Macree," the reaction was profound. Here were those burly Irishmen, some with tears streaming down their faces, saying: "Sing it again laddies!" or "Oh, how beautiful!" "Danny Boy" brought down the house! Our caps, placed on a chair beside us or on the floor, were soon full of pennies and nickels. We knew from that point on that we would never have to sneak into the movies again.

Despite our apparent success at entertaining, we visited the taverns only a few times. Our visits stopped rather abruptly, I think, once John's parents got wind of what was happening through the Irish circuit. My parents never found out about this activity until many years later, when I told my mother. She was amused then, but I am sure she, and particularly my sisters, would have been horrified at the time. I say this with a degree of certainty, since on one earlier occasion I created a family explosion by building myself a box and going into the shoeshine business. I was shining shoes at the 110th Street and Broadway exit of the subway one day, when my sister Johanna came up the stairs with a gentlemen friend. The results were traumatic!

Not long after the tavern episode, John's family moved and I lost touch with him. When I hear a glorious Irish tenor singing on St. Patrick's Day, I cannot help thinking that it might be the boy I sang with in those taverns more than half a century ago. Those songs made an Irishman of me at heart, and later, when I went into the army, it did not seem a coincidence that I entered service on March 17th, St. Patrick's Day. I went off to the tune of "the minstrel boy to the wars has gone."

The transient nature of city dwelling did not lend itself to extended friendships. While living on West 112th Street, I had another friend who was quite unusual. Ian Braley was exceedingly bright, with a bookworm's appearance, and though he was not much at sports, he was a tremendous intellectual challenge for me. The radio program *Information Please* was very much in vogue at the time, and we boys spent hours questioning one another in what today would be called Trivial Pursuit. We quizzed each other back and forth on world capitals, heights of mountains, kings of England, disasters, speed records, and a thousand other subjects, no matter what else we were doing or where we were.

I can still remember riding in the rumble seat of the Braley family convertible on a day trip to Poughkeepsie, New York, with both of us going at it incessantly, much to the amusement of Ian's dad, who was driving. The latter, by the way, is something of an American icon, although I was unaware of it then. Ian's father was Berton Braley, the poet, and the author of "The Thinker" and "Do It Now," which can be found in any anthology of "best loved poems."[7] I always wondered why Ian's dad was around the apartment so much of the time. Today, I realize he worked in his study at home. He was a soft-spoken gentleman, with a mustache, glasses, and a nice smile. Again, I lost touch with Ian as I grew older. He went off, as I recall, to Townshend Harris, the city's top academic high school, and I to the High School of Music and Art, Mayor LaGuardia's prized institution for talented children.

At first after moving to the West Side of New York City, I was enrolled in P.S. 165 Elementary, located between Broadway and Amsterdam Avenue on 109th Street. It was combined with Robert E. Simon Junior High School, to which there was a normal progression. Upon completing the 6th grade, I entered into "rapid advance" classes, which consolidated three years of schooling into two. I did reasonably well in these classes for quick learners, but was distracted to some extent by sports. The school had an excellent basketball team, of which I was an insignificant part. My size was a handicap, but not nearly as much as it would have been in the game today, with its towering players. I continued with my art, at one point painting a large mural for the school based on the popular movie *Captain Blood*, starring Errol Flynn. My art teacher encouraged me to apply to the newly opened High School of Music and Art. It was particularly selective, since it required not only high academic standing, but also exceptional talent in the arts. The examination and interview were rigorous and for me required an extensive portfolio of artwork.

The High School of Music and Art was coed and equally divided between the two talent areas, with about 500 pupils in each. Classes consisted of a full college preparatory curriculum, plus three regular periods of music or art. It made for a very long day of intensive instruction. The teachers were specially recruited and the equipment provided was of very high quality. When in later life I had to purchase my own oil paints, I was appalled at how expensive the ones I had been using were and how as a youngster I thought nothing of squeezing out gobs of Windsor & Newton brand tubes in cadmium and cobalt colors. Today a small tube might cost upwards of thirty dollars. I am sure the situation in the music department was the same, with students breaking gold harp strings without any idea of the cost. My years at Music and Art were memorable. In addition to an excellent academic education, I was instructed in painting, graphic arts, sculpture, ceramics, and metallurgy. I can still see myself standing at an easel, while listening to one of the school's several symphony orchestras practicing a Beethoven overture down the hall. It was glorious! There is considerable truth to the lament that: "It is too bad youth is wasted on the young!" As a boy, I was also aware that there was no match in all of New York for our pretty girl art and music students, many of whom went on to perform on the stage and in concert and opera halls.

There were some unhappy moments, however. Our school basketball team, while not on a par with the vast "factory" high schools in the city, did passably well in competition with a select few schools in its own league. We had no football team and a number of us sought to organize an unofficial one to play in a pick-up league just for amusement. One of the boys I recruited broke a finger as we were starting up. The result was disastrous. The boy was a highly talented pianist, whose parents were grooming him for concert performances, with all the monetary implications this might have had. I was called to the principal's office. His parents were there, and it all was very unpleasant. It might have been worse; today, they might have taken legal action. That was the end of the football team.

My French language teacher, an otherwise attractive woman in her late twenties, was a close friend of my sister Johanna, a French teacher, herself. At the outset of language training, which I recall to have been a mandatory subject, I would have opted for German, since I spoke it fairly fluently already. Johanna convinced my parents that German grammar, which was much more difficult than French, would be my undoing. Beside, she averred, any cultured person had to be grounded in French. French it was, then, with the net result that in evenings my parents would receive word through Johanna how poorly I had done that day in class, or how I had not done my homework and, generally, what an embarrassment I was to the family and to my sister. Johanna's subsequent efforts to tutor me achieved mixed results. I never did prove to be the stellar student she had hoped. She was right, however, about German grammar. I did have trouble with it in my freshman year at Columbia; but this was due to bad study habits, which were corrected when I returned after the war. She was also right about French; it proved to be a valuable asset to me later in the diplomatic service.

My sister Elsie, who during these years worked in administration at the Bell Telephone Company of New York, became quite actively involved with the West End Presbyterian Church on 104th Street and Amsterdam Avenue. The senior minister there was Dr. Edwin Keigwin, a Scotsman, who was an outstanding preacher. The church, which had a gymnasium as part of its education building, was host to Troop 599 of the Boy Scouts. Elsie's fiancé, Fred Stahl, also an employee of the telephone company, was a high-ranking official in the Scouts in New Jersey. When I became twelve years old, I enrolled, at my sister's urging, in Troop 599. Initially, the troop had considerable adult support and a membership of 60–75 boys, but with the departure of its able scoutmaster, John Plummer, in 1938, it began to fall on hard times.

As our membership dropped, I found that more responsibility was placed upon me. A year or so later, I was a Senior Patrol Leader and then a Junior Assistant Scoutmaster. By that time, I had also risen in rather desultory fashion through the scout ranks to Life Scout. Our troop was now enrolling poorer boys from Columbus Avenue. Much to the dismay of oldtime scouts, who were prim and proper in their procedures and the wearing of the uniform, the troop's appearance had become somewhat shabby. Some of us had complete uniforms, including the traditional britches and campaign hat, while others had only neckerchiefs and perhaps a shirt.

The boys, however, were a rough and ready lot, and we did things together that most scouts today would never attempt. We delighted in going on camping trips on weekends and holidays, mostly in the winter and spring months. We would take the subway or a bus to either the 125th Street or Yonkers ferries, cross the Hudson River and then hike the five, ten or more miles to a wooded spot along the Palisades. We were a motley crew, knapsacks, sleeping bags or tents on our backs, pots and pans hanging from the packs clanking as we went along. My friend, Al Gorman, the Acting Assistant Scoutmaster, who was seventeen and two years older than I, would lead the group, usually ten or twelve boys. When he could not go, I was in charge. At times in January and February, we would freeze in our pup tents and sleeping bags. During the autumn, we engaged in playing football, and in the summer many of us were out of town.

On one memorable trip, we took a bus thirty or forty miles to a heavily forested area in the Ramapo Mountains along the New York/New Jersey border. We left on the Friday afternoon of a long weekend. That night it started to snow heavily, and by morning we must have had over two feet on the ground. Our tents and lean-tos were more like igloos. Some of us had trouble with the fires, but we managed and actually had fun with the challenge of it all. Though we were unconcerned, some parents were not, prompting the State Police to search for us. Monday found us returning to "civilization," much to the consternation of the authorities and some parents. Our experiences on these trips hardened me and taught me survival skills, which later proved of great value in World War II.

It is hard to believe how uncomplicated things were then. We had no trouble going off into wooded areas on the outskirts of New York and camping. In 1975 after returning from an assignment overseas, I took my son, Matthew, who had been a Boy Scout in Germany and Egypt, on a weekend camping trip to a large scout camping ground in Virginia. I thought it would be like the old days. When we got to the camp area, however, the man at the entrance told us we needed reservations. When I said there were just the two of us and that I had been a scout leader and we would be no trouble, he relented. He told us that we could not build a fire, except in designated areas away from where we were camping. That night, a troop of scouts pitched their tents about fifty yards from us; it sounded more like a nursery than anything I had remembered. There were almost as many fathers there as boys. I guess that is a good thing, but the boys from old Troop 599 would have been chagrined at having daddy along.

The late afternoons of my junior and senior high school years were often occupied with trips from our apartments on the West Side to the family business, a distance of a mile and a half across town. I would spend an hour or two working there and then return home with a large shopping bag of groceries or food prepared in our restaurant. At other times, I would be allowed to remain home to join my friends playing in the street or in Riverside Park. However, there was always a price to pay for this privilege. I was told, "You can play after you hang out the wash" or "after you put up the curtain stretcher" — a task I hated because of its sharp nails — or "when you have cleaned the bathroom."

On one occasion in 1937, this mundane activity enabled me to view the opening of one of history's tragic events. I was on the roof of our six-story apartment house at 111th Street and Riverside Drive hanging out the wash. In those days before dryers most roofs had clotheslines. As I looked out across the Hudson River, I saw a large dirigible in the sky above the New Jersey Palisades, which I immediately recognized to be the *Hindenburg.* The swastika was clearly visible on the tail. Just at that moment, I noticed an electrical charge run from the nose to the stern, whether from heat lightning or some other source I cannot say. Other than having been interested in seeing the airship, I thought nothing more about it. That is until an hour later, when the radio news began to broadcast frantic eyewitness accounts of the *Hindenburg* bursting into flames at its mooring in Lakehurst, New Jersey.

Although my mother employed a cleaning lady for periodic heavy cleaning, my sisters before me and I in my time were expected to participate in this chore. My mother taught me to cook, scrub floors, clean sinks and tile, and do laundry. She also taught me how to iron and sew. There was no nonsense about this being woman's work, or that my male status exempted me from such activity. I learned, and I learned well.

I was also taught how to wash windows. In New York City, at least in Manhattan, most people lived in apartment houses. More often than not these edifices were at least six stories or taller. The way one washed the outside of windows was to open the lower half wide, slide out underneath it, sit on the window ledge facing inward and pull the lower or upper pane down across the thighs. The cleaning lady did it that way, my mother did it that way, and so did my sisters and I. Our several apartments over the years varied from five to eight stories above the concrete courtyards below. We never thought much about washing anywhere up to five or six windows at a time, first with water in which there was a bit of ammonia, and then drying the panes with crumpled newspaper. In later years, when I attempted to use this procedure on the upper windows of our three-story house in Chevy Chase, Maryland, my wife and neighbors seemed to go into cardiac arrest over the danger of it all. Oh, how times have changed!

In June of 1940, I embarked on a bicycle trip to Canada. Willie (Wilbur) Glass, my high school pal, and I planned our route for weeks beforehand, using American Youth Hostel (AYH) stops up through New England to the border. The idea of long bicycle tours was not new to my family. Two years earlier, Johanna, on her summer vacation from teaching, had been a tour leader on a SITA (Student International Travel Association) bicycle trip through Europe. AYH facilities at the time were often converted barns or sheds operated by farm families, often rudimentary bed and breakfast establishments for cyclists and hikers in those Depression years. As I recall, the price for an overnight stay was 25 cents, with an extra low charge for breakfast. At some places it was possible to obtain bedding and blankets, but I used a small sleeping bag.

As the time for departure drew near with the conclusion of the school year, I told my mother of our plans. She listened patiently, but evidently dismissed the idea as another one of her young son's fantasies. What made the proposed trip seem preposterous was that I had only a small five-year-old regular 24-inch-wheel Columbia with standard white wall tires, really just a "kid's bike." A touring bicycle, similar to the one used by Johanna, would have at least a 26-inch or a 28-inch wheel with thin tires along the lines of the English Raleigh type popular in those days. However, in contrast to Willie Glass's 26-incher, mine did not have balloon tires.

I look back on all the planning we did for that trip in amazement. I became a member of the AYH, wrote for tour books and other information, obtained maps, assessed my daily monetary needs, and carefully prepared and assembled my equipment. I required saddlebags, a handlebar basket, sleeping bag, poncho, rain gear, tools, tire- repair equipment, first-aid supplies, a hunting knife, and other sundries, as well as a minimum of extra clothing. I planned to sleep at times out in the woods or in the open, and I was not sure what to expect.

During the spring of that year, I saw a movie featuring Spencer Tracy called *Northwest Passage*. It was an historical film, depicting Rogers' Rangers making a perilous trek during the French and Indian War in 1763 from Fort Ticonderoga north to Canada, fighting all along the way. That movie made an indelible impression on me. Its theme music played in my mind for months afterward. And I was going to make that trek too!

Several days before we were to start, Willie told me his parents had absolutely forbidden him to go. Nevertheless, I was determined to proceed anyway. The one piece of equipment I did not have at the time was a sleeping bag. As an advance birthday gift, Johanna gave me $8, to which I added $3 to purchase the bag. When strapped tightly, it fit on the back carrier of my bicycle. Other items fit into the saddlebags or the handle bar basket. I had a fitful night before starting the trip.

The appointed morning, I arose at 4:00 a.m. and dressed quietly before going into my parents' bedroom to say good-bye. My mother awoke enough to ask what was happening. When I told her it was 5:00 a.m. and that I was off to Canada, she quickly dressed and accompanied me down the self-service elevator out to the front stoop of our apartment building. She never once said "don't go," or questioned my judgment. I told her, as I mounted the bicycle, that I would circle the block once, come back and wave to her, and then would be off. I can still see her waving to me in that early morning light. Years later, she told me that she thought I would be back before going too far, but on second reflection she remembered how she, as a sixteen-year-old girl, had left a good home alone to emigrate to America. I was her son and I would do what I set out to do.

I felt exhilarated as I swung out on to Riverside Drive and up along the Hudson River. It was a beautiful morning. Bearing eastward across Manhattan and the Bronx, I reached U.S. Route 1. That concrete highway in those days was well traveled with cars, buses, and trucks, but nothing equivalent to today's congestion. The route was lined with commercial establishments and gasoline stations. The trip went smoothly, with my speed averaging 10 mph, up to New Haven, where I branched north in the direction of Hartford. I traveled 114 miles the first day and was no worse for wear. The initial hostel I stayed at was in farm country and it provided a bunkhouse affording very primitive accommodations to half a dozen young people, mostly college students.

That night I met a young man, a senior at Brown University, who was going in my direction. After a full breakfast the next morning of cereal, eggs, and bacon for a minimal price, we agreed we would travel together provided I did not slow him down too much. His bicycle was far better suited to the trip. We enjoyed one another's company and, being a gymnast, he amazed me by doing back somersaults from a standing position. We journeyed northward through Connecticut, Massachusetts, and then over into Vermont. Our travel was more leisurely, covering considerably less distance than I had the first day. The next night we slept in a pine forest. In St. Johnsbury, northern Vermont, the hostel consisted of a group of small wooden cabins, one of which we shared. My friend and I were to part company the following day, he veering westward toward New York and I on to the Canadian border. As a farewell supper, he suggested Welsh rarebit. He fancied himself somewhat of a cook, and I had never eaten "rabbit," so it sounded like a grand idea. Little did I realize that rarebit was simply a cheese dish made with beer. Although I did not like it a bit, I assured him it was delicious and promptly got sick.

I did not go beyond the Canadian border, deciding instead to come back and spend time in the White Mountains and the Lake Winnepesaukee area of New Hampshire. The decision to travel in the mountains was not a wise one, for it was unbelievably tiring, walking the bicycle up five-mile stretches, only to hurtle down the other side at breakneck speed. My diet on the road consisted largely of milk and donuts or rudimentary sandwiches, which I made balancing the items on the seat of the bicycle.

After a relatively pleasant time traveling along the lake, I cycled back over to the Vermont–New Hampshire border to a hostel in Charlestown, New Hampshire. I arrived to find the place buzzing with young girls from a private school in Massachusetts. I remember it was a lovely summer afternoon and many of the group had gone swimming in an open spot along the Connecticut River, which flowed just below the property. The road in front of the hostel ran to a steel frame bridge across the river into Vermont. We had a most enjoyable time swimming in that fast flowing stream.

I recall telling one of the girls, in the event of being caught in the current, not to fight it, but to use it to carry her to whatever shore was afforded. I told her that I had had lifeguard training and experience with strong Atlantic Ocean currents, having spent my summers at the shore. At one point during this idyll, a discussion of the bridge arose. How high was it? Could one dive from it and swim to shore? Looking back on it now, the roadbed might have been 20–25 feet above the river. In any event, I found myself boasting that I could easily make the dive, spurred on no doubt by the appreciative young females present.

Not knowing how deep the river was, I dove and came up in as shallow a dive as possible. The current was swift and, true to my own advice, I flowed with it about 100 yards downstream until it deposited me on the opposite shore. I climbed up the very steep, heavily vegetated bank, pulling myself up on my stomach. Not focusing at the time, I immersed myself in either poison ivy or poison oak. That night my entire body from head to foot began to itch unmercifully. In the hope of obtaining some relief, I stayed at the hostel the next day, dabbing myself with calamine lotion.

Aware that the complexion of the trip had changed, I decided to head for home before the blisters that were appearing incapacitated me completely. I bicycled as far as Springfield, Massachusetts, but could go no farther. Summer heat and perspiration exacerbated the blistering and itching, making me miserable. I had just enough money to pay for a one-way train ticket back to New York City. I placed the bicycle in the baggage car and took the train home. The adventure came to a dismal conclusion when I was placed in St. Luke's Hospital for several days with a case of severe skin poisoning. On the other hand, the trip taught me that I, a fifteen-year-old, could function totally on my own. All in all I had traveled almost 1,200 miles—not bad for a youngster on a kid's bike!

Each season had its sports, but some games were played year-round. In the latter category were "stick ball" and "one-basket" basketball. Stick ball was played on the street with a broom handle and a rubber ball the size of a tennis ball, which was pitched under-handed and hit on the first bounce. Connecting with a good hard swing might drive the ball 200–300 feet down the street. Play would be timed to avoid any passing vehicles. Basketball was always a pick-up affair played down in Riverside Park. At times, we would play full court with ten men, but that was rare.

In autumn, we played football. "Two-handed touch" was sometimes played in the parks on grass, but in general it was considered sissyish to do so. On grass we played tackle football, no matter how badly equipped we were. I was well into my twelfth year before I received a hand-me-down football helmet and a pair of shoulder pads from my cousin, John Behr. The boys in our neighborhood organized into regular teams, with each player providing his own equipment. Only the jerseys were uniform and purchased from the same sporting goods store. The helmets varied but were all painted the same color. We played against other neighborhood teams in Van Courtland Park at 242nd Street in the Bronx, a considerable subway ride from home. We would travel all suited up, dragging along whatever extraneous gear we required. The games were always on Saturday, generally in the morning or early afternoon, rain or shine.

Toward the end of the season, at times, we would encounter snow. I usually played right halfback or running back, in today's parlance, but would also alternate at quarterback with a boy named Ronald Woodward. We used to come home from these games a mass of aches and bruises, with a few black eyes tossed in, for those were the days before face guards. Woodward and I in particular were damaged, because we were the ones who would run back punts and kickoffs. Arriving home, I would soak for hours in a hot bathtub to obtain relief.

Street hockey was another game we played in the winter, although its duration was limited by the oncoming snow, which tended to remain piled up along the curbs. We used roller skates of the four-wheeled type that clamped onto one's shoes and were fastened with straps around the ankles. Every boy had a pair, even if he didn't play hockey. Hockey sticks were not expensive and if we had no hard rubber puck, a block of wood sufficed. The rink was the asphalt pavement of the street laid out lengthwise. The goals normally were box-like areas chalked out on the pavement at each end. Some teams got fancy and constructed makeshift nets or used large open cardboard boxes, but these were a nuisance, since they had to be removed whenever a vehicle passed.

It is hard to imagine playing that game today with the number of cars and trucks traversing the streets, but in those days there was relatively little traffic and few cars parked along the curbs. To lay out the rink, we had to have an area where there were no cars parked, since the curbs served as the side boards similar to those in today's ice hockey stadium. Just to highlight how long ago the 1930s were, one of the annoying aspects of the game was to find that the Sheffield Farms horse-drawn milk wagon had passed through the street and that the unhappy animal had left its calling card. We played in street clothes, sometimes using our football jerseys when we played as teams. The games were very rough, with lots of body-checking. Hockey sticks gave many a black eye and bloody lip. The goalie, bless him, wore no more protection than the rest of us. Hockey, even more than football, led to fistfights, or even worse, to stick fights. In retrospect, it is good the season was short!

After the sale of our summer home on Long Island, I spent more and more time at my Uncle Hermann and Tante (Aunt) Meta's farm and gasoline station at Nanuet, New York. They were childless, and we became quite attached to one another. Their well-trained German shepherd, Rex, and I became inseparable. He could sense when I was coming to visit and would wait for me at the edge of the property. I spent extended periods with them during two summers. On weekends during the year, I would travel to Nanuet either on my bicycle or by bus. In good weather, I would cycle the 25 miles after school on Fridays, arriving before suppertime. My route would take me across the George Washington Bridge and then north through a series of small towns to Nanuet. My aunt would often have my favorite dish that evening, smoked pork tenderloin and kale. The ingredients were all cooked together in oatmeal. It sounds awful, but it was absolutely delicious! Neither my mother nor my wife, both great cooks, ever seemed to match Tante Meta's dish.

As part of the farm, my aunt kept goats, which were milked. Goat's milk has properties beneficial to people with certain types of infirmities and she did a lively business. I learned to milk the goats as well as the cows but found the former to be much more temperamental and troublesome. There was a chicken coop with hundreds of fowl and a large vegetable garden helped make the farm self-sufficient even in the depth of the Depression. The gas station took up most of Uncle Hermann's time, but unlike today, cars for most people were a luxury, not a necessity. Public transportation throughout the country was infinitely superior to what it is today. A bus from New York City passed right by the gas station and was relatively inexpensive. Cars would stop for gas on an average of every ten minutes, except on Sundays, when people would be on the road, visiting or simply joy-riding. I would help pump gas and assist in fixing flats, which were a persistent problem for all drivers of that period. In my spare time at the farm, I roamed the fields and woods with my air rifle, which was reasonably accurate up to a couple of hundred feet. I became quite adept at pigeon hunting.

I arrived at the farm one summer evening in 1939 to find that another one of my aunt's relatives had come for an extended stay, ostensibly to help out with the farm. Bruno was a tall blond young man from Germany about nineteen years old. He looked as if he might have stepped straight out of a "Hitler Youth" poster and, indeed, he was a model of all that organization represented. He would run around in his thin little black shorts and white undershirt doing calisthenics, spouting "Strength through Joy" (*Kraft durch Freude*) slogans. Bruno was unreal. He was a dyed-in-the-wool Nazi, if there ever was one! To complicate matters, my uncle and aunt had a paying boarder staying with them, a Jewish refugee from Czechoslovakia, who worked in the Lederle pharmaceutical plant in Pearl River. He was in his late twenties and played soccer for a local team in his free time. I always expected that some kind of collision would occur between the two, but fortunately it never did, and the refugee after a short while found quarters closer to his work.

I was not so lucky. I worked with Bruno for a week or so that summer, cutting hay in the fields with a two-handed scythe. We would then store the hay in the barn, with Uncle Hermann supervising while he kept one eye open for customers at the gas station. On one occasion Bruno got to be too much for me and we started to push one another and wrestle. To my amazement he was awkward and not very strong, and I had him on his back in a relatively short time. I shall never forget the look of pure satisfaction on Uncle Hermann's face as I finished Bruno off. To my surprise, Bruno did not return to Germany at summer's end, even though Hitler had taken his country into war. Instead, Bruno found employment out on Long Island, which seemed very strange. Subsequently, he did have trouble with the immigration authorities and had to go back when the United States entered the war. I always expected to learn that he perished in some SS division or other on the Russian front, but the last I heard, and this in the 1960s, was that he was a salesman somewhere in West Germany.

There was one return trip from Nanuet in 1938 I shall always remember. Climbing on the bus and waving good-bye to my uncle and aunt, I took a seat up front near the driver. It was a Sunday evening about seven or eight o' clock. The bus proceeded south through the towns of Pearl River and Hillsdale, picking up passengers along the way. When we came to Westwood, New Jersey, the driver stopped at a road crossing. I can still hear the hiss of the hydraulic mechanism as he opened the front door. A man ran up to the bus, leaned in, and shouted something to the driver that didn't make sense to me. I thought there must have been an accident. A woman came to the door and said we had been invaded and that the bus should not continue on to New York. She said the radio was announcing that we had been attacked by men from Mars, adding they were landing in New Jersey. The news created quite a stir on the bus, with some people wondering whether they should get out and return home. Others wanted to continue on to New York to their families. I immediately thought of my parents. The driver finally said with resignation: "All I know is that I have to get this Goddamn bus to the terminal on time!"

I do not recall anyone leaving the bus, and we continued on warily. As we arrived at the approaches to the George Washington Bridge, I looked anxiously out of the window to see whether it was still intact. Traffic was flowing over it as usual. The driver pulled up to the tollgate and said something to the attendant. All I could hear him reply was "Crazy, ain't it!" We arrived at the 167th Street bus terminal and people there were also concerned about the attack from outer space and wondering whether the subways would be safe.

By the time I finished my subway ride down to 110th Street and Broadway, passengers coming aboard were speaking about the "invasion" as a hoax and saying that the persons responsible should be prosecuted. Later that night, the radio news broadcasts were full of the incident and of the excitement it had created nationwide. It was then my family learned in detail of what had happened. An Orson Welles radio program had taken segments of H. G. Wells's book *War of the Worlds* and broadcast it as if it were actually happening, without adequate disclaimers or clarifications. The authorities reacted in a manner similar to today's emergency radio broadcast system announcing a nuclear attack. The affair prompted the Congress and the Federal Communications Commission to enact legislation and regulations to prevent such a thing from occurring again.

While I did spend more time with my aunt and uncle in Nanuet, my other relatives also played a significant role in the life of my family. We made numerous visits to Brooklyn to my Aunt Cilly, my other uncle, Hermann Tietjen, and their four daughters, Lucille, Eleanor, Cecelia, and Helen who were somewhat younger than I. I was a terrible influence, shooting off firecrackers, throwing rocks, or knocking balls through windows, to the great delight of the girls but to the mortification of my mother and the annoyance of the older relatives present. "What is he up to now?" was heard more than once during a visit. I loved Tante Cilly dearly; she must have had the patience of a saint to put up with me. She and my mother were very close and often, in the evenings, they would talk with one another on the telephone. These conversations were interminable and greatly annoyed my sisters, who might be expecting calls.

We visited Uncle John and his wife, Lottie, but they were considerably older and my memory of them is vague. We also went to see Uncle Fritz and his second wife, Helen, who was a great favorite of mine. His first wife died early, and Helen, who came over from Germany and worked for us for a while, later married him. Christmas was always a fine time for visiting. I can remember the wonderful presents I received. My aunts were always so thoughtful in their choice of presents for me. Unlike today when children are deluged with gifts, I would await the single present I would receive from each set of relatives with great anticipation. Their gifts were always innovative and ideal for a boy interested in drawing, painting, and various aspects of handicraft.

No discussion of this period would be complete without some reference to the efforts on the part of my parents and others to mold my character. My parents made sure that I attended church, in particular Sunday school. At the beginning, while I was young, it was at the First German Baptist Church over in East Harlem, which in those days was still a nice neighborhood.[8] I received a full submersion baptism there as a boy, probably never forgotten by those present. I was considered to be somewhat of a phenomenon, able to stay underwater several minutes at a time. Baptism was carried out in a large tank beneath a high platform, which formed part of the altar at the front of the church. When it came my turn and the minister submerged me, I took it into my head to show my stuff by staying under for quite some time. I then simply explained that it took more to cleanse me than other boys. Pastor Kaaz, our minister and a very kindly man, I am sure, did not know what to make of me. My parents did, however, and I felt the wrath of my mother's strap.

As the neighborhood changed in Harlem, the church dropped in attendance and finally closed; its members then joined congregations elsewhere. My sisters attended various churches: most notably the West End Presbyterian, where the renowned Dr. Edwin Keigwin preached, and Riverside Baptist Church, the magnificent Rockefeller-endowed edifice, where Dr. Harry Emerson Fosdick presided. During this period I was exposed to the great religious figures of the day, and now recount when speaking in ecclesiastical circles that I can remember hearing the sermons of these great men of faith.

The closing year at the High School of Music and Art was a transitional phase in my life and warrants an additional word about that exceptional institution. I mentioned earlier that a number of Metropolitan Opera stars got their start there. Roberta Peters immediately comes to mind. Even while students at Music and Art, some children were performing on Broadway at night. One of my friends was in the hit play *The Corn is Green* at the time.

Another, who was a hell-raiser in class, was a virtuoso violinist, capable of playing the most difficult Paganini pieces with pyrotechnic brilliance.

The art students were less noticeable. Most were very competent, but there were a few dilettantes in the crowd, the children of overweening parents, who "oohed" and "aahed" over every stroke their little darlings put on canvas. They were miserable in drawing and drafting classes, but blossomed in expressing themselves in modern art forms in painting. One or two of our teachers were taken in by these modern artists, but most were not. My friend, Willie, disgusted at one point with one of the teachers who encouraged "letting out one's innermost feelings," developed an art form he called his "spitball technique." He would scoop up gobs of paint on his palette knife, step back a couple of feet and splatter them on the canvas. The result would have made Jackson Pollock proud. His work became the rage of that teacher's class. It was a rage in a dual sense, since often he would miss the canvas and hit the rest of us!

My class graduation in June 1941 included a performance by the school's senior symphony orchestra. Considering the talent available, there were several orchestras, but the senior was outstanding. From time to time it was led by some of the great conductors of the day, including Walter Damrosch and a very young Leonard Bernstein. The guest conductor at the 1941 graduation was Erich Leinsdorf, still in his late twenties but highly regarded as the conductor of the Metropolitan Opera Orchestra. The incident I am about to recount is a highlight in the history of the school, and people always ask, "Were you there when Leinsdorf conducted *Egmont*?" Well, that was my year and here is what happened:

Picture a large school auditorium, a stage seating a symphony orchestra of well over one hundred students about to graduate, Leinsdorf on the podium in white tie and tails, a large crowd of dignitaries, city officials, and the graduating class and their parents. Seated in the front row with Dr. Steigman, the school principal, and the honored guests was Dr. Richter, the permanent conductor and mentor to the senior orchestra.

The program went along without incident to the point where the orchestra was to play the major rendition of the morning, Beethoven's *Egmont Overture*. The first few bars of the overture started out all right, but then Leinsdorf, who would later earn a reputation as being brash and cantankerous, did not like what he was hearing. He shouted "No! No! No!" and banging his baton against the stand, he brought playing to a halt. He then proceeded to hold class instruction, informing the various components how the piece should be played, to the mortification of everyone present. Dr. Steigman was stunned and Dr. Richter looked as if he were about to have a heart attack.

This was a final performance and such things were just not done! Leinsdorf then said: "Let's take it from the beginning." He went through this procedure three, possibly four times, until he was satisfied. In the meantime, he had taken off his coat and hung it on the stand. On the final go-round, the orchestra was so frightened and the adrenalin was flowing so freely, that they played like people possessed. The result was astounding! The audience erupted in tumultuous applause. Many of the parents present were musicians and they, as well as the rest of us, knew we had heard a singularly brilliant rendition.

2
Young Manhood

At the conclusion of my high school graduation ceremonies, my parents got up to leave the auditorium and I joined them from the place where I had been sitting with the graduates. My father was speaking about the program and noting how my sisters had received recognition for accomplishments in aspects of academic pursuit. I, on the other hand, had received a general award for athletics. He questioned whether I was college material. My sisters, Eleanor and Johanna, had both gone to Hunter College, the city's outstanding institution for girls. Having heard his remarks I addressed myself to them, retorting: "The bottom of the graduating class from Music and Art was as good or better than the top of other high schools in New York. Besides, I would never be dependent on my parents to put me through college." My father, who was really a kind man, had not meant to hurt me, but the damage was done and it set the stage for much of what was to follow in later years.

Angry about what had happened, particularly since I had finished without great scholastic effort about the middle of my class in the city's prize high school, I was determined to teach my parents a lesson. One of my older football-playing friends had mentioned to me earlier that he was thinking of finding a job by going down to the hiring hall on the Hudson River docks and signing on as a seaman. This now seemed like a capital idea to me and that is just what I did. I signed on the M.S. *Kungsholm*, a Swedish-American Line cruise ship of medium size and tonnage. I wanted to be taken on as an able-bodied seaman, an ABS, but I was still only sixteen and inexperienced and without seaman's papers. I was told that perhaps the next time I shipped out I could apply for my papers. I was taken aboard, instead, as a general utility worker, much the same as the kitchen help, waiters, or stewards. I was also told that if an opportunity arose, I might be used as a "wiper." Those men were employed in the engine room doing just what the title implied, cleaning oil off the engines, for the *Kungsholm* was a diesel motor ship.

While still, as they say, "wet behind the ears," without consulting my parents I was off for the Caribbean and South America. At one point much earlier I had mentioned an interest in going to sea to see the world, as I am sure other young people have done, but said nothing specific. Before departing, I did inform my mother of my intentions. However, it was some time before she heard from me again—and this was in the form of a postcard mailed from Havana, Cuba. In later life, I regretted having acted that way, wondering how I would have felt, if any of my children had been so headstrong. Once aboard the *Kungsholm*, I found that the lot I had chosen was a difficult one with long, hard hours. I worked a twelve-hour day for one dollar and food and lodging. I carried heavy crates, sacks of vegetables and fruit, large steel cans of milk, and other items up from the hold to the kitchens. With several hundred passengers aboard, plus a large crew, the amount of food consumed was prodigious. Working in the kitchens, I was wringing wet with perspiration most of the time. However, I had learned to work hard in my parents' business. I had carried heavy cakes of ice from the truck, big stalks of bananas, and 125-pound ice cream cans as a boy, so I was able to hold my own.

One of the more distasteful tasks working in the kitchens was the squeezing of oranges and lemons. This was before the introduction of concentrates. We did not have rubber gloves and the citric acid played havoc with one's hands after a while. It was particularly painful, should one have any cuts or abrasions. One incident was almost my undoing. About the third day at sea, I was ordered to haul out the garbage cans and dump the slop overboard. This was done in calm weather from an opening about ten feet above the waterline. The heavy metal cans were dragged along the steel deck to the opening, then lifted by hand and emptied into the sea. I finished dumping my second can, when I noticed that my shirt and trousers were covered with blood. In the initial exertion of lifting the cans, I had not been aware of the razor sharpness of the bottoms, caused by repeated sliding over the steel decks. The cuts were deep and very painful. No one had alerted me to this obvious danger; more experienced hands were aware of heavy gloves used just for this purpose. I was not afforded any great sympathy for my stupidity and suffered mightily for some time afterward, particularly when it came time to cut or squeeze citrus fruit.

Members of the crew were not permitted on the upper decks, nor were they allowed to fraternize with the passengers.[1] For the first time, I felt class distinction in society. I caught glimpses of the first-class dining room and of passengers in elegant evening clothes, the kind my mother and father wore when they went to the opera. Envy set in as I glanced at boys my own age neatly dressed at dinner with their parents, or even worse, at their pretty sisters seated primly amid glistening silver and sparkling crystal. This was to be a memory that came back to me many times, as I later made numerous first-class trips aboard ocean liners as a member of the diplomatic corps. I slept with other crew members in bunk beds in a large cabin in the very aft of the ship, above the drive shaft. Although there was a great deal of noise and vibration, we were generally too tired to notice.

There were some treasured moments, however. On good days in midafternoon, provided one's work was done, we were afforded an hour or so off to sleep or to do as we wished. It was then I spent as much time as I could in good weather up on the open forward deck at the bow. The deck held winches and other heavy equipment and was restricted only to crew members. I would go forward to the farthest point at the flag mast, sit on the deck, and with a rail stanchion between my thighs, dangle my feet over the side. I was a figurehead in the form of a young man, rising and falling as the bow of the ship pounded through the waves.[2] I was mesmerized as bursts of flying fish would dart out of the sea and skitter ahead of us. Often schools of porpoises would race the ship. They appeared as torpedoes just beneath the surface of the bright blue-green water, interspersing their runs with leaps while traveling at unbelievable speeds of eighteen knots or more. One would think I should have become ill from the constant elevator rides, first way up and then way down in a shuddering motion as the ship settled. It was glorious!

One day off Santo Domingo, about to enter the Windward Passage, I settled into my forward perch and saw what I thought was a large porpoise running just starboard of the bow. At closer look, I noticed large protuberances on either side of its head. I suddenly realized I was observing a hammerhead shark. I watched it for several minutes. Then wanting to share this phenomenon with my shipmates, I jumped up and ran back to the crew's quarters, but by the time some of them came forward, the shark was gone.

Our first port of call out of New York was Havana. The *Kungsholm* did not dock but lay off shore a few hundred yards, and passengers were ferried to land in launches. The crew had been promised a few hours' shore leave, which was to be taken in shifts. Only a few of us were allowed to go ashore the first afternoon and evening. Several men who were off duty but without passes were talking about how easy it would be to swim the distance. It would be a relatively simple matter to drop a rope from the lower fantail deck and make it to the shore. Reason prevailed, however, and the idea was abandoned, when someone brought back word that he had seen a pass list with our names on it. The next morning, a garbage scow came alongside. While observing its maneuvering, I looked down into the water to see the unmistakable forms of several good-sized sharks

lurking beneath the surface. What type they were I do not know. I doubt
if they were the man-eating white sharks generally found in the high seas,
but they might have been tiger sharks, common in Caribbean waters.

We did get shore leave later that day. A group of us went together, the
old hands leading the way and expounding on the watering holes and
highlights we should experience while in Havana. As we crossed one large
downtown plaza, I was struck by the number of soldiers in evidence. It
seemed that every street corner was a little command post. This was 1941,
and the dictator Fulgencio Batista was very much in power. We stopped at
a bar with sidewalk tables. "You haven't lived until you have had a couple
of Cuba Libres!" our leader, a Swedish sailor, informed us. Later, I was to
learn that in essence this is rum and Coca Cola with a slice of lime and a
bit of lime juice. I thought the drink tasted admirably and the second was
even better. After a while, one of the group wanted to visit his girlfriend,
who lived not far from there in a side street. We were invited to go along
in the event she had some friends.

We arrived at a small apartment building, which had a narrow staircase. Going up to the second floor, we knocked on a door and, indeed, the
girlfriend was at home. She appeared overjoyed to see her sailor and ushered us into the apartment, which had a rather large parlor indifferently
furnished with a sofa and a number of chairs. Soon several of her sisters
appeared and they also seemed pleased to meet us. I was by far the young-
est. The rest of our group ranged in age from about the late twenties to fifty. It was fascinating to see how people can communicate: Swedes with no
Spanish, speaking in heavily accented broken English; the girls with little
English jabbering away at each other in Spanish, with much giggling and
laughing. There were three of them and five of us. The girlfriend pointed
to me, evidently commenting on how young I was. Soon there was great
discussion about "Yahnny" (me) amid great hilarity.

One of the girls left the apartment and in about five minutes returned
with a beautiful young lady, who appeared to be about 15 years old, but
fully mature in figure. Well, I was a big city boy, and by this time I had a
pretty good idea of what was going on. This was a bawdy house, and in
a short time these guys were going to initiate me into the facts of life with
this lovely young thing for everyone's amusement. Under other circumstances, there certainly could have been worse fates than spending time
with this dark-eyed beauty. Just then, however, I bolted for the door and
flew down the stairs with a couple of my "pals" laughing in hot pursuit. I
outran them, wandered the streets of Havana for a time, and finally found
my way back to the pier and the launches to the ship.

Having returned considerably before the others, I went down to the
kitchens. I arrived in time to come upon a commotion involving several

crew members and ship's officers in a loud discussion. A few minutes earlier a crewman and a cook had been in an altercation and the latter had struck the sailor with a meat cleaver on the shoulder, virtually lopping it and his arm off. There was blood everywhere, despite best efforts to stop the flow. The Havana police came on board, and the cook and crewman were taken ashore. I never did find out whether the fellow survived. Subsequently, I was the subject of much kidding and ribald humor, as the bawdy house incident was related. One wag was willing to bet that some day I would be an Olympic sprinter, for he had never seen anyone run that fast!

In Colón, Panama, I got my first taste of what it would be like to be a "wiper." I did relief duty in the engine room. The heat was unbearable. July in Panama was bad enough, but to be below decks with boiling hot machinery was akin to being in a furnace. I was glad to be back in the kitchens, even if the Havana incident had left the cooks short-handed and foul-tempered. Panama impressed me with its poverty, tin shacks, and half-naked children. Spanish Harlem with its tenements was the height of luxury by comparison. The passengers, however, were whisked off to the fancy hotel and shopping areas, whereas we crew members, wandering through the squalid parts of town near the docks, could see life in the raw.

From Colón, the ship sailed farther down the eastern coast of Panama toward Colombia, dropping anchor off the San Blas Islands. I was struck by how much the scene that morning looked as if it had been filmed for a Somerset Maugham South Sea island movie. Native canoes came out from shore with fruit, trinkets, and woodcarvings, which the Indians eagerly sold to the passengers. Small boys dove for coins dropped from the upper decks into the sea. The water had to be pretty deep to accommodate an ocean liner, but more often than not they came up laughing and shouting with the coins in hand. It was an idyllic setting; a sparkling blue sea, white beaches on the islands in the distance, palm trees, and native huts. I was to see such sights later in the Philippines, Borneo, and Africa, but that morning is still clearly fixed in my mind.

Our stop in Port-au-Prince, Haiti, was a quite different experience and, although I was not aware of it at the time, hazardous for me. I wandered about alone through the town one late afternoon and early evening and found myself at its outskirts.[3] It was an area that had hut-like dwellings with palm-thatched roofs. I came upon a makeshift stall that served as a storefront, with rusty Coca-Cola signs and other advertisements attached to the wooden supports. The proprietress, an old woman, called to me in French I could not understand. She pointed to a crudely drawn sign that depicted a hand and playing cards and kept uttering "*bonne aventure.*"

Although my three years of high school French and all my sister's efforts were not doing much good, I surmised that she wanted to tell my fortune. Pointing to her palm and drawing lines on it with the index finger of her other hand, she made it clear that she was a palm reader. Sitting in her open hut, I was uneasy as the old woman ran her fingers over my open hands, sighing "oh" and "ah" throughout the procedure.

I learned that I was to become a great hunter or warrior and that there would be many pretty girls in my life. She must have known that I was a seaman from one of the ships in the harbor—travel to Haiti was not that common in those days—so what else would she tell a young sailor, if she wanted to keep him happy enough to pay her well? As I left her and headed back to the ship, I was struck by the surroundings, which appeared quite rural despite the proximity to the main part of the city. I was also conscious of what I can only describe as a pagan atmosphere and the pervasive influence of voodoo on the native population. I could hear native drums beating in the distance.

I came away from working on the ship with a love for the sea that has stayed with me all of my life. Over the years it was the source of a dream in which I would sail my own boat, a small two-master, a ketch, or a yawl, to far-flung ports in the world. Upon my retirement from the diplomatic service, I seriously entertained this idea and even took a course in seamanship and navigation, but my wife was less enthusiastic. Instead of buying a forty-foot sailboat, I settled on purchasing a recreational home on a mountain lake with a dock and a speedboat.

As a New York boy I was aware of the divisions between the haves and have-nots in this world. I now became acutely conscious of this reality and, convinced that if I wanted to be topside with the passengers enjoying life rather than sweating down below decks, I had better start making something of myself. Thirty dollars a month was not going to get me very far. When I returned, I told my parents that I planned to work the following year, hoping to earn enough to start college. I was almost two years younger than the average high school graduate as a consequence of having been placed in school early and participating in the rapid advancement program used by the New York City education system, designed to push quicker learners ahead.

In these latter years of the Depression, my parents had seen their confectionery and restaurant business languish as the upper Fifth Avenue neighborhood changed. While taken aback by my independence, they were pleased to see how I had matured. Jobs were hard to come by in those days, and my father arranged for me to work for a family friend, Bernhard Kranke, who owned a jewelry business in a high-priced neighborhood downtown.[4] Mr. Kranke had been a frequent guest at my family's

Sunday dinners and had enjoyed listening to my sisters' musical performances. I was impressed with my new job, especially when Mr. Kranke took me to lunch on my first day to Sardi's Restaurant, then one of New York's finest.

Dressed in a suit, white shirt, and tie, I mostly traveled from his establishment to different parts of Manhattan to deliver or pick up various items of jewelry. Primarily, I would go down to Maiden Lane, the jewelry district, with its numerous old office buildings, housing floor after floor of little lofts with men behind caged windows staring down through magnifying eyepieces at precious stones or gold artisan work. Here were Old World craftsmen plying their trade, as their forefathers had done in the cities of Europe. Many of them in this year, 1941, were refugees from Hitler's conquests—Poles, Czechs, Lithuanians, Latvians, and Estonians. Many were Jews. Anyone who appreciated fine workmanship or had admired the beauty of a Cellini bowl in a museum would also marvel at their skill and realize what a treasure Europe had lost. Given my high school training in metalwork and jewelry, I found it a joy to see these men at their benches.[5] I would travel about town with a large, black leather wallet chained to my wrist. In it were numerous manila envelopes containing watches, jewelry, or precious stones, each addressed to a repair shop or an artisan firm. I had always thought a jeweler was a person of unlimited talent, able to repair and make everything. So, this was his secret.

I learned a great deal in the short time I worked for Mr. Kranke, but my salary was little more than I made as a seaman, less if one factored in room and board. As I look back on it now, although New York had its crime problems then, it must have been a far different place than today. Either that was the case, or I was unbelievably lucky not to have been robbed at least once. I doubt if an unarmed boy of just seventeen today would take the subways around the city with a wallet containing valuables chained to his wrist.

While on one of my trips about town, I sought employment at the Lord and Taylor department store on Fifth Avenue and 38th Street, a few blocks from Kranke's jewelry establishment. I was hired for the munificent sum of eleven dollars a week as a stock clerk in the shoe department. There, I also had an opportunity to become familiar with shoe-sale advertising layouts in the local newspapers. I worked six days a week. While no heavy labor was involved, one had to listen to the constant complaints of the salespersons, mostly men, about our customers. On the other hand, I was astounded at the lengths to which they went to please some of our wealthy clientele. One buyer was a gorgeous woman in her early thirties. Though married, she had half the salesmen in the store traipsing through the place to look at or talk to her.

My life took on added spice when I would be sent fairly regularly up to the tenth floor with shoes or some other item for use in a fashion show. The backrooms there were a beehive of activity, with pretty young models running around in varying states of undress. The first time I encountered this situation, I must have evinced some embarrassment, for one of the luscious cuties pinched me on the cheek saying, "Oh, come on in, it's all right!" I quickly learned to feign embarrassment, since the more hesitant I became, the more the girls would tease me by exposing themselves. There was always great hilarity on these occasions. I never did tell them that I grew up surrounded by girls as the only boy among three older sisters.

As 1941 drew to a close, the country was in the throes of war. Pearl Harbor had shocked the nation, and the news that followed day after day added to the dismay. Everywhere the democracies were in retreat. The draft had been instituted the previous year, and as men were being called up, job opportunities beckoned for those still too young to serve. A visit to an employment agency one day resulted in my being placed, almost immediately, in a position with a Wall Street firm, not as a banker or a broker, far from it, but as a "runner." My work with Mr. Kranke carrying jewelry and valuables made me ideally qualified for a job transferring securities, and the pay was an 80 percent increase over my previous salary. I was back to carrying a big, black leather envelope chained to my wrist, only this time it contained stock and bond certificates. Whenever stocks and bonds were sold in those days, the certificates were physically transferred between brokerage houses.[6] My employer was J & W Seligmann and Company, a brokerage firm located on the upper floors of the American Express Building at 65 Broadway.

I would pick up or deliver the certificates to the N.Y. Stock Exchange, the Curb Exchange, which no longer exists under that name, or to individual brokerage houses and banks. I soon became familiar with the exchanges and all the great houses and banks on "the Street," many of them not physically located on Wall Street at all but in nearby areas. I always made it my business to be properly dressed while other older runners wore more informal clothing. As a result, at times I would be asked to undertake special tasks. On one occasion, I was asked to deliver a package to the Greenwich, Connecticut, home of one of the directors of the firm, who also headed a subsidiary company, Tricontinental Securities. I remember taking the train from Grand Central Station and being picked up in Greenwich by his chauffeur. I was struck by the large, lovely houses I passed and by how "WASPy" the community was.

Seligmann also controlled another firm, Union Securities. The overall CEO and chairman of the board was Francis Fitz Randolph, a slight, bald-headed man with a ruddy complexion and a crisp British mustache, who had been a major in the U.S. Army during World War I. He would arrive every day wearing a waistcoat and striped pants in his old-fashioned Rolls Royce, driven by a uniformed chauffeur. Although Broadway was a busy avenue, that Rolls Royce sat out in front of the building with the chauffeur in a special parking place all day at Mr. Randolph's disposal. I had no idea, then, that his dress would set a fine example for me later in the diplomatic service.

Finding a place for myself at a first-rate college had occupied my thoughts throughout my senior year in high school. Nevertheless, the nature of teenagers is such that I did not study enough to realize that ambition. After graduation and my declaration to my parents that I would put myself through college, I began to plan in earnest. The series of jobs I had taken on did not pay particularly well, but with some savings and a year of work I calculated I could manage payment for a year's tuition at the going rate for most private colleges. That did not encompass room and board, which would nearly double my estimate. I thought in terms of one year only, because America was already at war and I would be of draft age when I entered my freshman year. Even if I were accepted, I did not want to go to City College of New York (CCNY), a free school, nor did I want to attend New York University (NYU), which was private. The latter was considered the place where students went who could not get into CCNY, but whose parents could afford the tuition.

I had my heart set on going to an Ivy League college. I read everything I could get my hands on about the various institutions. I learned about the curricula and where they ranked in the eyes of the knowledgeable public. I came away with the understanding that Harvard was at the top, challenged for that spot by Yale. Next in line was a toss-up between Columbia and Princeton, followed by Brown, Dartmouth (considered at the time to be a "jock school"), Cornell, a state institution, and the University of Pennsylvania.[7] One heard about Stanford as being top flight academically but clear across the country and another world away. There were also a myriad of smaller private colleges such as Amherst, Williams, and Haverford, but my attention was not focused on them. The desirability of going to a coed college was never a factor, since most Ivy League schools had sister institutions nearby. My initial explorations made me appreciate how difficult it was going to be to fulfill my aspirations.

During those years, only five percent of American youth, mostly males, went to college. With their European backgrounds, my parents were totally unfamiliar with America's academic world and of no help in the application process. My sisters were products of the city's colleges and for some reason were not much better informed, despite the fact that two of them were teachers. My first contact with college authorities came as a result of learning that Bard College, in Annandale-on-Hudson, was offering art scholarships. Bard was then a unique institution providing a virtually tutorial education, with only a handful of students to each professor. It was somehow affiliated with Columbia University. Using my background at the High School of Music and Art as an entrée, I received an encouraging response to my application and was invited for an interview. I remember taking the train to Bard, located in beautiful surroundings on the east bank of the Hudson River about 100 miles north of New York City.

The interview went well, but I soon became aware that Bard was a very expensive school. Even with a scholarship, my funds could not begin to cover the cost. Furthermore, I would be immersed in a milieu of wealthy students and would be out of place. I remember being shown around the campus by a nice young man, who upon entering one of the residences pointed to his car parked outside. It was a sport model Duesenberg convertible, probably comparable to a Ferrari today. On the train ride home, I said to myself that there was no way I would be able to manage Bard, nor was I convinced that I wanted to be there.

As 1941 came to an end, I was feeling out of touch with the academic world. I decided that regardless of how difficult it might be, I should enter some preparatory program of studies in the evening. I might even be able to use this effort to obtain college credit. I enrolled in the evening winter/spring semester at CCNY, which did not require matriculation, and took two courses I thought would be useful, Latin and Calculus. My intentions were good, but my judgment was not. I was inherently poor in both foreign language grammar and mathematics. Furthermore, these classes were attended by serious, no-nonsense students in their late twenties and thirties, many of them refugees from Hitler's Europe. After a full day's work at my job, I found that I could not attend classes and complete all the homework required. At age seventeen, my approach to studying simply could not compare to others in the class, and I was soon left in the dust. After a few difficult weeks, I dropped out.

During the following months, I examined various possibilities for entering Ivy League colleges, but after a while I came to the conclusion that my best chance would be to go all out for Columbia University. Johanna, at that time, was working on her master's degree in French in the School of Education at Columbia. I remember the first time I spoke to her about applying for Columbia College. She responded all too matter-of-factly, saying: "You will never get in." Johanna had every reason to be discouraging. The university, even in those days, was a large institution, with numerous faculties and separate colleges, as well as a School of General Studies for which one did not have to matriculate. The undergraduate school, Columbia College, in contrast, with a student body of about 1,200, was the smallest in the Ivy League.

In addition to Johanna's association with the university, my sister Eleanor's husband, Alfred Bingham, was working on his doctorate there, and Alfred's father, Seth Bingham, was a highly regarded professor in the Music Department and a renowned organist and composer. If I played my cards right, the situation might not be totally unavailing. I obtained all the information I could about the college. I visited the admissions office, which was really only a short distance from my home. I told a very nice woman there that I was applying to out-of-town schools, but I had heard so much about Columbia's humanities program that I felt compelled to inquire. I remember discussing the "Great Books" program at St. John's at Annapolis with her. Our talk was most useful, and I came away with two key bits of information: first, that enrollment was already being seriously impacted by the war, the draft, and military recruitment, and second, that emphasis was placed on geographic representation. Columbia wanted students from all over the nation and did not wish to be overloaded with New Yorkers. I regarded these factors as one plus and one minus in my efforts to gain entry, hoping they would cancel each other out.

It would be useful here to discuss another aspect of my development that was to play a role in my admission to college. At one point during my senior year in high school, my sister Johanna decided to join the "Book of the Month Club." She may not have benefited much from this act, but the effect on me was profound. At the outset, the beautifully bound volumes intrigued me. The first book she received was *The Seven Pillars of Wisdom* by T. H. Lawrence (Lawrence of Arabia). I was especially drawn to the book because it had a foreword by Lowell Thomas, to whom I felt a special kinship since he owned the estate near a family friend's farm. Next, she received *The Tales of Sherlock Holmes*, which I also devoured. This was followed by a book about Roger Casement, the Irish revolutionary and his efforts, with German support, to oust the British during World War I.

By then, I was hooked and eagerly awaited the following shipment. Next came an exceptionally attractive collectors' edition of *The Complete Works of Keats and Shelley*, followed by the Greek tragedies of Aeschylus, Sophocles, and Euripides and the comedies of Aristophanes and Menander, as well as Plato's *Republic*, all of which, true to form, I also read. About this time, after a bit of extra research, I wrote a comparative analysis of the works of Keats and Shelley with relative ease. My teacher questioned me about the paper and I believe she was surprised to find me thoroughly conversant with my subject. I received an A+ on the paper.

In the spring of 1942, while working for Seligmann & Co., I submitted an application for admission to Columbia College. I indicated great interest in the College's humanities and contemporary civilization programs and expressed in my letter all that I could to sell myself. To my great joy I subsequently received a response inviting me for an interview. I took great care in my attire to appear as "Ivy League" as possible—a subdued tweed sports jacket, grey trousers, white button-down shirt, and a rep tie. The Dean of the College, Howard Hawkes, interviewed me. He was interested in my High School of Music and Art background, and I mentioned that I had been offered an art scholarship to Bard.

I talked about why Columbia was the place for me, about my interest in the humanities program, and about the importance of being a "renaissance man." When asked about reading, I said I had read the Greek tragedies and comedies and Plato's *Republic*. Trotting out the phrase "*mens sana in corpore sano*" from my Latin studies, I said I enjoyed sports and played football. I concluded by noting that my sister was working for her master of arts at Columbia and my brother-in-law for his doctorate, and that my sister's father-in-law was Professor Seth Bingham. Before I could overdo it any further, the dean told me that despite my poor grades, I had come from an excellent school and that arrangements might be made for me to take an entrance examination. The College would inform me of their decision.

I had no idea what I was in for! Among a recently found packet of letters from me that my mother had saved, one dated August 10, 1942, described the entrance examination. My mother had gone on holiday on Long Island for a week with my Aunt Cilly and my letter began by apologizing for not coming home that afternoon in time to carry my mother's luggage to the train station, as I had promised. I had taken the day off from work (it was a Monday), and had left early in the morning for the exam, confidently expecting to be back by three o'clock. I had anticipated the exam would take only an "hour or two." Instead, it took four hours and fifteen minutes, with additional time for an intermission.

The exam covered the waterfront, with particular emphasis on English and writing as well as physics and calculatory mathematics.[8] I thanked my lucky stars for those horrible weeks in the evening courses at CCNY that had helped me prepare. Though plenty of test time was spent on other subjects, I made no mention of them. I concluded my letter to mother by telling her how pleased Johanna was with me for having spent two hours scrubbing down the bathroom that evening.

I evidently did well on the examination, as I received notification a few weeks later welcoming me to the Class of 1946. I had just turned eighteen and America was in the depths of the war, every day bringing further news of defeats on the battlefronts. How long I would be in college now that I had finally managed to get in was a question I could not answer.

On registration day in late September 1942, I reported to the college gymnasium and was processed. I paid my tuition for the fall semester at the bursar's office. I do not think I had a checking account, so I must have paid with cash or a money order. The amount was all of $325. I still have that little blue cardboard bursar's office receipt, marked "paid" in my files.

I registered for the courses set by the college's mandatory curriculum. These included Humanities, Contemporary Civilization, German A-1, Solid Geometry, English Composition, Hygiene A-1, and Physical Education. The large number of required textbooks dismayed me, but that could be expected given the nature of the first two courses above.

What I did not expect was the "beanie" that tradition obliged us as freshmen to wear. I do not recall whether we had to buy the "beanie" or if it was given to us. It can best be described as a skullcap with a very short brim in front, light blue in color with a little white button on top. A girl I knew said it was "cute." If an upper classman caught a freshman without his "beanie" on, he was in for trouble. It was a silly custom, but my classmates and I went along with it out of pride in being a Columbia student and participating in the system. It was simply not a point of contention. Five years later, however, it was another matter, when I was a returning war veteran and an effort was made to make me wear a "beanie."

I settled into classes readily, but the volume of required reading, which amounted to several hundred pages a night, was daunting. My humanities professor had a penchant for giving weekly quizzes, which kept us all on edge. It seems to me that the author of the best seller *The Paper Chase* must have modeled Professor Kingsford after him. Our man was a slight, white-haired, irascible taskmaster with British mannerisms named Professor Kinney. He terrified us. I recall one question on a quiz, covering hundreds of pages of Homer's *Iliad*, that asked us to describe what was on Hector's shield, a detail so insignificant in that vast amount of reading that most of us could not even make a decent guess as to the answer.

I was not at my best in these courses. My study habits left much to be desired, and my focus must have been elsewhere—just where I do not know, since I was paying for this instruction with my own hard-earned money. Perhaps it was on sports, since physical education was the only subject in which I was getting an A. Freshmen, because of the war, were allowed to play varsity football, and some of us went through the motions but never saw any real service. I discovered however, that I was an unusually good wrestler. I had never been exposed to Greco-Roman wrestling before, and I learned a good deal from my instruction and competition, which I later put to good use in the army.

The year 1942 was a very unsettling time for my family. The upper Fifth Avenue neighborhood, where my parents' business was located, had deteriorated, and they were preparing to sell. The restaurant was still a money-making proposition, but the ice cream and confectionery components had been overtaken by the times.

Around this time, my parents brought into the business a couple who had worked for them previously as individuals and were now married. Otto and Elizabeth Schwabe moved into the apartment in the building next to the business that my family had at one time occupied. This enabled them to be more readily available, and they absorbed more and more of the load of supervising activities. The Schwabes had two children — a girl, Marian, a year older than I, and a son, Henry, two years younger. I saw a great deal of these children initially, but as time passed and my bonds with youngsters on the West Side where I lived grew, I saw less of them. I was away camping with the Boy Scouts one summer when I received word that Henry had drowned in a swimming pool accident. He was a kind and lovable boy, and his parents were profoundly shocked.

As Dad made arrangements to sell the business, Mother stepped in and urged that they simply turn their establishment over to the Schwabes, saying that the latter had worked long and hard for the Kormanns and that they had earned the right to be the proprietors. I am sure that the loss of young Henry weighed heavily on her mind. Mother said to me much later that "it was the Christian thing to do." My parents were glad that they had done this very generous act and were sure that God had blessed them for doing so by making their retirement days in Florida such happy ones.

My mother was a remarkable woman, small in stature, but with towering spiritual and moral strength. I learned more about what is truly important in life sitting at her feet than I can say. She had a habit that made a profound impression on me. I knew I could always find her early in the morning, before anyone else was stirring, in the kitchen reading her Bible and thanking God for all the blessings he had bestowed on our family. Her approach to life was so positive that it affected everyone around her, but she was also a supreme realist. She would say to me, "Don't ever expect life to be fair. Life is not fair." I heard from her early on those powerful words from Ecclesiastes, Chapter 9, Verse 11: "I returned and saw under the sun that the race is not always to the swift, nor the battle to the strong, neither yet bread to the wise, nor riches to men of understanding, nor yet favor to men of skill, but time and chance happeneth to them all."

Mother's answer to this was that we had to be larger than the things that happened to us. Nothing that occurs is half as important as the way in which we meet it. No one can be sure that disappointment, injustice, illness, rejection, or humiliation will not befall us, nor can we be protected from our own mistakes and failures. But the way in which we choose to meet life is ours. When integrity, courage, dignity and compassion are our choice, the things that happen to us lose their power over us. Many years later, I saw these wise thoughts phrased in an article by Dr. Ina Corrine Brown and I could hear Mother's voice as I read them.[9]

Mother and I were on a special wavelength. I was never able to explain this phenomenon, but I could always sense her presence, even when I was far away. There was always some indication that she knew where I was or what I was doing. This was particularly true during my military service in World War II and later in periods of crisis in the Foreign Service.[10] After our marriage, my wife Elsa would comment on this phenomenon as well. When such situations occurred, Elsa and I would look at one another and say, "Mother."

Autumn 1942 was a dismal time for me. Each day I commuted across town. As I arrived at Columbia, the large open field in the center of the college complex would be crowded with midshipmen training in the Navy's V-5 and V-12 programs. I knew that soon I, too, would be drawn into the military. I had registered for the draft at age eighteen the previous summer, but rather than enter one of the Navy officer programs at Columbia or seek some form of Army ROTC training elsewhere, I simply let matters take their course. That was to be the most foolish and regrettable decision of my life. No one really discussed the matter with me. I had no male relatives in the service and there was no family experience to draw on. No one gave me advice as to what the true consequences of my indecision might be, and I wandered blithely into a situation I was to rue for the next three years.

In December 1942, I visited the local draft board, inquired about the Army Air Corps, and expressed interest in duty with that branch of the service. I wanted to become a fighter pilot and I thought this an appropriate way to select the area of service I desired. I could not have been more wrong.[11] As the mid-term examinations came, I prepared to enter military service. My grades reflected my preoccupation, and my performance was borderline at best.

Late one day after classes, I took a long walk up Riverside Drive. It was a cold evening in early February and my route took me from 116th Street up to the George Washington Bridge. As darkness fell, I wandered out onto the bridge to the midpoint over the Hudson River far below. I gazed at the city lights of Manhattan and across to New Jersey. It was one of the loneliest and lowest points of my life. I saw nothing but a bleak and forbidding future ahead.

A few days later I received the "Order to Report for Induction" from the "local board composed of your neighbors," extending a greeting and telling me to report to the Nemo Theatre at Broadway and 110th Street on

March 17, 1943 (St. Patrick's Day) at 5:00 a.m. for "training and service in the Armed Forces."[12] I made a final call on Dean Hawkes of the College. He was very kind, in view of my poor performance, in wishing me well and hoping that it would not be too long before he would see me back on campus. It was a generous expression of concern, which I have never forgotten. I received a letter on Columbia stationery stating that I had been "granted a leave of absence from the College until the expiration of the period of national service."

The procedure for reporting for active duty at the time was to go from the assembly point at the Nemo Theatre to a train or bus terminal for transportation to one of the reception centers. I was to depart from Pennsylvania Station for Camp Dix, New Jersey, for processing into the army. I telephoned the news to Mother, at the time out on Long Island. She had been expecting that I would be called up. Virtually every other young man of my age was receiving a similar notification. Mother said she would come to New York City to see me off, and we made arrangements to meet at the train station, since there was no prohibition against relatives and friends accompanying inductees that far. I arose at 3:30 a.m. on the morning of March 17, 1943, and dressed in a tweed suit, which had a Columbia College emblem on the breast pocket. I wanted to make a good impression. Dad arose and watched me get dressed and eat breakfast. With tears in his eyes, he hugged me and stoically said good-bye. The Schwabes were away, and he had to be available at the opening of business.

I departed in the dark for the Nemo Theatre, carrying a small suitcase with toilet articles and sundries. The initial processing was routine and by eight o'clock we were at Pennsylvania Station. Mother was waiting for me at the appointed place—her train had come in a half hour earlier. The terminal building was crowded to capacity with commuters and servicemen and women. The place was bedlam! Airline travel was in its infancy, and the bulk of transportation was still by rail. Groups of soldiers, sailors, and marines stood about or moved through the vast noisy hall with relatives and loved ones saying farewell and weeping. The train for Camp Dix was to depart in about forty-five minutes, leaving just enough time for Mother and me to have a few final words together. I will never forget that moment. We found two seats on a long wooden bench near the center of that amphitheater-like building.

Mother was calm and not at all tearful. She told me that I would always be in her prayers. Serving my country was a great responsibility and I should acquit myself in such a manner that I would always be proud of what I had done. She then said: "Pray with me, son," waiting for me to get down on my knees in front of her, so that she could put her hand on my head. I was taken aback. We were seated on a bench with half a dozen other people, with hundreds milling about, many of them young men. We were not in her kitchen, where I had often knelt at her feet as she sat in her chair, Bible in hand.

I hesitated, but even as an unruly and rather irreligious youth I had learned that when Mother prayed, things happened. I got down on my knees and she prayed for me. The next five years were to find me at times in all sorts of danger. I am convinced that I came through virtually unscathed because of the prayers of that righteous woman. Throughout it all, I could sense that I was under her protective care and knew I would be all right. Could any son have been more blessed? Then I kissed her good-bye, passed through the iron gates, boarded the train, and began the adventures of my life.

3

"You're in the Army Now!"

The passenger coach was filled with men varying from eighteen to thirty years in age, with a few who appeared to be somewhat older. They represented a sociological cross section of New York City. I felt out of place in my tweed suit with its Columbia College crest on the pocket. To most of the others, I must have appeared to be a rich kid from Riverside Drive or Park Avenue. I found myself wishing I had taken off that pretentious emblem and worn more casual clothing. I had not realized that we would not be allowed to keep any civilian clothing once we were in uniform and that all my clothes, and my suitcase, would have to be mailed home after our arrival at camp.

At the start of our journey, the train was engulfed in darkness as it coursed its subterranean way through the tunnels under Manhattan and the Hudson River. It broke out into the open on the Weehauken Flats, an area that in those days contained smoking factories and foundries. Industrial waste steamed in pools of water along the tracks. I could see the skyscrapers of Manhattan disappearing behind us, and I sensed that it might be some time until I saw them again. After a few more miles, we rolled through the New Jersey countryside with its scrub brush landscape fronted by light industry and warehouses along the route.

An hour and a half after our departure, our train pulled into an open siding. I recall seeing a large sign that read "Welcome to Camp Dix." As cheery as this greeting was, what followed was less pleasant. Sergeants, forming the reception party, hustled us out of the coaches and endeavored to line us up. There was some confusion and much shouting and after a while we were marched off, carrying our baggage, to a processing building. My memory of all this is vague, but it seems to me that we were assigned to platoons and companies and allocated quarters, which were large tents with floorboards and wooden sides. The next day we were issued uniforms and equipment. Each man received a serial number that we had to memorize to the point of being able to shout it out on any occasion.

Woe betides the man, who in response to a sergeant's question could not immediately produce his serial number. My number, which I can recite in my sleep sixty years later, was 32865751. I was Private Kormann and would be so for the next several years.

We ate in a large mess hall and later proceeded to a building for physical examinations. I was in fine shape, pronounced a healthy specimen, and passed without a problem. I had been classified 1A by the draft board, now confirmed. I was surprised by the number of others who had flat feet, heart problems, and a variety of illnesses. They were moved to one side and, I surmise, declared unfit and sent home. I thought it would have been relatively easy, under the circumstances, to be selected out even by feigning disabilities. To most of the young men, however, it was a matter of pride that one should pass. At one point, I was directed into a cubicle with a person I presume now to have been a psychiatrist. He asked me a number of questions, concluding with one as to whether I liked girls, which struck me as rather strange and to which I responded, "I guess so." He then said, "Do you prefer boys?" thus snapping me into his meaning and engendering the retort, "Hell, no!" That was the end of my session with him.

We were then moved to an adjoining area for inoculations. It seems to me that we received at least four shots and a vaccination. We proceeded in a single line to a point at which several medical technicians lined up on either side of us. They injected or vaccinated us in both arms at once. I was later to see many a comic movie routine, most notably with Jerry Lewis, about this procedure in which the actor faints. Indeed, I can vouch for the accuracy of that script, because I saw more than one recruit in that long line grow dizzy and topple over. Matters were not helped, during this or later such sessions with the needle, when some wag with false bravado would shout "Watch out for the corkscrew needle!" or "Be careful of the one with the hook!" I do not ever recall receiving inoculations, and there were many, during my years in the Foreign Service, which were as painful as those that day. My vaccination really took effect and turned into a nasty swelling with a huge black scab. The shots stung and made my arms sore for days.

The following day, we were marched to the "supply room," which was a large warehouse with a long row of tables. Behind these were bins and shelves. We were issued two barrack bags—olive drab, a dull color always referred to as OD—to hold our effects. We then passed along the row of tables calling out our sizes, as we were given two pairs of ankle high Army shoes, several pairs of khaki-colored socks, two sets of OD boxer shorts and old-fashioned OD undershirts. Then we were issued a brown, wool, dress uniform blouse with brass buttons, a two inch wide military belt, two pairs of brown woolen trousers, two brown woolen shirts, two tan Khaki neckties, a hat with a visor, an overseas cap and a heavy, brown full-length woolen overcoat with brass buttons. Moving farther down the line, we received our fatigues: two pairs of green baggy twill pants, with matching shirts that could be worn inside or outside of the trousers. This outfit was completed with the addition of a floppy crew-style hat.

Finally, we were issued a mess kit, an aluminum canteen with cup, a musette bag (knapsack), a web (pistol) belt and a variety of toilet articles, including a safety razor, in a small canvas bag. We were subsequently instructed on how to pack our barrack bags. Each piece was to be rolled tightly and placed in the bag in a certain order. The rolling was to minimize wrinkles. I recall shortly afterwards putting on my dress uniform, which, nevertheless, needed pressing and was ill fitting. With the brown woolen shirt, khaki tie, baggy trousers and clodhopper shoes I truly looked like "Sad Sack," the soldier in the much read cartoon of the day.

Later, we were called out to formation. After berating us as to what a sorry bunch of recruits we were, the sergeant queried, "Has any one here been to college?" A number of us held up our hands. With a look of satisfaction on his face, the sergeant said: "This area is a pigsty, cigarette butts everywhere! I want you college boys to pick them up and show the rest of these excuses for soldiers how it should be done!" That was the last time that I was ever to raise my hand unless I was sure as to the purpose. I also learned never to volunteer and to keep a low profile. It was deemed a success when the sergeant did not know your name or asked whether "you belonged in this outfit?" This attitude was reinforced when I was shipped out to another camp to undertake basic training.

During my short stay at Camp Dix, we were drilled and exposed to a few rudimentary elements of military life: how to march properly, to salute, when and when not to say "sir," and to recognize the various bugle calls. But it was primarily a period of processing to determine where we might best fit into the army. One afternoon, we were taken to very large classrooms where Army General Comprehension Tests (AGCT) were administered. The tests were the multiple choice type, using a pencil to mark one or more slots, designated "a" through "f" for each question. Apparently the tests were graded electronically. The AGCT was designed to demonstrate one's overall knowledge and ability to reason. Although students routinely encountered tests of this sort in later years, I had never taken one up to that juncture.

I remember working rapidly in answering questions. At one point, however, I looked up and without seeing what others were marking, I noted by the amount of pages that I seemed to be much farther along than anyone else. I wondered whether I was doing things incorrectly or perhaps that I should be taking much greater care with my answers. This slowed me down, an act that could have had very unfortunate consequences. I should have focused on the obvious fact that this was not a room full of college students, but a cross section of America. Though I was aware that speed was a factor, it was in reality an absolute necessity. I came away with a good score, but it was nowhere near the best I could have done. When I learned how important the test was to a soldier's future, I went into shock. The test results went into a soldier's personnel file, and one had to have a certain minimum to be commissioned an officer. While I was much above that level, had I tended to my own business and continued to work rapidly, I would have been better off. I was not given an opportunity to be retested and was taught a lesson never to be forgotten.[1]

We were run through other tests. One such test involved putting on earphones and listening to rhythmic sounds. As perverse fate would have it, I scored exceptionally well and was earmarked as a potential radio operator. This designation was to plague me for many months and on two occasions affected my assignments.

As part of the paperwork on entry into the Army, we were asked to fill out forms for government insurance. Every soldier was required to take out a $10,000 term life insurance policy. They also gave us forms that, if we chose, would allot a portion of our pay, which at the time was $21 a month, to anyone we designated as a dependent. The government would then add a percentage to whatever we allotted. I saw everyone else filling out these forms and thought I should do likewise. I simply designated my parents as dependents.[2]

A month or so later in basic training, I received a letter from my mother stating that a gentleman from the government had visited my parents' apartment on Long Island as part of the allotment process. My mother had told him in no uncertain terms that she did not want me to allot money home, nor would she accept any contribution from the government, since none was needed. The receipt of this news angered me at the time. My fellow soldiers were providing for their loved ones; why should not I? Besides, I reasoned, if she did not want the money, she could put it in a bank account for my college education, when and if I returned. Today, I would have viewed the matter entirely differently and hope I did not cause my family too much embarrassment. As for the government visitor, he routinely encountered such cases.

The days that followed were marked by anticipation among the recruits as to where they would be assigned. They really had no idea whether they would end up in the Infantry, Artillery, Engineers, Quartermaster, Signals, Cavalry (Armor), or any of the smaller branches such as Military Intelligence or the Adjutant General Corps.[3] Perhaps some might be designated for the Army Air Corps, where I expected to be assigned. That expectation made me less apprehensive than the rest and thankful I had indicated to the draft board that I wished to volunteer for flight training. Looking back on the matter today, I doubt whether most of the recruits had any idea how fateful the processing at Camp Dix was. Those assigned to the combat arms and to some extent, the Air Corps, stood an infinitely higher chance of becoming casualties than the others.

At each formation, names were read off and the individuals involved were told to pack their effects and be prepared to ship out. In a few days, I heard my name called and joined a group ready to be transported. With one barrack bag over my shoulder and another under my arm, I climbed onto a truck and was driven to a train siding. We were loaded aboard railroad passenger coaches, with window shades drawn, and began a journey lasting four and a half days, traveling almost 2000 miles across the country. It was uncomfortable sitting in coach day and night, with minimal bathroom facilities. A bit of spice was added, at least for part of the journey, when we learned that a large contingent of Women's Army Corps (WAC) recruits were in cars elsewhere on the train. While there was much hoopla about their presence, we had virtually no contact with them and at one point their coaches were detached from our train, evidently to be routed southward to Camp Oglethorpe, Georgia, the WAC basic training center.

Despite the obvious attempt to maintain troop train security by drawing the shades, we had little difficulty, initially, in discerning where we were. We caught glimpses of signs on train stations through the cracks. Other references we saw, as we moved through the cars at mealtime, told us we were in Ohio or Indiana. At night, it was more difficult to get our bearings and at one point word was passed that we were in Minnesota. This struck me as rather strange considering that my final destination was to be Randolph Field in Texas or some other airbase in the Southwest. Throughout the trip, the train would move along at a good pace for a few hours and then come to a stop at a siding, sometimes for long periods, to everyone's great irritation. The circuitous routing, we were later told, was all part of the security effort to keep the enemy confused.

On the fourth night, around 11 o'clock, we made one of our interminable stops. This time, however, our drowsiness was shaken by considerably more noise and activity than usual. Peeking out from behind the drawn shade, one of the recruits spotted a station sign that read "Neosho," which meant nothing to any of us. "Where the hell is Neosho?" was a cry that could be heard from one end of the coach to the other. Within minutes, noncommissioned officers (noncoms), the military term for sergeants and corporals, came aboard the train and ordered us to grab our equipment and line up on the platform. I noted that the noncoms had orange piping on their overseas caps and crossed signal flags on their lapel insignia. A first lieutenant addressed us once we were in formation on the platform, saying, "Welcome to Camp Crowder, the home of the Signal Corps!" We soon learned that Crowder was in the Ozark Mountains, at the very southwest tip of Missouri, near the Oklahoma border. The nearest city was Joplin, Missouri, and that was many miles away and surely no metropolis. As one New Yorker put it, "We really were out in the boonies."

After an extended period of sorting out personnel and making assignments, we were loaded on specific 2 1/2 ton trucks for transport to various units. Our ride through the darkened camp, with row after row of barracks interspersed among drill fields, took about twenty minutes. It was bitter cold and I was thankful for the long, heavy, woolen overcoat I had been issued. We stopped in an area with many wooden two-story barracks. By then it must have been 2:00 a.m. We lined up in platoon fashion in front of a one story wooden structure with wide doors over which was a sign, "Supply Room." We were issued two white muslin sheets, a pillowcase, and two brown army blankets and were then marched over to a barrack and assigned bunks. The latter were steel frame collapsible cots upon which, rolled up, were stuffed cotton mattresses. We were told to make our beds "Army style" and to "hit the sack." It seemed that we had no sooner done so, when a bugle sounded "First Call," followed shortly thereafter by "Reveille."

It was 4:30 a.m. and pitch black outside. In no time, the noncoms were moving up and down the aisle shouting and urging us to dress rapidly. My bunk was located on the second floor; about halfway down the building from the staircase, which was near one end. As you entered the barrack on the first floor, the staircase was straight ahead. To the left, was a large room with two long rows of bunks, each perpendicular to the outer walls, with a long wide aisle down the center between the beds. Lining the aisle, at the foot of each bunk, was a footlocker. Along the outer wall, at times between windows, were combination shelf-clothes racks to accommodate each bunk user.

To the right of the barrack as one entered, were two steps down leading to the latrine. The second floor layout was similar to the first, except that there was no latrine and, instead, at one end there were two small rooms reserved for noncoms. Each barrack accommodated about 50–60 soldiers. The latrine had sinks capable of handling about 15–20 soldiers. Consequently, there was an immediate backup as everyone rushed to use the facilities at the same time. Formation was at 5:45 a.m. We were to dress, wash, shave, use the toilet, line up at the mess hall for breakfast, eat, return to the barrack, make the bed, and prepare our footlockers and clothing racks for inspection, all within this time.

The first morning was obviously far below the noncoms' standards and they did not hesitate to tell us so. I doubt if anyone had very much for breakfast that morning. Somehow, we were all standing on the company parade ground as the cannon went off at Post Headquarters far off in the distance and the bugler played the rising of the colors. We lined up in platoons and the sergeants took roll call. Out in front of the formation was a first sergeant and behind him three officers. A first lieutenant, our company commander, subsequently addressed us saying that we were now part of Company B, 34th Signal Construction Battalion, which was one of the finest outfits in the Army, and that we were going to make sure that it stayed that way.

The following days were filled with typical basic training instruction designed to turn recruits into soldiers. We spent many hours drilling, learning the manual of arms, and military practices. The noncoms put the fear of the Lord in us, for at the slightest infraction we found ourselves on "fatigue detail." The company maintained a roster for various duties, such as KP (kitchen patrol), latrine orderly (cleaning the bathrooms and toilets), garbage detail, guard duty, furnace detail (round-the-clock stoking the barrack, mess hall, and company headquarters furnaces with coal), and officers' quarters orderly. The latter was considered the cushiest of the lot, although they all involved long hours and at times backbreaking labor. Ostensibly, the roster was in alphabetical order. However, it was liberally supplemented by those named to "fatigue detail." Noncoms were exempted from such activities, and it did not take long for your name to appear on one of the lists.

I soon had a taste of each duty, and then some. At a fairly early stage, I spoke to our sergeant telling him of the mistake in my assignment and asked to talk to the first sergeant or company commander about the matter. He said he would see what could be done. I heard nothing more about the subject. A day or so later, I noted my name on the KP roster. I thought nothing about it at the time, got up at 3:30 a.m. and reported to the mess hall for KP duty and the seventeen-hour day that followed. Subsequently, at the first opportunity, I visited company headquarters to inquire what I might do about getting my assignment to the Air Corps straightened out. Within a day or two, I was back on KP. I was sure that in neither case was I alphabetically scheduled, nor had I been placed on fatigue detail. One did not have to be an Einstein to realize what was happening, and I soon gave up my quest, settling down into our rigorous training.

Besides the normal components of basic training, including rifle instruction, bivouacking, close combat drill, and several long marches, one of 25 miles, we entered into our branch training. The 34th was a pole-line construction battalion. Several of the sergeants were former employees of the telephone company, and the battalion commander, a major, had been a telephone company executive. It was not long before we were introduced to the fine points of telephone pole line construction. Today, they have trucks with large posthole diggers on the rear. We were expected, by hand, to dig holes 6 feet deep in rocky Ozark soil for telephone poles about 15 inches in diameter and about 25–30 feet high. In World War I, they imported Chinese coolies to dig the trenches in France and Belgium. Well, there were none around to dig miles of telephone pole holes at Camp Crowder.

Digging was interspersed with an even more intriguing activity: that of stringing lines. To do this, a trainee had to put on climbers and mount the pole. It was fascinating to watch a neophyte strap on the equipment, and then dig the sharp hooks into the side of the pole as he went up. He was warned all the way to embed the hooks solidly or the consequences would be severe. Invariably, someone would miscue and start to slide down the pole. At this point, either he managed to dig his climbers in and stop the fall, or loosen the climber's belt and jump completely back and free of the pole. Instinct, however, would have him endeavor to hug the pole, which was the worst thing possible. Sliding down a pole that had been "spiked up" and full of large wooden splinters was known as "burning the pole" and brought with it an agonizing and hospitalizing fate.

I spent much of my thought during this time ruing the day I had not applied for some form of officer training while I was at Columbia. I could not believe how foolish I had been. Officers lived in a privileged world of their own. One rarely had contact with them, with the exception of our platoon lieutenant. He was a clean-cut, rather frail-looking, young southerner, whom we called "Candy Ass." He had participated in the ROTC program at one of the southern universities. Seeing him at evening formation in his resplendent officer's uniform had me muttering to myself. At best, our noncoms were telephone construction workers. At worst, they were old time Army cadre, many of them shifty and unreliable. The boys in the ranks who seemed to do the best, under the circumstances, were hillbillies and farmers. They generally knew how to handle a rifle and were handy in repairing vehicles and other equipment. The city kids, and particularly college boys, did not fare well. I felt that I was somewhere in between. Early on, an incident arose that was to establish my reputation.

Sunday was the only day one could gain a bit of respite. There were no passes issued during basic training, so on Sunday afternoons we hung around the barrack, wrote letters, read, or maybe wandered over to the day room or to the Post Exchange (PX). One such afternoon, I was lying on my bunk dozing. Suddenly the foot of my bed collapsed, partially depositing me on the floor. There was a great burst of laughter from the others present and I realized that one of them had kicked in the collapsible end of my bed. Other than having been awakened and having had to straighten my bed out, I was no worse for wear and tried to take the joke good-naturedly. I had no sooner gone back to my repose, than it happened again. This time I saw the culprit, who could hardly contain himself, he was laughing so hysterically. He was a big—very big—6'4," 265-pound Midwestern farm boy. I told him to "knock it off or I would give him something to think twice about." Within minutes he was back again, kicking at my bed. This time, I jumped up and we started throwing punches. Our fighting quickly turned to grappling and my college wrestling experience came into play.

We ended up on the floor at the foot of a bed with his head up against one of the square 4"x 4" posts spaced down the center of the room to support the ceiling. I had him in a headlock with my arms around the post, pressing the side of his head and face into a sharp edge of the column. As I squeezed with all my might, he bellowed in pain. The commotion brought a noncom from an end room. To his queries, someone shouted, "He's going to kill him!" I was ordered to stop and was pulled off my opponent. After that, an uneasy peace settled over the room and I went about my business, not speaking to anybody. The word spread through the company, however, and from then on I was given a wide berth.

One aspect of off-duty life in the barracks I found to be a nuisance was the interminable card games and gambling. There would always be one corner of the room with soldiers playing, at times for high stakes, and always with some commotion, as a pot was won or lost. I tried my hand at a card game early on, but was no match for the very skillful card sharks, who always congregated at these sessions. It seemed that the company cooks, wherever I was assigned, practiced card playing as an avocation and many came away rich in the process. As a big city boy, I thought myself adept at shooting craps, but there as well, after dropping $11–$12 (which was more than half of my first month's pay before deductions), I quickly forswore any further such activity. Every once in a while, however, it proved entertaining to watch when these games involved really high-rollers and pots of hundreds of dollars and, a few times, even more.

Mother saved many of my letters from the Army, and I was able to piece together much of those initial experiences. They were filled with complaints about sore feet, KP and latrine duty, and many references to efforts to get out of the unit and into the Air Corps. I requested that she send me additional underwear, sweat socks, a pants presser, and a small travel iron my sister Johanna had used on her trips to Europe. These latter items indicated that I had already started a sideline, which was to earn me additional money during my service as an enlisted man. It began when we were issued our first unit shoulder patches, a red and white number "2" designating the Second Army. We were ordered to have them sewn on by the next morning's formation, which presented real difficulties for those endeavoring to use the tailor shop at the PX.

I blessed my mother for training me to sew and iron and promptly earned an extra $3–$4 that night, a lot of money for a $21-a-month private. I have always had a fastidious streak in my nature, inherited from my father. It annoyed me greatly, therefore, when my uniform appeared even slightly unpressed, thus detracting from a reputation of being a "sharp-looking soldier." Using a footlocker covered with an army blanket and the little pants presser and midget travel iron, I soon became the barrack tailor.

Our letters home were not censored at this point, as they later were once we reached the port of embarkation and went overseas. A letter of April 22, 1943, expressed my satisfaction over having been made the "company draftsman." I explained it was "a job that is half engineer and half surveyor and necessitates using the full capacity of my mathematics. It is somewhat of an improvement over digging holes." Looking at that comment today, I can only utter, "What mathematics?" Someone must have examined my personnel file and noted that I had an art school background and had taken "drafting." This seemed enough to qualify me for the job. I was set to work placing the appropriate markings on printed maps and drafting (simply drawing) others, which was fine. I had escaped that sweaty, dirty fieldwork.

As our basic training drew to a close, we were informed that our unit would be going out on maneuvers. In conjunction with that activity, I was to prepare maps of our bivouac areas and marching routes, all of which had to be hurriedly accomplished. Everything went well, up to a point. Our company had been in the field a day or two when the unforgivable occurred. The mess truck carrying hot food to soldiers, who had been living on cold field rations, attempted to ford a stream at my map-designated crossing point. Onlookers gasped as the truck submerged and stalled out in the middle. When the word of what had happened got out, I was not the company's most popular soldier.

In the latter part of May 1943, we were all routed out one night and ordered to pack rain gear and entrenching tools. We were loaded onto trucks and driven to a train siding, where we boarded boxcars for an unknown destination. Our train departed into the night and after several hours of an uncomfortable ride, we came to a stop and were ordered to unload. As the door slid open, we looked out on an expanse of water as far as the horizon. Here and there, one noted the upper portions of trees above the water and the roof of a house or two. We were in the middle of a vast flood plain, with the railroad track the only area not inundated. Our location was Oklahoma, about thirty miles northwest of Tulsa, in an area bounded by the Verdigris and the Neosho Rivers, the banks of which had overflowed in a year of exceptionally heavy rains. We worked for days, sandbagging the tracks, telephone poles, and railroad bridges along that narrow strip. At times, one would slip and lodge waist or chest deep in the cold water. It was a happy company of soldiers able to return to the barracks and a hot shower following that ordeal.

At the conclusion of the flood detail, the Army's administrative machine caught up with me. I was summoned to company headquarters and asked why I was in this unit when I had been designated for the Air Corps. I was told that I was to report the following week for a physical examination at the camp hospital, prior to being sent to Texas. Oh! Wonderful news! The very next day at formation, several names were read out, including mine, as part of an order transferring us to Lincoln, Nebraska. At first I thought it had something to do with my air cadet training, but I soon learned that I was being sent to the Army Specialized Training Program (ASTP).[4] As we were then made to understand, there was a shortage of officers and this training led to a commission. That was fine, but I still wanted to be a pilot. I was told in no uncertain terms, however, that ASTP was a high priority activity and took precedence.

In a day and a half, I was on my way to the University of Nebraska at Lincoln and back to college, wondering whatever happened to the time when I saw no way of ever getting out of the Signal Corps. After more than two months in the Ozarks and the rigors of basic training, I was almost overcome by the sight of the University of Nebraska campus, with all the pretty coeds leisurely strolling to their classes or sitting on the lawns. It was June and life was beautiful! We soon learned that we were in a STAR unit, which was an acronym for an assembly point. From there, depending on one's specialty, we would be sent to a college elsewhere in the country. We were to be categorized as engineering, language (German-Japanese), or medical trainees. It seemed logical to me that I would be chosen for German language training, since my records already indicated a background and studies in that area. The two weeks in Lincoln were pleasant ones, with little to do but wait for an assignment. My heart twinged, however, whenever I saw a contingent of air cadet trainees march by singing "Off we go into the wild blue yonder." In turn, our ASTP STAR unit would pass by them, bellowing out another tune at the top of our voices.

Some mention of singing in the services is warranted. In World War II, when a body of men marched, it was customary for them to sing. The more intricate the singing, interspersed with cadence counting, the sharper the unit. A commonly sung cadence was, "I had a good home, but I left. I had a good home, but I left, left, right, left." etc. At Camp Crowder, we often sang such songs as "I've Been Working on the Railroad," "She Wore a Yellow Ribbon," "Sunny Jim," "Clementine," and a host of others, some quite bawdy. One of our sergeants lost his stripes marching a platoon down a camp street past a senior officer's wife, while singing one of the lewd verses of "Sunny Jim." Singing did something for the esprit of a unit. It was an impressive experience later in my service to see, hear, and at times be part of a company of paratroopers in full battle gear coming down the road singing their "Airborne Song."

Soon rumors were rife that a contingent would be sent to a college in Rhode Island. My first thought was that it might be Brown University, which would be a real stroke of luck. My brother-in-law, Alfred, was an assistant professor there, and it would be wonderful to be close to my sister Eleanor and their family. Word was then passed that the group going there would be engineers. Consequently, I thought that would leave me out. It seems that I still had learned little about the Army. When the orders were read out assigning individuals to engineering training at Rhode Island State College, my name was among them. I was not in a German language–training program and I was not going to Brown, but things could have been worse. Eleanor and Alfred were a half hour away and it was only a two-hour train ride to New York City. For all practical purposes, I was back home!

Our contingent arrived at Rhode Island State in Kingston on a beautiful afternoon in mid-June. We were marched to a large dormitory building in the center of the campus named, inappropriately at least for soldiers, Eleanor Roosevelt Hall. It had been a women's dormitory with all the lavatory facilities that go with such a building, not a urinal in the place. It was a far cry, however, from a barrack and the life we had known in basic training, and we could not have been happier. Soldiers from other STAR units soon arrived, and before long our complement numbered about 400 soldiers, formed in two companies. We were issued textbooks and other materiel and promptly settled into a regimen akin to a military academy, falling out for formations at 7:30 a.m. and 1:00 p.m. and marching to classes.

The curriculum was that of any college or university placing an emphasis on engineering. Rhode Island State had a good reputation in that field. The ASTP course was highly concentrated, each semester three months in duration. I was pleased that in addition to a deluge of mathematics and science, there was a sprinkling of liberal arts courses. The curriculum was the same for everyone, with no electives. I had considerable difficulty with math and sciences, particularly chemistry, but for some strange reason, I did well in physics. In the final analysis, however, Rhode Island State was not Columbia or CCNY, nor was the student competition anywhere near comparable, and I managed as well as most.

On the other hand, I excelled in the liberal arts courses. I particularly remember an English composition class. In response to a homework assignment, I wrote a lengthy stream of consciousness piece in blank verse that I was almost afraid to turn in. I need not have been. The professor, a rather avant-garde type in his late forties, was absolutely ecstatic over my effort. He encouraged me to write further. The result was the same. After months in basic training, my mind was a wild mix of swirling thoughts and this was cathartic. I doubt if I have ever had more fun dashing off whatever I felt, being treated like a budding Walt Whitman or Carl Sandburg, and getting As to boot.

The Army leadership at the College made a distinct effort to retain as much of the ethos of military life as possible. There was a good deal of marching around, constant inspections, and strenuous physical training. Infractions of the rules were dealt with severely. A much-used punishment was to have a soldier march the campus quadrangle laden with full field equipment for hours on end. I was once meted out this "instruction" at a time when I had to wear overshoes and I can testify to its effectiveness. In addition to the sheer physical exhaustion of the punishment, there was the added embarrassment of being observed by everyone attending classes, particularly giggling coeds.

Two unusual physical training activities took place during my stay at Rhode Island State that I will never forget. The first was a game, invented by one of the coaches, designed to toughen us. Called "Murder Ball," it was played with a very large, heavy, leather medicine ball. The game had no rules to speak of other than prohibiting punching and could be played by any equal number of participants. The object simply was to move that ponderous ball over the opponents' goal line by any means possible in a group effort. Play stopped only when a goal was scored. The huge ball was too heavy to throw and the game soon became a pushing, wrestling, and shoving match, with elbows and knees flying everywhere. It was the rare soldier who did not receive a cut, lump, or black eye from this play and it soon filled the college infirmary with its casualties. I once spent a day in the infirmary with a mild concussion. Although a great sport while it lasted, the civilian authorities, irritated with the drain on medical resources, soon saw to the game's demise.

While we were there, the college was in the national spotlight for its basketball team. Coach Keany had developed a strategy for high scoring, and State was one of the first to regularly score points in three digits. It was among the top teams in the country at the time. Those were the days before the introduction of giant basketball players, and its star was a slight, average height (perhaps 5'10") player, whose name was Ernie Caverly. On one occasion, a group of us in ASTP got to play in a practice game against

State. We had two or three fair college-level players among us and a few like me who just enjoyed the game. Much to our surprise, we were about a quarter into the game when State began complaining about our rough-house tactics. I was playing guard, and my strategy was to meet Caverly as far out from the basket as possible and keep him from shooting, since he was a deadeye shot. At one point I must have been too rough, for Coach Keany ran on to the court and berated me, shouting, "What are you trying to do, cripple my boy?" I only played the first half, but my colleagues went on to win a game that was quietly forgotten.

My time at Kingston, Rhode Island, differed markedly from our earlier army training. We were generally free to depart the campus after the 1:00 p.m. formation and inspection on Saturdays until roll call at 7:30 a.m. on Monday mornings. A soldier could leave provided he had no demerits or weekend duty, and enough money. On average, that worked out to receiving a pass two or three weekends a month. There was always a rush to the station on Saturday afternoon to catch the train to New York or other nearby cities. It was wonderful to be able to see my parents regularly. On occasion, I would also visit my sisters, Eleanor in Providence or Johanna in Cambridge. The experience at Camp Crowder made me appreciate these privileges, but I had no real idea how precious they were until the army sent me overseas for years without seeing my family at all. Reading the letters Mother saved from this period, I was struck by how uninformative they were. There is very little discussion of the curriculum or any detail about persons with whom I associated or about life in the unit, other than a number of complaints about punishment meted out for infractions. It would have been interesting at that stage to recollect more about partici-pating in a program that attempted to emulate West Point.[5]

I spent nine relatively enjoyable months in the ASTP. It would have been more pleasant, had I not struggled with a condensed engineering curriculum. As time went on, it became more and more obvious that the program was not going to lead to the commission we had expected. Con-sequently, I endeavored again to pursue my candidacy for Air Corps pi-lot training. It might have been easy to do this from outside the service, but from the inside there always seemed to be a bureaucratic tangle and months went by without any results. Returning from leave over Christmas in 1943, I noted a request on the company bulletin board for volunteers for paratroop training and I spoke to the First Sergeant about the matter.[6] A few weeks later, we began hearing rumors that ASTP was to be disbanded. The war news was filled with reports of heavy fighting in Italy and the Pa-cific and there was a desperate need for infantry replacements overseas. It seemed highly illogical to me, however, that the government would spend all that money to train us and then use us as infantry replacements.

By February, we were taking our finals, considerably distracted by reports that we soon would be sent to the 78th (Lightning) Infantry Division, which was preparing to go overseas. Then we heard that we would go to the 26th (Yankee) Infantry Division.[7] All of this was very unsettling, not only for us, but also for the college authorities. Despite the problems posed by a large body of soldiers attending classes completely separate from the rest of the students, retrenching to a smaller civilian school was going to create difficulty for them, particularly because of the loss of federal funds. As for the male civilian students, I am sure they were delighted to see us go, while many a female heart would be broken with our departure.

One morning in late February, a list of names was read off, mine among them. We were told to get ready to ship out at a moment's notice, although most of the unit remained. The following day our group was taken to the station. We boarded a regular train going south. Our train passed through New Haven, New York, and Philadelphia. In Washington, we changed trains and boarded the Southern Railroad, and again the officer-in-charge said nothing. I was deeply puzzled. What was so secret about us and why were we not told where we were going? During the night, we passed through Richmond and then Chattanooga, heading west in Tennessee.

Mid-morning, we came to a stop at Tullahoma, a small town in the south central part of Tennessee. We detrained quickly and lined up on the station platform as we received our first glimpse of our future hosts: tough-looking noncoms in jumpsuits and fatigues. We all noted their ominous shoulder patches, a black circle framing a gold eagle's talon. Above that, also in black, was a strip that contained the word "AIRBORNE" in gold. "Holy mackerel," I thought, "The Sarge really acted on my conversation with him about the paratroops!" The noncoms, rather than walking, trotted up and down, and from then on everything was "on the double." We were hurriedly loaded onto a truck, commonly referred to as a six-by-six, and took off with a roar. Before long, the highway widened and we came to an MP post with a gate. Off in the center strip of the divided highway was a large sign, which read, "WELCOME TO CAMP FORREST, THE HOME OF THE 17TH AIRBORNE DIVISION."

The truck proceeded along the post road, past platoons and companies of men running in undershirts and fatigues. There was a large open parade ground that extended for a mile or more between the barracks areas. As we went by groups of barracks, we read signs indicating units such as "Battery A, 466th Parachute Field Artillery Battalion" and "17th Abn Parachute Maintenance Company." After driving for what seemed to be many miles, we stopped at the headquarters of the 194th Glider Infantry Regiment. Our group was processed and assigned to individual units within the regiment. I was placed in a Rifle Company in the First Battalion.

By the time that day was over, my mind was a jumble of wild tales about gliders, the murderous nature of the training, and the casualties the company had received completing that training. I was back to barrack life, only now in what portended to be a far more dangerous existence. The personnel in the company were a far cry from those in ASTP, or for that matter in the 34th Signal Construction Battalion. They were a much tougher lot. Where previously I had been digging holes and climbing telephone poles, my regimen now consisted of a lot of calisthenics, marching, rifle practice, bayonet drill, and hand-to-hand combat training.

I soon took my first glider flight, in a WACO CG-4A.[8] Driven out to a nearby airfield, our squad of twelve soldiers boarded the glider. I was astounded by how flimsy the glider was—nothing but metal rods covered with doped fabric and a plywood floor. A pilot and copilot, both Air Corps lieutenants, sat up front behind a large, grilled Plexiglas nose. A long thick rope, 375 feet in length, was attached to the nose and lay loosely on the ground, extending to a two-engine, salmon-colored C-47 aircraft. We waited in anticipation as the C-47 warmed up and started to roll. We felt a spongy tug as the rope tightened and we started down the concrete runway. Watching as we became airborne, we noted that the C-47 was below us, still on the ground. I thought that plane would never take off! Soon we were flying at 1500–2000 feet and the thought struck me that I had never been off the ground before and here I was in this contraption. I experienced all the initial sensations of flying and then some.

Looking out a small, porthole-like, side window, I noted the wings flapping up and down. The canvas sides made a high-pitched rustling sound. The pilots frantically pumped foot pedals and turned little wheels above their heads in the nose of the glider. I was beginning to enjoy watching the Tennessee countryside below, when the WACO lurched and I saw the towline whip away. The pilot had cut us loose. Someone shouted, "Here we go!" The glider took a sharp bank to the left, and we circled downward. Our heads had been filled the previous week with talk about glider crashes into trees, lakes, and buildings, so I did not know what to expect. The pilots busily made adjustments with their little wheels and foot pedals as the ground rushed up at us. We all held our breath. Suddenly, there was a loud "bam" and then a great deal of bouncing around, and we were back down on the runway. You could hear the sighs of relief as we finally rolled to a stop. We were ordered out of the glider, lined up, and marched off.

I thought to myself, "That wasn't so bad." Had I a bit more of the experience I was to gather later, I would have reserved judgment. On a beautiful day, with no wind, we had landed on a concrete runway. There were to be other days in practice that were not so nice, when I was to land in rough, open fields. Even that was by no means comparable to crash-landing under combat conditions in enemy territory at night, taking heavy anti-aircraft and machine gun fire.

I had been at Camp Forrest a few weeks when it was announced that a provisional parachute school was to be set up by the division, obviating the necessity of training at Fort Benning, Georgia. Soldiers of the 17th Airborne glider units watched with interest the construction of a wooden 34-foot tower, a mock-up of a C-47 fuselage, and a series of six-foot platforms. Ft. Benning's trademark 250-foot-high parachute tower, however, was missing. In late April, a request for volunteers was sent down to every unit and a fair number of us stepped forward. I intended from the outset to enter parachute training, so I was spared the nonsense I had previously experienced when attempting to transfer to different duty.

Gaining paratrooper status meant an immediate 100 percent increase in pay for a private such as myself—from $50 to $100 a month, a princely sum. Furthermore, had I known what I was to learn later in July, when I was assigned special duty with gliders, I certainly would have preferred going into combat using a parachute. In keeping with the saying that in life everything seems to happen at once, no sooner was I set for paratrooper training, than I was told that I was to be transferred from the 194th Glider Infantry Regiment to another unit within the division. My old nemesis, the auditory test at Camp Dix, had come to the fore again. The army needed code radio operators, and I was to be sent to the 517th Airborne Signal Company to receive jump and radio training as part of that unit. An interesting aspect of this instruction was that in combat, radiomen jumped with a fair-sized radio strapped to one leg, which was loosened during the drop and dangled on a rope below so that it landed separately, to prevent injury to the jumper. That might have been the case in theory, but in combat it turned out that, to avoid ground fire, paratroopers dropped at such a low altitude they had a difficult time dealing with the radio.

I had barely settled in at the 517th, when my radio operator training began. I may have done well in the auditory test, but in application I proved to be a washout. The da-dit-da and dit-dit-da beamed into the earphones had soothed me and I could not stay concentrated. Either my mind would wander or I would begin to doze. My heart was simply not in that activity, and I would use some of the training period for correspondence. In a letter to my parents on May 19, 1944, I explained that, "I am in the code room again. This is the only place I seem to be able to find time to write." I went on to state that the pre-jump physical conditioning was getting tougher and tougher and that I was scheduled to make three parachute jumps the week of June 5th. The afternoon of June 5th, when I made my first jump, was the same hour, given the time differential, that American paratroopers in England boarded their planes for the D-Day drop in Normandy.

Jump school consisted of a two-week period of intense conditioning involving interminable calisthenics, long marches, clambering over obstacle courses, and constant double-timing. There was a great deal of hazing. We did push-ups at the instructor's slightest whim. We were taught at the command of "JAB!" to immediately assume the crouched, bent-knee, legs-together, arms-close-to-the-body, parachute landing position. We never knew when an instructor would utter this command to a student, day or night, in the chow line or on the parade ground. Failure to respond instantly was punished by the order, "Give me 20!" or "Give me 30!" or sometimes more, push-ups. Later, after further conditioning, we were introduced to the jump platforms, the C-47 mock-ups, and the 34-foot tower.

The jump platforms were flat structures about six feet high, designed to help us practice parachute landings. Students in single file would run up the stairs on one side and, on command, jump off the front of the platform, landing in a crouched position on the balls of the feet, while twisting slightly so as to fall on the sides of the calf and thigh entering a body roll. We spent many hours on this exercise, until it almost became second nature to us. Next, we moved to the simulated airplane with its mock door. The students were generally divided into groups of nine called "sticks." There were two sticks to a planeload, seated facing each other along the interior and extending to the rear of the aircraft. We were taught on signal to "Stand up!" "Hook up!"—attach our static lines to the steel cable running down the center of the plane. "Count off!"—shout out numbers to indicate readiness. "Stand in the door!" and "Go!"—jump. These steps were thoroughly drilled into us until our responses became automatic.

The top of the 34-foot tower resembled the open door of a plane. A cable attached above the door angled downward and was fastened to a large strong post, 150–175 feet away. The student, wearing a parachute harness with a static line about 15 feet long, would jump at the instructor's command and fall freely until he reached the end of the line, which was attached to a pulley. Then, he would receive a vicious jerk and whisk down to the ground at about 20–25 miles an hour. At the end of this joy ride, he was to hit the earth in the proper paratrooper position.

One unforgettable incident I witnessed at the tower soon became the talk of the camp. We were taken out to the training area one morning, lined up in formation, and given instruction. After a few demonstration jumps and slides, a squad in single file climbed up the tower and proceeded to jump. I was surprised at the reticence of several of the students, since this contraption, really at most only three or four stories tall, was nothing like leaping out of an airplane. Subsequently, I learned that the proximity of the ground actually had a more unnerving effect on many people than great heights, which tend to lend an air of unreality to the situation.

As the first group went through, the rest of us sat in place on the dusty field, watching. Perhaps twenty-five or thirty jumpers had completed the exercise when, with a loud "twang," the cable broke, dropping an unfortunate fellow straight to the ground. The impact on the audience was profound. The instructors promptly called us to attention and marched us out of the area. We later heard that the victim had been critically injured and hospitalized, but we never found out if he survived.

My turn to jump from the 34-foot tower came the following day. Of course, we all wondered if the cable had been repaired properly or whether we were to have a repeat performance of the previous day's accident. Once I stood in the door at the top of the tower I realized that, indeed, the height took on a more awesome aspect. Nevertheless, I had no problem leaping out on command, receiving a spine-stretching jerk at the end of the static line, and whizzing along down the cable. I hit the ground with considerable force, but employing the parachute landing technique I had been taught, I rolled and bounced up no worse for wear. Before it was all over, I had made a number of jumps from the 34-foot tower.

As we approached the time when we were to jump from planes, we were taken out to a building located at the airfield used by the Division's Parachute Maintenance Company and taught by the paratrooper "riggers" to pack a parachute. Each soldier was to pack his own. I doubt if ever one could find a more attentive audience, as the riggers explained each of the fine points. The silk panels were folded like this, the suspension lines were laid out like that, rubber bands held the folded lines and so it went. This was before the introduction of nylon and we were told that it was important with silk to prevent dampness and static electricity. Either could cause a "streamer," a malfunction of the 'chute in which it came out of the backpack, but failed to pop open. A streamer was also known as a "cigar," because of the shape the closed parachute took as it fluttered above the falling jumper. We were also told at the time about an incident involving an intrepid lieutenant colonel who maintained that by keeping one's cool, it was possible to shake out a damp silk malfunction. To prove his point, he soaked a parachute in a bucket of water, packed it, and then jumped. There is supposedly a monument to him somewhere down at Ft. Benning.

I can assure you, that I packed my parachute with great care, but was distressed later when I was handed one with no way of identifying whether it was actually mine or not. Subsequently, all of our parachutes were packed by the Maintenance Company's riggers, which made me feel better, since I really did not trust myself to do the job and worried even more about doing it for others. In preparation for jumping, we were issued protective headgear resembling old-fashioned football helmets. They were discontinued not long after I completed my training and jumpers thereafter wore standard army helmets.

By the time jump week arrived we had been well conditioned physically and mentally. There was no question in our minds that we were the toughest troops on the face of the earth. I found a letter written to my parents at this point that was hilarious in its degree of braggadocio. This and subsequent letters were always full of misguided youthful assurances: "Don't worry, nothing will ever happen to me!" When my elder son, Brad, went through parachute school thirty years later, it almost seemed poetic justice that I should be on the receiving end, given all the anxiety I must have caused my mother and father.[9]

The day of our first jump, we were driven out to the airfield in trucks and formed in companies on the tarmac. C-47s lined up on the runway. Parachutes were distributed and we paired off, assisting one another in putting on the harnesses. Then, in single file, jumpers boarded the planes, while others sat in place on the tarmac waiting their turn. The number of aircraft was limited. Each plane would take off, fly to the drop zone, and return in about twenty minutes for another load.

As the first planes returned, taxied over to us, and stopped, I witnessed a human drama. One of our number exited the door of the second plane and walked across the expanse of the tarmac toward us. The jumpmaster strode along behind him. It suddenly dawned on me, as it must have on the others around me, that he had "frozen in the door" and been afraid to jump. The erstwhile paratrooper passed by all of us, and I was stunned to recognize my friend, a tall, handsome college boy who had come down from my ASTP unit. The look on his face was indescribable. I resolved in that moment, were they even to take the parachute away from me up there, I would rather go out the door without it, than face the shame of walking before that audience and the unbearable consequences of my action for the rest of my life. I never saw my friend again. He and others who did not jump were quietly shipped out of camp, whither I did not find out.

When our turn to board the C-47 came, we loaded quickly in the sequence of the positions we had been assigned in the two "sticks" of nine. I was positioned not far from the open door. Never having been in an airplane before but having been up in a glider, I wondered whether the sensations would be similar. It did not take long to find out. They were not. The plane's engines started with a whine, then a cough, and finally a roar. Unlike in the glider, you could feel the power as the entire fuselage vibrated and surged forward. With the door off, the noise was deafening. The propellers and the motion blasted wind into the cabin. To be heard one had to shout. Once more, I found myself fascinated by what I could see of the earth below through the small window at my back and a portion of the open door visible to me.

Before long, we received a warning that we were nearing the drop zone and we all stood up, hooked up, and counted off. The jumpmaster readied us with the command, "Stand in the door!" As a red warning light turned to green, a loud, clanging buzzer went off and the lead jumper left the plane. The rest of us pressed forward rapidly. I barely had time to place my hands on the sides of the door, fingers together, thumbs down in the appropriate manner, before the jumpmaster shouted "Go!" in my ear, and whacked me on the leg. Out I went into the prop-blast counting, "one thousand, two thousand, three thousand...!" Waiting for the parachute to open as I dropped in wind-blown space, my mind thought, "Should I pull my reserve chute?" Just then, I felt a terrific wrench. Looking up, I saw the sweet darling open as nicely as you please.

We made our training jumps at heights between 1000 and 1200 feet — high by combat standards — so I had a chance in the next 40–45 seconds to focus on the terrain below. It was a lovely sight, everything in miniature. The wind swished gently as I swayed to and fro. Unfortunately, with a parachute only 28 feet in diameter, it does not take long to come down. I landed in the middle of a plowed field with a good deal of force, but I was in fine shape. There was a mild breeze blowing. I pulled on the risers and spilled the air from my parachute, rolled it up and packed it in a bag, thinking, "Piece of cake!" Euphoric over my own situation, I did not pay much attention at the time to what was happening to other jumpers. A shout from a noncom alerted me to the fact that they were dropping around me. Having someone else land on you at parachute speed could cause serious injury. I moved quickly off the field to an assembly area, where we boarded trucks back to camp.

There was considerable discussion on the way back about other jumpers' experiences. One had encountered a "Mae West" (a suspension line over the top of the canopy) and another a delayed opening. This talk tended to deflate my own rosy outlook. However, there had been no fatalities, at least none of which we were aware. It was not unusual in those days to lose two or three men when jumping a regiment; the equipment was a far cry from today's standards.

The following three days were among the worst in my life. It started with the ride out to the airfield the next day after lunch. It was warm and sunny and we were fully loaded in trucks proceeding out in convoy for our second jump. When we came to a bend in the road, the convoy slowed down to about twenty miles an hour. Sitting on benches that ran along the inside of the canvas-covered vehicle, some of us dozed. A fellow across from me seated next to the tailgate appeared to be sound asleep. A practical joker leaned close to his ear and shouted, "Jab!" The sleeper in reflex action leaped up, assumed the parachute landing position, and fell over the tailgate out of the truck. The driver in the following vehicle swerved and slammed on his brakes. A combination of the quick action of that driver and the sleeper's rolling off to the side of the road in true paratrooper fashion prevented a serious accident that day.

Arriving at the airfield, we repeated the previous day's procedures. I was positioned in about the same place in the plane. When my turn came, I jumped, counted, felt my parachute open, and then it happened. I dropped sharply. Looking up, I saw another trooper walking around on the top of my canopy. He slipped off to one side and the next thing I knew he was in my shrouds like a bird in a cage. His parachute collapsed partially, as did mine, and they started to twirl around one another. In no time, we hit the ground. I landed with a vicious thud and went into a forward roll. I did not see the other fellow come down, but I heard him in pain after landing. Observers on the ground witnessed our plight and before I could get to him, they shouted for medical attention. I was badly shaken, and he was taken to the hospital. I later learned he had a broken leg.

Returning to camp that evening I was less sanguine about it all. The mood in the mess hall at supper was more somber than it had been the previous evening. I attributed this to a greater awareness of the jumping experience. The first time, we were really oblivious to what was happening, but now we could see the dangers inherent in the situation. I also learned that after I had left the plane, two others had "frozen in the door."

I slept fitfully that night. I would not have slept at all had I any idea what the next day would bring. We were taken out to the airfield early in the morning. Again, it was a sunny, late spring day. Parachutes were distributed, we paired off helping each other into the harnesses, and sat in formation, waiting to be taken aloft. We were told, weather and wind permitting, we would make two jumps that day. Boarding the plane this time, I was seated near the open door and had a fine opportunity to observe all that was occurring. At the proper time I exited counting, "One thousand, two thousand, three thousand! "I waited for what seemed to be an eternity and nothing happened. There was no vicious jerk. I sensed that I had fallen free of the plane and that my parachute had been pulled out of the pack, but there had been no opening "pop." I thought, "Oh, Lord no, I've got a streamer!" Then, I told myself that I was just scared and that I had compressed the time too much. The chute would open any millisecond. The mind races unbelievably in these circumstances.

Convincing myself that, indeed, I was in trouble, I started to pull the "D" ring of my reserve. As I did so, I received a tremendous wrench. My main chute opened. However, the pull caused me to yank the "D" ring loose. My reserve was spilling out and might well foul my main. I did my best to clutch the reserve together on my chest. Totally absorbed with my predicament, I was unable to grasp the risers to prepare myself for a landing. I was coming in backwards at considerable speed. As I landed, my feet flipped up and I took the shock on my back, head, and shoulders. I lay there for some time until supervisory personnel came. An officer asked me if I was all right and if anything was broken. I got up and fell down and then got up again. I seemed in one piece. The officer commented that he had seen me descend and asked why I had taken so long to pull my reserve. What if my main had not opened? It only takes about eight seconds to hit the ground that way. I was numb all over and had nothing to say. Although I did not know it at the time, that fall resulted in my requiring medical treatment in the following weeks and was to cause me grief for the rest of my life.

At the conclusion of the morning's training, we returned to camp for lunch. Driving back out to the airfield that afternoon, I was beginning to take a fatalistic attitude toward the entire procedure. I reasoned that I had been through my share of bad luck and that not much more could happen to me. Most of the other soldiers, although still apprehensive, were getting into the routine of jumping. As I sat in the plane on takeoff, I thought only two more jumps to go and then I would get my wings and the furlough that usually accompanies graduation from parachute school. Soon we were over the drop zone. At the jumpmaster's commands, we stood up, performed the exit drill, and then with a rush, virtually on top of one another, we went out the door into the prop-blast. I counted, felt the parachute open, and was about to take in the ride, when I heard loud cursing. Another jumper swung into me. Our parachutes collided and began a deadly twisting around each other, spilling air.[10]

For what seemed an eternity, we descended that way until we struck the earth, one slightly above the other. We hit hard, but in a forward motion position so that both of us were able to achieve a minimal parachute landing and a roll. I was unhurt and so was he. Shouting at each other, I said that I felt him "ride" me out the door. He was too close. His reply was that I had not "slipped away" (pulled on my risers to drop) fast enough. Though we let off steam in shouting, we both knew we had been very lucky.

At the close of the day, I was called to the Company Orderly room. One of the officers admonished me, saying, "What the hell is it with you, soldier? Every Goddamn time you get up there, something happens!" He could understand one collision, but two—something was wrong. I could only reply: "Sir, I did what I was supposed to do." Seeing that I might have been unnerved by the events of the past three days, he compassionately asked me whether I was going to be able to make the night jump all right. I retorted, "Yes, sir!" In my heart, however, I was not so sure.

To make matters worse, we were told that we would not be making the night jump until the day after next, a full 48 hours or more away. That jump was to be made with full equipment, and we were to wear steel helmets, instead of the protective headgear, to simulate a combat drop. Participating in training activities and at meals during the following days, I sensed that others considered me a jinx, some sort of a pariah. I felt terribly alone. I look back on that time today with amazement. I do not know how I was able to withstand the sheer terror that encompassed me. It could only have been my mother's prayers. Everyone was on edge about the night jump. There is something frightening about darkness and not being able to see where one is landing. I kept telling myself, as I am sure countless other paratroopers have done before and since, "If other fellows can do it, so can I."

It was June and darkness did not fall until late, when we loaded on to the trucks and drove out to the airfield. The night imparted an eerie quality to things around us. We were now used to seeing the C-47s lined up on the runway. But somehow, the engines warming up sounded louder, the flashes of firelight from the cowlings more forbidding. There were lights on the tarmac. Nevertheless, as we helped each other put on the parachute harnesses, we were especially careful to make sure that it was done correctly. Having additional equipment made everything more difficult. I worried particularly about my steel helmet staying on through the opening shock. There had been all kinds of stories the previous days about the heavy helmets coming off during a jump and "raining down" on the men who had landed below.

In single file, we climbed into the dimly lit aircraft, seated ourselves, and waited for take-off. It is not easy to fit oneself with parachute and equipment in a small C-47 bench seat. As the plane taxied down the runway and we headed aloft into the wind, I looked across at the tense faces of the other paratroopers in that half-light. Up forward, the cockpit door was open and the pilots talked laxly. The jumpmaster was businesslike as he peered out of the open door at the ground below. It was a fine clear night and he seemed to have no trouble identifying landmarks.

As we neared our destination, the warning light went on, and I flinched with the jarring sound of the buzzer. On command, we all stood up and hooked up. The buzzer sounded again, the green light flashed, and we shuffled rapidly to the door. As I came to it and exited, it seemed as if I were entering a large, dark, windblown, empty room. I am not sure I even counted, but I must have. I felt the parachute open and looked up. I knew it was there, but I could hardly see it. All I saw was a brilliant heaven, full of stars. The parachute appeared vaporous, and I could see stars through it. I was in a fairyland full of beauty and wonder and the air around was gentle, almost caressing. I was up there a long time and had a chance to drink it all in. Landing lightly on my feet, I felt like a fool for going into a roll and not simply walking away. That experience will live with me forever.

The day following the night drop, I commented to a noncom, who was an experienced parachutist, that I seemed to hang in the air forever during that jump. He explained that night air is heavy and full of moisture. Consequently, one descends more slowly. To further clarify matters, on landing the night before, I noted that, instead of the previously used white parachute, I had been given a camouflaged one. Perhaps, that is why I saw stars through the silk. It was not until more than a week later that all of the students passed the provisional parachute school. Rumor had it that before we had finished, there had been four fatalities. At a parade of the entire 17th Airborne Division, we were presented our paratrooper's wings. I doubt if I have ever been prouder of anything in my life. From this point on, I would be getting $50 a month extra pay, for which I would have to qualify by making a jump every 90 days.

A short time afterward, I left Camp Forrest for New York City on furlough. Everywhere I went at home, I was lionized, with people asking me in awe what it felt like to jump out of an airplane. It was a heady time. I was brought to reality periodically, however, when I encountered a highly decorated soldier home from overseas, or even more pointedly, a wounded veteran. My war, I realized, had not yet even begun. Coming back to camp after leave, I was again immersed in unit training, which for me also included radio operator school. It did not take long for me to convince my superiors that I was not suited for the latter. The question of what to do with me then arose. Given my choice, I would have transferred to the 513th Parachute Infantry Regiment, to my mind the elite organization in the Division. To the powers that be, however, I was a college boy and a jumper and those were qualities not to be parted with lightly. I was reassigned to the Message Center Section of the company, the communications hub of the division. There one routed messages, encrypted them when appropriate, and provided courier services between the units.

I was promptly exposed to the M209 converter, a machine the size of a small loaf of bread, which laboriously encoded communications. It seemed to me at the outset that this apparatus had little value for an airborne division, where the chances of capture after dropping into combat behind enemy lines were so high. Then, in a move that was later to have great portent, while still in the section I was simply detailed out to the airfield to work at "loading and lashing," since an airborne signal company could be expected to take considerable equipment into combat. At first, I thought I would be engaged with C-47s, but there was not much "loading and lashing" to be done with regard to those aircraft. It was in the gliders that one loaded jeeps, trailers, and artillery pieces. The British, I was told, were even putting a small tank into one of their larger gliders.[11] I would learn more than I really wanted to know about gliders. Although I had already flown in a WACO CG-4A Cargo Glider, I now became thoroughly familiar with them. Experienced personnel instructed us in loading jeeps, trailers, and other materiel. The WACO's large plexiglass nose was hinged at the top to allow raising it. Using a low ramp, it was possible to back a jeep into its interior. Once inside, a cable and pulley-type arrangement attached to the rear of the jeep would lift the nose and pilots' seats as it drove forward out of the glider on to the battlefield. We had ample practice loading jeeps and utility trailers into WACOs.

Going into combat, jeeps would be fully gassed and trailers crammed to the limit with equipment, ammunition, or gasoline. While actual loading was accomplished readily, the skill came in the lashing and seeing that the weight was properly distributed. If not tied down properly, a jeep or a trailer the size of a jeep could easily come loose in flight. Because of the air turbulence caused by the motors of the tow-planes, gliders tended to bounce around a great deal. Even the slightest rough weather played havoc with their flight. After a few days working on the ground, our crew was ready to put our learning to the test. We loaded a jeep into a WACO. After arrangements had been made with the airbase's troop carrier headquarters for glider pilots and a C-47 tow-plane, we were ready to go.

Throughout the war, there always was a great shortage of glider pilots. It was our understanding, whether true or not, that they were mostly washed-out fighter and bomber pilots. They served their country well, however, in an exceedingly dangerous assignment and sustained far higher casualties than the rest of their Air Corps brethren.

With the jeep taking up virtually the entire interior, we felt our visibility impeded. At least half of our group were jumpers, and the suggestion was made that we leave the little side door of the glider off, C-47 paratrooper-style, so that we could see the ground below. The pilots posed no objection to this, since they tended to block the forward view out of the plexiglass nose. We experienced the usual sensations of glider takeoff and soon were flying high above the countryside. This was not a short orientation flight, as had earlier been the case for me, but a simulated combat run. The only exception was that we were not to crash-land, but come down on the runway on our return. We were in the air about fifteen to twenty minutes watching the wings flap and listening to all the glider rippling noises, creaks and groans, when disaster struck. A loud ripping sound met our ears and the canvas material on the right side of the WACO peeled off, exposing the frame. We looked out into open space in disbelief.

The pilots immediately became aware of the problem and moved to bring us down on an emergency basis. Their efforts were hastened by further sounds of ripping canvas, which may have been caused by the air buildup from the open door. As we picked up speed, in excess of 125 mph, there was a danger that the wings might fold back and come off. We were also bouncing around severely. Thanks to our proficient lashing, at least the heavy jeep remained secure. The pilots were determined to make it back to the runway, rather than attempt an open-field, combat-style landing. Who could blame them for not wanting to crash-land with a jeep directly behind their seats?

Fortunately, we were relatively high when we dropped the towline. Also, we had been in a circling pattern not too far out from the airfield. With a gliding ratio of 12 to 1, the WACO made it back to a relatively smooth part of the field, if not the runway. Other than being jostled around a bit, we were safe. We thanked our pilots profusely. Whether the open door caused the problem or not, we were never sure. Nevertheless, there were no further such deviations in glider flights. I wish I could say that this incident was the only mishap I experienced in gliders, but it was not. Even in training, there were rough landings and parted towropes, all in preparation for what someday might occur.

An Airborne division, once dropped into combat, is faced with the problem of engaging the enemy under uncontrolled circumstances. Regardless of the paratrooper's specialty, whether an infantryman or a cook, he is expected to be able to fight. His life depends on that ability. Even Airborne generals, finding themselves alone after dropping behind enemy lines, had to fight as if they were ordinary soldiers. Great stress was placed, therefore, on hand-to-hand combat, rifle practice, hand grenade drill, and the use of the bayonet and trench knife. In my own case, I became an expert marksman with the rifle, the submachine gun, the hand grenade, and, later, the .45 caliber pistol. I also received a certificate indicating that I was a "qualified gliderman." That, I might add, was a skill that I did not particularly wish to have widely publicized.

After parachute school, we continued our rigorous training until the word came in July that we were to move to a port of embarkation, preparing to ship overseas. In those final weeks, however, there was an effort to be a bit more liberal in granting weekend and three-day passes. Some of my most vivid memories relate to these brief respites. Given a weekend pass, I would join other paratroopers in a rush to leave camp for the nearest cities, Chattanooga, Nashville, or others, some 80 or 90 miles away. More likely than not, I would have less than $10 in my pocket. In a letter to my parents written from Huntsville, Alabama, I stated that I only had 27 cents, but I was off for Chattanooga a hundred miles away. How was it possible to travel and live with such meager funds? The country was far different then. As a young soldier, I could stand on any highway and count on being picked up by virtually the first vehicle that came by. A serviceman was welcome in any YMCA, civic organization, service club, or train station canteen. Volunteer townspeople would see to it that sandwiches, doughnuts, coffee, and other refreshments were provided at these places.

Sunday mornings, I would visit a nearby church. The kindnesses those congregations showered upon me touch my heart to this day. Southerners were steeped in patriotism and provided far more than their share of recruits to the airborne divisions. Not taking a visiting young paratrooper home to dinner after church was unthinkable. I sensed that I was a substitute for absent sons. Yet, this was the old South, and some things made me uncomfortable. Seeing a black soldier drinking from a segregated drinking fountain in the train station or an elderly black grandfather escorting little children step off the sidewalk as I passed made a deep impression.

One aspect of our free time I could well have done without. Something about the paratrooper mystique lent itself to raucousness and brawling. There were fights with members of any non-airborne unit on the slightest pretext. I recall meeting a lovely young lady at a swimming pool on the outskirts of Nashville one Sunday. Escorting her back downtown afterward on the bus, I heard a commotion in the street ahead. The bus stopped, and a battered head appeared in the door shouting, "Any troopers in here? We need help fighting the Air Corps!" I was not about to leave my charge, but felt, as the bus proceeded, that in her eyes I must have sacrificed some of my manhood.

One by one, the towns in the area were put off limits to the airborne, first the smaller localities, then Nashville and, finally, Chattanooga. By the time we were ready to ship out, there was no place left! I was bumptious enough on a three-day pass traveling home to New York to tell a couple of burly Marines that the only reason they did not have paratroopers in their service was that they could not get enough volunteers. This affront resulted in a brawl that saw us taken off the train by the MPs in Washington, D.C. My accusation was also incorrect; the Marines did have several paramarine battalions. I lost a precious half-day in the guardhouse near Union Station as a result. It was a great way to be introduced to the city that was to become my future workplace.

Despite the spectacular performances of the airborne divisions in the Normandy invasion, they took heavy losses. There were additional plans to mount airborne operations in southern France in August[12] and in Holland in September.[13] The 17th Airborne Division, still in the United States, was to participate in the latter. By July, we were ready for transfer to Camp Miles Standish in Massachusetts, preparatory to being shipped out of the Boston Port of Embarkation. With that move, every letter we wrote was subject to strict censorship. The army was taking no chances: "Loose lips sink ships!"

The units in my division had been honed to a fine point, creating a sense of camaraderie. The division had been at Standish a few days when, as a welcome gesture to the troops, some units including mine were taken by trucks and buses to a Boston Red Sox game. We arrived shortly before the game was to start and it struck me that rather than watch the game, I could slip out and visit my sister Johanna, who lived in Cambridge not far from the stadium. An average baseball game would take at least several hours and I could be back in my seat in half that time. I had visited Johanna before, when I was stationed in Rhode Island, so I was acquainted with the area. Telling my buddies to cover for me, I left for the men's room and Cambridge.

Johanna was not at home when I arrived but just as I was about to leave disappointed, she returned and we had a brief visit together. I told her that I was on my way overseas, to inform Mother and Dad, and to send them my love. With that I returned to the stadium, where the game was still in full sway. All would have been fine, except that early in the game, word was sent to the stadium to bring every one back immediately preparatory to shipping out. I was in a quandary. I had no idea how to get back to Camp Miles Standish or for that matter even where it was located in relation to Boston.

Luckily, I found a military liaison office at the stadium. I told them that I had been separated from my unit after going to the men's room and that before I knew it, they were gone. My story was plausible, since soldiers ordinarily were permitted to enjoy a ball game without having to leave before it was finished. I was taken from one place to another until I finally boarded a bus that took me the many miles back to the MP post at the front gate of the camp. I had no pass or other papers, since ordinarily I would not have needed them. A well-lit cyclone fence surrounded the camp as far as I could see, high enough to discourage any attempt at entry. The MPs at the gate were suspicious. Evidently Camp Miles Standish, as a port of embarkation facility, was a likely point for desertion.

It took some time to locate anyone who could help solve my problem. Finally, an officer appeared who had been charged with the responsibility for moving out the division's remaining equipment. By this time it was late in the evening. I arrived at the barrack in which I had been staying and found it deserted. All my things were gone. I went over to the building that had been our orderly room and blessedly found one of our sergeants closing things down. He was surprised to see me. I told him that I had been separated from the company at the ball game and came back as soon as I could. He commented that I was probably listed as AWOL by now or that I might even be up for desertion. "You don't fool around when you are being shipped overseas," he said. He still had to turn in some materiel and then would be joining noncoms from Division Headquarters Company to be trucked down to the port. I would go with him.

Before I could ask him where he thought my things might be, the sergeant told me to go to the supply room, where anything left in the barracks had been dumped. I did so and fortunately found the two bags that made up my possessions. While most of my clothes and equipment had already been in the bags preparatory to moving out, some good soul had put in whatever was left. In a short while we boarded the truck and drove to the dock area, where I joined the rest of the company. My friends knew that I had not deserted but were concerned that I might miss the boat, which would have been a serious matter. I was relieved beyond words to be back with the unit, but I knew I was in trouble. I reported to the First Sergeant, who said that I had been listed as AWOL and that I would be put on company punishment. Things could have been worse; I might have been subjected to a court-martial.

Boarding the troopship struck me as something right out of the movies. Assembling at dockside, we were fed coffee and doughnuts by Red Cross volunteers. A band played, as we hoisted one barrack bag on our shoulders and another under our arms and headed in single file for the ship. I could swear that they were playing "Over There" as we went up the gangplank, but that sounds so corny, perhaps my memory is playing tricks. Nevertheless, in that very moving scene I am sure most of us wondered whether we would ever come back. Our troopship was the large United States Lines' S.S. *Manhattan*. Converted to U.S. Navy specifications and camouflage-painted, it had been renamed the U.S.S. *Wakefield*. It was spacious enough to take over 10,000 men. That included most of our division plus several small units. In addition, it was capable of higher speeds and thus traveled without convoy.

Once on board, we were assigned bunks consisting of canvas tightly stretched between rectangular steel frames, stacked one above the other, four or five high. You barely had enough room to slide in between the bunks. If the soldier above you was heavy, his rear end would almost touch your stomach. Soldiers slept in shifts to accommodate the large numbers on board. At night we ran under blackout orders. Portholes were covered and there were curtain guards on the doors to the decks. The ship traveled an erratic zigzag course at speeds of 20 knots or more, resulting in considerable vibration. Throughout the voyage we were concerned about prowling German U-boats, so great care was taken not to smoke on deck at night or to throw anything overboard.[14]

The punishment for my baseball game episode started as soon as I boarded, and I reported to the kitchens for KP duty. As humorous as it may seem now, I found myself peeling a mountain of potatoes. The work was hard, but nothing like what I had done as a youngster on the MS *Kungsholm*; and the pay was much better. The Lord works in mysterious ways, and I found that my punishment was actually a blessing. Meals on shipboard were not too generous and the troops always left a little hungry. Working in the kitchens, I could dip into food being prepared, just to make sure that it was seasoned properly. Besides being on the skimpy side, some of the meals struck me as a bit incongruous, unless of course you like chunks of hot dogs in a greasy tomato sauce for breakfast.

I was permitted an hour or two of free time after we'd been at sea for a few days. I would spend these up on deck in the fresh air. High stakes gambling often took place on the afterdeck. Normally, this would not have made a lasting impression on me. However, in this instance the central figure in the games reportedly was movie star Mickey Rooney, and curiosity as well as the large sums of money involved drew numerous onlookers. I always wondered why some of the officers did not step in and stop these games, for surely they were aware of them. I do not know what unit Rooney was with, but it was not our division and I never saw him, if indeed he was actually on board.[15]

About halfway through the trip, boxing matches were arranged on deck to entertain the troops. A ring was set up and volunteers were asked to step forward. It was a loosely organized affair, which went on for several hours with quite a few three-round matches. At one point, the matchmakers looked for a partner for a soldier who appeared rather elderly. He had gray hair and a thin, wiry build. One of my friends, who had been in an earlier bout, called for me to get in the ring with him. He soon was joined by others in shouting for me to do so. Feeling forced to comply, I climbed into the ring and put on the gloves. We boxed around for about a minute, each of us throwing feeler punches, when a smile came across my opponent's face. He seemed to hesitate, and then there was a blinding flash. I literally "saw stars" as I lay on the deck. Gathering my wits, I got up (I never heard the referee count) and the fight went on. I covered up as best I could and hung on until the end of the round. I was knocked down again twice at the end of the second round before they stopped the fight. The "old man" I had been fighting was a professional boxer and sparring partner. I do not think my friends were aware of my opponent's background, at least, I hope they were not.

The ocean crossing in midsummer was not particularly rough, judged by numerous such journeys since that time. Nevertheless, there was an inordinate amount of seasickness down in our hold. Close quarters, lack of ventilation, and limited latrine facilities made it miserable for those who could not get up on deck. We saw very little of the officers during the trip, and once again I thought of how foolish I had been not to have entered an officer training program while in college. Our voyage, by those days' standards, was not a long one. However, we were all happy to receive the news that we would soon reach our destination. We were not told where that would be, but most of us surmised that it would be Europe, more specifically the British Isles.

4
Under a Wartime Sky

We made landfall on the West Coast of Britain, which was enveloped in mist, and proceeded into the estuary of the River Mersey up to Liverpool. The city appeared dirty and dingy under the gray and drizzling skies. Gazing down from the deck waiting to debark, everything seemed so small. Railroad cars at the dockside were half the size of their American counterparts; automobiles were smaller, as were the houses in the distance. This was my first time in Europe and I felt like Gulliver. Only the British Army lorries, with their drivers sitting on the "wrong side," appeared large. Everywhere there were cobblestone streets. We were marched off to a rail siding and loaded onto typical European trains, with compartments and side aisles.

As we traveled south, the countryside was lush and green. Fields were smaller and enclosed by hedgerows. I saw thatched roofs and Franconian, some would say Shakespearean, architecture. There were little villages with winding streets that contained pubs, tobacconist shops, and green grocers. This was Great Britain as it was after World War I, before all the super highways, large commercial airports, housing developments, and high rises. In many ways it was still the England of Dickens.

Passing through train stations, it seemed everyone was in uniform. Even the young women wore the brown garb of the ATS (Auxiliary Territorial Service), the blue of the RAF (Royal Air Force), or the dark blue of the RN (Royal Navy). I was struck by the noise of the heavy hobnail shoes of the British servicemen as they moved up and down the platforms. Unlike the United States, everywhere here I sensed that this was a country at war. You could read the pain that bombing, rationing, and hardship had brought in the eyes of ordinary people, despite their efforts to go on with their lives without complaining. At the conclusion of a four-hour journey, we arrived at Swindon, an industrial city 80 miles west of London. We were loaded into trucks and driven first through cobblestone streets and then along a narrow, two-lane blacktop, all of it on the left side of the road.

At the conclusion of a twenty-minute ride, we entered a British Army encampment, which appeared largely unoccupied. We were in Chiseldon Barracks, the new headquarters of the 17th Airborne Division.[1] We unloaded in an area that was to become the company motor pool and marched the short distance to our barrack. It was a long, narrow, one-story, wooden building. Doors on either side made it possible to walk through the middle of the building. This structure had three sections: two large barrack rooms housing the troops and a small center room containing a toilet closet and the doors to the outside. In each barrack room were rough, wooden, double-decker beds constructed of two by fours. In the center of the room sat a pot-bellied stove, fired by coal. This was to be our home for the next four months.

As soon as we were assigned our bunks, we went to the supply room for bedding. We were issued a coarse, white, muslin mattress cover, which we filled with fresh straw. We soon learned that there was an art to this task. With too much straw, your mattress was lumpy and high, and you rolled out of bed; with too little, the wooden slats underneath cut into your body. The straw and the covering were to be changed once a month. There were no sheets. Each man was issued two army blankets and that was all.

It was a good thing that conditions on the ship had been so incommodious. Otherwise, the comparison with barrack comfort in the States would have been worse. The main latrine and washroom facilities were located down the company street about a block away. Since showers were heated only at certain times, units used them according to a schedule. The mess hall was a consolidated activity, feeding large numbers of men. The meals in England tended to be on the sparse side. We were always hungry. Packages from home containing cookies or other food items were received with great rejoicing and it was impossible not to share them with others in the barrack. KP here, as on shipboard, was looked upon more as an opportunity than a chore.

Shortly after our arrival in Chiseldon Barracks, five of the paratroopers in my section were ordered to report to the motor pool. We were told that we were going to be trained to become couriers. While the headquarters and a large part of the division were at Chiseldon, some of our units were located elsewhere. The 507th Parachute Infantry Regiment, which had fought with the 82nd Airborne Division in Normandy, for example, was now attached to us but encamped many miles away. Furthermore, we were to be part of the XVIII Airborne Corps, comprising the 17th, 82nd and 101st Airborne Divisions plus several independent parachute infantry and artillery battalions. Going one step higher, all these American units were incorporated into a newly established First Allied Airborne Army, which also included the 1st and 6th British Airborne Divisions, the Canadian Parachute Brigade and other smaller Allied units.[2] All this extensive organization spread out over western and southern England required efficient courier service.

None of us at that moment knew that we were in for a treat. We had been working odd jobs in the motor pool for several days when delivery was made of five powerful Harley-Davidson model 45 motorcycles, the type used in the United States at that time by the state police. When informed that these were for the prospective couriers, all of us reacted as if it were Christmas morning. I do not recall that any of us had ridden a motorcycle before, but we certainly were ready to learn. More by experiment than anything else, we started them and drove them around very slowly in the spacious garage. Then we took them outside onto the large dirt field that served as the parking lot. The ground was quite uneven. Before long, there were motorcycles roaring around and bouncing over bumps everywhere. Convulsed with laughter, observers witnessed a good many spills, but they also saw a happy group of soldiers. We practiced riding for a day or so and then were put to work.

The Division Message Center sorted deliveries into various "runs," and the drivers of the five "bikes" were assigned routes, which we exchanged periodically. I had an initial run that took me south through Marlborough, Devizes, and Andover to Salisbury. Another went north through Swindon and Cirencester to Cheltenham, and yet another went east to Oxford, Reading, and, at times, London. We traveled to many other places, but these were our primary routes. We rode regardless of the weather, which, by the time we reached late November and December, became less than pleasant, even quite dangerous.

Initially, our motorcycles were stripped-down models, but after a week or so we received windshields for them. In keeping with British procedure, we were instructed to place a blue and white insignia on the windshield, designating us as couriers on "His Majesty's Business" and not, under penalty, to be delayed. Of course, we all thought this was first rate, adding even more to our feelings of self-importance. We were also issued crash helmets, much like the ones used by British paratroopers. To set us apart from the latter, I conceived the idea of painting an enlarged pair of U.S. paratrooper wings on the front of our helmets. Everyone thought that was a capital suggestion and I was set to work as the artist in our group on this task.

We cut quite a figure; pulling into Headquarters with our motors growling, ready to deliver messages to far-flung points at top speed. I can still remember the feeling of exhilaration I felt roaring down the road and meeting the occasional convoy of military vehicles. If they were a U.S. paratrooper unit, I would pull up behind the truck, give the troops inside the "parachute salute"—a salute concluded by bringing the hand down with fingers spread imitating a parachute descending—and then speed on by with their cheers ringing in my ears. My courier runs took me through some of the loveliest English countryside. I had to take care coming up over a hill on some narrow lane not to run into a herd of cattle or a flock of sheep crossing the road. As picturesque as this may sound, it always posed a certain danger. On the other hand, taking the southern run to Salisbury, there was a place where I could pause in tranquility and see a view of the cathedral just as John Constable had painted it 150 years earlier. It was a wonderful way, day after day, to become acquainted with England. While at Chilbolton Airfield at sunset one evening, I recall jotting down a brief poem:

> To the heavens above us,
> oh, look and behold.
> The planets that laud us
> all harnessed in gold.
>
> What horses, what chariots,
> against us shall bide,
> While the stars in their courses
> do fight on our side?

I have always felt that I had seen these verses somewhere before, but where? They had also come to me during that night training jump. This time, rather than putting them down on a scrap of paper, I inked them in my sketchbook and later embellished the poem with a watercolor painting background.

Over and above the thrill of riding motorcycles, being a courier had other advantages, notably being on your own for many hours of the day in the civilian community. We soon became accustomed to stopping at bakeries or fish and chip shops, if we were ahead of schedule, and filling a saddlebag with purchases. Our return to the barrack would be welcomed by the rest of our comrades, with whom we shared these goodies. The courier going through Swindon would always stop for delicious hot buns at a bakery on a cobblestone street at the top of the hill as we entered the town. I have often wondered whether that shop is still there after sixty years.

There were some drawbacks to our job. Three out of five of us during our tour met with accidents of one sort or another, none permanently damaging. Wet, icy, or snowy roads posed a constant challenge. A particular hazard came from military vehicles on maneuvers, tracking up the roads with clods of mud or snow. Upon hitting these at high speed, the rider would at times lose control, ending up in a ditch or worse. I was lucky and suffered nothing more than a few minor spills.

My worst injury during these months was to my pride. I was instructed at one point to take one of our motorcycles having mechanical problems up to the vast U.S. Army supply depot in Cheltenham and exchange it for a new one. On the way back, I was speeding along contentedly on a rural road when suddenly a British Auxiliary Territorial Service (ATS) girl whizzed by me on a British motorcycle. Curious to see what she looked like, I gave my new acquisition the throttle and passed her. On the open road, the Harley had no peer for speed. Relaxing a bit, I felt I had shown this young woman my superior vehicle, when again she went by me even faster. In seconds, she was far ahead of me, and I was determined to catch her. She whipped around a turn into a little village with a street lined with sidewalks and shops. On her well-balanced, lighter motorcycle, she negotiated the turn with apparent ease, but my heavy Harley bounced up on the sidewalk, spilling me and sending pedestrians fleeing for their lives. My speedy nemesis was never seen again.

Soldiers at my level, or even at regimental level for that matter, knew very little about the grand scope of the war. When we arrived in England in the summer of 1944, we were unaware of the plans at Supreme Headquarters Allied Expeditionary Forces Europe (SHAEFE) to shorten the conflict by an airborne invasion of Holland that September. It was not until after the war that I actually learned the 17th Airborne Division was originally slated to be part of that force. A shortage of troop carrier aircraft curtailed the strength to two American airborne divisions (82nd and 101st) and one British (1st), plus a Polish parachute brigade.

Traveling about as I did just before that invasion, I noted great activity on the roads leading to the numerous airfields in the area. It was not, however, until Sunday, September 17th, somewhat before noon, that I realized what was afoot. The sky became alive with aircraft, as a vast armada of planes and gliders headed eastward toward the coast. For the next few days there was much talk in the barrack about our being committed to combat as reinforcements, as well as some complaints about being "left out of the show."

These latter comments were soon to be silenced, however. In addition to units of our division, Chiseldon Barracks also housed a field hospital to which I would routinely deliver messages. It was not long before casualties evacuated from Holland began pouring in. The facilities were crowded to overflowing and the sight of the wounded and dying lying on stretchers all over the grounds outside that one-story building will forever be etched in my mind. Those anxious for combat were given a further sobering up when, a few weeks after the battle, we were told that anyone needing additional equipment could choose from excess materiel down at the motor pool. Many of us went to see what was available. We arrived to find a truckload of clothing, battle gear, and other items in a huge pile that had been dumped on the ground in the parking lot.

As we rummaged through the "excess," it was immediately apparent that these were the contents of the barrack bags of troopers who did not make it back from Holland. All of the personal items had been removed and everything there was government property. Nevertheless, it gave us pause. Soon several of the boys spotted jump boots in their sizes, and others khaki paratrooper jumpsuits (prized possessions since they were no longer issued) and the reticence was overcome. I found a jumpsuit that fit me perfectly. It was in fine shape, except for two little jagged holes that could be repaired. The military hardens men. I look back in wonder at our callousness in rationalizing that our fallen comrades would have welcomed us putting those things to good use in fighting the enemy. (This experience is not a nice tale, but in recounting the occurrence, I have endeavored "to tell it as it is," so that the reader will share the flavor of those times.)

Every effort was made while we were in England to toughen the troops and ready them for prospective airborne operations. In addition to our duties within the company, we continued our military training. There were bivouacs, maneuvers, and trips out to the ranges for rifle practice and to the airfields for pay-qualifying, mandatory parachute jumps and glider rides. On one occasion at one of the airfields, I witnessed a terrible tragedy. A number of us were sitting around, waiting to be taken aloft, when we noted in the distance a formation of planes towing British Horsa gliders at about 2,000 feet up. Seconds later, we thought we saw a Horsa simply crack in half, spewing out its contents into the sky. Bodies and equipment rained down onto the far edge of the field, while we watched in disbelief. With that, we were summarily loaded into the truck and driven back to camp.

Despite the intensive training, I did receive several passes in the fall of 1944, which permitted me to visit London. I remember staying at facilities arranged for soldiers by the Red Cross. Most particularly, I recall that I slept between sheets for the first time since leaving the United States several months earlier. It was such a simple thing, but what a treat it was. However, my sleep was interrupted by V-2 rockets landing in areas not far from where I was staying. I would listen to the sound of the motors and then, when there was silence, count until they dropped and exploded. I was in a bedroom with the curtains tightly drawn when one hit in the vicinity. The entire place reverberated; but since the window was not blown in, I surmised it was really not that close after all.

As for sightseeing, the landmarks were all there, but so much was stored away for protection from the bombing that the museums, if I visited any, made no impression. There was always the cinema, often featuring Hollywood movies, and the theater, which at that stage I did not attend. Covent Garden was a big attraction for all of the servicemen. From my wartime acquaintance with it, I always thought of it as a large dance hall. My meals in London consisted of mess hall rations served at American facilities for those authorized to eat there, but also of fish and chips purchased at local stands. The latter were always sold wrapped in conical fashion in ordinary newspaper. English restaurant fare was largely the inevitable strong tea served with milk, which I grew to love, and watercress sandwiches on very thinly sliced white bread. As an alternative to the watercress, at times I might have anchovy or sardine paste sandwiches. Of course, rationing was in effect throughout the country, but as a soldier I always managed.

From where we were stationed out in the west country, we could see the sky light up night after night from German bombing of London and the surrounding area. Swindon, as an industrial city, was also bombed. Despite all the deprivations, the English were not about to become morose. An infectious attitude of cheerfulness prevailed among the common folk.

During World War II, the average English working-class family loved to dance. On Saturday evenings and Sunday afternoons, and often on weekday evenings, you could find them, "Dad" and "Mum" and their daughters and younger sons, enjoying themselves in the local community center or "Palais de Danse." Attending these sessions in Swindon opened a new world for me. There was always a live orchestra and dancing was a disciplined affair. Everyone moved in a counter-clockwise direction, smoothly and in rhythm to such dances as the quick step, tango, Lambeth Walk, fox trot, and waltz. There usually were quite a few pretty girls in attendance, so it was natural that American GIs would be drawn to these places.

I can remember how embarrassed I was when I first summoned enough courage to ask a girl to dance. Compared to others on the floor, I was awful, but my partner said, "That's all right, Luv, I'll show you." And that is just what she did! By the time she was done that evening, I was moving around the floor with confidence to the quick step, the two-step, and the tango. After a few more such dates with English girls, I turned out to be a reasonably accomplished ballroom dancer.

Our stay at Chiseldon Barracks was abruptly changed with the German counterattack beginning on December 16, 1944, precipitating the Battle of the Bulge. The initial defeats and heavy losses inflicted on American units prompted an almost immediate redeployment of our division to the continent. Word was first received early on December 18th that elements of the XVIII Airborne Corps, of which we were a part, were to be moved to France. That morning, General Ridgway, the Corps commander, and his staff, who were located in Marlborough a few miles south of Chiseldon, departed by air. Later in the day, orders were received to airlift part of our division to areas near the battlefront. Other units were to be promptly transferred across the Channel by ship.

The weather at the time was terrible, grounding the troop carrier planes and delaying their departure for several days. Consequently, the air and the ship contingents arrived at virtually the same time. As soon as we received word that the 17th Airborne Division was on the move, our company was a beehive of activity, preparing to leave by air and ship. A small detachment was to be left behind to look after equipment, store explosives, close down our facilities, and then rejoin the unit in France or Belgium. I was on the orders for that detachment.

Upon arrival in France, the Division was reassembled and moved up to the front. It was moved from the XVIII Airborne and attached to the VIII Corps, which was taking the brunt of the German attack around the town of Bastogne, a key road junction in Belgium.[3] German progress had been assisted by snow, fog, and bitter cold weather, precluding Allied air resupply and reinforcement. The 101st Airborne Division, fighting as a ground unit in the VIII Corps at Bastogne, had been surrounded in the German attack.[4] It held out magnificently against a larger force of SS Panzer and infantry divisions, succeeding in slowing the German attack along the entire front. On December 23rd, the skies cleared enough for several days to permit airdrops and gliders to crash-land within the Bastogne perimeter.[5]

Over Christmas, the Germans launched a final, all-out assault on the 101st but were repulsed and withdrew, with heavy losses. Shortly thereafter, on the 26th, an American armored column entered Bastogne, prompting General Patton to claim that his forces had "rescued" the defenders, much to the defenders' indignation.

A key part of the Allied strategy then was to cut off the German salient in the Bulge by having the VIII Corps move northeast from Bastogne to Houffalize, where it would link up with another American corps. The units assigned this task were the 11th Armored Division, the 87th Infantry Division, elements of the 9th Armored Division, and the 502nd Parachute Infantry Regiment, supported by the 17th Airborne Division in reserve.

The weather was miserable and extremely cold. A heavy snow had fallen, making movement difficult. Many of the troopers in our division had traded in their heavy, long woolen overcoats for the more stylish, jacket-length, twill mackinaws while in England. They were paying the price for that change now. They had already been bitterly cold in the long, open-truck ride over snow-covered roads to their current position.

It was General Patton's supposition, as the overall Army sector commander, that German forces would be retreating and relatively thin, since their advance had been thwarted. Instead, the 11th Armored and the 87th Infantry Divisions that attacked on December 30, under conditions of poor visibility and with minimal intelligence, ran head-on into the flanks of two German Panzer armies moving down from the north. Hitler was still determined to take Bastogne. In this engagement, the Americans were decimated, losing many tanks and taking heavy casualties.

Patton, thinking that he was dealing with a retreating enemy, was furious and threatened to relieve the commanding general of the 11th Armored on the spot for what he believed to be the division's poor performance in the face of an almost nonexistent enemy. The attack fared so badly and the remnants were so disorganized that the 17th Airborne Division was rushed to their aid. Hurrying forward blindly without being able to put out reconnaissance or use artillery support in deep snow and heavy fog, the 17th Airborne also ran into trouble. Pressed by General Patton, the 513th Parachute and the 194th Glider Infantry Regiments took on German divisions. They moved forward through the woods, in some cases with fixed bayonets, and captured the town of Hubremont, but then they were forced to withdraw by overwhelming German strength. When General Miley, the commander of the 17th Airborne, reported losses in a second attack on January 7 of up to 40 percent in some of his battalions, Patton commented in his diary: "This of course is hysterical. The loss for any one day of over 8–10 percent can be put down to a damn lie, unless the people run or surrender."

Subsequently, it was established that in fact the casualties, killed and wounded, in the 17th Airborne were appalling. An historian estimated that at one point they totaled about 1,000 a day, and this in a scaled-down division of about 10,000 men. Patton came to realize that his subordinate generals had indeed been telling him the truth. He later turned these terrible losses into a triumph in his diary, stating: "They ran right into the flank of a German attack. Had this not happened, things [at Bastogne] could have been critical. As it was, we stopped the attack in its tracks. Historians will claim that such perfect timing was a stroke of genius . . . [but] I had no idea the Germans were attacking."

Given a brief chance to nurse its wounds, the 17th Airborne went on the offensive again on January 13, led by the Normandy-hardened veterans of the 507th Parachute Infantry and the 194th Glider Infantry Regiments. Angered by the mauling they had received earlier, they swept the Germans before them. Each regiment vied with the other to see which could move faster, reaching the Ourthe River on January 15.

The foregoing descriptions of the Division's actions are taken from a superbly researched book by Clay Blair, entitled *Ridgway's Paratroopers*, published in 1987, which I read in preparation for writing this section of my account. In all the years prior to that time, I had no idea of the scope of the Division's hardships in the Bulge, nor how well in the final analysis it performed. My life as a private was simply one of responding to instructions from some sergeant, corporal, or an occasional officer. To say I had a worm's-eye view of the grand picture might be overstating the case! I have no definitive recollection of when I rejoined my outfit, but I had blessedly missed that freezing ride up to the front and the initial actions. Reporting to my unit, I recall crossing the English Channel in an LST (Landing Ship Tank). I no longer had my motorcycle. The heavy Harley would have been a liability on the narrow icy roads of the Ardennes. Furthermore, the noise it produced would have made me a leper among the troops in the battle area.

I reported in to the Message Center section. In addition to courier duty, I remember being on missions that in part had as their purpose moving up the company to new ground. At one point, I was deathly ill with the "GIs" (dysentery) and had to run, partially disrobed, from a latrine slit-trench to catch the rear of a hastily departing jeep when we were ordered to move out in a hurry. I can still in the depths of my memory hear the noise and reverberations of German 88mm shell bursts as they exploded and the fragments ripped through the trees with a spitting sound, as well as the sharp crack of a German Mauser rifle and staccato of a Schmeisser submachine gun.

Somewhere at this point an incident occurred that was to change my life. I was standing in a chow-line waiting to wash my mess kit in the field kitchen's two large metal cans, one filled with hot soapy water, the other with boiling rinse water, when a shell burst in the trees in the vicinity. I had a habit, probably more out of anxiety than anything else, of shouting out in German in such situations. My German was fluent so that when, in exaggerated fashion, I mockingly yelled derisive comments about the shelling at the enemy, everyone laughed. Shortly after that, as I was seated at the base of a tree, a heavy-set master sergeant I had not seen before came up to me and asked where I had acquired my German. I responded that I had learned it as a child and, up to about age six, had been more fluent in

German than in English. Furthermore, I had studied German at Columbia before coming into the Army. He explained in a thick German accent that he was with the Division's CIC (Counter Intelligence Corps) Detachment and had stopped simply to use our mess facilities.[6] He seemed impressed that I had attended Columbia and inquired whether I had any interest in being in Intelligence. I must have replied in the affirmative, for he took my name, rank, serial number, and organization. After a week or two had passed, I forgot about the matter.

There were no letters home covering this period. Conditions were such that I must have been unable to write, being constantly on the move. Flashes of memory related to specific incidents, however, remain. At one point, I remember taking away an unusual rifle from a German prisoner, who was being removed to the POW enclosure. It was an exceptionally long-barreled Mauser, delicately engraved. The rifling in the bore was precise. It was an old-fashioned bolt action, but obviously a fine sharp-shooter's weapon. After dragging it around for a few days on the floor of a jeep trailer, I was determined to see what it could do. From a forward position where I could observe enemy movement across a distant open area, I decided to take a shot or two using the standard German rounds I had picked up along the way. Taking aim with the adjustable windage sight, I fired several shots at enemy soldiers far off on the crest of a small hill. In no time, all hell broke loose! Stupidly, I had taken for granted that others would know that it was I doing the shooting. Instead, the sound of an enemy weapon close by aroused everyone. I was lucky to have escaped unharmed. It was an idiotic thing to do, and I got rid of that trophy in a hurry.[7]

The average soldier seemed to have a preoccupation with spirits, the liquid kind. We were always looking in cellars of houses or ruins we fought through to see if there was any wine or other beverages. Calvados, an indigenous apple brandy, aptly called "white lightning" by the troops, was much prized. We were told that the Germans were booby-trapping such caches, but it made no difference. A find would result in much whooping and hollering and general celebrating. I cannot recall where it was acquired, but I do remember sitting on the ground one day, leaning my back against the wheel of a jeep drinking a bottle of champagne while eating the little can of concentrated ham and scrambled eggs from a K-ration package. One of my friends, a connoisseur of such things, told me that we were not too far from Epernay, the heart of the champagne country, and that it was only proper that we should be imbibing the local product.

Our division was eventually pulled back off the line to Chalons-sur-Marne in France in preparation for future operations. We occupied quarters that had previously housed a German SS unit. The walls of the *Kaserne* (military camp) still had some of the signs and insignia on them, now redecorated with our superimposed graffiti. During the weeks we were in Chalons, I had my first real contact with the local population. I enjoyed the opportunity to practice my high school French, what I could remember of it. I made an effort to acquire a language dictionary and a primer. An initial order of business was getting our laundry done and our uniforms pressed. Dealing with the local laundresses was a service my colleagues asked me to provide. With the Germans gone, life returned to normal for the people of the town, and it was interesting to observe their customs. We were located in the vicinity of a school for little girls. They would arrive every morning dressed in uniforms, and during the day they would be marched about by their teachers, who were nuns. A considerable effort was made to impress upon us the need for good behavior while we were in France, and the military authorities came down hard on violators.

During the early weeks of March 1945 our training was intensified. Rumors were rife that we would be engaging soon in an airborne operation. There was talk about a drop on Frankfurt or Berlin, which I dismissed as wild speculation, since I did not see how there could ever be a link-up with ground units under such circumstances. Had I been privy to high-level war planning, I might have thought otherwise, for indeed there were such plans on the board.[8] It seemed to us at the time that the war was far from over in Europe. We still had not even crossed the Rhine, which should have been a clue as to what was actually in the offing. We had settled into our routine in Chalons, when on short notice during the third week of March, the company was given orders to move out. I endeavored to go into town to pick up the laundry and pressing I had left, which included the jump suit I had acquired from the parking lot "excess" in Chiseldon. I was told that there was no time, and under no circumstances should I leave.

In rapid order we packed our barrack bags and were loaded on trucks and driven to a railyard, where we boarded 40-and-8 boxcars. There was straw on the floor and the cars smelled of horse manure. We were reliving World War I history, and it was quite possible that those very boxcars, which appeared so dilapidated, had been used 27 years earlier to transport soldiers of the AEF to the front. As we traveled through the French countryside, I was upset about having to leave the laundry and pressed uniforms behind. I rationalized that we would be coming back to Chalons before too long, but we never did return. The doors of the boxcars were open as we traveled past farms and little French villages. Looking at the map, today, our journey took us from Chalons-sur-Marne through the outskirts of Paris southwest to Chartres. It was a distance, given some roundabout routing, of 200–225 miles, which we completed over a period of two days. At the time, however, we had no real idea where we were going and sleeping on the floors of those stinking boxcars was uncomfortable, to say the least. On arrival, we detrained and were moved to a large field, where a vast tent city had been erected. We were not told where we were and no one was permitted to leave our company area. It was obvious, however, that we were most likely not far from several airfields, because one could hear the constant noise of airplane engines warming up and aircraft passing overhead.

Considering the size of the encampment, a significant part of our airborne division must have been there. The weather was clear, not too cold, and we were reasonably comfortable in the large eight-man tents. The food was unusually good, based upon the Army's ten-in-one mess hall rations. Everything taking place, the entire atmosphere, seemed to tell us that we were going into action, this time as paratroopers. I was aware that not all of our company had accompanied us to our present location; some of the headquarters personnel were not with us. On Friday, March 23rd, several groups of us were taken over to an adjacent airfield. To my shock, I saw numerous WACO CG-4A gliders lined up alongside a line of C-47s. One of our sergeants directed us over to the WACOs and instructed us to load designated jeeps or trailers into specific gliders. That they were our company vehicles there could be no doubt, for I clearly recognized our unit's markings on the front and rear bumpers.

As we proceeded to load and lash, it became obvious to us that we were expected to ride with this equipment and we had better take care to do the job well. I remember agonizing that the last damn thing in the world I wanted to do was fly into combat in a jeep-laden glider. It was a flying coffin! Jumping was one thing; crash landing was something else! Besides, one might not even get to the drop-zone, for the chances of the tow-rope parting, the wings coming off, or the jeep tearing loose in a bumpy flight were all too real. Prior to that time, there had been the assumption that paratroopers would jump and others who were glider-qualified would be transported in that manner. I was qualified both ways and nobody was giving me a choice in the matter. When I returned from the airfield and learned another platoon of the company might jump, I envied them. At least when jumping, should the plane be hit, one had a parachute and a chance at survival. In a glider, which was flimsy and likely to break up, you had no parachute and the odds of coming out alive were slim.

At five o'clock that afternoon, we were fed a better than usual meal and were even encouraged to come back for seconds, which we did gladly. There was no question in our minds then that something was going to take place on the morrow. We returned to our tents and began checking our equipment. Rifle bolts clicked. Scraping sounds were heard, as trench knives and bayonets were sharpened. I adjusted the netting over my steel helmet, to which was tied a small first aid packet containing sulfa powder to disinfect wounds. I paid special attention to the M-3 submachine gun I had recently been issued to replace my rifle; somehow, I felt uneasy about it as a weapon. Earlier, I had sewn a 3x5 inch American flag on the right upper arm of my battle jacket. Several of the men were writing last-minute letters home.

It was still daylight when we heard the shout, "mail call!" We all gathered outside to listen to the mail clerk call out the recipients. It had been some time since we had had a mail delivery and sure enough, there were two letters for me, one from my mother, the other from my sister Elsie. Elsie's letter reflected her usual cheerful self, was newsy, and probably admonished me to write home more often. Mother's letter, on the other hand, upset me greatly. She always had a sixth sense about what was happening to me and I could tell she knew I was to go into combat. Her letter spoke about the Germany she had grown up in, that some of those good people must be there still, and that I should have compassion for my enemy and be merciful. I would be facing some boy whose mother worried about him and prayed for him, just as she did about me. I was furious. She had no idea that all of my training had taught me to "kill or be killed," and that a "second's hesitation can mean your life." What was she trying to do, get her son killed? Her intervention was the last thing I wanted to hear at this time. Things were bad enough. If there ever was a time I needed to be tough, it was now. I recall muttering to myself as I was sharpening my trench knife that Mother simply could not fathom my predicament.[9]

After a while, I settled down, but I had no success sleeping that night. Even had I not received Mother's letter, anxiety over what was to come and the continuous din from the airfield, where planes were warming up their engines all night, would have kept me awake. Many years after that night, while going through some old papers I had saved from the war, I found two "short-snorters" among those papers. One is a British pound note, the other a French franc note, both covered with the signatures of buddies with whom I served. The French note was signed that evening.

I also found a bit of verse I had excerpted from a poem by Bartholomew Dowling, entitled "The Revel," written about British soldiers in India during the nineteenth century. I remembered that I would recite it from time to time for my buddies, who shouted, "Hurrah!" over the bravado sentiments it expressed. In jotting it down, I gave it my own title:

The Night before the Battle
(Written March 23, 1945, in France with the 17th Airborne Division)

We meet 'neath sounding rafter,
And all the walls around are bare;
As they shout back our peals of laughter
It seems that the dead are there.
Then stand to your glasses, steady!
We drink in our comrades' eyes:
A cup to the dead already—
Hurrah for the next man who dies!

About three o'clock the following morning, March 24, 1945, we were awakened and fed an elaborate breakfast of steak and eggs, finished off with apple pie. No one said it might be our last meal, but I am sure that the thought was not far from everyone's mind. We then returned to the tents, completed preparations, put on combat gear, and moved out to the airfield. While waiting around to load, I noted that a couple of troopers were looking at a copy of the *Saturday Evening Post* I had received in a package sometime earlier. We all had enjoyed it, particularly since it was not an abridged version of the type the recreation services or the Red Cross supplied us from time to time. This copy had all the advertising in it, especially the pretty models and the latest automobile ads.

When we were taken out onto the airfield itself, I noted that the WACO we had loaded the jeep in the previous day was positioned behind a C-47, with another glider off to one side. Dual lines stretched back from the single plane to the two gliders. We were going to be pulled in tandem! The thought of that two-engine, propeller-driven aircraft pulling two heavily loaded gliders at the same time made my blood freeze. I was going from bad to worse and began to think that I would never get out of this affair alive. How in the world were those pilots ever going to keep the gliders apart? An explanation that one towrope was longer than the other, so that the gliders' wings would not collide, did little to assure us. What was to keep the wing from being ripped off by the other towrope? Evidently, gliders had been towed in tandem before or they would not be doing this. However, I had not encountered the procedure in the numerous flights I had taken in training. We later learned that the severe shortage of transport planes had demanded either using tandem pulls or aborting the entire operation.

Another innovation noted that morning was a new C-46 on the field, although it was not near any of the gliders. The C-46, which we had seen in England the previous December, was larger and more powerful than the C-47. It could carry 36 paratroopers, compared to the 18 we were used to in the C-47.[10]

On the positive side, a beautiful, sunny morning dawned. Far off on the horizon, we could see the outskirts of a city. I was told it was Chartres. We waited around for a while and then were ordered to board the gliders, based on the loading detail breakdown we had used the previous day. The Air Corps pilot and co-pilot were already in their seats, checking the controls. There were six of us altogether in the WACO, plus the jeep loaded with equipment and extra five-gallon gas cans. While we waited apprehensively, the C-47 in front of us gunned its engines, taxied slowly, taking up the slack in the towropes, and then started sluggishly down the long runway, with us bouncing along behind. "How is that puny old plane ever going to get this double load into the air?" I thought, "I can't believe this!" If I had qualms, those poor glider pilots must have been beside themselves!

It took us forever to get into the air and, for a while, I thought our pilot was going to release the towrope while we were still only 75–100 feet off the ground. We lumbered along slowly, anxiously keeping our eyes on the other glider. Our air speed could not have been more than 100 miles an hour. Everything shook and rattled and seemed to be coming apart. In the midst of this travail, I must have sensed that this was one of life's unforgettable moments. I looked out at the sky to see clouds still tinged pink with the dawn. Down below us were green meadows. Off to one side, I saw a French farmer and his horse peacefully plowing his fields. Just then, a few hundred feet below, we passed right over the top of Chartres Cathedral in all its magnificence. It was so close that I felt I could almost touch the tips of the spires with my hand.

As I gazed at the tense and sullen faces of the troopers sitting with me, I remember saying to myself, "Why me, Lord? What am I doing here?" The answer I guess can be found in a statement made by Chief Justice Oliver Wendell Holmes over a hundred years ago: "As life is action and passion, it is required of a man that he should share the passion and action of his time, at peril of being judged not to have lived."

From the position of the sun, we could tell we were heading in a westerly direction toward the English Channel. Many planes and gliders flew around us, but our only real concerns were that our "crate" would hold together and that our pilot and the one in the tandem glider would be able to maintain a separation. From the outset the flight was bumpy, and it worsened as we continued. Our roundabout course took us out to the Channel coast, where we rendezvoused with elements of the 6th British Airborne Division and then down over Brussels on the last 110 miles to the Rhine River at Wesel, Germany. We were in the air in that glider an interminable amount of time. I do not think any of us focused on just how long, but it must have been close to three hours. All the while we were being thrown about, as we prayed that the lashings on the jeep would remain tight. The pilots were close to exhaustion trying to keep the gliders apart. Some tandem-towed gliders did converge, causing them to crash or prematurely cut loose. Other gliders bounced around so much that their wings came off or the heavy loads came loose, causing them to plunge to the ground.

In one wave, twenty-one gliders were lost even before they reached the combat area. About a third of the way into our rough flight, the first of our group became airsick. A couple of us did not help matters by either smoking or chewing on cigars. I should point out that cigars tended to be part of a paratrooper's mystique; we smoked them to make us look tough. While I smoked them occasionally at that time, I almost always had one in my mouth, unlit. By the time we came near the drop zone, most of us were sick or queasy from the stench of vomit. The general paratrooper airsickness procedure was to separate one's steel helmet (pot) from the plastic liner (inner helmet) and use the former as a receptacle. That might have been fine in training, but in combat one had better have a full helmet on when the shooting starts. Consequently, the moment we came under fire, those who were ill jammed their liners into the steel pots and put their helmets on, vomit dripping down around the edges. It was a sight to turn a grown man ashen!

The pilot shouted as we came over Germany and neared the Rhine River. Looking down, I saw that the entire area seemed to be covered with smoke or haze. Within seconds, we started hearing sounds resembling pebbles tossed on a tin roof, interspersed with loud, thumping sounds. Bursts of light appeared in the fabric frame around us, with ripping sounds and splintering in the plywood floor. We were taking flak and small arms' fire. Everyone except the pilots crouched down in the jeep, hoping the chassis would provide some protection. I prayed that the jeep's full gas tank would not be hit, or the glider would become an inferno. We were totally helpless targets those final minutes.

Through the large Plexiglas nose, I could see the sky totally pockmarked with flak bursts and a plane farther ahead burning. Airsickness in those moments was forgotten. It seemed as if we would never cut loose! Finally, the lurch came, and the WACO went into a sharp bank to the left. We descended rapidly. As we came around for a landing, I saw we were coming down at the edge of a wood, aiming at a large plowed field crisscrossed with tracks made in landing attempts. The field was covered with gliders, parts of gliders and fuselages of planes scattered every which way. Some were broken in half, while others had tails sticking straight up.

We came down parallel to the edge of the woods, a wing hitting a downed glider while still off the ground. Flying forward virtually at air speed, we smashed into the earth in a belly-landing, bounced and careened and scraped along until the nose struck the trunk of a tree with full force. In the landing, we were all thrown about wildly. I was momentarily knocked unconscious. When I came to, I heard moaning and cursing. The realization that we were being shot at prompted us to push out the door and tumble frantically out of the glider. Once on the ground, I could hardly move. My left pants leg was ripped, exposing a very bloody and swelling knee. It seemed I had cuts, scrapes, and bruises everywhere. Actually, I may have been in better shape than some of the others, particularly the pilots, who took the brunt of the nose collision. There were no medics around, and for minutes we all lay hugging the ground.

In the collision, the jeep had flown forward, partially lifting open the nose of the glider and wedging it upward against the tree. Under the circumstances, there was no way to remove the damaged jeep from the WACO. The lifting of the nose, however, raised the pilots' seats and probably spared them from being crushed by the jeep. Looking out across the vast plowed field beyond the aircraft wreckage, one could see a road lined with several farmhouses. Off in the distance, tall high-tension-wire pylons stretched across the countryside. A parachute draped over the wires was mute testimony to what might have occurred. Smoke and the sound of exploding artillery and gunfire enveloped the area.

Back along the path our glider had taken, in a far corner of the field at the edge of the woods, was a German anti-aircraft gun emplacement. We must have come in directly over their heads, but too low, I thought erroneously, for them to have brought anything other than small arms to bear on our flight. However, the Germans used 88 mm artillery as both an air and ground weapon with deadly effect in either instance, hastening our decision to get off the field into the woods as quickly as possible.

A short way into the trees, we encountered a railroad track with a long, waist-deep trench running parallel to it as far as we could see. Dirt was piled up alongside the trench, and foxholes were scattered about in the woods. The Germans must have evacuated these emplacements for more secure positions deeper in the forest, for had there been a fight for them, casualties would have been lying about. We took stock of our position and saw to our injuries. After cleaning the deep gash in my knee with water from my canteen, I removed the first aid packet from my helmet and poured sulfa powder on the wound. That done, I was told to move north in the trench to reconnoiter, while someone else moved south. We had no idea where the rest of our company was, but generally our position would not be far from division headquarters. I was about 150 yards up the trench, out of sight of the others, when from over the piled-high dirt I heard foot-steps crashing through the woods coming toward me. I crouched down in the trench, my submachine ready for a burst. Bounding over the top of the dirt into the trench, I was suddenly confronted with someone wearing a smock and helmet similar to that of a German paratrooper. The instant he spotted me, he shouted, "Don't shoot, Yank!"

There were so many similarities between the German and British paratroopers' garb. It seems inconceivable to me that the latter did not place a flag patch in a conspicuous place on the battle uniform as we did. The regular British Army helmet, in contrast, looked like ours from WWI. As it was, there was a report of a firefight between our troops and the 6th British Airborne, which cost several lives. After commiserating with one another on how confused things were, the British paratrooper and I went our separate ways. I returned to our position to find that my group had moved out of the woods onto the plowed field and headed west. Why this decision was made I do not know. I could only surmise that it must have been toward an assembly point known to the pilot or a corporal who was with us. Others, who had landed in the interim, were moving that way as well. I followed, running and limping as fast as I could despite my injured knee, out to the wreckage of a WACO and dropped to the ground.

Looking around, I saw that I was lying among casualties of a direct hit. Not more than four feet from me lay a glider pilot, in his Air Corps pinks and green (dress) uniform with the top of his skull cleanly taken off, his brains spewing down onto his shoulder. Other bodies were scattered in and around the glider. The sight of your unit insignia on a dead man is always a sobering experience. Shaken by what I saw, I hastened farther out onto the field in pursuit of the others. I must have gone 30–40 yards over plowed ground when I became aware that I was under fire. Just ahead of me I spotted a deep track in the soft earth and I dove for it. The combina-tion of a furrow and glider track was just low enough to keep me from being hit. I raised my head at one point to see where my companions were and was knocked sideways, my helmet ripped from my head. I could see it ten feet from where I lay, but I dared not try to retrieve it.

From where I was lying, it seemed that the shooting was coming from the farmhouses, about 300 yards away. I am sure that with a rifle I could have put a few rounds through some of the windows. Under these circum-stances, my .45-caliber, M-3 submachine gun was useless, and I vowed to dispose of it as soon as I could. Shortly thereafter, adding to my anxiety, several phosphorous rounds exploded on the field, but I was not certain what or whose they were. With the din of battle and firing from the farm-houses, I failed to notice a WACO coming in until it was virtually on top of me. At the last second, I heard a rush of wind and a slapping sound as its right wingtip passed directly over me. It bounced and scraped to a landing about 150 yards away. My first thought was that now my assailants would focus on the glider and I would be able to move; but before I could even stir, dirt kicking up around me told me otherwise. I have no idea how long I lay there; it could have been five minutes, or it could have been twenty-five.

I was about to chance running again, when I heard loud airplane motors above me. Looking up, I saw a B-24 bomber flying low overhead. I could clearly see an airman standing in the open door pushing out supply bundles. The plane flew on, but was back again in minutes to make another drop. To my horror, it took a hit just as it was over the field. I watched as the airman in the door fell out, plummeting to the ground with no sign of a parachute. The plane, itself, lumbered on for a short while until I saw a huge fireball and thick black smoke. I can remember crying out in anguish, "He was trying to help us, and you bastards have killed him!" This time, I rose, grabbed my helmet and started running for the farmhouses. My helmet, however, would not fit together. I sought the cover of some wreckage and endeavored to fix it. Evidently, a bullet or some shrapnel had struck it just at the seam of the liner and the pot, twisting the entire thing off my head. It left me with a nasty scalp wound, which in the excitement I had not noticed. My entire neck and collar were covered in blood. My leg throbbed and my head hurt.

Lying there, I pondered what would happen next. Just then, I saw a wonderful sight. Out of a line of trees on the far northwestern side of the field, a jeep appeared. There were paratroopers all over it, sitting on the hood, hanging on the back. Others ran alongside. Farther back, spread abreast, came more of them. It was the 3rd Battalion of the 513th Parachute Infantry, which had been dropped in error far to the north of their jump zone. Riding in the jeep next to the driver was Major Morris Anderson, their commander. "Need a little help?" was his comment as he approached me. I was never so glad to see anyone in my life. Their appearance must have been noted, for the firing stopped. I told them where the shooting seemed to have originated. One of the men said there was a machine gun emplacement over there that had been raking the field. In no time, I was limping along in the company of some of the 513th men, angry and determined to clean out those farmhouses. When we got there, it was obvious that the position had been hastily vacated. German equipment and spent rounds lay about in two of the buildings.

Departing then to seek my own group, I passed close to the last house along the road. Pausing, I heard sounds coming from a storm cellar. I took a grenade I wore on my shoulder strap and approached the cellar trapdoor. Cautiously lifting the door slightly, while keeping myself out of the line of fire, I was prepared to toss in the grenade, when I remembered my mother's letter and her plea, "be merciful." Instead, I hesitated and then shouted down in German, *"Haende hoch! Sofort heraus!"* There was no response. I shouted out again. This time there was stirring and then the first person emerged. I was stunned to see an elderly grandmother emerge, then another woman, then four or five little children, until a total of fourteen women and children stood before me. I trembled at what I might have done. To this day, I still shudder at the burden that would have been placed on my life had I not received my blessed mother's letter.[11]

By this time, I gave up my effort to rejoin the others and simply accompanied the men of the 513th as they fought their way to their assigned deployment. On our way, we recrossed the landing area, entered the woods, and followed the trench past where I met the British paratrooper. Moving farther, we came to the German artillery emplacement our glider had passed over. When we attacked that position, we found that it too had been recently abandoned, but the 88 mm piece still appeared to be in operating condition. It was aimed in a flat trajectory, affording direct fire at incoming gliders. Eventually I did link up with my company early the following morning by continually asking paratroopers I met to direct me to division headquarters. I recall moving along a wide sandy path through a piney wood and encountering numerous German and American dead along the way, as well as groups of surrendering Germans.

Upon arriving at our company area, I promptly followed the example of others and dug myself a foxhole, since we were the targets of irregular German artillery and mortar fire. A sergeant, observing my limp, wounded knee, and bloody head, told me to report to the field hospital. With foolish machismo, I disobeyed his instructions, possibly visualizing the various inoculations I would be given. I did not focus at the time on the fact that treatment at the field hospital was registered. It was the basis for issuing a Purple Heart, which counted five points toward early discharge and subsequent preferential treatment as a veteran.[12] Over the following three weeks, I treated myself with sulfa powder.

Before the division attacked farther into Germany, several of us were ordered to return to the landing field to see if the jeep in our WACO was salvageable. After much effort, we got it out of the glider. Surprisingly, despite substantial outward damage, it functioned. As an ordinary soldier, I had a myopic view of what occurred on the day of our drop. After the war, I learned that Operation Varsity, as it was termed, was the most concentrated airborne invasion in history, involving 17,000 men of our and the 6th British Airborne divisions. While Operation Market-Garden in Holland may have been somewhat larger, that drop was staggered over several days and used landing areas extending twenty miles. Varsity, by contrast, landed everyone in daylight in about two hours in an overall drop zone of four by six miles.

We encountered a German force of 85,000, some of them parachute and SS units. Of the 1,305 American and British gliders used, only 148 WACOs and 24 Horsas were later salvageable. Of the 1,545 planes involved, 77 were shot down (including 15 B-24 bombers) and 475 seriously damaged.[13] Major General James M. Gavin, Division Commander of the 82nd Airborne, flying above the action as an observer, recalled: "It was an awesome spectacle. At one time, I counted 23 transports or gliders going down in flames, trying desperately to make it back to the west bank."[14] The British and American casualties in Operation Varsity numbered 1,070 killed and over 3,000 wounded. March 24, 1945, in terms of losses, was the worst single day for the Allied airborne in World War II.[15] It is noteworthy that four Congressional Medals of Honor were awarded to members of the 17th Airborne Division: one for action in the Battle of the Bulge and three in the Rhine drop.[16]

Hindsight questions were raised about Operation Varsity. It was considered by some as the most successful Allied airborne invasion of the war but at great cost. American troops had by that time already crossed the Rhine farther south. Britain's General Bernard Montgomery, after the failure in Holland in September 1944, remained bent upon pushing across the north German plain to Berlin. He kept pressing General Eisenhower for the opportunity to do so until the latter relented. Operation Varsity was the opening phase of that attack.

Among the material I had sent home to my mother that she had saved, I found two poignant mementos of this period. One was a yellowing copy of *Yank*, the Army's weekly magazine published for the troops, dated April 8, 1945. It contained an article about Operation Varsity. I had circled a passage in it in crayon about a young American captain who had landed in a tree just beyond the point where I had met the British paratrooper. Before the captain could release himself from his parachute, he had been killed. He was hanging high in the tree when I passed with the boys from the 513th. The article went on to say, "When a group of paratroopers on their way to clean out the woods passed, they saw the body and the bars on the shoulder that were simply indistinct strips of adhesive tape. As they passed, the paratroopers saluted." Next to the crayoned circle, I wrote the word "me," telling Mother and Dad that I was a participant in that tragic scene. The second item is a letter written to my parents sometime in early April 1945. It speaks for itself:

Thanks for your packages and letters. You will never know how much I appreciated them. The magazines and letters—which traveled so far and looked so battered when they reached me—each seemed to be a little link in a long chain stretching toward home. One copy of a magazine that I will never forget lies somewhere in the deserted fields of Germany among the decaying wreckage of planes, parachutes, gliders—and comrades. Its pages gave a last bit of joy and humor to friends during those difficult bumpy hours of that terrible airborne ride—for none of them came back.

The magazine, of course, was my *Saturday Evening Post* that those friends at the airfield in France had taken with them. Their glider took a direct hit on landing.

The next days saw us assaulting the industrial heartland of Germany. By March 27, 1945, the Allies' bridge across the Rhine at Wesel was fully operational. British armored forces crossed it and joined our division in driving forward. Those who were not riding on tanks moved in trucks and jeeps. My message center courier duty during this period can best be described as chaotic. I never knew, when having lost my way, I would run head on into a German roadblock. Traveling by jeep at night with no lights is an exhilarating experience. Wandering around on foot proved more precarious. I practiced routines I would use should I run into a German armed force. They varied from telling the Germans that they were surrounded and that they had best escape while they could to saying I would help them surrender. All of this would be done, of course, in my best German—as one interested in their welfare. Thank goodness that at this point, when the Germans still had plenty of fight left in them, I was never called upon to use these charades. In actuality, I came closer to being shot by GI sentries or point men.

Having vowed earlier to dispose of my .45-caliber M-3 submachine gun, I sought to exchange it for a .30 caliber M-1 (Garand) rifle or a carbine. I never again wanted to be in a position where I was totally unable to fire back at a long-range enemy. I was told that the M-3 was my issue weapon and that was all there was to say in the matter. I solved my problem by simply picking up a folding-stock .30-caliber carbine on the battlefield. This weapon, when folded, was only 25 inches long and fit into a canvas holster I could wear on my belt. Thus, with both weapons and the grenades I always carried, I was ready for any eventuality.

I always wore a grenade attached to my suspenders, General Ridgway-style. I recall one day being sent on a mission to a rear area by truck. In jumping out of the truck at my destination, the grenade I was wearing accidentally came loose from my harness and bounced on the pavement.

The rear echelon types standing around went into panic, diving for cover every which way. Familiar with grenades, and knowing it takes a substantial pull to separate the pin, I nonchalantly picked it up, refastened it on my chest, and sauntered away. When I later recounted the incident to my buddies, they thought it hilarious.

The 17th Airborne Division pushed on through the towns of Dorsten, Haltern, and Duelmen to the city of Muenster. In Haltern, my company ran into trouble trying to cross a stream. Today's map indicates that the Lippe River runs adjacent to the town. I remember the company taking heavy artillery and small arms fire as we approached the stream. Apartment buildings lined the side of the road right to the water's edge. We found that by going through basements we could blow passages from building to building and thus come to one end of the partially destroyed bridge. Endeavoring to get over the bridge, we took murderous fire, and a good friend was hit in the groin and lower abdomen in the effort. A German civilian (or a soldier in mufti) lay wounded on the far bank. His loud cries of *"Hilfe, Hilfe"* should have at least enabled our medics to get to him. However, any attempt to cross brought a hail of machine gun and small arms fire.

We were told that a fierce SS unit was determined to hold the bridge at all costs. Artillery was called in to pound the enemy positions. By nightfall, we had cleared the bridge. Our troops always believed SS units to be composed of "fanatic" Nazis who would fight to the death. In some instances, this reputation was deserved, more because of the individual leadership of particular units than anything else. I was to learn later, however, when it was my job to know in detail about Nazi organizations, that the SS had several branches and that some of the divisions in the Waffen SS, the military branch, were little more than ordinary army units. Toward the end of the war even their ranks were at times filled with draftees, older men, and teenagers. German paratroop units, on the other hand, which were part of the Luftwaffe, not the Army, were volunteers and tough adversaries. When I later interrogated German prisoners, it was interesting to note that they often had many of the same preconceptions about us. To them, American paratroopers were known as "devils in baggy pants," referring to the large side pockets in our jumpsuit trousers. We were considered an implacable foe that never took prisoners. The latter aspect, although largely untrue, was based on the rationale that in an airborne drop there was no rear area to which prisoners could be evacuated.

A non-airborne lieutenant joined our company during this period. Several of us were assigned to a patrol he led to seek out a new command post in a forward area. Four or five of us packed into a jeep and drove down a country lane, up to a manor house situated in a grove of trees.

It was apparent that a force of our infantry had swept through the area minutes earlier, for numerous dead were in evidence. We pulled up to the front steps and, before all of us could climb out of the jeep, came under fire. In these fast-moving days, it was not unusual for pockets of resistance to be left behind. Two of us raced up the spacious marble steps, past a German soldier sprawled dead, head down. We ran through the open door of the house, not knowing what we would find inside. The lieutenant and the others remained outside, crouched down behind the jeep.

As we entered the building, the strangest sensation came over me. I was certain I had been there before. Thinking it possible that the Germans were using the upper floors as a communications center, just as we intended to do, we moved cautiously. I found myself quietly whispering directions, thoroughly familiar with that baronial place. I knew the location of kitchens, the library, and the bedrooms on the upper floor. Realizing that there were French doors exiting to the gardens out back, I went to the front door and shouted out to those in the jeep to move around to the rear. They got there in time to see several German soldiers rapidly disappearing through the trees. I always intended to go back and find that house again, but could not for the life of me remember where it was.

By the beginning of April, we halted on the outskirts of Muenster. The German garrison there refused a call to surrender, forcing General Miley, our division commander, to order an attack. The sight of that city burning at night is fixed in my memory. It was a pity for both sides to have to take casualties at that late stage in the war. However, what is apparent now from history—that the entire war would be over in less than six months— seemed not at all likely at the time. I learned later that Major Anderson, the CO of the 3rd Battalion of the 513th PIR, who had come to my rescue only days earlier, was badly wounded in that action.

5
Assigned to Intelligence

For more than a week, we had been constantly on the move. We rested when we could, sometimes sleeping in vacated houses and on other occasions in the field. Late one night, several of us bedded down at the edge of a wood next to a 105 mm battery of the Division Artillery. I was exhausted and even sporadic cannonades could not keep me awake. I should have plugged my ears, for when I awoke at dawn I was virtually deaf. It took several days before the ringing in my ears stopped. On the lighter side, I recall coming to an abandoned farm on Easter Sunday. There were no Germans in sight. The farm animals were gone except for two scrawny chickens clucking around the barnyard. It was about noontime and the thought struck the three of us in the jeep that an Easter chicken dinner would suit us just fine. We chased those chickens up and down the yard for twenty minutes to no avail. One flew over the coop fence and was gone, so we simply shot the other one.

We plucked the bird as best we could, cleaned and roasted it. When it seemed done, we attempted to eat our meal. It was as tough as an old inner tube. Someone then suggested that we boil it, which we did. Roasted or boiled, it still tasted like rubber. We gave up and finally settled for our combat D-Rations—concentrated chocolate and fig bars, each about 4"x1"x1" in size. What an Easter dinner! Actually, I complained less than most soldiers in my company about D-Rations and really liked them at first. I found, however, that after a while my teeth started loosening. The medics told me I was developing trench mouth. At the end of the war, an investigation concluded that D-Rations were a totally inadequate diet.

I came to associate the attack on Muenster with a breakthrough in my fortunes as a soldier. Ordered to report to the First Sergeant one day, I was told I was being detailed to the division Counter Intelligence Detachment (CIC) and that "they want you there right now!"[1] When I arrived, I learned that the detachment was made up of a handful of "special agents" and a few administrative personnel. I was informed by the unit's commanding officer that our job was to counter the activities of enemy agents, arrest war criminals, and assure the security of our forces. The fact that I spoke German was a major reason for my selection. I was also a combat paratrooper, so a little danger should not bother me. Not quite sure of what I was getting into, I began some of the most interesting activities of my life.

Following the assault on Muenster, the 17th Airborne Division was ordered to circle back to the Ruhr in an effort to reduce a pocket that contained two German armies numbering well over 300,000 men, under the command of Field Marshal Walther Model.[2] I was briefed as thoroughly as circumstances permitted on my new duties as a CIC agent. I received materials describing the organizations of the Nazi Party, the NSDAP (*Nazionalsozialistische Deutsche Arbeiterpartei*). I learned about the SS (*Schutzstaffeln*), the SA (*Sturmabteilung* [Storm Troops]), the Nazi Party hierarchy, and numerous other groups. Upper levels in the U.S. government had prepared a list of Germans to be held for war crimes.[3] It included high-ranking Nazis responsible for the war, as well as individuals known to have committed atrocities. It was our mission to search them out and bring them to justice. High on the list were the top Nazi Party leadership, the Gestapo (*Geheimstaatspolizei*), the SD (*Sicherheitsdienst* [the security service of the SS]), and the SS Death Head units (*Totenkopfverband*), concentration camp personnel.[4]

We were given a last known location of those individuals thought to be in our area and then it was up to us to apprehend them. In doing this, we relied to a considerable extent on the local German police system, which in large part still functioned. As a matter of routine, CIC offices were usually located in the executive offices of area police administrations. As early as April 1945, an American directive, JCS 1067, forbade the employment of former members of the Nazi Party. Enough ordinary policemen not so affiliated were only too glad to cooperate in chasing down Nazi bigwigs and those ruthlessly wielding power under them.

The general scene was one of chaos, with German troops surrendering by the tens of thousands, refugees from the East pouring in by the millions, and thousands of foreign forced laborers seeking to return home. The overall security situation was precarious. Jails had been emptied of prisoners and even mental institutions had opened their doors. Pockets of resistance remained. Our division had all it could do to evacuate prisoners of war to enclosures, control the refugee flow, guard its own facilities, and secure public utilities and captured enemy stores. The manpower, even fully deploying the division's parachute and glider infantry regiments, could not cover the hundreds of square miles we occupied.

My life changed entirely in CIC. I was freed from military routine and given great independence. The detachment had specific tasks to accomplish, and I was expected to assist in carrying them out. I was still a private first-class at this time and was told to remove the single stripes from the sleeves of my jacket. CIC special agents wore Army uniforms with no designation of grade or rank, only two officer-type gold "U.S." insignia on their shirt and jacket collars, as well as officers' silver and gold piping on their overseas caps. We were called "Mister" or "Special Agent" and as a result were often thought to be American civilians. CIC personnel generally had civilian backgrounds as FBI men, lawyers, or investigators and tended to be older and more experienced individuals.

At one point, our commanding officer told me never to tell anyone my actual grade, particularly the Germans, since they were much impressed by rank. I was given the power to arrest Germans and other foreign nationals in carrying out my duties, and this even extended to American military and civilian personnel in certain cases, such as espionage or subversion. I soon developed certain techniques that proved quite useful in doing my job. I found that forceful, clipped German oratory immediately commanded attention. In situations involving American personnel, simply acting authoritatively, as if you had every right to be in charge, was surprisingly effective.

One of my first assignments was to apprehend a high-ranking Nazi official in the Duisburg area. He was the overall Nazi Party chief for the region. Accompanied by another member of the detachment, I drove one of our jeeps to the suburb in which he resided. The military situation was still quite fluid and outlying districts were not yet under our control. Many German soldiers were still armed, some putting up stiff resistance. We found the suburb without encountering any difficulty. The Nazi's home was a large villa on a street of beautiful houses, many of them damaged from bombing and artillery fire.

Ringing the bell at the outer gate, we waited to see if anyone was home, half expecting the place to be abandoned. Instead, a woman came to the door of the villa and called out, asking us what we wanted. When we told her, she responded that the person we were seeking was out of town. We told her that we were American military personnel and that we wished to come into the house. If our man was not there, at a minimum we were going to have to make an effort to obtain information concerning his whereabouts. The woman, who turned out to be his wife, was a formidable obstacle. A large Brunhilde type, she obviously was used to exercising authority. "Do you realize whose house this is?" she demanded, totally unaware of the fact that her world had turned upside down. Going through the house, we were awed by the Nazi leader's large home office. The entire wall was lined with magnificent Nazi flags and banners, all gold tasseled, many of them crowned like the standards of the Roman legions. There were signed photographs from the Party elite, including Hitler.

Our job of trying to find some clue as to our man's whereabouts was hindered as the woman followed us around and continually told us that we had no authority to be there and that she would see to it that we were severely punished. We left knowing only that her husband had gone to Berchtesgaden in Bavaria. That case was not one of our success stories. By comparison, when I went to Berlin, I learned how the Russians had rounded up the Nazi leadership. They simply went from villa to villa in posh suburbs and shot anyone suspected of being a Nazi, often including family members. As time passed, I found myself wondering whatever happened to "Brunhilde" back in the Duisburg area under the British, who during their years of occupation of that Zone requisitioned the houses of Nazi Party members, as we later did, for use by their troops.

We did better in our next pursuit. This time we were after a notorious midlevel member of the Gestapo. His last known address was near Oberhausen, again in an area not fully controlled by our forces. To get there we drove through what might best be described as a no-man's-land. We traveled through deserted bombed-out areas, always worried about mines or an unexpected meeting with holdout German soldiers or being shot at by snipers. At times we had to detour and backtrack to get over canals or creeks where the bridges had been blown. Finally arriving at a block of apartment buildings, we had difficulty in finding house numbers. Some structures were badly damaged, others totally destroyed. Uneasy civilians directed us to the proper building. We climbed several flights of stairs to our man's apartment. Neither my colleague nor I expected to find our quarry there, but hoped at least this time to come away with definitive leads.

A middle-aged, round-faced man in slippers came to the door. It was the Gestapo inspector. When he saw us, he attempted to slam the door, but with pistols drawn, we forced our way in. As we interrogated him in the kitchen, I could only think of the many times this evil man must have unceremoniously taken some poor Jew or quaking German into custody. Now ironically the tables were turned and justice was being served. I did not like this aspect of CIC work, however, and was always a bit unnerved by it. In searching his apartment we found two pistols, one a 7.65 mm Walther, the other a 9 mm Luger. Had we not surprised him, we might have had a shootout. We took the prisoner down to our jeep parked about a block away from the entrance to his building.

While walking a step behind the Gestapo inspector on the street, I checked to assure myself that the confiscated Walther I was carrying was unloaded. To do so, I pulled back the bolt and checked the chamber to see if it was empty. It was. I then let the bolt slam forward, pulled out the magazine, pointed the pistol down at the pavement and pulled the trigger. To my astonishment, it discharged with a tremendous bang and a ricocheting sound. Thoughtlessly, by failing to remove the magazine first I had put a round in the chamber. Without touching him, the bullet bounced up, putting a hole in our prisoner's trouser leg. I was appalled, my partner surprised, and the Gestapo man gibbering and terrified. I am sure he thought I had intended to execute him on the spot.

With the cooperation of a screened German police organization, we were able to track down numerous individuals on the wanted list as weeks went on. For the most part they were midlevel members of Nazi organizations, some of whom were surprised that we considered them culpable. Many were detained. As I was later to become more aware in Berlin, the truly notorious top leadership had no doubts about what would happen to them and thus made special preparations to elude apprehension, creating a basic injustice in the denazification program not at first apparent.

Numerous leading figures in local society also held positions in the NSDAP or its affiliate organizations such as the NS *Fliegerkorps* (Flyer Corps) or NS *Kraftfahrerkorps* (Motor Corps). For example, a regional school administrator might also be a member of the *Allgemein* (General) SS, basically a political organization, with his position in it an avocation. A *Hauptsturmfuehrer* (captain) in that body was different from one in the *Waffen* (Armed) SS, a fundamentally military structure, who later served as a full-time soldier. Then again, such a position in the *Totenkopfverband* (Death Head Group) SS usually indicated a full-time position of some authority in the concentration camp structure and the programs to eliminate Jews and opposition elements.

It was important, therefore, that I not only understand the structure of these organizations, but that I be aware of the activities they carried out. I could be relatively certain, when apprehending a member of an SS *Wachbattalion* (guard battalion) who had served at the officer or NCO level at a concentration camp such as Dachau, Buchenwald, Auschwitz, or several other notorious camps in Eastern Europe, that he would be wanted for war crimes. In the *Waffen* SS it was different. Here, the record of the unit or the individual had to be considered. In some cases toward the end of the war, these units were augmented with draftees. *Waffen* SS units serving in Poland and Russia, those comprised largely of ethnic Germans or Eastern Europeans sympathetic to the Nazis, often had records of atrocities. We were particularly on the alert to find members of the SS unit that had conducted the Malmedy massacre in the Battle of the Bulge.

I recall at one point questioning a midlevel member of the *Allgemein* SS who was the director of one of the large steel firms in the Ruhr. He was not the least bit contrite about what he and his Nazi cronies had done to millions of suffering people throughout Europe. He let me know in no uncertain terms that if I did not take care how I treated him, the British branch of his firm would see to it that I would be broken in rank and disciplined. I could hardly contain myself and was truly tempted to tell him that a private in the American Army was handling his august personage. A subsequent comment from a colleague to the effect that in view of the Russian forced laborers employed in his plants, arrangements might be made to turn him over to the Soviets. That prompted an immediate change in his attitude.

When I see tattoos today, I am reminded of the emaciated individuals who had spent time in concentration camps. They would display for us the numbers that had been placed on their arms. In grotesque contrast were the tattoos on the inner upper arms of SS men that they, however, endeavored to keep hidden from us.

On one of our forays into the countryside, we may have made history. We were driving south in our jeep on the main road to Duesseldorf one afternoon not long after our arrival in Duisburg. We had gone about five miles without seeing another vehicle when in the distance we saw a column of tanks coming toward us. Our immediate thought was that they were not ours, since they did not look like Shermans or British Churchills. From a distance they looked low slung, possibly German Panzers. Our hope was that they had not spotted us, as my colleague swerved the jeep off the highway and down a slight embankment. He turned it around to be prepared to make a fast getaway.

We quickly got out of the jeep, keeping low to the ground, to take a better look. I recall wishing we had field glasses. Just as we said in unison, "Let's get out of here!" a vehicle that appeared to be a jeep came up to the front of the column. After half a minute, it became obvious that they were Americans. We climbed back into our jeep and drove down to them, with me standing up and waving so that they would not take hostile action. When we reached them, a captain greeted us, asking us who we were. We told him we were with an intelligence detachment from the 17th Airborne Division. He responded that they were the advance element of the 13th Armored Division attacking north to link up with U.S. units. I informed him that as far as we could tell there was nothing between his outfit and the 194th Glider Infantry Regiment.

In no time, we were treated to the sight of tanks stretching down the highway with their hatches open and tankers waving and cheering. Evidently, the word had been sent down the line by radio of our meeting. After the war, I learned that Willie Glass, my boyhood friend and best man at my wedding, was in the 13th Armored Division. Had I known it at the time, I would have made an effort to find him. He was a tanker in one of those battalions farther down the column. The following day there was a report on our Armed Forces Radio that American units had closed the Ruhr pocket. Perhaps there was another link-up elsewhere, but I like to think that our meeting was the actual one.

Two CIC agents, on a rotating basis, were stationed at the bridge over the Rhine at Duisburg as part of the security effort to screen Germans and other foreign nationals moving to the west bank, France, and the Benelux countries. Initial MP and civilian guard screening would cull out possible security or other suspects for our subsequent questioning. In this task, we were exposed to hundreds of tales of escapes from bombings, concentration camps, or ravaging Russian troops. Had someone been there to tape these sagas, they would have provided plots for many movies.

As a precaution against the spread of infectious diseases and epidemics from Eastern Europe to the West, an installation for delousing was set up at the crossing point. This public health procedure always caused considerable upheaval. Aristocratic elderly women, forced from their homes and now refugees, would invariably become incensed when told by some MP that they would have to be deloused. Dealing with masses of humanity in extremis, with all manner of problems, can be the education of a lifetime.

I learned a great deal about the Nazi structure during this screening. It was particularly helpful to me later when in graduate school I wrote a thesis on denazification policy. Most Germans were in some Nazi-sponsored organization, whether a youth group, a labor front, or a professional or sport association. Occasionally we would encounter someone on our detention list or a person in a particular organization responsible for war crimes. I was always amazed how these people could declare their innocence, claiming they were only acting under orders or that they were unaware of what was taking place.

The most memorable incident of my duty with our division's CIC detachment came one day when a German civilian walked into our office in Duisburg and informed us that he knew where a secret cache of arms had been buried. In the waning days of the war, there was great concern about the possibility of a large-scale underground resistance movement that could pose a major threat to our forces. I informed our commanding officer about the report, which he took seriously, particularly in view of other data related to the formation of "Werewolf" cells in the area. Another agent and I drove the man to a field screened from the road by trees several miles out of town. He said he had noted from a distance that a contingent of men in uniform, as well as a number of civilians, had buried something there a month or so earlier. He had been afraid to go to the spot himself for fear of being observed.

Using shovels we had brought, we began to dig to unearth the suspected weapons and boxes of ammunition. We had gone down less than a foot, when my colleague uncovered a decomposing human arm. Within minutes the German, some distance away, also began uncovering bodies. It was a relatively cool and windy day, but even so I cannot believe how we could have been so empty-headed as not to have focused on the smell in the area. We were so preoccupied with the thought we were going to locate a Werewolf cache that we were oblivious to everything else. Instead, we had discovered a mass grave.

Reporting back to our office, we took steps to find out what we had uncovered. We learned from German police sources that there had been mass executions of forced laborers, mostly Russians, prior to the arrival of the Allied forces. We had stumbled upon one of the graves. An excavating detail was formed of Nazis held in detention. I was ordered to accompany soldiers of our division guarding the Nazis out to the site and to assist in putting the detail to work. This was one time I wished I had not known a word of German, so that I would not have been called upon. It had been determined that the execution order had been given by the Nazi city police administrator, who was among those selected to do the digging. Unlike my first trip to the place a week earlier, this day was warm and sultry. A German truck loaded with many, rude, pine-box coffins was also sent out to the site.

Early in the excavating, a sergeant in the guard detail came over to me and said that the SS police administrator had refused to dig and asked if I would say something to him in German. Of all the people there, he was the most guilty. I told him to get into the pit and dig out bodies with the others. He struck a pose and said, "*Niemals!*" meaning never. My reaction was instinctive. I took my .45 caliber pistol out of the holster and ordered him again. Evidently contemplating what a Nazi officer would have done under the circumstances, he thought better of his posturing. Jumping into the grave, he began lifting out corpses.

I came away from the incident shaken. There were men and women in that grave in the most horrible states of decomposition. The stench on a warm spring day was unbearable. It was one of the worst things I have had to witness in my life and I still see it in my mind's eye. The bodies were placed in the coffins and taken away for an appropriate burial. Subsequently, an order was given that a dozen or more of the coffins should be buried in a square in the center of Duisburg as a reminder of what the Nazis had done. On occasion I have subsequently wondered whether those coffins were still there. In 1996 at a 17th Airborne Division reunion, I was told by one of the paratroopers who had been in the guard detail that he had been back to Duisburg and found that the square had been paved over and was now the site of a multistoried parking lot.

We were functioning in the Duisburg, Essen, and Oberhausen sectors well before any military government was in place. I recall being involved in the process of finding a suitable mayor and other officials for Duisburg, to start the local administration and public utilities functioning again. It was a large city of perhaps 300,000 people. In retrospect, we were rather naïve in our efforts at reestablishing the governmental process. The Nazis were bad and had to be removed. Conversely, persons who had been imprisoned for political offenses by the Nazis had to be good, we thought. Membership in an organization called the Victims of Fascism (*Opfer des Fascismus*), for example, was considered to be an asset when seeking to work with the Americans. Subsequently, we learned it was a Communist front organization, but no one focused very much on that aspect at the time. I remember that some Germans, when asked whether they had been members of any Nazi organizations, put the matter to rest by declaring that they were Communists. A year later when I was in Berlin, we had learned better and were hard pressed to remove Communist elements in local administrations, particularly as Stalin's Soviet Union endeavored to spread its influence in Germany.

In June 1945 British forces replaced the 17th Airborne Division in the Ruhr industrial area, which was to become part of the British zone of occupation. With that my temporary duty with CIC came to a close. It was a sad day for me when I was told to report back to my company. I had enjoyed the excitement of being a "special agent" and all that went with it. I left after a little ceremony in which other men in the detachment were awarded Bronze Star medals. Not being officially part of the detachment, it would have been up to my own unit to take such action for me.

Within a day or two of reporting back to the 517th Airborne Signal Company, some of us were on our way by truck to France. Leaving Duisburg, we drove through the center of town, our truck column halting for several minutes directly in front of the *Rathaus* and police headquarters where I had worked. As I sat in the back of the truck members of the German staff I had supervised were passing in and out of the buildings. I was embarrassed lest they see PFC Kormann, who had cut such a big swath just days before, sitting in the truck with the rest of the soldiers. The drive took us through many destroyed towns. We could just barely traverse Aachen because so much rubble lay in the streets. Our convoy wound its way through Belgium, the scene of so much heavy fighting that past winter during the Battle of the Bulge. We passed through Houffalize and I saw nothing but ruins. There seemed to be nothing standing over four feet in height.

I do not think many of us fully comprehended what was happening at the time to the 17th Airborne Division. It had fought so well and sacrificed so greatly, first in The Bulge and then in the drop over the Rhine into the German homeland. When it was over, it had taken 6,292 casualties killed and wounded and had lost a regiment, the 193rd Glider Infantry. Its four Medal of Honor awards (the most of any airborne division in World War II) were all posthumous. Tragically, rather than try to reconstitute the 17th, the Army deactivated it, much to the dismay of its commander, pioneer paratrooper Major General William Miley. With the war over in Europe, what remained of the division was largely split up, with some of us sent to the 82nd Airborne Division slated for occupation duty in Berlin. Others were assigned to the 101st Airborne Division destined for the war in the Pacific. A number of high-point veterans were returned to the United States.

It took us two days to reach our destination, the small French city of Epinal, about 35 miles southeast of Nancy and the headquarters of the 82nd Airborne. We were now part of that division and entitled to wear its special honors on our uniforms, a Belgian red and green *fourragère* (braided cord) for our right shoulder, a Dutch orange lanyard for our left, and a Presidential Citation ribbon for the right side of our chest. With that and other ribbons from the 17th Airborne indicating that we had fought in three campaigns and an airborne invasion, our uniforms "lit up like Christmas trees." We were even prouder soldiers when we were told we had been selected to parade for President Truman, Prime Minister Churchill, and Chairman Stalin at the Big Three Conference in Potsdam, Germany.

At an afternoon formation one day in early July in Epinal, I heard my name called out. Reporting to the front, I was surprised and pleased when Major Hancock, the commander of my new company, read aloud an Official Commendation pertaining to my service with CIC. My buddies were impressed that I had captured numerous high-ranking Nazis and that it was recommended I be transferred to Intelligence. Reference was also made to my "fine speaking knowledge of German," which in view of our imminent assignment to Germany resulted in my being asked to teach classes in that language. I did so with pleasure, using simple Army phrasebooks as my texts. Soon the boys had fun calling me "professor."

A few weeks later, as we were departing for Berlin, I was further rewarded with a two-month assignment to a university in Shrivenham, England. I was the only member of the company given that opportunity. The Army, anticipating delays in demobilization at the end of the war, had set up university programs for the troops at Shrivenham in England and

Biarritz in France. Reporting to the university in July 1945, I was afforded a chance to register for three courses, for which I would later be given college credit. I chose German, anthropology, and art from among those offered. I had already shown an aptitude for two of my selections and felt that I would not be too hard pressed to succeed.

My sojourn at Shrivenham was thoroughly enjoyable. We were only a few miles from Swindon and my former haunts. Our weekends were free for trips to London and other places of interest. I met a lovely English girl at a band concert in Hyde Park on a visit to London and was invited by her parents on one occasion to spend the weekend at their home in the suburbs. With everything rationed, I was loath to impose upon them. They could not have been more gracious.

While I was at Shrivenham, an incident occurred that I did not consider humorous at the time but which makes me chuckle now in hindsight. When I first came to England in the summer of 1944 and was engaged in motorcycle courier runs, I would often bring back something from the bakery for one of the corporals in the headquarters. We became friends. He was considerably older than I, probably in his mid-thirties. One Saturday in 1944, when I had received a pass to town, he invited me to join him and his girlfriend to see a movie in Swindon. I cannot remember what the film was, but I have not forgotten what happened.

His girlfriend was an earthy, full-blown blonde, a Frenchwoman who had fled her native country at the outbreak of the war. She sat between us during the movie and throughout the latter half of the film spent the time placing her hand on my knee or thigh in such a way that I could not mistake her overture. I handled the situation as best I could, since my friend, I am sure, was totally unaware of what was going on and I did not want to cause a rift in his friendship with the woman or with me. I found some excuse to part company with them after the show. Thereafter, I saw the corporal at headquarters as usual but never said anything to him about the matter. I did not see the woman again, and the corporal and I subsequently went off with the division to war on the continent.

My course in art at Shrivenham University had progressed very nicely, when the visiting American professor, a recognized artist in his fifties, announced that we would be provided with live models for several sessions in the following two weeks. I thought nothing much about the procedure having been an art student. I came into class a few afternoons later to find a screen in the front of the room with a woman's clothes hanging over the top. Before long, out stepped the French blonde in all her Rubenesque glory. Easels were up all around the room and mine, fortunately, was near the rear. The professor came in, and it did not take much discernment to see that he and the model were bosom friends. At the end of class that day,

I saw the professor ride off on a motorbike with our model clasping him tightly as she rode behind.

The next several days while she posed, I tried as much as possible to blend in with the students in the back of the room. Once or twice, however, during pauses she would look at me as if she were wondering where she had seen me before. I guess I could have livened things up in class in the presence of the professor by saying something such as, "Didn't you used to be the corporal's girlfriend?" Then again, perhaps I could have quipped, "Been to any movies lately?" I was tempted, but thought better of it, not knowing how the professor might have reacted or what impact it might have had on my grade.

My studies at Shrivenham went well, and I received good grades. I was sorry to leave and did not look forward to returning to a soldier's life, although I was excited about being stationed in Berlin and hoping that action had been progressing on my possible transfer to Intelligence. The trip from England to Berlin in those days was an arduous undertaking. There were no quick flights from Heathrow to Tempelhof. I made my way by train to Portsmouth, then by LST (Landing Ship Tank) to Le Havre and from there by rail through Paris to Frankfurt. In Frankfurt, I boarded the special military train that went to the Helmstedt checkpoint and then through the Soviet Zone to Berlin.

The 82nd Airborne Signal Company, of which I was now a part, was quartered in Steglitz, a few blocks off Steglitzerstrasse on Gruenerwald-strasse. The houses were lovely old mansions belonging at one time to aristocratic German families. Entering one of the huge rooms that served as a mess, I remember how shocked I was to see a magnificent painting, perhaps fifteen feet long, of Kaiser Wilhelm I reviewing the German Imperial Dragoons, full of strategically placed cuts and bullet holes. It was a painting worthy of any museum and I hoped that it had been the Russians who had abused it and not our troops.

Occupation duty was a far cry from our responsibilities in the field during the war and even further from those with CIC. We spent a large part of our time serving as guards at headquarters buildings and other key installations. I had my share of guard duty and did not find it pleasant. Little did I know at the time, however, that in not too many months I would be walking in and out of those same buildings as an officer, receiving salutes from those guards. When that happened, I think they sensed a certain empathy as I returned their salutes.

Late summer, early fall 1945 in Berlin was an unsettled time. The city was administered on a quadripartite basis, with members of the Allied forces, including the Russians, moving freely about the city. On time off from company duties, we would go downtown to the Brandenburg Gate area or over to the busy Kurfuerstendamm, the nightclub and theater district, which had entertained the Wehrmacht personnel. It did not skip a beat in turning round to do the same for the victors.

At times, I wandered through the totally bombed-out areas around the Reichstag and the Chancellery, where Hitler had committed suicide. I remember walking one day from there to the Kreuzberg District not far away. I climbed up a pile of rubble about 50 feet high. As I looked around me, I could see nothing standing almost as far as my eye could range. Hitler spoke of a 1,000 year *Reich* (empire). Well, I thought, it is going to take 1,000 years before they can rebuild this place again. The smell of dead bodies was everywhere.[5]

Both the Allied military government and the Berlin city administration made stringent efforts to get public utilities and the transportation system working as soon as possible. What remained of streetcars and buses were put into service relatively early. Large sections of the subway, however, remained flooded and filled with bodies. In a last-ditch attempt to stop the Russians from entering the city through the tunnels, the SS had diverted the waters of the river Spree and the canals into these subways, despite the thousands of people seeking shelter from the bombing and shelling in them.

As a young soldier, I traveled with another paratrooper one evening to a theater that was just starting up deep in the Soviet Sector. The performance was rather lengthy and the city streetcar we had taken over there was no longer running when we came out. We waited for a while in totally deserted, bombed-out streets to no avail. An empty streetcar heading for the barn appeared, which we boldly flagged down. I talked with the motorman, who was no help. I finally told him in forceful German that he was going to take us back over to the American Sector and then return to the barn and that was all there was to it. He ostensibly agreed and headed off with us in the right direction. After about a mile, he stopped the streetcar in front of a building, which turned out to be a Russian military police headquarters. The motorman went in and brought out Soviet MPs. A heated discussion ensued, with the Russian officer in charge not at all sympathetic. The net result of this escapade was that we were held there until picked up the following day by American MPs and returned to our unit.

I was not due for duty until that evening and, as I recall, did not encounter any serious trouble for my folly. A year later, however, it might have been a very different story, for by then the Iron Curtain had come down and the two of us might well have disappeared. By that time, as well, I was busily engaged in a life-and-death struggle with the Soviet espionage services. The Soviets, I later learned, kept dossiers on CIC personnel, so I may have been even luckier than I realized.

No account of Berlin in those days would be complete without some comment on the economy. As the war ended, American soldiers were paid in Allied military scrip, exchangeable at a rate of 10 German marks to the dollar. The true exchange medium, however, was the cigarette, valued at approximately 200 marks a pack. Soldiers quickly found that they could exchange their cigarette rations for large amounts of money and did so. They could also purchase items such as cheap watches, preferably of the Mickey Mouse variety, and sell them to Russian soldiers for hundreds of dollars.

Once we gave the Russians the plates for the scrip, they printed enough to pay off several divisions of their army. Russian soldiers, in turn, paid their American, British, and French counterparts in scrip at fantastically high prices for their wares, to the detriment of Western treasuries. U.S., British, and French troops consequently sent home several times their pay each month. It was a wild time, with the black market dominating the lives of both the occupation forces and the Germans. The latter, by and large, saw any savings they had disappear while at the same time they bartered away what possessions they had for the necessities of life.

I came off guard duty one day and went over to our company mess hall for a cup of coffee. Walking around the back of the baronial German house to enter the kitchen, I spotted a tall, regal, elderly woman, dressed in what once must have been a fine long gown, scraping the inside of one of our metal garbage cans with a bread crust for the residual fat. When I started to walk over to her, addressing her in German, she hurried away with a look of embarrassment on her face now imprinted in my memory. I could only wonder whether at one time that palatial building in which we were quartered had been her family property.

During this period I had my share of spit-and-polish parading. General Patton once commented in Berlin that the 82nd Airborne Division's Honor Guard was the finest he had ever seen. As October 1945 drew to a close, I anxiously waited for some word of my transfer to Intelligence. Finally, I was asked to report to Berlin Headquarters for an interview with the Operations Officer of the 82nd Airborne Counter Intelligence Detachment. In the course of my meeting with him, who should enter the room but the same master sergeant I had originally spoken with in the chow line back in the days of the Battle of the Bulge. He told the captain of how he had recruited me and how I had distinguished myself in CIC work in the Ruhr. From that point on there was no question that serious steps were going to be taken to bring me on board as soon as possible; with all of Berlin on its hands the detachment was buried in work.

Shortly thereafter, I bid my friends in my old company goodbye, loaded my barrack bags in a CIC jeep, and drove to a fine house in the Zehlendorf district, where I was given a large well-appointed room of my own. The next day, I took off my PFC stripes, pinned the gold U.S. insignias on my collar and acquired an officer's overseas cap and trench coat. I received an ID that gave me officer's privileges, including the use of the officers' mess and clubs. I had finally opened opportunity's door and I was in heaven. This time, I was truly a Special Agent of the Counter Intelligence Corps.

January 1946 saw the departure of the 82nd Airborne Division for the United States, but its CIC Detachment remained behind in Berlin. We were declared essential, our work just beginning. With a heavy heart I saw my former company depart for home. Shortly thereafter I heard that the 82nd Airborne had been chosen to march up New York City's Fifth Avenue in a glorious "Victory Parade." Sadly, I wrote to my parents that I would not be back, but that they should go to the parade and see my friends march. I would be there in the ranks with them in spirit. I had made my bed in Berlin and now I had to lie in it.

The 82nd Airborne CIC detachment was broken down into several field offices located throughout the American Sector and was rapidly augmented with personnel from elsewhere in Germany. I was assigned to the Tempelhof Field Office. My duties were a continuation of what I had been doing in the Ruhr. In actuality, because of that, I had more experience than others in the office. My German also was better. Within a few months, the officer in charge of the Tempelhof Field Office was moved up to headquarters to be the operations officer and I, by now in reality only a sergeant, was placed in command. This was one of the anomalies of CIC. You were picked because you could do the job, not because of your rank, which was always kept confidential. Later, as a second lieutenant, I had captains assigned to my office and once, for a short while, even a major.

On occasion, I was given special assignments away from my office. Once, on reports that Hitler's notorious deputy, Martin Bormann, was believed to be hiding in the vast labyrinth that was the underground bunker complex beneath the destroyed *Reichskanzlei* (Hitler's palatial headquarters), I was ordered to dress in shabby German civilian clothes and camp out in that ruined subterranean area. I did so for days, armed only with a snub-nosed .38 caliber pistol, in the hope I might pick up some information or even on the wild chance that I might encounter him.

At one point down in those darkened passages, I heard voices that sounded authoritative coming from an area behind a heavy iron grid cemented into the walls. There was no way I could get through, and efforts to find another route in were to no avail. I reported the finding to my contact. After that, American troops cordoned off the entire area and a search was made of the passages. However, we succeeded only in routing out a number of German refugees who had fled from the East and taken shelter there.

Rummaging around in those ruins did have one benefit. In the rubble, I found a blackened, dusty, heavy metal plaque about 6 x 12 inches in size. It featured a raised side-view bust of Hitler and below him the Nazi swastika eagle in high relief. An inscription, also in raised print, stated, in translation, "IN COMMEMORATION OF THE COMPLETION OF THE REICHSCHANCELLERY, CONSTRUCTED FROM MARCH 1938 TO THIS DATE. DEDICATED TO THE WORKERS, JANUARY 9, 1939." I was not able at the time to establish where the plaque had been placed. However, I kept it as a fine souvenir and took it home with me when I left Germany. Later in 1954, when I was stationed in Bonn with the State Department, I felt I should inform the German authorities that I had the plaque, thinking perhaps it should be returned. I mentioned the matter to members of the Foreign Office but received a cold response. Nazism was something Germans wanted to forget. In 2001, I gave it to the Franklin D. Roosevelt Library and Museum.[6]

Martin Bormann was to be my quarry on another occasion, again without result. In a final report on the matter to CIC Headquarters, I concluded that he had last been seen alive near a Tiger Tank on a bridge over the Spree Canal. The tank was set ablaze by Russian troops as they battled in that downtown Berlin area, and Bormann died in the vicinity. Several decades later, workmen excavating for the foundations of a building found a corpse in a *Reichsleiter's* (Imperial Leader's) uniform a number of blocks from that bridge. Doubts remained, however, as to whether it was Bormann until DNA tests settled the matter in the mid-1990s. I finally had the satisfaction of knowing that I had been correct. For decades, there had been reports that Bormann was residing somewhere in South America.

From time to time I was given different identities.[7] I still have an official Berlin city identification card in my files with a photograph of me as a German police officer. There is also an unrelated U.S. Army authorization giving me the power to arrest both German and American nationals, as well as to carry the snub-nosed .38 caliber revolver I wore in a shoulder holster on some of these assignments.

In the early months of 1946, the emphasis was still on rounding up ranking Nazis and individuals charged with war crimes. Berlin, not only as the seat of government, but as the headquarters of the security services of the SS and the *Gestapo*, was a far more fertile field than other parts of Germany in which to apprehend individuals on the war crimes list. Although some of the notorious personages had escaped from Berlin or had been captured or killed by the Soviets in April and May of 1945 on their entry into the city, others were still in hiding. Berlin was also the refuge for numbers of SS concentration camp personnel from Eastern Europe who had fled westward with remnants of the German military. The CIC field offices sought them all out, and before long the Wannsee Detention Center was full. Some were then brought before the Nuremberg Courts and others were administered justice elsewhere. Once while on a business trip to Munich, I used the occasion to visit Dachau and the concentration camp. I came away numb, recalling the mass grave I had uncovered in the Ruhr and the cadaverous survivors from the camps I had questioned.

From the outset, our relationship with the Soviets was an uneasy one. Efforts at cooperation in apprehending Nazi leaders were attempted but yielded little results. One endeavor that I have never seen mentioned anywhere may be worth recording. My memory is a bit vague, but essentially this is what occurred. Our CIC Headquarters in Berlin let the word out that we would be interested in meeting with the NKVD, a predecessor of the KGB, to obtain certain Nazis on our wanted list we thought the Soviets might be holding. Elaborate plans were set up to meet over in Pankow in the Soviet Sector. The Russians reportedly were flying in an NKVD general from Moscow for the meeting.

We did everything to protect the identities of our personnel. The person who was designated to the Russians as our senior representative was impressive in appearance, but really only a nominal member of our unit. One of his "assistants" actually headed the group. All the names used were fictitious. The driver of the car was in reality one of the higher-ranking officers. Two meetings were held, but when Washington got word of what was going on, I was later told, it put a stop to the operation. I do not know where this incident ranks in the annals of Soviet-U.S. intelligence cooperation, but it certainly was a reflection of those extraordinary times.

Our office at Tempelhof was at times brought into unusual situations involving the Russians. I can remember receiving an excited call from the area German police chief to the effect that some Russian soldiers were creating a disturbance at a Catholic hospital in Lichterfelde, which was in our sector near the border of the Soviet Zone. Although a U.S. military police station was nearer to the scene, we had a closer working relationship with the German police because more of us spoke German. I took another agent with me to the hospital. We arrived to find several inebriated Russian soldiers with lust in their eyes chasing the nurses, who were nuns, around the place. The most bizarre aspect of this affair was finding two of the Russians, roaring drunk, in the hospital morgue strenuously having sex with female cadavers. By the time we were through, we had both the

American and the Soviet military police involved in a situation that today would have been grist for the tabloids.

Before long our efforts at rounding up Nazi war criminals were overshadowed by the Cold War and problems with the Russians. The latter soon became engaged in efforts to abduct German scientists with backgrounds in the nuclear or rocket propulsion fields and ship them off to the Soviet Union. They were not hesitant about kidnapping them from the Western sectors, and witnesses would give accounts of black limousines, the standard German police vehicle, pulling up in front of houses or apartment buildings and East German policemen and Russians—probably NKVD—in civilian clothes spiriting away their prey. Sometimes these abductions would be carried out in the dead of night, on other occasions in broad daylight. Through our informant network we would try to learn about prospective kidnappings and take steps to intervene. It was a dangerous business, one in which, when it was our office's case, I was usually directly involved. Often we would work with the British or French when intervening in their sectors, or at a minimum obtain clearance from them.

As 1946 wore on, our activity shifted inexorably to countering espionage. We were inundated by enemy agents, generally low-level East Germans working for the Soviets whose mission might be as simple as acquiring a U.S. Army Berlin Command telephone book or a schedule of military flights out of Tempelhof Airport. We in turn attempted to penetrate the sources of these and other activities, and an extensive intelligence network was established. Each field office developed its own group of "informants." The term "agent" was not applied to the latter, since they were involved in counterintelligence, but the activity was basically the same. While I was still in charge of the Tempelhof Field Office, an incident occurred that I will never forget, since it had all the potential for a large-scale human disaster.

At one point the field offices were asked to provide Berlin CIC Headquarters with a set of duplicate files relating to their informant networks, which were obviously very sensitive and highly classified. We were told Berlin had received a request for a composite set of these files from Frankfurt, the overall European CIC Headquarters. Why this was to be done I can only surmise, but it appeared to me to be administration for its own sake. A special plane was dispatched to Tempelhof Airport for the purpose of taking the files back down to Frankfurt. A lieutenant colonel from the European Command CIC Headquarters in Frankfurt was placed in charge of the project, and he arrived to escort the material, which filled a briefcase, personally.

I recall meeting the lieutenant colonel at supper in our officers' mess the evening before he was to return to Frankfurt. I learned from others that he was a person of some importance, reportedly the nephew of a very senior and powerful member of the U.S. Congress. He was quartered that night at the Columbia House Hotel officers' billets at Tempelhof Airport, which was near our field office.

The following morning I was at work when I received a call from headquarters informing me that the special plane was waiting, but the lieutenant colonel had not appeared. He had taken the briefcase with all the files with him overnight, since the plane was to take off early that morning. I was told to get over to the officers' billets on the double to see if he had overslept or if something was wrong. I ascertained that he was not in his room, in the dining room, or anywhere else in the building. His bed had not been slept in. There were no messages at the desk. He had simply disappeared. Nor was the briefcase anywhere to be seen. When informed, headquarters was apprehensive, and later that day it went into shock. The reverberations were felt all the way back to Frankfurt and Washington. Had he been kidnapped? Had he defected? The day went by with everyone engaged in an effort at damage control. If the Soviets had him and the briefcase, it was a catastrophe of the first order. Many lives were in jeopardy.

He turned up a day or so later. He had a drinking problem and had been on a binge over in the Berlin nightclub district. The briefcase had been left in an unguarded baggage room full of other pieces of luggage. It was the last place anyone would have looked. Considering its "Top Secret" classification, not to say its contents, it was inconceivable that the briefcase would not have been chained to the officer's wrist, much less out of his sight. The lieutenant colonel returned to Frankfurt under guard and the entire matter was subsequently handled discreetly. I never did find out what finally happened.

On another occasion, an informant provided Berlin Headquarters with information that had all the appearances of a higher-level case of espionage. We were told about a prospective contact between an alleged Soviet agent and a well-placed German working for the U.S. forces. The meeting was to take place in an apartment near the border with the Soviet Zone. In a surreptitious casing of the building, it was noted that a toilet for general use of the apartments on that floor abutted the living room of our suspect. Headquarters conceived a plan in which the building would be placed under surveillance so as to observe the arrival of the Soviet agent. As soon as he entered the suspect's apartment, the plan called for me, dressed as one of the German apartment dwellers, to climb the stairs to the given floor, enter the toilet, and listen through the wall to the conversation in the adjoining living room.

All went according to plan except that I could hear next to nothing, other than the flushing and related noises in the toilets above and below me. After a while, in disgust, I left the building and joined the sizeable group who had come to cordon off the area, leaving them to take both men into custody. As things turned out "Operation Outhouse," as it was dubbed by some wags, had no intelligence significance, but it did become the source of considerable ribald merriment.

In the late spring of 1946, the original 82nd Airborne CIC Detachment was disbanded and reconstituted to conform to organizational changes throughout Germany. We became Region VIII of the 970th CIC Detachment.[8] The latter serviced the entire European Command and was headquartered in Frankfurt. Region VIII (Berlin) was divided into subregions, with each of the field offices assuming that title. I became the Subregional Commander of Tempelhof.

Berlin was a wonderful place to be stationed after the war. It was a cosmopolitan city where many amenities sprang back into existence at a relatively early stage. With the large unemployed German labor force, we could obtain all types of services economically. Our small CIC officers' mess, for example, daily had its own musical accompaniment for meals featuring a pianist, a string ensemble, or both. There was a general acceptance of this situation and of the fact that most services and commodities could be obtained for a pittance with cigarettes. An effort was even made to see that the Germans were treated more equitably. Mrs. Lucius Clay, the wife of the U.S. Military Governor of Germany, was a driving force in setting up a barter center where the local population could bring items and receive a "fair" price for them. My future mother-in-law (to be introduced in the next chapter), fine Christian woman that she was, once obtained a used typewriter for the local church this way for two cartons of cigarettes, actually a very fair price by the standards of those times. A carton cost a soldier $1 in the PX, but was worth $200 on the black market.

The good living also had its detractions, often accompanied by considerable outlandish behavior. There were scandals involving high-ranking officers with mistresses, drinking, and unseemly conduct. Cases of high-finance black marketeering were brought to light, implicating both officers and enlisted personnel. Virtually everyone had a German girlfriend. The venereal disease rate among the troops soared. At one point commanders of the various military units were regularly assembled and told that their performance would be judged on how well they kept the VD rate down. Slides would be shown in these meetings with graphs depicting the VD levels in each organization. The U.S. administration stepped up efforts to bring this deplorable state of affairs to a halt. Cigarettes, which provided the troops with the wherewithal for much of the extravagance, were rationed and monitored. Wives and families were also brought over.

The situation in Berlin and an inadvertent action on my part were to play a role in my next assignment. I was having breakfast one Sunday morning in July 1946 when two officers visiting our unit from Frankfurt joined me. I had not met them before, knew nothing about them, and did not learn anything more during the course of our breakfast. At one point, a colleague came up to me and asked me something about my PX Ration Card. I remember handing him my card. He, in turn, expressed dismay that my cigarette allotment was mostly unused and had expired. I stated that I did not smoke cigarettes, only cigars, which were not rationed. His comment was, "Hell, why didn't you give it to me, rather than waste it?" A few weeks later, all, save a handful of us, were transferred to other CIC units down in the American Zone. Little did I realize at the time that the two visitors sitting with me that Sunday morning at breakfast were part of an inspectors' team intent on "cleaning up Berlin."

Our commander, the operations officer, and one or two others including me remained. There followed a wholesale shift of CIC personnel from other parts of Germany and the United States to Berlin. I was transferred from Tempelhof and promoted to Subregional Commander of Neukoelln. At about the same time, I was discreetly informed that action had been taken to give me a field commission and that I should report to Frankfurt to be sworn in. In a brief procedure a few weeks just after my twenty-second birthday, I was discharged as a "buck" sergeant and commissioned a second lieutenant, infantry. The infantry designation reflected a previous enlisted military occupational specialty (MOS) as a "rifleman." After three and a half difficult years, I had finally become a commissioned officer.

As I look back on it now, I cannot think of a more chastening preparation for an officer than having served as a private in the paratroops during wartime. Ironically, as soon as I left Frankfurt, I took off my gold bars and returned to using only the U.S. insignia on my officer's uniform or to wearing civilian clothes.

Neukoelln was a heavily built-up downtown area with many shops and apartment buildings, a combination middle class and blue-collar district and densely populated. Allied bombing had caused considerable destruction, and many buildings were reduced to rubble. Those left standing had damaged roofs and upper floors, with still inhabitable lower areas. Our office was on the second floor of a large, impressive old-fashioned bank building. The first floor housed a sizeable quadripartite military police station. The bank vaults in the basement had been converted into jail cells.

The Neukoelln office was staffed by half a dozen agents and as many German administrative personnel. The senior German staff member was a former police official whose background had been carefully screened. He was a taciturn, hard-working employee, whose knowledge, advice, and ability to deal with German officials proved invaluable. My second-in-command was a gregarious older first lieutenant from Texas. The office administration was in the hands of a warrant officer, who had emigrated from Czechoslovakia just prior to the Hitler takeover. The German staff did a lot of the routine clerical work in dealing with a population of over 300,000 people. Anything classified, however, was handled by an American NCO clerk-typist.

Our building housed two other American facilities. The area U.S. Military Government Office was located on the floor above us, headed by a major I was to know well and with whom I cooperated fully. An office of B Company of the 759th Military Police Battalion was on the floor below us. The company itself was housed around the corner, a block and a half away, in several apartment buildings and a large parking garage. The commander of that company, Albert Feldman, a pugnacious captain from Philadelphia, became a good friend. Shortly after I took over the office, I received a call from him telling me that a Russian troop train on its way to central Berlin's Anhalter Bahnhof had stopped on the outskirts of Neukoelln. The Russian soldiers from a division made up of Siberian troops had left the train and were engaged in wholesale looting of the apartment buildings along the tracks.

As I had a broad-gauged responsibility for the security of the area, he asked me to come along to see what was afoot. We drove to the scene in a jeep with an MP driver and a German civilian Russian interpreter attached to the quadripartite MP station. Arriving at the point along the tracks where the long boxcar train was located, we saw that it had apparently responded to a routine signal for an extended delay before proceeding farther to the station. The boxcars were loaded, and the side of the track was lined with hundreds of household items from nearby apartment buildings—chairs, lamps, tables, pictures, wall mirrors, pots, pans, and even a sofa or two. Many Germans stood off to the side in a state of high dudgeon. The Russians, during and shortly after the war, engaged in taking spoils as they traveled through Germany, but this was more than a year after the cessation of hostilities. It was also against Allied quadripartite regulations.

The Russian troops were of Asian, likely Mongolian or Tartar, background; a scruffy, mean-looking lot, they were all heavily armed with submachine guns. We sought out the Soviet train commander, who turned out to be a pudgy major with a broad smile displaying half a dozen steel teeth. Our captain told the interpreter to inform him that he was in the American Sector of Berlin, that what his troops were doing was illegal, and that they should return the items forthwith. By this time, a number of the Russian soldiers had gathered around to see what was happening. The major's response was to smile even more broadly and shrug his shoulders, as if to say, "What can I do? Boys will be boys. Anyway, who won the damn war?"

The exchange went on for several minutes without result. Finally, Captain Feldman told the Russian major through the interpreter that his troops would have to cease what they were doing and take the items back or he should consider himself under arrest. He would have to proceed with us to the Allied Kommandatura, where he would be turned over to Soviet General Kotikov. To reinforce his statement, Feldman took out his .45 caliber pistol and motioned to the major to accompany him to our jeep.

With all those heavily armed Soviet soldiers around, I could not believe what was happening. By this time, however, the major's smiling face had turned ashen. The mention of the Komandatura and General Kotikov put him in an agitated state. He began giving orders to the troops to remove their loot from the boxcars and then to get on the train. In minutes, everyone was aboard, and in a short while the train proceeded on its way. The side of the track for a hundred yards was littered with items dumped out of the boxcars. Chaos ensued, with apartment residents pouring out of the buildings to recover their belongings. I had been taught a lesson about dealing with the Russians I would not forget.

One morning, our senior German staff member came to see me saying that the local German police chief was outside and wished to speak with me. He was ushered in, accompanied by the handsomest dog I had ever seen, a beautifully marked, male black and white Shepherd just two years old. The chief explained that over the past months the German police had been forced to do away with their dogs, because they simply had no means to feed them. In these very difficult times after the war, large segments of the Berlin population were going hungry. Dogs were being used as a source of food. He could not bear to see this magnificent animal, which had been well trained, put away. Would I like to have him or find a home for him?

I took one look at the dog, called him to me, and that was that. I had a companion for years to come. I thanked the chief profusely and when he left, I ordered the dog to *sitz* next to my chair behind the desk, which he did. He responded to numerous German commands without hesitation. I took him to my quarters after work and fed him well. That night he slept beside my bed contentedly. Once or twice while sleeping, my hand must have hung down alongside the mattress and I felt his nose nuzzle into my palm. He was a wonderfully affectionate animal, who would subsequently accompany me everywhere. A very intelligent dog, I renamed him Socrates.

I had ample opportunity to meet members of the local German community. My interest in art brought me into contact with Georg Majewicz, a prominent artist, whose works were well known in Germany. His familiar painting, "The Crucifixion," hung in the Vatican's museum. Majewicz had survived the early days after the fall of Berlin by painting copies of Russian museum pictures for Soviet soldiers. His situation when I met him was desperate. I arranged to "study" with him in my spare time, and provided him with money, food, and cigarettes, helping him to refurbish his studio and obtain much needed art supplies. At one point Majewicz indicated he would like to paint a portrait of me with my dog, Socrates, and asked if I could let him have a photograph. I did so, commenting offhandedly that he could consider his effort a commission. He thereafter painted from the picture in a surprising way.

Just before I departed Berlin for home, Majewicz presented me with a large full-length portrait in the romantic, grand-museum style of a Van Dyke or a Gainsborough. The oil painting was encompassed in a massive gold frame.[9] I had been expecting something considerably smaller. There I stood, in paratroop officer's dress uniform, with Socrates at my side, on an airfield with C-47 planes in the background ascending into a dawn sky. What to do with it? The painting was rolled up and the frame disassembled, and it was all crated and shipped to my sister Elsie's residence in New Jersey, along with my household effects. Poor Elsie must have gone into shock when it arrived. Too large to hang in any ordinary room, too much of a worthy work of art to discard, it has been a problem ever since.

One day we picked up a low-level Soviet agent, a Yugoslav national, who was, to say the least, unusual. His name was Gorba and he had a remarkable gift of gab. His mission, apparently, was to collect information one might well have obtained by reading the newspapers or going to the library. He was held by the German police during the interrogation process. However, soon the police were complaining about women descending on the prison, each tearfully claiming to be his wife and begging for his release. I was treated to one of these sessions, as well. In virtual exasperation, we finally set the fellow free with an admonishment to mend his ways. Our generosity was tempered by the knowledge that the Russians would thenceforth be suspicious of him, fearing that we might have turned him into a double agent.

I had long dismissed Gorba from my mind when one evening in the Harnack Haus Officers' Club I saw a familiar face at an adjoining table. The man was in an officer's uniform I could not identify and was accompanied by an American nurse—a captain. Before long, I realized it was Gorba. But what was he doing in uniform, in the Harnack Haus dating an American officer? Our past interrogation had revealed nothing about his having had any military service whatsoever. The following morning we were back in the business of checking on Gorba.

As it turned out, he had been riding a motorcycle down the boulevard in front of the American 279th Station Hospital when he was involved in an accident. Admitted on an emergency basis, he had concocted a story for the staff that he was a Yugoslav officer with Marshall Tito's army and was therefore entitled to treatment as a member of the Allied Forces. During his hospital stay of two weeks he was treated royally and had a great time with the nurses. We endeavored to untangle matters by discreetly contacting his date, the American nurse, to tell her about Gorba's background. This was a mistake—she might just as well have been one of those German women who had visited the prison.

I finally had to call on the colonel in charge of the hospital and inform him of the situation. Gorba was again taken into custody, and again we were confronted with women begging for his release. I half expected to see the American nurse in this parade, but her colonel must have driven some sense into her. When the German prison doctor informed us that in addition to everything else Gorba had gonorrhea, that did it! This time, we simply turned him over to the Russians.

While serving in Neukoelln, I was involved in an incident that made international headlines. My German secretary transferred a telephone call to me one evening from a woman who was hysterically sobbing that her husband was being kidnapped by the Russians. I calmed her down enough to get an address from her, which turned out to be relatively close to our office. It was after the close of business, and I was the only agent in the office. Reacting to the urgency, I told my secretary to alert the American MP desk sergeant downstairs to what was happening and rushed out. With Socrates accompanying, I jumped into my jeep and drove the eight blocks to the address the woman had given me.

Sure enough, parked outside the apartment building was the telltale black Mercedes limousine. They were still in the building. With only my pistol and the dog, I climbed the stairs to a floor where an argument was raging and the prospective captive was fighting to fend off two men in dark civilian suits and an East German policeman. The struggling man was screaming that he was Swiss and that the Russians had no jurisdiction over him. I made my presence known by shouting in my loudest, most authoritative German, "American CIC, security police! What's going on here?"

Through the East German policeman, the NKVD explained that the man was a Russian deserter and had to be turned over to Soviet authorities. The captive refuted this, saying he was a *Wissenschaftler* (scientist) formerly employed by the Wehrmacht and that he had Swiss citizenship. After a few minutes of these conflicting statements, I declared that the matter would have to be settled by the four-power Kommandatura. I took the scientist by the arm, saying I was taking him to the quadripartite military police station and that the Russians should accompany us. While all of this was taking place, Socrates remained by my side, menacingly baring his teeth.

As I drove the scientist back to my office building, I reflected on how dangerous, if not foolhardy, it was to have acted alone. On the other hand, had I waited around for help, I might have been too late. At least I had told my secretary to alert the American MP desk sergeant. I returned to find that a jeep with MPs had departed to come after me. They must have taken a different route through the city streets, for our paths had not crossed. The black Mercedes and its occupants followed me back, stayed a short while attempting to regain custody of their captive, and then departed, leaving the Soviet element attached to the MP station in a visible state of excitement. The scientist was placed in one of the cells for safekeeping that night. He was greatly relieved to be in our custody, having thought that he surely would have been on his way to Moscow, if not Siberia.

I arrived at the office early the following morning to find the place in an uproar. A truckload and several other vehicles of Soviet troops, numbering forty or more, had come to take custody of the "deserter." They were in the process of taking him out of the jail cell with the assistance of the Russian MPs. The American desk sergeant, overwhelmed by it all, had just telephoned over to the Company B orderly room a block away, giving a situation report and calling for help. I intervened, demanding to speak with the Soviet officer in charge, but by this time the Russians had removed the scientist from the cell and were dragging him out towards the door.

At that moment there was a deafening scream of a siren from a large M-20 armored car. Its front wheels mounted several steps at the entrance of the building. With a whirring sound, it trained its cannon right into the MP station. This was followed by the screeching sounds of Captain Feldman's jeep and the shouts of his company of MPs coming around the corner on the double. If ever there was a tour de force, this was it. A heated argument ensued, with much posturing. Feldman was not about to give up the scientist. The Soviets were outnumbered, with reinforcements in jeeps with mounted machine guns continuing to arrive. The entire scene provided a spectacle for a crowd of Germans, who had gathered nearby. The Russians, after making numerous threats, finally left without their prisoner.

Within a few hours, the affair was the talk of official circles. Berlin Command wanted a complete report on the matter. Our representatives on the Four Power Allied Control Council for Germany and the Berlin Kommandatura also wanted to be fully informed. Evidently, it was a delicate time in our relations with the Russians and the last thing the Western governments wanted was a confrontation of this sort. Our office was instructed to be closemouthed about the matter.

The following day, an attractive young blonde woman correspondent from the *New York Herald Tribune* appeared at our door, inquiring about the confrontation. Her name was Marguerite (Maggie) Higgins.[10] She was already quite famous, having achieved her reputation in World War II as a woman who would go to any lengths to obtain a story. I had given strict orders to my staff not to talk about the subject and to refer all questions to me. I, in turn, told Higgins that all inquiries should be directed to Berlin Command. She was not about to be deterred. By questioning Germans and possibly some of the MP personnel, she managed to piece together the story. Her talent for making her reporting dramatic soon came into play, when the next day the *Herald Tribune's* international edition carried a banner headline reading, "Yanks and Soviets Clash in Berlin."

With the publication of the story, my phone practically jumped off the hook with angry calls from headquarters. I protested that we had been closemouthed, but to no avail. Higgins's femme fatale reputation had preceded her. Major General Frank Keating, the senior officer in Berlin, was going "to nail my hide to the wall," and I had better come up to headquarters right away. Arriving there, I assured everyone again that we were not responsible for the newspaper's story and in a bit of pique declared, "Who the hell saved the damn scientist from being kidnapped anyway?[11] Maybe someone should remind the general of that fact!" That outburst seemed to deflate the situation and I was never called on the carpet.

The incident was soon put behind us as the Soviets themselves created a furor among the population and in the press by entering into a unilateral campaign of stripping industrial assets from East Berlin and sending them to Russia. In addition to removing materiel, they also started forcibly taking skilled workers. Cynically, *Neues Deutschland,* the German language Communist newspaper, remarked that after all the damage Germany had done, the Soviets were entitled to these "reparations" and German workers should willingly assist in setting things right.

Kidnappings by the Soviets were a serious matter and, as I will recount later in this narrative, could sometimes strike close to home. Nevertheless, as grave as things seemed, there were—depending on your viewpoint— some humorous moments. For several months, an officer from the WDD (War Department Detachment), a predecessor of the Central Intelligence Agency, was attached to our CIC unit.[12] The individual in question was a bit odd, a closemouthed fellow who took himself very seriously. On one occasion, another subregion I happened to be visiting had taken charge of a black Mercedes sedan, similar to the ones used by the East German police. The commander of that office invited me to ride with him in the sedan back to our officers' mess for lunch. As we came within several blocks of our compound, we spotted the WDD officer on foot headed in the same direction. My colleague slowed the car to a crawl, pulled up behind him, rolled down the window, and, jokingly, in his best Russian accent, called out his name in hushed tones. My friend's purpose, above and beyond the levity, was to offer the fellow a ride.

To our astonishment, with one bound he leaped over a six-foot-high hedge into the adjoining garden and was gone. In no time, the incident became the talk of the headquarters, as the WDD officer reported an attempted kidnapping and we, chagrined, endeavored to explain what had happened. While most people roared with laughter over the affair, there were enough others in high places upset by it to make the situation unpleasant.

Although CIC was having its problems with the Russians as early as autumn 1945, other elements at upper levels charged with the occupation and governing of Germany were bending over backwards to cooperate with them. They did not take kindly to our initial efforts at counterespionage and countersubversion. Matters were made worse as the Congress, especially the House Unamerican Activities Committee, began a campaign of "uncovering" suspected communists in the U.S. government. These efforts were to set the stage for the later forays of Senator Joseph McCarthy. One of the accusations related to an official serving with the Military Government in Berlin, and our CIC organization was brought into the investigative process. The result was a tendency on the part of some persons in Military Government to regard us as part of a government witch hunt.

As time went on and our relations with the Soviets worsened, we grew aware of Communist expansionist tendencies. The Russians began increasing pressure to make the West's position in Berlin untenable. They interfered with our access along the Autobahn from Helmstedt to Berlin and held up travel of the special Allied train from Frankfurt. Incidents occurred in the air corridor. As one aspect of their considerable saber rattling, from time to time the Soviets moved masses of tanks in their zone to the border of the city, as if about to invade.

I recall one meeting at Berlin Headquarters, when the situation was deemed so serious that those of us with subregions bordering the Soviet Sector and/or Zone were given instructions by Colonel William Heimlich, the Berlin G-2, to patrol the perimeters. One would have thought that this would have been a job for the infantry or armored units. Instead, the job was given to intelligence, with the thought that we were the least likely to exacerbate matters. In a jeep with another agent, I patrolled the streets and fields of the border with the Soviet Zone one night, listening to the rumblings of Russian tanks on maneuvers in the distance. I wondered what our chances for survival would have been had those tanks, indeed, come crashing across.

There have been several references in this narrative to "denazification" and some further explanation of this program is warranted, since it related to aspects of Counter Intelligence Corps activity. A "Special Branch" of each Public Safety Section in U.S. Military Government Offices in Germany was established to ensure that no Nazis be returned to positions of authority, that they be relegated only to ordinary labor. As part of this, a vast vetting procedure was undertaken in which large numbers of Germans were required to complete *Fragebogen* (questionnaires) comprised of 150 questions.[13] Virtually any German having contact with the U.S. forces or state-run activities was asked to fill one out. CIC cooperated closely with Special Branch in this effort and it brought us into contact with all segments of society.

While much of this screening process was tedious, some of it could be quite interesting, especially, for example, when it came to the theater and the arts. Making contact with movie stars, actresses, ballerinas, "icecapades" starlets, and the like was far from an unpleasant task and on occasion provided an unusual entrée into the entertainment world, not to mention attractive escorts. During the course of such duties, one of the officers in the organization became deeply involved with a female acrobat, a woman in her late twenties. Theirs was an extended torrid affair, and "Mutti" ("Momma") as she became known, was somewhat of a fixture around his quarters. All went well until, as part of the policy to restore normal life among the overseas military, his wife and children were brought over. In the ebb and flow of those times, this was not an unusual situation. In most instances, after discreet, tearful farewells, husbands left their girlfriends and went back to their families.

However, this case was different. Mutti was convinced that she was the officer's only true love and that his life would be meaningless without her. Nothing he could say or do could make her think otherwise. I was sound asleep one night when my phone rang. It was the officer, beside himself, calling for my assistance. Mutti was banging on the front door of his house demanding to come in, while his wife and children were asleep upstairs. He begged me, as a friend, to come and take her away. After some hesitation, I agreed. Through my German police contacts, I quickly arranged to have a patrolman meet me at the house. The sight of the German policeman tempered her antics and soon we had Mutti in the jeep heading downtown. On the way, the policeman and I admonished her about the seriousness of her actions, threatening her with incarceration should she ever attempt to disturb the peace again.

Returning to my bed hours later, I wondered what had happened in the officer's household. Surely, the racket had awakened everyone and I could only guess, with a suppressed smile, at the story he must have concocted in explanation. I was not smiling two nights later, however, when the phone rang again with a repeat performance. If Mutti was anything, she was determined! This time we hauled her off to jail, where she was held for two days pending charges. The latter were subsequently dropped and, thank goodness, that was the last I heard of Mutti.

At a CIC Region VIII staff meeting at Berlin Headquarters one morning, a young newer member of the organization mentioned that he had received word through an informant that Mildred Gillars, better known to Allied servicemen during World War II as "Axis Sally," was hiding out in the French Sector. Gillars, an American expatriate considered a notorious traitor, had come to Germany before the United States' entry into the conflict. Born in Maine in 1900, she had studied to be an actress but had had little success at her chosen profession. While in New York City in the latter 1930s, she met and came under the influence of a professor at Hunter College with a German background. In time, impressed with Hitler, he chose to return to his homeland.

Discouraged by her inability to find employment, Gillars decided to try her luck in Germany as well. She traveled to Berlin, but did not fare much better there as an actress and only managed to survive by teaching English. Eventually, through a male friend she obtained a position translating for Radio Berlin, which led her into broadcasting enemy propaganda in English to our troops during the war. Gillars felt that at last she had an outlet for her talents and, apparently, was oblivious to the consequences of her actions. Romantic and a bit harebrained, she would broadcast scripts prepared by her programmer without question. Allied servicemen, particularly in North Africa and the Mediterranean theater and later during the Battle of the Bulge, were exposed to her broadcasts designed to undermine their morale. Among other things, she would play upon the soldiers' loneliness and homesickness, at times suggesting that their wives and sweethearts back home were being unfaithful. Her broadcasts popularized the wartime German tune, "Lili Marlene."

The mention of "Axis Sally" in our staff meeting drew the same jaded responses from old hands that one might expect from a further reported sighting of Martin Bormann, "Not again!" Gillars had been questioned by Allied authorities at one point very early on, but had then simply disappeared. The war had been over for many months and other efforts to locate her had been fruitless. Our new colleague persisted, however, in maintaining that his source was reliable. I do not recall what steps, if any, were taken to clear matters with the French, since no one really expected any result; nevertheless, arrangements were made to investigate the report. Thereupon, in relatively short order the agent returned from Tegel in the French Sector with a gaunt, middle-aged, washed-out blonde woman who was, indeed, Mildred Gillars.

She was confined overnight in the basement of the building next to my quarters, which served as the CIC Club. Frankfurt and Washington were alerted that "Axis Sally" had been apprehended. The news created quite a stir and preparations were made to send her down to Frankfurt and subsequently back to the United States for imprisonment and trial. While she was in our custody, instructions were given that she not be fed prior to our initial interrogation. I have a vague recollection that there was a fuss the following morning, because the sergeant who was guarding her had for some eyebrow-raising reason provided her with sandwiches. Gillars was eventually tried for treason in a District of Columbia court and in 1949 sentenced to twenty-five years in prison.

Years later, in 1973, when I was serving at the Consulate General in Munich, I read a newspaper account that Gillars had been released. She returned to Germany but was not received hospitably. Eventually, the unhappy woman made her way back to the United States and taught in a Midwest Catholic girls' school until she died in 1988.

1. Elsie Behr Kormann, the author's mother, at age seventy in 1955. A woman of deep religious faith and moral courage, she assisted her husband in establishing a thriving business in New York City before World War I.

2. John Matthew Kormann, the author's father, in a 1906 photograph. Born in 1879, he was an entrepreneur who built a confectionery and ice-cream making corporation in New York City.

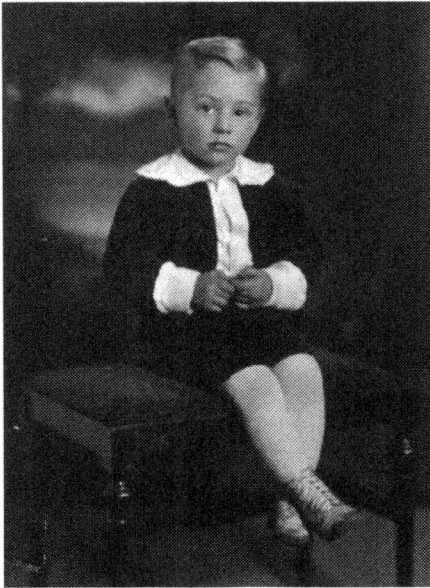

3. The author at age four, looking prim in a Little Lord Fauntleroy suit that belies his boisterousness. An only boy with three much older sisters, he was a handful for his parents.

4. Young John on his expensive rocking horse, which felt like a stuffed pony.

5. The Kormanns' summer home at the shore in Far Rockaway, Long Island, that no longer exists. That exclusive Atlantic beach area, which once contained lovely homes, has since been engulfed in city sprawl and apartment houses.

6. Certificate for 10 shares of Kormann Confections, Inc. stock, issued six months before the 1929 stock market crash heralding the Great Depression.

7. The football enthusiast with the family car in 1935. The author's mother is pictured standing behind a visiting aunt from Germany.

8. The 34-foot parachute training tower. One thousand . . . two thousand . . . three thousand – and ride the pulley! (US Army)

9. Stand up and hook up! Equipment check! Count off your numbers! Move to the door! Paratrooper exits a C-47. (US Army)

10. The USS *Wakefield* (formerly the luxury liner SS *Manhattan*) was loaded with over 8,000 members of the 17th Airborne Division, plus 2,000 other troops. The ship sailed across the Atlantic unescorted, as she would be too vulnerable to German submarines in a slow-moving convoy. (US Navy Archives)

11. Troops stacked five bunks high in the enlisted men's holds. With 10,000 men aboard, soldiers took turns sleeping. Personnel on deck were not allowed to smoke at night or toss anything overboard that might alert enemy submarines. (US Navy Archives)

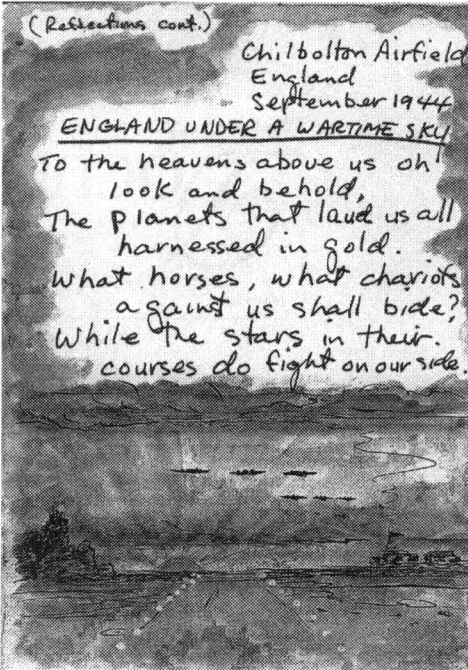

(Reflections cont.)

Chilbolton Airfield
England
September 1944
ENGLAND UNDER A WARTIME SKY

To the heavens above us oh!
    look and behold,
The planets that laud us all
    harnessed in gold.
What horses, what chariots
    against us shall bide?
While the stars in their
    courses do fight on our side.

13. The 17th Airborne Division was thrust into the Battle of the Bulge on Christmas Day 1944 to stop a German counterattack. Lightly armed airborne infantry engaged German "Tiger" tanks. At one point it was estimated that the division's casualties were 1,000 a day killed and wounded. Its heroic stand in the snows of the Ardennes at Dead Man's Ridge lives in the annals of American military history.

12. A poem and watercolor painting from the author's wartime sketchbook. In 2001, the page was framed and given to the British Airborne Museum at Aldershot, England.

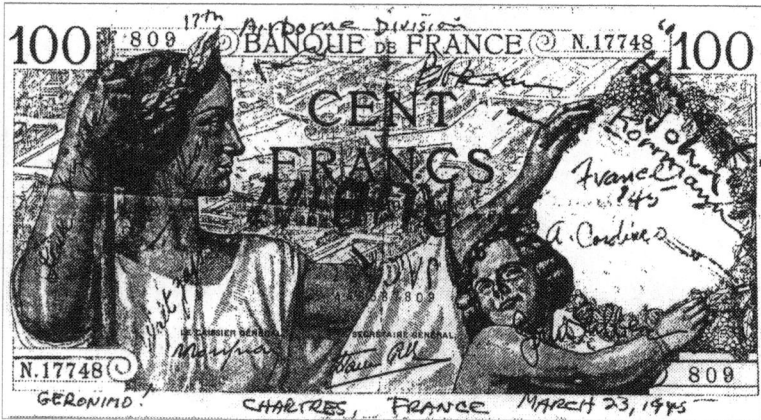

14. A "short snorter" using a 100 French franc bill signed by members of the author's airborne company on the eve of the 17th Airborne Division's drop over the Rhine River into Germany in "Operation Varsity."

15. An aerial view of Wesel, Germany, as American and British paratroops and gliders dropped into the industrial heartland of Germany. They met heavy opposition. March 24, 1945, was the worst day for the Allied airborne in World War II, when 1,070 were killed and over 3,000 wounded. (US Army)

16. Some paratroopers of the 17th Airborne Division landed in open fields; others hit power lines or came down in trees, all under intense fire from an enemy defending their homeland. (US Army)

17. Easy targets for anti-aircraft fire, some gliders crash-landed. Others received direct hits upon landing from German 88 mm artillery. Of the 1,305 gliders used in "Operation Varsity," only 172 were later salvageable. (US Army)

18. (Above) Troopers exiting the gliders were particularly vulnerable to being hit by enemy machine gun fire raking the fields. (US Army)

19. (Left) These paratroopers were killed while hanging in trees before they were able to get out of their harnesses. The author, running under a deceased officer during the heat of battle, recalls pausing long enough to render him a final salute. (US Army)

20. Paratroopers of the 17th Airborne Division on the way to attacking Muenster. The decision of that city's military commander to fight to the end resulted in numerous casualties on both sides. After capturing Muenster, the division circled back to close the "Ruhr Pocket," thereby assisting in surrounding 325,000 German troops under the command of Field Marshal Walther Model, who committed suicide rather than surrender. (US Army)

22. Socrates, a Shepherd dog highly trained by and obtained from the German police in Berlin, became a faithful companion for many years.

21. John Kormann, Special Agent-in-Charge of the Neukoelln CIC Field Office in Berlin in 1946. Neukoelln was a heavily populated downtown district bordering on both the Soviet Sector of Berlin and the Soviet Zone of Germany.

23. Above is a photo of the destroyed marble hall of Hitler's magnificent headquarters, the *Reichskanzlei* (chancellery), constructed in 1939 by architect Albert Speer to impress foreign dignitaries. (US Army)

24. While in the passages in the bunker under the *Reichskanzlei* on a futile mission to apprehend Martin Bormann, Hitler's deputy, the author came across the above plaque commemorating the dedication of the building.

U. S., RED TROOPS CLASH IN BERLIN

25. The banner headline, much reduced in size, from the *Detroit Times* of September 17, 1946, refers to an incident of which the author was the primary cause. He had foiled the Soviet NKVD kidnapping of a German scientist, rescuing him and taking him into U.S. custody. When a large body of Russian troops attempted forcibly to reclaim the scientist, a serious confrontation with an American MP company took place. It was a time of heightened international tension. *Herald Tribune* correspondent Maggie Higgins's dramatic, widely reported account of the affair created problems for Berlin Headquarters, Washington, and the author himself.

Marguerite Higgins

26. In 2003 Marguerite "Maggie" Higgins was featured on a U.S. postage stamp, part of a series honoring women in journalism. She had a reputation for going to great lengths to obtain a story.

27. Dr. Roger Wells, Deputy Director of Civil Administration for Germany (the author's future father-in-law), receives the Medal of Freedom in 1947 from General Lucius Clay, U.S. Military Governor of Germany.

28. Elsa, Dr. Wells's 17-year-old daughter, was a student at the American University of Berlin. She volunteered to teach English in Berlin's refugee camp for concentration camp victims, a heart-rending experience.

29. This portrait of the author was painted in Berlin in 1947 by German artist Georg Majewicz. Socrates stands alert, while in the background paratroop planes take off into a spectacular sunrise. The author, an artist himself, had befriended Majewicz, enabling him to survive during the difficult postwar years. The painting was presented to the author upon his departure from Berlin.

30. Mr. & Mrs. John Kormann, married June 11, 1949, in Ardmore, Pennsylvania, while Elsa was a student at Bryn Mawr College and John a graduate student at Columbia University.

31. Elsa remained behind to finish her senior year while her husband was on assignment with the State Department in Germany. She made him proud by graduating *summa cum laude*, number one in her class at Bryn Mawr.

32. Resident Officers and *Amerika Haus* Directors assigned to Bavaria in 1950. (Left to right) Rear: Paul Bethel, George Curt Moore, Edward Savage. 2nd row: William Schaufele, Caleb Baxter, William Dietz, Roland Haney, Merrill White. Seated: John Kormann, Richard Hamilton, Marion Baldwin.

33. Neumarkt/Opf, a city of over 25,000, heavily damaged in World War II. The author saw it as his task to do all he could to assist in the reconstruction.

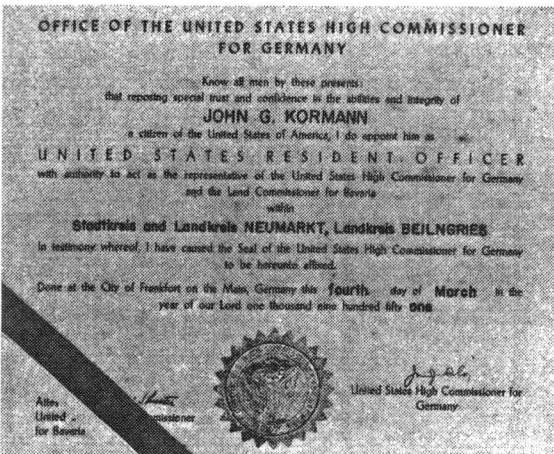

34. The document issued by the U.S. High Commissioner for Germany authorizing a Resident Officer to act in his name in the *Kreise* (counties) cited.

35. The Resident Officer and the County School Administrator sign the authorization for the construction of a new school with money obtained from counterpart funds.

36. Democracy at work! At town hall meetings, an American innovation, many decisions were reached, washed down by vast quantities of local beer. With 295 *Gemeinde* (communities) spread over 600 square miles in the three counties, the Resident Officer had much to do.

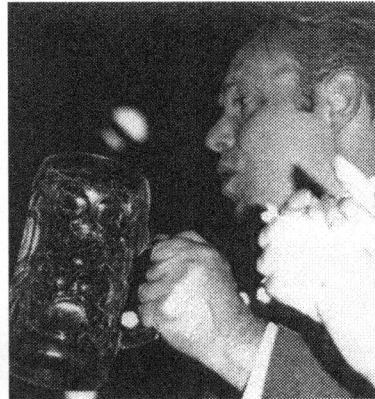

37. The author poses before the new Neumarkt Youth Center constructed with U.S. assistance.

38. Ten U.S. Resident Officers who returned to Germany forty years later, pictured meeting in Garmisch in 1988. The Germans honored them for what they had done to bring democracy to that country. At a luncheon given for them by the Bavarian Senate, they were called "living legends."

39. (Left) While with the U.S. Embassy in Bonn in 1954 as Chief Editor of the Amerika Dienst (official U.S. Press Service for Germany), the author and his wife took time off to vacation at Sitjes in Spain on the Mediterranean Sea.

40.(Right) Duty as a Public Affairs Officer in Hannover, German, in 1952-53 brought him in contact with the Pied Piper of Hamelin (*Hameln*) Festival. This story-book, medieval town of the famed rat-catcher near Hannover was a great tourist attraction.

41. (Left) The author as an Army Reserve Officer in the 1950s. "Special Operations" was a new concept, and he sought duty with the Special Warfare Center at Fort Bragg, North Carolina. He participated in drawing up doctrine for counterguerrilla and subsequently counterinsurgency and Special Forces operations.

42. (Below) A 1958 class of the Special Forces Orientation Course has its picture taken. (The author is front row center.) The Special Warfare Center in the World War II building seen here is a far cry from the large brick complex that exists today. (US Army)

43. Who said State Department diplomats are "striped pants cookie pushers"? The author was serving in Washington as a Political Officer before being assigned to the American Embassy in Manila in 1962.

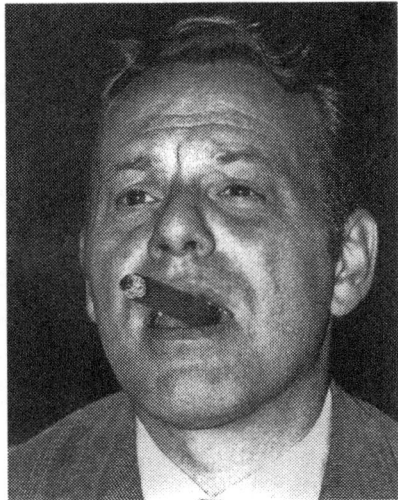

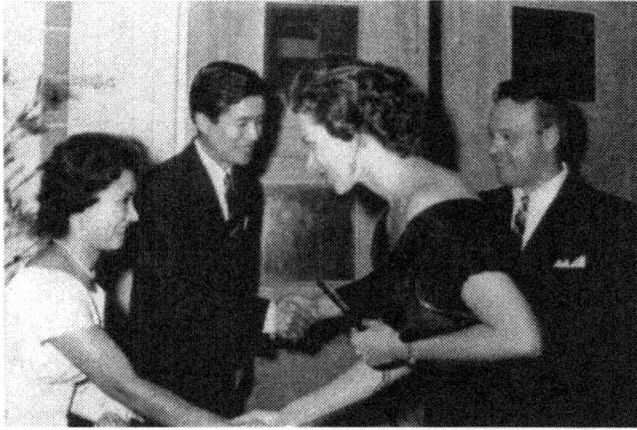

44. One of many receptions, cocktail parties, and dinners the Kormanns attended or hosted. This one was at the Japanese Embassy in Manila in 1963. In the diplomatic service, business is often transacted at these affairs, where one can meet with officials of the host country or colleagues from foreign embassies.

45. The Kormann children aboard the SS *President Cleveland* for twenty-one days en route to Manila in 1964. The children were entertained by special stewards throughout the trip in a Junior Sailing Club. Foreign Service life, with its constant uprooting and schooling in strange lands, tended to be hard on children.

46. Elsa Wells Kormann, photographed in Manila, not only served as a diplomatic hostess, but also taught history at the American School there. Despite all her representational responsibilities, she made a strenuous effort to provide a normal home life for her children.

47. (Left) This small rebuilt Piper Tripacer, with its 90-horsepower engine, flew the 3,000 mile round trip from Manila down the length of the Philippine archipelago to Sibutu Island, across to North Borneo, and up to Sandakan.

48. (Right) FSO Glen Fisher, the pilot, with the author on the island of Jolo in the southern Philippines. Flying over shark-infested seas, tropical rain forests, and hundreds of miles of mangrove swamps with 20-foot saltwater crocodiles proved to be quite an adventure.

49. (Left) While flying off the coast of Borneo, the author took a snapshot of a live volcano on a small island below. Malaysia and Indonesia were at war over claims to North Borneo (Sabah) at the time, and the trip enabled the author to prepare a report on the situation.

50. (Right) This photograph of a typical fishing village in the Sulu Sea was also taken during the flight.

51. The original drawing of a prize-winning cartoon by Filipino artist Larry Alcala given to the author. It appeared in the *Philippine Weekly Graphic* in August 1963 and depicts MALPHILINDO, an organization created to foster cooperation between Malaysia, Indonesia, and the Philippines, a pet project of Philippine President Diosdado Macapagal. While MALPHILINDO was the subject of much rhetoric, little was actually accomplished. The organization, as represented by characters in the costumes of the three countries, was seen as bolstering Philippine independence.

52. Secretary of State Dean Rusk having a final airport conversation with Philippine Foreign Secretary Salvador P. Lopez and U.S. Ambassador to Indonesia Howard Jones following the Southeast Asia Treaty Organization (SEATO) foreign ministers meeting in Manila in February 1965. In the background, the author, who was in charge of handling SEATO affairs for the embassy, appears concerned about departure arrangements. The United States was a member of SEATO, and its commitment to that organization provided the rationale for its participation in the war in Vietnam. (US Information Service)

6

Berlin's Treasure Trove

The winter of 1946-47 was one of severe hardship for the people of Berlin. It was bitter cold. Snow fell early that year. Most dwellings had little or no heat. Food was scarce and the black market economy had robbed the people of most of their savings. Hitler and his regime had left a disastrous legacy. While Germans suffered, the occupation armies lived in comfort, their officers enjoying a gracious lifestyle, generally free in the evenings to visit any of several officers' clubs. The Harnack Haus featured a fine dining room, immaculate service, a large ballroom, and a big-band orchestra playing most nights; the Town House, a bit less pretentious, had good food and always at least a combo; the Wannsee Club, in summer a yacht club, offered excellent meals year-round in a magnificent baronial villa, usually with a small orchestra. Then there were the Colony Club, the Tempelhof Air Base Officers' Club, and several smaller establishments. The enlisted men had similar facilities scattered throughout the city. German movie theaters were taken over for the use of the Allied forces and showed the latest Hollywood releases.

With the arrival of soldiers' families from the United States, little changed. The favorable ten-to-one exchange rate and the cigarette economy permitted Americans to hire Germans as household help, and wives, who back home might have been tied down with children, were free to enjoy themselves. For the rank and file of the military, unaccustomed to having servants, it was a good life of dining and dancing. All the German cultural facilities such as opera, theater, and concerts were available. Everywhere prices were ridiculously low. During the Nazi regime, a special box or choice seats were typically reserved for the Fuehrer and the Nazi elite at places of entertainment. Now these were made available to the Allied forces. The tradition of state-supported cultural activities assured a widely diverse program of events and a rich reservoir of talent.

In addition to the familiar repertoire of operas, musical pieces, and plays performed in America, Berlin boasted a wealth of material virtually unheard of at home. One could see and hear some of the lesser known works of the great masters and at times come away wondering why they had not received wider exposure in the United States. Colorful traditional operettas, a great favorite of mine, were very much in evidence and always great fun to see. My work was interesting, exciting, and at times dangerous. My off-duty hours were filled with wonderful things to do. What more could a young officer ask for? Little did I know what else awaited me.

On a cold snowy evening, Friday, December 13, 1946, my executive officer in Neukoelln, 1st Lt. J. Floyd Carter, and I dropped into the Harnack Haus Officers' Club to enjoy the orchestra, have a drink or two at the bar, and watch the couples dance. From there, we thought we might head down to Kurfuerstendamm and the nightclub district. As we entered the spacious, richly wood-paneled outer foyer, I noticed a beautiful young girl seated at a table off to one side of the room. She appeared to be collecting for a charity. During my year in Berlin, I had seen many pretty women. A young American officer who could speak German did not have much difficulty finding attractive companionship. The girl at the table, however, was different. She must be an American, I thought, probably a student visiting her parents on holiday leave from a private school or an elite Eastern women's college. As a former Columbia College boy, I could spot her type a mile away.

We watched her for a few moments and then walked to the table and inquired about her charity collection. She asked whether we would like to contribute to a program of Relief for Polish Refugees. Engaging her in conversation for several minutes, we learned that she was in Berlin with her parents, her father worked for the Military Government, and she was attending the American University of Berlin but would be returning to the States in the fall to attend Swarthmore College. I informed her that I had been a student at Columbia and had served during the war with the airborne. I was in a paratroop officer's dress uniform, "pink and greens," and jump boots, and wearing ribbons and *fourragères*. As a member of CIC, I wore no rank, but I let her know rather self-importantly that I commanded an intelligence subregion.

I could sense by the time the conversation ended that she considered Carter a far more pleasant person and me a conceited ass. At one point when she told us her first name, Elsa, I commented that it was also my mother's name. Carter and I then proceeded to the men's room. I remember telling him as we were washing up: "J. Floyd, when you go back out, take another good look at that girl. I'm going to marry her." Carter, who was a good bit older than I, with a wife and family back in Texas, smiled at me indulgently. "Come on, John," he said, "we haven't even started drinking yet."

From our seats at the bar we could observe the orchestra and the couples dancing. However, my thoughts were with the young lady collecting for Polish relief and before long I was back at the entrance to the club. Approaching the table, I asked her when she would close shop, adding that I had a jeep and, since it was snowing, would gladly drive her home. She replied airily, "No, thank you, my Plymouth is parked across the street." That response was enough to give me pause. She has an American car? No one has a private American car over here, I thought to myself, except maybe General Clay, the commander of U.S. Forces in Germany. Just at that point, a middle-aged woman, who had been standing at a distance, came over to us and, addressing me, said: "May I speak with you a moment?" Taking me aside, she told me that she was Colonel Shaeffer's wife and that "the young lady you were talking with is Dr. Wells's daughter and you would be well advised to keep your distance." Spotting my 82nd Airborne patch, Mrs. Shaeffer had sized me up as one of the wild young paratroop officers mothers kept away from their daughters. Although I was incensed, under the circumstances there was little I could do. I very politely thanked Mrs. Shaeffer, and shortly thereafter Carter and I left for the Kurfurstendamm nightclubs.

The following morning, I made it my business to find out who "Dr. Wells" was and where his family resided. With the intelligence resources available to me, I had a fairly good reading by the end of the next day. I learned that Dr. Wells was on General Clay's staff as deputy director of civil administration for Germany. He was an American professor, an expert on Germany, brought over to assist in the reconstruction of the country. His wife and two daughters had accompanied him, and they had shipped over the family car, a 1942 Plymouth.

The Neukoelln CIC Subregion was responsible for providing periodic reports for inclusion in the regularly published classified European Intelligence Summary, and I spent most of Sunday drafting our submission. On Monday morning I telephoned Miss Wells's home. Her mother answered and called her to the phone. I identified myself and said, "*Die Verkaufte Braut* is being given tomorrow evening at the *Staedtische* (the opera in the British Sector). I have two box seat tickets, and I am sure you will like it." I could just as readily have said *The Bartered Bride*, but I wanted to impress her with my German. "If you would join me, I will come by at seven o'clock and pick you up." After a few moments of conversation with her mother, she came back on the line and accepted.

I arrived at the appointed time at the Wells residence, a house on a quiet street in the Dahlem District. Mrs. Wells invited me in, and we had a brief conversation. Dr. Wells was still at the office. Elsa appeared shortly, and we departed for the Charlottenburg District in the British Sector. Upon entering the opera, I produced my tickets. We were promptly guided to the Royal Box, which had in earlier days been reserved for Adolf Hitler. In purchasing our tickets, once again our office's senior German employee demonstrated his talent in dealing with local officials. We had the best seats in the house, and I could only hope he had not told the opera manager I was related to General Eisenhower! The opera was a wonderfully melodic costume spectacle. The attractive lead singers had outstanding voices, and the large chorus and dancers provided an enthusiastic accompaniment. The stage sets were elaborate and realistic. It was a first-class performance. That was the beginning of a whirlwind courtship.

The following Saturday, I escorted Elsa to a housewarming party a fellow officer was holding for the arrival of his family from the states. Within a week, we were seeing each other almost daily. On a beautiful starry Christmas eve, Elsa and I walked miles in the snow to a candlelight service at a lovely little German church. Afterwards we returned to her home and sat up half the night talking. Christmas in Germany is a magical time, and as a young couple we were swept up in the romance of the season. Not everything went smoothly, however, and I remember how irritated I was that Elsa had a long-standing date with someone else for New Year's Eve. I am sure I was not particularly good company for the very pretty British Army secretary I escorted to a party that evening.

New Year's Day we were together again at the opera for a performance of Richard Strauss's *Salome*. Conscious of the admonition from Colonel Schaefer's wife, I made a special effort to win over her parents, who by this time were becoming a bit apprehensive as to what was happening to their younger daughter. I spent time conversing with Mrs. Wells, a professor of German at Bryn Mawr College in former times. I was helpful in a variety of ways, getting things done for them with the military authorities or with the Germans. Neukoelln florists soon began considering me their best customer. As was the German custom, I would arrive bearing flowers. On one occasion, I brought my future mother-in-law a magnificent spray of orchids three feet long. They were so spectacular that I have never seen anything like them since.

During my early courtship of Elsa, an incident occurred that could have had dire consequences. All these years later, I look back on it with a cold chill. I cannot see or hear the name of Raoul Wallenberg, the Swedish diplomat who disappeared behind the Iron Curtain, without thinking about it. In this book, I have made references to the Soviet NKVD's practice of kidnapping Germans from the Allied sectors of West Berlin. While generally this activity related to scientists or persons they ostensibly wanted for war crimes, they were particularly anxious as well to carry off anyone involved in intelligence activities. It is almost impossible to convey how possessed the Russians were with espionage, spies, and spying. They carried it to ridiculous heights, saturating the entire atmosphere in Berlin with it in those days. Our office in Neukoelln was inundated with reports about Soviet penetration efforts of American military government offices, the troop units, or German support establishments. Some of these had a basis in fact, and from time to time we apprehended a low-level agent or two.

One day in this mass of information, we received a tip that an operation was under way to pick up an American agent. To my staff, so used to these reports, it was "what else is new?" I recall we received the report on a Thursday or Friday; the kidnapping was to take place over the weekend, most likely on Sunday night, in the British sector of Wilmersdorf. Put off by the thought of spending many weekend hours in liaison with the British and then sitting outside for hours on a cold winter night in a useless surveillance operation, I chose not to act. As matters evolved, Elsa and the Wells family were away that weekend, and I found myself sitting around my quarters on Sunday evening. I wandered over to the room of one of my Neukoelln colleagues. His plans had fallen through, and he was as bored as I.

Before long we decided to check out that "oddball Soviet kidnapping report." As fate would have it, one of us had made a note of the address. Otherwise, we would have been stopped from going. We went over to the motor pool, climbed into my jeep, and with my dog Socrates drove over to Wilmersdorf, a trip of about twenty minutes. There had been no liaison with the British, nor did we notify anybody of our plans. In hindsight, what we were doing was quite unprofessional, hardly reflecting credit on me as a CIC subregional commander. We arrived at our destination at about 10:00 p.m., prepared to wait around until midnight and then go home. We pulled into the darkened street of apartment houses, cruised by the address in question, and parked farther down, still within sight of the entrance to the building.

The street was totally deserted; the Germans did not own cars and there were no Allied vehicles to be seen. If there was an American agent in that apartment building, he was not driving, which made the case even less plausible. Both the other agent and I were soon castigating ourselves. We were acting as if the Russians were going to meet us by appointment. What if they had been there already? Why would they not come in the wee hours of the morning? Should we really not be prepared to wait around until 1:00 or 2:00 a.m.? As we engaged in this debate of self-doubt, vehicle lights appeared coming toward us. Slowly, they moved up the street from the direction of the center of town toward the building in question.

With that, we were confronted with the problem of getting out of sight ourselves, should this indeed be an NKVD vehicle. Lights out, we slumped behind the dashboard in the closed-in jeep, hoping we would not be noticed were the car to cruise by us. Much to our relief, it simply stopped in front of the apartment building, almost convincing me that we could not be witnessing a Soviet intelligence operation. They would never be so careless as to fail to make a cursory inspection of the area. From the distance, we could distinguish three figures leaving the car. They moved about for a minute, and then entered the building.

Suddenly, it was no longer a boring evening, and we would have welcomed some help from the British or anyone else. The other agent and I were armed only with our pistols, I with my .45 and he with his .38 revolver. We also had the dog, and at least we were in uniform. We slowly drove closer to the building in the darkness and stopped. In a matter of minutes, the apartment house door opened and several persons appeared. Flipping on our lights, I gunned the jeep engine. With horn blaring and both of us loudly shouting at the people about to enter the car, we pulled up in front of a black, four-door Mercedes sedan, blocking its departure. Our object was to make it look as if we were the initial vehicle of a force about to descend on the scene. Identifying ourselves as American CIC, we caught our quarry completely by surprise. We confronted a Russian in the standard dark civilian suit and an East German policeman, obviously the driver. The Russian was holding a woman, who was still trying to dress herself.

Within seconds, another Russian civilian appeared escorting a man, also trying to get dressed. The other agent and I were dumbfounded to recognize him as a member of our Neukoelln office, a warrant officer special agent. Calling him by name, we put on a show as if the Russians had been caught red-handed in a trap and their supposed captive agent was a part of our "sting" operation. We told the East German policeman that they would be turned over to the British authorities. Surprisingly, there was no real display of weapons. Even the Russians escorting their captives made no show of arms. Our colleague, the warrant officer, seemed so overcome that he had made no attempt at resistance. However, he literally gave a great sigh and shook with relief when he saw us.

I announced that rather than wait for the British to arrive, we should proceed to their Wilmersdorf Headquarters, and I instructed the East German police driver to follow us. The NKVD men were glum and got into their vehicle, while their erstwhile prisoners climbed into our jeep. I watched through the rearview mirror as the Mercedes followed us for a few blocks, dropping farther and farther behind. Then their lights went out and they were nowhere to be seen. I had no intention of going to the British headquarters under the circumstances and had every expectation the Russians would make a run for it. How our man got himself into this position and who the woman was I could not at the time even guess. It was a mystery that had to be solved before I said anything to anybody.

My primary fear was that our entire Neukoelln counterintelligence operation had been penetrated. The warrant officer was one of our most trusted special agents and a close personal friend. It was just pure unbelievable luck that we had foiled his kidnapping. I could not understand why he had not been aware of the prospective Soviet operation, or why he had not put up fierce resistance, considering what the consequences of his capture would have been. More than likely he simply would have disappeared and never been heard from again. Perhaps an eventual agent exchange with the Soviets might have been arranged. Even that was doubtful, considering that it would have exposed the Soviets as acting without authority in the British Sector, a violation of the Four Power Agreement. This case had all the makings of an international incident that could have proved embarrassing in several respects, if the details became known, for the Russians, the Americans, the individuals involved, and not least for my office.

We drove back to the CIC compound and spent several hours that night and the entire next day at our office, endeavoring to ascertain what had happened. I was highly suspicious at first. The warrant officer, a bachelor in his late thirties, had an Eastern European background, having left Czechoslovakia around the time of the Hitler takeover. My initial thought was that he might have been blackmailed, with the Communists holding members of his family behind the Iron Curtain. However, he swore there were no such persons. Our attention then turned to the woman. Could she have been a plant? She had been his lady friend for some time, and he had been very discreet about the relationship, even to the point of visiting her apartment by taking the U-Bahn (subway). That explained why there had been no vehicle parked anywhere on the street. Unlike some of the German girls my colleagues dated, I had never met this woman.

I was beside myself trying to come up with an explanation as to how the Russians pinpointed our man. Finally, the best we could do was to surmise that, as part of a Soviet surveillance operation, he must have been followed leaving the office or the CIC compound and a pattern of visits to the apartment building then been detected. From that point on, our agent's own effort to be discreet worked against him, and, indeed, might have signed his death warrant.[1] I was relatively satisfied that my colleague and his lady friend were not working with the Soviets, and I so reported the matter to Berlin CIC Region VIII Headquarters. I suggested, nevertheless, that further steps be taken to interrogate the pair. At a CIC Headquarters staff meeting later in the week, I discussed the case and emphasized that it was imperative that the whereabouts of our people be known at all times. The revelation of the incident sent shock waves through the organization.

As the spring of 1947 approached, I turned my attention to returning to college. I had already been in the Army more than four long years. I was tempted again to take a civilian position with CIC at what then seemed a very high salary.[2] However, it was apparent that as a civilian in the Army structure, I would never be in command. Nor would it have been wise for that matter to accept the regular army commission I was offered. Either way, sooner or later I would be at a distinct disadvantage not having a college degree.

Examining my prospects, I had no great desire to return to Columbia. Had Elsa, who I was determined would be my future bride, not been a factor, I would have applied to Harvard or Yale. She was going to attend Swarthmore College for her freshman and sophomore years and then finish at Bryn Mawr. Swarthmore was a coed institution, which with Haverford (male) was affiliated with Bryn Mawr (female) as part of a triumvirate of academically outstanding Quaker colleges, all located within miles of each other in the Philadelphia suburbs. Her older sister Lois had spent two years at Swarthmore and finished at Bryn Mawr, and Dr. and Mrs. Wells had planned the same for Elsa. Both Lois and Elsa had attended Baldwin, a private school for girls, for the twelve years of their elementary and secondary education, and it was thought that a dose of coeducation and a stint of living away from home at Swarthmore would be good for them.

Dr. Wells was chairman of the Political Science Department at Bryn Mawr, but also taught courses on occasion at the other colleges, which made him thoroughly familiar with all aspects of Swarthmore. By this time, Elsa and I had come to an understanding that we were serious about our relationship. Consequently, I was not sanguine about her entering Swarthmore and sought to solve the problem by applying there myself. I find it hard to believe now that Elsa was still not quite eighteen years old at the time, and I twenty-three. I had been through the crucible of war, and she had seen far more working in the refugee camps in Berlin than women years older. Unlike other American teenage dependents in Berlin, she had volunteered to teach English to victims of the concentration camps, many of whom were still suffering the trauma of their incarceration.[3] Although attracted by her beauty, I must have sensed, correctly, that she possessed an inner goodness that was later to provide me a moral compass and second conscience.

Those months until my departure for home in late July 1947 remain enshrined in our memories as the "golden days." While my work was demanding, my free time was spent in a continuous round of theater and opera visits with her. There were dates when we went frolicking in the snow and ice-boating, and later sailing on the Wannsee. I played on our CIC basketball team, participating in Army area competitions. Elsa was one of our most ardent fans. At a luncheon given by the regional commander's wife for the families, she was invited along with the wives.

The course of events drew us closer together. On a Saturday in May 1947, Elsa's best friend in Berlin married an army lieutenant. Elsa was maid-of-honor. After the wedding and the noon reception, it was still early and four of us from the wedding party decided to go sailing on the Wannsee: Mary Lou Textor, the pretty blonde daughter of an army colonel, Jack Marshall, one of Elsa's former boyfriends, Elsa, and myself. We drove out to the U.S. military yacht club, signed out an open sloop about twenty-six feet in length, and, accompanied by Socrates, we set sail. It was a beautiful, blustery, sunny day, with puffy white clouds skipping across the sky. Berlin, being rather northerly, has a continental climate and the weather was still quite cool.

It appeared to be perfect sailing weather, and we were whipping along at a good pace, laughing and enjoying ourselves. Soon we were well out into the large lake. I was at the tiller and looking ahead when I noticed vicious gusts of wind rippling across the water. Several other sailboats were in my view. Suddenly, first one, then two of them capsized. Before I had a chance to react at all to loosen the boom, bring us about, or drop the sail, we went over as well. We were in the water fully dressed. Our spur-of-the-moment decision to go sailing meant we were in street clothes, not the comfortable boating outfits we might ordinarily have worn. The girls were in dresses, I was in uniform, wearing jump boots. There were no flotation devices on board, as they were not required. The temperature was in the fifties, and the water was cold. I shouted for everyone to hold on to the side of the boat and struggled to get my boots off, while sinking under the surface in my efforts to do so.

Taking stock of the situation, I became aware that the hull, floating at a ninety-degree angle with the sail in the water, would not support everyone hanging on at once. In this situation, the dog was a distinct liability. Unable to understand what was occurring, it attempted to clamber up on the nearest person or onto the hull, from which it invariably slipped off. To make matters worse, Marshall soon informed me that he could not swim, which seemed utterly inconceivable to me. What was this big, brawny, six-foot-four-inch guy doing out in a boat if he could not swim? Mary Lou was an excellent swimmer and Elsa was managing.

Alert persons back at the yacht club must have observed what was happening and soon a motorboat was rushing to the rescue. However, it sped first to the aid of the more distant capsized vessels, and we were in the water nearly twenty-five minutes before a boat came for us. During that time, Mary Lou and I mostly kept treading water, allowing Marshall to hold on to the hull. I made sure that Elsa was all right, while at the same time trying to deal with Socrates. Finally, the yacht club's German employees pulled us aboard the motorboat. They tied a line to the bow of our sloop, towing it on its side, and proceeded slowly back to shore. Upon returning to the dock, an examination of the forward stowage area of the capsized craft revealed that purses, glasses and their cases, and several shoes had miraculously been caught up in ropes and remained in the boat.

Frozen stiff and blue-lipped, we drove back to the CIC compound, where we dried off and fortified ourselves with innumerable hot toddies. I am struck, today, by how cavalier everyone was about the incident. The yacht club personnel took it in stride. The parties in the other boats were all rescued, apparently without serious mishap. There were no recriminations, and no effort was made to use the matter to call for better water safety procedures. We were very lucky.

My time in Berlin and the Army was winding down as July neared its end. It seemed as if I had been a soldier forever, and I found it hard to conceive of myself as a civilian, even more so, as a college freshman again. I wrote to my parents that I would be back home within a month or two. I had not seen them since June 1944—more than three long eventful years ago. I had written home about Elsa in earlier letters. My mother soon realized that her son had found an exceptional partner.

I had given Elsa my parachute wings the previous February, but I wanted her to have something more binding. Berlin, a medieval city, still had a few ancient craftsmen. I found a highly skilled goldsmith who fashioned two exquisite rings, each with a chrysoprase into which was cut an intricate crest. These lovely, emerald-like semiprecious stones were supported by delicate golden leaves in a work of art worthy of Cellini. Elsa has worn the ring every day since Friday, June 13, 1947, when it was given to her. There was no question in our minds that we were to be married.

As I was readying to leave, my Neukoelln staff and Army friends went overboard in hosting a series of farewell parties for me. During the course of my time in Berlin, our CIC Club had sent a truck down to Bavaria to load up on Delva Cognac and Frascatti Champagne, a vast amount of which had been found by the U.S. military in a Nazi warehouse. In addition to the club's shipment, individuals in the unit were allowed to purchase a "reasonable amount" at five cents a bottle. Ten dollars bought you enough to float a battleship. I had bottles stored everywhere, in my closet, in corners, and even under the bed.[4] Unprepared to take the liquor home, I made it available to my colleagues, who in turn celebrated my departure with even greater gusto.

My duty in Berlin had been memorable to say the least, and so it was only logical that even my final moments there should not go without incident. With much gaiety my friends drove me out to the Zehlendorf Terminal to board the military train to Frankfurt. As we came into the station, I was surprised to find Captain Feldman and his Company B, 759th Military Police Battalion lined up along the platform as a farewell honor guard. The train had just arrived from Frankfurt about fifteen minutes late. Normally, it remained at the station for about half an hour and then started on the return trip. Captain Feldman greeted me, wished me farewell, and asked me to review his troops, which I did to the accompaniment of shouts of military drill from his noncoms, the clicking of weapons, and the stamping of boots.

While this display was under way, the passengers from Frankfurt detrained. Two officers, standing at a distance, watched the proceedings with interest for a few minutes and then departed. I later learned to my chagrin that they were General Lucius Clay, three-star Commander-in-Chief of U.S. Forces and Military Governor of Germany, and his aide. Evidently, the general had at first thought the troops were a reception ceremony for him, not for some unlikely lieutenant. However, nothing came of the matter. I would really have been distressed had Feldman, who was a superb officer, been censured in any way over this gesture of friendship.

Unlike my movements in wartime when all my effects were contained in two barrack bags, by this time I had accumulated a lot of baggage. A large dog had to be shipped home, as well as army uniforms, military equipment, civilian clothing, minor items of furniture, a record player, a radio, pictures, and finally, a large rolled up portrait painting with a massive disassembled gold frame. Much of this was packed in large wooden crates addressed to my sister Elsie's residence in Teaneck, New Jersey. As if in preparation for her later role as a Foreign Service wife, Elsa assisted in my packing. After I departed, she saw to it that Socrates was crated and shipped home via Pan American Airways and that my effects were sent on their way promptly.

After a brief stay in Frankfurt, I was informed that arrangements had been made for me to fly home, departing from Rhein-Main Military Air Terminal. I was to be an officer escort for an army prisoner being sent back to Leavenworth military prison.[5] My flight would be to Westover Army

Air base in Massachusetts, via Lagens in the Azores. At Westover, I would turn the prisoner over to the MPs and then be free to go home on leave for thirty days before reporting to Ft. Holabird in Baltimore for a CIC debriefing and a subsequent discharge from the Army at Ft. Meade, Maryland.[6]

While I was not ecstatic about flying across the Atlantic handcuffed to a jailbird, I was glad not to have to spend a week or two aboard an army troopship. Luckily, I had packed my .45 caliber pistol with holster and belt in my hand luggage, thus avoiding having to be issued another weapon. On the day of my departure, I reported to the Provost Marshal at Rhein-Main, was given charge of a nondescript, enlisted man, the prisoner, and driven out to a C-54, four-engine, propeller-driven transport. The interior was devoid of comforts, with bucket seats. It looked very much like a paratroop C-47, but much larger. The flight to the Azores was interminable; it seemed as if we were in the air forever.

About an hour out of Lagens, we started having engine trouble. First one engine performed irregularly, and then a second, much to the consternation of the pilots. I was not really aware of it at the time, but Lagens was a difficult field on which to land and our aircrew were greatly concerned about bringing in a crippled aircraft. I, on the other hand, did not like the idea of being handcuffed to a prisoner under such circumstances. With considerable moaning and praying, the pilots managed to land the plane, and the prisoner and I learned how lucky we were to have come down safely.

The plane required repairs, which took two days. My prisoner was turned over to the base authorities for the period. All I can remember of Lagens Field was that it was unbelievably foggy and humid. Climbing into bed that night in the BOQ (Bachelor Officers' Quarters), the sheets were sopping wet, the walls covered with moisture.[7] I could not wait to leave. Although I was apprehensive about our plane, it performed well on the next leg of our flight to Gander, Newfoundland. It was in the Air Corps cafeteria at Gander that I ate the largest steak I have ever eaten in my life—an inch and a half thick and about ten inches in diameter. I might have expected something of the sort in Texas, but in this northern wilderness it was truly an unaccustomed treat. I came away feeling, "Oh, boy, I'm home!"

7
The Return to Civilian Life

I arrived at Westover Army Air Corps Base, turned my prisoner over to the Provost Marshal, and called my sister Elsie in Teaneck, New Jersey. She was happy to hear my voice. "I have a surprise for you," she said, and then first my mother and next my father came on the line. It truly was a joy to hear their voices after three long years of separation. Hanging up the telephone and anxious to be on my way, I arranged with the base headquarters to obtain a ride to the nearest train station for the trip from Massachusetts down to New York City. I was dressed in my Class A uniform, "pinks and greens," with full 82nd Airborne paratroop officer's paraphernalia, and I passed through trains and railroad stations with pride. People greeted me, and little boys saluted. Finally, I was back in the USA, all in one piece.

The city was just as I had left it. Walking through Penn Station, I noted the bench where Mother had prayed with me when I entered the army so many years earlier. Carrying my hand luggage, I took the escalator up to the street. Planning to take a taxi over to the bus terminal, I wandered down the street adjacent to the Hotel Pennsylvania. I was thinking how wonderful it was to be back when, suddenly, there was a burst of light and everything went blank. After that, I found myself looking up into a crowd of faces, with a policeman telling people to "get back!" I lay sprawled, half on the sidewalk, half in the gutter. My uniform was soaking wet. The officer was holding my overseas cap. I heard him say, "Are you all right, son?" in a thick, fatherly Irish brogue. I soon learned that I had been hit on the head by a brown paper bag filled with water, which evidently had been dropped as a prank from one of the upper floors of the hotel.

The American Legion Forty and Eight Society (referring to the World War I boxcars) was holding a convention in town, and they were a rowdy bunch. If that bag, dropped ten floors, had landed more squarely on my head and not partially on my shoulder, it might have broken my neck.

Had I gone through the war only to become a casualty at home? To this day, I am not fond of the American Legion.[1]

It was grand to be reunited with my family at Fred and Elsie's home. After a few days there, I accompanied my parents to their apartment out on Long Island. In the ensuing weeks, I met with numerous relatives and friends. Before departing Berlin, I had received word from Swarthmore College to come for an interview upon my return to the United States. Shortly after my arrival I contacted the admissions office and scheduled an appointment. Two weeks later I traveled there by train. The town of Swarthmore is located on a commuter rail line about ten miles west of Philadelphia. I was impressed with the lovely campus and the students, who seemed so far removed from the world I had just left. The assistant dean who interviewed me was a former Marine officer, and we got along very well. He took me in to meet the dean, an older, rather dour man. I came away thinking that the overall interview had gone reasonably well. Within a relatively short time, however, I received a letter from Swarthmore placing me on a waiting list for later admission, since the upcoming semester was already overcrowded.

I debated whether I should wait to enter Swarthmore. My education had been set back almost five years as it was. Would I now sit around even longer? With Dean Howard Hawkes's 1943 letter in hand, indicating that I had been granted a leave of absence for the duration of the war, I visited Columbia. It was late August and classes were to begin in a few weeks. The college had expanded in the previous two years to handle veterans on the GI Bill, and it too was overcrowded. Nevertheless, when I walked in, I was promptly welcomed, admitted as an "old boy," and told to report for registration for the fall semester. In addition to those courses I had managed to pass as a freshman at Columbia, I was given credit for my three semesters in ASTP and the courses at Shrivenham. My ASTP engineering program also took care of all the math and science requirements. What a fool I would have been not to have come back to Columbia! I vowed to show my gratitude by buckling down to my studies. Perhaps the greatest incentive for obtaining good grades however, was my determination to impress Elsa and the Wellses.

Dr. Wells was to have completed his two-year contract with the Office of U.S. Military Government in September 1947, and the family planned to leave for Bryn Mawr in time for the beginning of the academic year. They returned aboard an army troopship, arriving at the Brooklyn Navy Yard, where I met them. The following weekend I made my first visit to their home, a large, older house named "Dolgelly," right on the Bryn Mawr campus.

On a beautiful Indian Summer day, Elsa and I walked around the college. It was an idyllic academic setting: elegant Gothic buildings set among massive trees and a rolling landscape. Elsa then took me over to the Baldwin School, where she had spent twelve years of her young life. Here, again, I was impressed. Large Victorian buildings rested in the middle of green fields, upon which uniformed young women played field hockey. Around the extensive perimeter was a tall, wrought iron fence, with a massive gate at one corner and a long driveway leading up to the school. As a New Yorker, I had heard from time to time about the Philadelphia Main Line, with its Merion Cricket Club and posh private schools, and now I was seeing it firsthand.

Settling in as a civilian after years of military life was a chore. The dormitories at Columbia were already full, but I did not wish to room there in any case. Places around the university were virtually impossible to find, but after much searching, I came across a newspaper item advertising an apartment near Greenwich Village in lower Manhattan, a twenty-minute subway ride. Its occupant, however, would only vacate it to a person purchasing his furniture, which consisted of a few battered pieces, hardly worth keeping. For these, he was asking $600, a considerable sum in those days. The apartment was also on the fifth floor of a building without an elevator.

On the positive side, however, I would be taking over an apartment where the rental price was "frozen" by the city housing authority at $36 a month. It featured a fair-sized living room with a couch that doubled as a bed, a single bedroom with an iron cot, two hall closets, a kitchen large enough for a table, and a bathroom with a tub and shower. I had been drawing paratroop officer's pay and saving my money over the past many months and I had the cash on hand. Much to the occupant's surprise, after telling him I doubted the furniture was worth even $50, I said, "It's a deal!"

Once the apartment had been vacated, I saw how sparsely furnished it actually was. My move, then, was to obtain other pieces, particularly a bed or two for prospective roommates. Not desiring anything fancy, I went to the Salvation Army used furniture warehouse to fill my requirements. There I found any number of items that with a little repair work and painting would serve admirably. I even found a double-decker bunk bed guaranteed to make two veterans feel right at home. I spent several days working on the furniture after it was delivered. With dime store drapes hung appropriately and everything painted and polished, the apartment was quite presentable. There was an almost immediate response to cards placed on bulletin boards at Columbia on which I asked for two students to share the apartment with me for $10 a week each. Over the next three years, through college and graduate school, I had a series of five fine roommates.

Socrates arrived before I was able to establish myself in the apartment. After considerable difficulty in processing him through immigration and quarantine at La Guardia Airport, I took him to stay for several weeks with a relative in Queens, New York. She was a middle-aged married woman with no children who enjoyed his company. After that, the dog lived with us in the apartment and was a companion to us all. Eighth Avenue and 18th Street, where we were located, was a mixed neighborhood and not the safest area to wander around in, particularly at night. Walking the dog, however, was never any problem, for any potential mugger would take one look at that magnificent animal and rapidly head in the other direction.

Returning to classes at Columbia was strange. I was still required to complete the humanities and contemporary civilization courses I had started five years earlier, but now they took on added meaning. While there were quite a few veterans in my classes, the majority of students were still in their teens. Veterans on the GI Bill received $75 a month living expenses, $105 if they were married. Civilian clothing was relatively costly and most veterans would come to class wearing items of their former uniforms. I usually wore a leather airborne A-2 jacket with an army officer's shirt and trousers, which set me off a bit from the rest of the class. A number of the professors, who had been in the service, noted that I was a former officer, and their expectations of my performance in class served to make me work harder. Not knowing how well I would be able to perform, I had only registered for the usual five courses, amounting to fifteen credits.

Therefore, it was a pleasant surprise to learn as the first semester progressed that I was doing exceedingly well. I was even more pleased to find that at the end, I had been given two bonus credits for As—bonus credits were given for every six credits of As. This system was a bonanza I had not counted on and was to figure substantially in the rapid completion of my undergraduate schooling. As I look back on it now, one of the nicest things to happen to me at that time was to have kindly Dean Hawkes call me to his office one day, ask me whether I was the same young man with poor grades he had seen off to war, and then say he had just sent a notice to my parents that I was on the honor roll.

With Elsa at Swarthmore and me at Columbia, every other weekend for us was spent at the Wells's home in Bryn Mawr. When not there, I telephoned her every Saturday night. The relationship, however, caused me some problems. The wrestling coach, who was also an assistant football coach, remembered me from earlier times and was perturbed when I would not sign up for the teams. I wanted my weekends free and the two were incompatible. Matters really became awkward when, in the physical education class, I was put on the mats with a college heavyweight wrestling champion. While I could not pin him, he could not pin me either. From then on, while I continued to go out of town on weekends, I made an effort to avoid that coach.

I had come out of the army in good shape financially, the apartment was more than paying for itself, and I was managing on the GI Bill's $75 a month. While my trips down to Bryn Mawr were a bit of a drain, the roundtrip train fare was relatively cheap. Every other Friday afternoon saw me on the Pennsylvania Railroad en route to Philadelphia. I am amazed how different things look today on leaving New York, coming out of the tunnel on the Weehauken flats, and traveling farther into New Jersey. On an evening in 1947, Weehauken was ablaze with heavy industry, foundries spewing out flames, and the swampy areas of the flats around them phosphorescent with industrial waste that must have been highly toxic. All that is left of that today are vast empty flatlands. In 1958, I completed a large oil painting from memory of that earlier scene of nighttime factories and their effluence, which I titled simply "Pollution." Whenever I see it, I am reminded of those many train rides.

Settled into serious study, I regretted not having registered for more credits at the outset. My goal now was to finish my undergraduate work as quickly as possible. My major was in political science and public law, with a view toward eventually going either to law school or into the government. While I was toiling away in New York, Elsa was doing the same at Swarthmore. Despite being a very attractive coed, she was not particularly happy there. Her ties to me in effect took her out of circulation, making things a bit difficult. While some of our social life related to events at Swarthmore, I recall that we focused more around her Baldwin School friends' activities. Quite a few of them married early, and we went to a series of Mainline weddings, which were great fun.

My first two roommates attended classes at the university but were not matriculated in Columbia College. With less than 2,000 students, the College was only a small part of the university. One could also attend undergraduate courses at the School of General Studies, often referred to as the "extension school," on a nonmatriculated basis. Classes there usually met at night. I finished my college studies and was awarded an A.B. in February 1949, sixteen months after I started, by combining a maximum load of college courses with some from other areas for which I was given credit.

My three later roommates, all graduate students, Dick Pickering, Dan Sheingold and subsequently Bob Kinsey, were to see me complete college, a Master's degree, and the course work for a PhD. Finishing at odd times, I never participated in a graduation ceremony for either my Bachelor's or Master's degrees; the diplomas were simply mailed to me. In later years, however, I felt as if I had deprived my parents, if not myself, of the pleasure of having them formally awarded.

Living at 151 8th Avenue was a far cry from a typical student existence. We walked crowded city streets to our subway ride uptown to the campus. When at home in the apartment, we shared cooking and cleaning responsibilities. I made passable spaghetti and stews, and Pickering a superb pineapple upside-down cake. There were no fast food places in those days, so, from time to time, we ate at the Riss Food Shoppe, a diner-type restaurant on 8th Avenue, where the waitresses took a special shine to us as Columbia boys. It was in this downtown New York City setting that I was to be taught one of life's lessons.

On a sunny Saturday afternoon in November 1947, I decided to take the dog for a walk. With Socrates on his short German police leash, we strolled leisurely up 8th Avenue to 23rd Street and were about to cross when a taxi passed in front of us. The cab stopped a short distance farther in front of Cavanaugh's, one of New York's finest restaurants.[2] As it discharged its passengers, they immediately caught my eye. I stood transfixed as two gorgeous Las Vegas–type showgirls stepped out, followed by two New York characters out of Damon Runyon's *Guys and Dolls*. One was tall and thin, the other short and fat. I saw the rotund one tip the cab driver handsomely as the group proceeded toward the restaurant, attracting considerable attention as they went.

I had only been out of the service a few months, and I remember thinking bitterly that these two likely draft-dodgers had probably become rich while the rest of us were fighting the war. Now they were taking those beauties into a place I could not even begin to afford. I was standing on the corner at once fascinated watching them and cursing them in my mind, when suddenly the big tipper broke away from the group and rushed over to me. Taking me by the arm, he said, "Can I help you across the street, soldier?" He had seen me standing there accompanied by a Shepherd dog, hesitating. I was wearing sunglasses and my old Army leather A-2 jacket. Obviously, he thought I was a blind veteran. Too dumbfounded and embarrassed even to reply, I simply let him lead us across busy 23rd Street. Thereupon, he quickly returned to his waiting friends and they all happily entered Cavanaugh's. "Judge not, that ye be not judged" (Matthew 7:1).[3]

Columbia was a beehive of activity in the late 1940s. The war's end and the emergence of the Soviet Union and communism encouraged the growth of leftist/Marxist student groups on campus. There were rallies and protests, especially after General Eisenhower retired from military life and became president of the university. At one point a controversy arose over an article in *The Spectator*, the college's student newspaper. Eisenhower stepped in and shut it down, setting off a furor.[4] Residing off campus, I was determined to remain aloof, singlemindedly pursuing my studies. Nevertheless, I did get involved in one incident, which may have had consequences for me later. I saw a notice on a bulletin board one morning announcing that Gerhard Eisler, former justice minister of Communist East Germany, was going to be a speaker at a meeting sponsored by one of the leftist student organizations.

Eisler had been one of East Germany's top Communists when I was in CIC in Berlin. Consequently, I was curious to hear what he had to say, now that he had been ousted and come to America. By coincidence, a few days before going to that meeting, I had come across some material I had brought home from Berlin. In it I found a clipping from *Neues Deutschland*, the official East German newspaper, justifying the forced transportation of skilled workers from Soviet-dominated portions of Germany to Russia. I placed it and a few other items in my notebook and took them with me to the meeting.

The student organization had obtained the use of one of the university's auditoriums, and several hundred people attended. Initially, I thought Eisler might be critical of the East German regime. Had I reflected further on the matter, however, I would have realized that he would not then have had the sponsorship of that leftist organization. His address was a straight, down-the-line, pro-Soviet presentation. I squirmed in my seat as he told of how the East German Communist regime was admired and supported by the people. At the conclusion, there were questions from the audience. After a couple of planted questions designed to reinforce the speaker's position, I arose and asked: "How do the East Germans feel about their skilled workers being forced to go to Russia?" Eisler's reply was that no such thing ever happened. I responded that I had spent two years in Berlin after the war and had talked to people who had escaped from being taken. Again Eisler demurred.

Taking out the *Neues Deutschland* clipping, I asked him a bit sarcastically if he was acquainted with the paper and whether he understood German. I then quickly read and translated the headline and the thrust of the item. I asked how he could deny that these acts occurred when the East German government officially stated those laborers should be proud to work in Russia in repayment for all the war destruction Germany had caused. Finally, I declared, "Where was Minister of Justice Eisler when all of this was taking place?" By this time I had caused considerable unrest in the audience and organization stalwarts were shouting, "Throw him out!"

and "Fascist stooge!" Whereupon, I was forcibly escorted out of the meeting by a squad of student ushers.[5]

My courses were over for that day, and I made my way to the Broadway and 116th Street subway entrance to go home. As I was about to descend the steps, I was accosted by a man in his thirties dressed in a business suit. He politely asked if I would mind answering a few questions. Walking a few feet from the entrance, he produced an ID and stated that he was from the FBI. I responded, "Sure, glad to help you in any way I can." Evidently he had been at the meeting and was curious as to who I was. He said, "You really stuck a pin in the speaker's balloon." I told him that I was a student attending the College, but that I had formerly been an army intelligence officer, a CIC special agent in Berlin. He seemed pleased about our exchange. After he departed, I had a feeling that he was going to submit a report on my actions. Two years later when I entered the State Department, it may have played a role in expediting my FBI security clearance.

By the end of 1947, I had become a fixture around the Wells household. Elsa's older sister, Lois, had remained in Europe to work with relief agencies. The four of us—Dr. and Mrs. Wells, Elsa, and I—generally ate our meals in their spacious kitchen amid lively discussions about politics, academia, and the state of the world. During these discourses my future father-in-law and I often disagreed. He had the habit of constantly jumping up from the meal to refer to the encyclopedia, dictionary, or some other reference work, over protestations from the rest of us. Sundays would see us going together to the Ardmore Methodist Church. The Wellses played an active role in their church, he having served as Lay Leader and a Sunday School teacher and she as the head of the Women's Society and delegate to the General Conference of the Methodist Church. After church, we would lunch in a local restaurant.

Dr. Wells was asked to return to Germany for two months during the summer of 1948, and I took over the responsibility of driving Elsa and her mother out to Illinois on their annual visit to Grandmother Wells in Quincy and to other relatives in the Midwest. Compared to travel today, it was an arduous journey, even in a new Dodge with Fluid Drive. There were no interstate highways, only two lane blacktop roads. It was a hot drive, with no air-conditioning, requiring three days. Now one can make the same trip in one long day. I enjoyed meeting the relatives and spending time at the family's vacation home at McHenry on the Fox River northwest of Chicago. A few weeks after our return to Bryn Mawr in September 1948, Elsa's parents announced our engagement, with several articles appearing in the *New York Times* and the Philadelphia newspapers. Sensing all along their concern that marriage might mean Elsa would not finish college, I made every effort to reassure them she would.

The four and a half years I had spent in the army entitled me to the full forty-eight months of education under the GI Bill. The academic year generally was only nine months long. Consequently, a full university entitlement for the average student would permit a year, and possibly two, of graduate school as well, if one managed the system appropriately. With my previous Columbia freshman, ASTP, and Shrivenham University credits, however, even after undergraduate college I had as much as three more academic years available. There was no question, therefore, that I would pursue at least a Master's degree, particularly since Elsa in September of 1949 would just then be transferring from Swarthmore to Bryn Mawr College to complete her final two years.

I decided that I would enter the graduate Faculty of Political Science and that my degree would be in public law. In my college senior year at Columbia I had been exposed to the teaching of Professor Franz Neumann, a refugee from Nazi Germany with a brilliant mind. I chose him as my advisor. In our first consultation he suggested that with my background, I was the person to do a study on U.S. denazification policy in Germany. It was an extensive topic requiring considerable research and analysis, a subject worthy not only of a Master's, but an eventual PhD thesis. I was pleased with Dr. Neumann's suggestion. I already had some data on denazification available, as did Dr. Wells in his files, and I knew where I could find other original source material. In addition, my reading knowledge of German would be of great assistance as I did further research. Over the following months, I completed preparations for a thesis, submitted an outline and began writing.

Upon discharge from the Army in September 1947, I was asked if I would accept a reserve commission. After years of grinding duty during World War II as a private because I had not been alert enough to enter officer training, I quickly accepted . Also by that time I had matured to the point where I believed that as a citizen I had an obligation not only to myself, but to the country as well. I also felt I owed that to fallen comrades for the privilege of being allowed to return home alive. Although I soon found it a nuisance to travel one evening every other week up to the Bronx for Army Reserve drills, there were compensations. Reporting for two weeks of active duty in early June 1948 at the Intelligence School at Fort Holabird in Baltimore, Maryland, I found that my combat and Berlin CIC experience made me a valuable commodity. I was asked to join the faculty and later allowed to schedule active duty in subsequent years at my convenience. This meant that when my classes were not in session, I would go on active status and draw my officer's pay. It also resulted in some very interesting duty.

Among the subjects I taught were "Espionage Networks" — with an emphasis on the remarkable spy ring developed in Japan by the German Communist, Richard Sorge— and "Surreptitious Entry." Proficiency in the latter was to make me sought after by friends who had locked themselves out of their homes. While I was able to help by using other means, I always had to explain to them that it was illegal without special orders to have lock-picking tools in one's possession. Once with the cooperation of the MPs, I had to obtain the release of one of my students from a Baltimore jail for violating that prohibition.

Baltimore was a wide-open town in those days, with a bawdy strip called The Block and places similar to today's go-go clubs. On one occasion, I found myself in the company of a group of wild, fun-loving officers in one of these establishments, called the Oasis. The music was loud, the dancers fervid, and the rafters shaking. At one point in the midst of the revelry, a beautiful Marilyn Monroe look-alike came down off the stage and danced topless among the seated spectators. As she passed our table, she took it upon herself to plunk her bottom in my lap and, sitting there, ran her fingers through my hair.

I was startled. The audience went berserk, particularly when she then grabbed me by the ears and pressed my nose into her well-endowed bosom. At the very height of this hilarity, however, there was a piercing whistle blast and shouts as the police raided the place. To make matters worse, we were all in uniform. Unlike today, it was common practice not long after the war to wear the uniform off duty. After taking our names and organizations, the police simply released us. I am still not clear why they raided the Oasis, since activity of that sort on The Block had been going on for years.

The incident was the talk of the office when I reported for duty the following Monday morning. However, my compatriots in the affair did not seem to be particularly upset about the matter. About an hour later, I received a summons to "report to the colonel." The latter, a lieutenant colonel, was the head of the faculty at the school. He had been a paratrooper during the war, and once he spotted me as a reservist wearing airborne regalia, I was extended particularly cordial treatment. It came as a shock, therefore, once in his office to be given a dressing down of almost unbelievable ferocity: "How could an officer with your breeding, an Ivy League college man, disgrace the Intelligence School the way you have!" He continued, "In uniform with a topless woman on your lap, doing . . . well, I won't even mention what. . . . You are supposed to be an officer and a gentleman. . . . I am ashamed of you!" To say I was contrite would be the understatement of the year. I left his office devastated. Had I not been so mortified, I might have been more aware of things going on around me. Several of the officers and secretaries in the outer main office evidently had gathered around the colonel's closed door and eavesdropped on the tongue-lashing I was given.

Returning to my desk and sitting in abject silence, I could not help noticing that everyone in the room was having a hard time keeping a straight face, a few of them bursting into laughter for no apparent reason. It was then I sensed that I was on the receiving end of a grandiose joke that would be recounted for years afterward at Fort Holabird. Once over the shock, I was no worse for wear and in fact the incident tended to enhance my relationship with the colonel and the staff.

It was during that tour of duty I met an officer who could have profoundly affected my life. He, too, was a lieutenant colonel, a paratrooper in World War II and a person impressing me as being a "gung ho" adventurer. One evening at the officers' club he informed me that he had been working with organizations in the Pentagon to set up a special unit that could be dropped into enemy territory to effect the release of POWs or the destruction of high priority targets. With my intelligence background, paratrooper training, and combat experience, he averred, I would be well suited for such duty. If I were interested, I could be brought back on full active service. At the time, I simply went along with the colonel's discourse thinking it so much "bar talk." Three months later, after South Korea was overrun and UN Forces were engaged in a desperate struggle, I was to think otherwise.

One Sunday in March 1949, I was having lunch after church with the Wellses in the Horn & Hardart Restaurant in Ardmore, Pennsylvania, when Elsa and I were startled to hear her mother say, "Don't you children think it's about time you two were married?" I was eating a dish of vanilla ice cream at the time and a spoonful dropped on my tie. We were both surprised, assuming all along that there would be no marriage with parental assent until Elsa finished college. It was evident that Dr. and Mrs. Wells had discussed the matter and come to the conclusion that we would act responsibly with regard to our education and that there was no sense in keeping us apart any longer. With that, Mrs. Wells promptly contacted the family's Ardmore Methodist Church, since we had earlier agreed we would be married there, and a date was set for June 11, 1949. Elsa at the time was still 19, and I was 24. On the other hand, we had been going together for more than two years.

In some ways our wedding was hilarious, reflecting a life to come that was full of unexpected developments. Had Hollywood filmed a wedding comedy, some of the things that occurred at ours would have been high points. Thinking that I had brought it with me, the best man left his cutaway hanging in the closet in our apartment. On the morning of the wedding he had to return to New York to retrieve it, arriving back in Bryn Mawr with just enough time to change clothes. Coming from lunch at a nearby restaurant with my ushers a few hours before the wedding, I accidentally backed my brand new Ford convertible with considerable speed into a solidly built Packard sedan. The Packard's heavy, steel front bumper guard put a deep dent dead center in the rear bumper of my car. Luckily, it was so perfectly located that it looked as if the vehicle might have been designed that way. At the wedding, itself, either purposely or inadvertently, the best man had difficulty remembering in which of his pockets he had placed the rings. He fumbled for an inordinate amount of time, as the wedding guests squirmed in their seats. I was not much better, for as we were changing our clothes preparing to depart the wedding reception, I misplaced my wallet. That caused the guests to wait and wait, wondering what was going on up in the bedroom.

Our honeymoon planning left a lot to be desired. Owning a new convertible and visualizing lovely top-down drives colored our thinking. The automobile trip to Nova Scotia proved an arduous undertaking, particularly since we had not planned specific nightly stopovers. While there were some memorable interludes, I would not recommend an extended car trip to honeymooners, suggesting instead that they take a cruise or go to a resort.

The year following our marriage saw us busily engaged with our studies, Elsa at Bryn Mawr and me at Columbia graduate school. We found ourselves competing to see who would get the best grades, animatedly comparing As, much to the delight of our parents. In all fairness to my wife, however, she not only did her own work, but also typed my thesis, section by section, when I brought the drafts down to her on weekends. This set a pattern that was to continue later in the Foreign Service, as Elsa, superb scholar, researcher, and typist that she is, assisted me at my diplomatic posts.

Upon obtaining my Master's, I pushed on with the course work for the PhD. In the late spring of 1950, however, bored with continuous schooling, I thought I might test the waters with a view to obtaining a job in the government. After a working interlude, I planned to return to finish my Ph.D. My roommate, Dick Pickering, had already obtained employment with the Federal Reserve in Washington. I had taken the Civil Service examination at the Junior Professional Assistant (JPA) level and passed, but this meant nothing other than that I was placed on a list. I used the occasion of an Army Reserve tour of duty in Baltimore to travel to Washington myself and call on the CIA and the State Department. In this exercise, I was to learn a lesson in how things are done in Washington. Walking in the front door and dealing with the employment offices, I came away discouraged from both, having achieved little more than the submission of the standard application and personal history forms.

A week later, I decided to try again. After an extended wait, I was ushered in to see a personnel officer at the State Department. Reviewing my résumé, he concluded by telling me politely that they were not hiring at the JPA level at that time. The JPA entry salary was around $2,650 a year. Generally, officers with my qualifications entered into careers with the State Department by taking the Foreign Service Examination. This was something I had not considered at that time, since I was not interested in spending a large part of my life overseas. As I was leaving the building, I heard someone call me by name. It was Frank Wathen, a former captain who had been assigned to our Neukoelln CIC office for training back in 1946. He informed me that he was now employed at the State Department in the Office of Security.

Wathen, an affable Texan in his thirties, had been a lawyer before the war and was now putting his legal and CIC experience to good use. He suggested I join him for lunch. In between reminiscing about our times in Berlin, I told him about running up against a stone wall in my efforts to find employment. He was incredulous, saying, "With your background and experience in Germany, beside your language fluency, they'll hire you tomorrow. The department needs German-speaking officers in the worst way!" He went on to explain that the State Department had taken over the occupation of Germany from the Army and was in dire need of qualified officers to replace the military government personnel there.

After lunch, we returned to Wathen's office, where he telephoned someone in the Bureau of Administration. I could hear him touting my qualifications and saying, "This fellow would be a real find for the Bureau of German Affairs." Later that afternoon, I found myself back in the Personnel Office, where a more senior official interviewed me for a position as a U.S. Kreis (County) Resident Officer in Germany. The salary, $5,495 a year, was double the amount I was fully prepared to accept as a JPA earlier that morning.[6] At the conclusion of the interview, I was informed that steps would be taken to hire me, pending a security clearance. The entire process should take about sixty days. Needless to say, I thanked Frank Wathen profusely. To this day I am grateful to him for having launched me on a career in diplomacy.

On June 25, 1950, North Korea invaded South Korea. President Truman recognized that if steps were not taken promptly to halt the aggression, we would have learned nothing from World War II. American troops, who had largely been withdrawn from the Republic of Korea in a general postwar retrenchment, were ordered back. Led by the United States, as early as June 27th the UN Security Council condemned the attack and made the defense of the south a United Nations police action. Fortunately, the Russian seat on the Council was vacant at the time or most certainly they would have used their veto to halt these moves, as they did innumerable times thereafter.

At the outbreak of the war, I was engaged as a Reserve officer with the faculty at Fort Holabird. I do not remember whether I was actually on active duty the day the news came, but my Reserve status made me subject to call-up in any event. In August, I was ordered to report to the State Department for consultations. Preparations for hiring me were moving along reasonably well. I was told, however, that there was a possible hold-up on my security clearance. Using a former CIC colleague then with the FBI, I sought to find the source of the problem. Much to my chagrin, he confided to me that I had been a "bad boy . . . and a real live wire." I soon discerned what the trouble was when I returned to my New York apartment, which I had sublet for three months during the summer to an old school friend.

Visiting the elderly German couple who served as the superintendents for our building, I learned that my apartment had been the scene of some wild parties. I was taken aback as they described disconcerted tenants complaining about the noise; one partygoer had even blown up condoms like balloons and floated them out the window. The FBI investigator doing the background check must certainly have received an earful from other persons in the building. Luckily, I was in a position to take remedial action. I ousted the person who had sublet the apartment and saw to it that my friend in the FBI received an explanation.

After being informed that I was to report for duty with the Department of State on September 26, 1950, I put notices on bulletin boards at Columbia that my apartment was available for the rental freeze price of $36 a month, which was what I paid when I acquired it in 1947. In no time at all, I was able to dispose of the place, obtaining in return the same $600 I had originally paid for the furniture. However, I left my successor, a graduate student, a reasonably furnished apartment, taking with me only my boyhood student desk, which now reposes on the third floor of our Chevy Chase home. On moving day, Elsa and I drove our 1949 Ford convertible to Bryn Mawr with the top down so as to fit the desk on the back seat. In the rear of the car with the lid tied was a large steamer trunk I was soon to pack with all my belongings for shipment to Germany. Those were the days when automobiles were spacious. Stopping for fuel in New Jersey, I filled the tank with gasoline at 14 cents a gallon.

Both Elsa and I looked forward to going back to Germany. My prospective position with the Department of State as a U.S. Resident Officer sounded exciting and challenging. Our thoughts were full of memories of the wonderful times we had had together in Berlin, and we could not wait to return. Elsa, however, true to our promise to her parents, would remain at Bryn Mawr for her senior year. I, on the other hand, put my work toward a doctorate on hold, reasoning that an assignment in Germany would enable me to gather much valuable material toward my dissertation. After concluding my tour of duty, I planned to return to Columbia.

I drove to Washington several days prior to my reporting date. The first night I stayed at the YMCA at 18th and G Streets NW, but thereafter I found quarters in a furnished room in the home of a nice elderly woman in the Kalorama section off Connecticut Avenue. Processing through the State Department's administrative offices, I encountered one personnel officer who took a dim view of my military background. He dwelt upon my war and CIC experience, having fixed in his mind that I had a residual antipathy toward the Germans. I remember finally saying to him, "My mother was born in Germany. I spoke German as a child. What makes you think I dislike Germans?" Perhaps he was just testing me, but I found it very annoying.

I was placed in orientation training at the Foreign Service Institute, which was then located in a red brick apartment building on C Street NW, on the site of the current diplomatic entrance to the New State Building. Our class, numbering 25–30, was largely made up of newly appointed Foreign Service officers, most of whom were also designated to go to Germany as resident officers or directors of U.S. Information Centers, the Amerika Haüser. An elite group, largely the products of Ivy League schools and many with graduate degrees, they were in their late twenties and early thirties in age. The majority of them were married and their spouses, who would be accompanying them on their assignment, were enrolled in a special course for the wives. Many of the latter were graduates of the top eastern women's colleges ("the Seven Sisters"). There was no thought that they would have separate careers in the Foreign Service, but they were regarded as important adjuncts to their husbands' positions.

It was widely understood at the time that "a wife could make or break a man's career." The State Department was smug in expounding the concept that it could get "two for the price of one"! There is no question in my mind that some of those wives today would be candidates for the highest posts in the government. As I became better acquainted with my classmates, I learned that some were from distinguished Eastern Establishment families, one of them related to President Wilson. I recall a conversation I had with a colleague from Boston. He had been a pilot during World War II and had lost part of his leg, which was replaced with a metal support. In jest one day I tactlessly commented that with his family's influence, could he not have found himself a safer posting? His reply was that his family expected that he would acquit himself in the most honorable fashion and that it would have been unthinkable for him not to serve his country in the front lines. I have never forgotten that conversation nor the sense of *noblesse oblige* that existed among many of the officers with whom I was to associate.

There were some fascinating aspects to our orientation training, such as instruction in how to write the "despatch," the basic mode of written communication at that time between overseas posts and Washington. They were always addressed to the secretary of state and began, "Excellency, I have the honor to report . . . " I soon learned that great weight was placed upon reporting and one's ability to write well. Certain officers in the Foreign Service had achieved prominence through their despatches. Ability to conjure up an entire setting with a choice phrase was prized. I remember one written by a friend describing a difficult marathon negotiation that began, "It was a late night of dirty cups and cigarette butts . . . "

On the other hand, I also recall a test we were given in training: We were handed a three-page report describing an intricate scientific process involving the effect of certain chemicals on metal tubing. We were asked to condense the document for transmission by cable back to Washington, making it as short as possible. Some of us reduced the report to a page, the best to somewhat less than that. Our lecturer then stunned us all by remarking, "Do you know what this report is telling you? Precisely, in two sentences, it says: "'Don't use Drano. It rusts the hell out of the pipes!'" We were all properly chagrined.[7]

I look back upon some of our instruction now with a chuckle. In view of our imminent departure for Germany in a month's time, we were given a crash course in protocol and the customs of the Foreign Service. The wife of one of our diplomats, Romaine Alling, taught the course. I cannot recall whether in this instance the spouses joined us. I believe they did for some sessions. In any event, the wives not only received similar training, but more extensive instruction in the social customs of the diplomatic service, entertaining and running a household with servants overseas. The course created quite a stir among the wives, which husbands were bound to hear about upon coming home in the evenings.

Having served in Germany in an official capacity, I had a good idea of what to expect when governing a county and/or a small city. Mrs. Alling's lectures, therefore, seemed far-fetched. I listened amusedly as she told us how to make a courtesy call, which corner of our business/social cards to bend for this occasion or that, the proper way to address various dignitaries, how to enter an automobile, where to sit according to rank, and so forth.[8] While I dismissed Mrs. Alling's course at the time, I must admit that

I was grateful for it in later embassy and consular assignments, particularly in countries where diplomatic niceties are taken very seriously.

In early October 1950, the Department's Transportation Office informed our group that we would be sailing for Europe at the end of the month aboard the S.S. *America*, then the flagship of the United States Lines. As was usual for Foreign Service personnel at the time, we would be going first class. Household effects had to be packed for shipment to Germany, automobiles were to be driven to designated areas dockside for loading aboard our ship, and a variety of other arrangements had to be made. I purchased another large steamer trunk. It would go aboard ship with me, as would our Ford convertible.[9] The *America* debarked at Le Havre, and I would be driving via a brief stopover in Paris to Frankfurt.

We concluded our training and were given several days to pack and settle our affairs. My task was relatively simple. Unlike some of my colleagues, I had no house to sell or rent, no children in school, and no large-scale household packing to do. Elsa was remaining in the States and I only had myself to worry about. The shipping company had picked up my trunks, and all I had to do was to drive our car from Bryn Mawr to the dock in New York. It was then I received a call from the graduate student who had taken over my apartment. He told me that I had received a telegram from the Department of the Army and that it looked very official and urgent. I asked him to open it and read it to me. It was a call to active duty. Elsa and my parents-in-law went into shock. Mother Wells took it particularly hard. I can still hear that dear woman telling her husband: "Roger, you call Frank Pace (the Secretary of the Army at the time) and tell him that John has already put five years in the Army. That is enough!"

The war in Korea seemed to be winding down following our successful landing at Inchon. I had not heard of any large-scale call-up of reserves, and I wondered about the army's rationale for calling me up at this time. My mind wandered back to that "gung ho" paratroop lieutenant colonel who was attempting to form a special unit. With my effects already shipped, the State Department expecting me to report for duty in Germany, and the boat about to sail, I placed a telephone call to First Army Headquarters on Governor's Island in New York, the source of the telegram. My call finally was directed to the sergeant who had sent my telegram. At the time, I was assigned to a composite Army Reserve unit in New York City consisting of several hundred officers. He told me that "a few officers listed as students" had been sent telegrams. I responded that I was prepared to go, but that I was now employed by the State Department and two days away from sailing for occupation duty in Germany. After remonstrating that I should have notified the Army promptly upon entering into government employment, since that was an exempted category, he said a telegram canceling my orders would be sent that afternoon. I should proceed to Germany.

My parents, Elsa, and Mother Wells came to New York to see me off as I sailed on the S.S. *America* for Europe. I can see them and other family members and friends standing on the dock, as that magnificent ship, foghorn trumpeting, confetti rolls flying, and champagne corks popping, pulled away from the pier. There were tears in Elsa's eyes. We both knew it would be nine or ten months until we saw each other again.

It would be difficult for the average traveler today to conceive how luxurious first class was on the great ocean liners of that time. Our trip to Le Havre took almost a week. We sat down to each meal reviewing a massive menu, which permitted ordering virtually anything your heart desired. If one wanted filet mignon and oysters for breakfast, you had only to tell the steward or the waiter. In between meals, delicacies or bouillon were served while you lounged in a chair on deck. In the evenings, dress was long gown and black tie, or a costume befitting special occasions, such as masquerade ball night, or Hawaiian night. You were waited on hand and foot. Special stewards took care of the children so that the parents' time was free for other things. It was a gracious existence, a million light years removed from my Atlantic crossing six years earlier aboard a troopship.

There were twenty-six Foreign Service officers in our contingent, about half of them with wives, and some with children. A number of the "bachelors" were married, but for a variety of reasons had left their spouses behind. Added to this mix were a number of Foreign Service secretaries and assorted others. Among the latter were aging movie star Gloria Swanson, her starlet daughter, Michelle Farmer, and several attractive young women. Superb food and wines, dancing, and general merriment took its toll. One could sense that the wives were keeping tabs on the "bachelors" so they would not stray.

The Oscar-winning film *Sunset Boulevard* had just been released starring Swanson, and the steamship line made sure that it was shown while she was aboard. With much fanfare, Ms. Swanson introduced the film and afterwards afforded us an intimate view of its production. Most of the single men's eyes, however, were on her daughter, a stunning beauty. To say I had a great time on board would be an understatement. After a night of drinking, dining, and dancing, some of the fellows soon got into a routine of taking a middle-of-the-night swim in the ship's pool. On one particularly rough night at sea, we were playing water polo and the roll of the ship would cause the depth of the water to vary. At one moment you would be standing in waist-deep water, and then in the next it would be over your head. It made for interesting sport. I remember sobering up another time trying to hang on to the ball, while Bill Schauffele (later ambassador to Poland) kept holding me under water in an effort to take it away from me.

The S.S. *America* docked at Southhampton to discharge passengers for Britain and then proceeded across the English Channel to Le Havre. The harbor there had changed somewhat since the war, but destruction was still everywhere to be seen. Coming up on deck after being processed by the French immigration authorities, I watched as the automobiles, mine among them, were off-loaded. Three of my colleagues knew I would be driving my convertible to Paris and then on to Frankfurt and asked if they could join me. I was pleased to have their company. We sensed as we descended the gangplank that life's vistas were opening before us. For all of us, it was our first assignment in the Foreign Service. We were young, enthusiastic, and ready to meet any challenge.

8
Governing Occupied Germany

As my colleagues Ed and Charlotte Savage and John Black stood on the dock in Le Havre, I checked over my automobile. We realized our first challenge would be to muster up enough of our French to locate a service station and gas up the car. Finding our way out of the harbor area and onto the road to Paris proved less difficult than one might have expected, as was locating a petrol station. Our actual problem came in deciding which type of fuel to use and in calculating the price. Once in Germany, I knew that we would be using Allied facilities run by the U.S. military, which were similar to American service stations. We learned that my car used "super" and I bought the appropriate number of liters to get me to Paris and then on to Germany.

It was a nice autumn day and we drove through the French countryside with the top down. We passed through the historic city of Rouen with its magnificent 13th century cathedral. It was in Rouen that Joan of Arc was tried and burned at the stake in 1431. As we went through town, pedestrians stared at our open vehicle and its occupants. Our American Ford convertible was immense by European standards after World War II, a gas-guzzler beyond the means of most French drivers. We drove 85 miles more to Paris, through the outskirts with their open markets, and directly into the heart of the city. En route, particularly in the built-up areas, our hearts would stop beating at each intersection as small French vehicles sped through with no more than blasts on their horns. As we made our way to the American Embassy, we drove around the Place de la Concorde. It was an unbelievable beehive of vehicles cutting in and out, horns blowing and Frenchmen shouting at one another to the point of hilarity.

With cars whizzing at me and honking from every direction and my passengers laughing hysterically, I simply came to a halt. I had not stopped more than a second or two, when a gendarme, dressed in a resplendent uniform with a cape, came up to the front of my car. Banging furiously on my front right fender with his baton, he shouted at me in French to move on, calling us crazy Americans. Had my French been at the level of my German, I might have told him I would have to do so at the risk of my life, because no sane person would venture into that circle with its maelstrom of vehicles.

Embassy Paris, virtually on the Place de la Concorde, was an impressive building behind massive iron gates. Reporting in, we were told where to obtain overnight quarters. The embassy had an arrangement with the Hôtel de Crillon, located across an adjacent side street. The Crillon, a magnificent establishment, was formerly a palace and is today perhaps the most expensive hotel in town. Years later, in 1958, while at a UNESCO conference in Paris, I visited my sister Eleanor and her husband, Alfred, a professor on a year's sabbatical there. When I mentioned that I was staying at the Crillon, they almost went into shock. I mischievously did not tell them about the embassy's arrangement and that my lodging was covered by per diem.

The next morning, we were briefed by the embassy staff. After a few hours of sightseeing, we were ready to push on to Frankfurt the following day. Fortified by an early breakfast at the Embassy's restaurant/snack bar, we drove out of Paris on the road to St. Dizier, Nancy, and then Strasbourg. French roads in those years were two-lane blacktop, more often than not lined with trees. Driving was difficult and tiring and, I might add, dangerous. Europeans drive on narrow roads at speeds so high they make most Americans uncomfortable. As I recall, we overnighted in a small hotel in Strasbourg that evening and arrived in Frankfurt at U.S. High Commission headquarters early enough the next day to report in before the close of business.

We were informed that our group of twenty-six State Department officers and their families were being billeted in a hotel in Bad Nauheim, a village on the outskirts of Frankfurt. The hotel was the same one used by the Hitler government in 1941 to house the interned U.S. embassy staff. The war had been over only a little more than five years, and some of the Germans inquired about Americans held there with whom they had become acquainted. Several of those officers, among them Ambassador George Kennan, later went on to earn distinguished reputations in the Foreign Service.

Billeting the group together in one hotel turned out to be an interesting experience, a minor study in sociology. Little cliques formed. Certain wives assumed leadership. For several weeks pending assignments to the field, a large part of the officers' and wives' time was engaged in learning German and in briefings on the country and HICOG organization. In my case, I was simply put to work, since I had already spent more than two years in Germany, spoke the language, and was familiar with the structure of the American occupation. My first job was an assignment to the U.S. Information Center (*Amerika Haus*) Frankfurt as an assistant to Hans Tuch, the director. I needed very little training and simply worked along with Tuch, a fine colleague and a good friend.

In early November 1950, we began receiving our assignments to the field. Almost half of our number were selected to go to Bavaria, the largest of all the states in Germany and a former kingdom. We were given a short time to pack and report to Munich, site of the headquarters of the Office of the Land Commissioner for Bavaria (OLCB). The headquarters itself was situated in a series of large office buildings in a former German military compound, which had been renamed McGraw Kaserne. Bavaria had 142 rural *Kreise* (counties), 47 cities *(Stradkreise)*, which were counties in their own right, and over 90 Resident Offices.[1]

In the assignment process, a number of our group were designated *Amerika Haus* directors. Most of us, however, had our hearts set on being a Resident Officer (RO), or Herr Gouverneur as the Germans called us. I was a bit unhappy as the first RO assignment was given out to Bill Schauffele to take over the Pfaffenhoffen Office, while I was ordered to remain in Munich to replace Paul Deibel, who had gone on three months' home leave to the United States. In truth, my assignment was a bonanza. Deibel was the operations officer for the Field Division, which supervised all the Resident Offices in Bavaria. It was an excellent place to observe the overall scene, become familiar with office politics from the inside, and work intimately with my future bosses.

The chief of the Field Division was Kenneth Van Buskirk, a burly former colonel who had served under General Patton in the war. He was a gregarious, outgoing man, a natural politician and pragmatist. I liked him. From the confidence he placed in me, I think the feeling was mutual. We would kid each other as to who were the better soldiers, tankers or paratroopers. His deputy William Moran, a jovial and shrewd Irishman, was a lawyer who years later became a federal judge in Alaska. I learned a great deal in the months I served in Munich. I became acquainted with a good many of the resident officers and learned which offices were deemed efficiently run and which had problems.

The State of Bavaria was divided into five administrative districts (*Regierungsbezirke*), each of which encompassed 20-40 counties. The American Military Government and, subsequently, the U.S. High Commission found this German organizational structure effective and adapted the occupation to it. A district was generally headed by a chief/resident officer who supervised from 11 to 25 ROs, including senior ROs in charge of such large cities as Munich, Nuernberg, Regensburg, and Würzburg.

Each day I was acting operations officer provided me with new insights. Visits to Resident Offices I might have considered plush assignments, such as Berchtesgaden or Garmisch, idyllic Alpine mountain resorts, revealed that these places were actually not desirable assignments. High-ranking visitors seeking accommodations at overbooked hotels or wanting special arrangements plagued resident officers there. Other ROs having *Kreise* with large contingents of American troops were constantly in discussions with German authorities or the local press over incidents involving criminal activity on the part of soldiers, damage to property from military maneuvers, real estate transfers, and a myriad of other things.

I remember my secretary coming to me one morning saying, "Prinz Aloïs of Bavaria is here to see Mr. Van Buskirk." I went out to greet him and explained that Mr. Van Buskirk and Mr. Moran were at a meeting and that I expected them back shortly. Might I be of any assistance in the meantime? The prince, a distinguished-looking elderly gentleman, was quite agitated as he explained that a party headed by the commanding general of the American 1st Infantry Division and several other officers had gone hunting on lands that were his property. Evidently, when the local forester informed the general that he must first have the prince's permission, he had arrogantly dismissed the matter. Right after the war, the Allied occupation forces had tended to run roughshod over German sensitivities, but this was five years later. Traditionally in Germany, hunting and fishing are strictly regulated, with hunting in particular very upper crust and ceremonial. One is invited to hunt or fish, the former often a fashionable affair with the hunters dressed appropriately. It is done on property either owned or rented for the purpose, privately stocked with game or fish.

The prince told me that had the general sought his permission, he would gladly have given it, but the entire way in which he behaved was most discourteous. As I listened politely, Mr. Van Buskirk returned. It was obvious that he and the prince were old friends who had hunted together. After listening to the complaint, Van Buskirk said he would speak to the general in an effort to straighten out the "misunderstanding." The prince sought an apology, and I was curious to see how the matter would evolve. Van Buskirk later that day placed a long distance call to the general's headquarters. Rather than being apologetic or even the least bit contrite, the general berated Van Buskirk.

Somehow word of the telephone conversation got back to the prince, and he decided to take matters into his own hands. He called the queen of Belgium, who was his sister. She in turn brought the matter to the attention of Perle Mesta, the American minister to Luxembourg. Mrs. Mesta, before her appointment to Luxembourg, had been Washington's most important hostess and had countless political connections. Word soon reached various congressional leaders of the general's unseemly behavior and how it was "impairing U.S.-German relations." It so happened that the general was on a promotion list for a third star, currently awaiting consent by the Congress. Told that the promotion was being held up pending clarification, the Pentagon promptly contacted the general, asking, in effect, why he was courting retirement. A few days later, I watched as the general, hat in hand, marched into Mr. Van Buskirk's office, where the prince waited to receive his apology. It was quite a scene.

Bill Schauffele and his wife, Heather, had been ensconced in Pfaffenhoffen for a month or two when they issued invitations to members of our group in the area to a settling-in party. I drove the 35 miles up to the affair on a lovely Saturday afternoon over a snow-covered Autobahn. We were all interested to learn how Bill was faring as a resident officer; he was thoroughly enjoying the challenge of his new job. I did not know it at the time, but I was eventually to take charge of three counties northeast of Pfaffenhoffen. Heather had prepared a buffet, which had as its centerpiece a large, delicious smoked ham. Bill encouraged us to try his county's famous beer—Pfaffenhoffen was the center of Germany's hops-growing district.

The ham was salty and the beer excellent and most of us consumed a considerable quantity of the latter out of the tall German glasses. What most of us did not focus on, however, was that Pfaffenhoffener beer was known for its alcohol content—*zwei und zwanzigprozent*, as the Germans boasted—22 percent alcohol or 44 proof. Two large glasses were enough to settle (or unsettle) most of us. I recall being a bit numb afterwards and exceedingly cautious in driving home to Munich that icy night.

Before I left the Munich headquarters Van Buskirk gave me a very delicate assignment. It grew out of an affair with considerable notoriety. A number of the resident officers taken over in the transition from the Army's Military Government to the State Department's High Commission in 1948–49 were colorful characters. Among them was the chief of District I, which included all of Upper Bavaria. He was a big, strapping man who had once been a California State Trooper and later was tied into state politics. In the early occupation days, many of the American officers had German "girlfriends." The chief's had been, or perhaps still was, the wife of a high-ranking Nazi. The situation had been a source of embarrassment for the headquarters for some time, but even with occasional snide comments in the German press, nothing was done. It all exploded, however, on one occasion when he used exceedingly bad judgment. Matters came to a head down in Garmisch at the Winter Games, which was in the chief's district.

As was the German custom, a "Royal Box" was always reserved for top dignitaries such as U.S. Land Commissioner Dr. George Shuster and Bavarian Minister-President Wilhelm Hoegner and their wives. On this occasion, Mrs. John McCloy, the wife of the U.S. High Commissioner for Germany, was also present. The chief chose that time to attend the games, seating himself and his "girlfriend" in the box. The German audience recognized her, causing much snickering, all to the mortification of the minister-president and Dr. Shuster. The wives, including Mrs. McCloy, were very upset. Matters worsened the next morning when the German press had a field day with the story.

The atmosphere in our office following the incident was tense, as Dr. Shuster vehemently told Van Buskirk that it was time the chief was sent home. Shortly thereafter, the chief was informed that his position was redundant, since the senior resident officer for the City of Munich could cover it. I was to be sent downtown to District I to assist in the interim. My quarters were temporarily changed from an apartment in McGraw Kaserne to a room in the large city-center building housing the District I offices. This brought me into close contact with the chief, who also lived in the building. It was an awkward situation, particularly since he was acting irrationally.

By sending me down there, Van Buskirk obviously felt he had someone who would keep him abreast of the situation, while I would have been happy to have distanced myself. The chief, on the other hand, persisted in unburdening his problems to me, asking my advice. My response was that he had a "no-win situation." With his vast experience as a military governor and as a war veteran, I told him he should go back to California, where he had numerous contacts. Who knows what vistas would be opened to him in the state administration or elsewhere? He might even run for Congress. My reasoning seemed to strike a responsive chord with him. Soon he was telling me if he was not appreciated in Germany, he would go elsewhere and the sooner the better. When Van Buskirk queried me as to how things were going, I could tell him with some satisfaction that our "problem" was reconciled to leaving.

Unfortunately, however, arrangements had been made to have the head of the Public Health Division of the Land Commission for Bavaria visit the chief. A doctor experienced in dealing with mental health problems, he apparently had no real sense of the broader ramifications of the situation. Instead, in his most sympathetic manner, he urged his patient to face up to his troubles and deal with them with confidence. The chief then changed his mind and decided to stay, feeling it was his duty to do so. I met the doctor soon afterwards and shall never forget his comment to me about his patient. He lamented, "He is like a big ship, an ocean liner, sinking, but

I think I managed to keep him afloat." Land Commission Headquarters was livid when they learned about the reversal and the decision not to leave. Finally, after a number of unpleasant days, the former district chief was forced to depart under military police escort. I never did find out what became of his German "girlfriend."

I had been in Munich over three months when the Neumarkt Resident Office in the Oberpfalz became available. The city of Neumarkt was a rail-head, fifteen miles southeast of Nuernberg on the main road to Regens-burg. It had a population of 25,000, was a *Stadtkreis*, and was encompassed by Landkreis Neumarkt, a sizeable rural county with about 55,000 inhab-itants. In addition, the Resident Office had jurisdiction over Landkreis Beilngries to the south with an additional 20,000 people. In all, the entire area supervised by the Neumarkt office covered about 600 square miles, with some 300 *Gemeinde* (villages/communities). It had been well run by Elmo Marsh, a capable administrator. I jumped at the opportunity.

I had ample time to prepare for my new assignment. One Saturday, I made the hour and a half drive from Munich to my prospective charge. Fifty-five miles of the journey was on the Autobahn; I then drove east into Landkreis Beilngris for the remaining 30 miles north to the city of Neumarkt. The Resident Office was located in an old castle in the center of town, a short distance from a church built in the Middle Ages. Elmo Marsh, who was returning to a position in the United States, introduced me to the twelve-member German staff. The latter included a senior advi-sor, a public affairs advisor, and several specialists, among them a film librarian who traveled throughout the counties showing movies on sub-jects designed to promote an understanding of democratic institutions. The roster also included a senior bilingual secretary and several driver/ mechanics. There was a second Resident Office with a small German staff in Beilngries, where I would hold office hours two days a week.

Shortly thereafter, I gathered up my effects, most of which were still in the McGraw Kaserne apartment I shared with William Graves, a likeable member of our group. He was the stepson of Francis B. Sayre, a distinguished American and former U.S. High Commissioner to the Philippines. Bill as a teenager was aboard the PT boat that brought General MacArthur out of the Islands after the fall of Bataan. I lost touch with him over the years. He left the Foreign Service and followed in the footsteps of his natural father, becoming the editor-in-chief of the *National Geographic Magazine*.

On March 4, 1951, I received my official commission, signed by the U.S. High Commissioner for Germany, John J. McCloy, and Land Commissioner for Bavaria George N. Shuster, designating me the Kreis Resident Officer for Stadtkreis Neumarkt, Landkreis Neumarkt, and

Landkreis Beilngries. The following day, I moved into my new residence, the *Villa am Weinberg,* a palatial house on a mountainside overlooking the city of Neumarkt. There were tennis courts and a lovely garden on the property, as well as a large garage. The house was staffed by a cook, two maids, two gardener-handymen, and the driver of my official Mercedes/Opel car. From the balconies one had a fine view of the valley below and the surrounding Jura Mountains. The main cobblestone street of the town was visible, as was the church with its high tower and parapet. As I stood on the balcony, I wished that my wife, Elsa, were there to share the moment with me. However, it would be another four months until she joined me. Periodically over the following weeks, the cook, Fraulein Herrmann, a woman in her fifties, would inquire nervously, "The Frau Gouveneur will be coming soon, no?" I do not think that she had any idea that her new mistress would be an amiable young woman only twenty-one years old.

In no time, I was plunged into a series of meetings with the *Landraete* (German county managers), the *Kreisraete* (county legislators), the *Oberbuergermeister* of Neumarkt, and a myriad of other officials in the townships under my jurisdiction. There were many problems to be addressed. The City of Neumarkt had been heavily damaged in the final days of World War II, when an SS unit endeavored to hold the town in the face of advancing American forces.

Not long after my arrival, I heard the story of an earlier military governor who had been working with German officials to have a school rebuilt. There had been interminable meetings discussing how the job was to be accomplished. One morning the town awakened to find the American busily laying bricks at the site. Shamefacedly, the population went to work rebuilding the school. I was determined to follow that man's example. There were other schools to be erected and much to be repaired: bridges, roads, houses, and more. Neumarkt was in need of a community center. I soon learned that it was possible to obtain financing through counterpart funds established at the national level and administered through the High Commission offices in Frankfurt. I made it my business as soon as possible to submit projects for such financing and pressed local officials to begin taking action.

My ability to speak German stood me in good stead. I had developed an authoritative way of speaking during my years in Berlin, which served to belie my youth, and would often bring out the response, *"Jawohl! Herr Gouveneur!"* Traveling extensively throughout the counties, I endeavored to visit as many of the 300 communities as possible. My evenings were filled with town meetings far and wide. The consumption of beer by all at these gatherings was prodigious!

In mid-June 1951, I took a few days' leave and drove our car to Le Havre to meet Elsa arriving with our dog, Socrates, on the S.S. *America*. It was then I learned what a sacrifice Elsa had made to join me. Having graduated *summa cum laude*, number one in her class at Bryn Mawr, she had won the most coveted prize the college could offer, a yearlong European fellowship. It was a happy runner-up who saw her decline the prize to be with me in Germany. That was to be but the first of many loving sacrifices she was to make over the years to support me in the Foreign Service. Upon our return to Neumarkt, the local newspapers carried articles about Elsa's arrival, commenting enthusiastically about the attractive young woman who would be their "first lady."

I had not done any formal entertaining up to that point and decided that a large Fourth of July party would be ideal both to celebrate our National Day and to introduce Elsa to the German community. Working with the German staffs, we sent out 295 invitations to prominent persons and their spouses in the three counties. Believing that no Fourth of July party could be complete without fireworks, we hired a Neumarkt explosives and pyrotechnics factory to do the job. In addition to the obligatory local German beer, wine, and spirits, I decided to serve American cocktails popular at the time, Martinis and Manhattans.

Preparations took on a festive atmosphere as the day of the party approached. On a lovely, mild summer evening the guests began to arrive in droves. They soon congregated around the sumptuous buffet table, washing the food down with the intriguing American cocktails. As dusk fell, word passed that the fireworks were about to begin, and the crowd moved out onto the terrace and into the garden. The anticipatory chatter was suddenly drowned in a deafening explosion, a rush of air, and the tinkling noise of shattering window glass. As an attention-getter, it had no peer! This was followed by several lesser explosions also accompanied by rushing air and sounds of breaking glass, punctuated by brilliant bursts of color lighting up the sky. Those of us who could still hear and see after the ten-minute display could only be impressed. Several viewers down in the town said they thought World War III had begun. It was quite a show!

The fireworks alone would have been enough to cause participants to remember the party for decades. On balance, however, the cocktails may have made them forget they were ever there, for they worked with devastating effect. These libations, served in their little stemmed glasses, were passed off as harmless by guests anxious to savor the olives or maraschino cherries at the bottom. More than a few of them sat down or passed out on the lawn, causing a local newspaper to write the German equivalent of "it was one helluva of a party!"

My relations with the population were soon put to the test. An American Army officer called on me one day to inform me that Hohenfels, a large section of eastern Landkreis Neumarkt, was being considered for requisition as a troop-training area. He said the site was sparsely populated, about 3,000 inhabitants, and possessed terrain suitable for tank maneuvers. I was stunned, as indeed were the local German authorities, when they heard of the proposal. I promptly remonstrated to my headquarters in Munich and to the district chief in Regensburg. Over the next weeks, I endeavored to deflect the proposal, urging that the massive training area be placed elsewhere. For a while it appeared as if I might have had success in convincing the powers that be to locate it at Wildflecken near Aschaffenburg, which was also under consideration. The resident officer responsible for that region was naturally urging that it come over to us. In the end, we both lost and the names Wildflecken and Hohenfels have become bywords over the years to American soldiers serving in Germany.[2]

As it came time to remove the inhabitants, some in families with land plots dating back before the 1400s, I faced a revolution in the county legislature (*Kreistag*). However, it was the height of the Cold War and the borders with Communist Czechoslovakia and East Germany were within easy marching distance. I played upon this theme in an impassioned speech to the legislature, saying at one point, "If you don't want the American Army here, I am sure the Soviet Army would be only too willing to take their place!" A reluctant *Kreistag* went along with the requisitioning process and the arrangements to evacuate and compensate the inhabitants. There was considerable unhappiness in the relocation process.

The Hohenfels affair had an unusual sequel. A few weeks after the evacuation, when things had settled down, an American Army lieutenant colonel called on me. His name, LeMoyne, is imbedded in my memory. He told me that he had received orders to move his medium tank battalion stationed at Baumholder in Hesse to Hohenfels for training. However, before doing so, he thought it would be a good idea to visit the area first to see if he might encounter any civil-military problems. He was cognizant of the difficulties surrounding the requisitioning. When I asked him whether he had been instructed to come to Neumarkt to survey the situation, he said, "No, but I thought it might be a good thing to do anyway." He assured me that he and his troops would be sensitive to political/public relations problems and would do their utmost to be cooperative. I expressed my appreciation and told him that we would work together to make this first usage of Hohenfels by the American military a success. We agreed that the tanks would be brought by rail to the farthest possible point near the edge of town and that the shortest route would be taken to protect the city's streets.

A week later a long military train loaded with dozens of battle-ready M47 tanks on flatcars pulled into the Neumarkt rail yards. The tanks were driven off the flatcars and in single file proceeded down the cobblestone way to the intersection of the main street, which was the Regensburg road, toward Hohenfels. There, they spun a right turn and lumbered out of town. One has to have witnessed a tank battalion on the move to be aware of what a menacing and awesome sight it is. The roaring of the engines and the clanking of the treads are deafening sounds that can be heard on the battlefield for miles, striking dread in the heart of the average soldier.

LeMoyne, however, had a surprise for me. As I watched the procession, I laughed as the tanks passed. Their hatches were open and smiling young tankers waved and tossed cellophane wrapped hard-candy and chocolate bars to the delighted crowd. It was a public relations coup if I have ever seen one!

The battalion had been maneuvering and firing at Hohenfels several days when I received a call on a Sunday afternoon from a member of my German staff. He informed me the city was buzzing with a rumor that one of the tanks had crushed a little girl. I quickly endeavored to obtain the facts, but there was absolutely no truth to the story. My office contacted the press, telling them to check as well. Soon, a second story circulated to the effect that the local communist cell had put out the rumor to stir up anti-American sentiment.

It was with some anxiety that I awaited the return of the tank battalion to the rail yards for its trip home. However, that was accomplished over the same route, again with smiling tankers tossing candy. Without a hitch the tanks were driven onto the flatcars, and the train promptly departed. An hour later, my senior German advisor came in to see me. Prefacing his remarks with, "You will never believe this," he proceeded to tell me that a boy riding on a bicycle had fallen into a large fifteen-foot-deep hole, but that he was unhurt. It had occurred at the very intersection where the tanks had made their 90-degree turn toward the rail yards. Evidently over time, groundwater had washed away the earth under the cobblestone street and a massive sinkhole had formed. Surely the angels were on the side of Colonel LeMoyne and his men, for it was a miracle that one of those heavy tanks was not sitting at the bottom of that pit. It would have provided local communists much grist for their mill. Instead, despite the damage to the street, it was taken as a good omen.

Life as the *Herr und Frau Gouverneur* had its drawbacks. It was almost impossible to have a private life; we lived in a goldfish bowl. When Elsa and I would inconspicuously go to a local German movie anywhere in the counties, our cook, Fraulein Herrmann, or someone on the staff was sure to ask the following morning how we liked the film. Fraulein Herrmann grew magnificent strawberries in her garden. They were very sweet and large—often the size of lemons—and a real treat on our breakfast cereal or served in rich cream. Neither Elsa nor I at first thought to inquire what her secret was, but one day we were informed that she could often be seen with a dustpan diligently following behind the horses passing down her street. I turned the tables on her, however, when for Thanksgiving dinner I insisted on having turnips with the meal. At first she acted as if there were none to be had. When a short while later I spotted a farm wagon loaded with them, I again requested that she purchase some. I then learned that turnips were considered animal fodder and she as the *Herr Gouveneur's* cook was not about to let people know that I ate turnips. Much to her horror, I bought some from a neighboring farmer, who insisted that he would give me a wagonload gratis.

When the Office of the High Commissioner for Germany (HICOG) and the State Department took over from U.S. Military Government and the Army in 1949, we envisaged a major effort to coax the Germans along the road to true democracy.[3] In the period up to that point, various aspects of administration had been turned over to the Germans, such as the railroads, the postal administration, and public works. Earlier, military government officers ran local government, appointed officials, and supervised most activities. With the advent of the resident officers, a serious program designed to prepare rank-and-file citizens for self-government was undertaken. The citizens were to be brought into the decision-making process and the country was to be prepared for communal elections. We encountered initial resistance from officials such as local Buergermeisters wedded to the status quo. When the concept of town meetings (*Buerger-versammlungen*) was first explained to them, they viewed it as something the Germans had been doing for over one hundred years. After all, on Sundays following church, it had been customary for the whole town to gather to hear the Buergermeister read the latest government orders. However, there was never any discussion on these occasions and people simply did what they were told.

When informed that the gatherings were now to provide an opportunity to debate the matters at hand, the Buergermeisters were appalled. It was obvious that changing this pervasive attitude would present a Herculean challenge, although most counties had some form of citizen participation. I picked up where my predecessor had left off, spending considerable time on the road visiting the many little towns in my jurisdiction. Often these visits were in the evening for town hall or community planning board meetings. The planning board (*Arbeitsgemeinschaft*) was an innovation

I was to introduce to Neumarkt and Beilngries. Reluctant at first, Buergermeisters and other German officials soon eagerly participanted in both types of meetings. Many a heated debate was washed down with free-flowing beer. Afterwards, my driver, Georg Biehler, would have to drive me thirty or more miles over country roads in all kinds of weather. Arriving home in the early hours of the morning, he would often find me sound asleep in the back seat.

One of the good friendships I established in those years was with Landrat Otto Schedl, the county executive of Neumarkt. He was an exceedingly able official with a strong background in economics, and we worked closely together to solve community problems. The Bavarians are a fun-loving people; they enjoy their beer and a good joke. At one point, however, things got out of hand. On an evening during the Volksfest period, I was invited by Schedl and Theo Betz, the Oberbuergermeister of Neumarkt, to attend the festivities with them at the county fairgrounds. The celebration was in a large circus-type tent, seating perhaps as many as a thousand people. The Volksfest featured all sorts of carnival activities, including a roller coaster. A stage was set up in the tent for a large German "oom pah pah" brass band. When I arrived, the place was rollicking with singing, shouting, and the sounds of beer steins being banged on the long wooden tables.

Schedl and Betz had already finished a liter or so of beer and were urging me to catch up. During the course of the evening, the bandleader came over to the Oberbuergermeister and invited him to lead the band. Betz did a spirited job on a German march. The custom then was for the bandleader to present the "honoree" with a large full stein of beer, which he was required to finish "bottoms up." Betz obliged and was soon followed by Schedl going through the same routine. It then became my turn. The band launched into another rousing march, and I dutifully led them along. The crowd went wild. They carried on even more as I downed my beer.

Returning to the table, I found Schedl quite upset. He informed me that as a prank the band had had me lead them in the "*Badenweiler March*," Hitler's favorite march, which had since been outlawed by the U.S. Military Government. As an American, I had trouble telling one German march from another, especially when they were intermingled. The deed had been done, and I decided to take the prank in good grace. I sent word to the band "that they had been very, very naughty." As a punishment they would all have to drink a stein "bottoms ups." The crowd roared their approval, when they heard what I had done. The night concluded with Schedl, Betz, and me taking a wild ride on the roller coaster together.

I am sure had Elsa and some of the other wives been there, the boys would have been more circumspect.

Subsequently, comments arose hoping that I would not get in trouble over the "*Badenweiler March*" incident, which had been reported in a local paper. Neumarkt did not want to lose me as their RO. As it was, I did get a blast from Munich Headquarters. I responded that it had been a prank and all in good fun and that the Germans were not trying to revive Nazism, which, after all, was the reason for the ban.

Several large resident officer conferences were held during my tour of duty in Neumarkt. Those in Frankfurt brought together all of the officers in the three *Laender* (states) in the American Zone of Germany. However, the one I recall most vividly was one held at the Eibsee Resort Hotel at Garmisch in the Bavarian Alps. Only the officers from Bavaria and the Munich Headquarters Land Commission staff attended this conference. The setting was gorgeous; the lake sparkled in the sunlight at the foot of rugged, snow-capped mountains. Our time was spent reviewing programs designed to bring Germany along the road to democracy. Evening receptions and dinners were also attended by the wives, who were generally engaged during the day with their own programs related to encouraging German women to participate in community activities.

The most convenient way for us to travel to the conference site, which was a bit out of the way for the train, was to have our drivers take us there in our official cars, even though some of us had offices hundreds of miles away. At the conclusion of the conference, the ninety-two ROs each departed in his own black Mercedes or Opel Kapitaen limousine. It was almost a ceremonial event. The colorfully dressed hotel doorman would call out to the parking lot on a loudspeaker, "*Herr Gouveneur Brescia von Kreis Dinkelsbuehl's Wagen, bitte!*" or "*Herr Gouveneur Hamilton von Kreis Pegnitz's Wagen, bitte!*" etc. The cars would roll up the circular drive, and the chauffeurs would jump out to hold the door open for the officer and his wife, load the luggage in the trunk, and drive smartly away. Land Commissioner Shuster, witnessing this sight, was uncomfortable about it and said so in a subsequent staff meeting. From then on, we either took the train or drove ourselves.

During our stay in Neumarkt, we had a steady stream of visitors, many of them officials from various headquarters in Frankfurt or Munich interested in facets of our programs. In each case, whether youth affairs, the administration of justice, land reform, or other matters, Germany's future in the eyes of these callers rested in their area of activity. We did our best to keep them happy. Neumarkt and Beilngries, however, also developed a special reputation for drawing visitors interested in hunting and fishing, especially fishing.

On one occasion, I received a call from a major general, the chief of staff of the European Command, saying that his four-star boss was desirous of fishing our trout streams. An invitation was duly extended and the commander-in-chief and an entourage of generals arrived aboard a private train. Our German game wardens were used to such visits and did their best to make the visitors welcome. The American guests left after a fine sojourn. It was only then that I learned the lengths to which our local boys had gone to please. They had removed fish hatchery signs along sections of the streams, and as a result the fishermen had a field day.

In October 1951, we were visited by the noted journalist and author Robert Shaplen, who planned on writing an article for *Collier's* magazine on the occupation of Germany and, specifically, the resident officer program. He interviewed a number of the ROs, as well as Francis Lindaman, our district chief in Regensburg. The result was a lengthy article with numerous pictures entitled, "Democracy's Best Salesmen in Germany," which appeared in the February 9, 1952, issue. Elsa and I were featured prominently throughout the article.

It was during this period, as well, that we played host to Bernard Fall, a reporter for *Stars and Stripes*, the U.S. Army's newspaper. He spent two days with us observing the activities of my office and subsequently published an article on the subject. At the time, Fall was the boyfriend of Florence Cherry, the daughter of our minister back in Ardmore, Pennsylvania. She was also working in Germany then, and Elsa and I met with the two of them on several occasions. In the ensuing years, Bernard Fall established a spectacular reputation as an outstanding reporter on the Vietnam war. He wrote two books, *Street Without Joy* and *Hell in a Very Small Place*, considered definitive works on that conflict. At the height of his fame, he was killed working as a reporter in Vietnam.

In mid-December 1951, we were visited for three days by my parents-in-law. Dad Wells had again been asked by our government to serve in Germany, this time as director of the Historical Division of the U.S. High Commission for Germany in Frankfurt. He replaced noted political scientist Dr. Harold Zink, who was returning to academia. Mother Wells was a great hit at a Christmas party we gave for the Neumarkt and Beilngries staffs, playing German carols on the grand piano in our living room. It was a memorable Christmas in many ways that year. There was snow for several days before the holiday and the Bavarian countryside and mountains in the distance were blanketed in white. Christmas night fell crystal clear with a star-studded sky.

Walking out into the frosty air on our balcony, Elsa and I observed the lights twinkling in the valley and town below. We could hear singing from the monastery farther up our mountain. That night we went to mass in Neumarkt's 600-year-old stone church. It was the custom at midnight to trumpet in the Christmas from the parapet atop the high tower. The trumpeter sounded melodious notes in the four directions, which wafted and reverberated up and down the valley. In such a setting, Franz Gruber must have written "Silent Night, Holy Night." It is beyond my ability to recount in words the beauty of that exquisite setting; it remains one of our most cherished memories.

We also learned a culinary lesson that Christmas. Two other couples joined us for the holiday dinner. Fraulein Herrmann had purchased a magnificent goose for the meal. It appeared to us to be a very large bird. Had it been a turkey, it would have sufficed for a dozen or more guests. Unfortunately, as we were to learn to our dismay, a goose, having much fat, literally cooks away. We were unpleasantly surprised at our meager portions and worried that there would not be enough to go around. The staff, however, happily spread the enormous amount of goose fat on their bread for many days afterwards.

I had been in Neumarkt somewhat over a year when developments on the national scene brought about a change. With Allied assistance Germany had moved rapidly toward greater self-government, and the Resident Offices as such were to be phased out. Orders came transferring me to the city of Coburg on the northern border of Bavaria, a few miles from what was then the Soviet Zone (East Germany). I was both to close the Resident Office there and to assume the duties of director of the Amerika Haus. It seemed hard to believe that Elsa and I could have become so ensconced in Neumarkt in such a relatively short period. Our departure was a sad time for us but even more difficult for our very competent German staff, for they were soon to lose their jobs.[4] I did what I could to place them elsewhere, but all in all, it was a wrenching experience.

Although the German population was glad to see the vestiges of the American occupation depart, they viewed the resident officers in the latter days as their friends in court. Once cognizant that I would actually be leaving with no successor, German officials expressed a sense of loss. Landrat Schedl, Community Planning Board Chairman Sigmund, Oberbuergermeister Betz, and others were gracious in holding farewell parties in our honor and presenting us with mementos of our stay. As I look back on it now, that period was one of the most rewarding we were to spend overseas. Both Elsa and I were fully challenged as solitary Americans in a foreign environment. She found her work with German women's organizations exciting, leading her to prepare an outstanding report on the subject.

Our transfer to Coburg had been conditioned in part by the sudden illness and death of the previous resident officer. He died tragically of a brain tumor. Coburg, a medieval city of 45,000, is steeped in history. Its Wartburg Castle had housed Martin Luther, who sought the protection of the Prince Elector of Saxony after his flight from Worms. It was in the Wartburg that Luther had confronted the Devil, flinging an inkwell at him. The stains on the wall may be seen to this day in his room in the castle, which is now a museum. As the Resident Officer program phased out, I focused more in those final weeks on strengthening the activities of the Coburg Amerika Haus. But things were not the same. German employees, seeing the handwriting on the wall, sought positions elsewhere. Elsa even found it difficult to hire good household help, several of whom had left before our arrival. One of her less happy memories of Coburg is of washing the bed sheets by hand in the bathtub.

It was a time of transition, and before long I received new orders transferring me to Lower Saxony, to Hannover in the British Zone. With the signing of the Contractual Agreements in 1952, the Allied Powers had permitted Germany to move one more step forward in the process toward full sovereignty. A German government with a parliamentary structure was being established in Bonn. The Resident Offices had served as a transition from military government, and now a network of Public Affairs Offices was set up throughout the Western Zones of Germany. These were information and cultural relations establishments similar in some respects to those operating in conjunction with embassies around the world. They were felt to be compatible with West Germany's emerging status as an independent nation.

I was assigned to the American Public Affairs Office Hannover, as the information officer and deputy to my former district chief in Regensburg, Francis Lindaman. I assumed, among other things, the direction of the U.S. Press Service (Amerika Dienst) for Lower Saxony, which provided news and feature material around the clock to more than one hundred newspapers and other publications in that large state of six million people. An assistant information officer, Kempton Jenkins, ran a film program providing material to schools and cultural institutions throughout the area. The Public Affairs Office in the Hannover suburbs and the downtown Amerika Haus that functioned under it employed a total of eight Americans and fifteen Germans. The office had only been in existence a month upon my arrival. Negotiations for the lease on the building had yet to be completed. A parking lot for our vehicles was under construction and the finishing touches to the renovation of our offices were under way.

Administrative matters were complicated by having to work through the British Land Commission in matters of real estate. I made an early call on my British counterpart. He had been operating an Information Office for several years and viewed the overall situation for the Allies in West

Germany as winding down. He therefore felt our grandiose plans to open shop a waste of time, effort, and money. Nevertheless, he was impressed by the scope of our effort in setting up a full-fledged wire service to our constituents along the lines of an AP or Reuters. He was too discreet to say, "Those foolish Americans, all energy and money, but no sense!" (In the end, he proved right, for the office was closed a little more than a year after it opened.)

We encountered problems finding suitable housing for the incoming Americans. The British had requisitioned many houses in the postwar years, but as occupation staffing grew, these were not enough. Elsa and I were at first quartered in an apartment building in which there were German families. Each apartment was heated by a coal stove, tenants periodically visiting the coal cellar in the basement to fill a scuttle, which was then kept near the stove. We had not been there long enough to find a suitable servant, so Elsa and I routinely brought up the coal and kept the fire burning. It was a far cry from our pampered life in Neumarkt, but the German families considered themselves fortunate to have such an apartment. Who were we to think otherwise?

We did receive a shock, however, the first few days of our stay in the building. One evening we were disturbed by the noise of breaking dishes on the landing outside our door. My first thought was of *Kristallnacht* (crystal night) and the attacks against the Jews under Hitler. Was this breakage directed at us as foreigners? We had not encountered anything like this in all our time in Germany. After viewing the numerous broken plates on our landing, we simply remained behind locked doors until the following morning. When I mentioned the matter at the office the next day, I was told by German employees that it must have been a *Polterabend*, nuptial eve, and that someone in another apartment on our floor was probably getting married. The breaking of dishes on their doorstep was a way of wishing them good luck! The experience was a pointed lesson in demonstrating how important it is to understand the customs of other countries and cultures.

A month later, the British billeting office assigned us a furnished house in the Hannover suburb of Kleefeld on Muenchausenstrasse, a street of red brick houses in a middle class neighborhood occupied by English Land Commission personnel and several of our American staff. We were never quite sure whether the street was named after Baron von Muenchausen, the storybook teller of tall tales. Our Public Affairs Office was located in the same suburb, making travel to work very convenient. Nominally, we functioned under the American consulate general in Hamburg, 95 miles to the north, headed by Consul General Clare Timberlake. A branch office in Hannover was headed by Vice Consul Grant Mouser. While much of our daily provisions were procured on the German market, many things were not obtainable in that postwar era. Our American personnel would take turns every week driving the 120 miles up to the U.S. military enclave at the port of Bremerhaven, where there was a commissary and a PX.

Soon, I was busily engaged in setting up our office, supervising the installation of teletype equipment for the press service, and establishing contacts with German officials and the media. Lower Saxony is a large state, and our service was responsible for dealing with German press and radio facilities from Goettingen in the south up to Bremen in the north and from the Rhineland in the west to the Soviet Zone border in the east. This involved extensive use of the Mercedes and Volkswagen vehicles assigned to us. With the limited facilities the German media had at the time, they welcomed the Amerika Dienst material. Besides the teletype service, the Amerika Dienst in Bonn published a series of magazines and newsletters devoted to a variety of individual topics such as business, politics, cultural matters, and women's affairs. Our local employees kept a running tally of our items used in the major German publications, which we submitted to our headquarters in Bonn as a demonstration of our effectiveness.

Francis Lindaman was an able and considerate boss and we all enjoyed working for him. Kempton Jenkins, the assistant information officer, did a fine job of setting up a film program throughout the region. Wallace "Pic" Littell, the cultural officer, and Elizabeth Wilson, his assistant, effectively ran the Amerika Haus and a wide-ranging program. Bill Heyler, the administrative officer, made sure that the office ran smoothly. These were people who were to remain our friends over the years in the Foreign Service.

Each post in which we served generated particular memories: Littell and his wife, "B-Gay," encouraged us to follow their example and buy a German collapsible kayak, a *Klepper Faltboot*. It was a wooden two-seater with inflatable tubes extending along the gunwales. We used it to paddle on lakes and streams in and around Hannover. Jenkins and I made an unforgettable speaking tour throughout the region in 1952, an election year, and we addressed ourselves to the American political process.[5] Jenkins had been a quick study in German. His vocabulary was excellent and his delivery good, with a few rough edges, a bit of an American twang, and a great sense of humor. He had a habit, however, of taking American colloquial expressions and translating them directly into German, often with hilarious results. I remember him at the German police academy auditorium in Braunschweig referring to a political figure as "a really big snake" — a big time operator in English, but something quite different in German — which brought the house down. It was not long before our road show was as popular as Abbott and Costello!

Our association with the British was very pleasant. Tradition and formality still held sway. One could not enter the Officers' Club in the evening without wearing black tie or dress uniform. Ladies were appropriately attired in long gowns. We had been used to American clubs requiring coat and tie after six, but this came as a bit of a surprise to us. However, we were prepared, since Foreign Service travel aboard ships, which was first class in those days, required formal wear. Nevertheless, for the men it meant their tuxedos received a substantial workout, while the women were hard-pressed to augment their wardrobes of evening dresses.

Elizabeth II acceded to the English throne in February 1952, and the parade in honor of her birthday in Hannover the following June was quite a show.[6] The British commanding general was out to make the affair a memorable one. Regiments of colorful troops and elaborately outfitted military bands marched past an audience of men in dress uniform and ladies in long dresses with picture hats. There was quite a bit of ceremonial cannonading. The day turned out to be rather hot and as row on row of soldiers stood at attention for extended periods in the sun, the observer could spot one or two in that vast array fainting. No note was taken of these individuals and the troops simply marched around them, until later when the medics helped them up or hauled them off. After the parade, we joined the general, his staff, and their ladies in a large tent for refreshments. I recall thinking at the time that the affair had a movie-like quality and that I might as well have been in India a century earlier.

Elsa and I took a number of memorable trips in our 1949 Ford convertible during our tour of duty in Germany. By August 1952, I had accrued a sizeable amount of leave. Never having been to Italy, we decided to drive down through Germany to Munich and Garmisch and then over the mountain pass to Innsbruck, Austria. From there we went south through the Brenner Pass into Italy. The American Army presence in Europe in those days made it possible with planning to travel from one military installation to another. As authorized government personnel, we obtained food, lodging, and gasoline at minimal cost. At times even in out-of-the-way places, one would find a small American unit where one could eat in the club or snack bar and gas up the car. The latter was always quite a factor with a large automobile, since petrol on the civilian market was often as much as four times the military price. Driving through the Alps in an open convertible was a glorious experience.

Not wanting to traverse the Brenner Pass at night, we stayed in a lovely little *Gasthaus* high in the mountains on the Austrian side. Coming down into Italy, we proceeded through Bolzano over to Venice. I remember being quite upset as we drove around a plaza on the outskirts of Venice, seeking a route into town. I was informed that there was none, and we would have to leave the car in an open parking lot and take a *vaporetto*, a motorized launch—our equivalent of a bus—down a main canal into the city. Besides worrying about the security of a cloth-topped vehicle remaining in an open parking lot, we found that we simply had not packed in such a way as to facilitate an extended suitcase stopover. Once in town, our hotel turned out to be hot, musty, and incommodious. The canals in those postwar years were dirty and often foul smelling. But even had the drawbacks been infinitely greater, they would have been overwhelmed by the sheer grandeur of the architecture and art, as well as the unique charm of the waterways. Where else can one look out a hotel room window and see water sloshing against the building and gondolas passing a few feet below.

Driving through Europe, our American convertible always caused a stir. In Florence, I slowed down to gasp at the unexpected sighting in the center of a plaza of a statue by Donatello, familiar to all students in an art appreciation course. An Italian in a pint-sized vehicle, irked by my hesitation, leaned out the window, waved his fist at me and shouted, "Animale! Cannibale!" As if by instinct, I waved my fist and shouted, "Animale! Cannibale!" back at him. I wasn't quite in Rome yet, but I was prepared "to do as the Romans do!" Much to Elsa's horror, I went through Italy bellowing this war cry when appropriate, with the Italians accepting it simply as part of automobile travel.

We were overcome by the magnitude of great works of art everywhere we turned in Italy. I even became irritated over walls saturated to the ceilings with paintings, any one of which would have hung in solitary splendor in some museum in the United States. Rome, the Vatican, and the great cities of Italy are monuments to man's creative and artistic genius. Not to see them surely must leave a void in one's life. On our return journey, I recall stopping off in Viarregio on Italy's west coast. We stayed in a nice hotel on the beach that served us a delicious dinner of red snapper. The formally attired waiter proudly brought out a platter containing the entire decorated fish that was at least two feet long. That evening, we walked the beach at the very spot where the poet Shelley had drowned in 1824. We returned through Genoa, Lake Como, the St. Gotthard Pass, and Switzerland.

Homecoming was marked by unpleasantness. Our maid, Ursula, an East German refugee, had a few days earlier burglarized our house, leaving our dog, Socrates, to shift for himself inside. The place was a pigsty. Ursula, an attractive girl and former East German athlete, ostensibly had been talked into holding parties in our house by the German security guards patrolling the area. They must have been wild ones. A good number of the guards and other maids attending finished off the substantial representational liquor supply, as well as all the food in the house. Realizing that she would be in trouble upon our return, Ursula fled with virtually all of Elsa's winter clothing and our jewelry, including my father's solid gold pocket watch and chain, as well as five valuable 16th century silver talers. There were signs that she might have been planning the theft for some time, since she made a thorough job of it, stuffing suitcases with our things.

Ursula had been recommended to us by the pastor of the German Lutheran church and had seemed honest and a good worker. We had treated her very kindly, so we felt particularly let down. At the outset, British intelligence expressed interest in the case, fearing that Ursula might have been an East German agent and that I might have in some way been compromised. Having had experience in dealing with intelligence as a CIC officer, I set that matter to rest. I contacted the appropriate German police officials, informed them of my former working relationship with the police in Berlin, and in a kidding fashion said in effect in German, "OK gentlemen, let's see how quickly you can solve this one!"

A detective was assigned the job and, within a couple of days, he came to tell me that Ursula had been apprehended at the other end of the country, in Munich. The police had put out an all-points-bulletin for her. The detective was ready to go to Munich to follow up the case. We arranged to go down together in my car. Elsa came along to identify her belongings. Arriving in Munich, we learned that Ursula was in custody at the main police station. She had been picked up in a vice raid on a brothel frequented by American soldiers. My sweet wife was afforded the pleasure of visiting the place to identify and retrieve her clothing, jewelry, and other items left there. I arrived at the police station to find Ursula being interrogated.

Not realizing that the police already knew about the Hannover affair, she was in the process of telling the officers how a former employer had given her clothes and jewelry. Her back was to me and she was totally unaware that I was in the room, or even in Munich for that matter. At a key point in her tale, I came up behind her and said in German, "Ursula, Ursula, you know what you're saying is untrue. . . ." Immediately recognizing my voice, she turned around, broke down upon seeing me, and made a full confession. The detective accompanied us back up to Hannover. On the way we stopped off in the town where a bank official, for a paltry sum, had bought the five talers and my father's gold pocket watch and chain. Initially pleased, I am sure, over the valuable bargain he had made, he went into shock when our detective ominously stated, "You know what the penalty is for trafficking in stolen goods. . . ."

We soon had the talers back, but my father's heavy pocket watch and chain had already been melted down for the gold content. The banker was out his money. Subsequently, we learned that Ursula had received a prison sentence. There was a further report that she had earlier left East Germany with the police at her heels. The entire affair was a sad, sordid story.

Our office's relationship with the American consulate general in Hamburg and the vice consul's office in Hannover was tenuous. We regarded the large public affairs organization in Bonn as our headquarters. The latter, initially part of HICOG, was being amalgamated into the newly established American embassy. Duty in Hannover was my first real exposure to the traditional Foreign Service, which generally felt uncomfortable in the public affairs role. Most FSOs strove to work in standard diplomatic activities, preferably at key embassies around the world. They looked askance at being out of the mainstream, even to the point of avoiding service at consulates. Duty completely out of the diplomatic/consular track, such as in public affairs and information officer positions, was even more to be avoided.

I recall an earlier "revolt" of more than a dozen FSOs led by Kenneth Martindale, who decried their Resident Officer assignments as being out of their career paths. In later years, I wondered how many of my "revolting" colleagues liked their diplomatic and consular assignments in out-of-the-way places in third world countries. For many of us, the jobs we had in Germany as part of HICOG were among the most enjoyable of our careers. Where else could a junior officer exercise such authority, live in homes the equivalent of many ambassadorial residences, work in grandiose offices of their own, and have a Mercedes car and chauffeur at their disposal?

At this juncture, I was an officer with a limited appointment in the Foreign Service. After my tour of duty in Germany, I intended to return to the United States and finish my PhD studies. I had not yet given serious consideration to taking the examination and becoming a regular FSO. By autumn 1952, our public affairs program in Hannover was well established and our press service was being used by the media throughout Lower Saxony. My two-year tour of duty was coming to an end, and I was either to return to the United States permanently or take home leave and continue in my job. I was enjoying my work immensely and chose to continue.

In early November, not the best time of year for an Atlantic crossing, Elsa and I set sail aboard the S.S. *America* for home. We had a rough trip. Mountainous waves kept many of the first class passengers in their cabins. The waiters and the stewards as a consequence could not do enough for those of us who appeared in the dining room. Two other members of the Foreign Service were on board with their wives: George Kennan and Herbert Fales. Ambassador Kennan was on his way home after having been declared *persona non grata* by Moscow. Speaking to a reporter in

Berlin while en route to a conference in London, he had made an unfortunate comparison of living conditions in Russia to his wartime internment
in Germany. He may have thought his remarks were off the record, but
they appeared in the German press and the Soviets took umbrage. They
may also have sought an opportunity to rid themselves of such an astute observer of the Russian scene whose views were likely influential in
the Moscow diplomatic community. Kennan had been head of the Policy
Planning Staff in the State Department. He was the formulator of our government's policy of containment toward the Soviet Union and the author
of the famous "X" article in which he anonymously outlined that strategy
in the journal *Foreign Affairs* in 1947.

Our relations with the Soviet Union were always front-page news,
and the press were anxious to cover the story of Kennan's return. We had
not even entered New York harbor when reporters and photographers
clambered aboard from the pilot boat. Taking it for granted that my work
with the Public Affairs Office made me a press officer, Fales asked me to
run interference with the mobs of reporters expected. Ambassador Kennan kept to his cabin, and I indicated to the press that he would have no
comment until after his return to the State Department. However, as we
were about to dock and I was involved in our own debarking procedures,
I did see the ambassador speaking with reporters on deck.[7] It was unfortunate that Kennan did not complete his tour in Moscow, for I am sure he
would have served our country well.

As home leaves go, this was not a propitious one. My parents were in
the process of relocating to Florida, and the Wellses were still with HICOG
in Germany. We rented an apartment in a hotel on the upper West Side
of Manhattan and, interspersed with visits to relatives and friends, our
time was spent in New York City. After a two-month stay, we made the
return trip aboard the S.S. *America* to Bremerhaven. I recall being seated at
a dinner table that included the president and founder of the Stanley Tool
Company and his wife. A lovely elderly couple, they took a liking to Elsa
and me. Mr. Stanley at one point enthusiastically suggested I join his firm.
Now, whenever I see Stanley Tools, I am reminded of that trip.

It felt good to get back to work and into the swing of things. Hannover
was a major city with many cultural diversions. The first-rate opera house
featured international stars. We attended an unforgettable performance
there of *La Bohème* by the visiting La Scala Opera Company of Milan, with
Giuseppi di Stefano in the tenor role. There were also excellent theater of-
ferings and black tie evenings at the British Officers' Club. It was a most
enjoyable period.

About that time, Elsa learned she was pregnant with our first child.
She had been feeling ill and was bleeding. Upon examining her, a British

Army doctor confined her to bed for an extended period. She was worried and feared a miscarriage. I, on the other hand, believed that her concern increased the severity of the situation. After thinking the matter over carefully, I decided to tell her the biggest white lie of my life. Coming into the bedroom one afternoon, I told her happily that I had talked with the doctor and learned in confidence that she had nothing to worry about. She was fine. He had told me that British doctors like to be extra careful. Confining expectant mothers to bed was a good way of frightening them into being cautious and not undertaking too much. My ruse worked like a charm and Elsa was soon feeling better and able to move about the house. Her pregnancy was uneventful from then on.

We had a number of visitors during that period; the most notable were Roy Cohn and G. David Shine, Senator McCarthy's anticommunism investigators.[8] They would call at various American installations, particularly at information center libraries, endeavoring to root out "un-American" books and publications. They caused Pic Littell and Elizabeth Wilson some problems down at the Amerika Haus, and I was waiting for them to visit our facility. With my background of having battled the Russians in Berlin, I would have relished the opportunity to take them on, but they never came. Instead, fortune was to dictate a strangely different turn. Another visitor was Elmer Lower, the second-ranking officer in charge of the large public affairs program in Germany. We made an effort to demonstrate how effective our operation in Hannover was and must have impressed him.

Several weeks afterward, I was called to Bonn and told that I would be taking over the features half, as distinguished from the news half, of the Amerika Dienst, the U.S. press service for the entire country. I was to be responsible, as editor-in-chief, for daily wire service material and half a dozen German-language weekly and monthly publications devoted to such subjects as politics, economics and business, cultural affairs, youth activities, and women's affairs. What I was not told was that I was walking into a maelstrom. Ostensibly, my predecessor was simply leaving the job and transferring to the United States. I telephoned Elsa that evening and told her that I had been promoted into a job several grades above my present one. "Get packed, Honey," I said, "we are moving to Bonn!" Returning to Hannover, I made farewell calls on the key officials, publishers, and individuals prominent in the media.

Soon we were ensconced in a large, lovely apartment in the American embassy's housing project in the village of Plittersdorf on the outskirts of Bonn. Reporting into work the day after my arrival, I met with Robert Lochner, the director of the Press Division,[9] and his deputy, John Richmond, who introduced me to other American and German members of the staff. I was shown my new office, which was unoccupied at the time. Then I was taken to meet senior embassy members outside the public affairs sector, including the minister and the political counselor and his deputy. After that I returned to the office where I was to work and prepared to sit down at my desk, only to find it occupied. Taking it for granted that the individual was my predecessor, Joseph Franckenstein, about whom I knew nothing, I introduced myself, adding courteously that I hoped to do as good a job as he had done. I then wished him good luck on his trip home. He responded coolly that I must have been misinformed, as he was not going anywhere.

With that, I went back to John Richmond's office and asked, "What's going on?" He then informed me that Franckenstein was the husband of the noted author Kay Boyle, a target of the House Un-American Activities Committee,[10] and that he, himself, had been cited by Senator McCarthy as one of the communists in the State Department.

Franckenstein, Richmond added, had been relieved of his position and called back to Washington. He had not been expected to return to the office. "Go back," Richmond said, "and tell him that now you have officially taken over the position." I replied that I would find some other place to sit, since I was going to require a number of days in any event to familiarize myself with the job and get to know the German staff. In the meantime, personnel, the security boys, and Franckenstein could sort this one out.

Franckenstein remained adamant for several days, and I found myself an object of perverse curiosity. People were circumspect in my presence. Was I a McCarthy hireling? It was an uncomfortable situation, and circumstance, by chance, added to the difficulty. My mother-in-law had just returned from a visit to the United States, and we drove up to Rotterdam that weekend to meet her at shipside and bring her back to Bonn with all her luggage. Unfortunately for me, there was a party given for Franckenstein that Saturday, attended by Ambassador James Conant, and my absence was duly noted. After some time, Franckenstein departed under threat of removal by the authorities.

It was not an auspicious way to start a job, but soon I was deeply immersed in running the feature service. I faced constant deadlines, as well as personnel problems with the Germans engaged in translating, editing, and publishing the volume of material coming from America. At times humorous incidents arose from translations. The popular radio program in the United States, *The Voice of Firestone*, was elaborately referred to in one of the cultural editions as the "voice coming from the stone of fire." I caught the item and explained to the German editor that Firestone was the name of the rubber company sponsoring the show.

One of the most demanding tasks I was to have in the Foreign Service accompanied my duty over an extended period as an editor-in-chief of the Amerika Dienst. I was asked to edit the daily German press summary and hold regular early morning briefings for the embassy staff. This involved my perusing up to ten German newspapers and publications, highlighting major items, and digesting key editorials. I would get up at five o'clock in the morning to arrive at the office at six, and then read and take notes frantically. I became fairly adept at the job, but it was never easy. It also probably made me the best-informed person in the Embassy! However, several of my listeners in the Political Section would invariably come upon an item I had not covered to show that they were on their toes. I soon got used to that and won their goodwill by sincerely thanking them for their assistance. Some of these officers were to become notable figures: assistant secretaries of state, an undersecretary of the United Nations, and ambassadors.

One of the pleasant aspects of our transfer to Bonn was that we would be joining my parents-in-law there. As director of the Historical Division, Dad Wells was involved in a large-scale effort to document the work of the U.S. High Commission for Germany. The division, consisting of nine professional historians, produced 33 published monographs, varying in length from 100 to 260 pages, covering virtually every phase of the occupation. While I was still in Hannover, Dad contacted me about requests from Congress for a study on "denazification." He asked whether I would be willing to allow the division to use my Columbia thesis as a monograph. This would save time, effort, and money and satisfy the requirement. I agreed, and with a few format changes, *U.S. Denazification Policy in Germany, 1944–1950* was issued. It was nice to know that I had contributed in this small way to the recording of our country's monumental effort in post–World War II Germany. When contrasted with the Allies' treatment of Germany after World War I, which led to the rise of Hitler, the United States' later performance, spearheaded by the Marshall Plan, was remarkable. Our magnanimity helped make Germany the democratic and economic power it is today.

The story of the construction of the American housing project at Plittersdorf to house the vast number of employees, first of HICOG and then of the Embassy, is an interesting one. "Hollywood on the Rhine," as some congressional critics and press exposés dubbed it, contained those things one might expect to find in a large upscale housing project in the United States: a supermarket (commissary), cleaners, shoe repair, various shops, movie theater, clubs, a gymnasium, a swimming pool, and more. The one thing it did not have, in the early planning phase, was a church. My father-in-law was instrumental in seeing that one was added. When it was built, he became the first chairman of the Church Council of the American Interdenominational Church of Plittersdorf. When he departed in September 1953 to resume his position at Bryn Mawr College, he left that church as his legacy. It was taken for granted later that Elsa and I would be active in "Dad's church" and soon we were.

Initially, I was a member of the Church Council, but circumstance, as I will explain, propelled me rather reluctantly into the chairmanship. The church, at the outset, had been served by a series of U.S. Army chaplains and visiting clergy. Glen Wolfe, the head of administration for HICOG and later the embassy's counselor for administration, reacting to the urging of the church membership, sought to locate a full-time minister while on home leave in the United States. His choice, possibly reflecting his own predilections, was an Episcopal clergyman from the Virginia hunt country, who soon arrived with his wife to take up the post. Perhaps not appreciating how sensitive his position was with a congregation that ran the gamut of Protestant beliefs, he began to institute a number of changes in a church service that heretofore had taken a middle road between "high church" and "low church" worship.

The result was an uproar, with many of the more fundamentalist members of the congregation threatening to leave. The Reverend also did not help matters by his lifestyle and the requests he made for various expenses. He and his wife were seen to be frequent guests at cocktail parties, normal for the rest of us, but dismaying to some of the straitlaced churchgoers. The Church Council of fifteen members split along denominational lines in its attitude toward him. Distressed by what was happening to the church, I continually took the middle ground, arguing that we should be working with the Reverend, endeavoring to modify his approach to the services. Personally, I liked him but was a bit dismayed by his lack of insight. So strongly held were views about him that they spilled over into the day-to-day activities of the embassy. The wife of the deputy chief of mission was a member of the Church Council and one of the Reverend's strongest supporters. Ambassador and Mrs. Conant had their own views on the subject. After one heated council session in which a proposal was put forward to oust the Reverend, the chairman, who vehemently objected to him, resigned. Another member commented that his adherence to his church came before his job in the embassy.

It was the upshot of this deplorable situation in which I was asked—not just asked, but pressed—into taking the chairmanship. It was almost as if they were saying "He is Roger Wells's son-in-law and he will solve this problem for us." My first move was to call a congregational meeting, which in view of the furor the situation was causing, filled the church. At my request, the Reverend was not present. It was a session to let off steam and arrive at the consensus I subsequently presented to him. I told the Reverend that the congregation insisted on having a strictly interdenominational approach to all aspects of church activities. While many of the members liked him, myself included, we felt he would be uncomfortable with that approach. We were prepared, therefore, to release him from his obligations to us, should he wish, and go elsewhere at his convenience. The Reverend continued with us for several months while the Episcopal Church arranged for another assignment.

The church then went back to a system of visiting clergy. Forty years later, the minister of our Methodist church in Chevy Chase, Maryland, who had spent quite a bit of time serving in churches overseas, told me he had on occasion been a visiting preacher at Plittersdorf. To my great surprise, he knew all about that situation so long ago, even down to naming the people involved.

The summers of 1953 and 1954 will always be remembered as ones in which we spent weekends kayaking down the Rhine River. We would drive or have a friend take us up the Rhine River twenty to twenty-five miles, where we would unload our bagged, collapsible two-seater *Klepper Faltboot* from the car. Assembling and launching it, we would then paddle and float down the fast-flowing river to the banks of our housing project at Plittersdorf. On the way, we would be passed by barges and an occasional riverboat laden with singing Germans enjoying their day's outing. Care had to be taken to deal with the substantial wakes these vessels created to avoid swamping the open kayak. However, even when very pregnant, Elsa was always game to take the trip. On these glorious summer days, we would float by historic castles and vineyards on the cliffs above us. Stopping at our leisure at little inns along the shore, we would sample their wine and cheese or have coffee and a tasty torte.

It was in this setting that our first-born came into the world. Not wanting to make the long trip to Frankfurt or Wiesbaden to a U.S. military hospital, we examined the facilities at the Venusberg *Krankenhaus* near Bonn. We soon learned that the ranking doctor there was the world famous gynecologist Prof. Dr. Dr. Walter Siebke. When we approached him, he was pleased, and in those days perhaps a bit flattered, to take Elsa, an American diplomat's wife, as a patient.

Under his care Elsa blossomed, not just figuratively, but literally. As prenatal precautions, he prescribed a healthy diet, accompanied by a liberal guzzling of beer. I cannot ever recall Elsa being happier or looking better. She was active and busy to the last moment, hosting a reception for a large group of German ladies. I, on the other hand, did not feel too well. I had an upset stomach and was going through vicarious labor pains, to the point where Bob Lochner, my boss, even volunteered to take Elsa to the hospital. Pulling myself together, I drove Elsa on the evening of October 26, 1953, to the *Krankenhaus*. It was a stormy and windswept drive up Venusberg Mountain overlooking the city of Bonn. Lightning split the sky, casting us into a Wagnerian scene. It was atop the Venusberg that, according to Nordic legend, Siegfried, the great Germanic warrior hero, was born. As we neared a curve at the summit, I said to Elsa, "If it's a boy, I think the elements are telling us we had better name him Siegfried." I breathed a sigh of relief when Elsa responded, "Absolutely not!"

Arriving at the hospital, the nurses, who were nuns, immediately took Elsa into their care. I remained in the waiting room for half an hour, when the chief nurse came and told me that it would be quite some time before Elsa gave birth. She suggested that I return in three hours to see how things were going. I thereupon departed for Plittersdorf. Passing our American community movie theater on the way home, I noted it featured John Wayne in *The Wake of the Red Witch*, a South Seas adventure film. I thought this would provide a good diversion to keep me from worrying. At the conclusion of the movie, I would return to Elsa.

Returning to the hospital, I encountered the chief nurse, who said in German, "The baby has just arrived. It is a fine healthy child. With a twinkle in her eye," she added, "You always wanted a girl, didn't you?" I mumbled something appropriate while she guided me to Elsa's room. Once there, I found Elsa holding the baby. "Isn't he beautiful!" she exclaimed. It must have been half a minute before I registered, "He, he . . . it's a boy!" The chief nurse departed smiling, pleased with herself that her little trick had enhanced my joy even further.

Elsa and our son remained at the Venusberg *Krankenhaus* for ten days under Dr. Siebke's watchful eye and the nuns' pampering care, despite the fact that it was a perfectly normal birth, involving a very healthy patient and infant. What a far cry from today, when insurance companies force women to leave hospitals prematurely, putting mother and baby at risk. Once home, it did not take Elsa too long to lose the healthy forty pounds she had gained. Our son was an energetic little fellow, whose shaking and rocking would move his crib from one end of the room to the other. No, we did not name him Siegfried, although he did grow up to be a big, blond warrior. Instead, we sought to keep the Wells name active, calling him Wells Bradford Kormann as a tribute to his grandfather, Roger Hewes Wells, whose many fine qualities we hoped our young son would inherit.

Our life in Bonn resembled our later tours in the Foreign Service. By any standard, the American Embassy in those days was immense. Not long ago, I studied the Foreign Service List of those years and counted over thirty members in the political section alone. My workload at the Embassy was heavy, and we were further initiated into diplomatic entertaining.

Our apartment was spacious and beautifully furnished, lending itself well to dinners and cocktail parties. I look back now in amusement at a few of the things that occurred. On one occasion, we were invited to dinner at the home of an FSO colleague. His wife, an attractive, energetic young woman, was ambitious to see her husband move ahead. A lovely meal of several courses with accompanying wines was served. As dessert was brought out, the guests were stunned to receive small, individual flower pots complete with chocolate mousse representing soil, while the stems, leaves, and blossoms of the "plants" were confectionery. The dessert was a piece of ingenuity never to be forgotten.

Meeting the deadlines for the various Amerika Dienst publications was a grueling task, but our fine staff was up to the challenge. At times, our published material would be criticized, and I would be called on the carpet. I took this in stride, however, and must have become reasonably adept at defending our output. From time to time, I would be given assignments that may have had a significant impact on the course of events. I was asked, for example, to prepare a speech for Ambassador Conant to give at an American Reserve Officers' Association Convention in Wiesbaden. Since I was an Army Reserve officer myself, it was believed that I might have something apt to say. As matters developed, Germany was just coming into its own after the war and was wrestling with the problem of reestablishing its own military. Dr. Conant, who had a distinguished background as a scientist, educator, president of Harvard, and an inventor of Lewisite gas in World War I, was a man whose views counted for much. We decided to take this opportunity to lay out guidelines for Germany's rearmament.

I drafted a speech entitled "The American Citizen-Soldier Tradition." In it I described a military strongly under civilian control. A professional army responsive to that authority was augmented by a large body of citizen-soldier reservists ready to serve at their country's call. I remember indicating that of the 121,561 officers serving in the U.S. Army at that time, 91,323 were reservists. The draft speech included an explanation of our constitution and congressional powers, as well as institutions and customs designed to preclude a rise of militarism. The speech was well received and widely reported and discussed in the German press. It may well have helped shape the German *Bundeswehr*.

While stationed in Bonn, we were able to take two trips. One was to Spain, to the Costa Brava and the town of Sitges, the other to Switzerland and Italy. At Sitges we spent a delightful two weeks in a small hotel run by a German, who served superb meals accompanied by a running supply of local wines. I can still remember an English couple at the hotel who found the food too much for them. The husband would always lament to us, "I am used to plain food!" In his strongest Eliza Doolittle–Cockney accent, the word "plain" would always come out, "p-l-a-a-i-y-h-n !" As we neared the end of our stay, I was bitten in the groin by a spider that had lodged in my trousers overnight. The drive back to Bonn in our convertible then became a race against time. Elsa urged me to enter a hospital in Paris on the way, since I could no longer drive due to the swelling and the pain. However, I was determined to get home, and Elsa drove the final leg of the trip. Once there, the embassy doctor operated on me twice to remove infectious material, and I was bedridden for some time.

We will never forget being swept up in a wild ride on our trip to Italy and Switzerland. In the mountains in Italy, we were descending from a summit on a precipitous corkscrew-like road when we heard frantic honking of horns and gunning of engines behind us. Glancing back from our top-down convertible, I spotted two open sports cars of the Porsche or Alfa Romeo type behind us. The road was narrow and steep, with sheer drop-offs of hundreds if not thousands of feet. Far below in the distance we could see a fair-sized city. On the way down, we hugged the narrow road. There was no way I could, or would dare, pull my large American car close enough to the precipice to allow the racing cars behind me to pass. As we came to a cluster of houses, we could see crowds lining the road. There were banners stretched across the street from upper windows. As we drove past, a loud cheer erupted from the crowd and it soon became obvious that we were in the middle of a road rally, a race—the *Mille Miglia*. The crowd clapped and roared its approval as we went by, probably thinking, "Crazy Americans!"

At the first opportunity, I let the speedsters go by, and with angry gestures and shouts, they let their feelings be known. This mad adventure was to be repeated again before we finally reached the sanity of the valley below. One would think the authorities would have blocked off the road, but it was common practice in Europe in those days to run road rallies right along with normal traffic.

The American Embassy in Bonn was located along the west bank of the Rhine River several miles upstream from our housing project. During our tour we experienced some nasty flooding at the Embassy, which fortunately was constructed to handle that eventuality. After one unexpected overnight flooding, I remember seeing an elegant Chrysler convertible parked below my office window. It had been left there while the FSO owner was on a brief trip to Paris. The high-water marks could be plainly seen on the car's windows. Our second floor apartment in Plittersdorf was in a building on Steubenring some distance from the Rhine. Nevertheless, our steamer trunks stored in a basement room did on one occasion become casualties.

In March 1955, I received orders assigning me to Washington. In 1953, while I served in Bonn, the public affairs aspects of the embassy's activities had been transferred to the newly established U.S. Information Agency (USIA). I would have preferred to remain with the State Department, since my basic interest was in political affairs, but my position with the press service mandated the move. At this juncture a friend approached me with a view to joining the Central Intelligence Agency. He had known me in Berlin as an intelligence officer. During the recruitment process, I could not establish the level of the position I was to receive. For that and other reasons, I did not pursue the matter of joining the CIA.

A few weeks before my departure for Washington, a controversy arose over one of the public affairs programs. During the occupation days, counterpart funds had been provided to encourage the revival of the German publishing industry. At some point a grant was given to two German historians, Professors Arno and Anneliese Peters, who, with the cooperative effort of a long list of academicians, produced a synchronous history of the world, *Synchronoptische Weltgeschichte*. This work, a massive undertaking, traced history concurrently from all over the world, displaying every major event—military, political, economic, scientific, literary, and so on—taking place anywhere, by year, from the beginning of recorded time. The book was large, in colorful foldout chart format with minute print, and must have been exceedingly difficult and expensive to produce.

Just as the book was to be released, criticism arose, if memory serves me correctly, from a U.S. congressional source, charging that the authors were communists. The book, it erroneously averred, made much of events related to Marx, Lenin, and Mao Zedong without mentioning Jesus Christ. I remember thinking at the time that catching any lapses in that work would have been akin to editing and proofreading Webster's large unabridged dictionary. Such was the atmosphere at the time, however, that the embassy was called on the carpet, the book never distributed, and the copies carefully destroyed. Before leaving Bonn, I was instructed to explain the matter upon my return to Washington to Ambassador James Riddleberger, the director of the State Department's Bureau of German Affairs. I hasten to add that I had no direct responsibility for the publication of the book, but my return provided Washington with someone who could answer questions. I was also experienced in defending material put out by our press service. Nevertheless, I did not relish the thought that my explanations might have to be made to a congressional committee.

Our trip back on the S.S. *America* in the spring of 1955 was unbelievably rough, even for those used to sea travel. Elsa and I had each already made four crossings on that vessel. Ropes were strung everywhere to assist the passengers moving about the ship. Having worked at sea as a youth, I had no thought that I would ever become seasick. The first couple of days saw the dining room empty out. The few hardy souls among us, however, enjoyed meals of oysters, vichysoisse, filet mignon, truffles, and Baked Alaska, washed down with champagne, making up for the others' absence. Elsa did reasonably well for a while, although she was less swashbuckling in her approach to meals. What is the good of first class ship travel, I always say, if you can't eat as if you were royalty? The fourth day out was particularly stormy, and Elsa took to her bed.

Little Brad, now a year and a half old and a chip off the old block, seemed to be doing well. His appetite was hearty . . . and what went in, I understood, eventually came out. I say "understood" because I had never had much to do with the natural processes of babies. Those things were in Elsa's department, or, while in Germany, in the sphere of our dependable maid and nanny, Helga. After a particularly fine lunch, I went back to the stateroom to check on Elsa. Her moaning as she lay in bed seemed to indicate that she was not at all interested in what I had included in my repast or for that matter even what else was on the menu. As I tried to communicate with her, the baby was carrying on in a most unseemly manner. To be blunt, he was making a hell of a racket.

Elsa rolled over long enough to groan, "His diaper needs to be changed." Upon hearing that I promptly left the stateroom and sought out the stewardess. When I explained the situation to her, she eyed me up and down and said, "I don't do that sort of thing!" I was stunned. What did a stewardess do, if she didn't do that sort of thing? In the meantime, I could hear my progeny wailing; even over the roaring sea I could hear him. If the stewardess would not change him and Elsa could not change him, I would simply have to do it myself. I had not gone through the war and life's adventures to be daunted by having to change a baby. I went back to the stateroom, found a fresh diaper, and did the needful. As I struggled through the process, I was amazed at the residue in his dirty diaper. What had I sired?

Once cleaned up and changed, little Brad settled down comfortably, and I promptly became sick. My moaning and groaning in bed the next two days seemed, however, to have an ameliorating effect on Elsa. She was up and about shortly after I was stricken. The experience took the edge off what might have been a wonderful trip. The meals thereafter never regained their original savor. From that day on, male chauvinist that I am, I have not changed a diaper.

Sailing into New York harbor past the Statue of Liberty is always a thrilling experience. I had been working in Germany for four and a half years. Now I would get a chance to see how Washington functioned. With a month of leave before I had to report for my new assignment, there were many things to do. We wanted to spend some time in Bryn Mawr with Elsa's family and friends. My parents had retired and purchased a house in Debary, Florida, which we had never seen; we planned on visiting there for a period. Considering that I would be working in Washington for at least three or four years, we intended to buy a house. That would all take time. Finally, I had ordered a car overseas from the Studebaker Corporation under their diplomatic purchasing program. In so doing, to save the substantial freight charges, I had indicated that I would pick the car up at the factory in South Bend, Indiana, and drive it east.

This was our first real experience as a family returning from a foreign post, and it was relatively easy. Later, we were to have three school-aged children to take into account. Even Socrates, our dog, traveling with us on shipboard, had been no problem. Our return was also facilitated by having two sets of parents eager to take us in, while we went about our preparations for the transition. Many Foreign Service members were less fortunate. As our large ocean liner swung into its Hudson River dock, we spotted the eager faces of Mother and Dad Wells. They were soon to meet their first grandchild, and their faces were radiant. My sister, Elsie, and my brother-in-law, Fred Stahl, were there, too. It was a happy homecoming.

9
Washington: Challenges and Opportunities

We journeyed down to Bryn Mawr with the Wellses in their car. Socrates, as usual, nestled on the floor under Elsa's feet on the passenger's side of the front seat. "Dolgelly," the house Elsa had been raised in, was a welcome sight. Nothing had changed. The college grounds, always lovely in the spring, were ready to burst into bloom. The next day, as I prepared to leave for South Bend, Indiana, Elsa and I walked the campus discussing our plans. My car, a 1955 Studebaker "Champion" model, was to be ready at a certain date and I had informed the factory that I would be there to receive it. The purchase of the Studebaker was a lesson for me in American business practices. When ordering at the purchasing point in Frankfurt, Germany, months earlier, I specified that I wanted a black car with a red top. Two-tone cars were very much in vogue in those days.

A few weeks later, I received a letter from the factory saying they were sorry; they could not provide a black car with a red top, but I could have a red car with a black top. This struck me as ludicrous. I did not want a red car with a black top; I wanted a black car with a red top! The previous two years of editing the Amerika Dienst's economic weekly must have goaded me into making a substantive response. A long letter poured out of me in which I remonstrated that this was just one more example of why American automobiles would find it hard to be competitive in the European market. I went into an extensive analysis of how Studebaker, which was producing a sporty little model like the Champion, could sell its cars in Germany. The letter must have made an impression, for virtually by return mail I received a reply saying that a black car with a red top would be waiting for me at the factory.

After checking with the railroads, I decided that the most convenient way to reach South Bend directly would be via Greyhound Bus, a common and pleasant way to go in those years. The thought of air travel never entered my mind. The ride out could not have been more enjoyable. Departing early in the morning from Philadelphia, I reached my destination by late that night, with few intermediate stops. During the trip I was seated in the upper deck's front row with a full view of the road and the countryside. Once there, I overnighted in a nice little hotel near the bus station. Recounting this trip brings into focus how much things have changed. Today, I would never consider taking a bus to South Bend, if one were even to be found. Nor would I have sought lodgings in that downtown location. Crime and the flight from the cities of all but the poor would have made it unthinkable.

The following morning after breakfast I taxied to the Studebaker factory, where the receptionist told me I was expected and promptly ushered me into a manager's office. The manager telephoned to the executive offices on the upper floor of the building and in a few minutes one of the company's vice presidents appeared. After greeting me pleasantly, he said, "Mr. Kormann, let me take you to your car. It is on the showroom floor." We walked through an indoor area of assembled automobiles until we came to a large showroom, empty save for a shiny new black car with a red top. The vice president then explained, "Mr. Kormann, our assembly lines are set up to meet the demand for red cars with black tops this year. To reverse the drums would have required shutting down the lines, which is a very expensive operation." Before I could ask him how they did it for my car, he added, "We hand-painted this one for you; we hope you like it." I was thunderstruck. He then said, "We were very interested in your letter. We hope you can stay and join us for lunch in the executive dining room."

Stay I did, and I sang for my meal. I did my best, drawing upon all I knew about business practices in Germany and citing various contacts I had acquired through my work with the Amerika Dienst. I think the room full of Studebaker executives appreciated my efforts. I left with their best wishes, driving my new car and feeling good about the entire affair. Sadly, two years later, under heavy pressure from the Big Three American automakers, Studebaker relocated just across the border in Canada and not long after that went out of business. It was a fine company, with a highly skilled and loyal work force. Twenty years later in Cairo, Egypt, I was often pleased to see an occasional Studebaker driving about the city. With a dry climate and little rust, Cairo is home to many an old car.

I drove my new Studebaker back to Bryn Mawr nonstop. After a brief stay with the Wellses, I was on my way again to Washington. Checking into the old Francis Scott Key Hotel near the State Department on a Sunday night, I met with Ambassador Riddleberger the following morning.[1] He did not seem particularly concerned about the *Synchronoptische Weltgeschichte* flap, especially when I explained what a difficult task it must have been to edit that book, which no longer existed. Evidently, there had been no further noises from the Congress; as far as I am aware, that was where the matter came to rest. I often wondered whether the authors, whom I had no reason to believe were communists, succeeded in having their work published later.

When I reported in to the U.S. Information Agency at 1776 Pennsylvania Avenue, I learned that I was to be assigned to the Policy Staff, handling matters related to the satellite countries of Eastern Europe. I was surprised that I would be given such an assignment, having just returned from Germany. Personnel, I was told, had gone over my record, noting my experience in Berlin, the courses I had taken on Russia in graduate school at Columbia, and that I had taught classes on "The Background of Communism" at the U.S. Army Counter Intelligence School.

My new assignment entailed developing information policy with regard to Eastern Europe and providing day-to-day guidance to the Voice of America for its radio broadcasts. I was also to work with the other divisions of the agency, such as press, publications, motion pictures, and the newly emerging medium of television. I was expected to cooperate closely with the various desks in the State Department in developing positions to be taken by our media in their output. I came away thinking that I might not have wanted to be in USIA, but I certainly could not have asked for a more interesting or responsible assignment.

I next turned my attention to house-hunting. In 1955, the trolley lines were still in existence in Washington. Automobile traffic was tolerable and a reasonable amount of street parking was available without hourly limitations. Large open fields down near the Christian Heurich Brewery along the Potomac River, where the Watergate and the Kennedy Center now stand, were available for parking without charge. Friends I met told me that house prices and property taxes were lower in Virginia and that one "generally got more for your money there." With that in mind, I visited several real estate offices in the Falls Church area and selected a knowledgeable broker who drove me around for several days.

Earlier, while back in Bryn Mawr, Elsa and I had decided that we wanted a stone, two-story colonial-style house with a garage; and indeed we saw such places in the Philadelphia Main Line suburbs for $13,000–$15,000. Alas, such dream houses commanded almost twice that much in the Washington area. Welcome to the capital and the seat of government, where the constant turnover of owners drives prices through the roof! The broker showed me numerous houses before I narrowed the selection down to about ten. Elsa then joined me, and we finally decided on a new custom-built brick rambler with a carport in the Mantua subdivision near the town of Fairfax. That was considerably farther from Washington—14 miles—than we had thought we would be. The initial asking price was

$20,900; by the time I was through bargaining and offering a large down payment, it dropped to $17,990, which was still $3,000 more than I had expected to pay.

Our trip from Bryn Mawr to Florida with our little family was to be the first of many visits we were to make over the next sixteen years to my parents' house in Debary. Back then, the drive down blacktop roads was long and tedious. I had been a bit anxious about my parents' purchase of a home in Central Florida. There had been so many real estate scams there that I wished I could have been available when they entered into the transaction. I need not have worried. They had acquired a lovely single-level house with a large carport on an acre of property with majestic trees for a third of what I had paid for our rambler in Virginia. Seeing my parents, now in their seventies, sitting out in their garden and listening to the birds singing, brought joy to my heart. My parents had been in Florida for almost two years and were already well ensconced in a community that contained many retirees. My mother's vivacious nature and my father's courtliness assured that they would have many friends.

When one thinks of Florida, ocean beaches immediately come to mind. However, Debary was a 35-mile drive over deserted, backcountry roads to either Daytona or New Smyrna. The former was a built-up city, while the latter, 15 miles south, was still a small town with a wide stretch of beach upon which one could easily drive one's automobile. We soon settled into a routine of packing a lunch, driving over to New Smyrna and spending the day frolicking in the high surf. Mother Kormann would delight in having our favorite meals prepared for us upon our return. These were wonderful days, which we and especially our children would enjoy at vacation time as long as my parents lived.

The morning commute on a normal day via Route 50 to Washington by car from our home on Kirkwood Drive in Fairfax, Virginia, would take half an hour, and I would be at my office at USIA by 8:30 a.m. Andrew Berding, a renowned former journalist and USIA's deputy director for policy, was in overall charge of our office. Under him, E. Lewis Revey was responsible for Soviet Affairs. His two deputies were Barrett Reed (Russia) and myself (Soviet satellite states). Reed, a graduate of Columbia's Russian Institute, was an able and cooperative colleague. While I had a fair background on Russia, my knowledge of Poland, Czechoslovakia, Hungary, Romania, Yugoslavia, Albania, and Bulgaria, not to mention the three Baltic states, was limited. This, however, was one of the fascinating aspects of working in the Foreign Service. You were given a challenging assignment and you grappled with it, endeavoring to master it as quickly as possible. If you did not succeed, the selection-out process inevitably took its toll.

I could not hope to be as knowledgeable for example about Hungary, as the Voice of America's desk chief for that country, who was a Hungarian refugee. Yet with good judgment, managerial skill, and a certain detachment, I could provide policy direction. In doing so, I drew upon colleagues in the State Department and the National Security Council staff and on classified government directives. It was a constant battle, however particularly with VOA in its day-to-day broadcasting. Trying to keep Eastern European newswriters, many of them émigrés with axes to grind, from editorializing was like putting toothpaste back in the tube. Barry Zorthian, later to make a name for himself as our minister for public affairs in Vietnam, was my point of contact at the Voice. It is a wonder the telephone lines remained intact at the conclusion of some of our heated "discussions" about what could or could not be broadcast. Our diplomatic representation in most of the satellite countries was tenuous at best. It was not unusual, therefore, to have our ambassadors fire back cables complaining about broadcasts they felt made life difficult for them with host country officials. We were constantly treading a fine line.

On occasion a broadcast went beyond the bounds. The Romanian section at the VOA once put out an item so troublesome that immediate steps were taken to fire the desk chief. I remember intervening at the time, pleading that the person in question was an able and cooperative officer who would be difficult to replace. I suggested a cooling-off period before taking any action. Despite ruffled feathers in USIA, the State Department, and Embassy Bucharest, the situation was gradually defused. My working relations with the Romanian desk from then on could not have been better, particularly after Zorthian told the officer in question, "You can thank Kormann for saving your job." It was a gentlemanly thing to do, considering that Barry and I were constantly at odds.

The State Department's Office of Eastern European Affairs was staffed with a very capable group of officers. It included Jacob Beam as the office director and Walter Stoessel in charge of the Soviet desk; both were later to make names for themselves as ambassador to Moscow and to Warsaw. George Lister was handling Polish affairs; Charles Scherer, Czechoslovakia; Robert McKisson, Hungary and Romania; and Henry Leverich, Bulgaria.

With the death of Stalin in 1953, the Soviet Union entered into a period of transition. A high point was the 20th Communist Party Congress in February 1956, where Khrushchev delivered his "secret speech" denouncing the deceased Stalin. Moscow's efforts to redress world public opinion toward the Soviet empire were having the unwanted effect of loosening its grip on the Eastern European countries. As early as 1948, Tito had already begun going his own way in Yugoslavia. An ideological controversy arose over "differing roads to socialism." In June 1956, workers rioted in Poznan, Poland.

It was a delicate time in our relations with the satellite countries, made even more difficult by calls for the "liberation of Eastern Europe" on the part of our top leadership and the Congress. In Poland after the riots, reform elements succeeded in bringing Wladyslaw Gomulka back from prison to leadership. Gomulka trod a careful path between placating the reformers and not antagonizing the Soviets, thereby stabilizing a situation that could have erupted into large-scale unrest.

The case was different in Hungary in late October 1956. Hard-liners had remained in power when popular forces led by intellectuals and students took to the streets. Imre Nagy, a relatively popular former communist premier, ousted in 1955 by Stalinists, was propelled back into office. In an unstable setting with fighting in the streets, Nagy, spurred on by the insurgents, declared that Hungary would withdraw from the Warsaw Pact. Henceforth, it would be neutral. Nagy called on the United Nations to guarantee that neutrality. He also indicated that Hungary would adopt a multiparty system. The Soviet Union, which had earlier indicated a willingness to remove its troops from Hungary, then moved to crush what had become a revolution. Nagy took refuge in the Yugoslav Embassy. The Soviets then installed Janos Kadar as premier. Nagy was subsequently enticed out of the Embassy by a promise of safe conduct to Romania; the Russians arrested, tried, and executed him, along with two other Hungarians, in 1958. Some of these events played themselves out while I was policy officer for the satellite countries at USIA, amid much agony and frustration.

Colleagues at the State Department came up with temporizing guidance at best. I recall a toothless statement in an address by Secretary Dulles at the height of the trouble to the effect that we wished to see "governments of the peoples' own choosing in Eastern Europe." This occurred while émigré groups throughout the United States were up in arms, demanding that we come to the rescue of "freedom fighters" in Hungary. I felt the brunt of some of this anger. An unfortunate aspect overshadowing the Hungarian debacle was that it coincided with the launching of the attack on Suez in October 1956 by Anglo-French-Israeli forces. The United States and the United Nations suddenly found themselves preoccupied with a major war in the Middle East. Had that not happened, it is possible, though not likely, that the Russians might have been deterred from acting so forcefully.

In the end, however, NATO, and more specifically the United States, were not about to bring military force to bear on the situation. Without a serious threat of armed intervention, the Soviets felt free to act. The

Eisenhower administration received much criticism for having incited revolt with their statements calling for the liberation of Eastern Europe and then doing nothing while many courageous people died. As an aftermath, both Europe and the United States were confronted with a surge of Hungarian refugees. Many Americans, including members of Congress, felt that these people rightly had a claim to sanctuary in this country.

While serving on the policy staff at USIA during the Eisenhower administration, I had the opportunity to participate in working groups of the Operations Coordinating Board (OCB). The board had as its function the development of coordinated positions on a wide range of matters for the National Security Council and the president. Some of these, after approval, became NSC directives, which in turn would be implemented in coordinated fashion by the various agencies of the government. NSC directives were numbered according to the year, for example, NSC Directive 5601 or 5602. All were highly classified because they stated the manner in which our government would act in any given circumstance. While the NSC consisted of the president, vice president, and cabinet members involved in national security matters (State, Defense, and others), the OCB functioned at undersecretary or deputy secretary level and was chaired by the vice president. Subordinate working groups were generally headed by a ranking officer from the State Department.[2]

Numerous OCB working groups covered a variety of areas and subjects. Eisenhower, following the military example, wanted things well organized. Vice President Nixon was heavily involved in the process and, in my opinion, was exceedingly effective. Later, President Kennedy came into office attacking this "over-organization" and set about dissolving committees by the score.

I particularly remember being in a working group dealing with our relations with the Soviet Union and the Communist Bloc, specifically, drafting a paper covering cultural relations. Proceeding from a thesis that communism had within it the seeds of its own destruction, the paper averred that the more populations under communism were exposed to the "Free World," the more readily those seeds would ripen. It called for increased cultural exchanges with the Soviet Union and the Bloc, not only of persons but also of publications, films, and other media. The paper, taking a long view, envisaged the crumbling of the Soviet empire as the peoples of those countries were able to witness the freedoms and the standard of living enjoyed elsewhere. As time went on, a "revolution of rising expectations" would confront succeeding generations of Soviet leadership, producing a gradual "mellowing" of communism.

The draft became an NSC directive. It was not long before right-wing elements in the Congress got wind of the directive and attacked it openly as a vehicle designed by the "communists in the State Department" to open our borders to subversion. The chairman of our working group, FSO Fred Merrill, came under particularly heavy fire. Nevertheless, efforts at cultural exchange continued and, depending on the state of relations with the communist countries in any given period, increased or decreased over the ensuing decades. History, thirty-five years later, proved that NSC directive prescient.

I also recall participating in meetings of an interagency committee chaired by Erwin Seago, a special assistant to the secretary of commerce and the director of that department's Office of Strategic Information. The primary concern at the time was to stem the flow of communist propaganda material, much of it unsolicited, into the United States. The Seago Committee, as it was known, developed among other things a procedure whereby postal matter from communist countries would be held at the local post office. A card indicating that the material had been received would then be sent to the addressee requesting disposition.[3] This procedure was employed for several years, until it became the subject of a U.S. Supreme Court case arising out of an incident in Czechoslovakia, recounted in later pages, in which I was personally involved.

While I was on the East European policy desk at USIA, I had an opportunity to spend an afternoon with a future president of the United States. Senator John F. Kennedy had returned from a trip to Poland and was preparing to make a speech to be broadcast back to that country on the VOA. The Polish desk officer at the Voice and I were asked to come to the senator's office and assist him in writing the speech. While I was impressed with the trappings of his office, I found the senator himself rather lackluster. He sat in his high, leather swivel chair behind a massive desk, having little substantive to say and simply nodding from time to time regarding suggestions we would make. Later reports indicated he was in considerable pain from a back problem for which he took medication. That may have explained his demeanor at the time. However, I came away with the thought, perhaps unfairly, "It must have been his old man's money that made this fellow a senator."[4] I had difficulty in believing a few years later that he was the same person debating Richard Nixon on television.

The family settled comfortably into our home in Fairfax. Our daughter, Andrea Hewes Kormann, was born in Alexandria Hospital on Sunday, September 25, 1955, six months after our return from overseas. It was a difficult birth, complicated by personnel shift changes at the hospital. Thereafter, Elsa had her hands full with two young children and a house to care for. My hours at work were generally long, and I would often arrive home at 8:00 p.m. or later, after the children had been put to bed. Saturday mornings and at times on Sundays, I would be in the office. Elsa managed alone without a car, doing her shopping at night when the car was available. Not particularly adept at household repairs in the beginning, I soon learned. The first few months, even a fuse blowing was enough to send me into a quandary. Our house in those years was considered "out in the country," beyond municipal water lines, leaving us with a 30-foot-deep well, pump, and septic tank, and the problems such things can cause.[5]

We enjoyed the pastoral atmosphere of our home in Virginia and the many friends we made in the community. On Sundays, we attended the Fairfax Methodist Church. Its kindly elderly minister preached a fine sermon. On lovely Sunday afternoons, Elsa and I would take Brad and Andrea on walks through the surrounding fields and woods. We were a happy family. It was during these years that I returned to painting and completed a number of canvases. Our basement lent itself well to do-it-yourself projects, and I constructed a large toy castle, complete with drawbridge, moat, and siege tower. The following year, with the children's "help," I built an elaborate Christmas crèche. The castle was outfitted with numerous colorful little mounted and standing knights made in England, while the lovely nativity figures for the crèche came from Italy. These items over the years were to become family heirlooms.

We made numerous trips during this period to Bryn Mawr to visit the Wellses and spend time with Elsa's school friends. We also paid regular visits to my parents. Besides wonderful days at the beach, my parents' house in Florida lent itself to memorable experiences, particularly for the children. As we were sitting on the breezeway talking one afternoon, we heard loud grunting sounds coming from behind the house. When we asked excitedly, "What was that?" Mother, who could be rather imperturbable, responded, "Oh, that's the alligator back there in the swamp just beyond the property." After that, we kept a sharp eye on the children when they played in the garden.

On another occasion, I heard Dad shouting in the driveway. I came out of the house to find him standing with his back against a tree using his cane to fend off a four-foot "cottonmouth" snake. Grabbing a nearby steel garden rake, I rushed over and pinned its head to the ground between the prongs and eventually killed it. The snake was of the viper species and quite venomous.

It was during a summer vacation period in Florida in 1957 that my father died. Dad had a gourmet taste and Mother had made a particularly fine supper the evening before. Mother came into our bedroom at about six in the morning saying, "There is something wrong with Father." I went to him and found him lifeless. He had had a massive stroke and passed away during the night at the age of 78. Mother and Dad Kormann had been a loving couple; the previous year they had celebrated their 50th wedding anniversary. It was a godsend that, of all times, we were visiting then and could help Mother through this crisis.

In the closing months of 1956, I received a telephone call from Dr. Guy Lee, Dad Wells's former deputy in the Historical Division of HICOG in Germany. Guy had earlier been taken into the State Department as a Foreign Service officer under the Wriston integration program. He told me that he was the assistant director of the UNESCO Relations Staff and asked whether I would be interested in coming to work for him as a program operations officer. The position entailed functioning as a specialist in the social and natural sciences, as well serving as an executive secretary for UNESCO committees in those areas. Again, as I did when proffered the post on the USIA Policy Staff, I wondered about my qualifications for the job. However, I was anxious to get back into the State Department and if this was a way, so be it. As it turned out, my work in communist affairs made me better suited for the position than I realized.

The UNESCO Relations Staff (URS) had a dual function. It was the office that handled our dealings with the United Nations Educational, Scientific, and Cultural Organization, a UN Specialized Agency headquartered in Paris. The URS also served as the Executive Secretariat of the U.S. National Commission for UNESCO, an advisory body comprised of 100 leading Americans in virtually all fields of endeavor, including members of Congress, governors, corporation presidents, university heads, scientists, and movie stars. The U.S. National Commission for UNESCO met once a year in plenary conferences lasting several days in major cities around the country. These meetings would be followed in the evenings by special opera or theater performances, gala receptions, cocktail parties, and dinners. UNESCO functions were a mecca for the social elite, and hostesses would vie for the honor of inviting the celebrated visitors.

The membership of the commission was divided into various committees and subcommittees in the areas of education, social science, natural science, and the cultural arts. There were URS program operations officers for each of these specialties: John McAfee for education; myself, social science and natural science (the latter later taken over by Dr. George Mitchell); and William Mithoefer, cultural affairs. Guy Lee, our chief, was answerable to Max McCullough, the director of URS and the executive secretary of the U.S. National Commission.

I would call periodic meetings of the Committee on the Social Sciences and the Committee on the Natural Sciences to discuss the worldwide programs of UNESCO. The United States was by far the single largest contributor to UNESCO's budget, and it was important that the funds be spent wisely and in keeping with our national interests. The Cold War was at its height at the time and the communist countries and the Non-Aligned Bloc had their own agenda. Controversies in the United Nations itself also played themselves out in UNESCO. When held in Washington, my meetings would most often be at the National Academy of Sciences, the Social Science Research Council, or the Cosmos Club.

It was my responsibility, in consultation with the chairman of a committee, to prepare papers for discussion leading to the adoption of positions on various items on the agenda. For example, does the United States support UNESCO's entering into a multimillion dollar program on arid zone and saline water research? What should our position be on UNESCO's conducting a worldwide, nation-by-nation, survey of freedom of information? Should we push for the latter, knowing it will meet vehement opposition from the communist countries?

These gatherings were often spirited and insightful deliberations, and I came away feeling privileged to have been able to rub elbows with persons of great distinction. At times in preparing for a session, I would travel to Princeton, New York, Chicago, or elsewhere to discuss the more confidential aspects of our programs with the distinguished chairman or a committee member. Life largely became a series of conferences. Developing programs and reacting to others already underway in UNESCO brought my committees together on a regular basis. For this I coordinated with Ann Jablonsky and our administrative support unit to see that travel and lodging arrangement and per diem payments were made.

At one point I was under great stress, spending long hours preparing papers for a meeting on outer space research. The chairman was Athelstan Spilhaus, head of our science committee and an internationally acclaimed scientist. Invited were outstanding experts in the field from all over the United States. It was wintertime, snowing, and I did not feel well, but it was imperative that the conference, which was being held at the National Academy of Sciences, run smoothly. I managed to get through the meeting, obtaining from the participants the information and decisions necessary to staff out the position papers. In conversation on my way out of the building, I passed out on the front steps. Friends took me home, and I spent the next ten days in bed with viral pneumonia.

The Soviet Union was very active in UNESCO and we saw running battles over such issues as the admission of North Korea, East Germany, North Vietnam, or Communist China to the myriad of meetings held around the world under UNESCO auspices. We also constantly struggled over which country's nationals should be employed in numerous key positions of the organization. Guy Lee likely had these aspects of the job in mind when he brought me over from USIA, for I soon became the "communist/political affairs officer" for the staff. It was in this function, rather than in program officer activities, that I encountered my greatest problems and often raised the ire of other bureaus in the State Department.

Ordinarily our staff would have been part of the Bureau of International Organization (United Nations) Affairs. However, because it had "cultural" connotations and served as the secretariat for the prestigious U.S. National Commission, it was placed in the Bureau of Public Affairs, along with press and public relations and cultural exchanges. In many ways UNESCO was an unwanted stepchild. Unlike other UN Specialized Agencies such as the World Health Organization, the International Civil Aviation Organization, and the Food and Agriculture Organization, which were technically oriented, UNESCO served a conglomeration of scholars, artists, scientists, writers, and other individuals who took stands on all manner of issues and causes, many of them liberal and left wing. Of all the UN organizations, UNESCO was viewed as the most communist-infiltrated. It was also very active, holding meetings on a wide range of subjects all around the world, with a particular emphasis on promoting "peaceful coexistence." Colleagues in other areas of the State Department would constantly lament to me, "What is UNESCO up to now?"

Periodically I would be contacted by a Soviet diplomat named "Ivanov" (the equivalent of Johnson in English), who was a Counselor of Embassy, and invited to lunch, ostensibly to discuss UNESCO activities. The general procedure when meeting with the Russians was that you prepared a detailed memorandum of conversation afterward, which was then distributed to the appropriate offices in the government.[6] Ivanov probably labored under a similar requirement. The net result was that we had little substantive to say to one another. After a while he stopped calling me, and I stopped writing memcons. On the other hand, the Russians did liven up our activities, particularly regarding the Committee on Natural Sciences. I can cite no more telling example than an occurrence in October 1957.

For many months preparations had been under way by the United States to launch an object into space. The project was in the late stages and there was much discussion of the "satellite" to be launched. I place the word satellite in quotes because the term was a novelty for us in those days. The satellite was to be placed in the nose of a Vanguard rocket and fired into space from Wallops Island, Virginia.

Someone suggested that we provide a model of this object for display at a UNESCO meeting in Paris that coincided with some major aeronautical event there. I recall going to considerable effort to obtain a life-sized model from the Navy, the managers of the project. I was very pleased when I finally obtained the model, a basketball-sized sphere. Placing it atop my office filing cabinet one afternoon, I thought about how I would pack it for shipment to Paris and how impressed everyone there would be. Soon such an object would be whirling about the earth in orbit.

I discussed the requirements for shipment through the diplomatic pouch with the courier section of the State Department. My efforts were for naught, however, for within hours, the Russians announced the launching of *Sputnik*. Now my model became anathema—a reminder no one wanted of our failure to be first in space. My mind has blotted out what became of it, as it has the firing of the Vanguard rocket, which was to lift the satellite into orbit. That, too, I believe was a failure. Later, in 1958, with the successful launching of *Explorer I*, we were finally in space and the race was on.

The impact of *Sputnik* on America was profound, and we thereafter moved rapidly to strengthen a broad range of our scientific activities, even down to education on the public school levels. The distinguished scientists on our committee pondered what had happened. Taking stock of the situation, there was a consensus that America would eventually surpass the Russians in space exploration. While the Soviet Union, with the help of German rocket scientists, might have had the first drop on us, we were unequaled in the field of basic research, the key to success in the long run.[7]

Our URS office was also charged with the day-to-day support of the U.S. Representative to UNESCO in Paris, Dr. Henry Kellermann, and his staff. The views of our government and the U.S. National Commission on program and administrative matters were channeled on a routine basis through the Paris office to the UNESCO secretariat. It was a rare day that we did not send several telegrams or airgrams to Paris. The general procedure would be to take the completed communication to our front office for approval and then obtain the concurrence (clearance) of other interested or affected offices in the Department of State or elsewhere in the government. Our messages, regardless of subject matter, were always cleared through the International Organization Affairs (IO) and Public Affairs (P) Bureaus.

The clearance procedure was laborious and time-consuming, often engendering heated discussions with offices not in agreement with our views. At times, I would redraft a message to obtain the clearance of one bureau, only to have that position challenged by another. It could take a day or two or more before the entire procedure would be completed, especially if half a dozen concurrences were involved. I would find myself going from office to office in the latter part of the afternoon with a telegram, winding up in either the IO or P Bureaus at 6:30 or 7:00 o'clock in the evening.

While in some places I would run into a substantial brick wall, it was in P that most of my evenings were spent. Deputy Assistant Secretary E. Allan Lightner was my point of contact. A friend and at the same time my nemesis, he would constantly go over each message with a fine-toothed comb, leading me into endless discussions. In the end, however, he was generally supportive.

One evening when I was clearing a telegram to be sent to Paris, I became involved in an unpleasant incident. It was a lengthy message concerning the reelection of Dr. Luther Evans, an American, as director general of UNESCO. The concurrences of everyone except IO had been obtained, when I arrived at Joseph Sisco's office at about 6:15 p.m., forty-five minutes after close of business. Ordinarily he was cooperative, despite annoyance at my constant arrival with messages at late hours. That evening I encountered him rushing out the door. "Kormann," he said, "tonight I have an appointment; bring your damn message next time during business hours!" For some reason that evening all other IO Bureau officers authorized to sign off on my message had also left. Returning to the UNESCO Relations Staff, I stopped off at our front office. Frank Hopkins, our deputy director, was there alone. I informed him of what had happened, saying that I would send the telegram out the following morning.

He was visibly irritated, saying that it was important the message go forward. He instructed me to take it to the communications center without IO Bureau concurrence. I heard no more about the matter until several days later, when I encountered Joe Sisco in the hall. He greeted me with, "You SOB, don't you come to me with your telegrams any more!" I was taken back, since I should have been the one who was irritated, not the other way around. When I looked puzzled, he said, "Don't tell me you don't know about the memo to Wilcox!" I protested that I had no idea what he was talking about. He simply looked at me in disgust and walked away.

I then learned from Hopkins's secretary that he had sent a blistering memo through channels to Assistant Secretary of State for International Organization Affairs Francis Wilcox about Sisco's failure to act on our telegram. I was mortified, especially since I was dependent on IO Bureau colleagues for future cooperation. I never was able to reconcile myself with Sisco, who at that time was a middle level officer and could have had his career damaged by the memo. Fifteen years later, while in Egypt, I was assigned to assist him when he was Under Secretary of State Sisco and Henry Kissinger's right hand man during the period of "shuttle diplomacy." It was not the most comfortable situation.

The United States participated in the quarterly sessions of the UNESCO Executive Board, where we played a significant role. For these meetings there would be a delegation consisting of the U.S. Representative to UNESCO, Henry Kellermann, serving as the board member, and two or three of our staff from Washington. Over the years, I must have attended ten or more of these meetings, most of them in Paris, but also several in other countries. It became a matter of prestige for nations to play host to an EXBD session. The convening of a UN body in any given country was seen as conveying legitimacy. Germany at the time, for example, was not yet a member of the United Nations. When the UNESCO EXBD decided to hold one of its sessions in Cologne, the Germans spared no expense to be gracious hosts.

The Cologne EXBD Board meeting was replete with diplomatic formality, with receptions hosted at the ministerial level. From my HICOG days in Germany I remembered our efforts to "democratize" their foreign service. I could not help smiling, therefore, as I was introduced to polished German diplomats, some of them young, with "von" and "zu" before their surnames. Their foreign service apparently remained a mecca for German aristocrats, and perhaps that was not so bad. America did not always have the answer to all of Germany's problems. We never succeeded in "democratizing" Germany's two-track education system either. I listen with amusement today when distinguished American educators speak of the need in our country for higher-level vocational training separate from our four-year colleges.[8]

It had only been four years since my previous assignment in Germany and I felt quite at home. I was asked, perhaps as a consequence, to accompany UNESCO Director General Evans for a courtesy call at our Bonn Embassy to meet with Ambassador David K. E. Bruce. The ambassador sent his limousine to pick us up for the twenty-five mile drive south to Mehlem. En route, Dr. Evans told me how pleased he was to have been able to bring the EXBD session to Germany. It was the first UN meeting of any kind there and a major step toward facilitating full membership for Germany into the UN and the family of nations after World War II.

As he talked and we sped through the Rhineland countryside, I thought to myself how different this drive was from one I had taken through the same area fourteen years earlier in the closing months of that war. Then, as a young soldier, I rode in the back of a truck crowded with paratroopers en route to Epinal in France for transfer to the 82nd Airborne Division. Gone were the explosion-cratered roads, the artillery-flattened towns, and the streams of refugees carrying their pitifully few belongings. I wondered silently whether Dr. Evans really fathomed how far Germany had come.

Executive Board sessions in Paris were interesting, providing an opportunity for frequent contact with diplomats from many other countries. Formal exchanges in the meetings and long wine-sodden lunches in Parisian restaurants were the norm. It was here rather than in my earlier assignments that I received my first real taste of protocol and the usage of French as the diplomatic language.

At one Paris EXBD meeting to approve the organization's budget, I witnessed a remarkable and unfortunate occurrence. The budget had come under heavy fire during the previous year. Following accepted procedure, the director general of UNESCO at the time, Dr. Vittorino Veronese, a fine, distinguished Italian official and Luther Evans's successor in the post, addressed the assemblage with his proposed budget, a lengthy program statement. The conference room resembled that of the UN Security Council. The various national representatives were seated in circular fashion, their nation's name on the table before them. In a row behind them sat several advisors for each country.

Dr. Veronese was about twenty minutes into his statement, the text of which was already available to us, when suddenly a sheet of paper from his speech wafted into the air. My first thought was that a blast of wind must have whipped by the podium. Veronese did not try to recover the page. He kept speaking, but his voice was now a bit more high-pitched. A half-minute later a second page took flight. This time, I saw an arm making a tossing movement. Henry Kellermann turned around and whispered to me, "What's going on?" Before I could say anything, more papers were being thrown in the air and the director general's voice had risen to shouts.

We watched stunned as Dr. Veronese wildly threw pages of his text into the air amid cries of, "I cannot do this! I cannot go on!. . . It is too much!" Finally, Assistant Director General Adiseshiah, an Indian national, seated among a row of officials behind the podium, reacted. Coming up behind Veronese, he gently put his arms around the director general and, talking to him softly, led him to a seat. Within minutes a physician and hospital attendants in white coats appeared, and Dr. Veronese was taken from the conference hall and the UNESCO headquarters building, never to return. The Executive Board and all in attendance were in a state of shock. I had seen men break down in combat during the war, but coming as this did "out of the blue," the impact was profound. UNESCO thereafter continued for an extended period under provisional leadership until a new director general was elected.

During the heyday of the U.S. National Commission for UNESCO, it was interesting to observe some of its celebrated members in action. Corporation chairmen would always come to the meetings accompanied by an executive vice president or other senior official from their firm. While the chairmen would do the talking, the others generally served as the brains behind any report prepared. Often Commission members, both men and women, were exceedingly wealthy — possessors of or heirs to America's great fortunes. At one U.S. National Commission Executive Committee meeting, I remember noting at least two individuals in the room of perhaps twelve persons who had personal fortunes that today would be in the billions. We were discussing UNESCO programs they could have funded themselves for years.

I took a certain amount of vicarious pleasure in working with the Commission. If I could not be a multimillionaire, I did not mind at times living like one. C. Stanley Allyn, the chairman of the board of the National Cash Register Company, was one of the Commission's conscientious and thoughtful members. He was a grand, elderly gentleman, an entrepreneur of the old school, along with men such as Ford, Burroughs, and Harriman. On one occasion, he called a meeting of a committee at his penthouse apartment/office in the Waldorf Astoria Hotel in New York. At the conclusion of business, we adjourned for lunch in his large dining room overlooking the city. An elaborate and elegant meal complete with vintage wines was served by white-gloved waiters followed by expensive cigars.

At an annual U.S. National Commission meeting in Denver, Colorado, in 1959, I remember being told on short notice that I would have to introduce the guest speaker at a plenary session in the large auditorium. Why this fell to me I do not recall, but I found myself confronted with the task of presenting the American author and icon William Faulkner to a distinguished audience of one hundred Commission members and close to a thousand other people, including state and municipal dignitaries. I had two hours before my appearance at the podium. I put them to use by taking a taxi to the nearest library. Blessedly, I found a bit of resource material on Faulkner and came up with a thought expressed by that celebrated author to the effect that he did not consider himself a man of letters but "simply a farmer who loved to tell stories." With a bit of elaboration about his humility, this is the way I introduced him, much to the audience's amusement and Mr. Faulkner's pleasure.

That same conference, on the other hand, had its unpleasant side. I was scheduled to appear on a local TV station with Commission member Lew Ayres, the movie actor from *All Quiet on the Western Front* and the *Dr. Kildare* series, to discuss the activities of UNESCO. I called for Mr. Ayres with a taxi with more than an hour to spare for our appearance on the program. The cab driver, insisting he knew the station, took us to the wrong place on the other side of town. We encountered heavy traffic returning. By the time we arrived at the correct spot, the program was several minutes underway and since we were the only guests, the talk show host was desperately trying to fill in. Ayres was furious with me, despite the fact that I, too, was a stranger in Denver. Before departing the TV station, I suggested to the manager that when he had out-of-town guests on his show who do not know their way around, he send a car or a designated taxi to fetch them.

UNESCO felt it had a special role to play in bringing about peaceful coexistence/cooperation between nations. It is important to understand in this context that the term "peaceful coexistence" was Soviet phraseology. In the struggle for men's minds at the time it was unacceptable to the United States, if for no other reason than that the Russians had coined the term. I remember employing the phrase "peaceful cooperation" instead, which to me was more euphemistic. I do not know whether I was the first to do so, but I do recall introducing it in the UNESCO program context. Throughout the early years of the Cold War there was a distinct effort to keep from holding UN meetings in Eastern Europe as a way of showing displeasure over the Soviet-dominated regimes in those countries.

Consequently, when UNESCO decided in 1959 to sponsor an international conference of social scientists in Prague, Czechoslovakia, it caused a stir on our side. It would be the first of such UN conferences to be held behind the Iron Curtain. The topic suggested by Soviet supporters was "The Promotion of Peaceful Coexistence between Nations." We countered with the term "Peaceful Cooperation." Subsequently, both words were used together.

Member states were invited to send experts in the various fields of the social sciences. We were concerned that the affair would only provide a sounding board for communist propaganda and the views of the countries of the Non-Aligned Bloc. Four distinguished social scientists were asked to participate from the United States: Professors Walter Sharp of Yale, political science; Klaus Knorr of Princeton, economics; Everett Hughes of Chicago, sociology; and Harold Berman of Harvard, international law. I was assigned to accompany the group to the four-day conference to serve, in effect, as their political advisor and contact with the State Department and our embassy in Czechoslovakia.

Arriving in Prague, we were billeted in a newly Soviet-completed hotel on the main street just below the statue of St. Wenceslas, the city's landmark. In the process of registering at the hotel, the desk clerks took it for granted that I was, in communist parlance, the "political commissar" for our delegation, and they treated me as such. To make my life difficult, I was given a room on a separate floor away from our delegation. I had no sooner checked into my room than there was a knock on the door and an absolutely, stunningly beautiful young woman, with carefully manicured fingernails, introduced herself in halting English as the maid. (If she was the maid, I wondered what the rest of the staff looked like!) Seeing her, however, unnerved me in more ways than one. It took me back to my days in Berlin when, as an intelligence agent, I would be amazed at how crude

Soviet espionage ploys could be. On the other hand, they could also be extremely dangerous.

I had visions then of being identified, despite a dozen-year interval, as a former CIC field office chief. I was already behind the Iron Curtain and it would not take much to make me disappear. I was carrying a letter from the under secretary of state to Ambassador John Allison, our envoy in Prague, indicating that I was on an important mission and asking the embassy to provide me with whatever assistance I required. The letter, if read by the Russians or the Czechs, would immediately give credence to an impression they probably already had, that I was not really an American UNESCO staff person.[9] I took care not to leave the letter with my belongings. Inspecting the room carefully for two-way mirrors and other devices, I set little "indicator traps" for any persons going through my things when I was out of the room. They were always sprung when I returned.

Our Czech hosts went to great lengths to see that conference arrangements were carefully handled. Meetings were held in magnificent old Hapsburg Empire buildings and palaces. At the interdisciplinary sessions there was plenty of give and take in the discussions. The Indian delegation was particularly effective. It included two internationally known figures, V. K. Krishna Menon and V. J. Rau, who were articulate and quite outspoken. While at times the Indians were critical of the United States, the Soviet Union received severe censure for purporting to be one thing in theory, while in practice being a despotic system. Our delegation, headed by Dr. Sharp, gave a very good account of itself. I do not know how much further the conference sessions propelled the world along the road toward "peaceful coexistence/cooperation between nations," but they certainly were enjoyable and cathartic for the leading scholars in attendance.

A reception on the first evening for the conference participants was held in the vast main hall of the 17th century Wallenstein Palace, a site breathtaking in its splendor. The foreign guests were taken on several tours around Prague. While there was little the Czech Communist hosts could allude to as their regime's architectural achievements, it was obvious they took great pride in the treasures of earlier centuries. A cherished memory forever enshrined in my mind was the glorious Philosopher's Hall of the baroque Strahov Library, with its high walls of book shelves and ceiling with exquisite paintings. As golden rays of the late afternoon sun filtered through tall ornate windows onto the intricately inlaid, polished wooden floors, I said to myself: "This has got to be one of the most beautiful rooms on earth." Among the vast collection of ancient books in that library the curator showed us two old Bibles, one immense in size, the other scarcely larger than a postage stamp. He said that they were the largest and the smallest Bibles in the world.

As soon as my delegation responsibilities permitted, I made my way to the American Embassy in Prague. There I was met by Jonathan Dean, the political officer and an old friend from my Bonn and resident officer days in Germany. That evening our delegation was invited for cocktails with Ambassador and Mrs. Allison at the Residence. We all came away from that gathering with vivid impressions of how difficult and restrictive serving behind the Iron Curtain could be.

During one of my trips on foot to the Embassy, I got lost. I was following a street that had trolley lines and must have branched off in the wrong direction. I waited at a stop for a trolley car and, boarding it, asked the conductor in German for the street on which the American Embassy was located. I spoke no Czech and the chances of him speaking English I thought would be nil. With the years of German occupation, I was sure that language would at least be passably understood. That was a mistake, not because it was not understood, but because the Nazis had left such a bitter residue in the minds of the population.

As soon as I saw the sullen faces of the conductor and passengers in the front of the car, I realized my error. I then took a desperate chance and said in a loud voice, again in German, "Does anyone speak English? I am an American. I am lost and trying to find the American Embassy." The result was astonishing. The entire disposition of that trolley changed. It seemed as if everyone was ready to help. There were German speakers galore and even a few who were ready to try out their few words of English. I was told to remain on the car and where to transfer to another to take me to the Embassy. The incident left me with a wonderful feeling, which I happily related to our delegation and embassy friends.

At the conclusion of the conference, Professor Everett Hughes approached me with a large stack of printed matter on the communist educational system he had received from Czech governmental sources. He asked whether the embassy could send this material home for him. I told him that its facilities were limited and that anything sent out, even personal mail, went through the diplomatic pouch and was transported by courier. Nevertheless, I said I would inquire. The response I received from the embassy, with which I concurred, was that our already overloaded courier should not be asked to carry out a lot of communist propaganda material. I very politely conveyed this answer to Dr. Hughes, again explaining the circumstances. He then took steps either to mail the material himself or have the Czech conference organizers do it for him.

The sequel to the mailing of Dr. Hughes's material came to my attention many months later, when I saw an item in a Washington, D.C., newspaper to the effect that the U.S. Supreme Court had ruled on a case involving the receipt of postal material from communist countries. Everett

Hughes, who was cited as the plaintiff, evidently had been sent notification from the post office that printed matter from Prague had been received. In keeping with the governmental procedure set up in the Seago Committee meetings I had attended back in 1955–56, mentioned earlier in these pages, Hughes had been told that his material was being held back awaiting an indication of disposition from him. Perhaps annoyed by the delay or by having to go to the post office, he sued, challenging the constitutionality of the postal service's selectively withholding mail. The U.S. Supreme Court ruled in his favor and the procedure was discontinued.

I have promised myself that one of these days I will go through the law books to learn of the multistaged legal path of this case and the cost to everyone involved. What if we had simply decided to send that material in the diplomatic pouch, would we have spared the effort and cost of a Supreme Court case? Probably not, for in hindsight the Draconian measures taken in those earlier days, when communism was our greatest bugaboo, would eventually have withered under the test of constitutional scrutiny. For me, however, it was most assuredly a strange twist of fate to have been a participant in both the alpha and the omega aspects of this affair.

During my Washington assignment, I became more active in the Army Reserve. I had gone a number of years with minimal participation while overseas, only seriously attending drills during my final months in Bonn, where there was a regular unit. I found that being in USIA and the State Department made me a sought-after commodity by the Army when it came to going on fifteen-day tours of annual active-duty training. As a policy officer for the satellite countries of Eastern Europe with USIA, for example, the Army saw to it that I was brought on duty in the Pentagon to rewrite their country papers on Czechoslovakia and Hungary. It was a task that ordinarily would have required much more time, but for me it was a matter of pride to get the job done. It was a real busman's holiday, and I made it my business thereafter to avoid Pentagon duty, if only to obtain a change of scenery away from Washington.

Most of my subsequent annual Reserve training tours during these years were taken at Ft. Bragg, which with my airborne background was much more to my liking. I became associated with unconventional warfare activities and the newly established Special Warfare Center.[10] I enjoyed my duty with the Center and, when my fifteen days were completed, came away feeling that I had made a contribution, though sometimes in unusual ways. I remember being billeted in an old World War II–style wooden barrack that served as the Bachelor Officers' Quarters (BOQ). A section of the BOQ at the time was occupied by a group of field-grade officers from the Sudan. They were a friendly, outgoing bunch, who sometimes carried on uproariously after hours with the black maids servicing the building.

I received a summons one morning to come to the Center commandant's office. I arrived to find the colonel and several of his staff wrestling with a problem. Evidently complaints had been lodged over the Sudanese officers' behavior and there was a move afoot to send some or all of them home. I was asked, "How does the State Department feel about this?" When I inquired as to the reason that would be given for sending them back, I received a mixture of answers from "conduct unbecoming an officer" to "poor performance" in their training.

After thinking a moment, I responded that in the interests of the United States the most the colonel should really expect from the training of these foreign officers was to "win friends and influence people." If they go home with a good feeling about their time at Ft. Bragg and about the friends they have made, we will have achieved success. To send them home "under a cloud" will earn their eternal ill will, something the United States government could not afford. Unlike our country, those lieutenant colonels and majors will be running the Sudan when they go back. I guess the colonel agreed with me, for nothing was done about the matter. I have always thought it quite possible that Colonel Jaafar al-Nimeiry, later president of the Sudan who was trained in the United States, may have been in that group.

On one occasion, I was asked to assist in updating a guerrilla warfare manual for use by a new type of unit to be called "Special Forces." A slightly over-the-hill active-duty captain who had been with the 101st Airborne Division in World War II was already working on the project. I remember struggling with a section on how to make "shaped-charge" explosive devices from commonly available materials. In one case, a concave automobile headlight glass was to be packed with C-4 plastic compound. When placed against a wire cyclone fence and detonated, this device supposedly would fire an explosive stream ten or more feet, destroying a large power transformer inside an enclosure.

At one point I became dubious about our efforts, asking my partner, "How do we know this stuff will really work? We are playing with guys' lives!" Then and there we decided to test the theory. After informing our office at the Special Warfare Center of our intentions, we made arrangements to obtain a section of cyclone fence and an old 50-gallon steel drum to serve as a mock transformer. All we could find was one filled with waste oil. Rather than dump the oil, we felt the weight would give the target more solidity. A truck and two enlisted men were assigned to haul the material and help us set up the test, which was to be performed on a large open field not far from our building on "Smoke Bomb Hill."

We attempted to make our test as realistic as possible. Setting the detonator, we all ran and took positions a good distance away. It was our hope that the charge would go off aimed accurately at our "transformer," blowing a hole in it and making it inoperable thereafter. To say we were successful would be a gross understatement. Our charge went off with a flash of light. Simultaneously, a massive explosion and a rush of air, lifted me from my low crouched position and dumped me on my behind a good six feet to the rear. "Wow, that was some blast!" I heard one of the enlisted men shout. Instantly, I realized we had made a mistake in not dumping the oil.

Our group watched transfixed as a massive, black mushroom cloud rose high into the heavens from our test site. As we stood in numbed silence, we became aware of activity in the distance on all sides of us. A siren wailed, a clag horn sounded, and soon all manner of noisy vehicles with flashing lights were rushing in our direction. Despite our efforts to act businesslike, indicating that we were conducting an official experiment, there was no way we could mask our embarrassment before the fire department, the military police, and a curious crowd arriving in their cars. Spectators milled about asking whether there had been an atomic explosion. To make matters worse, that damn mushroom cloud hung up there forever, reaching a height that must have made it visible to half the state of North Carolina.

There were no more "tests," and the captain and I kept as low a profile as we could from then on. Nevertheless, until I left at the end of that week I was jokingly referred to as one of the "bomb boys." I expected that we might receive a word of censure from the post commander, but none came. I ran into the captain nine years later in the Tokyo Airport on my way home from the Philippines. He was returning from the war in Vietnam, a highly decorated Special Forces colonel.

During the course of the year, I attempted to keep my Army Reserve status in force by attending biweekly drills on Tuesday nights as part of a control group of officers who met in the auditorium of the Department of the Interior, a few blocks away from the State Department building. On days when I had drill, I would bring my uniform in the trunk of the car, change in a bathroom after work, and report for the two or more hour meeting that night. Unlike later duty, when I drilled one full weekend a month as part of a regular unit, I was not paid but attended only for retirement points.

The control group contained about fifty officers of varying grades. The drill generally consisted of lectures on military or related subjects presented by guest lecturers or members of the group. At times when our speaker failed to appear for one reason or another, a favorite tactic of the colonel in charge would be to call on a rather eccentric lieutenant colonel in the group named Fritz Kraemer to fill in. I did not know much about him at the time but was amused at his antics. He had a Prussian background, a slight accent, wore a monocle and often carried a swaggerstick. When called upon, he would come up to the podium and ask, "What would you like to learn about tonight?" He would rattle off a few topics on international affairs and then respond to the audience's preference.

I remember commenting at the outset to Milton Barall, a fellow State Department officer attending these drills, "This guy is full of hot air."[11] I soon changed my mind, however, when one evening Kraemer lectured us, off the cuff, on the potential problems between Iran and Iraq. Afterwards, I told him that I was with the State Department and was impressed with his presentation. He responded that he kept a vast file on potential trouble spots in the world and that he analyzed these with great care. He told me that he was employed as a civilian advisor to the secretary of the Army and it was his business to know such things. I also learned he had a degree from the London School of Economics and doctorates from universities in Germany and Italy.

Incidentally, he had been in CIC in Germany after World War II. I was surprised at how similar our Army CIC experiences and career paths had been. Thereafter, Kraemer and I had a friendly and cooperative relationship in which I would also lecture. He occasionally sounded me out to obtain a State Department view on matters of interest to him. His influence on me must have been greater than I sensed at the time for ten years later I found myself lecturing the same way under similar circumstances in my Civil Affairs Reserve unit. Only I did it without the accent, monocle, and swaggerstick, though not half as engagingly. What I did not know about Fritz Kraemer in 1958 was that he had been to Henry Kissinger during and after the war what Master Sergeant Severin Wallach had been to me in recruiting me for CIC. They changed our lives. Kraemer recruited Kissinger for CIC, later got him a job on the faculty of the Oberammergau Intelligence School, and finally influenced him to attend Harvard in 1947. I believe I met Sergeant Kissinger at Oberammergau, but little did I know that this fellow with the heavy German accent twenty-eight years later would not only be my boss but the secretary of state.

I had decided as early as 1953 that I did not want to return to academia, but rather to become a Foreign Service officer. To do that, I would ordinarily have had to take the Foreign Service exam or seek entry under the 517 Lateral Entry Program. My efforts to do either were complicated by fate. As indicated earlier, that same year, a decision was made to create a separate agency, the U.S. Information Agency (USIA), to take over the public affairs functions from the Department of State, and I was transferred automatically on paper. Concurrently, a process known as the Wriston Program was underway to integrate the remainder of officer personnel in the State Department into the Foreign Service officer corps, thus almost doubling the ranks of the latter.[12] Had I not been in USIA at the time, I would simply have been brought in as an FSO. Instead, I was confronted with a seven-year struggle to accomplish that aim.

The net result of the Wriston integration was to expand the FSO corps to a point where for years there was a glut of officers, and no new personnel were taken in. Thus, both the exam and lateral entry routes were closed to me. Despite returning to the State Department with the UNESCO staff, I was still only on board as a reserve officer under a limited appointment—much the same as when I was first hired for a Resident Officer assignment in Germany six years earlier. By the time the door did open a crack, I was beyond the thirty-one-year age limit for the standard exam. So I sought entry under the 517 Lateral Entry Program, which by then, since they took in a mere handful of persons, was dubbed the "517 Exclusion Program." Nevertheless, with persistent effort, a written test, and a several-hour oral exam by an almost hostile three-officer board, I finally became an FSO in 1960. I retained the grade I held in my limited appointment. Ten years had elapsed since I first joined the Department of State. Over the years entry into the FSO corps remained very difficult. In the following decades, as many as 20,000 applicants took the exam annually, with only thirty or forty of them finally receiving appointments. In some years there were none.[13]

Having acquired FSO status, I sought to move into the mainstream of the State Department. I was transferred to the Policy Planning and Guidance Staff (P/PG) of the Bureau of Public Affairs. From a personnel standpoint this made a great deal of sense, for in that job I would be on the opposite end of the pipeline from policy officers in USIA and working in a field where I already had considerable experience. The position I filled had a working title of special assistant to the assistant secretary for public affairs, at the time Andrew Berding, my former overall boss in USIA. In practice, however I was part of P/PG under the direction of Philip Burris. I was one of five officers dividing up responsibilities across a broad spectrum. My closest associate was John Baker, an extremely able Russian specialist, who while assigned to our Embassy in Moscow had been declared *persona non grata* by the Soviets. He had simply established too many contacts with students and other young people, and the communist government saw him as a threat. Baker and I shared a secretary and often backstopped one another.

In my new job I drafted policy guidance papers for State Department and USIA media output, but as was the case for other officers on the staff, I also took on a variety of ad hoc assignments. I was the department's point of contact for American private organizations invited to attend troublesome international meetings, such as the communist-sponsored "World Youth Festivals."[14] I was the representative on the interagency Committee on Commemorative Postage Stamps. In addition, all of us on the staff participated in various temporary working groups or task forces set up to deal with crises as they arose. During the Berlin Wall crisis, for example, I sat in on some of the action-level committee meetings, in one of which I caused a stir, thus fixing the matter firmly in my mind over the years.

In a Berlin Wall task force meeting chaired by the legendary Ambassador Charles "Chip" Bohlen, I asserted that the way to handle the crisis was to order the colonel commanding our infantry regiment in the city to take his tank support and knock down the wall, then only a short segment, before the Soviets went any further. I stated that I had been an Army officer in Berlin in 1946–47 charged with the security of the Neukoelln sector border. When faced with Soviet encroachments, we stopped them dead in their tracks at the outset. The Russians more than likely expected us to act this way and would back off when challenged. Partially in jest, I gratuitously added that if this did not work, you could always disavow the colonel's action, remove him, and later quietly give him a promotion.

My remarks did not sit too well with Ambassador Bohlen, who must have deemed me impetuous and Machiavellian. However, I feel sure the action I proposed would have succeeded at the very beginning of the wall construction. Later General Lucius Clay, the former military governor of Germany, also took a forceful line on a higher level, but by then more time had elapsed, and it was probably too late.

As the department's representative on the Commemorative Postage Stamp Committee, I had a grand time. It was the committee's job to assist in the selection of stamps to be issued. Before coming to this assignment, I had no idea of the pressures exerted by various groups and individuals to bring about the issuance of a desired commemorative stamp. Associations, ethnic groups, political organizations, and collectors of all sorts had something to say about the matter. During my time on the committee, stamps honoring numerous foreign heroes were issued in the "Champion of Liberty" series. There were pressure tactics from a dozen hyphenated American groups: Poles supporting a Paderewski stamp; Indians a Mahatma Gandhi stamp; Italians a Garibaldi stamp; Finns a Mannerheim stamp; Hungarians a Kossuth stamp; and so it went. Living with these pressures was part of the job, and it was interesting.

On the other hand, as part of the ceremony connected with the issuance of each stamp, I had to ensure the presence of a guest speaker, usually the secretary of state or one of his deputies. This also entailed writing a draft of the speech for that exalted personage. Generally, the ceremony would be held at the Post Office Department, but on occasion at some other site, for example, the St. Lawrence Seaway, when a stamp honoring the opening of that passage was issued.

In connection with each stamp ceremony, an attractive color program in booklet form would be prepared; each contained a bordered page with the new stamp cancelled in "first day cover" fashion. These, of course, were collectors' items and much prized by the recipients. During the period I was on the committee, I received a number of "first day cover" programs. Among these were stamps honoring Japanese-U.S. relations, Mexican independence, the Echo I satellite, Secretary of State John Foster Dulles, the World Forestry Congress, and an entire series on American credos, such as "Give Me Liberty or Give Me Death."

The most memorable stamp ceremony I was to participate in came with the issuance of the Mahatma Gandhi "Champion of Liberty" stamp. A new secretary of state, Dean Rusk, had just come on board in January 1961, and I arranged to have him speak at the ceremony before a distinguished audience at the Post Office Department. I wrote what I thought was an appropriate "humdinger" of a speech and sent it up to Rusk's office on the seventh floor. Coming days after his arrival on the job, it would be his first official, though rather unimportant, speech as secretary of state.

When I heard no more about my draft, I took that as acceptance, assuring myself that, indeed, I was one talented fellow. In driving down to the Post Office Department, the secretary said nothing about the matter. At the appropriate time after being introduced by the postmaster general, he went to the podium, took out my speech, carefully enunciated my salutation, and from then on launched off on his own. I was stunned as he began reminiscing about how he had sat on a bed in a room at Oxford in the early 1930s listening to and talking with Gandhi. The audience was enthralled; the Indian ambasssador beamed. It was quite a performance. I doubt if anyone had ever been taken down a peg so deftly as I was on that occasion.

Another stamp incident in the same series was less than pleasant. I received a call from the Post Office Department asking how the Finnish hero, Carl Mannerheim spelled his first name, with a "C" or a "K." My references indicated a "C," but to be sure I called the Finnish Embassy and spoke to the deputy chief of mission. I told him of the reason for my question and its importance. The stamp would be used in the international mails and, of course, some letters to which it was affixed would be sent to Finland and we absolutely wanted it to be correct. He insisted that it was spelled in good Finnish fashion with a "K" and his answer was relayed to the Post Office Department.

However, Mannerheim's parents must have had other ideas, for they had spelled it with a "C." A run of stamps thus had to be held back at the cost of thousands of dollars. I thought the matter would reverberate at top levels and was prepared to explain as best I could under the circumstances. However, the explosion never really materialized. The Post Office Department, having gone as far in the past as actually issuing stamps printed upside down, may have felt that this "in-house mistake" could be taken in stride. Nevertheless, the entire affair gave me some uneasy moments.[15]

As part of my shared duties, I drafted policy guideline messages, later termed "Infoguides." These were sent over to USIA and to all our posts abroad, laying out our public positions on a variety of major international issues. I would write them with the assistance of officers in the bureaus concerned, who would at times not only provide me with positions taken but the exact language to be used. These messages required numerous clearances and high-level approval before they were sent out.

On occasions where two bureaus had sharply differing views, I would do a "middle of the road" draft and endeavor to placate both sides. One such paper was on the Sino-Soviet split, the disengagement of Peking and Moscow. I recall it took a great deal of effort and research, not only in preparing the draft but also in dealing with the Bureau of Far Eastern Affairs. By the time I was through, I had become an instant expert on Communist China. With considerable assistance from Richard Davies in Soviet Affairs, we finally enunciated our government's official policy on Russo-Chinese relations.[16]

Davies, later my boss as an ambassador and career minister, also shared some notoriety with me in the debacle over the U-2 flight. During the first week of May in 1960, Davies, at the time public affairs advisor for the Office of Soviet Affairs, came to me with a proposed news release about a NASA weather plane that had strayed off course and was missing in the vicinity of the Russo-Turkish border. The inference, as I recall, was that it might have gone down somewhere in the Soviet Union.

The release seemed routine enough. From the P/PG and Bureau of Public Affairs standpoint, there appeared to be no problem. Airplane mishaps had occurred in the past and likely would in the future. I signed off on the release without the slightest idea that it was a "cover story" or of what was in store. Davies saw to it that it went down to Lincoln White, the State Department's press spokesman. By the time the week was over, the United States had a first-class crisis on its hands. Relations between America and the Soviet Union had been blossoming in an era of détente. Chairman Khrushchev had visited the United States. President Eisenhower would soon meet with him at a Summit Conference in Geneva prior to a visit to Russia.

The scene was set for significant moves toward disarmament between the two countries, but our side felt it needed more information about Soviet missile development. President Eisenhower had several years earlier proposed an "open skies" agreement which would permit a verification of the arms levels of each country, but the Russians demurred. Concern over their growing capability to launch intercontinental ballistic missiles then prompted our government to embark on a highly secret program of overflights of the Soviet Union. The U-2, a high-flying, sophisticated, photo-reconnaissance aircraft, carried out a number of these missions successfully.

The Russians, we later learned, were aware of the flights but were unable to shoot them down. Not wanting to admit their inability to deal with these violations of their territory, they remained silent about them. President Eisenhower personally ordered the termination of the program in April 1960, but at CIA's urging, a final flight to obtain definitive intelligence prior to the summit meeting was scheduled for the latter half of that month. A combination of circumstances delayed the takeoff from Peshawar, Pakistan, until May 1—a most unfortunate date considering its significance in the communist world.

Unlike previous flights, which flew erratic incursion courses, this one was to fly in a straight line from border to border. Near Sverdlosk, a Russian missile succeeded in hitting the U-2. The Soviets captured the pilot, CIA employee Francis Gary Powers, and recovered sections of the plane, photo equipment, and film. Khrushchev cleverly said nothing about the matter, allowing us to use a patently false cover story which subsequently enmeshed our unwitting, highest-level leadership in a series of lies. In fact, none but a handful of persons other than the president were aware of the program. What started with the release that I, among others, cleared, ended in a frightful embarrassment for our nation in the eyes of the world, when President Eisenhower admitted, counter to all expectations, that he had personally authorized the flights. The flight was a clear violation of international law. We were caught red-handed, and Khrushchev made the most of the situation. The Summit Conference and the Eisenhower visit to Russia went down the drain, as did our relations with that country for years to come. America was shocked and embarrassed. My office was both stunned and irritated that we had so palpably been caught up in a lie. At the time, I believed no one in the State Department, not even Secretary of State Christian Herter, knew about the U-2 program.[17] My colleague, John Baker, was so upset about the matter that he seriously considered resigning and had to be dissuaded. It was not our finest hour!

P/PG also approved the speeches of high-level officials of other government departments when they dealt with foreign affairs. I recall clearing an address by Admiral Arleigh Burke, the chief of naval operations, whose legendary World War II exploits earned him the nickname "31 Knot Burke." The address was to be given in Copenhagen at a NATO meeting. It was a strong speech with several anti-Soviet remarks in it, so I made a number of annotations in the draft. On the margin of one section, I commented, "The only thing we are not saying here is that we are going to bomb Moscow!" Most of these speeches were written by officers such as myself, but perhaps this one was not.

I was in bed several days later listening to the 6:30 morning news on the radio, when the unmistakable voice of Senator Strom Thurmond came on. He was criticizing "some bureaucrat in the State Department" for telling Admiral Burke how to run his business. From the references made, it was obvious he was talking about the speech and my comments. The senator appeared quite irritated and determined to do something about it. During the course of that day in the office, I expected that there would be repercussions, and I prepared myself to say that it was my job to deal with bellicose speeches that could cause foreign policy problems. If I ruffled feathers in the process, so be it, but I did feel uneasy about my gratuitous "bomb Moscow" comment on the margin. My boss, Phil Burris, merely noted that I was coming up in the world, taking on the redoubtable Senator Thurmond.

The most taxing single assignment I had while on the Policy Planning and Guidance Staff grew out of a request from Assistant Secretary Berding that I respond to a United Nations requirement for a formal report on the status of freedom of information in the United States. Wisely, the Bureau of United Nations Affairs had deferred acting on this request and passed it on to us with the indication that it was a "public affairs and press-type matter" that was more in our domain. I soon realized that it would take a PhD thesis to answer the UN's questions. The amount of research required was staggering. Mr. Berding said, "Take as much time as you need," but the report was due at the United Nations' offices in New York in a month. I called my wife, Elsa, a Bryn Mawr *summa cum laude* and brilliant researcher, for assistance. This was one more case in those days when wives labored gratis for the department.

We telephoned my mother-in-law, asking her to visit us and help with the children. Arrangements were made for us to have working space at the Library of Congress. When I arrived at the main building of the Library, I was taken to an office on an upper floor far back in the stacks. The sign on the door read "Vice President Nixon." The room was bare save for desks, empty shelves, and a few chairs. It was obvious that it was hardly, if ever, used. It had a window, which afforded a magnificent view to the west, looking out at the Capitol and over the roofs of congressional buildings and the city of Washington. Just outside that office in the stacks—row upon row of old books—were the writings of Thomas Jefferson, James Madison, and other great early Americans, a testimony to the days when men put their spare hours to productive use.

Sitting in that office alone one Sunday evening watching the sun go down over the city, I felt a sense of history and the splendor of our country as never before. I wondered whether, indeed, the chair I was sitting on had been used by Vice President Nixon or any of his predecessors. It was an excellent place to work, and Elsa and I, with the assistance of the Library staff, were soon well along in our research and writing. We labored night and day.

In a month we completed a highly detailed, 120-page document, *The Report to the United Nations on Freedom of Information in the United States*. It included, among other things, information on all facets of the media: legislation covering the flow of information, access to news, standards and codes of ethics, training of journalists, governmental efforts to assist the flow of information, copyright protection, and steps taken to inform the public about the United Nations through governmental and other sources. The work received favorable comment from the UN Secretariat and for us a letter of commendation from the under secretary of state. The task was indicative of the kind of assignment which can suddenly be thrust upon a Foreign Service officer. I certainly would not have been able to complete that voluminous report, which broke new ground in that area of scholarship, without Elsa's superb assistance. In truth, the report was probably more hers than mine.

In the elections of November 1960, the young senator for whom I had written a speech in 1956 became the president of the United States. Although earlier I had not been particularly impressed by John F. Kennedy, his debates with Vice President Nixon changed my opinion, and I voted for him. Subsequently, I was caught up in the euphoria his inauguration address created and was ready to "bear any burden" and "ask not what your country can do for you, but what you can do for your country." A tremendous snowstorm on the eve of that inauguration forced many of us who had to work late to sleep on couches in the office. The winter of 1960–61 was a hard one.

On December 28, 1960, I had also slept in the office rather than fight the heavy snowdrifts out to Fairfax at night. Coming home the following morning, I was barely able to barrel up a hill on the snowy road near our house. That day I was to drive Elsa to the Columbia Hospital for Women in Washington. She was pregnant, considerably overdue, and, on the doctor's advice, arrangements had been made to induce the delivery. With Elsa bundled up in heavy clothing, I proceeded to drive the De Soto convertible back to Washington. This time however, I was not so lucky. The car went into a sideways slide going down that same hill, landing us in a deep snow-filled ditch from which it could not be extricated. With some difficulty we walked the quarter-mile back to the house to try again, this time successfully, with the Wells's old Dodge. Our son, Matthew Tyler Kormann, was born the following day, December 30, 1960. It was a difficult birth, and had we to do it again, we would have waited longer, hoping nature would take its course.

With the change in administration, our office saw an influx of new faces. Roger Tubby, a well-known journalist, became assistant secretary of state for public affairs. I recall during the transition period coming into my office one morning and finding that a second desk had been added. When I inquired as to what was afoot, I was told that we were to receive an additional officer for whom there was temporarily no space. Shortly thereafter, I met my new colleague, an affable black officer named Carl Rowan, who in a matter of a few weeks moved into a larger office to take up his duties as Tubby's deputy assistant secretary of state.

Rowan was assigned to accompany Vice President Lyndon Johnson on his much derided world tour. I was in Mr. Tubby's office the day of his return. As Rowan came into the door, he was greeted with, "Good to have you back, Carl. How did things go?" Rather than respond with something such as, "You will never believe this . . . ," he burst into song. With a fine baritone voice, he began to sing verse after verse of a hilarious ditty he entitled "Around the World with LBJ," to the tune of "Around the World in 80 Days." It must have been some trip! Carl later was to move on to be our ambassador to Finland and, subsequently, director of the U.S. Information Agency.

Periodically, officers on our staff had to deal with matters related to unusually classified or technical subjects, which needed specific high-level security clearances. I recall having to take a sixteen-hour course of instruction in nuclear weapons orientation in February 1961 given by the Defense Atomic Support Agency in the Pentagon. That was a revelation. It was my first exposure to preparations made by our government to protect itself in the event of nuclear attack. I came away soberly aware of what atomic war might mean for our nation and, in particular, my family. That course, later Army War College instruction, and other training I was to have as an Army Reserve officer had a profound effect on my thinking for years to come. After visits to government nuclear emergency evacuation sites deep in the bowels of the earth, I developed my own crisis plans that subsequently resulted in my purchase of a retreat in the mountains of western Maryland.

During these years, I kept up with my Army Reserve training several evenings a month. I entered on two-week, sometimes three-week tours of active duty at the Special Warfare Center at Ft. Bragg, North Carolina. During one of these tours, I completed a Special Forces course. In April of 1961, I was promoted to the rank of major. At this point however, I ran into difficulty with our Office of Personnel. The Army, in an effort to make sure Reserve officers would actually be available in the event of mobilization, sent a letter to the State Department requesting that officers considered "critical" to State's operations be identified. I had the title of Special Assistant to the Assistant Secretary, and unbeknownst to me, I was placed on an unavailable list. I thereupon received word from the Army that I was to be removed from the Active Reserve and placed in the Standby Reserve, which would have made further promotion and continuation on to retirement less likely.

I was also dismayed at the thought of losing the change of scene and excitement that military duty provided. Concerned over this arbitrary action, I went to Personnel, told them that I had many years invested in the military and that their action would deprive me of my pension without due process. I added that since I would be eligible for a twenty-year retirement in less than three more years, I would put in a claim for the many thousands of dollars involved. I then contacted the Army and told them that I would be available. The State Department, possibly taken aback, never took further action. The matter rested, and I continued in the Active Army Reserve. A few years later, as State became more and more involved in politico-military matters, even to the point of setting up a full-fledged Bureau of Politico-Military Affairs, my Reserve status became an asset to both State and the Army.

In the fall of 1961, I entered into the department's three month Mid-Career Course aimed at preparing officers for higher-level policy and program direction responsibilities. This course taught leadership and management techniques as well as individual skills. I recall receiving instruction in public speaking, which over the years, I have found particularly useful. One bit of advice was priceless. The instructor urged us simply to slow down our rate of delivery and witness how much more control it gave us over our ability to speak.

The Mid-Career Course helped convince me of the need for more extensive training of government officers in public speaking and discourse. Programs and budgets of crucial importance to individual organizations were often argued out by personnel ineffective in the conference setting. I found this to be particularly true in interagency meetings when dealing with military representatives. When unable to persuade in the give and take of discussion, they would "stonewall" and simply refuse to clear a document or go along with compromise positions taken by others present. Later at the Army War College, I made it a personal obligation to stress to my military colleagues the importance of training young officers at the Military Academy and the Command and General Staff College to speak effectively to enhance their prospects in the "battle of the conference table." Without success there, I would argue, the resources to succeed anywhere would be lacking.

In early January of 1962, I learned that I was to be assigned as political officer to our embassy in Manila. I had thought that since I was fluent in German, I might be sent back to Germany, but I was pleased nevertheless to be in a traditional Foreign Service assignment. Manila was a large, Class I post in a part of the world I had never seen before. A number of misinformed persons asked me how my Spanish was and, indeed, for a time I thought of taking Spanish language training. However, a few more knowledgeable individuals told me that Spanish was spoken only by a limited number of upper crust mestizos. The masses spoke a variety of native languages, the most prevalent around the main island of Luzon and the city of Manila being Tagalog. English, however, was the *lingua franca*.

To prepare me for my assignment, I enrolled in the two-week Regional Seminar on Southeast Asia, which covered some of the salient aspects of the Philippine political structure and economy. Normally upon being assigned overseas, one obtains a copy of the Post Report, which provides considerable detail about living conditions, clothing needs, required equipment, and many other elements of information important to the families. Post Reports are prepared by personnel assigned there and generally provide a good insight into what might be expected by a newcomer.

The Manila report at the time was memorable in that it subsequently aroused the ire of the ladies. They were told to bring shoes with wedgie heels, since many of the receptions were held in gardens and high heels sank into the soft ground. This seemed logical enough to me, but it must have sent many a female out looking for shoes that had been out of style for years. Hats and gloves were also required for the wives. The women were also informed that black simply was not worn, since "the Filipinos are a happy people."

All that bogus information apparently reflected the views of the elderly, eccentric wife of the ambassador there at the time the report was prepared, who incidentally wore hat and gloves to go shopping in the commissary. Women who managed to find "wedgies" probably never wore them. Nor did they wear hats and gloves. Many probably regretted, however, not bringing their favorite little black cocktail dresses. The men found all of this rather amusing, but I assure you the wives did not.

For my part, I remember trying to find tropical-weight summer suits in February without much success and then ordering several from the T. I. Swartz Clothing Company in Baltimore, which in those days did a great deal of business with the Foreign Service. It was at a time when the lapels on men's suits were their very narrowest. Today, I have a number of these, including white dinner jackets, stored away, still waiting for them to come back in style. As things turned out, shortly after receiving the suits, a government travel freeze was declared, and I was held up until May before we could proceed to Manila. In the interim, I was assigned to the Philippine Desk, part of the time filling in for James McFarland, the officer-in-charge of Philippine affairs.

Spending those months in Washington proved of great value to me. It gave me insight into the department's reaction to incoming messages and its attitude toward various officers at the post. I established friendships with people who would be reading my reports, particularly McFarland and Robert Ballantyne, the economic affairs officer for the region.

During this layover, I became involved in a circumstance about which acquaintances still tweak me. New telephone books were distributed to our office one day, and I made the mistake of offhandedly telling McFarland that as a youngster I used to practice tearing the old ones in half. Incredulous, he insisted I demonstrate. Had that been all there was to it, everything would have been fine. However, several days later he came to me with a plea. He had informed his young handicapped son of the feat. The boy, in turn, had told all his friends at the school for disabled children he attended. Would I, McFarland asked, visit the school and tear a telephone book for his son's class. While I thought the world of Jim, this was a bit much, and I declined. He pleaded with me, saying I just did not understand how much it would mean to the children. Because of their handicaps, they were inordinately fascinated by acts of physical prowess.

The following week, I found myself on the stage of a school auditorium filled with children and teachers. As I stood there I thought how could I, a supposedly sensible adult and Foreign Service officer, possibly have placed myself in such a position. The principal introduced me to the cheers of the children. Looking into their expectant faces I remembered McFarland's words and concluded: who cares whether I am embarrassed or not, these kids are the ones who matter. I did my best to put on a show, telling them how as a boy I tried and tried until I finally was able to tear my first book. The important thing was to keep trying.

Then, with feigned exertion and a final lion-like roar, I tore a telephone book in half from the binding side. The place went wild. I doubt if there ever was a more appreciative audience. I concluded by taking pages out of the book and autographing them as souvenirs for the children. It did not take long for word of my school visit to spread around the State Department, particularly after the school sent it a letter of appreciation. Even to this day it is a source of merriment for old colleagues who quip, "Have you torn any phone books lately?"

While filling in for Jim McFarland on the Philippine desk, I had a bit of trouble with Averell Harriman, our envoy to Moscow during World War II and later governor of New York. He was currently the assistant secretary of state for Far Eastern affairs, which included the Philippines. He was in his seventies, but still very active. While on a visit to the islands, he entered into discussions related to a tobacco agreement between our two countries. He sent back a message about the negotiations in which he indicated that we should pass the information on to Congressman Cooley, then chairman of the House Agriculture Committee. I did so. A few days later a newspaper reported about the matter, citing Cooley. Ambassador Harriman upon his return saw the item and was extremely upset saying, "Who told Congress about this?" I indicated that I had passed the information to Chairman Cooley. He was furious at me, evidently forgetting the instructions he had sent from Manila. I wanted to get out the telegram and show him what he had said, but under the circumstances thought better of it. He was a great man, but at his age he had lapses of memory and could be very touchy.

I received an office visit one morning from an assistant naval attaché at the Philippine Embassy, a personable senior lieutenant in his late twenties. He was a graduate of the U.S. Naval Academy at Annapolis. When he learned that I would soon be on my way to Manila, he provided me with much helpful information and in no time we became quite friendly. He told me he would be returning home on assignment in a few months and looked forward to seeing me there and acquainting me with his native land.

During those final months in Washington, we put our house up for sale, deciding that with three children we would want a larger place. Disposing of a house can be an exhausting experience and one of the drawbacks of a life of continual moves in the Foreign Service. We finally sold our home in Fairfax, Virginia, for a few thousand more than the original purchase price. Twelve years earlier when we went to Germany, we had no children, furniture, or household effects. By contrast, after seven years of duty in Washington, we had accumulated a great deal. We also had to consider our two cars—a 1957 De Soto convertible and a 1953 Dodge sedan—since neither was suitable for shipping to our new post. We managed to sell both, the Dodge more as a gift to a neighbor.

I sought Jim McFarland's advice before ordering a new car for delivery in Manila. Receiving it there avoided the high stateside taxes. He counseled that I take a four-door sedan with air-conditioning that could double as an official car. Air-conditioners in automobiles were a relatively new and expensive option in those days, and I questioned his advice. We had never had one in our previous cars and had managed to survive blistering summer days during our visits to my parents in Florida. He pointed out, however, that we would always be driving with the windows closed, whether under the tropical sun on dusty Philippine roads or at a snail's pace through crowded Manila streets, where thieves reach in open windows to snatch wristwatches from one's arm. That settled the matter, and the Kormann family bought their first air-conditioned car, a black Chevrolet taxicab model. McFarland's counsel turned out to be a godsend.

The Wellses and Mother Kormann came to Washington to see us off. We all had dinner together, and the following morning Elsa, the children, and I were driven over to Baltimore's Friendship Airport. We boarded a propeller-driven plane for the long flight to the West Coast and our voyage by ship across the Pacific. After a short stay visiting sights in the San Francisco area, we embarked on the S. S. *President Wilson*, a large passenger liner and the flagship of the American President Lines. It was to be a passage of twenty-one days.

Sailing out under the Golden Gate Bridge at sunset into the vast Pacific Ocean is a memorable experience, one we were glad we could share with the children. We were out to sea only a few hours when we encountered heavy swells in what had appeared to be relatively normal seas, and a number of passengers, including Elsa, had their initial bout of seasickness. Travel aboard the *President Wilson* in first class, however, was the ultimate in luxury. A stewardess took charge of the children; they and other youngsters on board were looked after in special playrooms and entertained royally. They joined the "Junior Sailing Club," for which each child received a made-to-measure sailor suit from the ship's tailor. The children were fed at separate early sittings. Everything possible was done so that their parents could be free to enjoy themselves, feasting, partying, and dancing the night away.

In reading my wife's letters, written while on shipboard, I was again reminded of just how gracious ocean travel used to be. Incidentally, the ship's stationery she used had been placed in our stateroom imprinted "Mr. and Mrs. John G. Kormann" below the letterhead. At our first port of call, Honolulu, we were met by an old friend of the Wells family, Ingeborg Shields, whose husband headed the Chamber of Commerce. They were our hosts and saw to it that we all had a marvelous time. Stays in Yokohama, Tokyo, and Hong Kong proved interesting. On the leg down from Japan to Hong Kong, the ship encountered a typhoon and many a passenger said "amen" at the sight of land.

Hong Kong, in my opinion, is unrivaled in its scenic quality. We sailed into a harbor alive with ferries, sampans, junks, freighters, ocean liners, and naval vessels, including an aircraft carrier, a light cruiser, and several destroyers. Steep peak-like hills ring the harbor, while skyscrapers and other buildings crowd the city and extend up the hillsides. Activity bustled everywhere. With that visit and subsequent ones, Hong Kong became our favorite city in the Far East.

10
The Philippines: From Macapagal to Marcos

Our shipboard idyll came to a halt on our arrival in hot and humid Manila. A member of the embassy's political section came aboard to meet us and soon we were whisked into our new assignment, which unbeknownst to us at the time, was to last more than four years. The downtown areas of the city reminded me of Spanish Harlem in New York, yet with far more poverty and squalor. We promptly settled in an apartment building not far from the embassy's offices. I reported for work while Elsa hired household help and began her round of calls on embassy and diplomatic wives. I soon called on Ambassador William Stevenson, a tall, handsome man in his sixties who had once been president of Oberlin College. A staunch Democrat, he was a Kennedy Administration political appointee to the post. He and his wife Betty, nicknamed "Bumpy," were a gracious and engaging couple for whom it was a pleasure to work. Their daughter was the wife of the governor of New Jersey.

Even at this early stage we received numerous invitations and became immersed in Manila's diplomatic social whirl. My relationship with the deputy chief of mission, Minister John Gordon Mein, got off to a rough start. We were invited to a diplomatic dinner at his residence during our second week at the post. Foreign Service custom required that Elsa and I arrive ten minutes beforehand to assist in preparations and greet any early foreign guests. We departed with more than a half hour to spare for the ten- minute drive, but the taxi driver, who professed to know the area, took us to an incorrect location, completely out of the way, and we arrived twenty minutes late.

What made matters worse was that we had been invited by ourselves to an informal dinner there the previous week and the minister had been so kind as to drive us home. Later, with the arrival of our private car and our better knowledge of the city, there were no further such occurrences. We never forgot that lesson as we were thoroughly dressed down. Once we came to know them, however, we found Gordon and Betty Mein exceptionally fine representatives. It was with great sadness that we were later to learn of his assassination while serving as our ambassador to Guatemala.

The U.S. Embassy in Manila was one of the largest in the world, easily comparable to those in Europe. Our presence grew out of the former colonial status of the Philippines, which left many residual American business interests, a large number of U.S. citizens, and several important military installations.[1] Among the latter scattered on the main island of Luzon were Subic Naval Base, Cubi Point Marine Air Station, Clark Air Base, Sangley Naval Air Station, the Manila Naval Port Activity, and the San Miguel Communications Facility. Other U.S. government agencies maintained Asian regional support activities there. The total American presence ran into the hundreds of thousands. Personnel attached to the Embassy numbered about a thousand.

I was assigned to the embassy's Political Section handling external affairs, that is, the Philippines' relations with other countries, including the United States, as differentiated from internal affairs, which dealt with reporting on political and other matters within the country. I was pleased, for that was where my interest lay in any event. I replaced Paul Kattenburg, an extremely able officer, who was well liked by the Filipinos. Paul was later deeply involved in Vietnam affairs, demonstrating great insight into the problems to be encountered. His perceptiveness and outspoken views put him at cross-purposes with our national leadership, and he retired at age fifty to enter academia.[2] Southeast Asia was in turmoil during those years. The war in Vietnam was under way. In addition, Indonesia, under the capricious presidency of Sukarno, was embroiled in a dispute and subsequent war with Malaysia over Sabah (North Borneo).

It was a period full of exaggerated international maneuvering, which saw the creation of MAPHILINDO, an organization designed to foster cooperation between Malaysia, the Philippines, and Indonesia. Behind the scenes, the United States endeavored to influence Manila to mediate the dispute over Sabah. At the same time, we were engaged in diplomatic and other efforts to support our forces in the war in Vietnam. SEATO, the Southeast Asia Treaty Organization, provided the rationale for American participation in deterring communist aggression in Vietnam. The Philippines was a member of SEATO, and we worked closely with it on matters related to that conflict. Subsequently, when the post of secretary general of SEATO became vacant, I was very much involved in seeing to it that General Jesus Vargas, a Filipino, was selected.[3]

I soon became aware that much of my business was to be transacted not through visits to government offices or calls at embassies but at endless rounds of social functions. While this occurred at other posts as well, it was especially the case in Manila. At one reception, I might encounter a half dozen foreign diplomats and Filipino officials I could query in response to a cable from Washington. Handling external affairs generally required establishing closer relations with these individuals in a friendly environment. It was important, therefore, to settle into a house suitable for representational purposes as soon as possible. Nevertheless, it took us several months to find one, and then at a rental above our housing allowance. Our choice was a spacious, newly constructed villa with a garden in the suburb of San Lorenzo. It had large living and dining rooms, capable of holding 250–300 guests. The floors were terrazzo, with beautifully inlaid stone, a reflection of magnificent Filipino handiwork.

I was surprised at the extensive role played by women in the Philippines. They generally handled the money in the family and were the landlords. In buying or renting a house, one virtually always dealt with a woman. Many were factory owners, business proprietors, and professionals. A speaker at an embassy wives' group explained that this harkened back to previous centuries, when women had to conceal their men from the harsh hand of the Spanish occupiers. As a result "women became men and men became boys." On the other hand, men would act as if they wore the pants in the family, often resorting to macho displays and gun-toting cowboy antics.

After arduous examinations, four and three hours in length, our children, Brad and Andrea, were admitted to the fourth and second grades, respectively, at the private American School in Manila. Later, my wife taught American History and U.S. Government at the high-school level there. How she managed this is still a wonder to me, considering that she was running a household with several servants and involved in constant entertaining, charity work, and a vast array of social obligations. We soon became aware that the Filipinos were a gracious, warm, generous, and hospitable people. When we arrived, the average Filipino was well disposed toward the United States, growing out of the experiences of World War II. As I will elaborate later, however, the Vietnam War had a corroding effect on our position, particularly with certain sectors of the press and the intelligentsia.

During the summer of 1962, my Filipino friend, the young assistant naval attaché, returned with his family from his assignment in Washington. Elsa and I went down to the ship to meet them. We drove them out to their simple home in a downtown neighborhood and helped them get settled. I met with him a few times after that and recall his informing me that he was resigning from the Philippine Navy to take a job in the government. His wife was related to a member of President Macapagal's cabinet who evidently had been influential in obtaining the position for him.

I thought nothing much of the matter at the time, but two years later I was invited to a housewarming for the couple's new residence in the suburbs. It was a palatial place on a hill, with a fine view of the surrounding country. The outer foyer displayed a small waterfall cascading down the stones on one wall. This home and the Mercedes car parked in the driveway were a far cry from his previous ramshackle bungalow and dilapidated Ford station wagon. When I wondered whence this wealth had come, I learned that through family influence he had been given an important position in the government. I was told that, after all, this was the Philippines. Some time later on a trip to the countryside, I had occasion to talk with the mayor of a small town. Commenting on a story then in the press about President Macapagal and nepotism, I remarked that steps should be taken to curb the practice. My listener was surprised, responding, "How can I expect him to take care of me, if he won't take care of his own family!"

Corruption was pervasive in the Philippines. During my first year in Manila, the media were full of the Stonehill Case. Harry Steinberg, who had changed his name to Stonehill, was a former member of the U.S. Army. Staying in the Islands after World War II, he had amassed a fortune through selling military surplus and black marketeering. He was a wheeler-dealer of the first rank. Virtually every politician of importance was on his payroll or indebted to him in one way or another. A scandal broke when a close associate named Spielman turned state's evidence against Stonehill, who had the man killed. In the middle of the Spielman murder trial, Stonehill asked to be deported to Canada, a request promptly granted by President Macapagal. The latter had come to office on an anticorruption platform, but it was not long before he took the path of his predecessors. Mrs. Macapagal, like Imelda Marcos after her, was known as the "bag lady." It was through the wives that much of the money was funneled. Emmanuel Pelaez, who was Macapagal's running mate as vice president and reputed for his honesty and incorruptibility, was forced to resign that office as a consequence of the Stonehill scandal. However, he concurrently held the position of foreign minister, a post he retained. Other cabinet members also resigned as a result of the affair.

Early in our tour in Manila, we had one of our most memorable experiences. The Philippine Navy offered to provide a launch to take U.S. embassy employees on a Saturday picnic to Corregidor Island, twenty-three miles out in Manila Bay, a two-hour trip. So many families signed up, 120 persons in all, however, that a Landing Craft Medium (LCM) was provided instead. The LCM, a World War II vintage vessel, had a bow door to accommodate troops and tanks in beachhead invasions. Elsa, Brad, and I were among those who departed on the trip in brilliant sunshine and high spirits.

Upon reaching Corregidor, we experienced a considerable delay, because no one in the crew knew how to drop the anchor. We learned later that the skipper, a Philippine Navy senior lieutenant, had only taken a craft of this type out once before. About this time the weather changed, the skies darkened, and the rains began. Families gathered under a leaky tarp in the open craft's bottom awaiting word. After further delay, it was announced that we were turning back for the long trip home. The weather became stormy and the seas rough. To get out of the squall, many of the families crowded into the crew's quarters in a conning tower–type structure on one side of the craft.

Aware that the open, flat-bottomed vessel without heavy ballast could easily capsize in the wind given the inexperienced seamanship of the skipper, I insisted that Elsa and Brad stay with me on an open, upper perch next to the bow door. While this exposed us to the elements, at least we would be thrown into the open sea, should we roll over, while others might be trapped in or under the vessel. We remained there, soaked to the skin and shivering.

As we entered Manila Harbor two hours later, little did we realize our ordeal was far from over. The squall intensified with near gale force winds, and the skipper went to pieces. First he approached the Navy pier, but was afraid to come alongside for fear of severely damaging the LCM. He proceeded down to the ocean liners' dock, then back up to the Navy pier, then back downtown, too frightened to make a decision. Finally, to our astonishment, he headed wildly out to sea again. It was already late afternoon and the passengers were drenched and freezing; some were seasick, others near hysteria. The LCM, with no keel or ballast, was rocking precipitously. One of the young secretaries aboard, trying to get out of the weather and the two inches of water sloshing about on the bottom of the boat, fell down the tower stairwell to a deck below, injuring herself seriously.

By this time our embassy men were ready to take over. Minister Mein, who was aboard with his family, told the skipper to beach the craft across the bay at the U.S. Sangley Naval Air Station at Cavite, about a forty-five minutes' sail away. Efforts were made to raise Sangley on the radio and by blinker distress signals. Some time later, perhaps thinking we were nearing Sangley and the shore, the crew opened the bow door. We prepared to wade through the surf to the beach, only to observe to our dismay that, with night upon us, we were still almost a mile out at sea. Then out of the dark and rain, we saw a U.S. Navy air/sea rescue crash-boat approaching rapidly through the heavy seas. Despite both vessels pitching wildly, our stretcher case (she had lost a lot of blood) was transferred and rushed back to shore, accompanied by my boss, Political Counselor Max Krebs, the embassy's third-ranking officer. Half an hour later, a larger Navy vessel came alongside and, although the transfer, again, was precarious, everyone was taken aboard safely.

Once at Sangley, we were provided with shelter and hot drinks. Arrangements were made to ferry us in three powerful Navy launches back to Manila, which we reached at 8:30 pm, more than thirteen hours after our trip began. A day or two later, we learned that the LCM was still where we had left it. The anchor had been dropped to facilitate our departure, but the winch broke and the anchor could not be raised. Subsequently, the senior lieutenant was court-martialed for his ineptitude and, more likely, for having embarrassed the Philippine Navy. Had that LCM capsized miles out at sea, many embassy lives might have been lost to drowning, or possibly to the sharks common in those waters.

At one point, William Bruns, the officer charged with handling politico-military affairs for the embassy, was called back to Washington to sit on the promotion boards for several months, and I was designated to assume his duties in addition to my external affairs responsibilities. This was to set the stage for later occasions when I took over the job for extended periods. I enjoyed working with the Navy, Air Force, and the Joint U.S. Military Assistance Group (JUSMAG) and might ordinarily have been happy to have that position on a permanent basis. However, external affairs was where the diplomatic action was and the area coveted by FSOs. Having both jobs, while exhausting, was very satisfying.

During the ensuing months, I did a great deal of reporting. Ambassador Stevenson relied heavily on me to analyze the turbulent events taking place between the Philippines, Indonesia, and Malaysia. Not only during the workweek, but Saturday mornings and often on Sundays, I would be in the office discussing these matters either with him, Minister Richard Service, who replaced Gordon Mein, or Max Krebs. Sometimes all three would be present. After those sessions, I would draft a cable or airgram conveying the embassy's views as to what course of action the U.S. government should take. As I look back on it, I never worked in a more cooperative atmosphere. They were first-class officers who elicited the most out of me. When I took my drafts to them, there was no nitpicking; their suggestions were constructive and I benefited from their insight. Washington was also high in its praises of the embassy's reporting, which made me work all the harder.

From my years back in the Department, I had become aware that certain reporting officers established reputations for themselves. I now had an opportunity to emulate them. Their messages were well crafted and a delight to read; they were able to convey situations in a few pithy sentences. I recall drafting innumerable telegrams and airgrams related to actions our government should take with regard to various problems and crises in wartorn Southeast Asia.

Serving in Manila had many interesting aspects, and, in hindsight, amusing aspects. On the social side of business, the Filipinos were notorious for accepting invitations and then simply not appearing without excusing themselves or explaining their actions. There were other quirks, as well. In diplomatic entertaining, for example, a dinner party for fourteen is an ideal size. It allows for proper protocol seating at the table and sufficient, but not too many, guests for the cook and servants to manage. In the Philippines, however, that is a dangerous number.

A senior embassy wife, shortly after our arrival, told us of having given a sit-down dinner for fourteen. When one of the guests failed to arrive, the Filipinos present, among them a cabinet member, hesitated to come to a table of thirteen for fear of inviting bad luck. Finally, in desperation, the hostess went upstairs and prevailed upon her fourteen-year-old daughter to dress herself and attend the dinner. After that tale, the Kormanns, to allow for proper seating, planned dinner parties of 10, 18, or, in one instance, 22. This allowed the hostess to repay as many obligations as possible at one time, while also obfuscating the positioning of lower-ranking persons at the center of the table.

While we had our share of diplomatic dinners, our preference was for large cocktail parties and receptions. Later in my tour, when I might be called upon at the last minute to miss my own party because of some crisis or called out of town, my absence would not be as apparent. Elsa, however, still talks about my failure to appear at a reception to which we invited 250 guests. That time my absence was noted the following day in the newspaper column of one of the journalists we had invited, causing him to speculate as to what was afoot. In fact, the embassy had just received word that a coup was underway in Saigon and that the Philippines was designated an emergency evacuation site. I was needed to monitor the situation and respond to incoming messages.

No discussion of diplomatic social life would be complete or candid on my part if I did not address one of my strong peeves. A visiting American congressman late in the evening at a dinner once said to me, "You fellows have a grand job, going from one cocktail party to another." As blandly as I could, I responded that the dinner was the third social function I had attended that evening. At them, my drinking had been limited largely to ginger ale, and I had talked to about ten host country officials and foreign diplomats at earlier receptions and at the dinner on a matter of concern to our government. I added that after we were finished that night, I would be heading back to the Embassy to send a cable about what I had learned to Washington, so that given the international time difference, it would be there before the close of business that day, clearly inferring that he, on the other hand, would likely be returning to his hotel and going to bed. My wife might have also told him that it was no blessing to be away from home night after night, leaving our children in the care of servants.

As I had done during my other assignments, I continued to remain active in the Army Reserve. With a large community of Americans in Manila, many veterans of the military services wished to retain their affiliation. The Army Reserve unit was a thriving operation, well-led and organized. I was promptly enrolled in a section completing Command and General Staff College instruction. My position in the embassy as the official handling politico-military affairs was useful in establishing a relationship with key officers in the Reserve organization. On the other hand, my rank as a major impressed no one when I was assigned for my annual tour of active duty with the JUSMAG (Joint U.S. Military Assistance Group). Duty there was convenient and meant I could go home every evening as well as keep tabs on the office.

However, walking into JUSMAG headquarters as a major and being assigned duties of an officer of that rank were quite different from arriving as a civilian in my embassy capacity to meet with the general in command. While it permitted me to establish friendships with the officers there, it probably also did not enhance my authority when I dealt with them subsequently. Thereafter, I sought annual duty with commands elsewhere in the Pacific region. In another year, for example, I was assigned to Army Military Intelligence Group, Korea. Not only did my tour permit me to see that country, but to do so in grand style. After the colonel in charge of that organization and I had swapped World War II stories, he came up with the brilliant idea of suggesting to the military attaché at the American Embassy in Seoul that he take me along on his rounds visiting various Korean and American commands. The attaché's powerful, radial engine, Army "Beaver" aircraft enabled us to fly expeditiously all around the country, from the DMZ in the north to Pusan in the south. I had an excellent opportunity to meet South Korean officers, which might ordinarily have never occurred.

Before I left Seoul, I called on our Embassy and had an extensive discussion with Political Counselor Philip Habib. He was interested to have my assessment of MAPHILINDO developments and was intrigued that I had managed to obtain so broad an exposure to Korea in such a short time.

My participation in Command and General Staff College studies led to two of the most pleasant military assignments I have ever had. As part of our instruction, my two-week active duty assignments were to the Pacific Branch of the College at Ft. DeRussy in Honolulu, located on Waikiki Beach. While there, I had an opportunity to visit with my cousin, Susan Poremba, whose husband, Stanley, a Naval Academy graduate, served as an executive officer aboard a submarine based at Pearl Harbor. On one of our trips en route to Manila, he took us aboard his boat, which was quite a thrill, particularly for Brad.

At the Staff College quarters in Honolulu, I shared a billet with a captain who was a Hawaiian of Japanese extraction. He was a most engaging roommate with a wonderful collection of friends of similar background, who were also in the course. This group took a shine to me and I to them. One of them happened to be a celebrity in the Islands, a very popular singer. Our classes began at 7:00 a.m. and concluded at 2:30 in the afternoon, leaving ample time for the beach and many evenings (when, alas, we should have been studying) for nightclubbing. At the clubs, usually in some major hotel, our entrance would cause a stir the moment our celebrity colleague was recognized. He would be handed a ukulele and from then on, drinks would be on the house.

My effort to assimilate things Hawaiian did not fare so well, however, when one afternoon I decided to go surfing. I had never done so before. Arriving at a rental place on the beach, I picked out a surfboard with which I felt comfortable. The proprietor, however, took a look at me and said that for my weight and build, I should have a larger board. He then gave me a longer and considerably heavier one. Lugging that massive thing down to the water, I launched myself, along with other surfers, into the waves. Paddling out about 75 yards, I attempted to ride a wave in, with absolutely no success. I was not getting enough of a wave to stand. I thought I should be much farther out, where some of the other surfers were. Again no luck. Repeating this process another time, I became aware that I was out as far, if not farther than any of the other surfers, all of whom were catching waves back to the beach.

Deeming my surfing experiment a failure and forgoing any further attempt, I began paddling for shore. I found myself alone. The high-rise hotels were small objects on the skyline. It seemed as if I was making no headway on the heavy surfboard and then, suddenly, I heard the unmistakable sound of a steamship's foghorn. Glancing around, I beheld a terrifying sight. There, closer to me than the shore, I saw a stately ocean liner cruising by. I knew then that I was in serious trouble; a tide was impeding my progress and possibly moving me farther out to sea. For the next hour or more, with all the strength I had, I paddled furiously on that surfboard toward shore. Gradually, I could see I was making progress; the closer to land I came, the better my forward movement. Finally, I washed ashore.

I do not know how long I lay exhausted on the beach before I was able to get up and drag the surfboard back to the rental place, which had already closed for the day. I left it there propped against the doorway and went back the following afternoon for my deposit.

Although the surfing episode put a damper on my spirits for the moment, my Hawaiian friends soon had me back in better fettle. When it came time for me to return to Manila, they, along with our singing celebrity and his ukulele, insisted on driving me to the airport and seeing me off. Bringing leis and farewell presents, they again caused a stir in the terminal, resulting in my being given VIP treatment by airport officials. It was a heart-warming experience.

Early in 1963, Francis (Frank) Tatu, who had been the aide to the ambassador, was assigned as my assistant. He was a Chinese language officer, very able and knowledgeable. Having Frank available meant that I was not tied down continuously. It was during this period that Glen Fisher, an economic officer serving also as the minerals attaché, approached me, asking whether I would be interested in joining him on a flight to Borneo. We could take a week's leave over the Easter holidays, when the Philippines, a Catholic country, largely shut down. He had a single-engine Piper Tri-Pacer airplane and planned to island hop the thousand or more miles down the Philippines and the Sulu Archipelago. Below the Tawitawi Islands in the Celebes Sea, we would cross over to Borneo. The flight would then follow the coast north 350 miles to Sandakan, the principal city in the eastern part of former British North Borneo, now called Sabah. It sounded like a great adventure and an opportunity to do some good reporting.

Though I was all for it, there were some political ramifications. We would be going into a war zone, with Indonesia and Malaysia fighting over claims to the area. I told Fisher that the ambassador, much less Washington, probably would never approve of such a trip. However, I would broach the subject with Minister Service. I mentioned the trip to other embassy officers, who, to my chagrin, all smiled knowingly. Evidently, Fisher had been trying for some time to coax others into flying with him, with negative results. One not so reticent friend quipped, "He must have heard that you were a nutty ex-paratrooper and a likely candidate!"

Fisher had bought his second-hand Piper in the United States in damaged condition while on home leave. It had been taken apart, shipped out to Manila and rebuilt by Filipino mechanics. He had flown the plane when stationed at our Consulate on the central island of Cebu to our south. My colleagues pointed out that he had experienced a crash or two there. I discussed the proposed flight with Minister Service and he, in turn, with Ambassador Stevenson. Both took a dim view of the idea.

I learned that according to Philippine Aviation Authority records, no aircraft had flown out of the southern Philippines to Borneo since World War II, some twenty years earlier. There were no airports after Cebu and Zamboanga. Any landings on the long stretch south and then up the Borneo coast to Sandakan would have to be made on makeshift fields or beaches. With that the matter rested except for two local flights with Fisher in his plane and a session going over aeronautical charts for the abandoned trip. As I flew with him and got to know him a bit better, he impressed me as a methodical, skilled, and cautious pilot.

In the meantime, the conflict in Sabah continued, with reports of skirmishes between Indonesian and Malaysian forces. One dispatch we received discussed a trip upriver into the interior of Sabah by a British agent working for Malaysia. In the jungles, he had met with headhunting Dyak tribesmen and had come back bearing the "red feather," a token of their support. All of this to me seemed straight out of a Rudyard Kipling novel.

I had virtually forgotten about the Borneo trip when for some reason the ambassador changed his mind. Provided we were exceedingly cautious and exercised good judgment, we were told we could go. I could not believe my ears, especially given my second thoughts and the stepped-up fighting in Sabah. Perhaps the opportunity to obtain firsthand accounts was too enticing for the State Department or CIA.

Just prior to our departure, the British military attaché came to my office requesting assistance. He had learned of our trip and wondered whether we could provide information on a matter of concern to his government. A launch with several English men and women aboard had been captured in the waters off Borneo by a Sulu pirate named Amok. The captives were taken to one of the many small islands in the southern Philippines we would be flying over. Could we help in locating them or obtain any information about them? I told the attaché that we would gladly be of assistance, reporting anything we learned. He warned me that Sulu pirates were known for their ferocity. They had fired on a British gunboat and when it blasted them out of the water, the survivors made a raft out of the corpses of those killed and paddled three miles to the shore of a nearby island.

When I mentioned Amok to a longtime American resident in the Philippines, I was informed that the pirate's exploits were legendary. He added that *amok* in Malay is the origin of our English term "amok" (or "amuck"). It connotes a frenzied homicidal mania, peculiar to the Malays, as well as to the Moros in the Southern Philippines, during which they will rush out and attack everyone recklessly. The struggle by American troops against the Moros after the Spanish-American War resulted in the development of the large-bore, .45-caliber pistol. A bullet of that size was required to knock them down, stopping them in their fanatical attacks.

In addition to a thorough inspection and fueling of the plane, our preparations consisted of further study of the charts. Numerous markings denoted villages and other habitation along our route on the Philippine stretch, but virtually nothing but two or three isolated, widely dispersed designations of single houses along the hundreds of miles of Borneo coast. As for equipment and emergency provisions, we decided not to take any guns, since they would only create problems with local authorities or customs. We opted for two bolos (machetes) instead. Flying over wide stretches of open seas made lifevests and a life raft an absolute necessity. For provisions, we took canned meat and some high-energy items, such as fig newtons and dates.

We took off at dawn on April 9, 1963, for Cebu, a distance of 375 miles; much of it was over water, but usually islands were in sight in the far distance. Landing at Cebu City Airport in under four hours, we gassed up for the second slightly shorter but more formidable leg to Zamboanga on the island of Mindanao. On this stretch, once we were south of the islands of Cebu and Bohol, we would be over open seas with no land in sight for a long distance. Landfall would be the high coastal mountain range on northern Mindanao. The plane was performing well. En route Fisher instructed me on its handling and had me take the controls from time to time. We were both a bit apprehensive as land dropped away, but soon got used to it.

I can remember my reaction as we spotted Mindanao. I was happy to see land, but taken aback at the sight of the mountains. The Piper Tri-Pacer flew best in altitudes under 5,000 feet; over that it had problems. Some of these mountains were 10,000 feet high. Now it was a matter of finding passes between them. Fisher, with the sense of a bush pilot, maneuvered us through them. After that, we were flying over dense forests and slash-and-burn agricultural lands of this, the Philippines' largest island. The airport in Zamboango was little more than a dirt field at the time. Fisher brought the plane down nicely, scattering a herd of goats as we landed. We overnighted there as guests of a Catholic mission. The priest in charge was well known to Fisher and the members of our Consulate in Cebu.

Early the following morning, we were off again to the island and city of Jolo, 100 miles to the south. As we flew, we would note beaches and other areas on tiny islands ahead that might serve as possible emergency landing sites. Our landing in Jolo was on a rough piece of open ground, where a crowd of mostly children chased behind our plane. Local officials were surprised to hear that we planned to fly on to Kalimantan, as Borneo is known in Malay. Adding fuel from cans we carried with us, Glen and

I mused over the final and most treacherous part of the trip. Once we reached the halfway point of this stretch below the tiny island of Sibutu, our fuel level would be such that there would be no turning back. After that, it was open water over to Borneo and the flight up along a coast barely charted.

We had come this far and were not about to change our plans. With that thought, we flew ever southward over Bolipongpong and the Tawitawi Islands. Occasionally, we would observe island shores sprouting fishing villages with nipa huts on stilts out over the water or bancas (outrigger dugout canoes), with their brightly colored lateen sails. Other times, looking down into the blue-green water, I could spot dark shadows just beneath the surface. I would point out a particularly large one to Glen, with the comment, "That's got to be one big shark!"

At the point of no return, with the engine running smoothly, we veered west toward Borneo. Our anxiety during the next hour being so far from any shore, was nothing compared to making landfall! We were stunned at the sight of the forbidding coast of Borneo, shrouded in thunderclouds rising from the ground to thousands of feet into the sky. There was no way that small Piper plane was going to fly over those clouds or through them. Turning back now was out of the question. We simply had to fly northward along their seaward edge and hope for the best. This meant staying out from the coast, not being able to cut across a peninsula, and thus lengthening our flight and running down our fuel supply. My partner took the plane to near its maximum altitude and proceeded along the coast.

I was deep in thought pondering if we were ever going to make it to Sandakan, when, without warning, the plane went into a half barrel-roll dive. My heart dropped into my shoes. Fisher, ever keenly watching for a passage through the clouds, suddenly spotted an opening. Ambivalent about cursing him out royally for scaring the wits out of me, or praising him for being so observant, I watched as he maneuvered the plane inland, then northward. Below we saw nothing but hundreds of miles of mangrove swamps with serpentine streams weaving through them. Traversing one mile in those swamps, if you could move at all, you would likely cross the same stream ten times. I found myself straining to see if I could spot some of the huge saltwater crocodiles one associates with Borneo and East Indian islands.

After a while, we again came out over the coast. Although on the lookout for any signs of habitation as we flew, I saw none. At one point, we came to the estuary of a great river, the water from it muddying the ocean for many miles out to sea. Offshore, the water appeared to be filled with thousands of matchsticks. It soon dawned on us that we were looking at logs, and from our height, they had to be massive tree trunks, prime hard-wood from the jungles of Borneo further inland. A short distance out to sea we observed several ships—Japanese freighters—towing long stretches of that timber. Even in those days before our great concern with ecology, the sight sickened me. I felt even worse when later I was told that those logs might well have been turned into chopsticks. The Japanese used fresh wooden chopsticks for every meal.

As we moved up the coast closer to Sandakan, we passed over small islands with high cone-like volcanic peaks, one giving off wisps of white smoke. Even though we had sent a message ahead to the Sabah authori-ties, our landing at the tidy little airport created a bit of excitement. I was immediately struck by how British everything was. Arrangements were made to take us into town and to put us up in a small hillside hotel that seemed to be reserved for English expatriates and foreign businessmen. Hollywood would have been well satisfied to use the hotel as a set for a movie set in 1920s Burma or Singapore.

Sandakan itself was a miniature Hong Kong. Native policemen with Malay-Indochinese features in British-type uniforms, with shorts, puttees, and clodhopper shoes, stood on little raised platforms directing traffic at intersections. Schoolchildren in white shirts and black shorts played soc-cer. There was a cricket match underway on one of the lovely green play-ing fields. It was a very neat, clean, and orderly city, a far cry from Manila. Time, I thought, has passed this place by, and I had been transported back to another world. The following day we met with the resident, the gov-ernment official in charge of the area. Although Sandakan was now part of an independent Malaysia, he was an Englishman and, as I recall, was formerly the British resident for the district. He gave us a briefing and seemed pleased that we had come, likely taking our presence as an indi-cation that the United States looked with approval upon developments there. We, on the other hand, asserted that we were simply on an Easter vacation break from our embassy duties.

We spent the next day visiting various places around Sandakan, in-cluding a spotlessly clean fish market with a vast variety of sealife. We sounded out the local citizenry on their views of the current situation. That evening we were the guests of the resident for cocktails. Early the second morning, with the plane inspected and gassed-up we departed for home. I felt more at ease on the return flight. We knew what to expect, but were still awed by the vast expanse of territory showing no signs of habi-tation as we flew over. Throughout the trip we bore in mind the request from the British military attaché in Manila concerning the kidnapped Eng-lish citizens, but we had learned nothing new.

We had crossed the expanse of open seas between Borneo and the southern Philippines and were heading north over Sibutu Island when I happened to glance down. There, up a river estuary, lying on its side on a sand bar, was a boat. I shouted for Glen to go around and make another pass. No question about it, that was the launch the British military attaché had described. The area, however, seemed deserted. Had we even thought of landing, there was no place we could have done so and we flew on.

That evening we again overnighted in Zamboanga, only to awake the following morning to a cloudy day and a less than favorable weather report. To complicate matters further, our host, the friendly Irish priest at the Catholic mission, asked if we might take him with us to Manila, for he had business there. He was a big, heavy-set man, and while there was a third seat in the plane, our luggage and equipment made it a tight squeeze. The extra weight was going to cause us problems getting over the mountains in northern Mindanao.

We waited several hours. I could see that Fisher was worried and wanted to delay takeoff even further, perhaps until the next day, hoping for a better weather report. The priest and I, however, were anxious to leave. We prevailed. I was stupid and, given Glen's superb performance to that point, should have immediately supported his judgment. We reached the mountains and, with less than good visibility, Fisher sought to find a pass through them out to the sea to our north. We would fly into a canyon hoping to find a way through, only to come up against a mountain wall and have to make a vicious 180-degree turn around. Our Irish friend then was busy saying his prayers in the seat behind us. I soon joined him in prayer.

After several heart-stopping episodes, we found a pass and eventually were flying out over open water. Recalling how concerned we had been over that expanse of sea on the way down, after all we had been through, we now gave it little thought. That night Glen and I stayed as guests of Lyle Lane, the American consul in Cebu, the second largest city in the Philippines. The Irish priest visited friends at a local Catholic mission. Our last day's flight over the Visayan Sea, passing the islands of Panay and Mindoro, progressed smoothly. It was as if that small, 90-horsepower engine was purring the comment, "I told you I could do it, even with the extra passenger!"

Our families were happy to have us back. It was not until my return that the full impact struck me of just how risky it was to have flown in a small, single-engine aircraft over those thousands of miles of tropical seas, jungles, and mangrove swamps, much less weaving through mountain passes and thunderheads. Had we gone down in those Borneo mangrove swamps, I doubt if they would ever have found us. Glen Fisher proved himself to be a first-class pilot and his plane a little gem.

I was able to prepare an informative report upon my return, based on my conversations with officials and other persons we had encountered. The finding of the launch on Sibutu was reported to our colleagues in the British Embassy. When that story finally sorted itself out, the kidnapped persons turned out not to be English, the men were Borneo Chinese and the women, Hong Kong prostitutes.

Shortly after my return from Borneo, we received word that the officer who was to replace Bill Bruns in the politico-military job had died en route. I continued handling military affairs during a period where major incidents at the bases gave rise to Filipino demonstrations both there and at our Embassy. Some of the demonstrations against the Embassy were quite nasty, with a great deal of rock-throwing. For many years the United States had enjoyed high esteem in the eyes of the Filipinos. That changed with the Vietnam War, which afforded an opportunity to anti-American elements to incite the populace. I was to witness more than twenty demonstrations before my transfer in July 1966. This turn of events had a significant impact on Ambassador Stevenson, who seemed to take it personally. He looked haggard. For the next few months, I watched as he and his wife did everything they could to foster goodwill between our two countries, with diminishing effect.

These months were exceedingly busy ones for the entire Political Section. Max Krebs was a superb boss. As political counselor, he provided guidance and support, assuring that the External, Internal, and Politico-Military Affairs Sections worked smoothly and cooperatively. His morning staff meetings were brief but productive sessions. Not only were there problems with the military at this time, but major international efforts were also under way to bring the conflict over Sabah to a halt. Earlier in the spring of 1963, a "Little Summit" meeting of the Foreign Ministers of Malaysia, the Philippines, and Indonesia had been held in Manila for this purpose, giving rise to MAPHILINDO.

I recall writing a lengthy classified cable discussing the prospects for that organization and analyzing the situation at the time, which the ambassador particularly liked. I was surprised, though pleased, when he read six pages of it at a Country Team meeting, since several flag-level military representatives attending would not normally receive it in their communication channels. MAPHILINDO at its inception was something of a darling to the press and world opinion. In reality, however, like so many of these efforts, not very much resulted from it.

President Macapagal saw MAPHILINDO as a means for bringing the three states into closer cooperation. Ethnically, they had much in common.

However, politically they were far apart. Indonesia's dictator, Sukarno, viewed the organization as a vehicle for promoting his brand of neutralism. The experience of each of the countries under colonialism had been different: the Malaysians under the British, the Filipinos under the Spanish and Americans, and the Indonesians under the Dutch. Once the colonizers departed, their legacies remained. The British, perhaps with their development of a class of civil servants, best served Malaysia; they tended to curb some of the more corrupt practices found in the other two countries.

Although some vestiges of the American occupation remained when I arrived in Manila in 1962, I sensed that the Philippines was well on its way toward being a Southeast Asian nation with its own agenda. An undercurrent stirred in the press and among the intelligentsia that viewed the United States' large military presence as an embarrassment to national prestige. America's unavailing battle against a supposedly inferior force of indigenous fighters in Vietnam reinforced this feeling. A few Filipinos even likened the latter's struggle to that of their hero, Aguinaldo, and his insurgency against first the Spaniards and then the Americans.

On the other hand, business and vested interests in the country, the Catholic Church, and broad segments of the population feared the spread of communism. However, communism in the Philippines had little to do with the ideology itself. If asked, so-called communist leaders might describe themselves as adherents, but in actuality they understood little about Marxist-Leninism, or for that matter about Mao Zedong. They were not much more than bandits who cloaked their activities under a mantle of political opposition, taking advantage of the disparity of wealth, the social unrest, and the grinding poverty of the masses.[4] Earlier, President Magsaysay's efforts at land reform and counterinsurgency programs had wiped out this opposition, except for a hard core. Macapagal, on the other hand, did little to break the power of the large landowners or improve the lot of the Filipino masses.

The assassination of President Kennedy in November 1963 was a traumatic experience for the Philippines. The strongly religious Filipinos felt a special bond with the handsome, young Kennedy, first Catholic American president. The country went into a period of deep mourning. Somber music was played for three days on radio and television and masses of people attended special church services. Thousands of letters of condolence and gifts poured into the Embassy. Embassy wives were recruited to deal with the influx and prepare responses. Elsa not only participated in this effort but stayed up most of a night writing cancellations to 250 guests we had invited to one of our receptions.

A memorial service held at the American Military Cemetery at Fort McKinley on the outskirts of Manila drew the top levels of the Philippine government, the diplomatic corps, and over 3,000 members of the Filipino and American communities. It was a moving ceremony, there in that vast Arlington-like cemetery, with its 7,200 graves and magnificent marble monument listing their names along with an additional 10,000 Pacific World War II dead whose bodies were never recovered. The fact that some of those dead served with President Kennedy in combat in the South Pacific made the scene even more poignant.

Protocol, which normally serves as a social aid, on that occasion dealt me a serious blow. I had established exceptionally good working relations with Undersecretary of Defense Alberto DeJoya, then acting secretary. At the memorial service, the Philippine cabinet members were seated in the first row according to precedence. I assisted in greeting the dignitaries. My attention was called to a seating problem when Secretary DeJoya arrived. As he was representing the Defense Ministry, he expected to be seated next to the foreign secretary. To straighten matters out, I quickly found the Embassy's protocol officer, an American resident in the Philippines who had served several of our ambassadors. With years of experience in the job, she insisted that as an acting secretary, he could not be ranked before other actual cabinet members. Under the circumstances, since others had arrived and there were name cards on the seats, there was nothing I could do without a major upheaval.

To his great embarrassment DeJoya was seated in the second row. He lost face in front of a galaxy of high-ranking personages. The fact that I was unable to influence the matter clearly was a blow to my standing with him. The protocol officer may have been technically correct, but dealing with the Foreign and Defense Ministries was the embassy's bread and butter. It would have been a simple matter to overlook the fine letter of the rule at the outset. No one would have been the wiser, likely thinking that the order of precedence had been determined by the ministry, not the individual. From that point on, DeJoya, who headed the Defense Ministry for several months afterward, was never available, and I was forced to deal with other officials not having the authority to make decisions. Our embassy had been done a real disservice.

With the Johnson administration taking over, reports surfaced of an awkward situation arising between the new American president and his predecessor's free-wheeling and hard-charging younger brother, Attorney General Robert Kennedy. In early 1964, barely three months after President Kennedy's assassination, the embassy received word that Bobby and his wife, Ethel, would be visiting Japan and Korea and then traveling on to the Philippines, Malaysia, and Indonesia. In the latter countries, as we were to learn, he was ostensibly, to try his hand at mediating the dispute over Sabah. I was assigned to be control officer for the visit. During my career, I have been so designated for many visits, several of them momentous events, such as the Nixon swan song visit to Egypt and the Kissinger shuttle diplomacy, but this affair was unique!

The airport arrival portended much of what was to follow. No rock star could match the appeal that the Kennedys had with the rank and file of Filipinos. There was no controlling the masses at the airport that night. Crowds rioted, breaking through glass windows of the terminal, just to see him. They burst in on a second floor balcony and I was barely able to keep the ambassador's wife from being pushed over a staircase railing. We had great difficulty moving the attorney general's party to the awaiting cars and driving him to Malacanang Palace, where they were the houseguests of President and Mrs. Macapagal. When we finally bedded the visitors down and arrived back at the Embassy, it was well past midnight.

I went home, knowing that I would be returning at 6:30 the next morning to meet Ambassador Stevenson and accompany him to Malacanang Palace. Kennedy had requested that he be briefed at an early hour in his suite. We arrived at the Palace to find the attorney general fully dressed, conferring with his advisor and press assistant, Ed Gluckman. He greeted us curtly and directed us to a sofa. Kennedy and Gluckman sat in armchairs. Ambassador Stevenson began his briefing, one which I had heard him present to visitors on many occasions. As he was speaking, Kennedy suddenly got to his feet. Stevenson paused, but was told to continue. Bobby then paced up and down, at times sitting briefly. He appeared extremely energetic and dynamic. As he paced, I said to myself, "The only thing this guy isn't doing is sticking his hand in his shirt, or I would be witnessing an impersonation of Napoleon."

I made the mistake halfway through the all-too-familiar briefing of inadvertently glancing at the ceiling. Noting my inattention, Kennedy jumped on me with the question, "Have you anything to say?" Totally embarrassed and nonplussed, all I could blurt out was, "No, everything the ambassador is telling you is correct." Stevenson looked at me in wonderment, and I felt a complete idiot. I have had better moments!

That day was a wild melee of activities, from both my standpoint and that of my wife who assisted during shopping forays. Mrs. Kennedy brought her own hairdresser along to keep her coiffure presentable. I encountered reluctance and raised eyebrows from my Navy colleagues at Sangley Air Station when I asked for a helicopter to shuttle the hairdresser around after her. My solution to the problem was to say, "You tell the attorney general that his wife can't have it." There were no takers; the Navy brass were very politically savvy!

That night at about 10 o'clock, I was in my office trying to follow up on arrangements for the next day when I received a harried telephone call from Minister Service, who was at a formal dinner President and Mrs. Macapagal were giving for the Kennedys. "He is leaving . . . he is on his way to the airport!" Service shouted into the telephone.

Tired after a very strenuous day, I said, "Who is leaving?"

"Kennedy!" came the urgent response. "He wants his plane readied for takeoff right now!" I was told that the attorney general had risen from the table before the dinner had concluded. He simply walked out of the Palace in his evening clothes and headed straight for the airport, all the while giving instructions that his Air Force plane be prepared immediately to fly to Kuala Lumpur, although he was not scheduled to leave until a day and a half later.

I learned that during the dinner, someone had informed him that the holy month of Ramadan was to set in the following evening. Malaysia being a Muslim country, Tunku Abdul Rahman, the prime minister, would go into seclusion. If there were to be a meeting with him, it had to be the next day. Evidently, no one had told Kennedy about Ramadan, nor had anyone in his party taken the trouble to find out. I do not know where the State Department was in all of this. Arrangements were likely handled through the White House and the Department of Justice with a minimum, if any, consultation with the country desks of the State Department. Embassy Manila was not consulted, but simply told about arrangements. I was always amazed how high-handed and slipshod the doings of the mighty could be.[5]

Minister Service's telephone call set in motion a series of frenzied efforts. I had the appalling task of trying to round up the Kennedy party of ninety people scattered in nightclubs and other places about town. Thank goodness we managed to locate the pilot and most of the crew without too much trouble. During the midnight hours, Kennedy fumed while he impatiently waited at the airport until the takeoff was readied. As it was, he left behind a number of his entourage we could not locate in time. It was a nerve-racking and unpleasant experience for me as the control officer.

Up to that point in my career, I had never sent a message with the designator "flash," the kind that denotes the outbreak of war or an imminent nuclear attack. At Kennedy's instruction, I sent three that night. Our poor Ambassador to Malaysia in Kuala Lumpur must have been beside himself to arrange for that middle of the night arrival. However, there was a great sigh of relief from us when the attorney general and his party departed. I was told that Kennedy had been very complimentary about my handling of the visit. Nevertheless, it was far from a plus in terms of bolstering our relations with the Filipino leadership. I am sure the Macapagals must have been offended; one does not treat heads of state in that fashion.

During the frantic effort to locate everyone, I received a telephone call from our general services officer, Charles Williams, who was at the Malacanang Palace hurriedly packing up all the Kennedys' belongings and loading the many suitcases on an embassy truck. He reported with some irritation that he had completed the job, and then added sardonically, "but I fixed the SOB!"

In no mood for nonsense at that late hour, I retorted, "Chuck, what the hell are you talking about?"

He went on to tell me that in a final inspection of the Kennedy suite, he found one of Ethel's brassieres wedged between the bed and the mattress. The truck with the luggage had already departed for the airport; all that remained was the attorney general's briefcase, which contained documents and was to be hand-carried. "What was there to do," he said, "but put the brassiere in the briefcase?"

With visions of Kennedy opening that briefcase in the presence of the prime minister of Malaysia, I debated whether the ambassador or others should be alerted, but I remained silent and worried. After a week or two with no repercussions, I told them of the incident. Then we all laughed uproariously. It has been one of my favorite stories ever since.

We received an invitation one day from a Filipino friend we met aboard ship to be his guests at the Pampanga Ball at the grand old Manila Hotel. He was a distinguished, older gentleman, the chief justice of the Supreme Court and member of one of the wealthy ruling families. We did not think much about it at the time, but mention of the invitation to a long-time resident brought about an immediate gasp. The ball, we learned, was the social event of the year, where the upper crust of society displayed their jewels and regal ternos—puffed-sleeve gowns, many of which were exceedingly expensive and specially created in Paris.

Hearing that, I promptly inquired as to whether anyone else in the Embassy had received an invitation. The answer was no, not even the ambassador or the minister. The very day of my inquiry, the first of several unfavorable articles about the upcoming ball appeared in the press. It was said that such an ostentatious display of wealth was out of place in a city where poverty was everywhere. The mayor of Manila threatened to raid the ball. Students prepared to picket the hotel. Given the controversy, I asked the ambassador to decide whether we should accept the invitation, virtually certain the answer would be in the negative.

After considerable discussion in the ambassador's staff meeting, to my surprise I was told to accept. I was low enough in rank to avoid its being viewed as American embassy acceptance of the affair. On the other hand, in view of the turmoil caused, it would be useful to have someone at the event who could report about it firsthand. In retrospect, I am glad that was the decision, for it enabled Elsa and myself to attend one of the more memorable events in our service overseas.

I have often thought that there are times in diplomacy when one is akin to being an actor on the stage. This was one of them. Elsa and I carefully planned what she would wear. She chose a spectacular blue taffeta gown, set off with a floor length stole of the same material. As jewelry, she wore faux theatrical diamond earrings, with a magnificent matching clip on the dress. At any other affair one might question whether such jewelry could possibly be real; at this ball, it would be taken for granted that it was. Elsa could have been cast as a duchess in a Hollywood movie. As for me, men have life much easier; black tie was in order.

We arrived at the Manila Hotel to find the pickets out in force. This occurred despite reports in the newspapers that the ball organizers in response to public outcry were going to make it a more subdued affair. To some degree, it was. The meal was standard hotel fare. No hard liquor was served. Women supposedly wore their less costly jewels, although it certainly did not appear so to me.

The spectacle of the evening was the dancing of the *Rigodon d'Honeur* in which our hosts, the justice and his wife, took part. This dance consisted of parading in stately fashion up and down the huge ballroom, much like one staged at the 17th century court of Louis XIV in France. In a column of twos, led by the most distinguished members of society, they paraded to regal music, stopping, bowing, and then proceeding. The man's arm was outstretched, the woman's hand daintily placed on his wrist. The couples were spaced a dozen or more feet behind one another to accommodate the long trains of the ternos. The latter were something to behold. Some were encrusted with seed pearls and brilliants; others were completely beaded or made of handsome brocades. I was told that some of the gowns cost between $10,000 and $20,000 each—and that was many years ago! It was quite a sight!

Whenever possible, Elsa and I tried to arrange time together with the children. That was not easy given the demands put on both of us by my job, her household responsibilities and teaching, and the overblown diplomatic social life in Manila. The Embassy commissary, although well stocked by Foreign Service standards, still left much to be desired and required that we make periodic trips on the weekends or days off to the military PXs. Generally, we went to Sangley Naval Air Station at Cavite, a thirty-minute drive around Manila Bay. On other occasions we drove to Clark Air Force Base in Pampangas, a distance of sixty miles, or to Subic Naval Base over on Bataan, thirty miles farther.

The roads were poor and often crowded with pedestrians and animal-drawn carts. On these long drives, we could see Filipino families harvesting the sugar crop, the parents in the fields of seven-foot high cane, while youngsters sat on the backs of the carabao (water buffalo). Our children enjoyed these outings. We would have lunch in an officers' club or a snack bar and come home loaded with groceries and PX purchases.

Our family made great use of the embassy's own Seafront Club, which had a large outdoor swimming pool, tennis courts, and sports facilities. I took up tennis in Manila and after four years had progressed to being a decent player, noted for a powerful serve. My twelve-year-old son Brad found baseball more to his liking. He had difficulty, however, in convincing a young friend, Jimmy Connors, that there was anything else in life other than tennis. Connors and his mother had come down from Japan to stay in Manila during this period. She was singlemindedly set on breaking him into professional tennis even at that early age. With such dedication are Wimbledon champions made.

I took time to teach Brad how to pitch a baseball; I had him throwing fastballs into my catcher's mitt with such speed and accuracy that he became an easy choice for pitcher of his Little League team. The team was comfortably ahead on one occasion against a team at Sangley Naval Air Station when the coach substituted his son for Brad. To the dismay of everyone present, we then proceeded to lose the game.

The family remembers an incident that involved baby Matthew well. At age three, he was standing on top of a table on our patio one Sunday, when he fell backwards onto the stone floor, splitting open his head. Elsa and I arrived home from church moments later to find him covered in blood and the maids in a state of panic. Great spurts of blood shot from the back of his skull. I grabbed the nearest piece of cloth, pressed it firmly to the wound and rushed him out to the car. With Elsa holding Matt in her arms and pressing down on the makeshift bandage, we drove wildly from the suburbs to the nearest hospital in Manila. Although the facilities left much to be desired, a Filipino doctor took him into the emergency room, examined his skull, and sewed him up with satisfactory results.

We had two opportunities during our Manila tour to use the cottages at the Navy's recreation area on Grande Island at the mouth of Subic Bay. They were memorable weeklong vacations. We swam and snorkeled among myriads of tropical fish, spotting sharks and barracuda in the sea around the island. Our Klepper kayak was once raised out of the water as we passed over a giant manta ray, scaring the wits out of Brad, Andrea, and me. We confronted three-foot-long lizards on walks along jungle paths. Periodically, an aircraft carrier or other large U.S. fighting ship would glide close by in the deep channel alongside the island on its way in or out of the naval base. We had a glorious time there as a family.

I was once asked what was the most frightening experience in my life. Was it when parachutes delayed opening? Was it in combat during World War II or when angry mobs set our embassy on fire? My answer to this question is related to an event that occurred while vacationing on Grande Island. I still have the scene and the sheer terror that came over me etched in my mind. We were at the beach. Andrea had just come in from playing with other children, who were snorkeling in shallow waters offshore. She was enthusiastic about what she had seen. A fellow vacationer from the Embassy, an AID employee sitting on the beach nearby, overheard her. He was Pakistani, a naturalized American citizen with a Danish wife. Anxious to see the beautiful tropical fish Andrea had described, he asked if he could borrow the facemask and snorkel. Although we did not know him at all, we readily complied.

I took little note as the man floated about, at first parallel to the shore and then moving ever farther out. He was about fifty yards out when he suddenly let out a scream for help and sank beneath the surface. Seconds later, he was back up shouting again. Having served as a lifeguard in my youth, I jumped to my feet in a reflex reaction and raced into the water. I had gone half the distance when it suddenly dawned on me that this was not a drowning but more likely a shark or barracuda attack. We had seen both predators off the Navy Pier less than a quarter mile distant. My mind instantly conjured up a scene of bloodied water and a feeding frenzy into which I might be swimming. I hesitated, a thousand thoughts filling my mind.

The victim, farther out, thrashed and screamed. At that moment, I noticed a young sailor I had talked with that morning enter the water to help. He was an engaging boy, no more than eighteen or nineteen years old from a small town in the Middle West. I do not think he had any idea of the possible danger ahead. Seeing him snapped me back into reality. I shouted, "I've got him!" and motioned for him to stay back, fearing he would unsuspectingly swim into a shark or barracuda attack.

I swam on terrified, lifting my head and body as high out of the water as I could, constantly looking for blood in the water. Reaching the man, I attempted to take hold of him. A large, heavy-set person, he threw his arms around me like a madman. It took all my strength and brute force to break his grip before he passed out. I then turned him around and took him in tow. Meanwhile, my eyes inspected his limbs for signs of blood or torn flesh. The young sailor met me halfway and between the two of us we dragged the victim ashore.

Once there, I laid him out and, surrounded by onlookers, gave him artificial respiration. I was into this procedure for a few minutes when his wife arrived. "What have you done to my husband?" she screamed at me hysterically.

I responded, "He was snorkeling offshore and started to drown. He must have gotten a cramp."

"Snorkeling!" she cried." Offshore!" she screeched. "He doesn't know how to swim!" I was dumbfounded. How could anyone be so stupid as to go that far out if he could not swim. I was also incensed. This idiotic woman, rather than being grateful for my saving his life, was blaming me for "drowning" her husband.

I soon realized what had happened: with a mask and snorkel, as long as a person is breathing normally and lying on the surface, he will not sink. This fellow must have been floating along face down in shallow water watching the fish and the beautiful vegetation on the bottom. From time to time, he simply would stand up. After a while, not paying attention to his direction, he wandered far offshore. Then when he tried to stand in very deep water, he saw where he was and panicked. It was a very unpleasant episode. As rescues go, it was not much. Yet I know I experienced my most frightening moment in those agonizing seconds, when I told that young sailor to stay back and swam on, terrified.

Manila was the venue for a Conference of SEATO Foreign Ministers in April 1964. The focus of the meeting was on the war in Vietnam and what should be done to meet the threat it posed to the region. Secretary of State Dean Rusk attended with a large party of top-level State Department officers. To provide office space for them, the offices of the ambassador, the minister, and that entire floor, which also housed the Political Section, were vacated. Everyone was involved in the support effort, although as the embassy officer responsible for SEATO affairs, I had additional specific tasks, primarily reporting on the conference. Losing my office and my secretary was thus a real handicap. I also handled some of the control officer duties.

Secretary Rusk did his best to make the conference a productive one. He was distressed that his British counterpart saw fit only to send a deputy. He was even more irritated when the foreign minister of Pakistan, who was scheduled to appear, decided instead to remain in Djakarta at a conference of Afro-Asian countries. However, he was pleased that the French foreign minister attended. In addition to the conference sessions themselves, there were many things going on at once. These included Mr. Rusk's separate meetings with other foreign ministers, President Macapagal, and the Philippine leadership and, debatably even more important, similar activities involving William Bundy, the assistant secretary of state for East Asia, our immediate overall boss. I found that trying to stay on top of everything was good training for what I would encounter later on in Cairo.

Around the time the conference was taking place, former Vice President Nixon arrived in Manila as a private businessman. As this was a Democratic administration, there was a certain uneasiness as to how he should be received. The embassy decided on extending only the courtesies it would proffer to any leading American businessman. Joe Rand, the commercial attaché, met him at the airport; an Embassy briefing was arranged; and the ambassador extended hospitality. It is interesting to note that in conversations with Nixon at the time, which was many months before the 1964 elections, he clearly dismissed leading contender Bobby Kennedy as Lyndon Johnson's running mate. He correctly predicted it would be Hubert Humphrey. While being evasive as to his own candidacy for the Republican nomination, an associate on the trip intimated that Nixon was already planning what became his successful presidential run in 1968.[6]

One of my wife's letters describes the distaff side of that hectic period. During the SEATO Conference, Mrs. Rusk had 500 ladies to tea at the Embassy. Elsa and other wives assisted in this massive affair. We loaned our large silver coffee and tea service and other items for the purpose. The program of dinners, entertainment, sightseeing, and shopping was exhausting. She describes a large dinner we gave for some of the visitors from Washington, who arrived hours late because the conference session ran overtime. Despite concluding dinner at 11:00 p.m., some of our guests prevailed upon us to show them some of Manila's nightlife. Elsa lamented that we returned home at 2:30 in the morning, only to have to arise early for a busy day.

As if all the above were not enough, an American sailor was run over on Roxas Boulevard in front of the Embassy on one of those nights. I recall rounding up cars to ring our parking lot so that their headlights could illuminate the area enough for a Navy helicopter to evacuate the seriously injured man to the Clark Air Force Base Hospital.

By June 1964, we had been in Manila two years. We had the choice of remaining another year and then being transferred, or taking home leave and returning for another two-year tour. While the Philippine climate left a lot to be desired, we had settled nicely into our Manila home and made many friends. The children were receiving a fine education at their school and were happy. My work, though demanding, could not have been more interesting. It was the family's unanimous decision to opt for a four-year stay. With that, we prepared to fly back to the United States for over two months' leave, plus travel time.

Our plans called for us to spend a period in Jacksonville, Illinois, where Elsa's parents had relocated, and then go down to Debary, Florida, to be with my mother. At the end, after a sightseeing trip by car across the country to San Francisco, we would again embark on a President Lines' ship for the long return voyage to the Philippines. Before leaving Manila, we would sell our 1962 Chevrolet and order a new one, which I would pick up at the factory in Michigan, halfway around the world. Although we did not know it at the time, we were to drive our new car over 9,000 miles in the United States in what was to be the grandest vacation we ever had as a family.

My father-in-law, Roger Wells, retired at age seventy from his position as chairman of the Political Science Department at Bryn Mawr College. As a professor emeritus, he made his services available to a program that placed retired big name educators in lesser-known colleges. Dad had an illustrious career. He was a Harvard PhD and an authority on local government. Among other things, he had been chairman of a War Labor Board in World War II, president of the Pennsylvania Political Science Association, deputy director of Civil Administration for Germany, and an advisor to General Clay. He was also a holder of the Medal of Freedom. When his services were offered to MacMurray College in Jacksonville, Illinois, that institution jumped at the chance. For Mother and Dad Wells this would also be somewhat of a homecoming, both having been born and raised in Illinois, where they still had relatives.

When we arrived on home leave, they were comfortably ensconced in Jacksonville, a town of 22,000, which boasted two colleges, the other being Illinois College. I soon took a train to Flint, Michigan to pick up our new Chevrolet, which was waiting for me at the factory, and broke it in on the drive back to Jacksonville. We stayed with the Wellses for two weeks and then as a family drove to Niagara Falls, a sight we all wished to see. From there, we journeyed down to Washington, stopping en route at the New York country home of our Foreign Service friends, the Littells.

In Washington, I reported in for debriefings at the State and Defense Departments and the CIA. At State, I was pleased to learn that my reporting was held in high regard. Defense officials were particularly anxious to have my views on matters related to the military bases. As I look back on it now, however, perhaps the most portentous occurrence was when Bob McClosky, my old friend who handled press matters on the UNESCO staff, approached me to join the State Department Newsroom. He said my experience in dealing with the press was needed. I had also worked on the public affairs policy side, having provided guidance to the Newsroom as special assistant to his overall boss, the assistant secretary for public affairs.

In my own mind, however, I had spent ten years in public affairs and finally had moved over into the political cone, where I thought the action and real advancement opportunities were to be found, and where I chose to remain. Ten years later, Ambassador-at-Large McClosky, right-hand man to Secretary Kissinger, was to remind me of that decision when he came to Cairo during the Middle East shuttle diplomacy.

My widowed mother had been living in Florida a dozen years when we arrived in 1964. She was overjoyed to see her three grandchildren and us. She had made many friends in the community and was a pillar of her church. As part of the State Department effort to acquaint the public with its activities, speaking arrangements and press interviews are often scheduled for Foreign Service officers returning from interesting overseas assignments. Throughout my time in Florida, the Speakers Bureau programmed me to appear on TV talk shows and at press interviews in the Orlando and Daytona areas. While it was somewhat of a nuisance, the pleasure it gave my mother to see her son on TV and in the newspapers was worth every bit of the trouble. We were in Florida in late July and early August and it was hot, actually more so than the Philippines. However, our days at the beach in New Smyrna and Daytona made up for the heat and humidity.

Bidding my mother farewell, we drove to Illinois for a few last days with the Wellses and then began our journey across the western half of the United States. Our children were awed by the Rockies and the Grand Tetons. On a high mountain pass in the Rockies, we stopped at a snowy outlook and pelted each other with snowballs on a beautiful, sunny summer day. We went on to visit Yellowstone and Grand Teton National Parks. Brad and I fished in the high lakes and the clear running streams while the family picnicked. We all gasped as bear and elk wandered near us. Throughout the long drive to the West Coast, I marveled at how difficult it must have been for those pioneers crossing deserts, mountains and forests by foot and wagon train.

The modern world intruded, however, when we ate in a restaurant in Wells, Nevada. Slot machines filled every corner of the place. As an object lesson, I gave everyone a quarter with which to buy candy or play the slot machines. The children chose the slots, wishing to see the whirling oranges, cherries, lemons, and bells go round. I warned them that they would lose their money and there would be no candy. We all promptly proceeded to lose. When Brad's turn came, he dropped in his quarter, pulled the handle; after a few seconds the machine went berserk spewing out coins. He was much the richer, if not the wiser, and my object lesson flew out the window. Later, I mused that his luck may have had some connection with the fact that the town's name, Wells, was his given name.

After several enjoyable days in the San Francisco area, we boarded the SS *President Cleveland*, the sister ship to the *Wilson*, for the passage to

Manila. Our trip was a wonderful repetition of our twenty-one day voyage two years earlier. Nostalgia prompts me again to comment that cruise ship travel today is simply a shadow of the great ocean liner crossings of former times. Returning to a post on a second tour is generally a comfortable experience. Our house, a spacious villa, was waiting for us. Our cook, maid, and gardener had maintained the place and welcomed us with open arms. At work, I found the embassy confronted with the same problems. Frank Tatu, however, had done a fine job in holding things together in my absence. Shortly thereafter, in view of the upcoming elections, he was moved over to Internal Political Affairs, assisting William Owen, the chief of that section.

The Philippines was gearing up for a tempestuous presidential campaign year. In October 1964, Ambassador Stevenson was replaced by William McCormick Blair, Jr., a lawyer and associate of Adlai Stevenson, the losing Democratic opponent of Dwight Eisenhower in the presidential election campaigns of 1952 and 1956. A political appointee, Blair had previously served as our ambassador to Denmark. He was a friendly, likeable person in his early fifties. His wife, Deeda, a socialite in her thirties, was on the Ten Best-Dressed Women List. Her pilgrimage to Paris each year for the fashion shows was the talk of local society.

During this period, a series of assistants and I were busily engaged in obtaining Philippine government support on a variety of issues in the United Nations and in SEATO, as well as assistance for our forces' struggle in Vietnam. We were negotiating the Corregidor Memorial Agreement between our two countries. Tensions between Indonesia and the Philippines grew out of Muslim unrest in the Philippine south believed to be generated by Djakarta. The conflict between Indonesia and Malaysia over Borneo dragged on.

In February 1965, a Far East Chief of Missions Conference in Baguio, a city high in the mountains of Central Luzon was held at Camp John Hay, a rest center for the American military. During World War II, General MacArthur had accepted the surrender of the Japanese forces in the Philippines there. It was a lovely, well-maintained facility with ample quarters. I recall how luxurious it was, after coming up from the sweltering heat of Manila, to breathe the cool, crisp mountain air and have logs burning in the fireplace. The American ambassadors from all over the Pacific area attended the conference, including those from Southeast Asia. The focus was on broad-gauged policy. However, uppermost in everyone's mind was the conflict in Vietnam.

Assistant Secretary of State for East Asia William Bundy chaired the meeting, though his predecessor, W. Averell Harriman, now ambassador-at-large, was also very much in evidence. Admiral Ulysses Grant Sharp, the Commander-in-Chief, U.S. Forces Pacific (CINCPAC), attended, representing the military. I was one of three officers selected to be a rapporteur, along with colleagues Chester Beaman and Richard B. Owen, both of our embassy's Economic Section. The top-secret proceedings were wide ranging and in some instances of great significance, since they would determine America's actions in that part of the world.

The rapporteurs, working in shifts, did their best to keep up with the pace of discussions. We would take turns writing furiously while the other two sat back and followed the conversations. It was interesting to observe our Washington leaders, military chiefs, and a dozen ambassadors in action. I found myself amused watching Harriman. At times, he would appear to doze off during some drawn-out discussion, only to pop up with a pithy interjection when I thought he was in never-never land. I could swear at times he turned off his hearing aid when he was bored. While even years later I would not elaborate on what took place in the meetings, I recall one incident that made a lasting impression on me.

No stenographers, we rapporteurs found it difficult from the outset to keep up. Each day at the close of the sessions we were expected to transcribe our notes and have a detailed set of minutes available at the start of the next day. Using a small recorder, we decided to tape the proceedings as a reference to help us transcribe. We would subsequently burn the tape. The second day of the conference we presented the participants with a detailed and accurate account of the previous day's discussions.

At lunchtime, one of the ambassadors came to us taking issue with something we had attributed to him. Rather than simply revising the minutes to reflect what he wanted to say, we stupidly pointed out that he had indeed been quoted correctly. To prove our point, he could listen to himself on the tape. Talk about winning the battle and losing the war! Our diligence was to do us in. He promptly went to Mr. Bundy and the "fat was in the fire." How could we possibly have taped anything so top secret! The security violation chart would jump off the wall! Our remonstrances that we were going to destroy the tape as soon as we had finished preparing the minutes fell on deaf ears. I felt like saying, "What are we supposed to do then with the written minutes? Burn them before reading?" Discretion, however, prevailed. We went unaided, and our reportage the next day was not up to our former standard!

The United States during these years became more and more deeply enmeshed in the Vietnam quagmire, while the Philippines increased in importance as a support platform for that war. Clark Air Base served as the headquarters for the U.S. 13th Air Force and Subic Naval Base and Sangley Naval Air Station for the 7th Fleet. Merchant ships destined for

Vietnam crowded the ports of Cebu and Manila, using them as staging and holding areas.

President Johnson designated Henry Cabot Lodge, Jr., to be our ambassador to South Vietnam in 1963. Lodge, the son of President Wilson's nemesis in the struggle over the League of Nations, had himself been a Massachusetts senator and governor. He had achieved international recognition as the U.S. representative on the UN Security Council. It was with some interest, therefore, that I learned one morning in April 1965 that he and his wife would be stopping off in Manila en route to Saigon and that I had been designated the control officer for their visit.

I made the usual preparations, including among other things, assuming responsibility for all communications related to the visit, booking accommodations, arranging for vehicles, getting the embassy support staff to facilitate airport entry and departure, scheduling an ambassadorial briefing, making appointments for calls on Filipino and American officials, arranging for appropriate hospitality (reception or cocktail party), working out a sightseeing and shopping program for Mrs. Lodge and designating an embassy wife to accompany her, seeing to it that the Lodges' hotel suite was properly stocked (liquor, snacks, flowers, etc.), and preparing a detailed program of events and other information to be given to the visitors on their arrival.

In addition, I had to arrange my own work schedule so that I would be available to accompany Ambassador Lodge throughout his stay. He would be meeting not only with the Philippine foreign secretary but also with President Macapagal. Washington had instructed us that it was important that Lodge have every opportunity to consult with the Philippine leadership. Ambassador Blair told me to use his Cadillac limousine to meet the Lodge party at the airport. Besides Mrs. Lodge, the group included another ranking official, who served as an advisor or assistant to the ambassador.

On their arrival, our experienced and highly efficient Filipino staff "expediters" saw to it that we were whisked through the hectically crowded airport, and I deposited Ambassador and Mrs. Lodge in their suite in the Manila Hotel without incident. They were a gracious pair, he an exceedingly tall, handsome man and she an attractive member of upper-crust society. Had it not been for certain memorable occurrences I am about to recount, this visit would have been a routine one for me.

Some time prior to the Lodges' arrival, Elsa and I had received an invitation to dinner from Minister and Mrs. Service. It was to a sit-down affair to which very senior Foreign Ministry officials and their wives had been invited, and we dutifully accepted. I handled external affairs and would be expected to prepare messages on anything of importance growing out of the evening's conversations. However, as matters evolved there was a problem: President Macapagal, on short notice, invited Ambassador Lodge to have dinner with him alone at Malacanang Palace that first evening. As control officer, I had to escort our visitor and be on top of things.

When I pointed out my dilemma to Dick Service, he believed it important for me to be at his dinner and solved the problem by saying that I could pick Lodge up at his hotel and accompany him to the Palace. After depositing him, I could come back to the DCM residence, where Elsa would be waiting for me. There was no question that the Macapagal-Lodge dinner and ostensible subsequent discussions would go on for some time. Promptly after the sit-down portion of the dinner at the Services, I could return to Malacanang and wait for Ambassador Lodge. This plan, Service avowed, would serve everybody's purpose.

Early that evening, I picked up Ambassador Blair's chauffeur and Cadillac limousine at the Embassy. An escort of two Filipino motorcycle policemen was there also, flags fluttering resplendently from the handlebars of their machines. Well aware of how impossible it was to proceed through downtown Manila traffic without such an escort, I had arranged for them beforehand.

Arriving at the Manila Hotel at the appointed time, I telephoned the ambassador's suite and went up to get him. After a brief conversation with Mrs. Lodge, the ambassador and I took the elevator down to the lobby and the hotel entrance. The moment Lodge spotted the waiting motorcycles with their sirens and flashing red lights and the crowd of curious onlookers in the circular driveway, he shouted at me, "Get rid of them! I don't want them!" Stunned, I tried to explain that without them it would be impossible to fight our way through Manila's downtown traffic and arrive at Malacanang Palace on time. We would be late. He just looked at me and said sternly, "Get rid of them!"

I did, and our drive to Malacanang Palace was just as I had indicated. We arrived a good twenty minutes late. On the way there, Ambassador Lodge, not the least concerned about the traffic or delay, explained to me why he had insisted on doing away with the escort. "Do you know how I became governor of Massachusetts?" he asked. "Mayor Curley of Boston, who was running against me, always rode around with a fleet of roaring motorcycles, sirens screaming and lights flashing. He tied up traffic everywhere and made so much commotion that enough people tired of it to put me over the top and into office!"

Nothing was said about our late arrival at Malacanang, and Lodge was taken by a protocol officer up to join President Macapagal. I, on the other hand, jumped back into the limousine and without the escort made it back to Minister Service's residence. I was just in time to sit down to dinner. Elsa was there and possibly everyone took it for granted that I had been held up at the Embassy by some last-minute message from Washington. At the conclusion of the meal, I quietly slipped out and returned to the Palace.

Once there, I was informed that Ambassador Lodge had left a few minutes earlier. Shaken, I inquired as to his method of transport, since I was to fetch him in the ambassador's car. No one seemed to know. There was nothing to do now but go straight to the Manila Hotel and offer my profound apologies. On the way, I sat in the back of the Cadillac and castigated myself to the point where the chauffeur must have wondered what was happening. How could I have not insisted that my control officer's duties absolutely necessitated someone else taking my place at the minister's dinner.

Arriving at Ambassador Lodge's suite, I apologized profusely. "How did you get back to the hotel?" I inquired, thinking that the Palace must have provided a car.

"Oh, I took a cab" was his answer. I was dumbfounded and even more chastened. I bid Ambassador and Mrs. Lodge good night, vowing to do my utmost not to fail him again.

The following morning at 6:45 a.m., I called at the Embassy's communications center to pick up any cables that would be of interest to my visitor. I was told that he had already stopped by and read the pertinent traffic. "Not again!" I moaned. A full schedule had been planned for both Ambassador and Mrs. Lodge that day, and I promptly went over to the hotel to check on them. He was going over some documents, and she was propped up in bed reading the newspaper. They could not have been friendlier. I said, "Mr. Ambassador, I have not had this happen to me before. You are always one step ahead of me. From now on maybe I should sleep outside your door!"

Thank goodness, everything else related to the Lodge visit went like clockwork. I was as helpful as I could be to the third member of the party, arranging for accommodations and cars. However, he seemed to have his own agenda, and I suspected that he was tied into either CIA or the military. In any event, our relationship was a pleasant one. Seeing the group off at the airport, I found myself depressed. On other occasions, I felt comfortable that I had done a good job. This time I had really stubbed my toe.

However, I soon was to encounter one of life's ironies. Two weeks later, a message came in from Saigon asking whether I would be available for transfer to Ambassador Lodge's staff. That message presented me with a problem I was to confront throughout the rest of my career. Saigon was a post where I could not be accompanied by my family. They would have to return to the United States on their own, with all that involved. The job, I was sure, would be a real challenge and career enhancement opportunity. I also knew I thrived in a military environment and a war setting. However, life in the Foreign Service was difficult enough for the family without having an absentee father. Having seen some of the difficulties parents encountered with their children during the dozen years I had already spent in the Department of State, I vowed never to take an assignment where I would be separated from the children in their formative years. There were posts where children had to be sent away to school, but I would never accept such an assignment, despite the fact this might cost me dearly career-wise. With great reluctance, I backed away from one of life's crossroads and indicated to Ambassador Blair that I would remain in Manila.

As if to balance matters, within days, in May of 1965, I received word that I had been promoted to first secretary of embassy and supervising political officer, doing in fact the same job I had done for the past year. My promotion may well have come as a result of efforts on my behalf by my boss, Max Krebs, the political counselor.

Embassy officials generally were lionized by the Filipino community and particularly by politicians and influential businessmen, but there were usually ulterior motives involved. Political candidates might be anxious to have the appearance of the backing of the United States. Or, they might need assistance in an immigration or visa problem. There were a host of motives, not least, it was hoped, simple friendship. I had attempted from early on to distance myself from all but the latter of these efforts. Handling external affairs made it a bit easier for me. Nevertheless, after being in Manila only a week, I had received an invitation to a luncheon from Senator Fernando Lopez, thought to be the wealthiest and most powerful man in the land. Along with the invitation came a fine barong, the pima-cloth traditional Philippine dress shirt worn as an outer garment over the trousers.

I accepted the invitation and the barong with thanks, since I did not want to offend him, but did not wear it to the luncheon. Such a gift was considered a routine welcoming present. My relations with Senator Lopez throughout my tour remained simply cordial. For Bill Owen, Frank Tatu, and those working on internal affairs, it was more difficult; they had to maintain close contact and develop sources of information if they were to report on national politics effectively.

President Macapagal, despite his promises of reform, accomplished little. His efforts succeeded only in alienating powerful factions. Proposals to bring about land reform particularly aroused the ire of wealthy landowners. The peasants on the other hand were also disillusioned.

Corruption, lawlessness, unemployment, and inflation added to the sorry scene. Macapagal seized on xenophobic issues to appeal to the populace. He focused on Chinese businessmen who were naturalized Philippine citizens and, in a wave of discrimination, deported some of them. The atmosphere played into the hands of anti-American elements in the country and, coupled with Vietnam and other issues, laid the ground for periodic demonstrations against the Embassy and U.S. military bases.

In a move to play upon nationalistic fervor, Macapagal changed the date of the Philippines' National Day from July 4th, which had been retained since the colonial period, to June 12th, the day Aguinaldo had declared Philippine independence back in 1898. Macapagal later confided that as a diplomat abroad in his earlier years, he noted receptions at his Embassy on July 4th were sparsely attended, overshadowed by those of the United States.

There was much talk at the time that Macapagal, to obtain support of Ferdinand Marcos, had agreed back in the 1961 presidential elections to step aside for him in 1965. I was not sure whether that was true or not, although it is accepted as fact by many today. In any event, Marcos, who had been a dominant member of the Liberal Party, switched over to the Nationalistas to run against Macapagal in the latter's bid for a second term.

Ben Romualdez, Imelda Marcos's brother, and Frank Tatu were particularly good friends, and I recall seeing the Marcoses at various dinners and other social functions. Our boss, the political counselor Max Krebs, knew the leadership well and would caution us that the embassy must always remain neutral and above political partisanship. Max's very able successor, Richard Usher, was equally circumspect. It was generally assumed by the population, however, that the United States played a role behind these scenes.

In attempting to refresh my memory, I recently read two excellent works by *New York Times* correspondents: Raymond Bonner's *Waltzing with a Dictator*[7] and Stanley Karnow's *In Our Image: America's Empire in the Philippines*.[8] They reminded me of just how much we may have influenced matters advertently or inadvertently. Karnow states that Tatu informally made a number of campaign suggestions, for example, that Frank had suggested to Ben or Imelda that they ought to have a campaign song, perhaps one along the lines of the popular Broadway show tune "Hello, Dolly." I vaguely remember something of the sort occurring. "Hello, Marcos" became a great hit, and the future president and dictator later credited Tatu with helping him win the election.

There was a general feeling of disillusionment with Macapagal in the embassy. Marcos, although under a cloud for a murder he had committed as a young man, afforded some hope for the future. Many of us had reason to believe reports he was a highly decorated war hero were specious. Marcos talked a good game. He had the support of powerful elements, while Macapagal had alienated landowners and Chinese businessmen. Even the peasants, bombarded with rhetoric and clever campaigning, flocked to his side. Millions of dollars poured into his campaign. When Senator Fernando Lopez, who himself might have been a candidate for president, was persuaded, ostensibly by Imelda, to be his running mate, the scales in the election of November 1965 were tipped in Marcos's favor.

The election was unusually dirty and violent, even by Philippine standards. There was much last-minute pandering to the population in the rural barrios. Driving through small villages in central Luzon that lacked electricity, we would see lights powered by a portable generator strung up across the road. A crowd, attracted by that novelty and by a loudspeaker blaring music, would gather to listen to some local politician. Often bags of rice would be broken open and the contents doled out to eager recipients. It was not unusual to pass along money as well. On one trip, I recall seeing a road sign that was the height of irony. Based on good old American know-how it read, "Drive safely, the life you save may vote for Senator Marcos."

Marcos's victory by 600,000 votes set in motion a busy period for the embassy. There were requests for analyses as to how the change would affect all aspects of Philippine affairs. Word was also received that an American delegation headed by Vice President Humphrey would attend the inauguration on December 30, 1965. He would be accompanied by Jack Valenti, special assistant to President Johnson, and a coterie of other White House and State Department officials. Minister Service was designated control officer for the visit and I, his backup.

My first task was to draft arrival, departure, and other appropriate speeches for Vice President Humphrey and send them back to Washington for approval. I had written such speeches in the past while in the Bureau of Public Affairs. Certainly this task was not comparable, for example, to speeches I had to draft for Dean Rusk for the Foreign Ministers' Conference in Paris at the height of the Berlin crisis. Little did I know, however, that one of my efforts would become the cause of considerable ribbing. The arrival of an advance party and a Secret Service security detail with all their demands, at times out of proportion to the situation, was an initiation into later experiences I was to have in Egypt. For security reasons Vice President and Mrs. Humphrey were to be housed in the DCM residence, displacing the Services.

The official delegation itself came a week later on Air Force One. The American community and the embassy staff turned out to meet our visitors. Our ambassador, an old friend of the Humphreys, looked forward to greeting them. A Philippine Army band played stirring music, as the plane moved up to the airport receiving point, where a red carpet had been rolled out on the tarmac. I recall seeing an ebullient Hubert Humphrey alight, bound down the rollaway stairs, and proceed to the standing microphone. It was with some satisfaction that I heard him launch into my well-chosen words. I listened carefully as he recited my one-page arrival statement and was about to clap heartily as he came to its erstwhile conclusion.

However, my words only seemed to have whetted his appetite, and he continued on and on. Some time later, standing on the hot tarmac, I saw colleagues looking at me as if to say, "How could you possibly have prepared such a long-winded harangue?" When I later tried to explain to the ambassador, he responded casually, "You just have not met Hubert before." His loquacity aside, Hubert Humphrey struck me as one of the nicest men in public office I had ever met. He and his wife could not have been more gracious. In contrast, most of the rest of the delegation turned out to be demanding and disagreeable. I soon became immersed in the infighting between the aides to Humphrey and those of President Johnson, as represented by Jack Valenti, who would tell me to deal only with them, particularly when it came to messages from Washington, ostensibly intending to leave the others in the dark.

At the inaugural, seated in the stands behind Humphrey and Philippine Vice President-Elect Fernando Lopez, we were treated to a rousing speech by Marcos. He denounced the evils of the past and declared that he had been given a "mandate for greatness." Afterwards, many persons compared his inaugural address to that of President Kennedy in 1961. The American delegation was completely taken with Marcos, particularly Valenti and his wife, who had been a former secretary to Lyndon Johnson. Our embassy was generally enthusiastic as well, perhaps more out of a sense of wishful thinking than anything else. A photograph taken on the occasion features my frowning face close to Marcos at the height of his oratory. Although I shared in the day's enthusiasm, years later I wondered whether that look might have been prescient.

As I consider it all in retrospect, I am astounded by the hypocrisy of that inaugural address. Ferdinand and Imelda Marcos and their cronies were the exact opposite of everything they professed to be at the time.

One of Washington's concerns was to engender support from the new president for our military effort in Vietnam. Despite indications to Ambassador Blair that Marcos would be forthcoming on this matter, there was no mention of Vietnam in the inaugural. Indeed, in subsequent months we were to find ourselves "yo-yoed" by Philippine promises to send an over strength engineer battalion of 2,000 men, which we had secretly agreed to finance. It was not until almost a year later, after I had departed the country, that any real movement on this matter occurred.

The subsequent participation of PHILCAG (Philippine Civic Action Group) in the Vietnam conflict was negligible. By contrast, the cost to the U.S. government in financing this unit, even down to their pay, was exorbitant. A portion of the money was siphoned off to fill the Marcoses' pockets. On top of this, Marcos sought support to create ten engineer battalions to be used in civic action programs at home, thus bolstering his own political future. More than ever, continued use of the bases was tied to receiving increasing amounts of military equipment and foreign aid.

We were deluged with visiting congressional delegations (CODELS) during the final months of 1965. I recall that in December, four different ones arrived in Manila at the same time. Sometimes, a CODEL would be made up of a few members of a small congressional subcommittee; on other occasions, they would be large groups, such as the House Armed Services Committee. Often they would stop off after visiting Vietnam, since Manila was known as a good, inexpensive place to shop. A few of the larger CODELS would have a second Air Force plane accompany them to carry all their purchases. It was incredible the lengths to which the Air Force would go in currying favor with the Congress. The cost to the taxpayer of these junkets was enormous.

An important part of the control officer's duties in handling a CODEL was to see that each visiting member of Congress was provided with $50 a day expense money in counterpart funds. I would count the days each congressperson or senator was to be in town, multiply it by fifty and place that amount of dollars in envelopes for them. I would then pass out those envelopes upon their arrival. Failing to do so assuredly meant trouble. A few CODELS provided pleasant recollections: I remember a three-hour automobile trip I made with Senate Majority Leader Mike Mansfield to visit Magsaysay's widow. He was a wonderful man, a fount of information on the Philippines, and many other subjects. Spending time with him was an education in itself.

Then there was the visit of Senator Edmund Muskie, a fine fellow, who was later to be our boss as secretary of state. He had a lively time with a group of senators in one of the craft shops. Accompanied by much ribald humor, Muskie purchased half a dozen woodcarvings of a hand, fist clenched, one finger raised, suggesting to Americans an obscene gesture. In the Philippines, by contrast, the carving had a religious connotation. My wife, who was accompanying the group, was shocked. One hoped the "good old boys" back in the Senate, who were going to receive these tokens, would accept them good-naturedly.

Of the thirty-odd CODELS visiting Manila during my four years there, the worst was a senator from Maryland, Daniel Brewster. I was assigned to handle him as part of a larger group of senators from the Armed Services Committee. A message from Brewster's office a week prior to his arrival said that he wanted to visit Corregidor Island and that a helicopter should be made available for the purpose. On the appointed day, the main body of senators arrived in the morning from a previous stop without Brewster. We then received a message indicating that he would be coming separately a bit later.

When he did not arrive by 3 o'clock in the afternoon, the Navy said it would be too late to make the flight that day. Shortly thereafter, Brewster arrived. He was furious at not finding the helicopter waiting and demanded that it return. I called Captain Ed Spruance, the chief of staff at Sangley, who remonstrated that it would be too risky to undertake such a trip. The helicopter would have to land in the dark at the Embassy on its return, endangering those on board, as well as others on the ground.

Brewster, however, would not be denied. Against his better judgment, Spruance released the helicopter, which flew back to Manila to pick up Brewster, Captain Richard Lazenby, the naval attaché, and myself for the flight out to Corregidor. A half hour before dusk, we landed on the uninhabited island, with its dense vegetation and ruins redolent of World War II. Brewster, a man in his early forties, had been a Marine during that war and was interested in examining the fortifications. He was fully aware that we were all concerned about getting back safely. No matter, the senator wandered about, taking his time. Finally, the pilot had to insist that we leave. Back in the air, Brewster was vociferous about having to depart before he was ready.

At this point Captain Lazenby, a very reasonable man, had had enough. I heard him say: "Senator, my name is Lazenby. I am a member of the Lazenby family of Maryland, and I am ashamed to call you my senator!" Astounded, I thought, "What a gutsy thing to do . . . but there goes one Navy officer's career." Brewster was a bit subdued by Lazenby's words, but then just seemed to shrug the matter off. However, he appeared to be a person who might later inflict retribution. The Senate Armed Services Committee gives its assent to an officer's promotion.

It was dark when we arrived back at the Embassy. The helicopter hovered near the Chancery. On the ground, I could see embassy personnel scrambling to move cars and circle them around the parking lot. Headlights were turned on to assist the pilot in landing. We came down blowing branches out of palm trees and scattering gravel and objects on the pavement. Other than that, no damage was done. On the Embassy roof terrace adjoining the ambassador's office, however, the situation was quite different. A reception for the other senators and their wives was in full sway to which numerous distinguished guests had been invited. The blast from the helicopter's rotors blew away tablecloths, glasses, and, worst of all, many ladies' hairdos.

I took Brewster up to the reception, but quickly ducked out before the ambassador could collar me for fear I would be shot on sight. Descending to the first floor to Dick Lazenby's office, I found him trying to telephone Washington to report what had happened. He obviously was distraught. Assuring him that I would go to the mat for him with the ambassador and the Navy, I told him I was proud of what he had done. Then, screwing up my courage, I went back up to the reception to find Senator Brewster in conversation with Ambassador Blair and several other persons.

A lively discussion was in progress about American World War II dead buried at the Fort McKinley Military Cemetery. I came in just as Brewster was opining that rather than bringing them to McKinley from all over the Pacific at great effort and expense, the dead should have been buried where they fell. This brought a very strong rejoinder from Ambassador Blair, who was supported by those present. Others had evidently taken the measure of the senator from Maryland, and rather than being upbraided for my participation in blowing the party away, I was the recipient of sympathy, as indeed was Lazenby. I felt sorry for Brewster's wife, who, I could tell, was long-suffering. I later learned that he was not reelected to a second term.

In addition to the continual congressional visitors, the embassy played host to trade delegations, businessmen, academicians, and celebrities of all sorts. It was an exhausting burden on embassy personnel. However, there was never any trouble in getting someone to act as control officer for a visiting Miss Universe group or a Miss America. I was taught a lesson in logistics and cost analysis while serving as control officer for an annual visit of the National War College class. The group of about fifty officers arrived aboard an Air Force four-engine jet, yet the message from Washington requested that I arrange for a plane from Clark Air Base to fly them from Manila to Subic and Clark and back. Had they come to the Philippines by commercial aircraft, I could see the sense in this request. When I queried the Pentagon on the matter, I was unceremoniously informed to do as I was told. The Air Force at Clark would provide a four-engine prop-driven C-54, which burned far fewer gallons of a less costly fuel for these local stops.

One of my more satisfying tasks during my Manila tour was the negotiation of the Corregidor Agreement, which established a permanent memorial on the island to those who fought and died there in World War II. American forces evacuated from Bataan held out on the island for months under the command of General Jonathan Wainwright until forced to surrender in May 1942. In February 1945, the Americans recaptured the island, often referred to as "The Rock," in an attack spearheaded by the 503rd Parachute Infantry Regiment. To capitalize on the element of surprise, the 503rd was dropped on the 400-yard-long parade ground on top of Corregidor. There they engaged defenders determined to fight to the last man. Intelligence estimates, which had placed the Japanese garrison at 600 men at most, proved to be woefully wrong. The battle was one of the most vicious of the war, with bayonet attacks and hand-to-hand combat.

In the end, of the 5,000 Japanese troops stationed on the island, only 50 survived. Some of the paratroopers training at the time I did, were assigned to the 503rd and were killed there. The Corregidor Memorial Agreement, therefore, had a special meaning for me. Over a period of weeks, working with Ambassador Rafaelita Soriano on the Philippine side, we brought it to realization. Foreign Secretary Mauro Menendez signed the document for his country and Ambassador Blair for the United States on December 22, 1965. Afterwards, I was graciously given a signed photograph of that ceremony in which I am pictured. It was inscribed, "To John Kormann, who did the work."

The spring of 1966 saw us involved in another Chiefs of Mission Conference at Baguio. Again, I was a rapporteur, dealing with our ambassadors from all over East Asia and a dozen high-level officials from Washington. On its heels was another SEATO Conference. The workload never let up. In the world of the common Filipinos, the president with the "mandate for greatness" was in office, but it was still too early to foretell whether there would be any change for the better. The population was increasing by leaps and bounds, from somewhat over 20 million when I arrived to almost 30 million by the time of my departure. Squatters and people living in poverty were everywhere, while 400 rich families controlled 90 percent of the wealth of the country.

The division between the rich and the poor in the Philippines was never more keenly felt than in functions raising money for charity. My wife has vivid memories of affairs she attended under the sponsorship of First Lady Imelda Marcos and her predecessor, Evangelina Macapagal. Invitations would be extended to the wives of the elite for an elaborate luncheon with entertainment. The women would come exquisitely attired for this social event at which contributions would be solicited. When all was said and done, next to nothing would be turned over to the charity in question, with the preponderance going to cover the cost of the party. Most likely, some money would be skimmed off the top, enriching the sponsors.

Once at a Christmas party at Malacanang Palace, Elsa noted that packages were being distributed to the "poor," based upon the recipient's having been issued a ticket. Well-dressed individuals, some with several tickets, would step up and claim a package. At one point, however, when an obviously needy, blind woman came forward without a ticket, she was pushed away by the guards.

My duties at times involved me in unusual projects. The effort to restore the sailing ship *Kailani* comes to mind in this regard. I was visited one day by a Captain James Kleinschmidt, USCG, who was affiliated with the Seaport Museum in Mystic, Connecticut. He had come to the Philippines to see if he could acquire the large commercial sailing ship built in the United States and then see to its restoration. The vessel, a bark, was constructed at the shipyards in Bath, Maine. It had a metal hull and, among other things, had sailed along the west coast of South America during the latter part of the 19th century carrying guano, nitrate fertilizer. After many years and vicissitudes, including two world wars, it finished out its life demasted as a cargo barge in the Philippines and at that juncture was a derelict.

I recall dealing with the Foreign Ministry on the matter of obtaining the hull, while efforts were under way in the United States to obtain funds for the reconstruction. The project proceeded as Kleinschmidt came out to the Philippines for an extended stay to initiate the work. It was thought by some Filipino officials that a reconstructed *Kailani* might make a handsome gift to the United States in conjunction with a future state visit by President Marcos. At the height of the early optimism, I had visions of my son, Brad, being able to sail as a cabin boy on the ship's voyage back to America. However, my tour of duty ended before any real progress had been made. Despite all the effort, the restoration project fizzled. The last I heard, the hull had been cut up and a few pieces sent to a maritime museum in San Francisco.

I had expected to be reassigned in October 1966 and had made reservations for a leisurely sea voyage home on the SS *President Wilson*. I was therefore surprised to receive word in April that I was to be transferred to Benghazi, Libya, departing Manila the end of June. I was to take up my duties at my new post in October. My first thought was that these orders made no sense. I was not an Arabist; I had no experience in North Africa, or the Middle East for that matter. When Elsa mentioned the move to Helen Service, the minister's wife, she commented jokingly, "What did you do to be sent to Benghastly!" I had, of course, heard of the place, primarily in conjunction with Rommel and the fighting in the North African desert during World War II.

After the initial shock and some inquiries, I learned I would be the principal officer at a post that was basically an embassy. Libya was a bifurcated country, where the capital had rotated between Benghazi and Tripoli every two years. Our ambassador currently was in Tripoli; however, the major ministries, such as foreign affairs and defense were in Benghazi. I concluded that the assignment would be a real challenge and sent my acceptance to the Office of Personnel in Washington.

The early assignment meant realigning plans. I had kept up faithfully with my Army Reserve duties while serving in Manila. Soon I would be eligible for promotion to lieutenant colonel, and it was important that I take my annual tour of fifteen days' active duty, which I had scheduled for that summer. I was able to arrange matters, but it meant that I would have to interrupt my home leave in the United States and fly back out to Hawaii to attend the Command and General Staff College course at Fort DeRussy. I had enjoyed being a part of the Army Reserve unit in Manila, where I had associated with officers having a wide variety of backgrounds, everything from American overseas business leaders to individuals who had been in Japanese captivity during the war. One captain, who continually sought me out because of our paratrooper backgrounds, turned out to be a soldier-of-fortune, a gunrunner with a price on his head. A mercenary, he had been supporting rebels on Java and Sumatra, and the Indonesian government sought him. I was contacted by our intelligence people and told to keep an eye on him.

By the time I was ready to depart, I had virtually become a fixture at the Foreign Ministry. My constant visits to Ambassador Rafaelita Soriano, the officer-in-charge of American affairs, made me well known. There was always some instruction from Washington that had to be carried out. Often it would be to seek Philippine support on a resolution up for a vote in the United Nations or on some other perhaps more troublesome matter. There were good days and some very difficult ones. However, my relationship with the Foreign Ministry, and indeed with the Defense Ministry and the Filipino military, had been very positive. I liked the people I dealt with in those places, and I believe the feeling was reciprocated. We had made many wonderful friends in Manila. It was particularly hard on the children to leave. Our servants were close to their hearts and would be terribly missed. Such, however, is life in the Foreign Service, and we geared our minds into a departure mode. When the time came, there were many *despedidas*, Philippine farewell parties.

The Kormann family departure from Manila had none of the leisure we had envisioned. With a boat trip out of the question, we were scheduled to fly on July 1 to the United States via stops on Guam and Hawaii. The day before we were to leave, a typhoon, massive beyond all expectations, struck Manila. There had only been perfunctory warning. We were in the final stages of packing, when roofs in the neighborhood were blown off and torrential rains flooded the area. Without air-conditioning, electric fans, or lights, existence becomes unbearable in that heat and humidity. At transfer time, there are always a thousand errands to run at the Embassy and elsewhere, yet I could not leave the house. Downed power lines crisscrossing the area flipped and sparked in the flooded streets, making explosive sounds. To venture into that wetness threatened electrocution.

Our family and the servants simply rode out the storm in the house. Without a basement as a refuge, I ordered everyone to take shelter in the study on the ground floor. It was a smaller room with more substantial walls in the event the building collapsed. Tying back drapes and curtains, I opened all the windows, as well as the doors between rooms, to allow the wind to pass through the house. Not to do so brought the danger of the walls or windows being blown in. In addition, a difference in air pressure in a tightly closed up house could cause it to explode or implode.

Although everyone was terribly frightened, there was no panicking as the wind and rain whipped horizontally through the rooms at well over 100 miles an hour. It blew in one direction for half an hour, followed by a period of ten minutes of dead calm while the eye passed overhead. Then came half an hour in which the torrent blew back the other way. Through it all, the house shook and shuddered violently, acting as if it would be lifted off its foundation. For me the experience was a demonstration of everything I had learned about typhoons and hurricanes and their unbelievably powerful, circular, rain-laden winds.

The telephones also were out of order, making it even more imperative that I somehow get to the Embassy. The utility company finally shut down the power lines and one hoped it was safe to venture out. Leaving the family to continue packing under the most miserable of conditions, I climbed into our car for the drive to the Embassy. The heavily flooded areas in the suburbs were nothing compared to what I encountered at intersections nearer town. Water was over a foot deep and in some places more than that. As I maneuvered through the torrent-filled streets, I would encounter jeepneys crowded with Filipinos. Their high wheelbase enabled them to pass through the waters more freely. However, driven with reckless speed, they created waves which sloshed up over the bumpers and doors of automobiles.

The water over the base of my car doors was rapidly seeping in, and I feared that I would join the many other vehicles stalled along the way. Everywhere, stranded occupants were walking, pants rolled up over their knees or dresses held high, holding shoes in the air. You could hear them cursing at jeepney drivers, whose careless attitude was causing thigh-high waves and geyser-like splashes. By some miracle I managed to reach the Embassy compound, but not before I had seen amazing sights. As I drove along the Manila Bay waterfront on Roxas Boulevard near the Embassy, I saw a large ship, a 4000-ton freighter that had been blown up over the sea-wall, its stern and propellers hanging up over the edge of the roadway.

There was destruction everywhere. Trees had been uprooted, buildings partially destroyed. The Embassy had suffered damage from the winds, and waves had come over the seawall causing flooding. The aftermath of the storm preoccupied the staff as I tried desperately to complete my departure processing. Most of my household effects had been picked up by the moving company several days earlier and were now somewhere down on the docks. I had no way of knowing where they were or what condition they were in. I learned that Manila Airport had been badly hit and that all flights in and out had been cancelled. We were due to fly out on Pan Am the next day, but that now seemed unlikely.

Leaving a post is normally a traumatic experience, but under these circumstances it was a nightmare. Even simple matters such as remaining in touch with my wife as questions arose was impossible with the telephones out of order. We finally managed to depart two days later on a propeller-driven plane, the first Pan Am flight out after the typhoon. As if to perpetuate our misery, we felt the aftereffects of the storm during the trip across the Pacific. The fasten-seat-belt sign was on during the entire eighteen-hour flight. We had several nasty exchanges with the stewardesses when we had to insist that the children be permitted to go to the bathroom.

The turbulence caused many passengers to be ill. My daughter Andrea fared poorly. A large group of Filipino laborers were aboard destined for Guam, which apparently did not suit the stewardesses, who were noticeable only by their absence. It was even difficult to obtain a glass of water for the children. Unlike ship travel, which was first class in those days, State Department officers below the rank of ambassador traveling by air did so by coach. That flight on Pan Am from Manila to Hawaii, where we stopped over, was one of the worst we were to experience as a family in the Foreign Service.

Our home leave during the summer of 1966 was a busy one. Arriving in St. Louis in early July, we were met by the Wellses and returned with them to Jacksonville, Illinois, where Dad Wells was enjoying his duties as a visiting professor at MacMurray College. Their pleasant little home at 860 West State Street housed the Kormann clan for two weeks, before we departed for Florida and a stay with my mother. After I returned from a tour of military duty in Hawaii, the final weeks of our home leave were spent in Washington in a rented apartment, while I attended a Middle East

Orientation Course at the State Department's Foreign Service Institute. Earlier, it had been decided that I would take Arabic language training at the post. Edwin Wright, one of our professors, had spent many years in the Middle East. At one point, he encouraged us to see the movie *Khartoum*, then playing at the Uptown Theater on Connecticut Avenue in Northwest Washington. It starred Charlton Heston and Laurence Olivier in a wild Technicolor drama about the massacre of General Charles Gordon in the Sudan in 1884. Wright said it would give us an insight into that part of the Arab world. I saw the film, little realizing that in less than a year I would in many ways be reliving that drama.

I was informed by persons who had served in Benghazi that it would be wise to use as much of my household weight allowance as possible to take along provisions for the tour. Once at the post, much of our food, particularly meat, would have to be ordered from Denmark and took months to be shipped. There were no supermarkets in Benghazi and household items and ordinary Western clothing were scarce, expensive, or nonexistent. For an American family of five, it took quite an effort to calculate what was needed for a two-year supply of canned foods, breakfast cereals, toothpaste, soaps, detergents, toilet paper, and a host of other things. Elsa and I went over vast lists of items available through the White Rose Company in New York and the S. S. Pierce Company in Boston. We placed substantial orders, which were shipped in large crates to the dock for loading aboard our ship, along with the Chevrolet car I had purchased.

In late September 1966, we drove to New York for the initial phase of our trip to Benghazi. This time we were sailing on the American Export Lines' SS *Constitution*, a large luxury liner, which plied an Atlantic and Mediterranean route, calling at Lisbon, Gibraltar, Majorca, Sardinia, and, lastly, Naples, our destination. It was a pleasant trip that made up for missing out on our sea voyage home from Manila. There was one early untoward incident on board, however, occasioned because of the Foreign Service members aboard. When it came to seating for the late, more formal dinner sitting, the maitre d' took it into his head to place those traveling first class at government expense along the side of the dining room at small tables. He announced in a voice that could be overheard that the cruise passengers paying their own fare did not want to sit with us at the larger tables.

I learned that a ship's officer afterward informed him that the persons he was referring to in this case were members of the diplomatic corps, which in many countries of the world was represented by the aristocracy. The point was driven home when our group, which included several strikingly attractive couples, appeared elegantly attired for dinner each night in an array of long gowns, mink capes, and dinner jackets. Unlike other passengers, we were going abroad for an extended period and had the advantage of steamer trunks filled with the formal clothing required for diplomatic entertaining. Much to the chagrin of the maitre d', it then appeared as if our group wished to remain aloof from the rest of the passengers.

The Consulate General in Naples arranged for us to stay at a large, older hotel in the center of town. In retrospect, one tends to forget the many details and vexations that accompany overseas travel. I had to see to it that the family and our considerable baggage were moved from the ship to the hotel. Arrangements had to be made to transfer several steamer trunks and large containers of provisions to the small, 1,000-ton Italian vessel, the SS *Citta di Livorno*, for the onward trip four days later across the Mediterranean to Benghazi.

Then there was the matter of taking our car out of the hold of the SS *Constitution*, checking it over, and obtaining papers from the local authorities to enable us to drive while in Naples. Most of this business was transacted in my very limited Italian. We spent three delightful days in Naples, driving along the scenic Italian coast down to Sorrento and eating in colorful little restaurants. We thought about climbing Mount Vesuvius, which dominates Naples and the cities to the south, but friends told us it was a hot, dirty, ash-filled trek. Instead, we visited Pompeii and were glad we did, coming away impressed with the ruins. Here, as we had done in Gibraltar and later in Malta, we hired a horse and carriage with a driver guide, an excellent way to see the sights and always a thrill for the children.

53. The Chiefs of Mission Conference in Baguio in February 1965 brought together high-ranking officials from Washington and American ambassadors from all over Asia. Senior military officers attended, including the Commander-in-Chief of the U.S. Forces in the Pacific (CINCPAC). The meeting, chaired by William Bundy, Assistant Secretary of State, reached key decisions on the war in Vietnam. Ambassador-at-Large Averell Harriman is at Bundy's right. The author, serving as a rapporteur, is seated next to the flag.

54. The signing ceremony of the Corregidor Memorial Agreement between the United States and the Philippines on December 22, 1965. Foreign Minister Mauro Menendez and Ambassador William McCormick Blair are affixing their signatures to the document. The author represented the United States in the negotiations and is seen assisting Ambassador Blair. The photo is inscribed, "To John Kormann, who did the work." (U.S. Information Service)

55. Vice President Hubert Humphrey and his wife, Muriel, represented the United States at the first inauguration of Ferdinand Marcos as President of the Republic of the Philippines in December 1965. Left to right are Ambassador Blair, the Vice President, the author, Mrs. Balir, and Mrs. Humphrey. (U.S. Information Service)

56. President Marcos receives the applause of the crowd at the inauguration. He gave a rousing address, calling the Philippines to greatness, which some compared to President John F. Kennedy's inaugural address. Many had high hopes that Marcos would, as he had promised, end corruption and be a model democratic leader, but some had their doubts. Among the latter was the author, whose questioning grimace may be seen slightly to the left of Marcos's right hand. In the row before Vice President Humphrey are (from left) former Philippine president Garcia and President Marcos's wife, Imelda. (U.S. Information Service)

57. The Kormann family on home leave in 1966 with the author's mother at her residence in Florida. The State Department had arranged a number of speaking engagements and TV talk show appearances during the period. Although a detraction from vacation time, the pleasure it gave to his mother to see her son on TV more than made up for the inconvenience.

58. The journey from Naples to Benghazi in Libya was made aboard a small, aged 1,000-ton freighter, the *Citta di Livorno*. The family car, a new Chevrolet sedan, was hoisted and dropped into a small, open area on the deck. Ropes used to lash it down were eaten by a dozen goats taken aboard during the rough Mediterranean crossing.

59. The American Embassy Office in Benghazi, Libya, as it appeared in 1966. The structure had been a heavily secured former Italian bank building with a vault-type front door and barred windows. The Principal Officer's official car is parked in the foreground.

60. Members of the April 1967 expedition searching for the *Lady Be Good*, the World War II B-24 bomber that vanished in the Libyan Sahara Desert in April 1943. Returning from a bombing run over Naples, Italy, at night, it overshot the airstrip on the coast and ran out of fuel 440 miles deep into the desert. Although the searchers pictured here had exact map coordinates, the plane was in a slight bowl-like depression just deep enough to keep it from being seen.

61. Standing on the wing of the plane with other members of the expedition are Ambassador David Newsom (wearing white cap and light-colored trousers) and the author to his right. When the plane was first located in 1958, the fuselage was intact, the radio worked, and there was water in the canteens. With fuel exhausted, the crew had bailed out, and the plane landed itself on automatic pilot. All ten crew members perished.

62. The author made the above pen sketch at the *Lady Be Good* site on the back of a piece of green-colored, doped canvas from the fuselage of the plane. The dry desert had preserved the interior; aircraft manuals and papers lying about were in perfect condition. It was an eerie experience to sit at the controls in the cockpit.

63. The expedition traveled 180 miles farther into the Sahara to the village of Kufra, the birthplace of King Idris I, ruler of Libya and head of the Senoussi tribe. Above, one of the expedition's Land Rovers stands before the crenellated walls of a structure that could have appeared in a movie about Beau Geste and the French Foreign Legion.

64. At the outbreak of the 1967 Arab-Israeli War, the American Embassy Office in Benghazi was attacked. The mob is seen on the roof attempting to raise the Egyptian flag. To assure the destruction of a large amount of secret files, codes, and classified equipment, eight members of the staff and two members of the Military Advisory Group (MAG) fought off the mob in a hand-to-hand struggle using rifle butts and tear gas. Locking themselves in the code room vault, they completed the destruction even while the mob was setting fire to the building. After an ordeal of fire, smoke, and tear gas, the embassy team was rescued by British troops.

65. The second-floor office occupied by the Ambassador or the Principal Officer/Consul, which looked out upon the cathedral square. It is pictured here months before the 1967 war. Early on during the attack, the floor of the office was filled with rocks and cobblestones thrown through the windows by the mob. Once in the building, the mob set the office on fire.

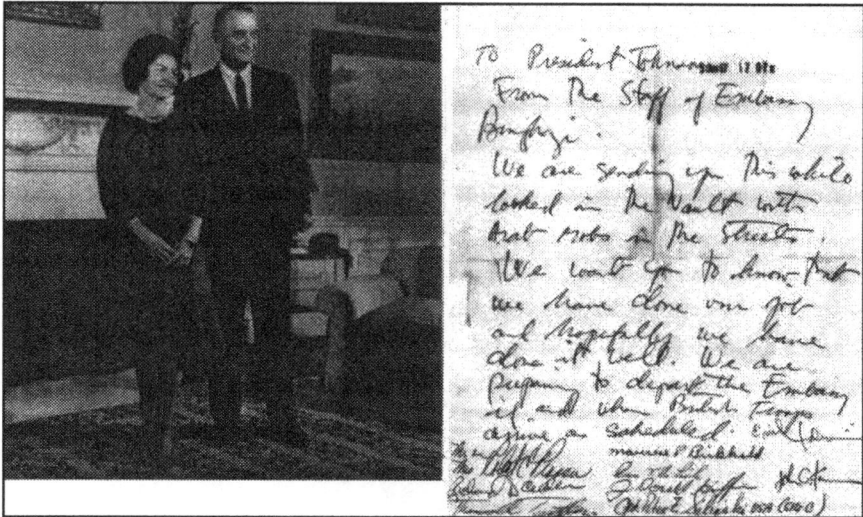

66. When word was received that a second attempt to rescue the Americans locked in the vault at Embassy Benghazi had been aborted, the author took down a picture of President and Mrs. Johnson hanging on the code room wall and wrote a final message on it addressed to the President. It was then signed by all present as a gesture of courage and defiance. The photograph with its message is now in the Lyndon Johnson Library in Austin, Texas. (U.S. Information Service)

67. The staff of American Embassy Office Benghazi received the Department of State's Superior Service Award on December 7, 1967. The author was also presented with the Medal for Heroism. In a separate ceremony (not shown), the Army awarded medals to Captain Peter Sielinski and Corporal Emil Fabrocini of the Military Advisory Group. Present in the picture, taken six months after the attack, are (from left): front row: Telecommunicator Richard Calder, the author, Telecommunicator Maurice Birkhold; back row: Public Affairs Officer Constantine Savalas (who arrived in Benghazi after the attack), Political Officer Thomas Twetten, and Communicator/ Records Supervisor Donald Griffin. Not shown are Administrative Officer Robert Prosser and secretaries Ann DeLisle and Doris Prosser. (U.S. Information Service)

68. The British departing Libya in February 1968. The Landing Ship Tank (LST) pictured took aboard the final load of troops and equipment from Benghazi. The last words to the author from his good friend, Colonel Alastair Martin, the Cyrenaica Area Commander, were: "It is all yours now, John!" In retrospect, that may have been a prescient comment about what lay ahead for America in its role in the Middle East.

69. Returning from Libya in 1968, the Kormann family flew to England to board the S.S. *United States*. That sailing marked the end for them of the era of Foreign Service personnel travel by ship. Air travel became cheaper and less time-consuming. With the change, however, came jet lag and the loss of a bit of elegance and a more leisurely pace of life.

70. "Rollingwood," the house in Chevy Chase, Maryland, the Kormanns bought in October 1968 after their return from Libya.

71. Newly appointed U.S. Ambassador to Liberia Samuel Westerfield visiting the Firestone Rubber Company in Akron, Ohio, in October 1969, accompanied by the author, who was Officer-in-Charge of Liberian Affairs at the State Department. Chairman of the Board Raymond Firestone (center) hosted a luncheon for the visitors and took them on a tour of the plant. Firestone at the time was still a major force in Liberia. Pictured at far right and left are company officers.

72. Economic Officer Frank Tucker and Political Officer John Linehan of the American Embassy in Monrovia, Liberia. Their plane was forced to make an emergency landing in the jungle when returning from the Firestone Rubber Plantation near Harper, Liberia. Prior to taking off, an elderly woman (possibly a witch doctor) was noticed dancing around and scooping up handfuls of dust, which she periodically tossed on the plane. When told to stop by the author and his colleagues, she turned and pointed the Voodoo curse sign at the plane and its occupants.

73. While the limited scale of the picture above makes it difficult to recognize individuals, it does give an idea of the size of this class at the Army War College, which has as its purpose the broad-gauged training of the most senior officers in the military and the government. Given the many thousands of candidates throughout the armed services, the 228 officers shown represent an elite. The class of 1973 consisted of 188 Army officers, 16 Air Force, 10 Navy, 6 Marine Corps, and 8 civilians from agencies with national security responsibilities. Among the future four-star generals and admirals in the class of 1973 are Norman Schwarzkopf, commander in the first Iraq War, and Carl Vuono, the Army Chief of Staff at that time. Earlier graduates included Generals Pershing and Eisenhower. (Army War College)

74. The coat of arms of the U.S. Army War College. The motto, *Prudens Futuri*, translated from the Latin is "Provident for the Future" or, more loosely interpreted, making provision for the future. There were earlier versions of the coat of arms, but the one shown, which is used today, was adopted in 1924.

75. A Kormann family picture taken for the U.S. Army War College Yearbook in 1973. Elder son Brad was in his second year at West Point. Daughter Andrea and younger son Matthew were in school in Chevy Chase, Maryland. (Army War College)

76. In April 1974, the author acting as deputy to the American ambassador, reopened the American Consulate General in Alexandria, Egypt, after a more than seven-year hiatus. The Consulate office, where the flag is being raised, was in temporary quarters. The beautiful downtown Consulate, heavily damaged by mob action during the 1967 Arab-Israeli war, remained to be restored. (U.S. Information Service)

77. Secretary of State Henry Kissinger being introduced to a member of the Egyptian parliament by the author. During the period of "shuttle diplomacy" to settle issues arising out of the October 1973 Arab-Israeli War, Kissinger visited Cairo numerous times on short notice. (U.S. Information Service)

78. President Richard Nixon is given "red carpet" treatment on his arrival in Cairo in June 1974. He and Mrs. Nixon, Egyptian President Anwar Sadat, and American Ambassador Hermann Eilts are at the start of a long receiving line of Egyptian officials and military officers, followed by Americans headed by Helen Eilts, the ambassador's wife.

79. At the height of the Watergate scandal, President Nixon endeavored to bolster his image as an international leader by traveling abroad. Egyptian President Anwar Sadat guaranteed him a tumultuous welcome. The road from the airport was lined with two million people in a tremendous display of hospitality. (U.S. Information Service)

80. Colonel John Kormann serving as a Reserve officer assigned for mobilization as a Deputy Director, Special Operations, Office of the Deputy Chief of Staff for Operations in the Pentagon in 1975. He was also subsequently attached to the 82nd Airborne Division in a support capacity. (U.S. Army)

81. A 2004 ceremony dedicating an impressive memorial on Sacrifice Field, Fort Benning, Georgia, in conjunction with a 17th Airborne Division Association reunion. The memorial is a tribute to the division's four Medal of Honor recipients and its 6,292 casualties, killed or wounded, in World War II. The author gave the memorial dedication address. (17th Airborne Division Assn.)

82. "Soldiers Three." Father and elder son Brad (USMA '75) welcome Matthew (ROTC '82) to the Army. The author's sons have served in keeping with George Washington's admonition that it is "the basis of our system that every Citizen who enjoys the protection of a free Government owes not only of his property, but even of his personal service to the defence of it."

83. George H. W. Bush, in a photo given during the author's service on the 1980 "Bush for President" National Campaign Staff. Earlier, in 1975, he had worked for Bush as the Department of State's representative on the Intelligence Community Staff, when Bush was Director of Central Intelligence. The author retired, after 35 years of government service, to join Bush in his campaign against Ronald Reagan for the presidential nomination. (Ron Wright)

After leaving the government, the author returned to his earlier training as an artist. He painted landscapes in oils on large linen canvases, at times encompassing both modern and traditional styles. The paintings focused on unusual light, sky and cloud formations, and brilliant color. Two examples:

84. "Outward Bound South Pacific," a 60" x 34" oil painting on linen. The painting combines a modern abstract, illusory rendition of the Golden Gate Bridge on a dramatic, realistic background of sky and sea.

85. "Lord Byron Journeys in the Dolomites," seen in its museum frame, is a 24" x 18" oil in the traditional, allegorical style of historical painting. The horse-drawn coach winds through mountains under luminous skies.

86. In 1983, the Kormanns purchased "Eagle's Tarn," their vacation home on Deep Creek Lake in the mountains of westernmost Maryland. It has been a great source of family togetherness, often accommodating up to fifteen people. Pictured is the speedboat and dock a distance below the house on the lake.

87. The author being initiated into the "Round the Horn Society" by an ancient Norseman, on a 5,000-mile cruise from Valparaiso, Chile, to Buenos Aires, Argentina, in 1999. Despite stormy weather and heavy seas, the ship passed Cape Horn twice, from east to west and then in reverse, before proceeding to the Falkland Islands in the South Atlantic Ocean.

88. World War II German and American paratroopers meeting on March 24, 2000, in Wesel, the site of the Allied airborne drop across the Rhine River fifty-five years earlier. Erich Heiken, vice president of the *Fallschirmjaeger Verband,* and the author, then president of the 17th Airborne Division Association, shake hands. Heiken in jest told the author: "John, I had you in my gunsight as you were coming down. I'm glad I missed!"

88. The Kormann family at the 50th Wedding Anniversary of John and Elsa on June 11, 1999. Fifteen members are pictured. Thomas Matthew Kormann, the eighth grandchild, was born the following year.

89. The author and his wife reflect that life may not have been one long, golden ballroom dance, considering the Foreign Service and military vicissitudes recounted in this book, but it certainly was worth the price of admission. Here they close with a final tango.

11
Benghazi: The Libyan Adventures

On the afternoon before our departure from Naples, I drove the Chevrolet over to the S.S. *Citta di Livorno*'s dock. It was a miniscule vessel compared to the SS *Constitution*, with an open deck area amidship of about 35 by 30 feet. I watched in terror as lines were slung under my car and a crane hoisted it up onto the open deck, where it was deposited and tied down for the trip to Benghazi. Elsa and the children were even more taken aback when they boarded the following day, as we ensconced ourselves in two of the ship's seven tiny cabins.

The other nine passengers on board were English, most sailing to Malta. An exception was an engaging young British Diplomatic Service officer assigned to the Consulate General in Benghazi. Our children were fascinated by his well-trained companion, a cat. This remarkable animal went to the bathroom by perching on the toilet, all very sanitary. I cannot remember, however, whether it was trained to flush!

We ate our meals at a long table in the wardroom with the captain and the first mate, who were affable individuals with a limited command of English. When seated at the table on the stretch between Naples and Malta we numbered fourteen. Although we were apprehensive as to what the meals would be like, they turned out to be quite good, Italian style. An incident that has become part of the Kormann folklore took place the first night at sea. One of the dishes the cook prepared as an early course I found particularly tasty; it resembled French-fried onion rings. When I subsequently inquired as to what it was, the Captain said, "uuktoopooso." At first, I did not understand him; then it dawned on me he meant "octopus."

Only a limited portion of fried octopus rings remained on the platter when two tardy diners, elderly, English, lady schoolteachers, took their seats. Once at the table, they eyed the dish preparing to sample it, when I cheerily commented, "Oh, have some octopus! It's absolutely delicious!" With that statement, a look of abhorrence crossed their countenances and they pulled back. The platter, thereafter, remained untouched until some-time later I announced, "Well, if no one else would like any more of this, I'll finish it. I hate to waste food." When we returned to the cabin, Elsa was furious. "You did that deliberately! You kept those ladies from touching that platter because you wanted it for yourself! Shame on you!" I found myself slinking away under her verbal barrage.

We had been under way only a few hours when we encountered a squall. Seas the SS *Constitution* would have taken in stride bounced our smaller vessel around unmercifully, and several passengers became sea-sick. Early on we learned from one of the passengers that the *Citta* had been sunk during World War II but had been refloated, repaired, and re-furbished. I hoped for our sakes that they had done a good job. I also worried about the car on the open deck but found that it had been roped down securely.

Our first port of call was the ancient city of Siracusa (Syracuse) on the southeastern coast of Sicily. In addition to taking on cargo lowered into the hold, we took on a dozen or more goats, which were simply herded onto the open deck where my car was located. The railings on either side of the ship kept them from going overboard. After a day at sea, however, they must have missed the green pastures of home and started snacking on the ropes tying down my Chevrolet. When I mentioned this problem to the first mate, he responded that we would be in Benghazi long before the goats chewed their way through.

The trip across the Mediterranean on the tiny, clanking *Citta di Livor-no* with my family imbued me with the sense that we were now truly in the Foreign Service. I might just as well have been an American consul, traveling to some exotic post a hundred years earlier. Our stop in historic Malta, with its vestiges of the Crusades and centuries of war, reinforced this impression. However, nothing had prepared me for our first view of Benghazi and the North African shore. On a crystal clear morning at sea, far off on the horizon, we spotted a vast bank of low-hanging, reddish colored clouds. My natural inclination was to think that I was witnessing a prairie fire. The air, even far out at sea, became heated. I was told by the ship's crew that it was the *ghibli*, a sandstorm. Laterite rock turned to dust in the desert by whipping sands gave it a red appearance.

Buried under those clouds somewhere was Benghazi, a city of 140,000 people. An hour later the storm had abated enough for us to discern the city's skyline, which was dominated by a double-domed cathedral built by the Italians after their occupation of Libya in 1911. I was told that Ameri-can flyers during World War II, using it as a landmark, often referred to it as "Mae West," after the bosomy screen actress. In time, the *Citta* made its way around the breakwater into the port area. As we pulled alongside the dock, we found a delegation from Embassy Benghazi waiting to greet us: Political Officer Thomas Twetten and his wife, Kay, Administrative Officer Anthony Santiano and his wife, Sigrid, and two local employees. With a staff ready to assist, I had none of the problems I encountered in Naples.

We were driven to the Residence, a three-story structure in the center of town, a block from the Corniche, the boulevard along the seawall. The interior of the Residence was beautifully furnished and very spacious, with several living rooms and a large dining room. However, the bedrooms were distant from one another on separate floors, a concern with children. Living on Sharia Istiklal (Independence Avenue) also presented problems; it was a main street in the middle of the city with no place for them to play. While the family unpacked, I proceeded to the office. Descending the Residence's marble staircase and opening the massive wooden front door, I encountered a soldier of the Cyrenaican Defense Force (CYDEF) on guard. A walk of one block took me to the office, a two-story building, formerly an Italian bank. It faced out on a large open plaza at the opposite end of which stood the towering cathedral.

As I entered the building, I was struck by the barred, ground-floor windows and the heavy, outer iron gate protecting the door of a massive, steel vault-type Mosler safe with a combination lock. These features were to play a prominent part in a drama that would take place six months later. The Libyan receptionist in the front hall greeted me respectfully. Members of the staff escorted me up to the ambassador's office on the second floor, which I would now occupy as the principal officer and American consul. The room was quite large, with a curved bank of windows behind an impressive desk, flanked on the left and right by consular and American flags.

My secretary, seated in an outer office, was a small woman I judged to be in her late forties or early fifties. I had a brief, pleasant conversation with her and learned that she had arrived in Benghazi a few months earlier from an assignment with our embassy in Rabat, Morocco. It had not been my intention that first afternoon to remain in the office very long. I was concerned about my family and their adjustment to their new surroundings. However, before I could leave, my secretary announced a visitor, the Catholic Bishop of Benghazi, the first of many courtesy callers. He, however, had an ulterior purpose. He had been petitioning my predecessors, and now me, for the return of the Residence, which initially had been a palace and then an Italian school for girls. The property had been taken over by the British during World War II and the church, which once ran the school, wanted it back.

My response to the Bishop was that I would convey his request to Washington. Questioning the staff about the matter afterward, I was told that it had a long history and that the State Department's Foreign Buildings Office had repeatedly sent back negative replies. It was now my obligation to try again.

Returning to the Residence that evening, I found my wife again facing a strange household staff and having to assess their competence. They were a cut below the skilled, hard working, English-speaking Filipinos at our previous post. Elsa, at one point, found them dusting books in the bookcase simply by dropping them in stacks on the floor to "shake them out." She did not catch them at this process soon enough, however, and some fine old volumes had their bindings broken. One of these was an original 1886-autographed edition of Englishman James Bryce's noted work, *The American Commonwealth*. Dusting was a constant undertaking. The red dust from the *ghiblis* was so fine that it would even find its way between pages of closed books and stain them.

Being principal officer at what was a part-time embassy had certain advantages. The quarters were furnished at a level suitable for diplomatic entertaining, with an extensive amount of gold-bordered embassy china, as well as silverware and crystal. Our own china and silverware could thus happily remain stored away in their packing and thus avoid the inevitable breakage.

My first few days at work were largely taken up making calls and receiving visitors. Among the first to visit me was Colonel Alastair Martin, the commanding officer of the British troops in Cyrenaica. Great Britain had an arrangement with King Idris by which an armored regiment, the 5th Royal Inniskilling Dragoon Guards, was stationed near Benghazi at Wavell Barracks. The British also maintained a military headquarters, as well as a Military (Assistance) Mission, at D'Aosta Barracks on the outskirts of the city. Colonel Martin was an engaging person, and we took a liking to one another from the outset. He was an old line officer, who had served in China in the 1930s. He extended the use of D'Aosta's Officers Club and the British Beach Club to my family and me. I was a bit taken aback when he asked whether I played polo and invited me to join his officers in the sport. After he left my office, I felt that I was again in a place time had passed by. I might just as well have been in British India a century earlier.

Colonel Martin's call was followed later that same day by a visit from the British military chaplain, the Padre. He wore a uniform set off with a clerical collar and appeared somewhat diffident. I was surprised, therefore, by his comment, "We will see you in your pew on Sunday," equally a question and a statement of fact. While my family was accustomed to attending services wherever we were assigned, in the church here maintained for the British troops and open to the English-speaking community a pew was set aside for the "American Ambassador." There was a brass plate designating it as such on the back of the pew.

As soon as I indicated my assent, the Padre seemed pleased and added, "You will, of course, take the services on your special days." Noting the puzzled look on my face, he explained, "On your Thanksgiving and holidays as such." This was the first time I had encountered this aspect of the British practice of noblesse oblige. In the Anglican Church, the leaders in the community, whether civilian or military, were expected to participate in the services, reading the lesson and even on occasion giving a homily. In my case, since there was a sizeable American membership in the congregation, it would be up to me to serve in the chaplain's place.

Functioning as a quasi-spiritual leader of the American Christian community was one of many curious aspects about my tour in Benghazi. My penultimate predecessor at the post had been Jewish. An exceptionally able and friendly officer, he had told me in Washington that there was little social life in Benghazi, particularly with the Libyans. I found this not to be the case. Arab acquaintances later told me they stayed away when word got out that he was Jewish. It made me wonder whether in those early days the State Department was trying to make a point in assigning him to an area so steeped in Muslim fundamentalism.

The population of Cyrenaica, Eastern Libya, was largely made up of peoples belonging to the Senussi tribes. Though many had moved to the cities and villages, they retained vestiges of their Bedouin life. They were deeply religious, conservative in their faith, and had a great sense of independence. Once I had established friendship with them, they were very loyal. I grew to like them and believe the feeling was reciprocated. They demonstrated their friendship toward me to the point where it surprised my colleagues.

The Senussi were an 18th century Muslim puritan sect who proselytized throughout North Africa. When Libya became independent in 1951, King Idris, a Cyrenaican and the grandson of the founder of the sect, was declared its ruler. His ascension met with objections from many Tripolitanians, who were not Senussi and were more sophisticated and Europeanized. Idris's rule over Libya as a whole was an uneasy one, backed by the police and the military.

Another one of my early perfunctory callers was the Russian consul. A nondescript man about forty years old, he made a profound impression on my secretary. She came into my office that morning with much flustering to announce his presence. I received him and we engaged in half an hour of general conversation. Being the newcomer, I probably learned more from him than he from me. In the back of both our minds, I am sure, was the obligatory memorandum of conversation we both would have to write about our meeting, he for Moscow and I for Washington.

That meeting, however, set in motion an unusual series of events. After the Russian consul departed, my secretary, still agog, exclaimed, "Oh my, did you see his eyes? What wonderful eyes . . . he is so handsome!" I had seen many Russians in my day, and this one seemed quite ordinary, dressed in Moscow's typical dark sack suit. She, however, carried on to the point where it made me wonder whether she was in full possession of her faculties.

During the following week, I was told by Political Officer Tom Twetten that she seemed preoccupied with the Russians and had received invitations from them to social events at their compound. I ascribed her actions more to the loneliness of an old maid than to anything nefarious. She likely would not have carried on in front of me had it been otherwise. Nevertheless, my background as an Army counterintelligence officer flashed a danger signal, and I proposed to do something about her assignment as soon as possible. This was the height of the Cold War and Benghazi was a sensitive post. My secretary handled secret material. Our office received highly classified messages from the State Department, the CIA, and the Pentagon, as well as from NATO Headquarters, the 6th Fleet and other American missions. The vault file room was extensive, as the building had originally been an embassy.

James Blake, our deputy chief of mission in Tripoli, whom I had not met before, passed through Benghazi a short time later. I called his attention to my secretary and stated that arrangements should be made to transfer her, preferably back to Washington. He seemed surprised that I was so definitive, particularly since I had been at the post such a short time. I told him that I found her a nice enough person, willing and competent in her secretarial skills, but that she was an incident waiting to happen. Jim said he would inform the ambassador of my concern and that was where the matter rested. A month later matters were brought to a head when she ran into difficulty in Tripoli, after which she was reassigned to Washington. A disturbing aspect of this affair was that the woman had been transferred from Rabat to Benghazi as a consequence of her involvement with the Soviets at that post. It was thought that this action would take care of the problem.

Our consulate staff in Benghazi consisted of a dozen Americans. We also had a thirty-five man Military Advisory Group (MAG) headed by a lieutenant colonel. Most of our personnel, those with families, were quartered in or near a suburb of Benghazi called Belaun Farms. There was a fair-sized American community there, as well as the American School operated by the ESSO (later EXXON) Company for its employees.

ESSO had substantial oil holdings in Libya and was in the process of building a $2 billion natural gas liquefying plant at Mersa Brega, halfway between Benghazi and Tripoli on the Mediterranean coast. Along with others from the embassy, our children attended their American School, for which the school received tuition payments from the State Department. The principal and the teachers, recruited in the United States, came largely from Texas and Oklahoma, where most of the ESSO company's employees had formerly resided. Classes ranged from elementary through ninth grade. On the whole, the curriculum and instruction were quite good. I was able to evaluate this since my position automatically placed me on the school's board of directors.

A month after our arrival, I paid my first visit to Tripoli to attend a Country Team meeting at the Embassy. I did so by flying Libyan Airlines, which operated medium-range jet aircraft. To drive meant traveling 700 miles along the desert coastal road. For a business meeting, that simply was not practical. Later, however, I was to make the drive several times with my family to obtain supplies at the Wheelus Air Base PX and commissary.

At the meeting, I met Ambassador David Newsom, the embassy's various section chiefs, and the officer commanding Wheelus Air Force Base. As the discussions progressed, I was struck by the importance of Benghazi and Cyrenaica in the scheme of things and the fact that I was the only one at the meeting who could speak for that vast eastern half of Libya. It was there that the oil strikes were taking place. It was there that American drilling and equipment companies were locating, and because of this activity, the United States was enjoying a $2 billion yearly balance of payments surplus in its trade with Libya. I returned to Benghazi eager to prepare a series of reports bringing Tripoli and Washington up-to-date on developments in my region.

By now Elsa and the children had settled into their daily routines in this strange new country. From the outset, we were swept up in a round of social activities. We received invitations from other diplomatic and consular missions, as well as from business people. Although Benghazi was considered a far cry from London or Paris, we soon learned that standards of entertainment were not that far removed. A number of my foreign colleagues were experienced diplomats and had served in many countries around the world. I recall a dinner party at the home of the Wakefields, our British counterparts, which was elegantly prepared and served. They had brought one of their servants with them from a previous assignment in Cairo. He wore a turban and a magnificent gold-braided robe. Had someone introduced him to me as the Sultan of Balihoochistan, I would have accepted it as fact. He made quite an impression moving around the dinner table meticulously serving each course.

Another time, the Brigadier commanding the British Military (Assistance) Mission invited us to dinner. At one point during the formal meal, the guests were stunned to hear a loud roar, followed by another. Shaken, several of us in agitated fashion inquired of our host," What was that?" To which he placidly responded, "That is a lion." "A lion!" we exclaimed. After a moment's pause, the Brigadier added with a twinkle in his eye, "You *are* in Africa, you know." We were baffled to say the least. The mystery was soon solved, however, when we learned that the house was only a short distance from the Benghazi Zoo.

Throughout that initial period, I made an effort to call on key Libyan officials, including those in the Royal Diwan (household), the Ministries of Foreign Affairs, Defense, Interior, and several others. In addition, I made it my business to establish good relations with the governor of Cyrenaica, the mayor of Benghazi, the area chief of police (*hakimdar*), and the head of the Cyrenaican Defense Force (CYDEF). I had learned early on, during my days after World War II in Berlin, how important it was to be on good terms with the police and the security forces. My contacts with them were to stand me in good stead during the turbulent days to come. Lieutenant Colonel Robert Campbell, our MAG chief in Benghazi, was helpful in introducing me to a wide range of senior officers in the Libyan Army.

A typical call, usually lasting about half an hour, would begin with a set pattern of reciprocal phrases in Arabic, inquiring about one another's health, family, etc. Tea or coffee (*shai* or *ghowa*), which had the consistency of syrup and was very sweet, would be served in tiny cups or glasses. As an alternative, one might be offered *gahzooza,* a sugary orange soda pop. More often than not the conversation would be conducted in Cyrenaican Arabic; only a limited number of officials, generally older ones, spoke English. I generally would use my beginner's Arabic,[1] backed up by the interpreting of Salah Butalag, my senior Libyan advisor.

It was the custom to pay brief calls on officials on Muslim holidays as a gesture of courtesy and friendship. One might arrive at their offices or homes to find several other callers there at the same time. While the visits were a sign of respect, they were also quite trying. Carrying out half a dozen or more of them during a day and, perforce, imbibing at least one sickeningly sweet drink in each place often left me with a queasy stomach.

On the occasion of a scheduled visit to Benghazi of Ambassador Newsom, Elsa and I decided it was time for us to host our first major reception. With Salah Butalag's assistance, we prepared an invitation list of 300 guests that included Libyan officials, members of the diplomatic and consular communities, business people, American and foreign, Libyan, British, and American military, and individuals from a variety of other categories. Included mistakenly on the list was a Libyan royal personage of dubious reputation and legitimacy. He was known as Abdullah, the Black Prince. Salah had referred to him as a man of wealth and influence who had his fingers in many facets of the economy, possibly also in the black market. I did not know at the time that most embassies considered him a social pariah.

The reception had a fine turnout; the Residence filled to capacity with guests happily in conversation and enjoying the refreshments. At a mid-point in the evening, there was a commotion at the entrance. Quickly moving to see what was afoot, I encountered several burly figures in long robes with unsheathed scimitars in the doorway. They cleared a passage into the reception for a large dark-skinned man in a magnificent robe wearing the khefia, the traditional Arab headdress. His appearance caused a great stir among those assembled. Ambassador Newsom, recognizing him, appeared stunned and whispered to me, "It's . . . it's the Black Prince. He's never invited. Didn't they tell you?"

I had sent an invitation list to Tripoli, but no one evidently had picked up on the matter. With the comment, "Well, he's here now," I went over and greeted my guest and did my best to make him feel welcome. All the while, his guards, still with scimitars drawn, eyed everyone warily, prepared to whack off a head or two, should it become necessary. Fortunately, when Ambassador Newsom, who was our houseguest, subsequently mentioned the matter to me, he did not seem particularly upset. The incident, however, turned out to be beneficial. After the 1967 Arab-Israeli war, when many Libyans shunned relations with Americans, Prince Abdullah remembered my invitation, extended a friendly hand, and was always ready to render me assistance.[2]

November 11, 1966, is a day my wife and I recall with a certain amount of amusement although it did not seem at all humorous at the time. The occasion was the Remembrance Day ceremony for Allied World War II dead at the Commonwealth Military Cemetery on the outskirts of Benghazi. It was held there every year on Armistice Day at 11:00 a.m. under the auspices of the British Army's Cyrenaica Area Command. The invited guests were seated in rows amid the crosses on that autumn day under the brilliant North African sun. The British military were resplendent in dress uniforms, their wives formally garbed, wearing picture hats. Peter Wakefield, the British consul general, sitting directly in front of me, was attired in his black, gold-braided, diplomatic uniform, replete with a magnificent, white-plumed, Duke of Wellington cocked hat. A very tall, handsome man, he was an impressive sight.

The ceremony, basically an Anglican Church service, included several hymns, sung to music provided by the 5th Royal Inniskilling Dragoon Guards' Regimental Band. As the service proceeded and the chaplain began his homily lauding the fallen, a single, lonely, dark cloud appeared on the horizon in an otherwise perfectly clear sky. In time, it floated above us. As the chaplain finished, we launched into a final hymn. I tended to dismiss initial raindrops, thinking this is Libya, the desert. It doesn't really rain here.

Under the circumstances, no one had brought an umbrella. Suddenly, the cloud burst and there was a downpour of unbelievable intensity. We had just finished the first verse of the hymn, as Niagara Falls pummeled us. I looked around to see whether anyone was running to seek shelter in their cars. However, with stoic English resolve and stiff upper lip, not a soul budged, and we sang eternally on during the deluge, bubbling out the remaining five verses of that hymn. To make matters worse for me, Wakefield's large cocked hat collected water as if it were a rain bucket, and every time he looked up from his hymn book the back of his hat, a natural spout, dumped even more water on me.

As the crowd left the ceremony, they were a dismal vision to behold. Had we all been thrown into a swimming pool, we could not have been more drenched. Women's clothing clung to them in revealing, embarrassing fashion. Picture hats flopped, soaked and misshapen. Uniforms were saturated to the skin. An officer poured water out of his saber scabbard. When we finally reached home and dried out, we found that Elsa's dress and broad-brimmed hat were ruined, as was her wristwatch, the case filled with water. My dark suit and tie shrank and lost their shape. My own Omega Seamaster watch, which was supposedly waterproof, was cloudy under the crystal but fortunately continued to function.

In retrospect, we may have fared better than some of the other participants, who were wearing ceremonial clothing. Even the four years in Manila, with its tropical rains, had not prepared us for that day, and I wondered later whether there was a lesson to be found arising from the experience. Alas, I found none, other than perhaps one should always carry an umbrella and wear rubber clothing in the desert.

From the time of my arrival in Benghazi, I had a sense of unrest with regard to the security situation, perhaps because of the guards constantly on station at the Residence and the office. Two years earlier, there had been student demonstrations. The CYDEF had shot and killed ten demonstrators on the street near our house, and scores had been wounded. Benghazi felt the repercussions of Egyptian President Nasser's stirring up the Arab world. The University of Libya was located a short distance down Sharia Istiklal from us and students often wandered past our door.

The Residence would be right in the thick of things, should any trouble develop. Remembering the bishop's request to have the building returned to the Catholic Church, I kept my eyes open for an alternate site.

As luck would have it, in December 1966 ESSO decided to vacate a complex it had been leasing as a guesthouse in the Belaun Farms suburb. ESSO was moving many of its employees to a housing development it had constructed at the Mersa Brega liquefied natural gas plant. Their Belaun Farms guesthouse was spacious, with numerous bedrooms and bathrooms. It had a high wall around it for security, and it had a garage. The place seemed ideal for our purposes. After talking with our Embassy in Tripoli, I cabled Washington, urging that we take advantage of the opportunity. I particularly stressed security and the volatility of the Arab-Israeli controversy, which could easily spill over into our area. The almost two thousand Egyptian workers involved in the construction of a pan-Arab Olympic stadium in Benghazi were easily stirred up by Nasser's diatribes against Israel and the United States.

Several weeks later, I received an order to undertake discussions with the Libyan owners of the guesthouse and, after some negotiating, we came to an agreement. It was one of the most fortuitous steps I was ever to take, one which received the repeated blessings of the Catholic bishop. He was ecstatically grateful when he heard from me that, after all these years, his church was to have its property back.

As the year drew to a close, I decided to couple business with a few days' leave and drive to Tripoli with my family in our Chevrolet car. The 700-mile journey along the desolate, often sand-covered, coastal road was an adventure in itself. There were no gasoline stations or rest stops and little habitation, save the tents of roving bands of Bedouins. I had to be careful driving at night, since stray camels took to sleeping on the blacktop pavement still warm from the sun.

Enough fuel could be carried in five-gallon cans for the trip. There was a small U.S. Coast Guard LORAN station facing the Mediterranean about halfway along the route. The handful of men manning this lonely outpost were always glad to receive the few American visitors passing through. We were their guests overnight. Happily, they had just been supplied with provisions by a C-130 flight from Italy. We enjoyed a breakfast of pancakes and sausages, finished off with stateside ice cream. It was a special treat for our children.

In Tripoli, I took care of several business matters at the Embassy and then, as a family, we did Christmas shopping at the Wheelus PX and Commissary. We also visited nearby sights, such as the magnificent ancient ruins of Leptis Magna and Sabratha. The remnants of these cities and that of Oea, ancient Tripoli, are rich in Phoenician, Punic, and Roman history.

Before leaving on our trip to Tripoli, we had obtained a tall, balsam "Christmas tree" from the government-run agricultural farm and decorated it with ornaments we had used over the years. I had the bright idea to sprinkle a mixture of dampened Ivory Snow soap flakes on the tree to give the appearance of snow. Instead, I caused everyone to sneeze and made the place smell like a laundry. It was the general wish that we should arrive back in Benghazi in time to spend Christmas at home. However, there was so much to do and see in the three days we were in Tripoli that it was Saturday, the 24th of December, before we were ready to depart. I decided, therefore, that we would drive straight through so as to arrive about 3:00 or 4:00 a.m. on Christmas morning. While that may seem arduous to some, we had on numerous occasions driven through the night on trips down to Florida to visit my parents. The children were used to sleeping in the back seat as Elsa and I drove on through the blackness. However, this drive was to become enshrined in our family's memory as no other.

After a late start that day, the drive was a tortuous one. In several sections the winds had shifted the sand dunes along the road, so that they covered the pavement. At night it was particularly difficult to discern the roadbed. Going off in the sand in a cumbersome, low-wheelbased American car could easily result in getting stuck. We were picking our way along an hour after dark on a particularly desolate stretch when it began to snow. Of all the things I was prepared for, that was the least expected. The North African desert can become quite cold at night and this was early winter... but snow... not just snow... a blizzard!

As the windshield wiper worked furiously, I questioned my judgment. With almost no vision, we moved along at a snail's pace, feeling for the roadbed through the tires. There was the ever-present danger in front of us of sleeping camels or the bodies of those that had been struck. Twice the glaring headlights of large Italian trucks lunged at us out of the snow and darkness. These transports barreled past us with reckless abandon, virtually forcing us off the narrow, two-lane road. Commonly used throughout Libya, those trucks testified to the influence the Italians still had in their former colony.

It stopped snowing as we drove through the isolated great Marble Arch erected on the road by Mussolini to mark the empty border between Tripolitania and Cyrenaica. The night then cleared and stars floated over the barren desert. It was freezing. As I drove along, with Elsa dozing and the children asleep in the back seat, I found myself becoming irritated by a light shining at the very top of my windshield. It bounced up and down in keeping with the motion of the car. Sometimes the light was hidden by the roof; at others, it appeared in the darkened, upper, tinted glass of the windshield. It was as if a stranger were shining a small, pocket flashlight at me.

Having had enough of that, I stopped the car and got out to see what was vexing me. It was as if I had stepped into another world. I had been told of the beauty of the desert at night, but this was almost beyond comprehension. The sky was saturated with stars, and there in the east was the source of my annoyance, the largest star I had ever seen. It was positively huge, with four pointed rays. Incredulous, I stood there saying to myself, "This is unreal!" But there it was on that cold, beautiful night, hanging low in the east in the direction of Egypt and the Holy Land.

With reverential tones, I called to Elsa to waken the children. Aroused from sleep, they joined us on the road. Andrea, without hesitation, said, "It's the Christmas star!" "Of course," Brad responded. "It's Christmas Eve!" The star pointed the way to Benghazi, and for the rest of the night it guided us home. I have spent considerable time since then, endeavoring to pinpoint what we saw. One thing is certain: I have never over the years seen anything in the heavens to match its brilliance.

Despite being in a strange, far-off land, our Christmas was joyous. It was highlighted by a fine church service we managed to attend on Christmas Day and several parties given by the British community. Before Benghazi, I had always had the impression that the English were stiff and reserved. As I will recount in several places in this chapter, I could not have been under a greater misapprehension, at least regarding their military and overseas communities.

New Year's Eve at the D'Aosta Officers' Club was a swinging affair, with ordinarily sedate couples on the dance floor doing everything from the Charleston to the Twist. At a party given during the holidays by the staff of the British Military Hospital, I was introduced to a libation, which I had heard about but not imbibed, called a "French 75," after the World War I artillery piece. This concoction consisted of a glass of champagne into which a cognac-soaked sugar cube was dropped and was as lethal as its name implied. A British Army nurse quipped at the time, "We only serve these at the hospital!"

One of the time-honored events that takes on more significance in out-of-the-way ports such as Benghazi is the occasional visit of American naval vessels. Sailors needed a respite from being at sea, and part of the duties of our Foreign Service personnel was to arrange for port calls. In the Philippines with the 7th Fleet headquartered there, the U.S. Navy had simply taken care of such matters. I received a cable one day indicating that the commodore of a destroyer squadron and his flagship planned to call and that I should take steps to obtain the necessary clearances and suggest a suitable program for the officers and the sailors.

To say the least, I was apprehensive about a bunch of sailors running around in such a conservative Muslim city, where it was forbidden even to look at women and drinking alcohol was against the law. However, I complied with Washington's instructions, while indicating the need for the Navy to take special care. The visit opened the door to a new world of naval protocol for me. The flagship was an older swaybacked destroyer.[3] The commodore paid a formal call on me at my office, which was reciprocated by my visiting the ship, where I was ceremoniously piped aboard. According to maritime etiquette, upon the departure from the vessel a consul is given a seven-gun salute.

The first evening, we held a reception for the commodore and the ship's officers at the Residence, to which a variety of appropriate guests were invited. The commodore in turn hosted an open house aboard ship, serving hot dogs and soft drinks. The Navy, I learned, by regulation never serves hard liquor aboard ship. As part of the recreational activities, a basketball game was arranged between the ship's personnel and a team from the University of Libya. In a closely matched game, the Libyan team won in the last minute. I was never quite sure if this was part of a Navy strategy to foster goodwill.

Other than one sailor's incurring the wrath of the authorities for trying to enter a mosque with his shoes on, the visit, which lasted two and a half days, went swimmingly. I was able to send a message to that effect back to the State Department, with a copy for the Navy.

Several weeks later, a newly commissioned British frigate visited Benghazi.[4] The Wakefields went through a similar drill. Elsa and I were invited to their reception, as they had been to ours. That is about where the similarities stopped. We were guests at an elegant black-tie dinner aboard that sleek, formidable man-of-war. The soup amazed the guests. When it was placed before us, we noted that the left half of the soup was white, while the right was red. In the upper white corner there was a small crouton in the shape of a cross.

Noting our reaction, the captain, our host, explained that we were about to partake of Maltese soup. Indeed, what we were looking at was a miniature replica of the Maltese flag. "What keeps the two halves from flowing into one another?" was the question on everyone's lips. "Ah," the Captain replied," that is a British Navy secret." There followed a superb multicourse meal with fine wines. Afterwards, on a lovely evening, the guests danced under colored lights on an awning-covered deck to music provided by the crew's orchestra. When all was said and done, I was left with the feeling that although the United States was unchallengeably the mightiest nation on earth, that time it came away looking like the country cousin.

When I arrived in Libya in the fall of 1966, the oil discovery boom, which had begun in the late 1950s, was in full sway. Petroleum companies from the United States, Britain, Italy, France, the Netherlands, and other countries were all vying for drilling concessions and vast areas of Libya were being subdivided. British Petroleum (BP), in conjunction with Nelson Bunker Hunt of the billionaire Texas oil family, were early discoverers in their Concession No. 65. Oil was flowing freely from wells deep in the desert. Subsequently, BP Exploration Company (Libya) and Hunt constructed a 350-mile pipeline to a terminal at Marsa al Hariga near Tobruk.

As the American representative in Cyrenaica, I received an invitation to the ceremonial opening of the pipeline on February 14, 1967. I arose at 5:00 a.m. that morning for the 300-mile flight to Tobruk. The lavish ceremony was held in a huge tent with many costly carpets on the floor. The food and refreshments for the several hundred guests were typically Bedouin. Elderly King Idris, the Crown Prince, members of the Royal Household, and many government leaders attended, as well as numerous desert sheiks. Hunt, his brothers, and their wives arrived in a large private jet from the United States. Other overseas guests were brought by chartered aircraft. The entire affair was something out of the Arabian nights.

The ceremony afforded me my first opportunity to observe King Idris at close hand. He seemed frail and removed. After speeches by the Libyan minister of petroleum affairs and the chairman of British Petroleum, Hunt presented the king with a massive solid gold key to a special housing development in Tobruk. The key, which appeared to be a foot long and enclosed in a magnificent velvet-lined case, was virtually a heavy bar of gold bullion. It struck me as possibly an ingenious way of proffering a bribe. Immediately after my return to Benghazi, Hunt called on me at my office, visibly upset. He had made an offer to buy the New Orleans Saints football team and was beside himself trying to find out where the negotiations stood. Expletives flew, as he described his efforts through the Libyan telephone system to reach the United States. I did my best to assist him.

I had come to know Ambassador Newsom well. He was conscientious about staying in touch with this area of his responsibility. He would visit us about once a month, and we finally set up a special room and bath for him in the Residence. He was a considerate guest, and Elsa and I enjoyed his company. At times, he would arrive with Mrs. Newsom and their children. On one occasion, he came on a Muslim holiday (Eid), and we made the rounds of courtesy calls on high-ranking Libyan officials together. After a number of calls, I had enough *shai* and *gahzooza* to make a horse sick, but he was still raring to go. He was the consummate ambassador, and I admired him greatly. In March 1967, I received a call from him proposing that we undertake a two-week trek into the Sahara down to the Kufra

Oasis, where King Idris was born. En route to Kufra, he indicated, we would stop at the *Lady Be Good*, the World War II B-24 Liberator bomber that had been lost in the desert for many years. Having been intrigued by the story of the *Lady be Good* and pleased to have a chance to travel in the Sahara, I greeted the entire proposal with enthusiasm.

The story of the *Lady Be Good* is fascinating: The plane took off for a raid over Naples from an airstrip at Soluch, south of Benghazi on April 4,1943, and never returned. The wartime assumption had been that it had gone down in the Mediterranean. Instead, on its return from Naples a tail wind had caused the navigator to misjudge the flying time and he had not noticed the coastline. From the air, the sands of the desert at night appear very much like the sea. Thinking he was still over the Mediterranean, the pilot overflew the Soluch tower radio beam and continued outbound on into the desert. Eventually running out of fuel, the nine-man crew bailed out. The plane, on automatic pilot, came down gradually, landing itself on a barren, flat, pebbly surface. The rest of the story is one of hardship, horror, and death in the Sahara.[5]

On May 17, 1958, more than fifteen years later, it was spotted by chance 440 miles deep in the Sahara Desert by a plane from an oil exploration company. Although both the British and American military authorities were informed of the sighting, nothing was done about it, since numerous Allied and Axis aircraft had been downed in the Mediterranean theater during World War II. A story about the B-24 in a Tripoli English language newspaper months later, however, roused public interest. When a ground party from the D'Arcy Oil Exploration Company arrived at the plane in late February 1959, there were no bodies to be found, perpetuating the mystery.

Media attention given the "ghost plane of the desert" spurred on the investigation. In the ensuing months, strenuous efforts were made by the U.S. military to locate the crew without result. Finally, on February 11, 1960, nine days after a CBS Armstrong Theater television special on the *Lady Be Good*, the pitiful remains of five crewmembers were discovered 78 miles north of where they had landed. A diary recounting the daily horror was among the items recovered. Eventually, three other bodies were found: One sergeant had struggled on 11.5 miles farther and another 37.5 miles. Later, remains covered by a partially opened parachute indicated that at least one member of the crew, the bombardier, had died instantly and been spared the agonies of his comrades. One body still lies hidden in the desert. Despite the crew's desperate efforts, mostly over open rocky ground, there was no possibility that they could have made it to the coast. A few miles farther and they would have entered the great Calanscio Sand Sea, with dunes 150–200 feet high stretching for hundreds of miles.

Our travel, twenty-four years later, would be at the exact time of year the tragedy occurred. Temperatures in the Sahara might range from 135 degrees Fahrenheit during the day to less than 40 degrees at night. Arrangements were set in motion over the following weeks to prepare for a safari of eight persons and a CYDEF guide. We would travel using two Land Rovers, a Jeep, and a small Dodge Power Wagon truck. Among our group were the ambassador, the defense attaché, a U.S. Air Force officer who was liaison to King Idris, a Mobil Oil geologist, two officers from our MAG in Benghazi, and myself.

The plan was to have the contingents from Tripoli and Cyrenaica gather at Agedabia 175 miles south of Benghazi on the coast and from there proceed down into the desert. I remember scratching around for suitable clothing for the trip and finally deciding to use my old Army suntans, desert boots, and a wide-brimmed hat with a parachute silk scarf hat/neckband. I had a pith helmet made in India but thought better about wearing it for fear of being kidded, as indeed our Mobil geologist was when he turned up in one.

In going over the list of supplies, I noted that we would be eating Army C-rations. Extended periods living on C-rations during World War II had given me an aversion to them, so I made it my business to supplement this fare with some canned goods of my own. Placing them in a pillowcase, I included a number of my favorites such as chow mein, chicken à la king, lasagna, and a variety of soups and canned fruit. When we met in Agedabia, I learned that I would be riding in Ambassador Newsom's Land Rover with the CYDEF guide.

Taking on the role of "trail boss," Newsom checked the vehicles and went over our supplies prior to starting out. When he came across my pillowcase with the canned goods, he exclaimed, "What's that?" I told him what it was and explained how I felt about C-rations. He was annoyed, telling me that every extra ounce of weight might mean the difference between success and failure in getting through the desert sands. I removed the pillowcase from the vehicle and began to dispose of the contents by the side of the road, when he had a change of heart. "All right," he said, "take it with you. But the minute we see we are overloaded, dump it!"

We started off with the ambassador at the wheel, me in the front passenger seat, and the CYDEF guide in the back. Our first day's drive took us over ground with varying surfaces, often gravelly with marble-sized stones (*fesh-fesh*). At other times the terrain was sandy and, on occasion, rocky. Generally, the land was flat to slightly undulating. The first night we stayed in an oil company camp near the El Gialo Oasis, which had prefab buildings and conveniences I had not been expecting.

From then on, things went downhill. The following days when we made camp, we cooked in the open and slept on the ground. As we entered the Great Calanscio Sand Sea, the vehicles started getting stuck in the sand and we would have to shove tracks under the wheels to extricate them. The tracks, which we carried on the roofs, were sections of metal flooring used to construct temporary airstrips in World War II.

We soon learned how important it was in deep sand to keep the vehicle moving at about 30 miles an hour. Slowing down, and above all stopping, risked being mired. Newsom had recently purchased his Land Rover and was enjoying taking it through its paces as we came upon an area of especially high dunes. Serving as the lead vehicle, we were racing up one dune when the Libyan CYDEF guide became agitated, yelling in Arabic for us to stop. It was only a short distance from the top and to stop meant the Land Rover would surely become stuck. Nevertheless, so violent were the guide's protests that we did, feeling the wheels sink down.

The guide jumped out and ran up the steep incline to the dune's crest and pointed downward. Joining him, we saw that we were standing on a cliff, looking down 100 or more feet. We had encountered a "slip-faced dune," a deadly peril to desert travelers.[6] Our Land Rover likely would have gone down that precipice end-over-end, and quite possibly killed the three of us. On that occasion, our Libyan guide served us well and we were extremely grateful to him; but when our safari later lost its bearings, he proved woefully inadequate. Efforts to raise Benghazi, Tobruk, or any place else on our radio proved useless. Instruments carried by the Mobil Oil Company geologist were not working properly either, perhaps due to magnetic distortion.

Deep in the dunes and not sure where we were, we made camp that evening. I could see that the ambassador was worried. Determined not to let our situation disturb me, I laid out my sleeping bag and started cooking my supper on a little sterno stove. I had not yet had to dispense with my pillowcase, so I took out a package of soup mix and cans of chow mein, noodles, and lychee fruit. My colleagues were heating C-rations. As the aroma of my soup and chow mein wafted through the camp, Newsom came over to ask what I was cooking. "A Chinese dinner," I replied. Taken aback, he pointed to a can with Chinese characters on it saying, "What's that?" To which I responded, "Oh, that's lychee fruit—tastes like Queen Ann cherries in sweet syrup, only better. Comes from China. I found them in the market in Benghazi." Seeing the look on his face, I could hardly contain myself. When all was said and done, everyone sampled my chow mein and lychee fruit, and I was hard pressed not to become the camp cook.

One member of our group brought several items on the trip to test for use in survival situations. We had finished eating, it was getting dark, and we were preparing to bed down when he went off to climb a nearby dune. I watched him as he reached the top. Suddenly, there was a pop and a red flare shot high into the sky, followed by another. For a moment, I felt as if I were at sea on the Titanic. These wandering thoughts were interrupted by a highly agitated Ambassador Newsom standing near me shouting, "What's he doing? Get him down from there!" We were lost, but I suspect that the last thing Newsom may have wanted was to indicate any such thing or to be "rescued." He may have envisioned headlines, "U.S. Ambassador Missing in Libyan Desert; State Department Concerned." Had I been in his place, I would have felt the same way. I am sure he was determined to extricate us from this predicament without any notoriety. Despite the seriousness of the situation, however, I found myself laughing.

Several times our vehicles became stuck in the deep sands of the Calanscio Sand Sea, but we became more and more adept at freeing ourselves, using gravity to assist us. When stuck going uphill, the solution was to back up and then swing around until the rear wheels were higher than the front. We would drive in a circle between the dunes to obtain speed and with a sling shot effect get up over a difficult dune.

Exiting the Calanscio, the terrain resembled the surface of the moon. We still did not have our bearings nor had we made radio contact when we came upon the remains of an encampment. Blackened ground testified that fires had been made at the spot, but in the desert it is difficult to tell how long ago they had been set. Examining the encampment to ascertain who had been there, it appeared that it had been an oil exploration party. We hit the jackpot when we came across a seismic stake they had driven into the ground, providing us with grid coordinates. Pinpointing them on our maps, we saw to our shock that that we were only a few miles from the Egyptian border. Had we continued on our path, we might well have wandered across with unforeseen consequences.

For those who have not ventured into the Sahara Desert, I should try to conjure up a vision of how vast it is. We traveled for hundreds of miles without seeing a single living thing, not even an insect or blade of grass. We broiled under the sun by day and froze at night. The desert is infinitely varied, ranging from lunar landscapes to sand dunes. There are high buttes or mountains around or through which passage must be found. On one occasion we came across the eerie burnt-out hulks of World War II tanks, vestiges of their tracks' maneuvering still visible in the hard ground. The British Long Range Desert Force had battled the Italians in these far-flung reaches of the Sahara.

Once we became aware of our exact location, we headed southwest for the *Lady Be Good*, which we knew to be at 26 degrees 42.5 minutes north latitude and 24 degrees 01.5 minutes east longitude. Arriving in that area late one afternoon, there was no plane to be seen on that barren, ostensibly flat, stretch of desert, not even when standing on the roof of a Land Rover and searching the far horizon with binoculars. Finally, we succeeded when the party split up and crisscrossed the area. Searchers in the other Land Rover came back exuberantly blowing their horn, letting us know of their find not far from us.

The aircraft lay in a shallow bowl-like depression, just deep enough to keep it from being observed. I was astounded to see it was still in good condition, considering that it had crash-landed twenty-four years earlier. The fuselage, other than a break amidships, was all there. The cockpit was completely intact. The scene sent shivers up my spine. I had to force myself to enter the aircraft; I am sure my companions must have had similar emotions. Once inside, it was as if I had revisited my war years. So much of it reminded me of the C-47s and CG-4A gliders I had flown in. There were manuals and other items lying about. When the plane was first visited sixteen years earlier, it was reported that the radio still worked and the canteens left behind by the crew still contained water.

As I walked around the plane examining various parts, I disturbed an engine cowling, only to note that I had caused it to drip oil. We overnighted out of the desert wind in the lee of the *Lady Be Good*. I recall that I slept fitfully, hearing engine noises and seeing apparitions. Everyone with a camera took pictures. A group photograph was taken for posterity of us all, standing on the wing of the plane. Before leaving, I removed a loose section of the doped green fabric of the fuselage and completed a pen and ink drawing of the scene on the backside.

The next destination of our trek was the oasis and village of Kufra, 180 miles to the southwest. By now we were experienced desert travelers and took the terrain variations in stride. In the vicinity of Kufra, rock outcroppings and high buttes extended for miles on either side of us, forming a natural channel in our direction. Nearing the oasis, we saw a stretch of date palms, a small lake, and numerous adobe houses. There was a larger structure with crenellated walls, affording the appearance of a French Foreign Legion fort. Hollywood might well have used this spot to film *Beau Geste*.

We were greeted by local officials and afforded the hospitality of sleeping in primitive guest quarters. As planned, three members of our party continued south 75 miles toward the border of Chad to Awiknat and the range of mountains that rose beyond there.[7] The rest of us awaited their return in Kufra. During their absence, the ambassador and I met with our hosts. Sharing a meal with them, we sat on carpets on the ground out in the open. The meal was a mixture of greasy lamb, goat, and rice, piled high on a very large, battered, slightly rusted Coca-Cola tray. We scooped out portions with our fingers, as flies buzzed around us. I shall never forget the look of horror on the face of Colonel James Moore, the defense attaché, when he was invited to join us. He graciously declined and beat a hasty retreat.

It was decided early on that after our hot, dusty journey, we simply had to take a swim in the lake, which looked so very inviting. Never thinking we would need bathing suits on the trip, we had brought none and so were forced, the ambassador included, to dip in our undershorts. We must have been quite a sight. Once in the water, it turned out to be so saturated with salt that we simply floated on the surface, without any chance of sinking. We came out positively crusted, which was unpleasant and irritating to the skin.

The party journeying to Awiknat returned without incident, the better for having missed our swim. Arrangements were made to have a C-47 fly down to Kufra to return the ambassador to Tripoli, dropping me off in Benghazi. We had to get back to work, he said. A sandstorm, however, forced a delay. When the plane finally arrived, the pilot complained that in addition to being delayed by the storm, he had difficulty in locating Kufra in that vast desert landscape, likening it to finding a pinpoint in the ocean. While I was spared making the arduous trip back to Benghazi overland with the others, I found myself missing those added days of adventure.

Returning from the trip, I was immersed in completing a series of reports. We had planned as a family to take some annual leave in Europe during the month of June, after we had moved to the new Residence. I arranged just prior to that time to have our Chevrolet car shipped over to Athens and held there in a garage pending our arrival. (That was before one could readily rent cars overseas.) It was to be an arrival delayed many weeks. My negotiations for taking over the ESSO Guesthouse had been concluded in late March, and repairs and modifications to the structure were now finished. Anxious to move the family out of the city and into their new home as soon as possible, I hired local movers, but there were delays due to a labor dispute and the job was only just being started. I then took steps to use our office truck and some Libyan workers to complete the move, settling the family in the final weekend in May.

The Middle East situation became more volatile daily. The local press and radio, full of Egyptian President Gamal Abdul Nasser's diatribes against Israel and the United States, were arousing the Libyan population, especially the university students. I ran into sporadic demonstrations around town as I went about my official duties. Looking back, some of these moments were humorous, others far from being so. During that period, we attended a cocktail party given by the elderly French consul in his spacious apartment overlooking the city. His wife was living in France at the time. The doors to his balcony were open, and during the party one could hear the demonstrators.

I was talking to a very attractive, single Englishwoman in her early thirties, while basically having an ear cocked for shouts in the streets below. At one point I casually asked her, "And what do you do?" thinking she worked for one of the British firms. Looking me straight in the eye, she responded, "Oh, I am Monsieur the Consul's mistress." To her mischievous delight, I gulped, nearly swallowed the olive in my glass, and spilled some of the drink on my tie.

I recall receiving a very formal engraved invitation from the British brigadier, commander of the Military Mission, and his wife to a "Black Tie Pajama Party" at the Beach Club. Not knowing what to make of it, I had my secretary call to make inquiries. She returned to comment, acidly, "It means just what it says, you come in pajamas, instead of a tux, wearing a black bow tie. Women in nightgowns." I was dumbfounded. I knew the Brits were great partygoers, but this was beyond the pale. I could not wait to go! It turned out to be a lively, fun-filled affair. In a letter my wife wrote to her parents at the time, she mentioned that party. Relating it to the unrest in Benghazi, she remarked with considerable prescience, "They fiddled, while Rome burned!"

A week later, on Friday, June 2, 1967, I attended a late afternoon reception given by the Italian consul general on the occasion of his country's national day. I was busy in conversation with a Libyan official when the Soviet consul rushed up to me and, almost gleefully, told me that a large unruly mob was demonstrating in front of my office. The word quickly spread among the guests. In one of life's more dramatic moments, I bid my host farewell and rushed out, calling to Jaabha, my driver, to take me to the vicinity of the embassy. Telling him to keep the official car with the American flag flying from the fender out of sight, I made my way to the building on foot.

Two Libyan CYDEF guards were still at their post by the entrance. Moving through the noisy crowd, I came up to them. They recognized me and signaled for the staff inside to let me in. Political Officer Tom Twetten, who had been in charge, briefed me on the situation, indicating that there had been no serious damage to the building. After an hour, as darkness set in, the mob moved off, leaving me to finish a cable to Washington reporting the incident.

The following day, Saturday, June 3, 1967, my colleague Consul General Peter Wakefield and his lovely wife, Felicity, hosted a large Queen's

Birthday reception at their Embassy. There was much pomp and circumstance. The British military, with their dress uniforms and regimental band, were very much in evidence It was a grand affair, but in retrospect a sad one. I did not know it at the time, but this was the end of an era; one would no longer see its like again in Libya, which in a sense had been a British protectorate since World War II.[8]

As I moved through the assembled guests talking to diplomats, Libyan officials, and businessmen, there was a sense of foreboding. The British military with whom I talked indicated that they were in a state of readiness, and special steps were being taken as we spoke to protect Her Majesty's Embassy. The Middle East political pot was boiling and might soon spill over. How soon, we were about to discover.

*We had an exceptionally competent staff in Benghazi. George Naifeh, the public affairs officer, and his wife, Marion, both of whom spoke Arabic, were the best the Foreign Service had to offer. Sadly, they were being transferred elsewhere in the normal course of their duties. Everyone, the Libyans in particular, were very sorry to see them go, and there were numerous farewell parties for them. On the day of their departure, my wife and I rose very early to accompany them to the airport. After wishing them Godspeed and watching the plane ascend into the sky, we drove back to Benghazi in the official car. On the way, we dropped Elsa off at the new Residence in the suburbs.

The day was Monday, June 5, 1967, a day I shall never forget. I arrived at the office around 9:00 a.m. to encounter Libyan staff members in great excitement rushing out of the building, while a guard detachment of five CYDEF soldiers took positions at the door. I was told that war had broken out between Israel and the Arab countries, and unruly mobs were already in the streets. Running upstairs to my office, I met Tom Twetten, who calmly gave me a situation report. I gave instructions to the staff to call the Emergency and Evacuation (E & E) Committee together and to secure the building. While we had done some burning of classified material in the previous weeks, urgent measures now had to be taken to deal with the vast amount still in the file room.

In the final analysis, despite the fact that the ambassador was in Tripoli, Benghazi was a de facto embassy, with all that went with it. It was a repository for top-secret messages and documents from Washington and posts all over the world. Should this material or the code machines fall into unfriendly hands, the consequences for the United States could be disastrous. I immediately ordered the files to be burned, using the file room incinerator, as well as five emergency fifty-gallon drums on the roof.

The E & E Committee met promptly, and within fifteen minutes coordinated instructions were passed on to everyone. Key persons on the

E & E Alert List were to be telephoned. The thirty-five members of the Military Advisory Group were to have played a key role in the defense of the Embassy, but a telephone call from Lieutenant Colonel Campbell informed me, minutes after he had left the E & E meeting, that he had run into mobs on returning to his headquarters. He said it would be unwise to try to force a passage to the Embassy with his men at this time. However, a station wagon loaded with weapons for us had departed earlier. Indeed, while we were on the telephone, it arrived, accompanied by Army Captain Peter Sielinski and Corporal Emil Fabrocini, who had come along to help defend the Embassy. Footlockers with rifles, pistols, grenades, tear gas, and gas masks were quickly carried inside. The station wagon sped away, just as a mob of several hundred Arabs came running around the corner.

The doors were slammed shut. Weapons were passed out in the entrance hall with the admonition that no shot be fired without my permission. I strapped on a .45 caliber pistol. With Robert Prosser, who had replaced Anthony Santiano as administrative officer, I made the rounds of the building, checking its security. I was grateful that in an earlier life it had been an Italian bank. It had strong, barred windows, a heavy iron grill, an outer door, and a massive, vault-type steel inner door opened by combination lock.

In addition to myself, nine members of the American staff were in the building, as well as a Peace Corps volunteer, Richard Johnson, who was helping to telephone persons on the E & E Alert List. The latter were being told to relay instructions down the line to the American community to stay indoors, listen to the radio for BBC and British Armed Forces broadcasts, and await further instructions. My good friend, John Tomazos, the Greek consul, as well as two Libyan employees, were also in the building, having been trapped by the appearance of the mob. Tomazos had stopped by seeking advice on how he might protect the Greek community.

At first, the 500–600 demonstrators were content to wave a large bed sheet-like banner with a pro-Nasser inscription in Arabic, while they jeered the CYDEF guard. Suddenly, they became violent. The cobblestone streets around the Embassy and the cathedral square had been torn up prior to being repaired. Large piles of cobblestones and rocks were lying about. In minutes, the CYDEF soldiers went down under a barrage of rocks and then scurried off without firing a shot. Everywhere, there were sounds of windows breaking and the smashing of shutters. The building received a tremendous pounding. In no time offices were badly damaged, the floors covered in rocks. Office equipment was smashed. Antennae on the roof were knocked askew. From what we could see of the mob, they were not just the students we had seen demonstrating in the streets in past weeks.

Many appeared to be foreign workers, likely Egyptians, who were among the two thousand of their countrymen engaged in building the pan-Arab Olympic stadium and other projects in and around Benghazi.

Radio Cairo was broadcasting erroneously that American planes were bombing Cairo, and one could sense the mob's hostility. Shortly after we came under attack, we lost our electric power and had to switch over to an emergency gasoline generator to operate the communications equipment. The telephones also ceased to work. There had been no indication from government authorities of any proposed cut-offs. Possibly these facilities had fallen into the hands of the rioters. Still at this point, it appeared as if the Libyan government was doing what it could to protect us.

However, we were in a violent part of the world and when serving in such places, one prepares for these situations. In cooperation with the British military, a two-way radio had been placed in a cabinet behind my desk. Periodically, two British soldiers from the signals detachment would come by to assure that it was in operating condition. Nevertheless, at the fateful hour, it did not work, and we were unable to reach British Cyrenaica Area Command Headquarters.

The communications vault's incinerator was woefully inadequate. Our main effort to destroy files then rested with the five fifty-gallon steel drums on the roof. Several file loads were hurriedly carried up there and dumped in the drums. Destroying all the classified material in the file room was going to be a long, laborious, and dangerous process, since anyone on the roof moved under a shower of stones from below.

Before much could be done, however, I arrived on the roof to see attackers appear on top of a higher adjoining building. They began hurling rocks down on us. A ladder was lowered, which some of them used, while others simply dropped down the twelve feet to our level and rushed toward us. A hand-to-hand struggle ensued. I gave the order to clear the roof and we fought our way to the stairwell, slamming the steel door shut. Captain Sielinski was placed on guard at that entry point.

A short while later, Sielinski reported that our assailants had tried to force the steel door to the stairwell and, unable to do so, had departed. Before leaving, however, they had cut the halyards on the vertical pole from which the American flag flew and it was left draped down against the front of the building. He requested permission to retrieve the flag and run it back up the pole. I dismissed his request, saying it would be counterproductive and only incite the mob further.

Venturing out onto the roof again to retrieve the fifty-gallon drums, we were spotted. Fortunately the drums were still in place, but in recovering them we were bombarded with rocks from the adjacent building. The drums were hauled down the stairs and placed on an interior courtyard balcony which could only be entered from the communications vault on the second floor. Using burning kits and thermite grenades, the feverish effort to destroy safe-loads of highly classified material began again.

With the antennae damaged, we were having problems in maintaining contact with Embassy Athens, which was relaying messages for us to Washington, Tripoli, and other posts. A direct telephone line in the vault to the British military headquarters functioned for a brief time; but it too soon went dead again for most of the day. Suddenly out of the blue, one of the office phones rang. It was an American oilman calling from deep in the desert to find out what was happening. I explained our situation and asked him to forward messages to our Embassy in Tripoli. We arranged to have him call back periodically, since even with that phone we could not call out.

On a normal sunny day in June, temperatures in Benghazi can go well above 100 degrees, as desert winds blow warm air and sand into the city. The building, now buttoned up, without electricity, and filled with smoke from burning files on the inner balcony, became a furnace, and I knew it would only get worse. One could see that staff members feared not only for their lives, but for those of their wives and children on the outside. We had received word that "half the city was ablaze from the burning of Jewish shops and properties."

I then did something I was often queried about later. Captain Sielinski came to me once more with a request that we retrieve the flag and raise it to its full height. Any sensible Foreign Service officer might again have dismissed this as foolishness. However, I was troubled by his request and the effect it might have on others present. In combat as a paratrooper in World War II, I had seen how important it was for soldiers to feel that they were acting bravely. I knew what defiance and a bit of bravura could do for them when under mortal stress. A display of courage can be infectious and inspiring, just as an act of cowardice can be demoralizing.

I went into my office and closed the door. It was in ruins. The windows were obliterated. The floor lay buried deep in rocks, which continued to crash in violently, scattering glass and debris. Kneeling down in a far corner trying to protect myself, I sought guidance. I do not know how long I was there, possibly two, three, or more minutes. I then came out and told Captain Sielinski to raise the flag, which he did with considerable daring. The psychological impact I had hoped for was obvious, as everyone, with resolve etched into their faces, worked on with grim determination.

A reinforced CYDEF contingent of forty soldiers with automatic weapons arrived, accompanied by a large riot truck with a water cannon. Their presence enabled the Greek consul, PCV Johnson, and the two Libyan employees to exit the building. Six CYDEF soldiers with axe-handle clubs were admitted into the building; four were placed on the roof. That was none too soon, as just then another assault was launched against the roof. I arrived at the top of the stairwell with Tom Twetten and Bob Prosser to find the CYDEF soldiers retreating down the stairs. Outside, Captain Sielinski, with an axe handle taken from the CYDEF, was desperately clubbing intruders to keep them away from the entrance. Joining him in a wild melee on the roof, we were buffeted by rocks as we fought to bring our people in and then secure the door. One attacker lodged himself in the door only to have it closed with bone-shattering effect on his leg.

By noontime, the mob around the Embassy had worked themselves into a fever pitch. Waving an Egyptian flag, they routed the large contingent of soldiers, who obviously had orders not to use their weapons. The mob was then bent on destroying the riot truck, which was employing its powerful water cannon. Undeterred, they began to rock the vehicle furiously. Battered, windshield gone, the driver in a last hysterical effort to avoid being tipped over, drove off crazily through the crowd.

The mob then, with a vengeance, stepped up their attack on the Embassy. A long, steel sewer pipe was brought up and used as a battering ram. The entire building shook under the onslaught. We were now under severe attack. I ordered everyone into the second floor communications vault except Captain Sielinski and Corporal Fabrocini, who assisted me in a quick survey of the building. The click of a rifle bolt again prompted a shout from me that no shots were to be fired without my order.

We found that the mob had pried apart the iron bars on several ground-floor office windows and were entering. A twelve-inch-high, glass-brick transom above the front entrance door also was almost battered through. The roof stairwell door was giving way. Staff members stood at the vault opening, ready to secure. I was at the foot of the wide marble staircase when the breakthrough occurred. Fanatical, knife-wielding intruders rushed screaming down the hall. They were covered in blood, cut as they were pushed through broken windows by the mob.

Putting on gas masks and dropping tear gas grenades, we engaged them on the stairs with rifle butts in a hand-to-hand struggle. In seconds tear gas filled the area. We fought our way up to the second floor and moved into the vault. Securing the steel combination door, we locked in ten persons: Twetten; Prosser; communicators Donald Griffin, Maurice Birkhold, and Richard Calder; secretaries Doris Prosser and Ann DeLisle (both of whom had elected to remain); Captain Sielinski, Corporal Fabrocini, and myself. There was battering on the vault door for several minutes, but then the tear gas must have severely impeded those efforts. It soon also began to saturate the vault, where in the blistering, bake-oven heat, it made breathing extremely difficult. Eyes and skin burned.

Agonizingly, there were only five gas masks for ten people, and these had to be shared among the men, if the work of destroying files was to be completed. The two women were moved into a separate telecommunications room, where an additional door provided a modicum of protection. They were seated in a corner and covered with wet blankets.

My greatest fear, which I kept to myself, was that the gasoline for the generator, which was located down in the patio, would be discovered, sloshed under the vault door and ignited. Minutes went by, and this did not happen. Nonetheless, my heart sank as outside smoke wafted in, and I knew the building had been set afire. While this was occurring, the frantic effort continued to empty safes and burn files on the small outside balcony overlooking the patio. Load after load would be placed in the fifty-gallon drums and ignited with thermite grenades, sending belching columns of flame and black smoke high into the air from the center of the building. In hindsight, this must have added to the impression that the Embassy was engulfed in flames.

It was imperative that fires in the building be controlled, if we were not to perish. As noises outside the vault diminished, the door was cautiously opened and, gas masks on, several of us went out. Locating additional fire extinguishers, we spread out through the building. The fires were largely on the first floor and confined mostly to woodwork, furniture, and drapes. The tear gas, when mixed with the smoke and heat, was so intense that it helped to keep the mob out of the building while at the same time making them think that we had succumbed. Instead, the fire extinguishers were brought into play, spraying down walls and putting out flames where possible.

Signs of the blind fury of the mob were everywhere, with blood on the floors, walls, and furniture. One tear gas canister had skin and blood clinging to it; evidently one attacker had grasped the discharging grenade. As the afternoon wore on, the staff continued burning files and sending messages. With his quiet courage, Tom Twetten was a great asset, methodically working with Griffin, Birkholder and Calder to see that messages were sent and files destroyed. We encountered difficulties encountered making the equipment function, and at times we went off line, but the ingenuity of the communicators overcame almost every problem. Bob Prosser seemed to be everywhere when help was needed.

There were several more intrusions, as small groups of attackers climbed into the building, only to be forced back by the heat and residue of tear gas. Corporal Fabrocini, acting as a sentinel, remained at the head of the stairs, gas mask on, for five hours. He would signal when it was clear to come out of the vault to check the building and extinguish fires. On four occasions we received word of planned British rescue attempts, only to have them postponed. This was unusually hard on Mrs. Prosser and Miss DeLisle, who bravely endured without gas masks.[9]

We had a few erratic telephone contacts with the British Headquarters. Colonel Martin at one point pleaded with me to hold on, saying that an effort to reach us could cost lives. He was a fine, competent officer and I knew he was doing his best. He told me that armored vehicles had been stopped 200 yards from the Embassy. One armored car had been destroyed by pouring gasoline down the hatch, setting it afire with an officer and five soldiers inside. Colonel Martin added that Her Majesty's Embassy and the British Council had been set afire and that the U.S. Information Center had been sacked and burned, as had our former Embassy Residence. Blessedly, I had moved Elsa and the children to the new Residence out of town the previous week.

Our last message was sent at 5:55 p.m. in preparation for a 6:30 p.m. evacuation, arranged with the British forces. By then the destruction of all the classified material had been completed. Cryptograph machines had been selectively rendered inoperable, so that they could be repaired, should there ever be a chance we might return. Any item we did not want to fall into unfriendly hands was burned. In another sporadic telephone call, Colonel Martin told me that rescue efforts again had to be delayed. It seemed that we had finally reached the breaking point. The waiting now was particularly hard on the women. The intense heat of the burning building, hours in tear gas without gas masks, and the smoke in that acrid vault had us to the point where we were roasted, blackened, and barely able to see. Our throats were raw, our lungs seared and painful.

I was so proud of my colleagues. They had done the impossible. At this low point, in an effort to keep spirits up, I took a photograph of President and Mrs. Johnson from the wall. Breaking it out of the frame, in a grandiose gesture I wrote a brief letter to the president on the back, saying no matter what happens to us, we had done our job and done it well. I had everyone sign it, while thanking them for a magnificent performance. The photograph was then date-time stamped in good communication records fashion.[10]

At 8:00 p.m., a British force under the command of Major Jonathan Hall-Tipping finally arrived. That time was selected to take advantage of a Libyan government curfew imposed at 7:30 p.m. By prearranged plan, the staff exited hurriedly through a battered ground floor window to a waiting British lorry. Clambering out between the pried-open iron bars and broken glass, I saw a convoy of vehicles through the black smoke. The major was in the lead jeep with several British soldiers, one sitting on the back holding aloft a large Union Jack fluttering in the ash-filled breeze. It had been an unreal day, one taken from some movie scenario. I found myself listening for bagpipes. We were a miserable sight, cut, battered, bruised, and burned, but for the time being we were all safe.

Sitting in the back of the lorry as we rode through litter-strewn streets, it seemed as if much of the city was ablaze. Buildings were on fire and shops burned out, their goods looted or scattered in the streets. As we reached the outskirts of town and darkness settled in, I looked back to see the entire sky illuminated by fires. A large lumberyard owned by a Jewish merchant was blazing furiously, sending sparks high into the night. Benghazi had been turned into an inferno, and I realized how lucky we were to have escaped. My thoughts were also with Elsa and the children. I planned somehow to get to them and keep them with me.

Arriving at D'Aosta Barracks, I was met by Colonel Martin, who was apologetic about having to delay attempts at our rescue. That fine gentleman had the lives of everyone to be concerned about and had handled the situation with great skill. I was deeply grateful to him. The British had seen to it that Elsa and our three children had been picked up and taken to D'Aosta Barracks, where they were ensconced with the families of British, American, and other nationals in a large warehouse/garage. They were bedded down on concrete floors, but blessedly all were safe.

Had my family still been in the Residence downtown, they might very well have been killed. The massive, ten-foot-high wooden door of that building had been battered in. Finding the house empty, the mob became even more enraged, viewing it as testimony that the Americans were forewarned of the Israeli surprise attack. After demolishing the interior, they set the place afire.

My job was only half done. I felt strongly my responsibility for the many Americans still in the city and elsewhere in Cyrenaica. At 2:00 a.m. that night, I called for a volunteer to accompany me into Benghazi to bring out U.S. citizens who, because of their location, were deemed most in danger. Foreigners had been instructed on British emergency radio broadcasts to remain out of sight in their homes. Captain William Walsh of the MAG offered to join me and drive a station wagon. In addition, a Libyan Army sergeant stationed at D'Aosta Barracks rode with us. Driving through the burning city, we were repeatedly stopped at roadblocks manned by nervous, trigger-happy Libyan soldiers. We passed smoldering buildings and shops as we navigated through the debris-laden streets. As we neared our Embassy, we saw the blackened, burned-out hulk of an armored car and the destroyed private vehicles of our staff.

Pulling up in front of an apartment building illuminated only by fires from Jewish shops a short distance away, I went into the building, leaving Captain Walsh at the wheel and the Libyan sergeant on guard. The city was without electric power. Flashlight in hand, I climbed the darkened stairs, knocking on doors. My efforts were finally rewarded, when on the fourth floor a door was cautiously opened by an American woman. Addressing me by surname in the candlelight, she said, "Thank God, I knew you'd come. We are all packed. The suitcases are in the next room." In that moment, I was deeply moved. Her words were as fine a commentary as I have ever heard on the faith our citizens place in their Foreign Service.

We made several sorties into the city that night bringing out Americans. Some incidents were particularly nerve-wracking. At about 4:00 a.m., we drove to a petroleum tank farm on the edge of the city to pick up the American manager and his wife, who lived at the site. We arrived at the gravel road leading into the place only to find that a barrier had been erected. Rumors were rife that saboteurs were intent on blowing up oil wells, pipelines, and other facilities. Telling Captain Walsh to remain with the vehicle, I started down the road in the dark on foot. The Libyan sergeant was no longer with us or I would have had him accompany me.

I had gone about fifty yards, when I heard the unmistakable click of a rifle bolt. Suddenly I was transported back to my World War II days, only now I did not have the password. I found myself confronted by a young Libyan soldier, who appeared terrified. Finger on the trigger, he jabbed at me with the point of the rifle. It suddenly struck me, however, that rather than just jabbing, he was also shaking so much that the weapon could easily have discharged. Speaking in my rudimentary Arabic, I tried to calm him down, telling him I was a friend and identifying myself. I said that I had come to take the Americans to the *Hakimdar*. The latter was the Libyan chief of the Security Police, whom I knew well. While I had no intention of going to the *Hakimdar*, just the mention of his name was enough to allow me to pass down the road to the house. In a matter of minutes, the manager and his wife were accompanying me back to the station wagon.

The next forty-eight hours were to witness the staff repeatedly endangering themselves to rescue American citizens from the rioting, burning city. We feared particularly for the several Peace Corps volunteers in outlying regions of Cyrenaica; but one by one, they found their way to Benghazi and D'Aosta Barracks. The personnel in our office in Baida ninety miles to the east, having been forced to flee, also reported in. The British, with long experience in dealing with hostilities in distant lands, handled the situation well. Troops of the Devonshire and Dorset Regiment from Cyprus were brought in as reinforcements to protect their installations and citizens. Some were sent to Tobruk, where the British airbase at El Adem was located. Others joined with the 5th Royal Inniskilling Dragoon Guards and the headquarters of Cyrenaica Area Command in Benghazi.

D'Aosta Barracks, which ordinarily quartered the 400 troops of the Command soon was housing over 1,500 civilians of various nationalities under wartime conditions. Military order prevailed, and for three days my family found itself queuing up for meals and engaging in KP and house-keeping duties. Sleeping on concrete floors did little for their disposition, but then there was the adventure of it all! Our staff did what it could to care for American citizens.

A myriad of problems arose. I remember being confronted by a hysterical American woman whose child had been bitten by a cat, raising the possibility that it might be rabid. With no anti-rabies serum at D'Aosta and turmoil all around, there was little likelihood we could obtain some in timely fashion. Fortunately, the child did not develop rabies, we learned later.

The overall situation in the country was chaotic. The Libyan government was ambivalent. Its relations with both the United States and Great Britain had been good, unlike those of Egypt, its neighbor to the east. Egyptian strongman Gamal Abdul Nasser, with the backing of the Soviet Union, had become increasingly hostile toward the West, fostering a pan-Arabism which the Libyan population generally supported. At the outbreak of hostilities, King Idris departed the country. One might have expected that Libya would have broken relations with the United States, particularly after he left, but it did not.

In an effort to support the Arab cause, however, the Libyan Army dispatched an armored contingent from the military barracks in Benghazi to Egypt. The operation turned out to be a fiasco, with virtually all of the tanks breaking down before they reached the Egyptian border 350 miles away. Some Libyan troops, however, did arrive in Egypt, but were not treated very cordially. Nasser accused Libya of paying only lip service to the Arab cause.

The evacuees were under instructions from the British military not to try to return to their homes. Many had fled with just a suitcase and were anxious to recover more of their belongings. As my responsibilities afforded me the opportunity to move about, I resolved to return to the Residence to retrieve the family silver, our wedding album, and a few other precious items, if indeed they were still there. Using an official car, which my driver, Jaabha, had taken out of town on the morning of the outbreak of war, I drove out to the Belaun Farms area. My son Brad, just then going on fourteen, accompanied me. Everything at the Residence appeared normal, even to one of the usual guards stationed outside the gate. He recognized us as we drove up. I greeted him in very friendly fashion, as if naught had happened since last I saw him and went into the house.

Nothing had been disturbed. The halls and several of the rooms were still filled with unpacked boxes from our move. We soon found the items Elsa had instructed me to bring out. The problem now was how to carry out the box of silver and other things without being stopped by the guard, who likely was under instructions not to have anything removed from the house. On occasional weekends in the past, Brad and I would play basketball at the American school. We would leave the house, basketball in hand, often carrying a bag with equipment or clothes. Imitating that procedure, we filled the bag with the flatware and other items and walked out the front door joking and tossing a basketball back and forth. I bounced a pass over to the guard, who laughingly threw it back to Brad, while I locked the front gate. We drove off for D'Aosta Barracks, where my wife greeted us, overjoyed that we were able to retrieve a few of our valuables.

The Libyan government's decision to fall in with its Arab brothers had immediate consequences for our situation in Benghazi. Dependents were being evacuated from the Middle East, and we were seized with the problem of moving several hundred of them out of Benghazi. It would have been expeditious under the circumstances to have them evacuated by the U.S. Navy. However, that would have brought the 6th Fleet into play, and there was a reluctance to involve that resource for a variety of political reasons. After a series of messages, using British facilities, between our Embassy in Tripoli, Washington, and myself, it was decided to evacuate dependents using the U.S. Air Force.

I visited two areas on the outskirts of town to locate a suitable landing strip so as to avoid Libyan interference if we used Benina, Benghazi's international airport. Each possibility had drawbacks. It was then concluded that given the general confusion among the Libyan authorities, we would simply bring the planes into Benina Airport and deal with the repercussions and legalities afterward.

My sense of satisfaction over our evacuation plans was given a serious jolt when Colonel Martin informed me during the morning of June 8, 1967 that he had received word Egyptian MIG fighters and Algerian ANC-12 troop carriers loaded with 1000 paratroopers had landed at the airport and might be parked there for an undetermined period. Evidently they had come in overnight. I promptly called Ambassador Newsom in Tripoli to report this development. His reaction was one of profound concern, saying that the airlift was on its way. He added ominously that the planes were just then reaching the point of no return. If they were to be called off, it had to be done immediately.

I recall saying to him, "What do you want to do?" I shall never forget his reply: "Well, John, you are the man on the spot. This is your decision to make. Do you want the planes to be turned back? If so, tell me now." I agonized for the next thirty seconds. It seemed an eternity. What would happen if the planes were shot down—with women and children on board...

with my family on board? Newsom waited. I finally heard myself say, "Bring them in. We'll handle it."

I reviewed the situation with Colonel Martin, who informed me that there was an Englishman working as a traffic controller in the Benina Airport tower. He could be counted on to be helpful and planned to be on the job when the planes arrived. Then Colonel Martin and I decided that his army radio operators could contact the planes in the air as they approached Benghazi, instructing them to land at the farthest point of the airport away from the tower, the MIGs, and the ANC-12s. They would be told to come in along the fence where we would have the evacuees waiting, ready for a hurried boarding. I made several telephone calls to Embassy Tripoli informing them of the plan and passing on radio frequencies to be relayed to the planes.

In the meantime, with the assistance of the British Army, hundreds of people were prepared for evacuation. Buses and lorries were loaded at D'Aosta Barracks for the drive out to the airport. After a number of delays, we approached the airport from a side road away from the terminal, entering through an opening in the fence near a service area. I was in the lead bus and instructed the driver to wait at that point until our radio operators had received word from the British air controller in the tower to move across the field and await the airlift, which would soon be under way.

With the "go ahead," we quickly drove out on the runways, right past the parked MIGs and ANC-12s, pulling off far down the field on a mixed surface of grass, gravel, and dirt. Parked up against the fence, we waited anxiously. We were as far as we could be from the terminal. Although my wife and several others were aware of the potential danger in the situation, most of the evacuees seemed not to be. In minutes we spotted three planes on the horizon. The buses were quickly unloaded, as the planes came straight in. I identified them as a C-124 Globemaster and two C-130 Hercules. Having flown in the latter, I knew they had rough terrain and short take-off capabilities. I was not so sure about the Globemaster and held my breath.

The touchdowns on the rough surface along the fence, though bumpy, were without incident. As the planes taxied to us, I noted the large print above the U.S. Air Force insignia on their fuselages. It read "Tennessee Air National Guard." I was amazed. Here were "weekend warriors" from Nashville on a training exercise coming to our rescue in North Africa. As a Reserve officer who had put in countless hours of duty, I said, "God bless them!" I promptly spoke to the major in command piloting the Globemaster. His first utterance was, "Aren't those MIGs and Communist planes out there on the field?" I assured him they were, saying, "You had better get loaded up fast and get your rear end out of here, before they realize what is happening!"

With engines idling, the three planes were hurriedly loaded with several hundred evacuees, each carrying a suitcase. I accompanied Elsa and my three children into the cavernous interior of a C-130 and strapped them into the paratrooper-style bucket seats along the plane's fuselage. It was a terse, tearful farewell, and they were off, the planes kicking up clouds of dust, as they roared into the sky close behind one another. The entire landing, loading, and takeoff had taken less than ten minutes.

On the ground, we watched anxiously as they disappeared out of sight, heading out in the direction of the Mediterranean Sea and away from Libyan territory. After a few minutes, noting no activity on the field, our now passengerless convoy retraced its drive across the airport, past the MIGs and ANC-12s and back to D'Aosta Barracks. The operation was carried out with such speed and audacity that there was no reaction from the Libyan aviation authorities until long afterward. It had been our initial understanding that the airlift was destined for Spain. Early in the flight, however, they were redirected to land at Naples, Italy. That night, I received a cable through British channels from my friend Bill Lehfeldt at the U.S. Consulate General in Naples that my family and other evacuees were safely ensconced in hotels in the city.

Our staff spent a week living at D'Aosta Barracks as the Arab-Israeli "Six-Day War" played itself out in the Middle East. We were all anxious to get back to our homes, even though things would not be the same without our families. In some cases two members moved in together. I went back to the Residence. Nothing had been disturbed, the sole change being that the soldiers on guard now had bayonets fixed to their rifles. I shifted for myself the first afternoon and evening, making my meals and eating alone in an empty house.

That night I was awakened by loud crackling noises outside my bedroom. My first thought was that the house had been set on fire, but I smelled no smoke, felt no heat. I jumped out of bed and rushed out into the hall, flipping on the light switch. There was dead silence. I stood there in the hall piled high with yet-to-be unpacked cardboard boxes from our move. There was not a sound. Thinking I must have been dreaming, even though I was sure I heard the noises after awakening, I went back to bed. Within minutes the crackling began again. This time fully awake, I moved stealthily as I entered the darkened hall. The noise continued. It stopped the instant I turned on the light. Unmistakably, the sound came from the packing boxes. Mice, I thought; we had a good share of them in Libya.

Taking one of the boxes marked "lamp shades," I opened the top, turned it over and dumped the contents on the tile floor. It had been my expectation that a mouse or two might scurry out. Instead, the floor was instantly covered with a myriad of two-inch-long cockroaches. They had been rummaging around and possibly eating the crumpled newspaper used for the packing. In seconds, they had scattered. I killed a few, but the task at that hour seemed hopeless, since surely the other boxes were also infested. I returned to bed. The crackling noises disturbed my rest for a while, but the thought struck me that they could have been scorpions, which from time to time we had seen traversing our living room. Then I would have had a more serious problem. On that positive note, I went to sleep.

The following morning was spent spraying down the boxes with insecticide with the help of a faithful servant, Othman, who turned up for work the moment he heard I was back in the house. In a few days, our office resumed operations in a house in the suburbs, close to the homes of most of the staff. There was considerable reporting to be done, but with the encoding machines gone, we had to send and receive messages via "one-time pad." This required the laborious encoding or decoding of each letter of the alphabet by hand, cutting communications to an absolute minimum.

Despite the fact that relations between the United States and Libya had not been broken, the population itself was quite hostile and our movements had to be restricted. Even limited encounters with the Libyans provided ample opportunity to note their bitterness toward us. A visit to the market took on a combat zone atmosphere, where one would be spat upon or severely jostled. Ten days after the attack on the Embassy, I sent a message to my friend, Brigadier Abdulwanis al-Abbar, the *Hakimdar*, asking to see him. Word came back that I should visit him at his home the following evening. The implication was I should come as surreptitiously as possible, using a vehicle that was not readily identifiable. When I arrived at al-Abbar's house, he greeted me alone in his living room.

Much had occurred since last I had seen him. He was anxious to know why the Americans had attacked Egypt in support of Israel? Why had we bombed Cairo? When I told him we had not, he did not believe me, saying the Israelis were no warriors and were incapable of mounting such an attack. I assured him, as a former military officer, that they were. They were highly trained and had first class-equipment, much of it American. At that stage little was known in the Arab world of Israeli capabilities. However, I think he remained unconvinced, wedded to the view that planes from 6th Fleet aircraft carriers had done the bombing. Egyptian propaganda had been very effective. We parted friends, agreeing to meet periodically.

I also met with Consul General Peter Wakefield. The British Embassy had been attacked, but suffered less damage than ours had. British troops in the end had been our source of protection, and I thus gauged returning to our Embassy on Wakefield's actions. In the meantime we continued to function in the suburbs. On June 15, 1967, Libyan Prime Minister Hussein Masiq announced that British and American bases in Libya were to be closed and military forces removed from the country. Shortly thereafter, Ambassador Newsom and British ambassador R. G. Sarell were called in and told to relay the demand to their respective governments.

King Idris returned home to announce that Libya would participate in an Arab summit in Khartoum to unite the Arab countries against Israel and imperialist (meaning American and British) aggression. Foreign Minister Ahmed Bishti left for Kuwait for a foreign ministers' conference backed by Iraq to coordinate Arab policy against Zionism and imperialism. The 1967 war, which pushed the Libyans into the orbit of states critical of America and friendly to the Soviet Union, would have far-reaching consequences for years to come. For us in Benghazi, the removal of Cyrenaica Area Command and El Adem Air Base was to provide a front row seat to the unfolding drama of the demise of the British Empire.

As soon as I could, I made arrangements to fly to Tripoli to confer with Ambassador Newsom. When I arrived, I found that reports of what had transpired in Benghazi had been received with awe, not only in Tripoli, but in Washington and elsewhere. Although there were attacks on many posts, including Tripoli, none had been as severe or dramatic. Our actions had taken on heroic aspects. I found letters waiting for me from the assistant secretary of state for African affairs, the director of North African Affairs, the officer-in-charge of Libyan affairs, the director of the Peace Corps, and several others commending our staff. Some compared us to courageous figures in history. It was all very flattering, but I knew we had been very lucky. Much of what I did on June 5 could have backfired.

I apprised Ambassador Newsom of the situation in Benghazi and Cyrenaica, indicating it would take some time for things to settle down. With proper handling, however, we could reestablish our working relationships with the Libyans. I was sure that I could make some inroads in the not too distant future. I must have looked a bit worn down, because after a while he said, "Look, not much is going to happen in the next few weeks. You have earned a rest. Why don't you take some leave and join Elsa in Naples? It will do you good." I was surprised, thinking how could I possibly leave in the middle of a crisis. But the ambassador was right; there wasn't much I could do, and I had a first- class deputy in Tom Twetten, who would be more than able to take over. With that, my mind quickly turned to what I would have to do to retrieve our private car in Greece and drive to Italy to see my family.

On June 24, I flew to Athens. We had originally planned to take leave in Europe during the month of June. My friend, John Tomazos, the Greek consul, had arranged for our car to be shipped on a Greek freighter from Benghazi to Piraeus, the port of Athens. The car, a four-door, full-sized Chevrolet less than a year old, had been spared the Benghazi attack. However, such was the state of world affairs that there had also been in the interim a coup attempt and rioting in Greece. Flying to Athens, I pondered how life in the Foreign Service was full of unforeseen hazards.

As soon as I dropped off my suitcase at the hotel, I proceeded to the address given me for the garage. Once there, I was met by the Greek owner, who asked to be remembered to Tomazos when next I saw him. To my great relief I found the car, without a scratch on it, safely parked in a corner of the garage. After completing some arrangements, I was ready the following day to drive the 125 miles from Athens across the Peloponnesian peninsula to the port of Patras. That night I stayed in a little hotel on the Gulf of Corinth, where the proprietor was impressed with the size of my American car, but scornful of its fuel consumption. I drove into Patras in time to purchase a ticket for a cabin, meals, and car space on the ferry crossing the Ionian Sea to Brindisi, Italy. The overnight trip took about twenty-three hours and was quite scenic, sailing past historic Corfu and other islands by day.

Arriving in Brindisi in the afternoon, I was anxious to be off for Naples and started out as soon as I drove off the ferry and gassed up. In hindsight, wanting to see the family warped my judgment. The 250-mile drive alone at night over the rugged Apennine Mountains on narrow, winding roads was dangerous and nerve-wracking. I was fortunate that nothing untoward occurred. There was great stirring in the hotel when I unexpectedly rolled in at 3:30 a.m.. It was a wonderful reunion. The next few days were spent driving down the glorious Amalfi coast to Capri and visiting sites we had not seen earlier.

The State Department had afforded our Benghazi dependents the option of moving to Athens or returning to the United States until things settled down in Libya. Elsa, fearing that our separation might be lengthy, was concerned about the children's education and believed it best that she return home to place them in private schools. With that in mind, we decided to drive to Garmisch in Bavaria for a week, stopping off en route in Rome. At the end of two weeks, I would put the family on a plane in Munich for the flight to St. Louis, where they would be met by Mother and Dad Wells. We had an enjoyable vacation as a family, culminating in halcyon days in the Bavarian Alps.

I was troubled, however, as I put them on the plane at the Munich Airport. Elsa was terribly distressed about my returning to Benghazi, which she viewed with grim foreboding. I did my best to reassure her, but I must admit her concern bothered me the next two days on the long drive down through Germany, Austria, Yugoslavia, and northern Greece to Athens. There, I arranged for the car to be placed on a ship, while I boarded a flight back to Benghazi. Before leaving, however, I visited with the Twetten family; they had opted to stay in Athens awaiting return to Libya. I could report that they were bearing up reasonably well.

As expected, not much had occurred in my absence. Relations with the Libyan authorities, while proper, were cool when compared to those before the war. The British brigadier commanding the U.K. Military Mission had been asked to leave the country. Evidently his earlier "no nonsense" approach to training Libyans had come back to haunt him. Some months earlier Lieutenant Colonel Campbell of our MAG, in frustration over his own efforts to train them, told me that he was contemplating following the brigadier's example. He was tired of Libyans simply wanting the Americans to repair military equipment when it broke down, rather than learning to fix it themselves. I told him not to take any drastic action saying, "We are here to win friends and influence people. Political aims supersede military ones."

During the next few weeks, I cautiously endeavored to expand my contacts with the Libyan authorities. The third week of August, I moved the staff back into our damaged, downtown Embassy. Administrative Officer Bob Posser and his local personnel, including a German and a Greek national, had their hands full in contracting to restore the building. Slowly, however, we were digging out. In a letter written to my parents-in-law on August 27, 1967, I indicated that I was sitting in my office with its boarded-up windows and badly damaged furniture and walls. I had just written an entry into the Consular Log Book describing the attack and how the staff had responded to the crisis.[11] That volume, like so many of our messages during those fateful hours, now rests in the National Archives for future researchers to read.

For both political and economic reasons, I had classified our cables "Limited Official Use Only," mindful that we wished to avoid anything that might have embarrassed Libya and caused a break in diplomatic relations. There was Wheelus Air Force Base to consider, as well as our business interests. We had enjoyed a $2 billion balance of payments surplus in our trade with the Libyans, growing largely out of their purchase of oil-drilling equipment. As it turned out, relations were not broken. I was told afterward that had our messages not been classified, the incident would have received widespread media coverage.[12]

Without our wives, entertaining during this period had largely come to a halt. Roaming around in the evening in our large house made me miss my family all the more. Othman was there during the day. He was a good soul. Not the greatest houseboy, he was nevertheless loyal and hard working. Given the hostility toward Americans at the time, he might have stayed away, as some other servants did. By American standards, Othman lived in impoverished circumstances with his large family in a village about a two hours' walk from the Residence. He was also burdened with caring for a severely mentally ill son. Wishing to spare him the long walk mornings and evenings, I bought him a secondhand bicycle.

For a few weeks, he rolled in and out smartly on his new acquisition. Then I noticed he was walking again. Thinking he might have had to sell the bicycle, I inquired about it. He responded that the bicycle was *mafeesh*, meaning broken. That evening, I sent my driver, Jaabha, with the car to pick it up to see if it could be repaired. Examining the bicycle, I found that a 3/4-inch bolt and nut holding the front fender in place had dropped off, thus interfering with the turning of the wheel. In less than a minute, I screwed on a simple bolt and nut and the bicycle functioned perfectly. Othman had been walking more than ten miles a day, unable to deal with this rudimentary aspect of modern technology.

I might add here that already as a matter of course, my wife kept a jar in our kitchen into which the servants were to place "upon pain of death" any nails, nuts, bolts, screws, or other parts found on the floors or anywhere else in the house. This simple procedure saved many an appliance, cabinet door, and lock that might have been rendered inoperable for want of that part. Previously these items had unthinkingly been swept up and thrown out in the trash.

As the weeks went by, the situation settled down enough to press for the return of the families, and most came back. However, in two cases women who had suffered traumatically did not, resulting in steps to transfer the husbands as well. At the end of August, Elsa and the children returned to Benghazi after arduous flights from St. Louis via New York and Rome. Once back, life slowly began to return to normal. We adopted regular office hours, and limited entertaining began. We made efforts to revive the American School, although some teachers did not return.

On one of his visits, Ambassador Newsom mentioned that he was thinking of flying the American flag on his official car again. He said I might wish to do the same. "It would demonstrate our presence, show that we were back in business." I was tempted to say, "This is not Tripoli, with its more Westernized inhabitants. We have wild-eyed Senussi tribesmen around here!" However, I held my tongue, and the following week the flag flew on my car. From then on, without my saying a word, Jaabha would avoid congested areas. When that was not possible, I would see him wide-eyed, watching me in the rearview mirror as I slumped farther and farther down in the back seat to make myself less of a target.

At one point, Peter Wakefield asked me why I was baiting the tiger. It obviously put pressure on him to do the same and not too long afterward, he followed suit. Had it been up to me, I would have taken my lead from the British. We were extremely grateful for the unstinting aid we had received from the British Army during the crisis and were determined somehow to show our gratitude. I sent a message to the State Department in an effort to have a bronze plaque made up thanking Colonel Martin and the British forces for rescuing us, feeding hundreds of Americans, and assisting in the evacuation. In doing so, I ran into a bureaucratic maze, culminating in a final response to the effect that there were no funds or procedures for obtaining such a plaque. In disgust, I arranged to have it done privately through a commercial firm in Tennessee. Every member of the staff contributed to its cost. Later, in mid-November, at a reception at the Residence for 250 guests, the plaque was presented to Colonel Martin, who accepted it on behalf of the British Army.

The demand that British bases in Libya be closed out and the forces removed was received with acquiescence by Prime Minister Harold Wilson's Labour government, which was searching for ways to reduce expenditures and overseas commitments. The United States, on the other hand, was concerned about the possible loss of Wheelus Air Force Base, which served as a prime training facility for NATO forces. With the vast empty Sahara Desert to its south — Libya was 93 percent desert — there was nothing in Europe to match it for aerial bombing practice. We hoped that Britain would move slowly, possibly allowing for a change in the situation. In my conversations with the British, I put forth this view whenever I could. However, it seemed that the die had been cast and the decision was made to move dependents back to England in November, with the final departure of the forces in January and February of 1968.

There was no question that Cyrenaica Area Command would be missed by our staff. With it would go D'Aosta Barracks, the Officers' Club, tennis and squash courts, the Beach Club, the church and chaplain, not to mention many friends. Our stand during the attack on our Embassy, particularly the flag-raising incident, evoked many "good show" comments in British Army circles. My own military background, particularly the fact that I had dropped into Germany during World War II along with their 6th Airborne Division, was also appreciated. I was invited to be the guest of honor at a "dining in" of the 5th Royal Inniskilling Dragoon Guards. There was formality and ritual as the meal was served with the regimental silver. The "Skins" traced their heritage back to the 17th century, with battle honors that included Blenheim, Waterloo, and the Crimean War. It was a most interesting evening.

As if sensing the passing of the colonial era, the dress parades at D'Aosta took on additional splendor. I shall long remember the Inniskilling Guards with their colorful regimental band marching past the reviewing stands. Visitors and wives, the latter in Sunday long dress and picture hats, applauded as they went by. The departure preparations set me in motion to see what the American community might recover from the facilities the British would be vacating.

Foremost in my mind were the church and the Beach Club. The church was on property outside D'Aosta Barracks and proved no problem. Services simply went on, attended by members of the British and American business communities. The congregation faced the problem, however, of finding a clergyman. I had my share of filling in as a lay minister in the meantime. I still have a sermon or two in my files from those times. The Beach Club with its fine convenient beachfront, restaurant, and other facilities was another matter. The Libyans eyed that prime property, as did several other groups, including Air France, which had a less desirable beach. I told Ambassador Newsom that I would like to see if I could obtain the Beach Club for the American community. He authorized me to try, but was not optimistic as to the outcome.

I intended to approach the mayor of Benghazi on the matter, indicating that if acquired it would be open not only to the Americans but to the British and other nationalities as well. Foreigners in bathing suits at the beaches had consistently been a problem for the Libyan police. Although Libya boasted miles of white sand shoreline along the Mediterranean Sea, we had to be careful where non-Muslim women and children bathed. Arab men, completely unaccustomed to seeing women and children unclothed, reacted unpredictably. At times they would come on to the beach and stare at them for long periods.

One Sunday at the Beach Club, my family sat down on the sand at the farthest end of the property. Before long, I noticed a Libyan in Western clothing peering at us from behind an abutment about twenty yards away. I motioned for him to go away, but he would not. When I went over to him, I found him masturbating. It just happened that a British major and his family were the next group over from us on the beach. He was a massive Scotsman, the Command's provost marshal in charge of the military police. Seeing what I was about, he came over as well. Between the two of us, we escorted the man over to a jeep and took him to a nearby Libyan police station. He was simply released with a warning.

The newly installed mayor of Benghazi, Muhammad Bin Younis, was an idealistic, able young lawyer on whom I would call frequently. He was well versed in the Sharia, the Islamic Law. Over a period of time I laid out the case for making the Beach Club available to us, describing how it was in the city's interest and good business to assist the foreign community and prevent incidents such as the one mentioned earlier. Generally, however, given the hostility of the Arab world toward the Americans, dealing with the Libyan authorities was a painstaking process.

Returning from Tripoli on one occasion on Libyan Airlines, I was seated next to an attractive young lady in her mid-twenties. She was Australian and traveling to Benghazi to join her Libyan husband, whom she had met and recently married back home. Never having been outside of Australia, she was excited to see her new home and meet her husband's family. I sensed she knew nothing of Arab customs or what her future would be like. I was torn between remaining silent and telling her not to get off the plane. Under the circumstances, all I did was urge her if at all possible to contact the Australian consul and try to remain in touch with him. The last I saw of her she was whisked into a white Mercedes by an older veiled woman, probably the mother-in-law, covered head-to-foot in the traditional long black barracan. Two other veiled, similarly dressed women already in the car, likely were other wives.

Cyrenaica was a very conservative region where women were kept in their houses out of sight. Whenever I visited a Libyan official at home, the women were always spirited away before I entered. On the few occasions when an upper class and "more modern" lady visited my wife, her husband would enter the Residence first to assure that no man was present. Shopping for food and other essentials was done by the lowest-ranking women or servants in the household. Tattoos on women's faces were considered marks of beauty. On occasion in the souk, one could spot a bit of tattooing around an eye of a woman, the only uncovered area. More than once over the years, my thoughts returned to that young Australian woman, wondering what her fate might have been in a harem completely cut off from the outside world.

While reminiscing about foreign customs, I should relate another incident affording an insight into Libya as it was then. I was sitting in church one Sunday morning when the visiting minister announced from the pulpit that my presence was required elsewhere. Believing that there was some emergency, I hurried out to the narthex to find my secretary in a state of great agitation. Her houseboy's wife who had been giving birth to a baby had started hemorrhaging badly and been taken to a hospital. Without a blood transfusion she would die, and they needed volunteers. Consequently, my secretary and an American girlfriend were going down to the hospital to give blood. Would I accompany them?

Dubious about the entire affair, I nevertheless agreed. I had never been in the city hospital in downtown Benghazi. I was only familiar with the missionary hospital on the outskirts of town run by American Seventh Day Adventists. It was frequented by a large number of Libyans, and I soon found out why. The sanitary conditions downtown were appalling. As we passed through the waiting room, I saw the woman's husband and a group of relatives waiting. When I asked whether they would be giving blood, I was told they would not. Whether this was out of fear, superstition, or taboo, I do not know.

Confronted with the dirty equipment about to be used on the girls, I put a stop to the procedure and promptly drove them out to the Adventist Hospital. There, blood was drawn and immediately sent down to the city hospital. The woman survived, and my secretary and her friend were spared a possible case of hepatitis or worse. It is worth noting that despite all the good the Seventh Day Adventists were doing for the Libyan population, they were viciously attacked during the war and among the first we sought to rescue. Dr. Clifford Luddington and his staff remembered that assistance and were always ready to render us a service.

Six months after the attack on the Embassy, in December 1967, I received an excited telephone call telling me that my name was on the wire services. At a large annual awards ceremony in Washington attended by many notables and complete with music by the Air Force Band, Secretary of State Dean Rusk had presented me *in absentia* with the "Award for Heroism" for "calm and effective leadership as the officer-in-charge of Embassy Benghazi" during the Arab-Israeli War. I also learned that I was the only living recipient among the four top awardees. We placed above such luminaries as Governors Averell Harriman and Henry Cabot Lodge and Senator William Benton, who were given "Distinguished Service Awards" at the same ceremony. Those medals were followed by a hundred or so lesser awards. The Benghazi staff was given the "Superior Service Award." The two members of the MAG had been decorated separately by the U.S. Army.

In February 1968, I witnessed the departure of the British forces from Libya. They had been there since the Allies had taken over Tripolitania and Cyrenaica in 1943, after ousting the Italians and the Germans during World War II. The British then governed those areas by military administration until independence in 1951, when Libya became a constitutional monarchy with King Idris as its sovereign. A treaty of alliance and friendship between the United Kingdom and Libya in 1953 provided the British with bases and the king with certain protective arrangements.

The lowering of the Union Jack at D'Aosta Barracks was carried out with pomp and circumstance. After one last parade, the flag was lowered.

The troops were moved down to the port of Benghazi to load on LSTs (Landing Ship Tanks). The front ramp doors were dropped and vehicles drove aboard.

I can still see the final scene clearly, there on the waterfront. A number of well-wishers had come down to say farewell and see them off. The American flag on my official black Chevrolet was fluttering in a stiff breeze, as Colonel Martin came over to me. Rendering a salute, he said with some resignation, "It's all yours now, John. Good luck!" Returning his salute, I replied, "Things won't be the same without you, Alistair. All the best to you, my good friend." Shortly after that he went up the ramp, the LST pulled away, and with it went a page in history. It was not until years later that I saw him again, as his guest at the Army-Navy Club in London.

After the departure of Cyrenaica Area Command, I again contacted Mayor Bin Younis about the Americans taking over the Beach Club. I had heard rumors concerning strenuous efforts being made by other parties to secure that choice facility and was beginning to think we had lost out. To my surprise and pleasure, Bin Younis telephoned me a few days later saying that he was making the Beach Club available for our use. As I recall at the time there was not even a mention of payment.[13] The rejoicing throughout the American and remaining British communities at that news was great.

I liked the Cyrenaicans, and this must have somehow come across to them. Gradually in my personal relationships, I made a good start in reestablishing prewar ties. As a result, from time to time I would be taken into their confidence. I recall at a Country Team meeting at the Embassy in Tripoli Ambassador Newsom spoke with considerable pleasure about arrangements that had been concluded to send the new Libyan prime minister, Abdulhammid Bakkoush, on a visit to the United States. It was to be a real indication that relations were improving. I found myself commenting, "My sources in Cyrenaica tell me Bakkoush will be out of the job before he gets to go." This remark produced icy stares from all assembled and irritated the ambassador. I was careful not to say anything when a short time later Bakkoush was indeed removed from office and did not make the trip.

The embassy maintained a guest house at the ancient Greek, later Roman, city of Cyrene, about ninety miles east of Benghazi on the Jebel Akhdar, the high green plateau that ran along the Mediterranean Coast. The ambassador and staff used this place as a recreational facility, because the air, even during the hottest days, is clear, clean and fragrant with the smell of pine. Baida, a town close by, was selected by King Idris as his new capital and hundreds of millions of dollars of Libya's oil wealth were being expended in construction projects there. When business would take me up to Baida, I stayed at the guesthouse. On occasion, I took my family along and remained a few extra days. These visits provided us with memorable experiences.

Cyrene, oft mentioned in the Bible, was founded in 630 B.C. The ruins of the acropolis, temples, theaters, cisterns, baths, tombs, and other features are still visible, spread out over a large area. The well-known statue of the Venus of Cyrene, now in the British Museum, was unearthed there in 1913. However, for my family the true gem in the area was the Greek city of Apollonia, the port city of Cyrene, ten miles to the north, off the plateau, and down the steep escarpment on the Mediterranean coast. Wandering among its fascinating ruins and along the stretches of white sand beach was pure joy. Unlike the tourist-clogged places of Greece and Italy, one could walk in solitude, save perhaps for a lone shepherd boy in the distance, minding his flock.

The sea now covers a large section of Apollonia, but much is still visible through the clear blue-green waters of the Mediterranean. On a warm, sunny day Elsa and I, accompanied by the three children, swam out several hundred yards offshore with masks and snorkels to visit these ruins. The sea was calm. The houses and streets, partially buried in the sandy bottom, lay visible beneath us. Diving down into "our Atlantis," we would excitedly point out new discoveries. Matthew, barely seven at the time, enjoyed himself immensely, mask and snorkel making it possible for him to swim out and stay afloat such a long distance from shore.

Returning to the beach, the children searched among the marble baths and cisterns for shards, finding pieces of ancient pottery, including jar handles possibly two thousand years old. What they found filled two shoeboxes, enough items to provide them with "show and tell" material for many a future classroom project. Unlike other places in the world at the time, there was no real control over these antiquities. Libya was truly an antiquary and archeologist's treasure trove.

Libya was also the repository for a great deal of unexpended munitions from World War II, when the Allies fought the Germans and Italians back and forth across the country. At times when we visited the Beach Club, my son Brad would go snorkeling offshore. He came out of the water one day telling us he had seen what appeared to be a large Grecian or Roman jar. It was fifteen feet down, buried in an extensive growth of vegetation about fifty yards out. When I went to examine his find, it turned out to be an unexploded shell from a warship. I was glad that I had dug around it cautiously. Munitions after many years can be unstable. We reported it to the British military demolition squad.

Another time, an American businessman came to the Residence on a Sunday. When I greeted him at the door, he handed me an American hand grenade, which his son had brought in from the back yard. The pin was still in place, although not too securely. Grenades were nothing new to me, but the demolition boys and I shared the view that neither father nor son was too bright. They should have left the grenade where it was and telephoned me or the disposal squad.

During my tour in Benghazi I had problems keeping up with my Army Reserve training. Unlike in Europe and the Philippines, there was not a large enough enclave of Americans in Benghazi or at a nearby American military facility to support a Reserve unit. The closest was in Italy. As a consequence, I resolved to obtain the fifty points' credit necessary to remain active through correspondence courses, which ordinarily combined with a fifteen-day tour of active duty served in lieu of attending drills during the year. I had been in grade as a major for over six years and was due to come before a promotion board. To my dismay, there was a bureaucratic hitch in the forwarding of my correspondence course credits to the board, which left me with a record of not having completed my training at that very critical juncture. With the war and all the related problems, I had no opportunity to stay on top of the situation. I was informed in November 1967 that I had been passed over for promotion to lieutenant colonel.

As fate would have it, Colonel Robert B. Nett, the chief of Army Reserves for the European Command, which included North Africa, visited Tripoli some time thereafter and learned that the officer in charge in Benghazi was a member of the Army Reserve. Colonel Nett was a holder of the Congressional Medal of Honor, and the attack on Embassy Benghazi and the award I had received piqued his interest. Shortly afterwards, out of the blue, I received an invitation to attend a three-day conference on Reserve affairs he was holding in Garmisch, Germany. I attended the conference and was able to provide some insight into the manner in which officers in positions such as mine could make a particular contribution to the Army. From then on Colonel Nett took a personal interest in me, culminating in his sending a glowing recommendation to the board that I be promoted the next time around.

In April 1968, I received orders to take a fifteen-day tour of active duty at U.S. Army Headquarters in Heidelberg. There, my background was put to the test in reviewing and developing military contingency plans for North Africa. I had hoped that Elsa might accompany me to Germany. She would have jumped at the opportunity, but with the children in school and the ever-present undercurrent of volatility in the Arab world, she felt it necessary to remain in Benghazi. It was just one of the many sacrifices my wife made for the Foreign Service. Mindful of that, I resolved to bring her back a worthy present from Germany. I found an exquisite porcelain figurine of a colorful hussar mounted on a white horse. With great care I took it aboard the flights back to Libya, and it has been on display ever since.

We perforce did a great deal of official entertaining during our years abroad. Many of these occasions are stories in themselves. Events tied to the Kennedys always come to mind. In Manila, the assassination of President Kennedy caused us at the last minute to cancel a reception for 250 guests. History repeated itself in Benghazi in June 1968, when Robert Kennedy was assassinated and a period of mourning was declared. In Manila, the Filipinos dearly loved John Kennedy and sympathetically accepted our cancellation. In contrast, Robert Kennedy's strong support of Israel made him anathema in the Arab world. The fact that the gunman was viewed as an Arab patriot made the situation even more delicate.

It was not until July 4th that we rescheduled a large reception, as it was customary to do on our National Day. We invited members of the Royal Household, a number of cabinet ministers, two former prime ministers, a host of high-ranking civilian and military officials, the diplomatic corps, and an assortment of business leaders and other notables. Ambassador Newsom flew over from Tripoli for the affair, arriving aboard the four-motor C-54 plane the Air Force provided for his use. To mark our Independence Day, I believed a brief speech was called for and invited the ambassador to do the honors. He responded that since it was our party and important for me in my contacts, I should give the speech. It was a thoughtful and gracious gesture.

I drafted an address I gauged to be a bit more than five minutes. It was boilerplate stuff, designed to foster good relations between Libya and the United States. Salah Butalog, my political advisor, then translated it into polished Arabic and coached me at length in the proper accent and gestures, as I read it aloud. I have a fair ear for sounds and mimicry. Over a succeeding hour, I virtually committed the translation to memory.

At the appropriate time during the outdoor reception, I came to the podium. Using a microphone, I welcomed the guests and gave the English version of my speech. Although most people knew I could speak rudimentary Arabic, it was expected that Salah would simply translate. Instead, I launched forth in spirited fashion in Arabic, gesturing as I went along. I could see eyes widening in astonishment. As I concluded, a tape stirringly rendered the Libyan and American national anthems. While they were sounding, a breeze swept across the area and the two flags at either side of the podium stood out dramatically. I could not have asked for a better bit of staging. The downside of that performance was that Libyan officials later took my command of Arabic to be far better than it was.

With the exception of three to four months during and after the 1967 Arab-Israeli War, there was a constant parade of visitors through Benghazi. Some were quite colorful, such as billionaire oil tycoon Armand Hammer. He arrived with his guests at the airport in a matched pair of converted B-25 World War II bombers. Hammer had in tow Senator Albert Gore Sr., the father of the former vice president. Hammer's Occidental Oil Company had brought in a huge well in the desert about eighty miles south of Benghazi.

After lunch at the Residence, Mrs. Gore and Mrs. Newsom, who was accompanying her, decided they wanted to visit the souk. My wife was concerned, since the situation in Benghazi was still quite hostile and at a minimum Western women were quite likely to get their fannies painfully pinched. Elsa made it her business to stay behind them, as they wandered through the market. Later, I was tempted to put in a request that she receive a "Purple Heart" and a commendation "for selfless gallantry." I doubt if our guests had any idea of what she had experienced.

While many visitors came on official business, such as inspectors, State Department officers dealing with Libya, trade missions, and members of Congress, a good many others did not. Word was getting out about the abundance of significant Greek and Roman ruins, and some government officials found excuses to detour their trips through the area. In doing so, however, they were soon shocked at how expensive everything was in that oil-rich country and how limited facilities were. As a result we found ourselves having to put up and feed more of these visitors than might normally have been the case at other posts. Occasionally sandstorms or an airline strike would keep them even longer than intended.

I remember being upbraided by an inspector, who by regulation could not be hosted by persons he was inspecting, complaining to me about the ceiling of his room leaking at the overpriced Berenice Hotel, the only Western-level establishment in town. After telling me how water dripped on his bed all night, he remonstrated, "This place is worse than Mogadishu!" The latter at the time had the reputation for being foremost on the list of unpleasant places in the Foreign Service. He actually took me to task for not asking for an increase in our hardship allowance.[14]

To be sure, living was difficult in Benghazi. Most Western food and drink items had to be ordered and imported months in advance. There would be times when for days we would have no running water during the dry season. On other occasions, we would have periods of torrential coastal rains when the street in front of the Residence would be a riverbed with foot-deep, fast-flowing water. During these rains, the poorly insulated wiring on the electric-line poles would spark violently, firing off sporadic rifle-shot sounds throughout the day or night as the current short-circuited. Finally, there was always the chance of sandstorms with the wind changing and air blowing in from the Sahara Desert.

As my assignment in Benghazi wound down, I sensed that I had truly been in the Foreign Service and in many ways had shared the hardships of predecessors generations past. The situation in Libya during 1968 had seemed relatively stable on the surface. However, the Arab-Israeli War had brought with it a considerable diminution of the power and influence of King Idris. He was more and more regarded as a tired old man out of touch with the times. The real power seemed to be with Colonel Shalhi, the chief of staff, and other senior officers of the army.

Vast amounts of wealth were generated by oil discoveries and extensions of exploration leases. Billions of dollars were being expended on construction projects, encouraging corruption and shady dealing. The situation, at least to some of us in Benghazi, seemed ripe for a coup. When it came, most observers thought it would be the senior officers of the army who would take charge. There was no thought at the time that an unknown young captain in the Signals Branch named Muhammar al Quadhafi would be its leader or that the revolution would be spearheaded by junior officers. Perhaps the most surprised man of all would have been my friend, the chief of signals, Lieutenant Colonel Ahmed al Mahdfi, Quadhafi's boss.

In hindsight, many commented that we should have cultivated the junior officers. However, given the strict hierarchical structure in Libyan society, that really was not practical. Contacts with junior officers would have immediately aroused the ire of their commanders and been counterproductive. When the revolution came a year after I left, George Lane, my successor, dealt with the repercussions while I watched it evolve from Washington.

During the early weeks of August 1968, I received several reports about a prospective assignment in Washington. The first word was that I might be assigned to the National Security Council staff, a duty that was considered career enhancing. Then a friend mentioned that I was being considered for a War College appointment. While the latter had the disadvantage of taking me out of the day-to-day action, I would have gladly accepted it, given my Army background. When the orders finally came through, I learned that my new post would be to replace Robert Sherwood as officer-in-charge of Liberian and Sierra Leonean affairs. It was a straight political officer assignment in the Bureau of African Affairs. We had a large American embassy and important interests in Liberia, as well as deeply rooted historic ties. Sierra Leone, on the other hand, had been a British colony and protectorate. The job appeared challenging, and I looked forward to it.

There was the usual round of farewell parties as we prepared to depart Benghazi, and I was surprised and pleased at the number of Arab friends attending. I made arrangements to fly with my family to London, where we would spend a few days and then board the SS *United States* at Southhampton for the ocean voyage to New York. For those never having served overseas, I should comment here that packing up one's household effects, including furniture, can be quite an experience. When the Libyan shipping company's packers arrived, I noted that the Arab foreman, who spoke passable English, was surly and did little to disguise his dislike for the Americans and the British. On other occasions, the foremen had generally been Greek or Italians. When I offered to pack a few of our more delicate and valuable items, he informed me sharply that his company then would not be responsible for insuring them. However, I did point out a few items, such as the porcelain figurine I had recently acquired in Germany, requesting that he take special care with them.

Nevertheless, when our shipment arrived in the United States months later and we unpacked, we found that beautiful figurine in with the pots and pans. It was in a box without the slightest wrapping, between two heavy iron skillets. There was not a scratch on it. Someone looks out for Foreign Service families!

There is always a good deal of uncertainty in foreign travel. In this instance, it revolved about two large steamer trunks we sent ahead by air to the docks in Southampton for placement aboard the ship. They contained the family's clothing and other items for the three months until our household effects reached home, as well as our wardrobe for shipboard. Would they arrive in timely fashion at the dock, would they be lost and not arrive at all?

Our flight to London from Benghazi via Rome on Libyan Airlines was not that unusual save for the antics of the Air France pilots who flew the planes under contract. With the verve of fighter jocks, they would whip those medium-range jet transports around during landing and takeoffs like none other I have experienced since. I had been told that London was an excellent place to purchase antique Persian carpets and 19th century oil paintings. As a consequence, the family now has a 125-year-old Kashan and two Flemish seascapes. Of course, we had no idea at the time that two decades later we would be back in London to witness the wedding of our daughter Andrea to an Englishman, a Winchester School Scholar and Cambridge University graduate.

After a train ride through the English countryside, we boarded the SS *United States* in Southhampton. Checking on our baggage, the ship's bursar informed me that his listing contained no record of our two steamer trunks and that we would have to sail without them. I spent the next frantic hour before departure on the dock checking with the U.S. Lines shipping office, but to no avail. Finally once again aboard ship, I asked to be taken to the baggage hold. After rummaging around for some time in that cavernous place, I spotted our trunks in the cabin-class storage area. They were soon sent up to our first-class staterooms amidst much rejoicing by the family. Had they been left behind in Europe, we might have had a devil of a time retrieving them.

The SS *United States*, flagship of the American merchant fleet, held the "Blue Ribbon" for the fastest crossing of the Atlantic at that stage. Although luxurious in appointments, she had a steel-like quality throughout. One could sense that she could easily be converted to a troopship. The trip to New York took less than five days, but we found the vibrations and the pounding that accompanied speed unpleasant. Our Atlantic crossings on the older, slower SS *America* and SS *Constitution* seemed far better. Little did we realize at the time, however, that this would be the closing of an era for us as a Foreign Service family, our last ocean crossing by ship. Air travel had become more cost effective, and time allowed to move between posts became based on that means of transport. With flying came jet lag, the disappearance of a bit of elegance, and the loss of a more leisurely pace of life.

12
The State Department and African Affairs

Arriving in New York in late August 1968, we set in motion plans we had made for a three- or four-year tour of duty in Washington. We had sold our house in Fairfax, Virginia, in 1962 and our car in Benghazi before coming back to the United States. With the school year about to begin, we were pressed to enroll the children wherever we could. We thus decided to proceed to Elsa's parents in Jacksonville, Illinois, and place them in school there, since we did not know how long it would take us to buy a house, or indeed whether that house would be located in Virginia, Washington, D.C., or Maryland—preferably Maryland. It was a trial making all these arrangements, but then life in the Foreign Service accustomed one to a certain amount of turmoil.[1]

After a brief visit with my parents-in-law, I left Elsa to deal with three sets of Jacksonville school authorities. By this time Brad, going on fifteen, was to be placed in high school, Andrea, thirteen, in junior high, and Matthew, eight, in elementary school, each school in a different location. Flying back to Washington, I reported in to the State Department for a series of debriefings on Libya and meetings relative to my new assignment as Officer-in-Charge of Liberian and Sierra Leonean Affairs. I settled into temporary quarters in a rented furnished apartment in Arlington, Virginia, and purchased a secondhand, six-year-old Ford Fairlane car, since the 1969 Pontiac convertible I had ordered from overseas was not yet ready at the factory.

During this period, I entered into serious house hunting with the assistance of an able female real estate agent. Narrowing down the possibilities to ten, I called my wife to come east and join me in the final selection. Our choice was a large, Georgian brick colonial built in 1941, with a detached two-car garage, in the Rollingwood section of Chevy Chase, Maryland. Its original owner had been a Methodist bishop. Later Cuvier Metzler, the builder of our house and many of the custom homes in Rollingwood, lived in it for fifteen years. Our dealings, however, were with the current owners, a pair of psychiatrists who had been in bitter divorce proceedings and were anxious to sell. While aspects of the purchase negotiations in late October 1968 were far from pleasant, the house turned out to be a wonderful home for our family over these many years.

At the department, I was not fortunate enough to overlap with Robert Sherwood, my predecessor on the Liberian/Sierra Leonean desk. Others in the West African Affairs Division assisted in easing me into the job, notably Roy Melbourne, the director, and Christopher Martin, the Ghanaian desk officer. As time went on, Martin and I filled in for one another whenever one of us took leave or went on official travel. A series of junior officers serving as our assistants also provided continuity.

During 1968–69, the political situation in Liberia was stable. President William V. S. Tubman, who had come into office in 1944, was an able and shrewd politician. Over the years, he had built up a powerful base through patronage and astute appointments. Establishing control over the ruling True Whig Party, he continued in office until his death in 1971. He was more sensitive than his predecessors had been to the sharp division between the tribal people and the Americo-Liberians, the descendants of freed slaves from the United States who had colonized the country beginning in 1822. The Americo-Liberians brought with them skills they had learned in the New World and, as an elite, dominated the indigenous population. Some, following in the footsteps of their former Southern masters, sought to establish a planter aristocracy.

The Americo-Liberians, never more than 5 percent of the country's population, largely displaced the inhabitants of the coastal areas, driving them into the hinterlands and subsequently bringing them back as a cheap source of labor. Maintaining ties with American missionary societies, they set out to establish a republic on the model of the United States. They adopted a constitution drafted by the dean of the Harvard Law School and established a Senate, a House of Representatives, and a Supreme Court. For a flag, they followed the American pattern, choosing one with a single star on a blue field with red and white stripes. The majority of Liberia's then over one million indigenous population belonged to sixteen tribes, each with its own language and customs. Thus separated from the start from the Americo-Liberian colonizers, it was not until recently that the vast gap between them was narrowed.

Fundamental economic development, education, and social change still have a long way to go. In a bloody coup in 1980, Army Master Sergeant Samuel K. Doe and a group of noncommissioned officers of tribal origin overthrew the government. In so doing, they killed Tubman's successor, President William Tolbert, and executed numerous officials, charging them with corruption and other crimes. During the ensuing years the hold of the Americo-Liberians has loosened, but the country has remained in a state of chaos and internal strife.

During my fourteen months on the desk, a dozen years before that first violent upheaval in 1980, I sensed that all was not right with Liberia. While I was constantly told that Liberia was a model country in a strife-torn continent, I had my doubts. I was also uncomfortable with what I saw when I visited there. I found the Americo-Liberians, who were everywhere in the government and Foreign Service, less than agreeable. In diplomacy, they carried protocol to ridiculous heights.

Their ambassador in Washington, with whom I dealt at the time, tended to be pompous and demanding, as indeed was his imperious wife, who would have little to do with the American black community. Later, at the time of my appointment as politico-military advisor for Africa, that lady, my wife recalls, attended a women's tea party at our home. Upon learning that I was no longer in charge of Liberian affairs, she was highly irritated and left early, questioning why she had been invited and implying that she was wasting her time. What she probably did not realize was that in my new position I was charged with handling the sizeable military assistance and training programs for Liberia.

The United States had substantial interests in Liberia and in that sense our governmental programs reminded me of my time in the Philippines. Monrovia was a Class I post with a large embassy. We maintained regional communications and printing facilities there. It had large AID and military assistance programs. We had already poured in over $350 million in economic and military support. There were important business interests in the country, primarily the Firestone Rubber Company. Outside the State Department the general view at the time was that Firestone totally dominated our relations with Liberia. An early call on me by Firestone's Washington representative made me doubt that supposition, which in actuality was not true. Firestone, at the time, was placing less and less reliance on the latex coming from its vast plantation in the southeastern part of Liberia. The development of synthetics during and after World War II had sharply reduced the dependence on natural rubber produced in Liberia and elsewhere in the world.

Liberia was, however, a country of prime concern to the shipping interests of many nations. Its "flag of convenience" arrangements provided means for many vessels to circumvent taxes and restrictions of various sorts. During those years, Liberia was registry to perhaps the largest number of ships in the world, while having virtually none of her own.

In early 1969, I paid my first visit to Liberia. Ben Hill Brown was our ambassador there at the time, and I had a number of very informative meetings with him and his staff. I observed the embassy's functioning and

gained insight into personnel problems. Accompanied by embassy officers, I made the usual calls on Liberian government officials, who were all
formally dressed in Western coat and tie, despite the equatorial heat and
humidity of their offices.

Part of the program laid out for me included a visit to the Firestone
Rubber Plantation, some 250 miles southeast of Monrovia. It was a trip I
shall not forget. I was accompanied by Political Officer John Linehan and
Economic Officer Frank Tucker, friends from previous assignments. For
the flight down to Harper, the town nearest the plantation, we flew in a
small single-engine Cessna aircraft piloted by a local American resident.
On takeoff, we were afforded a panoramic view of Monrovia. The pretentious presidential palace and government buildings stood out in the drab
surroundings. The American Embassy compound on a cliff overlooking
the ocean was easily recognized. Flying along the coast with the sparkling
blue sea beneath us on a bright sunny morning was exhilarating.

After two hours, we arrived at the town of Harper without incident.
The nearby airfield proved as primitive as any I had encountered in the
southern Philippines. Its only features were a dirt runway and a small,
single-room, cinderblock "terminal" with a listless windsock on the roof.
Climbing out of the plane, we saw that we were the only aircraft on the
deserted dusty field. We had waited twenty minutes wondering whether
there had been a mix-up in arrangements when a utility vehicle driven by
a Firestone employee arrived.

After locking the plane, the four of us, including the pilot, were driven
inland to the plantation. We traveled for miles amid rubber trees up to the
manager's large, lovely home on a mountaintop overlooking a broad expanse of tropical forest. That evening at dinner the manager and his wife
could not have been more congenial hosts. At sunset out on a veranda,
sipping cocktails, we were captivated by the view and the sounds of Africa.

The following day we observed the gathering of latex from the trees
and the initial processes in rubber production. The Firestone overseers
explained that the native workers were paid well and lived in conditions
far superior to those of other tribespeople in the region. I saw numerous
small, red-brick, one-room huts in which they dwelled with their families.
All this was thirty-five years ago, and there undoubtedly have been many
changes.

Most vivid still in my mind was a scene in a shed we passed through
while watching the rubber-making process. A single black worker was engaged in preparing the latex for the next step. The latex was spread out
in large flat sheets about two inches thick. Evidently, they were too big
for whatever was to come next, and his job was to tear them by hand into

more manageable pieces. The worker was an incredible vision of rippling muscles as he tore this extremely tough material. At the time, and over the years since, I have thought about that man with foreboding. If ever he were to break out of his toilsome life in anger and revolt, heaven help those in his path.

Our visit to the Firestone Plantation was a brief one, just long enough to give us a flavor of equatorial Africa, the rubber-making process, and the life of those engaged in its production. We bid farewell to our hosts and were driven back down amid the miles of rubber trees to the little airfield at Harper. I was not alone in worrying about our plane being left unattended, but as we drove onto the field it seemed to be all there. A single old woman in native garb was moving about near the plane, perhaps, I thought, curious about this machine that could rise birdlike into the heavens. As we came closer, we could see that every few moments she would bend over, scoop up a handful of dust, and toss it on the plane. While dirt on the wings and fuselage were an annoyance, flinging it on the motor cowling was a matter for real concern.

With shouts and hostile gestures we drove her off, as she hissed at us. During this set-to, I snapped a picture of the scene. That really upset her, and it became apparent to me she was some form of local witch doctor we had come upon in the process of driving away the evil spirits our plane represented. I was further convinced when, as she backed away from us, she gestured at us with the pointed left index finger, stroked by the right index finger. It was the Voodoo sign of a curse I had learned about as a young man during my visit to Haiti.

Making light of her antics after she departed, we readied the plane and took off for Monrovia. We were in the air about an hour, flying along smoothly, when the first of the motor hesitations began. I believe I was not alone as my mind harkened back to that old woman. Whether the cause was dirt in the engine or her Voodoo curse, we knew we were in serious trouble. Beneath us the West African coast and jungle stretched interminably. There was no place we could reasonably land the plane, much less take off again. Our only hope was to limp along in an effort to reach an iron ore mining plant known to have a landing strip, but that was many miles ahead.

Sputter along we did, our hearts in our mouths with each engine hesitation. Finally, the pilot brought the plane down on the plant's dirt landing strip. We spent several hours as, with some assistance from the plant's mechanics, he worked on the motor. With trepidation we then took off once more for Monrovia, landing hours later than expected. That evening back at the Embassy, my colleagues and I reflected on the incident. We revisited hair-raising experiences from other assignments, shrugging them off with the comment, "life in the Foreign Service!"

Before leaving Liberia, I had another experience that lingers in my memory. I was picked up for a meeting with the chief of the U.S. Military Assistance Group by an American Army major piloting a small two-seater open-sided helicopter. It was as precarious a ride as I have ever had, with only the seatbelt, under full strain, keeping me from falling out as the major wildly jockeyed the helicopter around. Had my hands been free to hold on to something, the situation would not have been as bad, but I was clutching a briefcase containing classified documents with one hand and a hat with the other. I could sense that the major was having a hilarious time "scaring the striped pants off a State Department cookie pusher." Comments on my part to "Take it easy!" had minimal effect.

When we landed, I quietly informed him I would recommend that he be sent back to helicopter training school. If he was trying to shake me up, he was doing so to a combat-experienced paratrooper, an Army Reserve lieutenant colonel. I added, had my briefcase with classified military documents fallen out of the helicopter, we both would have been in very serious trouble.[2]

On that trip to Africa I had an opportunity to visit my other charge, Sierra Leone. Americans generally tended to know something about Liberia from church and missionary connections, but Sierra Leone, which had been a British colony and protectorate, was shrouded in mystery. The Portuguese early on had established a fort and subsequent trading posts near what is now Freetown, the country's capital. The area became a center of the slave trade, which flourished for close to 300 years. As Portuguese power waned, British, French, Dutch, and even Danish traders established themselves there. After slavery was declared illegal in England, a party of 400 unemployed, freed blacks and a few white Englishmen were sent with government support in 1787 to establish a self-governing colony in Sierra Leone. The British authorities negotiated with local chiefs to obtain land for these settlers, while English abolitionists in London assisted them by drafting a constitution.

The settlement suffered numerous vicissitudes. In 1789, it was attacked by one of the chiefs' tribesmen and destroyed, but it was reestablished the following year by some of the survivors. In 1792, a thousand former slaves from the thirteen American colonies who had escaped from plantations to fight with the British in the American Revolution, fled to Nova Scotia, from which they were sent to Sierra Leone.

Another group of 550, called "Maroons," arrived eight years later. They had been slaves during the Spanish rule of Jamaica. When the British took over the island in 1655, they had sought refuge in the mountains and fiercely maintained their independence until surrendering in 1796. After being deported to Nova Scotia, they opted to go to Sierra Leone. The Maroons were far better suited to the climate and harsh realities of tropical Africa. Still, by 1807 only half of the colony's original 3,000 black settlers had survived. However, the British navy's capture of ships engaged in the slave trade provided the colony with a growing source of inhabitants, as Freetown became the repository for their cargoes.

The British granted the settlement a charter in 1801. A typical crown colony regime was established, with a white governor and a group of white administrators answerable to the Royal African Company's Board of Directors in London. For the Englishmen sent to administer Sierra Leone, the price was heavy. Known as the "white man's graveyard," disease and debilitation took its toll. During the first fifty years, with one exception, the average tenure of the British governors was less than one year, which did little for the colony's stability. Half the Anglican missionaries sent to the colony died within ten years. Subsequent years witnessed numerous efforts on the part of the local inhabitants to achieve greater autonomy. From a coastal settlement, the colony expanded into the interior, until a century and a half later it consisted of a colony and a hinterland protectorate, a total area of 28,000 square miles with a population of three million.

Tribal differences played a large part in society. Of the eighteen ethnic groups, the Mende and the Temne account for more than half the population. The Creoles, descendants of freed slaves, while only 2 percent of the population, were better educated. As in Liberia, they dominated the government and key facets of the economy. Sierra Leone became independent from British rule in 1961, but the years between that time and 1968 when I took over the desk at the State Department were far from smooth. Several political parties jockeyed for the position of prime minister and control of a house of representatives functioning under the Commonwealth system. In a chaotic situation, the military intervened. Martial law was declared in 1967 by a group of army officers calling themselves the National Redemption Council (NRC). The latter's regime was ended in April of the following year by a revolt of noncommissioned officers and enlisted men who restored tenuous civilian rule. This was the situation when I landed at the airport in Freetown in 1969.

I was met by Willard De Pree, the chargé, and taken to the Embassy to meet with the American staff and receive the usual briefing. Ambassador Robert Miner was on home leave at the time. On this occasion, however, there was no meeting with government officials. Shortly before my arrival, the embassy received a report that a potentially violent army coup might be in the offing. Instead of meeting with Sierra Leonean officials, the day after my arrival I was taken by car on a daylong orientation visit to the hinterland, accompanied by George Trail, the political officer. Returning that evening to Freetown, I was told that the security situation had worsened and steps had been taken to obtain a seat for me on the first available flight out of the country. There was a good chance, however, that all flights might be canceled and that my stay in Sierra Leone might be considerably longer than intended.

Early the next morning, not knowing what to expect, Chargé De Pree and I drove to the airport. The trip involved a drive through town and a ferry ride across an estuary. Everywhere heavily armed soldiers in jeeps rode about and guards checked our movements. A sense of anxiety permeated the air as I cleared customs, bid good-bye to De Pree, and boarded the plane. Once in the air en route to Washington, I breathed a sigh of relief. Despite the fact that my trip to Liberia and Sierra Leone had only been a little more than a fortnight in duration, I came away with impressions that were to be helpful during the following months as I dealt with problems related to those countries. When cables came in from Monrovia and Freetown, I could visualize the persons, places, and evolving situations.

I thoroughly enjoyed being an officer-in-charge of a country desk. It was a sought-after position for a person at my level in the political cone, as it was termed in those days. For someone with a military background, it was much like being a line officer given command of your own battalion or regiment. There was, however, some disparity between countries and the corresponding responsibility entailed. An officer-in-charge of Great Britain, Japan, or the Soviet Union at the time carried a heavier load than one accountable for Bolivia or Chad. However, there were always situations that might make even small countries vitally important. One has only to think of Kuwait, Somalia, or Serbia and the commitment of American forces in these places.

Desk officers were privy to activities and insights not generally shared with others. Often these dealt with personnel matters. For example, senior officers such as the assistant secretaries of state responsible for entire geographic regions were often not in a position to evaluate the performance of ambassadors and, consequently, relied heavily on the views of desk officers. Then, too, a cable or letter from the department to an embassy praising a report or some action might well have a significant impact on an officer's efficiency rating. I recall at one point the State Department decided to get hardnosed in its efforts to make room at the top for promotions and key assignments. It instituted a policy of retiring ambassadors who were up for reassignment if in ninety days there was no position available for them.

I was at a routine assignments meeting in the Office of Personnel one morning when I learned of the new procedure and was informed that one of my ambassadors, a career diplomat, was thus to be retired even though he had not reached the then mandatory retirement age of sixty. My reaction was to tell the gathering of personnel officers that my area was not about to be a test case. I remember saying forcefully, "Not on my watch, you don't!" The ambassador in question was found an assignment as a diplomat-in-residence at a university and was extremely grateful to have been able to serve a few more years in that capacity, thereby increasing his pension.

As officer-in-charge of Liberian and Sierra Leonean Affairs I had an opportunity to get to know both sets of ambassadors. I recall flying out to Akron, Ohio, in a Firestone private jet with Sam Westerfield, our newly appointed black ambassador to Liberia, for a meeting with Raymond Firestone, the company's president. While the company still had vast interests in Liberia, one could, as indicated earlier, sense that its activities there were being phased down. Westerfield, before receiving his assignment, had been a deputy assistant secretary of state in the Bureau of African Affairs, and my relationship with him had been a particularly friendly one. He asked that I be sent out as his deputy chief of mission, a request that caused some consternation. Liberia was a Class I post and called for a minister-level officer in the job, which was two grades above mine. While I was flattered, State Department personnel policy simply could not countenance such a move.

Ambassador Westerfield then invited me to several social functions in the black community of Washington. It was a privilege to meet these distinguished figures, great names in government, business, academia, and the arts. It made me reflect on how foolish Liberians and leaders in other African nations were at that time to hesitate in accrediting blacks as ambassadors to their countries, inferring that it gave their countries second-class status.

Westerfield's tenure in Liberia was a relatively quiet and stable one, unlike the years of upheaval and slaughter that were to follow. Sierra Leone, on the other hand, never settled down. Once during a government turnover, the Sierra Leonean ambassador, an impressive and cordial gentleman, found himself stranded in Washington. He returned home sometime later only to be executed. As years went by, Sierra Leone became a country despised for civil wars and unbelievable cruelties and atrocities against its population, including the maiming of children.

During that first year back from overseas, my family had settled nicely into our home in Chevy Chase, Maryland. The children transferred from their temporary classes in Jacksonville, Illinois, to comparable grades in local schools without much difficulty. In some ways, given their overseas experience, they were ahead of their classmates, but in others they had much to make up to fit in with the American lifestyle.

During his time overseas my son, Brad, had dreamed of playing American football. However, when he approached the football coach at Bethesda-Chevy Chase High School, he was given very short shrift, since he had no experience playing the game. Brad went out for soccer instead and at the end of the season was named to the metropolitan Washington area all-star team. You can imagine Brad's satisfaction the next year, when the same coach came to ask him to join the football team and he could respond that he preferred to play soccer. Our daughter, Andrea, gifted academically, began to make a name for herself at Leland Junior High School, while young Matthew attended the Rollingwood Elementary School a few blocks down the hill from our house.

Now back in the United States and anxious to retain my status as an Army Reserve officer, I sought placement with a local unit. I hoped also to assure being considered for a possible future promotion. I was about to ask to be assigned to a control group, a catchall outfit where one met for an evening twice a month simply for participation credit, when a colleague suggested that I approach a civil affairs unit training over in Riverdale, Maryland. They drilled one weekend a month and were on much-sought-after paid duty status. Realizing that there was little chance of my being placed on such status, I nevertheless approached the colonel in command asking only to participate in drills for attendance credit. This to him was a gift horse, and he concurred.

It soon turned out that I was the only officer in the unit with actual experience in civil affairs as a military governor (resident officer) in a war-ravaged occupied area. I was also a State Department official who had served in the overseas region for which that unit had responsibility. As fortune would have it, within a short time I was a lieutenant colonel in a responsible position on paid status assigned to the Army Reserve's 354th Civil Affairs Area (B).[3]

In late 1969, a year and a half after my return to the Department of State, I was asked to take over the position of politico-military advisor for Africa. Earlier that summer, David Newsom, who had been our ambassador in Libya, had arrived to assume the post of assistant secretary of state for Africa. He knew I had a military background and would be a logical candidate to replace James Ruchti, recently assigned to Stuttgart, Germany, as consul general.

The politico-military advisor was charged with a wide variety of duties, including liaison with the Department of Defense and the Joint Chiefs of Staff and supervision of the military assistance programs to seventeen African countries. Arranging for U.S. Navy ship visits to African ports and overflight clearances of military aircraft was part of the job, as were matters related to American bases and satellite tracking stations. Status-of-forces agreements, the activities of the military attachés, and the Marine guards were all aspects of interest to the politico-military advisor.

Before he departed for Stuttgart, Jim Ruchti briefed me thoroughly, over the course of several weeks, about various problems I might encounter. He took me to the Pentagon to meet my counterparts in the Department of Defense's Office of the Assistant Secretary for International Security Affairs. George Bader, the director of the Africa region, headed a staff of competent and cooperative officers at the colonel and lieutenant colonel level. However, given the differences in missions of our governmental departments, we were bound, at times, to be at odds.

One of Ruchti's problems that engaged me early on was that of Diego Garcia, an island in the Chagos Archipelago, a thousand miles south of Sri Lanka (Ceylon) in the Indian Ocean. The U.S. Navy had been negotiating with the British to establish an American base there. Great Britain controlled the area as part of the British Indian Ocean Territories (BIOT). At the time the Government of India and others were exerting considerable pressure on the State Department to have the Indian Ocean and bordering countries declared a nuclear-free zone. There was also considerable sentiment expressed in the United Nations along these lines.

All this amounted to the classic tug-of-war between the military seeking to establish bases for its forces and the State Department attempting to limit potential problems. At about the same time, the U.S. Air Force was endeavoring to locate an airbase on the Island of Aldabra off the east coast of Africa, a pristine area treasured by environmentalists and often compared to the Galapagos Islands. When an international outcry shelved that attempt, the Air Force sought out Farquhar, another island in the BIOT, but with much the same outcome.

One might question the rationale for these efforts. Simply, it was part of the global positioning of our military during the Cold War to deal with the challenge from the Soviet Union. The Navy required a well-situated base in the Indian Ocean to service its nuclear submarines, so that in the event of hostilities they would be poised to fire ballistic missiles over the Indian subcontinent into the heart of the enemy's defenses. At the time the Russians had as many as twenty naval vessels patrolling the Indian Ocean. The Air Force, on the other hand, needed a base to facilitate its around-the-world movement of military aircraft. In hindsight, given America's current superpower responsibilities and recent conflicts involving our forces, the efforts of both the Navy and Air Force to secure bases make sense.

Arrangements for a base on Diego Garcia and initial construction concluded in 1972 during my term as politico-military advisor, but not without problems and clamor. Some two thousand people, including four hundred families, were moved off the island to new homes. All this was accomplished with British cooperation in relocating them on Mauritius and the Seychelles. To this day, however, complaints about that action and resulting legal cases are still pending.[4] Diego Garcia now provides an excellent deep-water naval base as well as an airfield handling the long-range B-52 bombers, which were flown from there during the conflicts in Iraq and Afghanistan.

I was soon also caught up in the annual military assistance budgetary scramble, trying to secure resources for Africa. Congress appropriated the funds, from which a large amount went to Israel, with the remainder apportioned according to specific policy objectives and obligations to nations around the world. The location of a military base was a determinant. Cold War threats were considered, as were a variety of other factors.

Ethiopia, where we maintained Kagnew, a large American military communications facility near Asmara, in what is now Eritrea, was one of our more significant programs. Kagnew was an important relay base in our global communications system during the Cold War when our troops were fighting in Vietnam. By the time I took over in 1969, we had already provided the Ethiopians with over thirty jet fighters (F-86 and F-5); a squadron of transport planes (C-47, C-54); a number of helicopters; an 18,000-ton naval seaplane tender; ten large coastal patrol boats, scores of tanks, armored personnel carriers, and artillery; and a vast quantity of small arms and other items. We had equipped three 8,000-man army divisions and brought over to the United States almost 3,000 Ethiopian army, navy, and air force personnel for everything from pilot to staff college training. Morocco was also the recipient of a large amount of assistance. The U.S. Air Force maintained three Strategic Air Command (SAC) bases and a fighter base there, while the U.S. Navy had a naval base and a communications facility at Kenitra.[5]

In addition to the grant aid, our government conducted a Foreign Military Sales (FMS) program.[6] Obviously where countries could afford to pay for hardware, they were encouraged to do so. For example, when I was in Benghazi, I was aware that Libya, an oil-rich nation, participated in both programs. It received grant aid in part as compensation for use of Wheelus Air Base in Tripoli by the U.S. Air Force and NATO, while at the same time it purchased jet fighters and a quantity of other materiel through FMS channels. (The delivery of fighters was to become a bone of contention a few years later, when Muhammar al Quadhafi took over the country.)

George Bader and his Africa Region Directorate labored over these programs in the Department of Defense; and I with the assistance of a very able Marine Corps deputy, Lieutenant Colonel Richard Critz, struggled with them at State. After everything was decided upon and the allocations concluded, the various military service procurement systems delivered the materiel. We also provided assistance or sales in varying amounts to Cameroon, Dahomey (Benin), Ghana, Guinea, Ivory Coast, Liberia, Mali, Niger, Nigeria, Senegal, Sudan, Tunisia, Upper Volta (Burkina Faso), and Zaire (Congo).

During those years, half of the more than forty African nations were under some form of military rule. In essence, America's approach to military assistance to Africa was one of ambivalence. We never felt comfortable providing arms to these emerging nations, beset as they were with vast problems of political, economic, and social development, and were reluctant to see expenditures made for the furbishing of military forces that could more appropriately be used for nation building.

Nevertheless, the United States realized that modest military establishments were required to maintain internal security and to provide against external threats, whether real or imagined. This recognition was undergirded by the awareness that African governments that desired arms and training would not be deterred and that if we were not forthcoming, other countries, perhaps even those with interests inimical to our own such as the Soviet Union, would readily step in. Then, too, our government believed that by providing assistance we might exert a moderating influence, discouraging the acquisition of more expensive and inappropriate equipment.

We always feared becoming embroiled in the internal struggles of African countries, or that our actions might lead to arms races on the continent. Secretary of State William Rogers stated in a March 1970 report: "We want no military allies, no spheres of influence, no big power competition in Africa." Even so, from time to time, we did become involved in African struggles to a limited extent. Subsequently, the development of intercontinental ballistic missiles (ICBM) and Polaris/Poseidon missile-firing submarines made the requirement for SAC bases in Morocco unnecessary. While the United States never had vital national interests in Africa, it needed to ensure trade and access to natural resources, as well as to enable our citizens to travel about the continent.

Another one of our tasks was to arrange for visits to African ports by ships of the U.S. Navy as they sailed the oceans of the world patrolling regions significant to our national interests. Ships can be at sea only so long before they require refueling and provisions. Sailors must be afforded shore leave if morale is not to suffer. In addition to ports in the

Mediterranean some of the lesser-known, exotic places included Djibouti on the Red Sea, and Mogadishu (Somalia), Mombassa (Kenya), Zanzibar (Tanzania), Victoria (Seychelles), and Diego Suarez (Madagascar) on the Indian Ocean. (I had never before heard of Diego Suarez, but learned that it was a superb deep-water harbor and a French naval base on the north-ernmost tip of Madagascar. For years in the 17th century it had been a pirate stronghold.)

Political unrest, sanctions, and strained relations necessitated a con-stant struggle to assure that ports were available to our naval vessels. Some wonderful stories grew out of these visits. In one instance, an Amer-ican destroyer arriving at a port in conjunction with a certain country's independence ceremonies entered enthusiastically firing the traditional 21-gun salute. The population, not used to such protocol niceties, mistook the situation, and thinking that a coup was taking place, panicked and ran for the hills.

The vessels of COMIDEASTFOR (Commander, Middle East Forces) headquartered in Bahrain routinely called at African ports, as did those of the 6th Fleet in the Mediterranean. Unlike the latter area, our naval presence in the Indian Ocean in those days was not particularly impressive. COMIDEASTFOR's flagship guarding the oil supply lifelines was an old swaybacked tender, the U.S.S. *LaSalle,* which was supported by a small number of destroyers. I recall at one point briefing Vice Admiral Marmaduke Bayne upon his taking over this command. He was a fine officer, with such an intriguing first name.

Supporting our military operations in Vietnam periodically presented difficulties. At the height of the Vietnam War we sailed the aircraft carrier U.S.S. *Saratoga* from Norfolk to Southeast Asia on an emergency basis. It was not possible to use the Suez Canal. Furthermore, sanctions had been imposed against South Africa for its policy of apartheid. A vessel of that size ordinarily would have called at Cape Town for refueling, but under the circumstances that was barred to the Navy. The additional expense of having to send a fast fleet oiler to accompany the carrier at the cost of mil-lions of dollars sorely vexed the Pentagon.

Other incidents remain vivid in my memory during my assignment as politico-military advisor for Africa, particularly one related to the sale of five F-5 jet fighters to Libya. The fighter jets were bought and paid for prior to the al Quadhafi takeover, but they had not yet been delivered. A question arose about the phlegmatic leader and how he might put those planes to use. The America-Israel Public Affairs Committee (AIPAC) was dead set against delivery. Up to that point, al Quadhafi had not appeared to be particularly anti-American. It was my cynical view based on some experience that the Libyans, who had shown themselves to be poor pilots, might very well fly those planes into the ground. They had demonstrated their capability of doing so in the past. Furthermore, these short-range fighters were incapable of reaching Israel.

National Security Advisor Henry Kissinger was against delivery, while Secretary of State William Rogers was in support of doing so. I had a not-so-tactful discussion with Assistant Secretary Newsom over the planes, saying at one point, "When you were in Tripoli, you, as ambassador, signed the purchase agreement. How can you renege on it now?" He irritatedly replied, "You don't have to tell me I signed it. I know that, but there are more things involved here." He was looking at the broad political picture, and from his standpoint was probably right, in hindsight. This was one of those back-and-forth issues between Rogers and Kissinger, and I am afraid my heart was with Secretary Rogers. The planes were never delivered, and our relations with al Quadhafi were indeed negatively affected, but given his subsequent actions they probably would not have been a good idea.

In 1972, I went on an official trip to a number of African countries, stopping off in Senegal, Nigeria, Ghana, Zaire, Rwanda, Kenya, and Ethiopia. While most stopovers were brief, there were extensive discussions in Zaire and Ethiopia. Zaire was having serious problems with border incursions along Lake Tanganyika. We had been asked to provide patrol craft of the Swiftboat type used in the Mekong Delta in the Vietnam conflict. How to deliver these large items to the African interior posed a problem. The Lockheed-Martin Aircraft Company had just brought the massive new C-5 "Galaxy" on line. It was deemed capable of handling a load that size, and arrangements were concluded for delivery.

Zaire's mineral-rich province of Katanga was in a state of unrest, so I took the opportunity to stop off in Lubumbashi, formerly Elizabethville. I was surprised at what a pleasant posting it was for our consul there. Far from the visions of the African hardship assignment I had conjured up, he resided in a lovely house opening on an expanse of green lawn and a large swimming pool. I might as well have been in Hollywood. While there, I was given a chance to go down deep into the local copper mines. In doing so, I brought back several souvenir pieces of malachite, a byproduct of those mines, which I had made into jewelry for my wife and daughter.

In Addis Ababa, there were discussions with the ambassador and the brigadier general, who was the chief of our MAAG mission, relative to augmenting equipment given to the Ethiopian Air Force. From Addis I flew to Asmara to consult with officers at the Kagnew Station communications facility. The independence movement in Eritrea, where Kagnew was situated, was becoming increasingly violent, posing a security threat. Little did I realize at the time that our activities in Ethiopia would be coming to an end as that country would do an about-face. It would come under a regime oriented toward Moscow, while an Eritrean insurgency that blossomed into an all-out war would lead to the closing of Kagnew Station.[7]

On occasion the military services and the State Department did not see eye-to-eye. We had a problem with their desire to carry out responsibilities in a "hands-on" fashion. Commanders were taught to know their areas of jurisdiction by personal front-line inspections reasonable under normal circumstances. But when a four-star general in charge of one of the overseas regional commands visits, it gives rise to a variety of assumptions, not to mention expectations. The case of General John Throckmorton, the Commander-in-Chief of Strike Command (CINCSTRIKE), predecessor of the current CENTCOM, comes to mind. He had responsibility for the Middle East and Africa in our country's worldwide military command system. We received word that he was planning to travel to a number of African countries, taking his staff with him. They would travel in the general's military equivalent of the largest four-engine commercial aircraft at the time, a Boeing 707.

Visions of that large plane loaded with three-star, two-star, and one-star generals landing in some small African country, where the newly coup-installed president might be a captain or a sergeant, gave us fits. It was a sure recipe for trouble. At a minimum, the African president would expect a new military assistance package or an increase in an existing one. Why else would this galaxy of "stars" be coming to his country? Funds for military assistance to Africa were very limited. Furthermore, it was an activity over which the CINC had only a marginal say. However, being so bold as to suggest that the visit be low-key, that the generals go out in civilian clothes aboard commercial aircraft, the way our ambassadors do, one might as well have tossed a skunk into a church meeting.

We made our views known, but ran into stiff resistance. I urged our political advisor at STRIKE Headquarters at MacDill Air Force Base in Tampa, Florida, to see if stops in certain countries could be eliminated and the high-level entourage cut to a minimum. Instead, the political advisor, who had previously been our ambassador to one of the African countries, came back with a long message to Assistant Secretary Newsom justifying the trip as planned. The political advisor, of course, was dependent on the CINC for his efficiency rating. Throckmorton, who functioned directly under the Joint Chiefs of Staff, complained to them and the Defense establishment, and the situation became increasingly unpleasant. To straighten matters out, General Throckmorton and some of his officers were asked to join Assistant Secretary Newsom and me for lunch in the State Department's Executive Dining Room. I doubt if I have ever seen my boss more authoritative and, by the time the lunch was over, our guests certainly got the message. The visit went off well, as low-key as possible under the circumstances. My only regret was that I, through the POLAD or my contacts in Defense, was not able to prevent the situation from coming to a head.

In dealing with matters related to CINCSTRIKE, I made several trips down to Tampa. On the last one, I used the occasion to visit my mother in her lovely little house in DeBary. Over the years, whenever we were stationed in Washington, we would visit her for part of my annual leave. With the children sleeping on a mattress spread on the back seat and the built-up foot space of the car, we would drive through the night, arriving in the afternoon of the next day. Once there, our time would be spent largely going over to the Atlantic shore at Daytona or New Smyrna beach. The children loved swimming in the rough ocean waves. We would drive our car right out onto the hardened sand to some idyllic spot and spend the day. Returning in the evening, Mother would always have a fine meal waiting for us. I had no idea on that drive over from Tampa that I would be with Mother for the last time. She seemed a bit sad and frail when I took her out for dinner at a popular local restaurant. There was a loving tone of finality as we parted. As she was a person of remarkable inner strength, I thought little of it at the time.

Mother telephoned me from the hospital in Sanford two days later, saying she had been there overnight. Her doctor wanted her examined for the deep chest cough that had consistently plagued her. Worried, I said I would come down again immediately. She responded, "No, I will be all right." I should have known by her tone that she was saying her time had come. Soon thereafter I was notified that she had died on November 20, 1971, at the age of eighty-six. The family drove down for the funeral of a woman widely loved in the community. She had been a driving force in establishing the First Baptist Church of DeBary. The little town turned out en masse for the church and burial services.

It was with a deep sense of bereavement that we drove back to Chevy Chase afterwards. Her prayers had kept me safe through years of war and our family secure through typhoons at sea and violence abroad. They had sheltered us in sickness and in health, and now she was gone. The sadness I felt was almost unbearable. In the ensuing years, however, as we continued in the Foreign Service, we always felt her presence. In the midst of danger or trouble, when for inexplicable reasons we would come away unscathed, either my wife or I would say, "Mother Kormann."

The Vietnam War was at its height during these years. At times, I would drive to my office in the State Department and on the way down encounter large numbers of protestors. It was the era of the flower children, burning of draft cards, and unrest in the schools and universities.

By 1970–71, the situation in Vietnam had become ever more controversial with the incursion of our forces into Cambodia. President Nixon's decision to bring large numbers of American troops home, while at the same time endeavoring to build up the South Vietnamese military by a massive influx of weaponry to enable them to fight on alone, to me was a recipe for defeat.

The influence of Henry Kissinger and the National Security Council (NSC) staff was keenly felt. It seemed they, not the secretary of state, were running foreign policy, and it was resented. Given that situation, I decided to make the most of it by getting on good terms with a staffer at the NSC who handled, among other things, African matters. When I had some problem with my counterparts over in Defense or elsewhere, I would telephone my friend in the NSC and discuss the ramifications of the case, implanting my views. Later, I would mischievously say, "Well, you know the NSC thinks . . ." with a very helpful result.

I had also learned by that time of Kissinger's background and his relationship with Fritz Kraemer, my old friend, the lieutenant colonel I had known in the Army Reserve unit back in 1957–62.[8] In a number of ways, Kraemer had shaped Kissinger's future. The latter had come a long way since the days when he was a sergeant in the Army CIC back in Germany after World War II. Inwardly, I guess, I resented his capacity to push around highly experienced diplomats without having had any real hands-on foreign affairs experience of his own.

Going up to Capitol Hill to explain a program under criticism by the Congress is surely one of a Foreign Service officer's more difficult tasks. Senator J. William Fulbright, the chairman of the Senate Foreign Relations Committee, once took Assistant Secretary Newsom and me over the coals about our military assistance program for Morocco. An investigative journalist, Seymour Hersh, had written scathing articles about the program and our relations with that country. I came away deeply disappointed with the senator, who over a long career had sponsored fine legislation and served our country well. On this occasion before his committee, however, he held forth in long soliloquies that were little more than ego trips, while everyone present marked time. Power corrupts even the best of people if exposed to it long enough.

Although power was not a question with me, at times I must have been difficult to work with myself. The funds available for the African program were so limited that I tended to be tenacious in guarding against other bureaus' siphoning them off. I recall one of our disputes being taken up to Under Secretary for Political Affairs U. Alexis Johnson for resolution. The representative from the other bureau and I argued it out before the under secretary, who in his wisdom finally simply compromised, dividing the disputed amount between our two areas. He concluded our meeting saying, "Now each of you has something with which to be satisfied." To which my comment was, "Not really," since they were my funds we were dividing. I am afraid that fine old gentleman was a bit perturbed with me.

Our son, Brad, graduated from high school in June 1971, and we assisted him in his efforts to obtain admission to a suitable college. He had been placed on the waiting list for Duke University, when Lieutenant Colonel William Healy, a colleague in my Army Reserve unit, approached me suggesting that Brad seek an appointment to the U.S. Military Academy at West Point. He was an area contact officer for that institution. I talked with Brad, and we decided to take a chance, even though we knew there would be a hundred or more young men competing for our congressman's two appointments. Our approach was systematic. On his mother's side, he could state in his essay that her grandfather and great grandfather going back to the Civil War had been military surgeons and he wanted to continue that tradition. His father was a World War II veteran and an Army Reserve officer. He had good grades and was a star athlete. Unlike most other young men at his interview, he came conservatively dressed wearing a blazer, white shirt, and rep tie.

Brad was Congressman Gilbert Gude's (8th District, Maryland) first choice for an appointment. As part of the entrance procedure, he received a certificate indicating that he had been awarded a scholarship to the Academy, which was to be given to the principal for presentation at his high school graduation. When that day approached, I noted that the envelope containing the certificate still had not been delivered to the principal, despite our reminding Brad several times to do so. Finally, my daughter, Andrea, took me aside and said, "Dad, he is never going to deliver it. The kids would simply boo him out of the place." Such was the anti-Vietnam War sentiment at the school. I should have sensed what was going on, for earlier I was aware that Brad and several members of the football team had forcefully stopped some of the students who were attempting to burn an American flag. A local newspaper had reported the incident. Those were sad days for our country.

Brad's entry into the U.S. Military Academy during the summer of 1971 is indelibly fixed in the minds of our family. Together, we drove the 236 miles from home to West Point to give him moral support. We had a general idea from movies and folklore that a plebe's life was one of hazing and misery. But Brad was tough and he could take it. Arriving at the scheduled time, he reported to the drop-off place, the massive iron gate, which was the entrance to the football stadium. As Brad passed through, he gave us a sad little smile, the gate clanked shut, and he was gone. It was as if he had been placed in prison. Elsa turned to me and wailed, "What have you done to my son!" It was a bitter trip back to Chevy Chase, one filled with recrimination. However, that was only the beginning of trials to follow.

We were not permitted at the outset to visit Brad for three months, and when we finally did, it was a shock. Having survived the "beast barracks" period, he stood before us cadaverous and hollow-eyed. He had lost 25 pounds from what had been a slim muscular frame. His mother's natural reaction was to take him home. But neither Brad nor I would have any of that. What was required instead was a plan to support him as best we could. A decision was made to visit him on Sundays, whenever he had a pass for a few hours. For months, thereafter, we drove those hundreds of miles up to West Point and back every other weekend. As time passed, Brad grew more accustomed to the rigors and, supported by good friends he found among the other cadets, he managed, despite the fact that having entered at age seventeen, he was younger than most of his classmates.

Those years working on African affairs and politico-military matters were interesting and rewarding. They gave me an unusual opportunity to deal with other federal agencies and, in particular, the defense establishment. As a by-product, I was able to use the knowledge and experience gained to benefit the Army Reserve civil affairs unit to which I was then assigned. It had responsibility for the Middle East and Africa and would engage in extensive training exercises related to potential international problems. With my background, I was asked to prepare an exercise that would be played out over the course of a year or more. It was my view that a future war between Iran and Iraq was likely, and I authored a scenario designed to test the United States' civil affairs capacity to respond to the aftermath of a conflict between the two countries.

There was always a certain danger in these exercises that the media might become aware of them and speculate that "the United States is preparing for war in . . ." To avoid this, I made the scenario appear so outlandish that no one would take it seriously, while at the same time providing a situation that would put our forces to the test. The exercise was called "Operation Sinkhole." It involved a sudden, huge, deep opening of the earth on the Iran/Iraq border that sucked in thousands of people, with hundreds of thousands of related casualties. It postulated civil unrest, a complete disruption of government activity, and millions of refugees. "Operation Sinkhole" provided excellent training during the year and subsequently in a mock exercise at our annual two-week summer camp at Indiantown Gap Military Reservation. I recall playing the role in the exercise of the overburdened and distraught American ambassador to Iran.

As an indication that publicity concerns with regard to these activities were fully warranted, one of the unit's subsidiary organizations, a civil affairs company engaged in a project involving Tanzania, did cause trouble. Before long a telegram from our embassy in Dar-es-Salaam alerted the State Department that the Tanzanian government was alarmed, fearing the United States was preparing to send troops to that country. An item had appeared in the press about our Army training for hypothetical deployment to Tanzania. On that occasion, I hastened to inform the company commander about the repercussions their project was causing and it was dropped forthwith. It is always difficult to deny these stories once they get started.

I had served in the Bureau of African Affairs for four years, and it was time for me to consider moving to another assignment. I was pondering my prospects one morning, when my secretary announced an Army major who had made an appointment to see me before going out to Kinshasa as an assistant military attaché. We had a pleasant exchange about his duties, and he departed on his way. Some weeks afterward, we received a shocking cable from the post indicating that while swimming at a spot used by the embassy for recreation along the Congo River, the major had been dragged underwater and eaten by a giant crocodile. Such was life in service overseas.

13

A Year at the Army War College

I had always desired an assignment to one of the defense colleges. The one in Washington, then known as the National War College, would have been the most convenient, since placement there meant I would not have to disrupt the family with a move for a posting lasting only a year. As things turned out, I received an assignment to the U.S. Army War College at Carlisle Barracks, Pennsylvania. Without my knowledge, a good friend serving in the Personnel Bureau, Richard Owen, had mentioned my name believing that with my politico-military and Army Reserve officer background I would be an ideal choice. I have been forever grateful to him for that favor.

During those final weeks as I closed out my politico-military advisor duties, Dick Critz, my deputy, took over, enabling me to travel to Carlisle to meet with Ambassador Hermann Eilts, the diplomatic advisor at the War College. He was pleased that I had been assigned as one of the two State Department members of the Resident Class of 1972–73. When I mentioned that I was hesitant to sell or rent our house for just a year and move my family to Carlisle, particularly since it was my daughter's senior year in high school, he became concerned. He informed me that part of the training involved social activities and one's wife was expected to be a participant. I countered by indicating Elsa and I had discussed the situation and were fully prepared to take an apartment on the post, just as any other married couple would. She would be available for anything required of her. We would simply maintain our household in Chevy Chase, where my very responsible seventeen-year-old daughter would be in charge when my wife was away. My twelve-year-old son was levelheaded and would be helpful. Elsa thus committed herself to commuting back and forth between home and the college. It was a driving distance on the Interstates of 114 miles, or 92 miles taking a backroads short cut.

Arriving at the War College in the late summer of 1972, I was assigned a two-bedroom apartment in Young Hall, a long, red-brick, two-story building facing out on the parade ground. The other occupants were officers at the colonel or lieutenant colonel level and their spouses. Many had children. However, those with larger families were assigned houses on the post or rented them in town using their housing allowances. They were an attractive group of people. Many of the officers were highly decorated veterans of the war in Vietnam. A few had served in Korea. The class president, a senior colonel, and I were the "oldies," having been in World War II. The average age of the 228 members of the class was forty-one. The student body consisted of 188 Army officers, 16 Air Force, 10 Navy, 6 Marine Corps, and 8 civilians from government agencies involved in national security affairs. The Army officers, for example, were considered the absolute "cream of the crop," those under consideration for promotion to general. Bearing in mind that the Army has thousands of officers, one can readily see how elite a group it was. The choice of candidates for the Navy, Air Force, and National War Colleges was much the same. In each, the preponderance of students came from the host service, with a selected few from other areas. The National War College, later renamed the National Defense University, had more of an overall military and civilian mix.

After years of military service, I immediately felt at home with the administrative procedures established to assist students and families into their quarters. There were supply rooms from which to draw furniture and bedding, post regulations, and an "Army way" of doing things. Also available were a Post Exchange (PX), a commissary, a theater, a gymnasium, and all sorts of sports and recreation facilities. When moving vans rolled in with the belongings of my classmates, you would see packing crates from Korea, Japan, Germany, Panama, and other places around the world where they had been stationed. As my first day at Carlisle Barracks drew to a close, the sound of a cannon, a bugle blowing "Retreat," and the lowering of the flag brought back many memories.

The curriculum at the Army War College was designed to prepare an officer to function at the top levels of the government and the military services. At the outset it examined the world situation and the United States' strategic position with regard to challenges and means to meet them. The Cold War was at its height at the time and consideration was given as to how best to deal with the threat from the Soviet Union and the Communist Bloc. Strategic alliances such as the North Atlantic Treaty Organization (NATO) and other defense arrangements were appraised, as was the impact of the United Nations on our country's policies. The early months' activities laid the groundwork for the preparation of a national strategy. Having spent years in graduate school and in the Department of State dealing with aspects of what I was about to study, I was on familiar ground in that phase of the course.

For purposes of instruction, the student body was divided into committees, each one a class of about twenty officers. The committee not only met in the classroom, but also socially on evenings and weekends. Officers and their wives took turns entertaining. Those with houses were the more likely hosts. It was a good way to make friends and develop the social skills expected of a general officer and his wife. At the same time it placed a few students in a position similar to mine at a slight disadvantage. Officers working at the Pentagon or elsewhere in Washington, who knew they would be returning there and did not move their families, were labeled "roadrunners," after the Walt Disney cartoon character. In some cases, wives who had jobs simply could not afford to come up to Carlisle. Recalling my promise to Ambassador Eilts, Elsa and I determined to camouflage as much as possible the fact that we still maintained a residence in Chevy Chase. In this Elsa, and to some extent our children, put on a fine performance.

Prior to our arrival at Carlisle, I was asked to complete a biographic statement form, which was then incorporated into a large directory containing information not only about my classmates, but the officials in charge of the College, the professors, and other key individuals on the post.[1] In it one found small head shots not only of the officer in question but of the spouse as well. The directory was given to us at the outset and proved to be a useful document in acquainting us at an early stage with others in our academic community. Imagine my surprise when on my first morning one of the officers I encountered walking to class greeted me with the salutation, "Airborne!" Evidently, he had read my bio and knew that I had served as a paratrooper in the 82nd Airborne Division. My reply was the traditional, "All the way!" He was in uniform at the time, wearing an 82nd Airborne shoulder patch, and I, in civilian clothes. Little gestures such as this particularly welcomed me, a State Department outsider, to the club.

I soon grew to know the members of my committee, as well as the officers and wives living in my apartment complex. It was a relatively short walk across the parade ground to Root Hall, where our classes were held. To assist us in our studies, each officer was assigned a small office on an upper floor of that building, where we were to spend many hours reading and preparing presentations. Students were given a good deal of homework and expected to participate fully in class discussions. In addition to the books and resource material issued to us, the War College had a fine library. The faculty was a combination of military officers who had achieved advanced degrees and status in the academic world and civilian professors. In addition, the college's program offered a series of regular lectures by outstanding visiting scholars. I had the sense that no expense or effort was spared to provide the prospective leaders of our military and government establishments with the very best training. A number of my classmates were themselves recognized scholars and authors of published works.[2] Some of them were to become well-known in the coming decades.

I was soon immersed in studies related to national defense decision-making and executive management. We were given an opportunity to examine a variety of issues concerning the making of policy at the highest levels of the government. Stress was placed on the officers' presenting facets of problems in class for general discussion. We were informed at a relatively early stage that each student would be required to submit a thesis at the end of the year. Students were encouraged to take time in considering the matter and to choose subjects with which they had some familiarity, particularly ones that might be potentially useful to the military services or the government in general.

Having a son in his second year at West Point at the time influenced me on one or two occasions to make a related point during classroom discussions. Over the years I had attended many meetings involving members of the military services. At times my office would be at odds with them. It was in these "battles of the conference table" that courses of action, military assistance budgets, or other matters were settled. Once in a while, we found ourselves confronted by a member of the military, who was not able to present his position persuasively, lacking the rhetorical skill required. This generally created an impasse leading to bureaucratic contention and loss of time. With that in mind, I found myself wondering whether the Military Academy, with its emphasis on engineering and technical subjects, was giving my son the English language, discourse, and indeed debating skills required to function effectively in the government arena. As tactfully as possible, I pressed this point, I must say, to a very receptive audience, including a friend, Dave Palmer, who was later to become a three-star general and the Superintendent of West Point. Many of those officers had come from Pentagon assignments and knew exactly what I was talking about.

There were many enjoyable moments during my year at the War College. I was amused at the playful aspects of inter- and intra-service rivalry that would come to the fore at times. The Army would spoof the Air Force, and the Navy would find ways to needle the Army or the Marines. It was all in good humor and comradeship. It was the custom during the year for each of the services to host a gala Saturday night party at the officers' club. Sometimes this would coincide with a particular day, such as the birthday of the founding of that service. These were often formal affairs, with the officers attending in their splendid mess dress, while I wore a tuxedo and Elsa a long gown.

The officers and their ladies were indeed a handsome and attractive group. The Army as the dominant service also hosted galas honoring the individual combat arms with an "Infantry Ball" or an "Artillery Ball." On these occasions, as with the other services, those attending were at times also presented with party favors. I still have a letter opener on my desk, a miniature bayonet and an exact replica of the real thing, which is inscribed on the blade, "Infantry Ball, AWC, 1973."

While at the War College, I endeavored to keep contact with my Army Reserve unit. On weekends at home that coincided with drill at the armory in Riverdale, I would drop by to chat with Brigadier General Chester Finch, the commander, and with other officers. I also had a great fondness for the enlisted personnel in the unit and spent time with them. It was a feather in the hat of the unit to have someone attending the Resident Course at the War College, despite the fact that I was there not as an Army officer but as a State Department official. There was only one other Army Reserve officer in our class. He was there in uniform, having come from an assignment in the Pentagon, where he had worked in the Office of the Chief of the Army Reserve.

It was difficult to keep a sense of family solidarity during this period, but Elsa and I did our best, with Brad at West Point and me away in Pennsylvania. Matthew and Andrea were coming along well. In fact our daughter was turning out to be an academic star. One of my regrets during that year was that I was not at home to witness the full ramifications of her performance. A television station in the Washington area featured a live Saturday morning quiz program, *It's Academic*, which brought together teams from local high schools in a semester-long tournament. It had all the rivalry and color of a football game, including cheerleaders, as teams from three schools answered a moderator's questions before an audience in a large TV studio theater.

I was surprised and pleased to learn that Andrea, along with two boys, had been chosen to represent Bethesda-Chevy Chase (BCC) High School. At one point, when it seemed they would be defeated, since they were far behind on the final program, I watched my daughter correctly answer an entire category of questions, bringing her team to a last-minute victory and the area championship.[3]

My relations with the commandant of the War College, Major General Franklin M. Davis, Jr., were very cordial. As one of the two State Department members of the class, I was asked on several occasions to assist when foreign dignitaries visited the college. I would be included in luncheons to fill out the complement of guests. General Davis knew that I was an Army

Reserve officer and had served as a paratrooper in World War II. He, himself, had been an officer with our XVIII Airborne Corps in the Ardennes campaign (Battle of the Bulge) and was well acquainted with the actions of my 17th Airborne Division. He was a fine officer, a military intellectual, who, sadly, lost his elder son, a paratrooper with the 101st Airborne Division, in Vietnam.

General Davis learned that I was up for promotion to colonel that year and asked me about it. I indicated that, given the very limited number of selections, my chances were marginal. He was surprised, saying that with my overall background, plus being one of the very few Reserve officers who had attended the Resident Course at the War College, I would be a real asset to the Army. Subsequently, I heard that he had taken steps on my behalf with the Pentagon.[4] Sure enough, when the congressional promotion list came out that June, my name was on it.

Elsa, the faithful service wife, attended the various official and social functions during the year. More than once, she drove up from Chevy Chase in bad weather, including snow. On one occasion, she broke down going over the narrow, winding, mountain road between York Springs and Carlisle. The radiator of our Pontiac convertible blew a thermostat and the engine overheated. Luckily, there was a makeshift garage repair shop nearby and some helpful local mechanic managed to get the car functioning again. The word of Elsa's efforts spread through our class, and at one of the social functions she was surprised to receive an "award." Two of the officers, Dave Palmer and Jerry Curry, concocted a handsome, framed certificate awarding her the "Order of the Road Runner." It featured a long, cleverly worded citation and an embroidered patch depicting the Disney cartoon roadrunner. Elsa was deeply moved and has treasured the award ever since. Both Palmer and Curry later also touched on the lives of our sons, Palmer as superintendent of West Point and Curry, after retiring as a major general, as the deputy administrator of the Federal Aviation Administration, where Matthew worked as the senior watch officer in the Operations Center.

As we entered the second half of our academic year, preparations to complete a thesis began in earnest. I believed that I could best contribute to the effort to further politico-military relations by completing a study of the program I had spent years engaged in before coming to the War College. I therefore chose as my topic: "United States Military Assistance to Africa: Organization, Problems and Prospects." I had been the officer responsible for this activity in the Department of State from 1969 to 1972 and was in a position to provide insights that might otherwise not have been committed to print. The study was unclassified and consequently some care had to be taken not to offend foreign governments or disclose elements of confidential programs.

My writing was based on daily experience, discussions with a variety of knowledgeable government officials, two trips to Africa, and access to documents not available to the public. The study analyzed America's approach to providing arms to a number of struggling, newly emerging African countries. Our attitude had a degree of ambivalence, since one knew that if the United States did not supply arms, the Soviet Union, China, or others would. Contrasting grant assistance programs with credit sales, I projected future trends. I also examined the uncertainties of the congressional budget cycle, the changing character of the Military Assistance Advisory Groups (MAAGs), and the impact of the Cold War.

Unlike my days at Columbia, when the brunt of preparing the final typed version of the thesis fell upon the student, the War College, blessedly, provided each officer with secretarial assistance. Copies of the completed studies were placed on the shelves of the War College's library, the library at the Pentagon, and possibly the Library of Congress, although I am not certain of the latter. In my case, a copy was also given to the Department of State's library. Some time later I found it there along with a copy of my publication *U.S. Denazification Policy in Germany, 1944–1950*.

The government spared no expense in training its future leaders and this was apparent in the field trips we took during the year. Arrangements were made for us to visit the United Nations, where we met with our ambassador and his staff, as well as with representatives of other countries. We visited the Canadian Parliament and the president of Panama. We were flown by helicopter the length of the Panama Canal, from the Atlantic to the Pacific, and later briefed in the control building of the Gatun Lock as ships passed through. Some of us were taken to Norfolk Naval Base in Virginia for a tour of an aircraft carrier and discussions with officers of North Atlantic Command. We observed a special suppression and bombardment exercise at Eglin Air Force Base, Florida.

We visited the deep underground, nuclear-protected, alternate government site at Thurmont, Maryland. Similarly, on a trip to Colorado, we toured the Strategic Air Command (SAC) Headquarters deep in Cheyenne Mountain. While in Colorado we also went to Fort Carson, where we were given a demonstration by the 4th Mechanized Infantry Division. I recall that at the conclusion of a briefing on guided weapons at a battalion command post there, one of the officers departed the building, climbed into a nearby medium tank, and roared off, cannon blazing away, onto the firing range. My thought at the time was that it was like seeing a knight of old mounting his charger and going into battle.

Some of us also visited nearby Letterkenny Army Depot in Pennsylvania, while others went to Redstone Arsenal in Alabama or Fort Knox, Kentucky. In each case, where one of the services was involved, whether Army, Navy, Air Force, or Marines, they did their best to impress us, recognizing that in a few years some of their visitors would be playing a key role in determining their future.

Naturally, my classmates were aware that many of them would become general, or flag-level, officers. The latter term is used to denote officers from any of the services entitled to fly a flag with stars denoting his or her rank. A major general in the Army flew a red flag with two stars, for example, a vice admiral in the Navy, a blue flag with three stars, and an Air Force officer of equivalent rank one in light blue. Their personal stationery also featured a miniature flag with the appropriate number of stars.

Many of my colleagues and I wondered who would rise to the highest levels in the armed forces. It was an interesting guessing game, at which I must say I was not the best. While it was not too difficult to surmise those with a good chance to attain the lowest flag rank, picking those who would go to the very top was another matter.

The class of 1973 was one upon which "the stars fell." Carl Vuono, a very able member of my committee, later was Army Chief of Staff during "Desert Storm," the war to oust Iraq from Kuwait, while Norman Schwarzkopf was the victorious commander in that war. At the college, Schwarzkopf seemed a gregarious and easy-going fellow, but he subsequently turned out to be a brilliant, very tough leader. Several of my friends became three- or four-star generals. In contrast, some of the others whom I considered to be just as bright, if not more so, retired as colonels. On the whole, those who moved up were from the combat arms—the infantry, artillery, armor, or the equivalent in the other services.

During one of my committee's class discussions related to logistics and personnel, I asked a question as to how an officer was selected for attendance at one of the war colleges. It seemed as if I had struck a nerve. Obviously, the candidate had to have a stellar record in terms of efficiency ratings, commendations, and other items in the personnel file. Such things as command experience, decorations for bravery on the battlefield, and unusually fine performance in difficult assignments played a role. But there were many officers with those qualifications at the time; it was also useful to have a very senior flag officer interested in your career. Perhaps not so strangely, it helped to have an assignment in personnel, or at least a good friend there just prior to or concurrent with being selected for a war college. In a show of hands on that occasion, a significant portion of my committee had come from assignments in the personnel bureaus. It made me think of how lucky I was to have had Dick Owen serving in the

State Department's Bureau of Personnel at the time of my appointment. In truth, however, his call to me asking whether I would be interested in attending the Army War College came as a complete but welcome surprise.

From time to time, there were discussions at the War College about the Army Reserve, its make-up and deployment. I was always especially interested in the reactions of these career officers, the majority of whom were West Point graduates, to Reservists. There were enough officers in the course who had come into the Army through college ROTC programs and a variety of other means, however, to make the discussions somewhat guarded.

On one occasion, I had to come to the defense of the Reserves. It was during a slide presentation about Army personnel strength to the entire War College class in the large auditorium. The Tables of Organization (TO&E) of Reserve infantry, artillery, armor, and other outfits were shown. When a civil affairs unit was put up on the screen, one to which I just happened to be assigned at the time, there was a loud exclamation from the audience. They were aghast that there were twenty lieutenant colonels and colonels but relatively few enlisted personnel. I had to speak up to point out that the unit they were viewing was intended to provide the military government for a nation of many millions of people in the event of war. Those colonels were men with civilian skills in civil administration, public utilities, finance, public safety, health and other vital areas needed to run a country.[5] I added that from my experience, there were more generals and colonels than that in Berlin alone during the occupation days in Germany after World War II.

During the second week of March 1973, I received the sad news that one of my earliest friends in the Foreign Service had been murdered in the Sudan. G. Curtis Moore had been the deputy chief of mission and chargé d'affaires at our Embassy in Khartoum. Curt, along with our newly arrived ambassador, Cleo A. Noel, and a Belgian diplomat, were taken captive in an attack by Palestinian Black September terrorists at a farewell party being given for Curt at the Saudi Arabian Embassy. The terrorists occupied the Embassy, awaiting word as to whether their demand for the release of seventeen Palestinian prisoners in Jordan would be acted on. A toughly worded comment by President Nixon that "we don't negotiate with terrorists" may have had the effect of convincing the terrorists that their demands would not be considered.[6]

The captives were provided with material to write last messages and wills, then summarily executed. Curt was admirable to the end. As he was being led to his death, he even paused to thank the distraught Saudi ambassador for the party. The nation mourned as he and Ambassador Noel were buried at Arlington Cemetery. Sally, Curt's brave and lovely wife, carried on alone with his children. As I reflect on the numerous friends I have lost over the years in the Foreign Service, it is apparent that diplomacy has become an ever-more perilous profession. As is often noted, more ambassadors than generals have been killed in today's dangerous world.

I have reflected over the years on one incident at the college. It was an outgrowth of the National Security Seminar, an exercise held at the end of each year to which high-ranking members of our government, cabinet heads, congresspersons, and others are invited. That particular year, Army Chief of Staff Creighton Abrams and Under Secretary of State U. Alexis Johnson were among those present. A week before the presentation at the seminar, our class was divided into a number of committees to solve the problem of how to deal with a full-scale attack by Soviet forces through the Fulda Gap in Germany. We were faced with a massive breakthrough of Russian armor. Over several days, the committees pondered the problem and prepared solutions varying from our forces standing and fighting to pulling back to England or retreating to regroup beyond the Pyrenees in Spain. These committee solutions were the product of discussion and consensus, after which one spokesman for each committee was chosen to make the presentation on the day of the National Security Seminar to the distinguished visitors and the entire college in the auditorium.

Frankly, I cannot recall what our committee's solution was, although ours was a special group consisting of those with particular qualifications. It was nothing unusual, a logical positioning of our forces. As part of the various presentations, Dave Palmer, as the spokesman for his committee, offered a solution which had our forces retreating to Spain or something of that sort. In any event, it may have been wise, but to a military man, it seemed pusillanimous. At the conclusion of the exercise, General Abrams rose to comment. In a high state of irritation, he exclaimed that he had just come from the Army Command and General Staff School at Fort Leavenworth and was appalled at what was being taught there. Now, at the Army War College, supposedly the elite training ground for the very finest officers in the Army, he finds Lieutenant Colonel Palmer spouting nonsense. It was a tirade I shall never forget. Several times, he mentioned Palmer by name. To say the least, the Army chief of staff threw our class and the faculty into a state of shock that morning.

I left the auditorium at the conclusion of this affair bewildered and proceeded up to my office in Root Hall before going to lunch. As I passed Dave Palmer's office, I saw him sitting at his desk, with his head in his hands. I sought to console him, telling him not to make too much of the incident. I found out that he had dissented from his committee's solution, but it was the majority view, and when he was chosen to make the presentation, he did so like a good soldier. Dave was totally dejected, saying that for General Abrams to criticize him so harshly in public meant his career was over. My response was that he was one of the finest officers I had met at the War College, "head and shoulders over most of those here." I did not think for one moment the Army would not recognize that fact. However, as time went on after I graduated, I watched apprehensively to see whether Dave's name appeared on the promotion list to brigadier general. I was on a tour of Reserve duty, lecturing at the Command and General Staff School at Fort Leavenworth about four or five years later, when I saw his name on the list. I uttered a "thank goodness!" He was on his way to becoming a three-star general.

As the academic year drew to a close, we made the traditional effort to preserve school memories by encapsulating aspects of life at the college into a Class of 1973 Yearbook. There were photographs of all of the students and their families, as well as numerous pictures of activities, many of them hilariously depicted in cartoons.[7] I served as a member of the editorial committee putting the yearbook together and found it an enjoyable experience. There was much poking fun at classmates, faculty, and administrators. I never fail to be amused, even after all these years, on fingering through the pages. On a somber note, however, the Yearbook was dedicated to the many officers killed in Vietnam who had attended the War College. The war was still raging then, and we were all aware that some of our class would receive assignments taking them into combat.

Graduation was a busy time for all, as we prepared to move to new assignments. For some of the officers it was promotion time as well, and many of those who were lieutenant colonels received their "eagles." It was reported that I was on the Army Reserve list for promotion to colonel, as well, and there were congratulations all around. Several of my colleagues upon learning about my promotion, gleefully commented that "sometimes even diplomats receive proper recognition." I was informed that my thesis was among those which had been selected by the College for special commendation and that I had placed among the very top students in the class in an unofficial ranking. One of the traditions initiated many years earlier was to have a large, heavy, bronze plaque cast containing the names of all the graduates in each class. These plaques are affixed side by side along a front wall on the outside of Root Hall. My name, "John G. Kormann, USFS" (U.S. Foreign Service) is there with the Class of 1973 for future generations to see, along with some of the distinguished generals and admirals who were my classmates.

No sooner had my graduation services been concluded at the War College than I returned to Chevy Chase to attend those of my daughter, Andrea, from Bethesda-Chevy Chase High School. We were proud to learn that she had placed at the top of her class, had been admitted to

Dartmouth College (the students' then most desired choice), and had also been named Montgomery County "Youth of the Year." My parents-in-law came east from Illinois during this period to witness these joyful events.

Several months prior to concluding studies at the War College, my thoughts had turned to my next assignment. It had been a long time since I had served in Germany and with Elsa's and my fluency in the language, I believed that a tour with our Embassy there might be beneficial to both the State Department and my family. As matters evolved, however, I was told that I would be assigned to South Africa as consul general in Durban. All things considered, this was a good posting and I was prepared to accept, when I learned that the incumbent there had opted to stay on for another tour. My assignment was then changed to Germany, not to the Embassy but to the very large American Consulate General in Munich as political officer. I was told that I would be the deputy and number two ranking officer there. I had hoped to go to Bonn, but at least I was returning to Germany, with all it had to offer us as a family.

14

Munich, An Interrupted Tour

Upon our arrival at the Munich Airport in July 1973, we were met by consulate personnel and taken to our quarters, a very large and lovely apartment on the Koenigenstrasse, a short distance from the American Consulate General. The apartment overlooked the Englishergarten, a beautiful park replete with a little lake and swans. The Kormann family in Munich now consisted of my wife, Elsa, our younger son Matthew, and myself. Our two other children were back in the United States — son Brad at West Point and daughter Andrea at Dartmouth. We had last served in Germany eighteen years earlier and were in for a number of surprises.

Most apparent was the aura of prosperity. Germany in the meantime had once more become an industrial powerhouse. The residents of Munich appeared energetic and well dressed. Downtown was bustling with people hurrying about. Shops were well stocked. There were traffic jams, many of the automobiles high-priced Mercedes and BMWs. For someone who had witnessed the post–World War II years the change was dramatic. When we left in 1955, German salaries were only a fraction of those of Americans. Now, they were comparable. Prices for items in the shops, however, were considerably higher than in the United States.

Because of a labor shortage, Germany was importing workers from the Balkans and the Middle East, particularly Turkey. In the post–World War II years, American military families were used to having German maids, gardeners, and other household help. Now, the situation had to some extent reversed itself, and some wives of low-ranking American military enlisted personnel were now working for German families.[1] For diplomatic officers accustomed to business entertaining elsewhere overseas, the lack of servants and the high cost of everything came as a shock. I was glad that we had arrived from a Washington assignment and the War College, where we normally had neither servants nor entertainment allowances.

Nevertheless, I was soon to find myself at a considerable disadvantage in the course of my political officer duties. In the second week on the job, I was invited to lunch at one of the hotels by a local labor leader who was extremely well informed about Bavarian politics. Our bill, for what seemed to me a nominal meal, cost well over one hundred dollars in German currency, a high price by American standards at the time.

It did not take me long to enter into the various aspects of my political officer duties. Germany was a familiar scene for me and the political parties had not changed much. There was a crop of newer, younger faces, but many of the issues and problems remained the same. To my pleasant surprise I learned that some of my old German friends had moved into positions of prominence. I was particularly pleased to hear shortly after my arrival that Otto Schedl, the former Landrat in Neumarkt, with whom I had worked closely on a most cordial basis, had moved upward in political circles to become a figure of importance in the Christian Socialist Union Party (CSU). Otto had since been Bavaria's minister of economic affairs, then finance minister, and subsequently the vice minister president. He was considered Bavaria's "economic czar" and a "power behind the throne."

I telephoned his office soon after learning that he was in Munich, leaving my name with his secretary. In a short time he returned my call, and there was a happy reunion of two old friends. As soon as our family had settled in to our spacious, well-furnished apartment, he and his wife joined us for dinner. It seemed like old times, despite the fact that it had been twenty years since I had departed Neumarkt and we had said farewell to one another.

My political officer duties were straightforward. They were to maintain contact with officials of the Bavarian government and key members of the various political parties and report on their activities. I prepared regular reports, keeping Washington informed of the trend of events. The CSU was the dominant party at the time. I also kept my eye on the activities of the American military in Bavaria and stayed in touch with the officer who served as a liaison with the German state government and my office. The man who held that position turned out to be Kenneth Van Buskirk, the former chief of the U.S. High Commission's Field Operations Division back in the early 1950s and my old boss. He had stayed on all these years, living in the same house on Lake Starnberg.

Entering his office, it was as if I had seen a ghost. The power and authority of his old position were gone. We were no longer the occupiers endeavoring to "democratize" Germany. The U.S. Army, however, knew a good thing when they saw it. Colonel Van Buskirk's contacts and goodwill built up with the Germans over the years were great assets and the Army was wise enough to put them to good use. The colonel's eyes lit up when he saw me. He had learned of my assignment and was extremely pleased to see me.

Much of the property held by our forces had been turned back to the Germans, and what was left of our military was concentrated largely in a vast barracks and housing development on the outskirts of town.[2] The American elementary and high schools were also there, and we made arrangements for Matthew to be enrolled. For the military children the distance to school was minimal, but for Matthew it meant traveling many miles from the center of town. Initially his mother drove him to school, but in a relatively short time he learned to use the streetcar (tram). He found that being an outsider among military children had its drawbacks. I thought he might gain greater acceptance by going out for football with one of the Little League–type teams set up by the Army for its children. As in other sports run by the military it was highly organized and equipped. The coaches, at least in my view, tended to take an overly serious attitude to what, in essence, was the play of early teenage boys. Regular games were played in a stadium with girl cheerleaders and all the panoply of college contests back in the United States. His mother and I attended a game and watched as Matt was banged around by tough, larger Army kids. He took it well, but I had second thoughts about the wisdom of letting him continue for fear he might be seriously hurt.

To compensate for Matt's loneliness and missing his siblings, we decided to provide him with a dog. This turned out to be one of the most fortuitous decisions of our lives. Elsa visited the local German pound seeking an animal in need of a home. She was shocked to find that the attendants were less than cooperative. They simply would not agree to giving a dog to Americans, because our military had a reputation for abandoning them when transferred. Perhaps, had I intervened and pressed our case as a diplomatic family, the answer might have been different. However, rather than do that, she simply diverted her search to the U. S. Army veterinarian, and sure enough, found a selection of abandoned dogs.

Elsa focused on a sibling pair of black-and-white spaniel-type animals. She chose the male, although their attractive markings were similar. The dog was just a year old. We found that it had been trained by its previous owner, was totally housebroken, and extremely intelligent. I could not see for the life of me how anyone could have parted with that animal. Our previous dog, Socrates, a Belgian Shepherd, had been trained by the German police and had been a superb family companion. This mixed-breed dog had all the qualities of a Scottish border collie and was to be Socrates' equal. We named him Pericles after the noble Greek, Perry for short, since he promised to be an exceptional pet.

I ran him through the dog trainer's paces soon after we acquired him. He would "sit" and "heel" upon command, "come" when ordered, catch a tennis ball thrown high in the air, and do a variety of other tricks. Most startling, however, was his inbred tendency to perform as a sheep dog. A few weeks after joining us, our family and some friends, adults and children, were playing in the park, running around laughing and chasing one another. Suddenly, Perry gave a "yip," took off at top speed, and began racing around us in a circle, attempting to herd us together. It was quite a performance!

Soon after arriving in Munich, I had sought out the possibility of an assignment with an Army Reserve unit. Many American civilians worked with our forces in southern Germany, and I was sure there would be one in the area, and indeed, there was one in Munich. But I soon ran into problems. Apparently there were no positions available at my grade level, even though I was still only a lieutenant colonel. My promotion to colonel, which was to take effect in another eight months, would in those circumstances have made assignment virtually impossible. There I asked to be able to attend drills as a visitor for attendance credit to retain my standing in the Reserve, which was much the same as completing correspondence courses. I had done the latter in Libya, for example.

However, several months into my stay in Munich, I was called by the colonel commanding our Reserve unit and asked, "Who do you know?" I was startled to be told the commander of the Army Reserve for the European Theater had inquired about me and simply told him to make a place for me, period! The long arm of the Army War College network was at work. I subsequently learned that a general, a War College friend, had been appointed to a very senior position in Germany and had, without my knowledge, asked where I had been assigned. I was given a position on the faculty of the 3745th U.S. Army Reserve School, where I could bring to bear some of the knowledge I had gained in War College training.

My political officer duties with the Consulate General in Munich were more limited than those I had been accustomed to over the years. They were a far cry from the sweeping opportunities to be involved in day-to-day relations between our government and the host country, such as in the Philippines. There I had sent back cables reporting on efforts to mediate war between Malaysia and Indonesia or on activities to support our forces in Vietnam. Compared to Libya and hostilities in the Middle East or Manila and tempestuous political situations, Munich was a sea of calm. An exciting day now might include an interview with a Socialist Party candidate about his chances of winning a seat on the city council. I found myself wishing that I had been assigned to our Embassy in Bonn.

While I hoped for greener pastures, Elsa was supremely happy. Munich is a beautiful city with an abundance of cultural amenities. One could see the Bavarian Alps in the distance. The bells of the various cathedrals tolled throughout the city. The air was always crisp and fresh and the water from a tributary of the Isar River, rushing down from the Alps, coursed merrily through the Englishergarten across from our lovely apartment. There were operas and operettas, concerts and stage plays, and several wonderful museums, as well as a number of magnificent palaces. So very much had been restored since the dark days following World War II that it was a treat simply to be alive in that lovely place. Nevertheless, I had become so accustomed to living in a sea of activity and problems that I was bound to be restless despite all the wonderful surroundings.

Our 1969 Pontiac convertible had been in excellent condition, with low mileage, when we received word of our transfer to Germany. Rather than order a new car to be shipped over to Munich, we decided to take it with us. We remembered from our earlier assignment how much pleasure driving in an open car in southern Germany had given us. While Europeans were paying very high prices for gasoline, we knew that we would be using Army facilities and paying a reduced rate, so having a large American car was no hardship. During our six-month stay in Munich, however, war in the Middle East affected the supply of oil to Europe. Germans were temporarily subjected to rationing, as indeed were we.

On one occasion we drove the sixty miles up to Neumarkt to visit our old villa. It had been turned back to the executives of the dynamite factory. The building, garage, and tennis court were all as we had remembered them. However, Neumarkt had grown appreciably and was now a large bustling city. Visiting City Hall, we entered the Oberbuergermeister's office and found Theo Betz still sitting behind his same desk. Otto Schedl, the Landrat, had moved on, but Theo, it seemed, would be mayor forever! He had a grand time talking about earlier days.

Brad and Andrea visited us in Munich, and we spent a pleasant time as a family in Garmisch in the Bavarian Alps. Garmisch at that time had not changed much over the years. It was still largely the lovely, little Alpine village and ski resort it had been during my Resident Officer days back in the early 1950s. The U.S. military presence, however, had been reduced considerably and the number of hotels operated by the Army was limited to two. There were no longer separate establishments for officers and enlisted personnel. The Germans were now using the larger hotels previously reserved for Americans. Wealthy Germans were much in evidence, and I sensed that our military personnel were simply being tolerated, if not looked down upon. Part of the problem, I am afraid, came from the tendency of Americans to dress very casually, if not sloppily.

As my wife and I were walking one evening in Garmisch in the vicinity of the casino, a large Mercedes pulled up, disgorging a group of affluent Germans in black tie and evening dress, intent on entering that luxurious establishment. Spotting an American couple with their children (obviously a vacationing young U.S. Army officer and his family) about to pass by, one of the elegantly gowned women remarked to the others, "*Hier kommen die Ziegeuner* (gypsies)." Elsa and I fully understood her quip, although, thankfully, the Americans did not. Had the group not dashed into the casino, I would have been furious enough to have shouted at them in German, "Be glad that these 'gypsies' are here, or you might now be in Siberia!"[3]

As another indication of how times had changed, Elsa told me she had attended a meeting of the German-American Women's Club in Munich. The ladies supported a number of charitable causes, including those for the handicapped, the poor, and the homeless. At this particular meeting, the drive was to support "*die arme* (poor) *Americanishe* Boy Scouts." She hoped she was not alone among the American women feeling embarrassed, as the German ladies graciously contributed to this worthwhile cause.

Shortly before Christmas in 1973, I received a cable from Cairo from Ambassador Hermann Eilts asking me whether I would be interested in joining him as his deputy. He had been sent to Egypt by Secretary of State Henry Kissinger preparatory to a possible reestablishing of diplomatic relations between Egypt and the United States, which had been broken since the Arab-Israeli War of 1967. In the interim, President Gamal Abdel Nasser had died and been replaced by Anwar Sadat. Sadat had launched an abortive war against Israel in October 1973 with Russian assistance but now was reaching out to the Americans. I informed Consul General Edward Doherty of Ambassador Eilts's request. He graciously said it was up to me if I wished to be transferred but was obviously not pleased about the matter.

I used my prospective transfer to initiate a series of farewell calls on leading Bavarian politicians, thus enabling me to prepare a number of reports. Germany's former defense minister Franz-Josef Strauss, long a power in national politics, had been difficult to approach.[4] Although he resided in Munich, he was inclined to feel that any dealings with Americans should come at the Bonn embassy level, not with consular officers. I called his office and told his secretary that I was being transferred to our mission in Cairo as the number two during that period of high-powered Kissinger shuttle diplomacy and that I would appreciate having his views on the Middle East crisis. The response to call on him was immediate. Thereafter I prepared an analysis of the situation from the German point of view.

We spent Christmas awaiting further word from Washington and Cairo. As unsettling as that was, the holidays in Munich nevertheless were a joy. Elsa, Matthew, and I would wander downtown into the *Kristkindelmart* with *Gluhwein* to warm our innards and the sounds of German carols in the air. Light snow was on the ground and colored lights sparkled from the trees and market stalls. The smell of roasting chestnuts and bratwurst filled the senses. It was a happy time, so far removed from those days of hunger and hardship after the war. A generation had grown up untouched, yet in my memory I could recall clearly how their parents and grandparents had suffered, first under Hitler's madness and then in the aftermath that his diabolical machinations had wrought.

To me that holiday season had an unreal quality. Christmas and New Year came and went as our move was delayed on word from Cairo that our arrival in the middle of Secretary Kissinger's current shuttle diplomacy negotiations would not be convenient. The secretary had descended on the post with an entourage of close to one hundred persons, and the small administrative staff had been overwhelmed. Having experienced high-level visits, I sympathized with the staff and felt a sense of guilt. While they were struggling, in Munich it was *Fasching* (Mardi Gras). In that strongly Catholic area it was a time for wild celebration, with the city boasting the holding of 3,000 balls. Elsa and I attended two before we left.

It had been more than five years since I had been in an Arabic-speaking country and I believed that I should again enter into language study. While that seemed more practical in Cairo than in Munich and thus best deferred, at a minimum I could bring myself up to speed on recent events in the Middle East. The October 6, 1973, war, known by the Israelis and most Americans as the Yom Kippur War, is referred to by the Arabs as the Ramadan War in consequence of the respective holidays occurring at the time. The Munich newspapers had been full of accounts of the battles involving Egypt and Syria against Israel. Although the Arab countries achieved initial successes, the Israeli Army had managed to recover from the surprise attack. It had encircled Egyptian forces on the Egyptian side of the Suez Canal, driven the Syrians from the Golan Heights, and was on its way to Damascus when a cease-fire was called for by the UN Security Council on October 22, 1973. Subsequently, the United States became involved in bringing about a disengagement of forces, with Secretary of State Kissinger shuttling back and forth between Middle Eastern capitals.

A transfer in the Foreign Service brings with it a certain amount of vexing activity. Packing, disposing of items not needed at the next post, selling or renting one's house, and arranging for schooling for the children were all part of the myriad of things to do. Going through it all again in only a matter of months makes it all the more tiresome. This time, however, there was no house to worry about, but we were faced with the disposal of our car, since it was not deemed suitable for use in Cairo. Instead of taking our Pontiac convertible, we ordered a sand-colored four-door Chevrolet Nova to be delivered as soon as possible after our arrival in Egypt.

I was chagrined to have to contact the colonel in charge of the Army Reserve unit to inform him of my prospective transfer so soon after he had gone to great lengths to find me an assignment. That pill, however, was sweetened when I consented to sell him our car for a very reasonable price. I was glad not to be there when within a few weeks his son demolished that beautiful vehicle in an accident in which, thankfully, the young man was not seriously injured. While Matthew was happy to leave his Army school, Elsa was not pleased to have to interrupt her studies at the overseas branch of Boston University in Munich leading to a Master's degree.

We departed Munich for Cairo in February 1974, taking with us in the hold of the KLM flight two large steamer trunks and our newly acquired dog Pericles, for whom we had a special doghouse/crate made. Our flight had an hour and a half stopover in Vienna, where we were met by Franz Weiss, an Austrian first cousin on my father's side, whom we had not seen since the early 1950s during our previous assignment in Germany. Franz, a Catholic priest, had in the interim moved up within the local hierarchy, becoming a *Konsistorialrat*, a member of the church council who had as his charge the administration of a geographic district or properties.[5] We had a brief but cordial visit together in the airport before proceeding on to Cairo.

15
Cairo and Shuttle Diplomacy

Despite our diplomatic status and the assistance of Egyptian "expediter" personnel employed by our U.S. Interests Section in Cairo, clearance through the airport was more involved than usual. The dog was subjected to a separate clearance process. However, the registration document and health and inoculation certificates we produced satisfied the various inspectors and we were grateful not to have to place the dog in quarantine, which in the case of some countries might have lasted several months. As soon as we had cleared through customs we were to be taken to meet with Ambassador and Mrs. Eilts at their residence for dinner. The invitation was extended to Matthew as well. The dog, the trunks, and our hand luggage were to be deposited at the deputy chief of mission's residence in Maadi on the outskirts of town.

The trip in from the airport was to be one of many I was to make in the coming months. Driving into the center of that bustling city of six million souls, we experienced the traffic, sights, sounds, and smells of a Middle Eastern metropolis. Had we not spent years in Manila, in many ways similar, we would have been more astonished than we were. The ambassador's residence was located on an island section in the middle of the city. It was pleasant to see the Eiltses again. So much had transpired in the months since our departure from the Army War College the previous June. They had been ensconced in Carlisle in October, when word came that Secretary Kissinger wanted to interview the ambassador for a possible assignment to Cairo.[1] President Sadat had become disenchanted with the Russians and their military aid program and as early as 1972 had taken steps to reduce the Soviet presence in Egypt. America saw an opportunity to improve its position.

At dinner, Ambassador Eilts gave me an initial briefing on the status of our relations with the Egyptians and on my role in the functioning of the U.S. Interests Section, established under the flag of the Spanish Embassy when diplomatic relations were broken following the 1967 war. The

Interests Section was still housed in the chancery of our former embassy compound, however. Cairo in earlier days had been a Class I post, the largest in the Middle East.

After dinner, we were driven to the DCM residence in Maadi, a distance of about ten miles from downtown Cairo. The house was a large three-story stone building with a roof garden. A high cinderblock fence topped with broken glass enclosed a vast garden containing tall mango trees adorned with small electric lights. The overall area appeared to be the size of a small city block. I was a bit taken aback, thinking at the time the place would make a worthy ambassadorial residence, since it obviously would lend itself to entertaining hundreds of guests.[2]

Upon entering the gate, we were met by servants whom the Interests Section administrative officer had retained: a cook, a houseboy, a maid, and a gardener. Our houseboy, Hassan, an elderly man, was dressed in an ornate, gold-embroidered blue robe, a *gallabieya*, the traditional garb for one who serves meals or is in attendance in the main quarters of the residence. It is customary for the owner of the house to provide the servant(s) with money to buy the *gallabieya*. We were relieved to find that the house was completely and tastefully furnished, including official chinaware and silver flatware. We had been informed that would be the case and had stored most of our furniture in a warehouse in Munich, but one is never quite sure what one will find at post.

I reported for work immediately the following morning fully aware that the Interests Section's small staff was short-handed and overloaded. My office adjoined the ambassador's, separated by a room in which his and my secretaries labored over typewriters. Secretary Kissinger had departed a day earlier, and the staff members were seeking to catch their breath and prepare for the next onslaught of shuttle diplomacy. Kissinger at this time was endeavoring to bring about a disengagement of Egyptian and Israeli forces and to lay out boundaries behind which they would withdraw. Before long I was to be a sideshow bit player in these dramas, but at that stage I had no idea what I was in for.

The total complement of personnel on my arrival numbered about twenty Americans, including administrative, consular, secretarial, and other personnel. In addition to serving as the ambassador's deputy, I was to be both political and economic counselor, supervising those two sections. Assisting me, I must say, was the finest group of officers I have ever encountered in the Foreign Service. Arthur Houghton and April Glaspie were the stalwarts in the Political Section and Edward Peck and John Craig in the Economic Section. Bryce (Mac) Gerlach functioned as the administrative counselor, ably supported by A. Elizabeth (Beth) Jones, a young woman of remarkable organizational talents. Four of these officers were to go on to be ambassadors and one (Jones) an assistant secretary of state for Europe.

As matters stood, Ambassador Eilts had his hands full supporting Secretary Kissinger's negotiating efforts. He served as a conduit for communications to President Sadat and for relaying Sadat's responses to Washington and/or the secretary, wherever he might be at any given moment. He was very much involved in the day-to-day negotiations going on between Cairo, Damascus, Tel Aviv/Jerusalem and Washington, and his advice and experience were highly regarded. Given the amount of cable traffic going out and coming in day and night with the State Department and other embassies, as well as in back-channel messages, it was a monumental task. It was thus up to me to see that normal Interests Section activities ran smoothly. This is not to say that Ambassador Eilts was removed from the scene. Far from it. He kept a watchful eye on me, particularly regarding personnel matters, as I sensed he may have felt I was a bit tough on the staff at times.

Despite endeavoring to acquaint myself with what was happening in the Middle East during my final days in Munich, I had no real feel for the situation. I was aware that on October 22, 1973, the ten Arab members of the Organization of Petroleum Exporting Countries (OPEC) had voted to cut off oil supplies until Israel withdrew from territories it had conquered during the 1967 Six Day Arab-Israeli War. The result had been gas rationing, which affected us in Germany. Worldwide pressure then led to a Geneva Conference to deal with issues arising out of the Yom Kippur War. The conference, which began on December 21, 1973, was co-chaired by the United States and the Soviet Union. It included Israel and the Arab states involved in the war (although Syria refused to attend) and was intended to bring about a permanent peace settlement.

The mood in Egypt upon my arrival was one of public approval for President Sadat. While Egypt had not gained a victory, far from it, Israel's confidence had been severely shaken. The Israelis had felt secure since 1967 after constructing the Bar Lev Line, with its very high sand berm along the east bank of the Suez Canal. But as the time for the attack came, the Egyptians with Soviet assistance crossed the Suez Canal and simply employed high-pressure water hoses to blast a gap in the sand for their tanks to go through, overrunning surprised Israeli forces. In short order two Egyptian armies had moved beyond the 1967 War cease-fire lines and into the Sinai.

Although the Israelis initially reacted poorly in the first days of the war, they soon turned the situation around. They had virtually encircled Egyptian forces on the western side of the Suez Canal when the war was halted by a UN Security Council cease-fire order. However, the psychological impact of the Egyptian attack had been profound, and Sadat was regarded as a hero throughout the Arab world.

It was not long before I was plunged into Secretary Kissinger's efforts to stabilize the situation and effect the withdrawal of Israeli forces from Egyptian territory west of the Suez Canal. He had made several visits to Egypt before I arrived, and the staff had dealt efficiently with the problems involved; thus I was not particularly concerned when I was tasked with running a preparatory meeting not long after my arrival.

Arrangements were made on short notice to house the secretary and his large party on the top two floors of the Nile Hilton Hotel. Our difficulties in handling the visit came not so much from the official party itself as from the Secret Service, the support staff, and the media. The latter included a number of well-known journalists and television personalities. The sheer size of the influx of visitors, at times amounting to ninety or more persons, presented a problem. Besides Kissinger, the official party during the shuttling usually included Under Secretary Joe Sisco, Assistant Secretary for Near Eastern Affairs Alfred "Roy" Atherton and his deputy, Harold Saunders, Ambassadors Ellsworth Bunker and Robert McCloskey, Lawrence Eagleburger, Winston Lord, Robert Oakley, and Peter Rodman.

The Special Aircraft Mission (SAM) plane transporting the group was the Boeing 707 President Johnson used when he was vice president. It had been especially configured for him and had a conference table and a hydraulically operated seat that could be positioned to suit the user. It also had a couch and shower for the secretary, a staff area, and space for accompanying members of the media, who usually numbered fourteen. These included some of the well-known TV and press personalities at the time: Bernard Kalb or his brother Marvin, both of CBS, NBC's Richard Valeriani, ABC's Ted Koppel, The *New York Times*'s Bernard Gwertzman, and The *Washington Post*'s Marilyn Berger, the only woman in the group, who was envied by others for her ability to gain access.

A day or two before the arrival of the shuttle, a group of Secret Service agents would descend on us intent on checking out the security situation and electronically sweeping any place Kissinger might be during the stopover. This, of course, gave rise to incidents involving the hotels and official Egyptian facilities. With our administrative staff, it was my procedure to meet with the Secret Service agents beforehand, among other things, to caution them about being courteous and solicitous of the feelings of our Egyptian hosts.

Generally the security agents assigned to the secretary handled themselves well, although there were some complaints about people being shoved about in the effort to protect him. My old friend from UNESCO days, Bob McCloskey, who had been the State Department's spokesman and had since become an ambassador-at-large, was regarded as the prima-ry person for dealing with the media. Nevertheless, I had some problems with them, since complaints were ultimately directed to me. I remember Ted Koppel, in a state of high dudgeon, threatening me over a relatively minor inconvenience.

The American Interests Section ran quite well as a part of the Spanish Embassy. One had no real sense that the Spanish in any way impinged on our functioning; on the contrary, they had been most helpful. Had it not been for the letterhead on the official stationery, I might as well have been in a small U.S. embassy or consulate anywhere else. As the days went on, however, the burden of work grew, not only because of shuttle diplomacy, but also as normal intercourse with Washington increased. President Sa-dat had signaled that he was prepared to reestablish diplomatic relations, and governmental agencies back home began preparing to reinstitute their representation in Egypt. Cairo had been our largest embassy in the Middle East and Departments such as Defense, Agriculture, and Justice were anxious to reclaim properties to house their attachés and other staffs. I was surprised to learn, for example, that the fine house assigned to me as the DCM had formerly been the residence of the agricultural attaché.

In conjunction with the shuttle descending on us on February 28, 1974, an early bit of Egyptian hospitality was memorable. The Ministry of For-eign Affairs arranged a late dinner at the nightclub on the top floor of the Sheraton Hotel for the Kissinger party to which Ambassador Eilts and I and our wives were also invited. They served a fine meal with appropriate beverages. At one point, spirited Arab music filled the air and a delight-ed Egyptian Foreign Minister Ismael Fahmy watched as the famed belly dancer, the voluptuous Nagwa Fuad, undulated on to the dance floor di-rectly in front of our ringside table. The wilder her movements, the more appreciative the audience became.

Secretary Kissinger was having a grand time with it all, as indeed were the rest of us, that is most of the males in the group. The wives, on the other hand, looked uncomfortable. The following morning, the ac-companying American media had a field day in reporting the story, as did the local Arab press. The Egyptian population read about the affair with humor and a sense of satisfaction. Shuttle diplomacy and the overall crisis situation must have been moving along pretty well if the diplomats could carry on that way.

In those early days, we worried about the Soviet presence in Egypt, which was still substantial, despite President Sadat's determination to turn toward the West. He had come to realize that if any progress was to be made toward a peaceful settlement of outstanding issues he had to work with, the United States was the only nation capable of influencing or pressuring Israel. The Soviets, nevertheless, were determined to play a role in the overall picture, if only in their capacity as a co-chairman of the Geneva Conference. This was the situation when Russian Foreign Secretary Andrei Gromyko arrived in Cairo during that Kissinger visit. There was joking at the time about whether he would receive equal treatment from Fahmy and be taken to see Nagwa Fuad and, if so, how he would explain that bit of decadence back in Moscow.[3]

Coincident with that February 28, 1974, shuttle visit, diplomatic relations between the United States and Egypt were formally reestablished. After the party at the Sheraton Hotel, Administrative Officer Dick Smith and I worked through most of that night to get the Chancery ready for a flag-raising ceremony the following day at which the secretary himself did the honors.[4] The Embassy compound was enclosed by a high wrought-iron fence; two large American eagles adorned the massive gates at the entrance to the Chancery. At one time they had been golden, but they had been smoke-damaged in 1967 and over the years become badly tarnished, almost to the point of appearing black. At 2:00 a.m., Dick and I were still out there scraping, cleaning, and putting a coat of primer on them so that later in the morning they could be gilded before the arrival of Kissinger and Fahmy.

In a very moving ceremony on Friday, March 1, 1974, the Spanish flag was lowered and the Stars and Stripes raised on the tall flagpole on the grassy area in front of the Chancery. All of us who stood there had lumps in our throats. Kissinger and Fahmy then delivered brief remarks, and a new era in U.S.–Egypt relations began.

During the following weeks, Ambassador Eilts, who was busy with the negotiations, asked me to go up to Alexandria to officially reopen our Consulate General there. The building itself, which had been damaged from mob action in the 1967 Arab-Israeli War, was a large and beautiful white marble edifice. When I arrived, it stood empty and locked. In the intervening years, a small Egyptian staff had functioned in the former consul general's residence. Reopening the old building without completing a lot of repairs was simply out of the question. As a result, we had a small ceremony that culminated in my raising the flag on a pole out the window of our temporary quarters. The *State Department Bulletin* at the time carried a sad little picture of that flag-raising ceremony.[5]

The very nature of the shuttle negotiating process, which entailed going back and forth between Middle Eastern capitals, created difficulties for us. We would be told when Secretary Kissinger would be arriving, only to have the schedule changed any number of times. This played havoc with hotel arrangements, which were often made then canceled at the last minute. American businessmen occupying rooms in the Nile Hilton would find themselves ejected and forced to search for suitable quarters elsewhere in Cairo at a time when Western-type accommodations were scarce.

One of the Foreign Service's duties was to assist American business-men, and I am afraid, at least on these occasions, we failed miserably. My heart went out to those unfortunate souls, but there really was nothing I could do. As the DCM, I was the lightning rod on these occasions. Twice I was told that my name would be passed to the complainant's congress-person for disciplinary action. The individual most vexed, however, was the German manager of the Nile Hilton. He and I were good friends, but after numerous such goings on, he finally balked and refused to displace the occupants of the two top floors of his hotel during one of the shuttle visits. I pleaded with him, saying he had no choice but to comply. Still he refused. Reluctantly, I called the Egyptian Foreign Ministry with my prob-lem. He was promptly threatened with arrest for endangering national security. What a way to cool a friendship!

The shuttle negotiation process took on a pattern. Kissinger would arrive from Israel, for example, with a proposal related to disengagement lines. There would be meetings to discuss the subject with President Sa-dat, Foreign Minister Fahmy, General Mohamed el-Gamasy, or other key Egyptian officials at different places around Cairo, Alexandria, or at As-wan. Quite often there were tête-à-tête sessions involving only Kissinger and Sadat or Fahmy that would run late into the night. I have memories of Kissinger's attendants all sitting in the vestibule way past midnight at one of the palaces—usually Sisco, Saunders, Bunker, McCloskey, Eagle-burger, Lord, Oakley, Rodman, Eilts, and myself. From time to time the inner sanctum door would open and Kissinger would come out with a request for a map or something or other. As the low-ranking man on the totem pole or the person familiar with our office, I was "Jack Fetchit" and would go wherever necessary to obtain the item or bit of information.[6]

The shuttle process with its whirlwind pace seemed designed to keep up the pressure on the negotiators to find solutions. I made it my business to take special care of Ambassador Bunker. He was a distinguished white-haired diplomat in his eighties, frail, but very conscientious. The schedule, and indeed the entire process, took on a frenetic aspect, and I was really quite worried about his ability to withstand the rigors. He was a member of the group as a consequence of his position as our Permanent Represen-tative at the Geneva Talks with the Russians.

At times, we met at Sadat's residence in Alexandria, ninety miles north of Cairo. On occasion, we would fly there in Soviet-made Egyptian Air Force helicopters. The look of concern on some of our party's faces as we took off and the pilots jockeyed the helicopters about spoke volumes.

There were times when we met in convivial places, such as Sadat's garden in Alexandria, his offices at the Barrages in Cairo, or in the President's Rest House in the shadow of the Pyramids at Giza. The Egyptians were a hospitable people, and the negotiations were at times interspersed with sightseeing or banquets. From what I gathered, the stopovers in Israel, on the other hand, tended to be far less relaxed, more all-business affairs, and consequently even more stressful.

The hospitality aspect on occasion presented problems for our administrative staff. It would fall on me, for example, to decide who from our side would attend a dinner given by the Egyptians at which there was room for less than the full party. I knew better than to involve Ambassador Eilts in these situations and simply accepted the ire of some of the lesser-ranking members of the delegation, whom I hoped would forget, after they had risen to positions of prominence, that I had perforce slighted them. While this created some awkward situations, in only one instance did the person involved not accept graciously being left off the guest list.

As a result of the 1967 Arab-Israeli War, considerable damage had been done to buildings in the Embassy compound. The U.S. Information Agency library was a shambles, and ruined buildings stood between it and the Chancery, which was largely intact. I debated with myself at the time whether to approach the ambassador with a plan to use the Marine detachment in an overall clean-up program. I decided against doing so, since at that point it might interfere with efforts to put forward claims with the Egyptian government. As it was, I found that I would be spending considerable time on the claims growing out of President Nasser's earlier expropriation of properties owned by American companies or individual citizens. A lawyer from the Department of State's Office of Legal Affairs made several trips to Cairo in this regard while I was there. I was the other half of his negotiating team in talks with the Egyptians about settling the claims. It was my job to follow these matters and keep Washington informed by cable on a regular basis about developments.

I had to adjust to the ambassador's work schedule, which was seven days a week. He held staff meetings at different times during the week, as well as on Sunday mornings. I complained to him at one point, saying that my wife was irritated with me for not going to church on Sunday morning at the British Anglican cathedral in Cairo, as much of the American community did.[7] He seemed a bit surprised and allowed that if I felt the need, I certainly should take time off to go.

On days when we were not involved with shuttle visits, my driver would pick me up at my house in Maadi around 7:00 a.m. in his official black four-door Chevrolet sedan and drive me the ten miles on the boulevard along the east bank of the Nile River into town. Upon arriving at the Chancery, I would visit the communications center and gather up the morning's cables from Washington and other posts around the world. More often than not, there would be an instruction to visit the Foreign Office to discuss some matter. There was always an issue being voted on in the United Nations, itself, or in one of its Specialized Agencies, such as the WHO, UNESCO, or FAO, in which our government wanted Egyptian support. The Law of the Sea or a resolution dealing with Israel were perennial issues at the time. Regarding Israel, it was obvious that we were not going to get Arab support, but I would go through the motions anyway. The director of North American Affairs at the Foreign Office, Ambassador Mahmoud el Tohami, who became a good friend, was always gracious in telling me that his government would give the matter "most serious consideration," when we both knew they were not about to vote with us.

On subjects for the highest level, the ambassador would take the issue to Foreign Minister Fahmy or President Sadat. Often Political Officers Arthur Houghton and April Glaspie or Economic Officers Ed Peck and John Craig would visit the Foreign Office to carry out the chore. Washington always awaited our answer and was unhappy if we were tardy in our response.

Once we had reestablished diplomatic relations and taken on the role of an embassy, the staff expanded somewhat. Certain functions could not be handled by State Department officers, and soon we were augmented by military personnel. Air Force Brigadier General George Guay arrived. An extremely competent officer, he had worked on the National Security Council staff with General Brent Scowcroft and knew Secretary Kissinger well. His appointment to Cairo was indicative of the importance the White House and the Department of Defense attached to our relations with Egypt. He was followed by Army Colonel William Graham, a highly able Arabic-speaking officer. Later with the addition of Navy Captain Peter Block, we had the beginnings of a complete Defense Attaché Office.

The person perhaps most pleased with the arrival of the military families was my wife, Elsa. Prior to our posting in Cairo, a State Department directive had been issued forbidding the use of wives for representational activities. There had been numerous complaints on the part of Foreign Service wives, who at one point had been rated on their husband's efficiency reports as to how well they performed such duties. Elsa could relate many "horror" stories of how early in my career she had been put through the paces by the wife of an ambassador or DCM. Over the years, the climate had changed and many wives were currently working. Now that Elsa was the one in need of assistance, alas, the rules had been changed. Seeing her plight, several of the military wives, bless them, stepped right up and volunteered to assist in the entertaining and charity work expected from spouses of diplomatic corps members overseas. Many of our embassy wives, regardless of the directive, still helped out, but there was an onus on asking them to do so.[8]

Early in 1974, I became involved in activity related to the reopening of the Suez Canal. Sunken ships and damage to facilities along the Canal during the 1967 Arab-Israeli War had made passage impossible, resulting in a loss in Egyptian revenue of well over a billion dollars. Next to textile exports, the Canal was Egypt's largest income earner. President Sadat was therefore anxious to undertake a clearance operation with international assistance as soon as possible. World shipping, too, was desirous of seeing this vital waterway back in service. It was estimated that at the time of closure approximately 15 percent of the world's seaborne traffic passed through the Canal. The economic impact on Egyptian cities such as Port Said, Ismailia, and Port Sudan was also severe, since many jobs were affected.

The effort now was to remove the mines and other explosives, a dangerous activity, and clear away the ships blocking strategic passages. I made several trips to the Canal in the company of an admiral sent out from Washington, as well as a U.S. Navy captain from the Naval Systems Command who supervised the salvage. Once under way, the overall effort was international and included naval units from Britain, France, the Soviet Union, Egypt and ourselves. The funding for this cooperative undertaking, amounting to close to $300 million, came largely from the World Bank and several of the Arab states. The Canal was reopened on June 5, 1975, eight years to the day after the outbreak of the 1967 War.

In late April 1974, the Kissinger party arrived while President Sadat was sojourning in Alexandria. The secretary had flown in from Algiers and was intent on discussing aspects of the Syrian-Israeli disengagement with him. We arranged to have the entire group flown up to Alexandria by Soviet-made Egyptian Air Force helicopters. On that flight Assistant Secretary Roy Atherton and I discussed the hazards of life in the Foreign Service. I had made a trip up to Alexandria by train a short time earlier to check on our consular office and other facilities there.

We could never be certain where President Sadat would be, and we needed to be sure that any support requirements could be met for just such events as a visit from the shuttle party. As matters evolved, the Egyptians were fully prepared to host the visitors, placing Safa Palace overlooking the Mediterranean at our disposal. Alexandria is a city with an ancient and glorious history and Sadat was determined that the Americans should be exposed to some of the antiquities. The Egyptians, with their sense of drama, had colorful honor guards, lancers on horseback, placed at strategic points around ruins.

The sightseeing, which was part of many of the shuttle visits, was often quite strenuous. It involved climbing up and down flights of stairs and walking distances over rocky, dusty ground. In Alexandria, the tour included stopping at the excavation of a Roman amphitheater. Kissinger delighted in leading these forays, with Sisco and the rest of us following on behind. On that occasion, particularly, I stayed close to Ambassador Bunker helping him up and down stairs. He gamely struggled to keep up with the others. The pace and the long hours of activity wore me out, and I marveled at how a man in his eighties was able to manage. I was always glad to get back to Cairo to make it home during a respite for a shower and a change of clothes. If I managed three hours of sleep a night during a shuttle visit, I was doing well, for I felt it my obligation to be the first up and the last in bed during those times.

I was so busy during those first few months of my tour in Cairo that I had little time to think about my obligations as an Army Reserve officer. I had been sent a copy of a glowing efficiency rating I had received in Germany, prepared in the Office of the Chief of Army Reserves in Europe. General Edward Meyer, the reviewing officer, stated I was well qualified to be a general. It was indeed a compliment to receive such a recommendation from an officer on the fast track to top positions in the Service (he subsequently became chief of staff, the highest uniformed position in the Army). In the meantime, I had been given a new Reserve assignment, a mobilization designation (MOBDES—to the Office of the Deputy Chief of Staff for Operations (G-3) in the Pentagon in the event of a wartime mobilization. I was to be a deputy director for civil affairs in Special Operations, an assignment that suited my background and qualifications.

At the height of shuttle activity, my wife handed me a letter one day from the Department of the Army saying that I was one of several officers being considered for the position of deputy chief of the Army Reserves. It was a full-time active duty position, currently calling for an officer in the rank of colonel, but with every likelihood it seemed to me of being raised to brigadier general at some point in the future, which indeed turned out to be the case. Had I indicated interest and actually been accepted, I would have either had to retire from the Foreign Service or obtain a (highly unlikely) extended leave of absence. I still had more than five years to serve to complete the maximum pension-allowed time of thirty-five years in the Foreign Service. That took into account my four and a half years' active duty in the military during and after World War II. Pensions at the time were computed on the basis of 2 percent each year up to a maximum of 70 percent of one's final salary. I was in a fascinating job in Egypt, and, after giving the matter some thought and discussing it with Elsa, I sent back a letter indicating that while I was pleased to have been considered, I felt that I could best serve my country where I was.

Not long afterward, Ambassador Eilts and I had a conversation about the future of Embassy Cairo. Before 1967, it had been a Class I post, the most important in the Middle East. We had received word that Washington was giving consideration to sending out someone to take over the deputy chief of mission position. It was a plum, calling for a minister-level officer, and high-ranking officers were walking the halls back there looking for positions. We were told that Richard Murphy, who at the time was our ambassador to Mauritania, would be assigned. As to what would happen to me, I was offered the choice of becoming consul general in Alexandria or remaining in Cairo as the counselor for political and economic affairs.

Alexandria is a large modern city, which had a population at the time of close to three million people. It is full of grand old buildings and has a lovely waterfront facing the Mediterranean. I was sorely tempted to take the offer. However, it meant uprooting my family again. Matthew would have been in three different schools in less than a year, and it just did not seem right to subject my wife and son to another move. Besides, it likely would be many weeks until Dick Murphy would be on board and the embassy was faced with more visits from Secretary Kissinger. There were even reports of a possible trip by President Nixon to the Middle East. All in all, I would be of more use in Cairo. After discussing the matter with Elsa and Matthew, I indicated that I would remain where I was.

The Murphy assignment was one more indication that Cairo would be expanded considerably, although Eilts himself was determined to keep it as small as possible. It was his logic that the fewer the people, the fewer the problems, and indeed there is much to be said for that view. For me, however, struggling to deal with manifold duties, the more assistance we could receive, the better. We would expand sooner or later, as many agencies in Washington with overseas interests were clamoring to reopen their offices in Cairo. Little did I realize, however, that the Cairo embassy would become one of the largest in the world, with over a thousand employees. I might have had an inkling, though, given an incident over which I still chuckle.

One afternoon, the ambassador came into my office and said, "It's about time we thought about an AID (Agency for International Development) program for Egypt." Things were proceeding well politically, and certainly Egypt was in dire need of assistance in many areas of its economy. (At the time there was no thought of military assistance; that would come later.) The ambassador then added, "Why don't you draft a cable laying out some thoughts as to what an AID program might look like." My first reaction was to think about the size of the program he might be contemplating, so I said, "What kind of money are we talking about?" He responded, "Oh, about $250 million to $300 million."

I almost fell out of my chair. For one having administered military assistance programs in the $25 million range for an entire group of African countries, I was stunned. With that the ambassador departed, leaving me to mull over what to do next. I was no aid expert. I was the Economic Counselor, however, in addition to other things, and I would simply have to do the best I could under the circumstances. Though I had some general idea of Egypt's needs, my problem lay more in the timing. When Eilts said draft a cable, he wasn't talking about a long-term project; he meant something to go out tomorrow or possibly the following day. The normal communication for long think-pieces in those days was an airgram, not a cable.

I went through our files, background material, area studies, and the National Intelligence Survey on Egypt, pulling together as much information as I could. My secretary said goodnight at about 7:30 p.m., leaving me with piles of books and documents on my desk. I called home and said that something had come up that would keep me in the office most of the night. (That was not unusual, since during shuttle visits at times I came home in the wee hours of the morning.) By midnight, I had a good idea of where our assistance might best be placed.

My overall recommendations ran the gamut from agriculture and transportation to strengthening several of Egypt's basic industries, particularly textile production, as well as assistance for the educational system and other areas. The underlying thought was that seed money, bolstered by the advice and assistance AID personnel could provide, would launch projects of real benefit to Egypt. It was close to 5:00 a.m. before I had typed out the makings of what was, at least in my view, a reasonable aid program. Then I went home, showered, took a brief nap, ate breakfast, and went to work as usual.

I gave the draft to my secretary so that she could type up the many pages on clean cable forms. Around 11:00 a.m., I handed the cable to the ambassador when he came out of his office to speak with someone. He simply took it without a word and went back into his office, closing the door. I had every expectation he would find enough in that draft with which to take issue to give rise to extensive discussion. Instead, in about an hour he came into my office, handed me the cable, having made almost no changes, and said, "Send it."

Send it I did, thinking surely Washington with its entire bureaucracy of aid experts would pose questions, have other ideas, or balk at some of my proposals. A week or so went by until we received Washington's answer: They were making arrangements to send out a team to look into implementing the package! Well, my friends, that is how an aid program for Egypt, subsequently amounting to $2 billion yearly and employing hundreds of officials, got started.

The most noteworthy event during my Cairo tour involved the visit of President Nixon, who at the time was thoroughly enmeshed in the Watergate scandal and approaching the time when he would be forced to resign. Perhaps as a way of stemming the tide, the White House sought to arrange what it hoped would be a successful tour of Middle East capitals. In early May 1974, we received a cable requesting us to sound out President Sadat on the matter. I recall sitting in the ambassador's office when a telephone call came through from Sadat saying not only would Nixon be welcome, he would be given a banner reception. I do not remember his exact words, but it was with a sense of elation that the response was sent back to Washington, where it was gratefully received.

Unless one has been through a presidential visit, one has no real conception of what is involved. Soon we were inundated with people from Washington preparing the way. There were Secret Service advance parties, White House staffers, communications specialists, Air Force, and Defense Department representatives, all anxious to carry out their duties. I had nominally been the officer in charge of Vice President Hubert Humphrey's visit to Manila in 1965, but this affair was in a league by itself, especially when it became apparent that the Egyptians were intent on making it "one never to be forgotten." The Egyptians thought highly of Nixon as a consequence of America's shuttle diplomacy efforts to bring peace to the Middle East. They simply could not understand why there would be moves to impeach a president whom they regarded as being so very able, and there was a genuine effort to demonstrate their support for him.

I went through the drill already ingrained as a consequence of the Kissinger shuttle visits to brief the advance parties and laid down certain guidelines. I chaired several meetings attended by key persons on our staff and members of the various advance parties. While I did the talking, others such as Beth Jones and Mac Gerlach did the yeoman's work of programming activities, setting up schedules, arranging for vehicles, and carrying out the multitude of detailed matters required for dealing with a large presidential party and a hundred or more members of the American and foreign press. I endeavored to assist wherever and whenever I saw potential problems and accepted the criticism when things did not go as planned.

Other colleagues in handling presidential visits have remonstrated about the high-handed manner in which White House aides on occasion dealt with embassy personnel and host country officials. My outstanding example was a young U.S. Navy lieutenant commander tasked with assuring appropriate accommodations for the Nixons while they were in Egypt. This was a Head of State Visit and the first time an American president had come to Egypt since Franklin Roosevelt in 1943.

I knew that the Egyptians were accomplished hosts. Nevertheless, to make sure that all went well, I accompanied the naval officer and Beth Jones of our staff over to meet the very distinguished woman from the Egyptian Office of the Presidency in charge of arrangements for housing high-ranking dignitaries at the various palaces. She was the wife of an ambassador, charming and cultured, and what is more, related to Mrs. Sadat. She guided us about the magnificent Qubbah Palace, showing us the quarters where President and Mrs. Nixon would be staying. The commander, at times in very preemptory tones, would comment that this or that would have to be changed or moved about in those opulent rooms to suit the Nixons before they arrived. I was taken aback by what I was hearing and endeavored to act as a buffer, but to little avail. Our guide, on the other hand, could not have been more gracious or agreeable. She may very well have been furious, but she had the good manners not to reveal her feelings.

As we were leaving the palace, I informed the commander that the woman he was dealing with held an important position in the Egyptian hierarchy and that she was related to President Sadat's wife. He seemed not to be fazed in the slightest. After another session of that sort, I finally explained the situation to Brigadier General George Guay, our defense attaché.[9] A day or so later, the commander called at my office to apologize in the most contrite fashion for having placed me in an awkward situation. Evidently, George had read him the riot act, saying he would not have dared act that way had the DCM been a military officer of equivalent rank. Not only that, George had also mentioned the matter to General Scowcroft in Washington during one of his telephone calls. The commander was promptly ordered to shape up, given the importance President Nixon attached to his visit to Cairo.

Nixon's arrival in Cairo on June 12, 1974, was an affair to remember. It was a hot sunny day as we waited at the airport for Air Force One to arrive. The Egyptian government had indeed gone all out to welcome their distinguished visitor. We had passed through crowds of a million or more people lining the route to the airport. Banners across the road displayed pictures of Sadat and Nixon, and large signs reading "Long Live Nixon," "Nixon the Peacemaker," and "We Trust Nixon." Everywhere there were Egyptian and American flags.

At the airport, a long red carpet had been laid out. An honor guard and a battalion of soldiers in dress uniform stood ready to be reviewed. President and Mrs. Sadat, a host of Egyptian dignitaries, the diplomatic corps, and the staff of our embassy were waiting to greet President and Mrs. Nixon when the plane rolled to a stop before the red carpet and a platform with microphones. There were the usual arrival ceremonies, cordial statements by both heads of state, and a long receiving line. My wife and I were struck by how tired and pale both President and Mrs. Nixon looked as they proceeded down the line and shook our hands. Mrs. Nixon appeared far frailer than I had expected. I do not think they had any idea of the tumultuous welcome they were about to receive nor, for that matter, did I.

The embassy staff, working with White House advance teams and the Egyptian Foreign Ministry, had planned down to the smallest detail the order of the vehicle cortege and the seating according to protocol of the presidential party and Egyptian dignitaries. The two presidents rode in an open limousine, waving to the crowds, much to the dismay of the Secret Service. As the dozen or more vehicles escorted by a phalanx of policemen on motorcycles headed toward downtown Cairo, it soon became apparent that we would be facing a mob scene all the way in from the airport. Vast crowds of happy people pushed in toward the vehicles, trying to reach in the windows to shake hands or touch us. It was a situation in which one might easily have panicked. The vehicles toward the rear of the cortege simply could not stay together with the others. It literally took almost two hours through the crowds to make a trip that normally would have taken less than a half hour. Our vehicle broke away from the parade after entering the city and used less traveled streets so as to get me to the Embassy more quickly to take charge of aspects of the program.

During the course of that afternoon, the two leaders met at Tahra Palace, a large governmental office complex in the center of town. It provided Sadat with an opportunity to lay out his vision for dealing with the Middle East impasse. Nixon, on the other hand, responded with positions along the line that Secretary Kissinger had been pursuing during shuttle diplomacy. One of my concerns during this entire affair was the care and handling of Kissinger, who, although present, had perforce been pushed into the background. On all other occasions everything had revolved about him. He was our boss, after all, and the last thing I wanted was for him to feel we had neglected him in any way. I made sure that the ambassador understood I was concerned about that aspect of the Nixon visit and that I would do my best to deal with the situation.

During all my rushing around at this time, I had little chance to take note of what was happening to my family. The previous day, June 11, 1974, was our twenty-fifth—silver—wedding anniversary and I had not been home at all. That was certainly no way to cement a marriage! The Foreign Ministry planned an elaborate state dinner at Qubbah Palace on that first evening of the Nixon visit to which the ambassador and I and our wives were invited. Arriving home just in time to dress for this formal affair, Elsa informed me that our son, Matthew, was running a fever of 104 degrees. I found him in bed in a terrible state. We put him in a cold bath and iced him down. Although dressed to depart for the palace, under no circumstance was Elsa prepared to leave Matthew in the hands of servants while he was so critically ill. She urged me to go and simply point out the circumstances of her absence to Ambassador and Mrs. Eilts. As it turned out, Matthew had come down with dengue fever, and Elsa missed an event of a lifetime. She has always regretted not having attended Sadat's state dinner for the Nixons, but dutiful mother that she is, she knew she had acted wisely.

My driver was waiting for me at the gate to our house, and we proceeded to Qubbah Palace. Nearing the palace grounds, I spotted the first of the ornately dressed lancers on horseback. Lancers lined the long drive every few yards through the palace grounds. Qubbah Palace is a vast Versailles-type edifice constructed in the eighteenth century, when Egypt was a kingdom and such buildings were equated with the projection of royal power. Entering the palace with its expansive reception halls, one is impressed by the magnificent carpets and massive, sparkling, crystal chandeliers.

It was a lovely cool evening, and the state dinner for the Nixons, to which four hundred guests had been invited, was held in the palace gardens. The trees were aglow with colored lights. A company of waiters in ornamental regalia wearing turbans and *gallabieyas* glided among the many tables carrying large heavy trays with regal chinaware and silver serving dishes. While Egypt may nominally have been a republic, guests were enveloped in a milieu of eighteenth century royal splendor.

I was seated at a table with, among others, Henry Catto, the State Department's chief of protocol. Ambassador Catto, no stranger to sumptuous affairs, at one point commented to me, "I have never seen anything like it!" Indeed, it was an affair out of the *Arabian Nights*! I kept thinking, "How do you top this?" knowing only too well that the following day our embassy was to be responsible for hosting a return dinner at Ras-el-Tin Palace in Alexandria.

After a splendid meal enhanced by musical entertainment and a performance of belly dancing by Nagwa Fouad, the two presidents gave short speeches. President Nixon was gracious in thanking his host, and President Sadat used the occasion to make a point I have never forgotten. He said, "There is no other road to a durable peace without a solution to the Palestinian problem." As I write this section of my reminiscences thirty-one years later, hostilities still exist between Israel and the Palestinians, with the former expanding Jewish settlements in the occupied territories and the latter in desperation resorting to suicide bombers' blowing themselves up in Israel. And Sadat, prescient statesman that he was, is dead, the victim of an assassin's bullets.

The entire time I was in Egypt observing the process of shuttle diplomacy, I shared this view of Sadat's, always wondering, as haggling went on over kilometers and boundaries, when the United States would begin to deal with that overall obstacle to future peace. At one time, while serving in Libya I was told, "The Palestinians are the Jews of the Arab world." It seems as if that must be so, for under American and Israeli policies they are destined to suffer and remain scattered.

In preparation for the Nixon visit to Alexandria, several of our embassy staff had traveled up to that city the previous week. Employees at our small office there assisted us in checking out the facilities at Ras-el-Tin Palace, a magnificent structure comparable to the finest royal houses in Europe. A huge building, the palace stretches out onto a peninsula in Alexandria's harbor. Our concern in handling a dinner in such an environment was compounded by the fact that much of the food for the meal was being flown in from Europe and the United States. We went over the quarters with Secret Service and advance team members, dealing with all the details that make presidential visits a nightmare for those charged with seeing to their success.

If the Nixon entry from the airport into Cairo was a tumultuous affair, it was matched by his triumphal journey by train through the Nile River delta up to Alexandria. Sadat had said that the American president would be welcomed by the people of Egypt and indeed he was. The two presidents, riding in an ornate royal coach with open sides, were greeted by ecstatic crowds all along the ninety miles of track from Cairo to Alexandria. The *fellahin* (peasants) of Egypt might well have been greeting a pharaoh! On a slightly more skeptical note, many in the exuberant crowds were carrying signs in English, a tell-tale indication of the extent to which the Egyptian government had gone in its welcoming efforts.

Although I had been involved in the preparations for the Nixons' visit to Alexandria, while they were actually up there I was back in Cairo working with John Craig on an agreement between Egypt and the United States related to cooperation in the areas of economic, scientific, and cultural affairs. We were under tremendous pressure to complete a document that could be signed by the two presidents the next day at a meeting they were to have at Sadat's Rest House out by the Pyramids in Giza.

Although a young officer, John was superbly able. I recall Ambassador Eilts's comment when giving me the task. "Get Craig to help you." He had been on Eilts's staff in Saudi Arabia and the ambassador knew how capable John was. We worked through the night on a lengthy document entitled "Principles of Relations and Cooperation Between Egypt and the United States." While the final copies were being typed up the following morning, we searched for impressive binders and ribbons to give our effort the required appearance of an agreement to be signed by heads of state.

We had copies of the documents ready for signature when Sadat and Nixon arrived at the Rest House, a rather small building with a patio on which many of us sat or stood gazing at the Pyramids, while the two leaders conversed inside. Then, with the press and Egyptian and American officials looking on, the two presidents signed the agreement. Later that day the Nixon party in Air Force One and the press in a back-up plane took off for Saudi Arabia. The embassy staff breathed a sigh of relief. It had been not only a tiring three days, but two weeks of hectic communications, advance teams, and preparations leading up to the visit. At any other post, one might have been able to relax for a while, but we never knew when Secretary Kissinger might decide on another shuttle stopover.

The physical toll that such visits took on our personnel was substantial. While in the throes of one of these affairs, the six-year old son of a communicator came down with a case of the measles. He was an adorable blond boy, the joy of his parents, an attractive young couple. The father, overloaded with work in the communications center, had had little time to focus on problems at home. Complications rapidly set in, and suddenly to everyone's dismay the little boy was dead. My wife and I immediately went over to see if there was anything we could do for the parents. It was heartbreaking to see them sitting on the bed, totally crushed, in a state of shock. How does one ever find the words to say in such circumstances? The dedication of our Foreign Service personnel is a priceless asset to our government and the American people.

As if the presidential visit was not enough to tax our limited staff, a three-man team of inspectors from Washington arrived at the post coincident with that affair. The team was led by Richard Usher, my old boss and former political counselor in Manila. We barely had time to speak with the inspectors, although I did make time to have Dick out to lunch at our house in Maadi. It was obvious to him that the embassy was woefully short-handed. I knew how Ambassador Eilts felt about increasing the representation at the post and was thus circumspect.

At one point Dick asked, "How do you feel about being the DCM, political counselor, and economic counselor all at once?"

I simply replied, "It keeps me busy, but I couldn't ask for a better job." Nevertheless, the inspection team in their final report to the Department of State included a strong statement that Cairo was understaffed.

In late May 1974, I prevailed upon Ambassador Eilts to permit me to take my annual mandatory two-week tour of active duty as an Army Reserve officer as soon as we had concluded President Nixon's visit. He was not happy about the prospect, but earlier we had taken Edward Peck on board as an economic officer. I knew Ed from my service in the department. He was an extremely able, broad-gauged senior officer who could easily fill in for me in the interim. Arrangements were made through our Defense Attaché Office to notify the Department of the Army of my availability.

Shortly thereafter I received orders to report to the Pentagon for duty the last two weeks of June with the Office of the Deputy Chief of Staff of the Army for Operations (G-3). After a long commercial airline flight to Washington, I reported in on a Monday morning to my position as a deputy director for Civil Affairs on the General Staff. I was assigned to work with Colonel Jarold Hutchison, a War College classmate. The Army, among other things, promptly put me to work giving a series of joint service briefings for officers in the Pentagon.

I made presentations labeled Critical Issues in the Relations between Egypt and the United States, Prospects for a Military Assistance Program for Egypt, and the Status of Suez Canal Clearance Operations, which had been given the military designation "Operation Nimbus Star." I believe that tour of duty was as mutually beneficial a use of time as I have ever experienced on active duty.

While in Washington, I was contacted by Richard Murphy, who had just returned from his assignment as ambassador to Mauritania. He was anxious to learn more about Egypt and the activities of the embassy, as well as something of the living and working conditions at the post. He came to the Pentagon and, over coffee in the snack bar, I gave him my impressions of Cairo. I told him that my job was challenging and exciting, and for a Foreign Service officer there were few better assignments anywhere. I could not have been more positive about the work or the post. After all, I would have been foolish to have said anything else, since Murphy was soon to take over my DCM duties and become my boss.

Upon my return to Cairo, I told Ambassador Eilts of my meeting with Murphy. I thought no more about the matter, expecting Murphy to arrive in a few weeks, when word was received that he had been named ambassador to Syria. I always suspected thereafter that Eilts believed I may have somehow discouraged Murphy, so that I might have remained longer in the DCM position. As matters evolved, not only did Murphy assume his duties in Damascus, he went on to become a distinguished assistant secretary of state for Near Eastern and South Asian affairs. An old acquaintance from my days in Germany, Frank Maestrone, was subsequently assigned to the Minister position in Cairo.

Although time with my family was limited, we all tried to make the most of our opportunities. The Pyramids and the Sphinx at Giza were just on the outskirts of town, but it was many weeks after our arrival before we had a chance to visit them. We took the usual camel rides, and Matthew was thrilled in those days to climb the huge stone blocks of Cheops. Now that is no longer permitted. It was not until six months after our arrival that we acted on suggestions that we go horseback riding in the desert. There were several stables out near the Pyramids where one could hire horses, and we did so, usually very early in the morning, thus avoiding the heat and permitting me to arrive at work on schedule.

As indicated earlier, our house in Maadi was admirably suited for entertaining. The large stone building was in some respects reminiscent of a Moorish castle, with spacious living and dining rooms and a vast garden. The ambassador's residence downtown, by contrast, was somewhat limited. Both he and I were very much aware of this situation. During those early days I thus endeavored to assist him with as much of the routine entertaining as appropriate under the circumstances. In cleaning out files not long ago, I came across guest lists for receptions with attendees in the hundreds. A few of these affairs entailed some exciting moments.

Once, immediately after a reception in honor of a visiting U.S. cotton textile delegation, a fire broke out in a house just beyond a far wall of our garden. The local fire department came and attempted to put out the flames by deluging the building with water from powerful fire hoses. Much of the water sprayed over the wall, flooding a substantial area of our property. The lights in our tall trees were still on from our outdoor reception, and I called to Matthew, who was in the garden a long way distant from the wall near the fire, to flip off the switch at the circuit box, since water was spraying up into some of our lighted trees. Doing so sparked a bright flash, and Matthew was knocked to the ground and nearly electrocuted. The 220-volt current burned a deep gash in his right hand between the thumb and forefinger. A hurried telephone call brought Dr. Walter Miner, the U.S. Navy captain heading the Naval Medical Research Unit (NAMRU) in Cairo, over to treat our son and calm some very worried parents.

Despite the interruption in relations between Egypt and the United States after the outbreak of the 1967 Arab-Israeli War, NAMRU remained in Cairo and continued to function. Its research work in studying tropical diseases, particularly schistosomiasis or "snail fever," was a boon to world health and of particular importance to Egypt. It was estimated that 60 percent of the peasant population in the lower Nile Delta was infected with some form of the disease. The construction of the Aswan Dam, with its resultant constant water level, unfortunately increased the incidence of schistosomiasis. Egypt was also rife with other illnesses such as amoebic dysentery, typhoid, tetanus, and hepatitis. I was to become well acquainted with hepatitis before my departure from Cairo. NAMRU was a great credit to the United States and I took pleasure in acting as the Embassy liaison with those fine members of the U.S. Navy.

Another bit of memorable entertaining took place during a visit of Secretary of the Treasury William Simon. Elsa hosted a luncheon for his wife, the wives of others in the American delegation, and the spouses of a number of important Egyptian officials. Visits of key cabinet officers invariably involve a security detail, and Mrs. Simon on that occasion was guarded by a female member of the Secret Service, who blended nicely into the gathering. All went well until the guests proceeded into the dining room, when the agent's concealed, loaded pistol fell out and clattered across the marble tile floor. There were gasps all around, while my poor wife, the dutiful hostess, made desperate attempts at small talk. That was a hard act to follow! The Egyptian ladies went home afterwards with quite a tale to recount.

While in Egypt my son Matthew was enrolled in a secondary school that had the elevated title of Cairo American College. It was located in Maadi, a short, convenient distance from our residence. One of my unofficial duties was to serve as the embassy's representative on the school's board of directors. I had served a similar function in Libya. The Cairo institution was well run, and while it had some of the problems I had experienced elsewhere, it fared much better in recruiting faculty. Cairo, with its cultural advantages and big city lure, was not Benghazi.

One of the mixed blessings of serving abroad in many countries is having servants. While Americans at home may look with envy on this aspect of Foreign Service life, it does not come without drawbacks. In many places in the underdeveloped world, it is extremely difficult for an American family to function without the assistance of household help. Often modern appliances are not readily available or suitable for use. The demands of representative entertaining at most posts require employing servants. In Cairo, dealing with servants became an art form. We were faced at various times with a highly temperamental cook who was ready to quit before dinners with numerous foreign guests or bickering between the cook, maid, houseboy, and gardener. Our wives were often out of sorts having to deal with these situations, and their distress would in turn affect their husbands.

Once, as a consequence, I became suspicious of our gardener, Sabah. He was forever requesting money to buy fertilizer, seed, or some other item, although I saw little result from his efforts. We had some magnificent mango trees in our garden, loaded at one point with fruit. The harvest should have been enough to fill a room. However, rather than being surfeited with mangoes, we had only a nominal amount for the enjoyment of our family, much less enough to supply some of our friends. After speaking with others in the Embassy, I came to the conclusion that Sabah was selling the mangoes to dealers in the local market. When I confronted him with the matter, he responded, "Big birds come at night and eat them." My answer was, "You are for the birds! What happened to all the mangoes?" Again he said, "Big birds."

Convinced that I was being hoodwinked, I went out into the garden late that night. Sure enough, Sabah was partially right; the trees were full of huge fruit bats, not birds, devouring what was left of our mangoes. Had I had time to focus on the problem, rather than being overloaded with my duties, next time around I might have devised some way of keeping the bats out of the trees. Perhaps use of bright lights could have been the solution.

While we were in Cairo, we were visited by two of my sisters with their husbands. It was the first time in our numerous years overseas that members of my family came to stay with us, and we were admirably suited to house them. Not only did we have space in our residence, but we also had a small guesthouse on the grounds. The first to arrive were my eldest sister, Eleanor, and her husband, Alfred Bingham. Eleanor had gone through life being the center of attention. Attractive, effusive, and effervescent, she caused a stir wherever she went.

Rather than put Eleanor and Alfred up in the guesthouse, we chose to billet them where they could be closer to the dining room and the care of our servants. When they came down to dinner that first evening, the dining room with its long table was set as usual with embassy china and silverware. The meal was not much more than a normal one, with wines served by the cook and by our houseboy, Hassan, in his usual evening dinner finery, a long, blue, brocade, gold-trimmed *gallabieyah* and turban. When Eleanor saw this splendiferous apparition, I thought her eyes would pop out of their sockets. Remembering how impressed Elsa and I had been in Libya, when we were entertained by British friends who had brought their bedecked servants from Egypt, I readily understood Eleanor's reaction. As Hassan swept out of the dining room she asked, "WHO was that?" I nonchalantly replied, "Oh, just one of our servants."

Unfortunately, the press of my work afforded me little time to be with my relatives. Though Alfred became ill for several days, they did visit the numerous sights around Cairo that tourists frequent. Subsequently, they flew down to Luxor and the Valley of the Kings before departing.

My sister, Elsie, and her husband, Fred Stahl, arrived several weeks later during the summer of 1974, accompanied by their longtime friends and neighbors, Austin and Edna Mehrhof. We put Elsie and Fred up in our residence, while the Mehrhofs were ensconced in the guesthouse. I had a bit more time on that occasion and we had an enjoyable stay together. After the foursome returned from visiting the antiquities of Upper Egypt, Elsa and I planned a special celebration for them before their departure for Moscow, the next stop on their tour. We hired a felucca, an Egyptian sailboat, for an evening cruise on the Nile. These sturdy vessels ply their way up and down the Nile. Several gaily-painted ones docked on the river near Maadi were available for outings. The Stahls, the Mehrhofs, Elsa, and I, loaded down with coolers and picnic baskets, boarded a felucca for a sail on the Nile that none of us would ever forget. It was a beautiful evening, with the sun setting behind the palm trees, the Pyramids visible in the distance. We drank cocktails as the boatmen handled the felucca's lateen sail, gliding silently along watching the stars come up.

A good part of my duties consisted of preparing schedules and making appointments for visitors to Cairo, official and otherwise, including senators and representatives, former ambassadors, important businessmen, media personalities, and luminaries of stage and screen. Cairo had been off-limits for the years between 1967 and 1974, when we had no diplomatic relations, and suddenly there was a surge on the part of Americans to see the Pyramids and the wonders of Egypt. Others came to reopen business dealings. A few of these visitors still stand out in my mind, among them former senator and presidential candidate George McGovern, child movie star and former ambassador Shirley Temple Black, singer Pearl Bailey, and Senator and Mrs. Howard Baker. The Bakers were exceptionally cordial visitors. I also had an opportunity once again to meet the commander of one of my old World War II units, General James Gavin of the 82nd Airborne Division.

Senator McGovern's visit might best be described as a hassle. I recall going out to the airport to meet him only to find that he and his entourage were not on the plane. Returning to the Embassy, I spent the next few hours endeavoring to find out what had happened. Evidently our visitors had not made connections and the U.S. Air Force was brought into the picture to fly them on to Cairo. In the interim, I had made trips out to the airport to meet other commercial airliners. Once in town, this group provided me with other surprises.

The morning after their arrival, the senator was scheduled to confer with President Sadat. I went over to the Hilton Hotel to pick him up and accompany him to the offices at Barrages where he would be meeting Sadat. As I was about to knock on the door of his room, it swung open and

I was confronted by the senior representative of the Palestine Liberation Organization (PLO) in Cairo. It had been the official policy of our government not to recognize the PLO, and here was their top man coming out of the room of a person of McGovern's standing on the American political scene. I was dumbfounded.

Dealing with the PLO was a song-and-dance matter throughout my time in Cairo. We were forever running into that organization's representatives and were at pains to act as if they did not exist. At one point, the Egyptians suggested that Ambassador Eilts establish contact with the PLO, but Washington would not hear of it. What little contact was made was carried out elsewhere through other means. The influence of the Israeli lobby and Congress were strongly felt on this issue.

Once in the room with Senator McGovern, I urged that we depart promptly for our meeting with President Sadat. A very kind and permissive man, he was at pains to wait for his assistants, who, although they knew of the appointment, were out visiting the Pyramids. Wait we did, arriving late at the Barrages. The president, however, was his usual gracious self, though I was thoroughly irritated and embarrassed. I had rarely seen a more disjointed operation than this group. No wonder they missed connections.

I remember Ambassador Shirley Temple Black with a sense of sheer embarrassment. She spoke to me over long distance telephone one morning about a clock she had sent to Cairo for the Sadats. It was evidently not working and needed some repair. After she explained her problem to me, for some witless reason I responded, "Don't worry Madame Ambassador, I will fix your clock!" She did not think my bit of brainless humor was funny at all. Several years later I told John Linehan, who had been her DCM in Ghana, about my gaffe. He said that Mrs. Black had been a very able ambassador and he had enjoyed working for her. That made me feel even worse about the matter.

Singer Pearl Bailey's visit to Cairo was a series of mishaps. She came out as a representative of President Nixon's Arts Council and was accompanied by her troupe and members of her family. Neither the U.S. Information Agency in Washington nor its cultural affairs officers in Cairo had any input into her program. At a performance at the large, open-air auditorium near the Sphinx normally used for the "Sound and Light Show," everything seemed to go wrong. The lights malfunctioned, a brisk wind blew the piano player's music into his face, the bass player broke a string, and the audio system only worked intermittently. Bailey's choice of songs such as "Rainy Day Blues" in a country so bereft of moisture and one about "a man from Galilee," which conjured up thoughts about Israel, mystified the Muslim Egyptian audience. Finally, in a sequence acceptable in America, but not in Egypt, she persisted in coaxing Mrs. Sadat up on the stage. The president's wife, the very soul of shyness and self-effacing graciousness, was mortified. These are some of the things that occur when Americans perform abroad in countries where there are cultural differences. However, our embassy staff, while unhappy with what had happened, truly felt sorry for Pearl Bailey. She was the epitome of kindness, spending most of her three days in Cairo calling at such places as the school for the blind and children's wards in hospitals.

The visit of Senator Howard Baker and his lovely wife Joy was a pleasant experience for Elsa and me. Among other things, the four of us had a wonderful time having lunch on board a Nile River cruise ship. I learned much about the functioning of the Senate that one is not ordinarily privileged to know. Senator Baker, a Republican from Tennessee, a few years afterward became the Senate Majority Leader and subsequently chief of staff to President Reagan.

General James Gavin had come to Cairo on business. In the intervening years since World War II, he had retired and in the early sixties had been appointed by President Kennedy as our ambassador to France. Subsequently, as a military strategist, he had warned against America's expanded involvement in the Vietnam War. General Gavin was pleased to learn that I had served as a paratrooper with his 82nd Airborne Division. I endeavored to be helpful to him while he was in town, though he was anxious to speak with Ambassador Eilts. The latter, unfortunately, was unavailable at the time and I was disappointed not to be able to arrange a meeting for my old commanding officer.

It is difficult for me now to separate out the various Kissinger shuttle visits to Cairo, interspersed as they were over my stay there. We spent a good deal of time at the airport, either waiting for his plane to arrive or to depart. On one occasion, the secretary was preparing to depart in his Air Force version of a Boeing 707, and we were all waving good-bye. Ambassador Eilts and Egyptian Foreign Minister Fahmy were standing at the foot of the stairs. Earlier, before starting up the stairs, Kissinger had given Fahmy a parting embrace. As he was about to enter the plane, the secretary turned around, seemingly to come back down. My first thought was "What now!" Then, in a loud voice with a strong Germanic accent, he shouted down to Eilts, "HERMANN, ven I know you, like I know Fahmy, I vil hug you too!!" The many bystanders broke out in laughter.

On another occasion the departure gave us a shock. The ambassador and I were standing on the tarmac at Cairo Airport. We had just put Kissinger and his entourage aboard the plane and were waiting around for it to take off. The large aircraft, with its distinct blue and white markings and American flag on the tail, taxied to the end of the runway. It was a blistering hot day, about noon. We and the staff were anxious to get off the tarmac, out of the sun, and back to the Embassy. The plane, however, remained at the end of the runway. Ten minutes went by, then twenty, with all of us there perspiring unmercifully.

Then word came back that there had been shooting aboard the plane. Flabbergasted, my first thought was of a possible assassination attempt. After several anxious moments, we learned that a member of the security detail, upon seating himself, had accidentally discharged his Uzi submachine gun. No one had been injured, but the bullets had punctured the fuselage of the plane. What to do now? We all expected the secretary and his party to disgorge from the plane and be our guests again until a backup aircraft could be brought into play. Much to our surprise, however, after another fifteen minutes the plane took off. I was subsequently told that the holes had been plugged with chewing gum. Whether that is true or not, I never did find out and have always suspected that someone was pulling my leg.

In June of 1974, Secretary Kissinger was accompanied by his wife of two months, Nancy Maginnes. A tall, blonde, very composed woman, we all considered her a welcome addition to the shuttle team, since she seemed to have a mollifying effect on her husband. Kissinger could be a trial, often thoughtless of the demands he made on those around him. I remember late one night, it must have been about two or three in the morning, finally getting him bedded down in a room at one of the palaces when he came out complaining bitterly about his pillow. I cannot recall where I found a substitute, but I did, much to the relief of those of us waiting to leave and get some sleep.

Henry Kissinger and I came out of the same background in World War II. We were both privates in the Army, he in the 84th Infantry Division and I in the 17th Airborne, when we were approached to join the Counter Intelligence Corps (CIC). In his case it was Private Fritz Kraemer and in mine Master Sergeant Severin Wallach who were instrumental in changing the course of our lives.[10] Kissinger and I both spoke German and each of us was at one time involved in appointing the mayor of a town in Germany, he in Krefeld in Hesse, and I in Duisburg in the Rhineland. As a sergeant, he was later an instructor at the European Theater Intelligence School in Oberammergau in the Bavarian Alps. I vaguely recall visiting the school and being directed to see Sergeant Kissinger about something or other. When in Cairo during times such as described in the preceding paragraph, I was tempted to say, "Hey, Sergeant Kissinger, do you remember me? I am Lieutenant Kormann!"

One of the difficult aspects of life in the Foreign Service is being separated from one's children. I did my best throughout my career to be stationed at posts that had appropriate schools. That was possible up through the high school years. College attendance, however, was another matter. As parents, Elsa and I worried about our son and daughter back in the United States. Generally, we kept abreast of one another's activities by half-hour-long discussions on audiotapes, which we sent back and forth. Periodically, we also spoke to them on the telephone, but commercial connections from Cairo generally were not very good. Friends in the Embassy's Defense Attaché Office suggested that as an Army Reserve officer, I could readily use military lines to call West Point to check on my cadet son, Brad. There was a special connection via Naples our military had set up to service Suez Canal clearance operations. I used it from time to time with good results. Getting through to Hanover, New Hampshire, and Dartmouth College to speak with Andrea was more difficult.

Both Brad and Andrea came to Cairo that first summer. West Point afforded my son little time off, but he managed, using military transportation. He made the most of his stay, sightseeing, before I arranged for him to fly back to Rota, Spain, aboard the plane of an admiral who had come for discussions with Egyptian officials of the Suez Canal Authority. From there he traveled up to the U.S. Air Force's base at Torrejon near Madrid for a Military Airlift Command (MAC) flight to Dover, Delaware. Andrea, on the other hand, arrived aboard a TWA flight accompanied by a classmate from Dartmouth. Among other things, the girls had a hilarious time riding camels out at the Pyramids. A picture of that activity is a scrapbook favorite.

Another friend of Andrea's arrived a bit later, in time to enter Cairo's American University. He was a top graduate from Dartmouth and had been doing further work at Harvard. It was his desire to enter the field of petroleum economics. He had been studying Arabic and believed that he could best prepare by immersing himself in the language in Egypt. Andrea wrote asking that I take him under my wing and assist if he needed help. Upon his arrival, Elsa and I invited him to dinner and thereafter I kept a watchful eye on him. He enrolled promptly at the university in an intensive Arabic course that had four or five other students, all Japanese. Our American student kept up his studies for a while, but soon realized he simply could not keep up with the Japanese, who had all started at his level of competence, or less, in Arabic. He had to drop out and not long afterward returned home.

While I was somewhat surprised that a student of his caliber, coming from the best of American schools, could not keep up, I was reminded of our experiences in Manila. There my wife, as a teacher of American history, found her best students were Chinese. Similarly, I was stunned to witness a Vietnamese acquaintance learn to read, speak and write English fluently in three months. A further indication of the ability of many students of Asian background to excel academically may be seen in the enrollment figures in some of America's top universities. It makes one wonder what the future holds for the evolving nations of Asia.

The months of the summer of 1974 were very busy as I attempted to deal with a variety of responsibilities. Delegations from Washington arrived to discuss textile matters, reparation payments for nationalization under President Nasser, U.S. aid to Egypt, the promotion of commerce and investment, oil exploration, military assistance, the Law of the Sea, and a variety of other matters since forgotten. The several UN Specialized Agencies were all represented in Cairo and we endeavored to stay in contact with them. Lieutenant General Ensio Siilasvuo, who headed the United Nations Middle East Emergency Force was someone I went to see several times to convey messages.

In the end, I was pleased to be able to step back when Frank Maestrone arrived in mid-September to take up his position as minister and deputy chief of mission. I could not have asked for a more able and congenial supervisor. The work, however, took its toll. I had become so rundown and weakened that I contracted a severe case of hepatitis. Up to that point, I had never really been ill for any length of time. Even in places like the Philippines and Libya, where others became sick, I remained unaffected. This time, I was incapacitated and bedridden for three months, but nevertheless remained at the post.

Christmas 1974 was a sad time for our family. The bout with hepatitis affected my memory and my sight, leaving me virtually blind for a number of weeks. Ed Peck arrived and surprised us with a magnificent Christmas tree he had acquired from the Egyptian state agricultural farm, a particular act of kindness the Kormanns will always remember. It was a massive pine, fifteen feet in height, which we placed in the atrium entrance of our house. Ed and Ann Peck were good friends in our time of need.

My Egyptian doctor decided at one point that it would be wise for me to be hospitalized, and I was sent for a week to the American University Hospital in Beirut, Lebanon, which was then considered the best in the Middle East. Later, I was informed by the State Department doctors that I should have been sent home. Not only did I become a casualty at that time, but Elsa did as well. We spent a week together in the hospital, she with a hernia and I with hepatitis.

We were in the hospital in Beirut during the arrival of the initial victims of the violence that was to reign in Lebanon for decades to come. The basic arrangement for governing Lebanon, with a Maronite Christian president, a Sunni Muslim prime minister, and a Shia Muslim president of the Chamber of Deputies, broke down as the Muslim population increased and hundreds of thousands of Palestinian refugees entered the country from Israel and its occupied territories. PLO commandos, after having been driven out of Jordan in 1971, were a forceful presence in Beirut at the time, and the American University Hospital, I was later to learn, was at pains not to antagonize them. Consequently, it took in their wounded members despite the fact that they made no payment. My wife remembers hearing hospital personnel talking about PLO Chairman Yasir Arafat being down in the lobby of the hospital as the first cases were brought in.

During the late winter and spring of 1975, I settled into my position as counselor of embassy for political and economic affairs with a sense of relief. Arlene Stone, my secretary, was a sympathetic assistant. She had witnessed the crushing load we all had labored under during the early days and was concerned about my health. Egypt, despite Middle East political turmoil and shuttle diplomacy, was now a sideshow to events in Southeast Asia. At one point, I recall frantic messages coming in from our embassies in Phnom Penh and Saigon related to the catastrophic, collapsing situations in Cambodia and Vietnam. They were for Secretary Kissinger, who was down at the Palace Hotel in Luxor meeting with President Sadat. Perhaps unfairly, I could not help thinking as I read the telegrams: "Nero fiddled, while Rome burned!"

As the end of the 1975 fiscal year approached, I received word from the Pentagon that I had been scheduled for a two-week tour of active duty with the Army. The embassy's staffing situation had improved considerably over the previous year. Roger Merrick had been added to the Economic Section to assist Ed Peck and John Craig. April Glaspie was the stalwart in the Political Section, while Beth Jones had been moved over from the Administrative Section. Bill Poole had also been added in the latter months. I had no qualms, therefore, about talking with Minister Maestrone and Ambassador Eilts about taking two weeks of military leave in the United States. The fact that my son, Brad, would be graduating from West Point during the period that I would be in America, gave my request added meaning.

I returned to Washington on military orders, accompanied by Elsa and Matthew, traveling at our expense. The long flight from Cairo to the United States via Athens was arduous, but we were happy to be back in Washington once more. Upon our arrival, we soon found quarters in an apartment motel in Virginia. Having had duty with the Special Operations Staff in the Pentagon the year before, I was familiar with the procedures and acquainted with the officers with whom I would be working. Major Stephen Olynyk, an old friend from my former Reserve unit in Riverdale, Maryland, had returned to active duty on a permanent basis with the

Army General Staff in the Pentagon and was charged with assisting me in taking over my duties.

Throughout most of my military career, I had been involved in "special operations." These were activities outside of the normal combat arms track. They included such things as guerrilla warfare, counterinsurgency, Special Forces, psychological operations, some aspects of intelligence, and now civil affairs. My early years in Germany convinced me of the importance of civil affairs. The adage "win the war, but lose the peace" took on added meaning for me at this time when in Cambodia and Vietnam we had won neither the peace nor the war. The United States was expanding its power into far-flung areas of the world, and it seemed to me that the Army had to broaden its thinking. Despite Great Britain's shrinking empire, I had been impressed by the way their military and civilian authorities cooperated in administering foreign territories. I saw how efficiently they had meshed in Libya during the period of the British protectorate when King Idris was in power, and later in the Arab-Israeli War in 1967.

On this tour of active duty, I recall speaking to officers on the General Staff about the importance of including instruction on civil affairs in the curriculum at the Fort Leavenworth Command and General Staff School and the Army War College. At the time, there was only one under-strength civil affairs battalion on active duty with the 82nd Airborne Division. The preponderance of qualified personnel of that type was lodged in the Reserve. I had no complaint with this arrangement, aware that the Army's basic purpose was to fight wars, but at the same time it was vital that the leadership see to it that the Reserve was always fully prepared to interface with the active forces on short notice. Funding for this purpose in the final analysis might well be far more beneficial than the acquisition of the latest weapon. The future would reinforce that thought vehemently.

The highlight of our return to the United States at that time was Brad's graduation from West Point. We drove up from Washington on a beautiful late spring day to a motel in the vicinity of the U.S. Military Academy in preparation for the ceremonies the following morning. We were joined by other members of my family, including my sisters, Eleanor and Elsie, and their spouses. Andrea came down from Dartmouth, and young Matthew was there with Elsa and me. Brad met us, resplendent in his traditional gray uniform with senior's chevrons and a burgundy company officer's sash. The parade of cadets and the pomp and ceremony of a West Point graduation are things never to be forgotten. President Gerald Ford gave the graduation address.

Brad went through the Academy at a time when rough treatment was the norm. With the later acceptance of women, much of the hazing is now, for the better, no longer part of the routine. He had endured everything, despite having entered at a younger age than most plebes. In his final year, he volunteered for airborne training and went through parachute school. He had chosen as his branch of service the infantry, as I had upon my commissioning. A father could not have been prouder of his son. Brad entered the Army at a difficult time for men in the service. The United States had just been driven out of Vietnam. In the eyes of the nation the military was in disfavor— all the more reason now to stand up and be counted. In his time in the military he was to see innovations and serve as the commanding officer of one of the first female basic training companies in the Army.

Returning to Cairo, Elsa and I were again immersed in a busy round of visiting delegations and Middle East political activities. I had by then been overseas two years in Germany and Egypt, a normal assignment period. Earlier, when completing the Office of Personnel's assignment preference form, I had requested that my next posting be back in Washington. I did that with the realization that both Elsa and I now had health problems. Cairo had been hard on both of us.

The department responded by offering me an assignment with the interagency Intelligence Community Staff, a body that supported the Director of Central Intelligence in his role as the overall coordinator of intelligence activity in the government, including that of the Departments of State, Defense, Justice, and Treasury and the FBI. That position is often loosely referred to as the director's "other job" when he is "wearing his presidential hat."

Our final months in Cairo enabled me to finish several reporting projects and to participate in a whirlwind of farewell engagements. Ambassador and Mrs. Eilts graciously hosted a large reception in Elsa's and my honor, as did colleagues from other embassies. We had made numerous friends among the Egyptian and foreign diplomatic communities and were sad to be saying good-bye. Mac and Ruth Gerlach, our old friends from Berlin back in 1946–47, held an unusual party for us in a tent out in the desert. My family is still amused by a picture of me taken while I was undulating in a wild sequence with an Egyptian belly dancer at that affair.

Ambassador Eilts, members of the Cairo staff, and a circle of other friends saw us off for the long flight to the United States. By that time international affairs had entered a trying period. Terrorism had become a factor and airline travel was just beginning to feel its effects, presaging what was to come.

16
Coordinating National Intelligence Operations

Arriving back in the United States from my assignments in Germany and Egypt in 1975 contrasted with our previous returns. We came back to a house we owned. There was no trip down to Florida to spend time with my mother, who had since passed on. Matthew could enter school normally in September, Andrea was away from the family in her sophomore year at Dartmouth, and Brad, a newly commissioned lieutenant, was now stationed at Fort Drum, near the Canadian border in upstate New York. One aspect had not changed, however, and that was our trip to Jacksonville, Illinois, to visit Elsa's parents. We found them healthy and in good spirits. Dad Wells, now in his eighties, was still as active as ever. Despite his retirement, he was involved in academic affairs with the local colleges. His interest in matters of social concern prompted him to found a group to rehabilitate persons with drug and alcohol problems. The group set up a center in a small building on the outskirts of town. That austere establishment was to grow over the years until it became the large Wells Center, serving fourteen counties in Illinois.

Following a two weeks' stay in the Midwest, I reported to the State Department to undertake my new assignment with the Intelligence Community (IC) Staff, which had its offices in Langley, Virginia, at the headquarters of the Central Intelligence Agency. In my discussions with our personnel office, I queried why I had been considered for an assignment in the intelligence field outside of the State Department. Had someone examined my military background and learned of my years of experience and that I was "branch qualified" as an intelligence officer, authorized to sign after my name, "Colonel, MI (Military Intelligence)"? Had they discovered that I had attended the extensive Intelligence Officer's Career Course and Advanced Course"? No, they hadn't, but they were pleased to learn that their assignment was such a good fit.

I was not too surprised to learn that they had no inkling of my intelligence background and just assumed that, as a Foreign Service officer, I would be able to handle any assignment I was given. I came away think-ing that for once the bureaucratic process might just have put a round peg in a round hole. Ironically, after several attempts over the years by CIA colleagues to recruit me overseas, the State Department itself was placing me in an assignment where I would be halfway there.

We had sold our car in Cairo, and I was now hard-pressed to find transportation. I had ordered a new Mercury Monarch to be delivered from the factory through the diplomatic buying service and in the interim had rented a car. However, in view of the requirement that I now drive from our home in Maryland over to Virginia every day, we needed a sec-ond car. The Pontiac convertible we bought in 1969, of which Elsa and I were so fond, had gone out of production. None of the major companies manufactured convertibles. To satisfy our desire, I bought a used 1969 Pontiac GTO convertible and with it a ticket to some adventures.

The GTO, dark blue in color with a white canvas top, was one of the last of the great "muscle" cars. It had a "stick shift and four on the floor," with a huge 400 horsepower engine that required high-test gasoline. The GTO was to become a classic car buff's dream, but for us it was more of a nightmare. We had more breakdowns in that automobile in the ten years we possessed it than in all the years of our life before or since. For every minute of exhilaration on a beautiful sunny day on the open road with the top down, we had comparable moments in the repair shop or sitting on the side of the road waiting for a tow truck. However, as if to make up for the problems it caused, ten years later, in 1985, the GTO was sold to a collector for four times the price I had paid for it.

Driving via the Washington Beltway to CIA Headquarters, I antici-pated the difficulties I would have entering that security-conscious es-tablishment. The procedures I encountered then, however, were a far cry from those one would endure today. I finally made my way to the area of the building and the floor where my office in the Human Intelligence Collection (HUMINT) Section was located. There, I met my two other col-leagues in the three-man unit representing the Defense Department and the CIA respectively. Our basic function was to promote coordination and efficiency between our parent agencies and other government organiza-tions in the collection of intelligence from abroad. The CIA member, be-ing the most senior in grade, served for the time being as the chief of our little group, supported by an administrator and three secretaries. As I had expected, my background as an Army intelligence officer assisted in my transition. I was to find the work interesting and a substantial change from my previous assignment in Cairo.

My first day on the job, I was taken to meet the assistant director of central intelligence for the Intelligence Community. Ushered into his spacious office, I was dumbfounded to be greeted by a man who had been a neighbor fifteen years earlier in Fairfax, Virginia. I had known that E. Henry (Hank) Knoche had worked in the intelligence field, probably for CIA, but not much more than that. His son and Brad played together as youngsters. It was a pleasant introduction to my new position. Knoche was the number two to Lieutenant General Simon Wilson, who as a deputy to DCI William Colby was in overall charge of the IC Staff.

Colby had his hands full at that time with his other responsibility as director of the CIA, which was under severe attack from Congress and the press. Revelations of activities during the Vietnam era and Watergate were surfacing, as was the Agency's supposed role in the assassination of Patrice Lumumba in the Congo and the overthrow of Salvador Allende's Marxist government in Chile. The CIA was accused of financing a variety of nefarious projects by means of a "secret budget." The Agency, it was said, was simply "out of control."

The Senate established a Select Committee on Intelligence under Senator Frank Church of Idaho to get to "the bottom of the mess." The House of Representatives set up a similar committee under New York Congressman Otis Pike. Colby, in an effort to be forthcoming with the Congress, had done the unforgivable, in the eyes of the professionals in the Agency, by telling all and spilling "the family jewels" to the Church Committee.[1] It was in this atmosphere that I began my work over in Langley.

Our HUMINT Section was a small but key part of a larger contingent of 25–30 officers dealing with intelligence collection across the board. This intelligence ranged from communication-intercept traffic, aerial observation, satellite reconnaissance, and various scientific techniques to overt and covert human reporting sources. While I was in that position, the size of our group and the overall IC staff were to grow exponentially as the threat from the Soviet Union increased during the years 1975–79. Relations between the United States and the Soviet Union had deteriorated with the cooling of détente, to some extent because of the 1974 Jackson-Vanik Amendment, which fostered the emigration of large numbers of Soviet Jews to Israel. Senator Henry Jackson, who purportedly had presidential ambitions, seemed to be courting the support of the Israeli lobby and the important Jewish vote.

Congress held a "most favored nation agreement" in abeyance to induce the Russians to go along with the amendment's provisions. At first Moscow seemed willing to comply, but as Senator Jackson and his staff increased the numbers of Jews to be allowed to emigrate, the Russians took umbrage and balked. As a result they told us bluntly what we could do with our most-favored-nation status. Ill will had been created between our two countries, effectively ending efforts at détente. Henry Kissinger, in his autobiography *Years of Renewal,* writes of the problems he had on another occasion with Jackson and his staff, particularly Richard Perle, whom he cited as a formidable opponent.[2]

I might mention in this context that I had had a session with Perle a few years earlier while I was a politico-military advisor in the State Department. I encountered him one Sunday at a weekend drill of my Army Reserve unit. At the time, he was the senior staff member at the Senate Government Operations' National Security Subcommittee and had been invited as a guest speaker on the Middle East. Listening to him, it struck me that he was far from realistic about the military capabilities of the Arab countries, when compared to those of Israel.

After he had finished his remarks, I rose and indicated that it was my business to know something about the Middle East military balance. I commented briefly on the overall situation and stated, "If the Arab states attacked Israel, it would be a debacle. It would take the Israeli Army and Air Force less than a week to turn the situation around," which indeed is what happened not long afterward in the 1973 Arab-Israeli War. (Curiously, the following Monday morning, I was sitting at my desk when a State Department colleague came up to me and said, "John, you are living dangerously! The word is out around the department that you took on Dick Perle.")

While I had been welcomed to the IC Staff by my old friend and neighbor, Hank Knoche, I was to become particularly fond of his boss, Lieutenant General Simon ("Sam") Wilson. Perhaps it was because we were both World War II paratroopers. Wilson had been a member of Merrill's Marauders, a commando unit that served in Burma. Two combat teams serving under Brigadier General Frank Merrill had distinguished themselves harassing Japanese supply and communications lines. Wilson was an able administrator, who reminded me to a considerable extent of Vernon Walters, the CIA's deputy director and also a lieutenant general. Walters, with his superb language skills, played an important role in some of the notable events of the day. Both were highly talented Renaissance men.

Wilson regarded me, I believe, as somewhat of a curiosity, removed from the mold of the stereotypical Foreign Service officer. On one occasion, he asked me to accompany him to the "farm," the training center for CIA personnel in Virginia. We flew in a small private plane the U.S. government owned or leased. He was interested in some of the new developments in intelligence collection and in view of my responsibility for coordinating reporting from overseas and improving training, he wanted me to come along. While I was aware of much of what we saw, some far-out aspects of the training left me pondering their usefulness.

I had just become used to Bill Colby as the DCI when he was replaced by George H. W. Bush four months later in January 1976. Sam Wilson retired and Hank Knoche moved up to head the IC Staff. Knoche was subsequently chosen by Bush to be his number two man in the CIA and eventually as acting director.

While many of the projects, reports, and other matters I dealt with daily were classified "secret," my position as such was not. I was chairman of an interagency advisory group to improve intelligence reporting from overseas posts, with specific emphasis on the orientation and training of reporting officers from the CIA, the State, Defense, and Treasury Departments, and the FBI. We met once a month to discuss various aspects of training with a view toward improving them. To share information about procedures, the advisory group would sometimes hold its sessions at the training facilities of the various agencies to obtain a firsthand view of their activities.

A more immediate and critical part of my responsibilities on the IC Staff was to monitor the employment of reporting officers around the world. I did this in cooperation with an officer in the State Department who had a similar function. It was our job to preclude wasteful overlap and to see that we had adequate staffing to deal with the needs of overseas posts, as well as to fulfill the requirements of the various agencies concerned. Generally, we authorized assignments of individual officers going abroad. While it might seem that such activity would give rise to interagency conflicts, we were able during our tenure to work through a limited number of impasses without any serious friction.

At times overseas, State Department and CIA personnel found themselves with the same contacts in the host government and in the civilian sector. This could be troublesome, and my job was to preclude such overlapping by urging coordination, which usually resolved the situation. On several occasions during my assignments abroad, I was in close contact with CIA officers and found them very capable and useful in carrying out my duties. They assisted me over and above the basic activities they provided for their own organization. One of these individuals, a superb officer, later became the deputy director for operations at CIA, heading the clandestine services, and another the deputy director for administration.

George H. W. Bush's tenure as Director of Central Intelligence lasted barely a year, but he did much to improve morale in the intelligence community, which was then at an historic low after the Church Committee hearings. There was a sense that he respected and appreciated the ability and dedication of professional intelligence officers. He had a particular knack for making you feel that he was out to look after your welfare and that he was "one of the boys." He also worked tirelessly as a former congressman to improve relations with the Senate and the House of Representatives, briefing them regularly. It came as a disappointment to me, therefore, when he was not retained as DCI by President Carter as the latter took office in January 1977. I was not surprised decades later when they named the CIA Headquarters in Langley after George H. W. Bush.

Failure to reappoint Bush was also a blow to the concept that persons in the DCI position should be apolitical, providing a sense of continuity in an area so vital to national security. Hank Knoche then took over as DCI for an interim period prior to the arrival of four-star Admiral Stansfield Turner, a Naval Academy classmate of President Carter. Turner had a reputation as an innovator. He had been Commandant at the Naval War College when I was at the Army War College in 1972–73, and there were numerous stories about his turning the former's curriculum upside down. My military colleagues at the time were thankful he was not at Carlisle. Consequently, there was a certain amount of apprehension as Admiral Turner took office.

My HUMINT colleagues were concerned during Turner's tenure that too much emphasis was placed on technical and scientific collection, to the detriment of traditional overt reporting and the elicitation of information from clandestine (espionage) sources.[3] While that may have been the case, my own efforts for him seemed to be deeply appreciated. At one point he sent me a fine personal letter of commendation related to an extensive project I had completed for him.

From time to time while on the IC Staff, I was given assignments that required me to travel. In 1977, my responsibilities warranted an overseas trip to Stockholm, Berlin, Frankfurt, Paris and London. Stopping off in Berlin after an absence of thirty years and dealing with personnel in safehouse quarters gave me an eerie feeling. I felt as if I were back in CIC just after World War II. The streets and buildings where I had encountered Soviet NKVD agents were still there. As I walked one evening in the Wilmersdorf District of the old British Sector, I shuddered recalling just how close we had come to losing my CIC colleague on that cold wintry night in 1947. Had we not acted, he and his lady friend surely would have been kidnapped and perhaps never heard from again.[4]

I took the occasion to return to the Berlin suburb where our CIC headquarters had been located. Those buildings in the Zehlendorf District had long since been turned back to the Germans. Amazingly, there was no sign that the area had been a bustling CIC compound, replete with various agents' quarters, a mess hall, club, motor pool, and parking lot. The lovely old mansion in which I was quartered had not changed. I wondered who now occupied the place. It was my understanding that the owner, a ranking Nazi, and his family had been shot in the garden by the Russians upon their entry into the city. I could not bring myself to ring the bell; it was better to let the ghosts of the past lie undisturbed. Berlin was full of memories.[5]

These were the years of the Jimmy Carter presidency, and I recall a general sense of dislike for him and his administration on the part of government employees. The "Georgia Mafia" accompanying him into office tended to disparage those in government and their work. President Carter was not well served by these individuals. When it came to election time four years later, many public servants who might ordinarily have voted Democratic opted for Reagan and the Republicans.[6] That was unfortunate for Carter who, as an individual, was a very fine person, as demonstrated by his many humanitarian actions after leaving office. No president since Harry Truman has risen so markedly in the esteem of Americans and, indeed the world, after leaving office as has President Carter.

There were two occurrences during the Carter administration that remain fixed in my mind. The first related to a paper I prepared while on the IC Staff that was sent over to the White House for action. It was a brief document requiring a "presidential determination," commonly referred to as a "PD." I had on rare occasions in the past prepared PDs while in the State Department, for example, one related to releasing F-5 fighter planes to Libya—aircraft for which the Libyan government had paid. PDs were usually worked over by a staffer on the National Security Council and after a time came back simply approved or disapproved. On the occasion in question, the PD came back with little notations in the margins. That was not unusual and I thought little of it, until I focused on the "J. C." initials following the comments. The president had actually gone over the paper carefully, giving me the benefit of his views. Considering his vast responsibilities, this struck many of us as remarkable, but the president was subsequently criticized for being a micromanager.

The second occurrence dealt with the abortive attempt late in Carter's term to rescue the American Embassy hostages being held by the Iranians. I followed that situation closely, first as part of my job with the IC Staff when the hostages were taken, and then later outside of government. Several of the Foreign Service officers held, including L. Bruce Laingen, the embassy's chargé d'affaires, were my friends. When the full story of that failed rescue debacle was disclosed, I was dismayed. Reflecting on my own experience in crisis situations in Third World countries and on my training in Army Special Operations, it seemed to me that the basic approach to this daring operation was wrong. There was a lack of understanding of the surroundings into which the rescue force was to be injected, rural Iran with its ill-informed, backward peasant population. The "derring-do" aspect of the operation should have been tempered by a more subtle approach. Rather than shooting at the first sign of having been spotted after landing, the force should simply have gone about its business calmly. When queried by local Iranians as to what they were doing, the answer should have been that they were an earthquake response team or engaged in some other humanitarian activity.

One thing I have learned is that communications tend to be poor in that part of the world, and confusion is a normal state of affairs. Generally, it will take some time for the authorities to figure out what is going on. A case in point was my decision to fly U.S. Air Force planes into the international airport in Benghazi, Libya, during the 1967 Arab-Israeli War to evacuate Americans, despite its being occupied by hostile Algerian and Egyptian military aircraft.[7] Using weapons, on the other hand, creates a flow of adrenalin, which often leads, as indeed it did, to panic and confusion with untoward results. Subsequent analyses of this overblown joint-service military operation found that it was doomed from the start. It is my belief, however, that had it been kept simple, with a shrewd Farsi speaker at the helm, rescue might, I emphasize might, have been possible. Instead we suffered a tragic and considerable loss of American life and equipment.

A substantial amount of my time with the Intelligence Community was spent trying to bring about coordination among the various agencies with representatives at our embassies abroad. I briefed ambassadors, deputy chiefs of mission, political and economic officers, attachés, and other personnel prior to their departures overseas. Speaking to groups at various training facilities such as the Foreign Service Institute and the Defense Intelligence Agency became routine. I stressed the importance of Country Team cooperation and good reporting. More often than not, I did this in the company of my two IC Staff colleagues from the CIA and Defense Department. A matter that was always stressed was that at posts overseas the ambassador is the personal representative of the President of the United States. It was of paramount importance, therefore, that the ambassador be kept informed of all relevant activities. Officers might from time to time have differing views, but the ambassador set policy. Communications emanating from the embassy should have his approval. I say the above things, however, cognizant that other organizations in our government had their own channels of communication.

During these years, when I was on the IC Staff in Washington, I once again became engaged in duties as an Army Reserve officer. Upon my return from Cairo, I contacted the 352nd Civil Affairs Command with a request for an assignment and was promptly welcomed back to my former unit. At the time, paid training positions were scarce and I considered myself fortunate to be transferred from my unpaid mobilization slot in the Pentagon. I later heard that another officer, Colonel Wayne Jackson, had been seeking that vacancy but was disappointed when the Command became aware of my availability. As fate would have it, Jackson remained with the Pentagon and some time later was assigned to command our unit, and with it received a promotion to brigadier general. A fine officer, he was forever grateful for that turn of affairs.

There were four Civil Affairs Commands in the Army Reserve, each assigned to specialize in a given area of the world. The focus of 352nd was on the Middle East and Africa, areas with which I was familiar. I made an effort to convince colleagues in the active army of the need for training military personnel in civil affairs. The future pointed to greater involvement of the United States in the activities of other nations around the world. A penchant to "spread democracy" and overthrow authoritarian regimes, particularly when they were seen to be left-leaning or friendly toward the Soviet Union, presaged future actions on our part resulting in military intervention. Military operations are generally followed by peacekeeping and nation-building. For this our military should be prepared. The very motto of the Civil Affairs Branch of the Army states its case, "Secure the Victory."

From time to time, I spoke with Army War College classmates, and at one point even with the Army's deputy chief of staff for operations. The preponderance of civil affairs units were in the Reserve, with only one understrength battalion assigned to the 82nd Airborne Division at Fort Bragg, North Carolina. My concern was that this was unrealistic should the United States become enmeshed in any extended military operations in far off parts of the world. Either the Reserves would have to be called up for very lengthy periods or the Army would not be able to perform the vital civil affairs activities required.[8]

An opportunity arose when the U.S. Army Command and General Staff College (C&GSC) at Fort Leavenworth inquired in 1977 about the possibility of having an officer from our Reserve unit give a lecture on civil affairs. Our response was not only would we do that but we were prepared to provide the College with a full-length course on the subject. Shortly thereafter, my staff and I went to work preparing the course, which totaled 30 hours of instruction followed by a field exercise. Arrangements were then made for me and subsequently other officers to travel to Fort Leavenworth on tours of active duty to provide the series of lectures to the C&GSC students—officers at the captain and major level who had been selected for more senior positions. It was an eye-opener for them just to contemplate the kinds of activities they might encounter as the hostility phases into an occupation. Civil affairs units contain personnel capable of dealing with public administration, public safety, displaced persons and refugees, property control, labor and manpower, civilian supply, public welfare, communications, food and agriculture, education, public transportation, economics and commerce, arts and monuments, religious affairs, and other aspects related to the indigenous population.

With efforts over the years to constitute an all-volunteer force coupled with a diminishing defense budget in relation to overall government spending, I came to the conclusion that there was little chance of increasing to any substantial degree the numbers of civil affairs personnel in the active army. The latter was constantly decreasing in size, while its responsibilities around the world increased. The emphasis was on a "lean and mean fighting machine" with superb, costly, high-tech weapons. Civil affairs skills would perforce remain in the Reserve, leaving the problem of possible extended call-ups of reservists in case of war or military interventions of any sort.

By the summer of 1979, I had served a total of thirty-six years on active and reserve duty, five of those years as a colonel. The chances for promotion to brigadier general at the time were slim, and I was ready for retirement. The 352nd Civil Affairs Command held a heartwarming ceremony for me. I was particularly touched by the lengths the enlisted personnel went to express their affection. I think they sensed all along that I had been a private in the rear ranks once and understood them. Upon my departure, I was urged to remain in contact and to be available for consultation, which I have done.

I had acquired a broad range of experience in the military. I had been a soldier and paratrooper, a special agent rounding up ranking Nazis and war criminals, and a counterintelligence officer battling the Russians in Berlin. I had participated in the early development of the army's strategy for dealing with guerrilla activities and communist insurgency around the world. I had worked with the Special Warfare Center and Special Forces at Fort Bragg, and assisted in developing doctrine for those of us in special operations and civil affairs.

During my thirty-six years of service, I had been in uniform on actual active duty in one way or another for about a dozen years—almost five in and after World War II and the remainder in the Army Reserve. It had been an exciting and interesting part of my life, and I was grateful to have been able to couple it with my career as a member of the Foreign Service. My military experience throughout served to support my work for the State Department and, conversely, an understanding of the political and diplomatic aspects of situations involving the use of our armed forces at times was of benefit to the Army Reserve.

With the collapse of détente, demands for intelligence coverage of the Soviet Union increased and steps were taken to expand the IC Staff. In mid-1977, I was informed that an officer who had just completed a tour of duty as an ambassador would be assigned to our office. The Department of State was experiencing a glut at the top in its personnel system and very senior officers "were walking the halls" without positions, while at the same time the promotion process was being blocked. The IC Staff was a natural outlet. The newly assigned ambassador then became chief of the HUMINT Section. My duties, however, remained the same. Our office, thereafter, continued to have rather distinguished ambassadorial-level officers heading our section. One went on to be assistant secretary of state for East Asian affairs and another had been deputy assistant secretary for Europe. In the meantime, our office expanded with other personnel from the CIA and the Department of Defense. Perhaps as an indication of growing importance, the IC Staff was moved from CIA Headquarters in Langley to its own building in the immediate vicinity of the White House in downtown Washington.

An interesting aspect of my years in the Foreign Service entailed encountering, from time to time, people I had known earlier who had moved on to key positions in government. Perhaps the strangest of these occurred one day toward the latter part of my duty on the IC Staff. The ambassador then serving as head of our office notified me that the official to whom he reported, the newly assigned assistant director for the Intelligence Community, Theodore Shackley, wanted to see me. I had prepared a paper that had come to his attention and he wished to discuss its contents. During my meeting with him, he kept eyeing me with that look of "where have I seen you before?" It suddenly dawned on me that a Corporal Ted Shackley had been assigned to me for training as a special agent more than thirty years earlier, while I was in command of the Berlin Neukoelln CIC Field Office. He was with us for a few weeks and then, because he was fluent in Polish (his mother had emigrated from Poland), he was sent out to the displaced persons' camp to interview, and possibly recruit, refugees from the East.

Soon Shackley had also placed me, and a discussion of what had happened to mutual acquaintances ensued. In the years since Berlin, he had moved from CIC over to CIA and had become a legendary, if not notorious, figure.[9] He had been CIA station chief in Laos and Vietnam during the height of the war there and had been involved in a number of questionable activities. Prior to coming to the IC Staff, he had been assistant director of operations, CIA's clandestine service. I gathered from others that DCI Admiral Turner had eased him out of that position.

During the discussion with Shackley concerning old CIC acquaintances, I asked him about the German refugee, Master Sergeant Severin Wallach, who had been so helpful when I was an enlisted man in the paratroops in World War II and who had suggested during combat that I apply for a transfer to intelligence. Later in Berlin he was helpful in bringing me into CIC. I learned from Shackley that my benefactor had in the ensuing years also come over to the Agency. He had served in a number of places, lastly in Latin America. Other than that he was no longer in government service, Shackley knew nothing of his whereabouts. I would have welcomed the opportunity to contact him, especially meet him in person, and thank him for having changed the entire course of my life. Had I not met him, everything—education, career, marriage, and family—might have been different.

My association with Shackley was relatively brief, for I retired not long afterward. A year later, I learned that he too had retired from government service and had entered the business world. Subsequently during the Reagan administration, he was mentioned in press stories about illicit dealings. He was linked with Edwin Wilson and Thomas Clines, former CIA members under Federal investigation for involvement in illegal arms shipments to Libya and for the Iran-Contra affair. I remember being surprised at the time by these revelations. Clines at one point in 1976–77 had been the CIA representative on the interagency group I chaired to improve reporting from overseas.

During my years with the IC Staff, much emphasis was put on the collection of intelligence by technical means—satellites, U-2 and SR-71 overflights, communication intercepts, and the like. While there were a number of additions to the personnel of the HUMINT Section, I had the impression that our area, the use of human reporting from overt and clandestine sources, was being overlooked. In particular, reporting from clandestine sources overseas, difficult at best, should have been enhanced. Penetrating the Soviet Union, our major concern at that time during the Cold War, was a formidable task. It seemed to me that one tends to shrink from doing the difficult things, always seeking to find other ways to deal with situations.

In the final analysis, however, while technical means can provide information regarding capabilities, they rarely provide clues to what an adversary intends to do. That must come from human sources. America, for a variety of reasons, is only marginally adept at clandestine operations. We are an inward-focused people with a general lack of interest in foreign cultures and languages, despite our large immigrant population. The latter could and should provide a rich recruiting ground for developing strength in clandestine operations as new adversaries and situations come to the fore.

Certainly there has been ample evidence in the last two decades of the value of human intelligence collection, in terms of success on the part of both the CIA and its adversaries. With regard to the latter, one might cite the case of John Walker, who gave the Russians valuable information regarding American ballistic missile submarines. Perhaps the most spectacular example of human intelligence collection success in recent years, however, was the recruitment by the French of Lieutenant Colonel Vladimir Vetrov, an engineer working in the KGB's Directorate T, which had as its mission obtaining and analyzing Western technology.

According to an article in the *Washington Post* on February 27, 2004, President François Mitterand had informed President Reagan at an economic summit in Ottawa in 1981 about Vetrov's recruitment. Directorate T maintained hundreds of agents throughout the world who collected intelligence, and Vetrov was assigned to evaluate data coming in from them. He not only photographed over four thousand documents, which he provided to his French contacts, but also supplied a list of the many items the Soviets were seeking and the names of over two hundred of their agents.

The article indicated that a plan was devised to provide the Russians with a broad range of technology, skillfully doctored in such a way that when used in their equipment, it eventually led to breakdowns, occasionally with catastrophic results. By the time the Soviets realized what was happening, they were devastated, because large sectors of the economy had been affected. It was impossible to tell which equipment was actually flawed. The article pointed out that clever insertion of bogus software into gas pipeline programming technology, for example, caused pumps and turbines over time to create unacceptable pressures on the pipes and valves.

The *Washington Post* article went on to indicate that the result in one instance was an explosion so great that it caused serious concern in our North American Defense Command (NORAD). They feared a nuclear detonation had taken place and that there might have been a possible missile lift-off in a place where no rockets were known to exist. The impact of this activity, the article stated, on the Soviet economy, on currency earnings from overseas, and on the nation's infrastructure did much to bring about that country's collapse. Sadly, Colonel Vetrov, who was ideologically motivated to assist the West, was exposed by the KGB in 1983 and executed.

I had been with the IC Staff for three years when I received a telephone call from the State Department's personnel office asking me to drop by to discuss a unique assignment. I was informed that I was being considered for a position as the State Department's representative with the Sinai Peace Force. My experience in Egypt and military background made me particularly well suited for the job. In recent years, a brigade of the 101st Airborne Division had been rotated in and out of that desert outpost as part of the peacekeeping arrangement between Israel and Egypt. It was an unaccompanied assignment; there were no provisions for families. My wife and high school–attending son Matthew could reside either in the United States or in Rome, Italy, with provision for me to make frequent R & R visits. While fascinated by some aspects of the job, I was persuaded to say, "Thank you, no."

As 1979 was coming to a close, the nomination process for the presidential election of 1980 was in full swing. President Carter, the incumbent, was the natural Democratic candidate. By then, California Governor Ronald Reagan, George Herbert Walker Bush, my former boss as director of Central Intelligence, and several other aspirants were battling it out for the Republican nomination. I had always been intrigued by the political process and the more I thought about it, the more I now saw an opportunity to become involved at the national level. With Bush running, I had a candidate I actually knew and admired participating in a closely contested presidential campaign.

My combined State Department and active military service totaled thirty-five years, just the amount Foreign Service regulations set as the maximum time one could accrue for retirement purposes. I could have stayed on. However, here was an opportunity to gain the experience of a lifetime. I wrote a letter to James Baker, Bush's campaign manager, offering my services. I told him that I had considerable public policy and press experience and mentioned my association with his candidate. I received an immediate telephone call welcoming my offer. Early in 1980, therefore, I retired and joined the "George H. W. Bush for President" national campaign staff.

Due to the nature of my assignment to the IC Staff, I submitted this chapter for clearance to the CIA Publications Review Board. They helpfully suggested a number of deletions and alterations to prevent the disclosure of classified information and requested the inclusion of the following disclaimer:

All statements of fact, opinion, or analysis expressed are those of the author and do not reflect the official positions of the CIA or any other U.S. Government agency. Nothing in the contents should be construed as asserting or implying U.S. Government authentication of information or Agency endorsement of the author's views. This material has been reviewed to prevent disclosure of classified information.

17
An Education in Politics: The 1980 Bush and Reagan Campaigns

Early one morning in January 1980, I reported in to the George H. W. Bush for President National Campaign Headquarters at 732 North Washington Street in Alexandria, Virginia, a short distance across the Potomac River from the nation's capital. Upon arrival, I met Campaign Manager James A. Baker III; his administrative assistant, Margaret Tutwiler; David Keene, the political strategist; Peter Teeley, the press and public relations chief; and other members of the staff. A few were on the payroll; others were volunteers, many of whom had hopes for positions in a Bush administration, should their candidate be successful in his bid for the presidency.

I soon found that I was not the only person from the Foreign Service and CIA who wanted a taste of national politics. Moncrief (Monty) Spear, an old friend from the State Department, was working with a group dealing with issues likely to figure in the campaign. In addition, there were two colleagues who had been with the CIA and one with the U.S. Information Agency (USIA). Quite a number of young people were having the time of their lives in what seemed a made-for-television drama. They exuded a general air of excitement in what they were doing. Most of the volunteers had no experience in government on the national level. A few had been involved as volunteers in local politics. The paid staff had been through campaigns before and were specialists—campaign and political strategists, pollsters, and public relations and media people.

Bush's quest for the Republican Party nomination for the presidency had strong underpinnings. After President Carter had unceremoniously removed him from his position as DCI, he returned to Houston, Texas, and found himself at loose ends. It seemed all along, however, that with the experience he had gained as chairman of the Republican National Committee and in government, he had his eye on a run for the highest office in the land. Bush had many contacts and had made many friends. He was an inveterate note-writer, always dropping a word of congratulations or good wishes to individuals for this or that. Note-dropping was a trait

I witnessed in a number of successful people I had worked with over the years.

As early as 1976, the wheels had already been set in motion in Texas for a 1979–80 Bush campaign. Friends from President Ford's administration helped organize political action committees (PACs) for him. Texans Robert Mosbacher and James Baker became his finance manager and campaign manager respectively. Texas bankers and oil executives helped bankroll initial activities. By 1978, Bush had a well-coordinated effort underway. In May 1979, when he announced his bid for the presidency, therefore, it was no great surprise to many in the Republican Party.[1]

Shortly after I joined the campaign, we went into the Iowa caucuses. Considerable preparation had been done, for a victory there would have great psychological impact, if not actual political importance. Jimmy Carter had scored his first big success in Iowa and it had propelled him into the ring as a serious contender. Rich Bond on our staff, who did much of the advance work during the primaries, spent weeks out in Iowa before the caucuses. "Bush Brigades" were set up to tour all the precincts and the candidate himself worked the state tirelessly.

The Reagan campaign, on the other hand, evidently suffered from overconfidence. Their man had done exceedingly well in the Midwest in the 1976 presidential primary campaign, actually beating Gerald Ford, an incumbent president, by a considerable margin. Reagan was remembered fondly in the area for his radio sportscasting days. In a debate before the voting, Bush appeared with John Anderson, Robert Dole, Phil Crane, Howard Baker, and John Connally. A number of observers thought Baker came out best, but such was our campaign's groundwork that when the votes were counted, we prevailed. Reagan had simply watched the debate on TV at home in California.

When Bush won Iowa, there was a sense of elation among our head-quarters staff. But the victory by 2,182 votes over Reagan was in a sense a pyrrhic one. I think it took the well-organized Reagan camp by surprise, stirring them up to greater effort. Reagan had strong appeal with the hard-line conservatives of the Republican Party, while Bush, with his more moderate positions, drew in more middle-of-the-road supporters. Certainly Bush's views were closer to my own. I had generally been an independent voter over the years. Our campaign came out of Iowa echoing our candidate's declaration that we now had momentum! Bush, himself, referred to it as "Big Mo!"

That was a phrase he later was to regret, since it opened our campaign to derision as being lightweight, juvenile, and "preppy." The press commented that Bush was just an Ivy League rich kid and so were many on his campaign staff. I must admit that while not rich, I was Ivy League and so were some of us who had come out of the State Department and CIA to work for him. I am not sure of the sources—most likely an opposition strategist—but the term "wimp" in reference to Bush came into play with devastating effect.

At the very outset of my time with the Bush campaign, I sensed a dislike for the Reagan camp. If the feelings of antagonism were this strong in a situation involving two candidates within the Republican Party, I wondered what would things be like once the nomination process was over and the contest with the Democrats began. At one point we accused the Reagan campaign of using "dirty tricks" and took them to court in Alexandria, Virginia. I remember being assigned to sit in on the court proceedings and listen to the arguments of the lawyers. My ostensible duties, however, were largely in reviewing the press and developing releases for the media. On a few occasions when I saw a chance to insert a stratagem designed to make Bush look good, I took the matter up with Pete Teeley or, at times, Jim Baker.

Stefan Halper headed a section that dealt with policy and foreign affairs matters, and I recall talking with him a few times. However, rather than being involved in areas such as these, I tended to be used in a variety of operational matters as they arose. I recall one day accompanying Jim Baker to the Interdepartmental Auditorium on Constitution Avenue in Washington, D.C., where he was scheduled to speak to a group. I have long since forgotten who they were. When we arrived, we learned there had been a mix-up and we were an hour early. It made no sense to go back to Campaign Headquarters in Virginia, so we sat around and talked.

During our conversation, I inquired about his previous experience as under secretary of commerce in the Ford administration. In the natural flow of talk, it seemed a given that as Bush's campaign manager, should the latter become president, Baker would likely be appointed to some high-level post. With considerable diffidence he said he might be made under secretary of the Treasury. I had no idea then (and I wonder whether he had) that in a year he would be President Reagan's chief of staff, later secretary of the Treasury, and eventually Bush's secretary of state. I had worked in my time with a number of very capable senior officials, but none struck me as more able than James A. Baker, III.

I recall how once I embarrassed myself with him. I had come across something in the press which I believed to be exceedingly useful to our campaign effort and was prepared to tell him how we might expand on it. Going into Baker's office I proceeded to tell him how helpful the item was. He let me go on for a while and then with a slight smile quietly said, "John, I planted that story."

You would think that at the national campaign level, you would see a great deal of the candidate himself, but that was not the case. Bush was constantly on the road campaigning. He rarely came into headquarters, but would telephone in regularly to be brought up to date on events. I particularly remember briefing him very early one Sunday morning on events taking place overseas at the time, though I do not recall where he was telephoning from. There was always a constant flurry of advance people going out to various states prior to the primaries. With regard to assistance Bush received from his children in the campaign, I recall seeing quite a bit of Bush's son, Marvin, and to a lesser extent, Jeb, at National Campaign Headquarters. On the other hand, I was totally unaware of any role played by George W., his eldest son.

Bush received a serious setback during the campaigning in New Hampshire in February 1980. A debacle during the debate in the town of Nashua dealt our efforts a particularly hard blow. Controversy arose over who should be included in the debate. Bush was seeking to make it a one-on-one with Reagan, as had originally been scheduled, when four of the other candidates appeared. When Reagan moved to include the other candidates, the moderator, Jon Breen, wanting to remain with the two-man format, attempted to have microphones shut off. Thereupon, Reagan grabbed hold of the microphone and uttered his famous retort: "I'm paying for this microphone, Mr. Green (sic)!"

That action drew thunderous applause from the audience, effectively settled the question, and did much to dispel reservations some had about Reagan being too old to take charge as President. By contrast, the press had a field day making Bush appear small and petulant. Earlier, when the Federal Communications Commission ruled that the *Nashua Telegraph* could not cover the $3,500 cost of the debate, since it would be an illegal corporate contribution, the Reagan campaign had indeed funded the debate and thus did "pay for the microphone." In hindsight, it was a very wise move! Reagan went on to defeat Bush in the New Hampshire Primary on February 25, by 49 to 23 percent, with the remainder of the votes divided among the other candidates.[2]

The 1980 campaign progressed to other primaries, with the division between the hard-line Reagan conservative camp and the Bush moderates becoming ever more delineated, especially over such issues as an equal rights amendment for women and a more open-minded view towards abortion. The introduction by us of the term "voodoo economics" for Reagan's proposed fiscal policies particularly rankled the other side. Bush fared better in states with large urban populations, but Reagan had a strong hold on Republican Party stalwarts throughout the country.

I recall being in a meeting one morning prior to an upcoming primary. Jim Baker was saying that our funds were so low that we might not be able to participate there. By implication that would mean our national campaign was effectively over. I remember asking how much money we needed. His response was a figure of $85,000 or thereabouts. My incredulous comment to the effect, "We can't raise that amount of money?" brought a look from Baker that I will never forget. He was telling me in no uncertain way not to pursue the matter. That episode also told me that something was in the wind and that Bush might no longer be a serious candidate for the presidency.

However, we did win in Pennsylvania, Massachusetts, and Michigan. But Reagan at the same time won in Oregon, which by a rough tally gave him almost enough delegates to clinch the nomination. Although I did not have many dealings with him, David Keene, our political strategist, almost from the outset struck me as a reluctant camper. He was a relatively young but experienced, hard-boiled politico, a staunch conservative who seemed at odds with our campaign. Earlier he had worked for Reagan and Bob Dole. I had the feeling that he, more than Baker, would be the man to tell Bush to drop out of the race to enhance a chance of becoming Reagan's vice presidential choice. Later, I wondered whether I was right about that.

The other candidates had departed the race one by one, with the exception of John Anderson, who chose to run as an independent. Keene left our campaign after the South Carolina primary. The word was that he had been consorting with the Reaganites and that he and Bush no longer saw eye to eye. Our campaign, generally, did not do well in the South. A loss in May in the Texas primary, Bush's home state, was particularly telling.

As the Reagan juggernaut continued to roll, a certain tension was noted in our headquarters. Things were not going well and as the time for the California primary approached, Jim Baker went out to the West Coast. Financially, our campaign was in poor shape and there was considerable discussion among our staff as to what was going to happen next. Paid staffers had taken salary cuts, and I gathered some were receiving no money at all. I was told that Baker had held a press conference while in California in which he intimated, off the record, that we might be folding shop. Nevertheless, when he called a meeting at our headquarters in early June to tell us that it was all over and Bush would be dropping out, it came as a real shock to most. It was particularly hard on the young volunteers who suddenly found themselves at loose ends. One woman in her early thirties, a single mother, was visibly upset that the government job she had counted on receiving had suddenly evaporated. She was in tears. I remember asking, "That's it?" to which the reply was, "That's it!"

Publicly, Bush stayed in the race for a while to collect federal campaign matching funds. We were almost $400,000 in debt and he had promised to pay salaries owed to the staff and other obligations, which he eventually did. For me, the preceding months had been interesting and instructive. I was a bit disappointed that we were not going to battle it out at the Republican Convention in Detroit on the fourteenth of July, but it had been a great experience and I learned a great deal about American politics. I left our Alexandria campaign headquarters that June ready to immerse myself in my next chosen activity, which was returning to the artwork I had left early in my career. Reflecting back, so bitter had our battle been with the Reaganites that I saw no way of our people ever getting together with them. There had been some very vicious moments. Again, I was to learn a real lesson in American politics.

Despite the bad feelings, Bush seemed to be a natural choice as a vice presidential candidate, since it would bring together the moderates and the conservatives in the Republican Party. However, consideration in the Reagan camp was being given to enticing ex-President Ford into becoming Reagan's running mate. This apparently was thought by some to be a "dream team." Ford himself seemed amenable, but a series of statements he made did not sit well with Reagan and ultimately quashed his chances. In an interview with Walter Cronkite, for example, Ford spoke about a team in which Reagan would handle domestic matters and he foreign and defense affairs. When Cronkite referred to such a working relationship as a "co-presidency," Ford did nothing to dispel the idea.[3] Common sense would tell you any presidential candidate with even a bit of ego would react negatively to the prospect of sharing the Oval Office. Other than Bush, therefore, only Senator Howard Baker appeared to be a possible, but more distant, choice come convention time.

At the mid-July 1980 Republican Convention, Bush spoke glowingly about party unity and urged his delegates to get behind Reagan as the nominee. Reagan, after the rough campaign, probably had no real liking for Bush. Experienced political hands in the Reagan camp, however, apparently convinced their man that Bush rather than Howard Baker would do the most to assist in beating the Democrats in November. When the time came, Reagan chose Bush to join him on the ticket, much to the unhappiness of hard-line conservatives. It was later reported that Nancy Reagan was displeased about the choice; she preferred family friend Senator Paul Laxalt of Nevada. No longer in the throes of politics, I watched these things transpire on my TV set at home in Chevy Chase, Maryland.

In mid-August, I was busy at home working on an oil painting, when I received a call from someone I had known in the Bush campaign. She told me that many of my former colleagues had now moved over to the

Reagan camp. Arrangements had been made by Jim Baker during his June visit to California to have Bush delegates seated in the convention in July and they had supported Reagan. After all, she noted, we were all Republicans, and since Reagan and Bush were now the candidate team, we should work to put them in the White House. This also was an opportunity to demonstrate Bush supporters' loyalty to the party and appreciation to Reagan for having made our man his running mate.

I was uncomfortable with the right-wing Reagan crowd. However, after mulling the matter over, I reasoned that if I wanted to experience American politics, I had only been half-schooled. The real political race, Republicans vs. Democrats, had just begun. With that in mind, I reported into the Reagan for President National Headquarters off Columbia Pike in Arlington, Virginia, prepared to complete my education.

When I arrived, I was surprised to find many of the "Bushies" already there. I found myself teamed up with Monty Spears and Constance (Connie) Horner analyzing the media and preparing suitable responses for our candidates. To some extent, this was an operation involving late night and early morning hours, if we were to cover the press and media properly. Part of our concern, as I recall, was that John Anderson's independent candidacy was sapping support not only from the Carter/Mondale camp, but from Reagan/Bush as well.

Everyone was also conscious of a possible "October surprise." President Carter might succeed in arranging the release of the hostages the Iranians were holding captive. Later, it was revealed that negotiations had been under way to release Iranian assets that had been frozen and to provide spare parts for American military equipment in the Iranian arsenal as inducements for the release.[4] I recall preparing a paper for William "Bill" Casey, later CIA director, one Sunday analyzing various press reports dealing with the hostage crisis, which made me wonder whether our side had any private contact with the Iranians. It brought to mind regulations against persons out of government negotiating with a foreign power on matters involving the national interest.[5] While desirous of bringing the hostages home as expeditiously as possible, there was an obvious disadvantage to our campaign should the Carter administration succeed in doing so before the election.

On the surface, there was an effort to engender a spirit of cooperation in the headquarters. However, I sensed that the Bush volunteers tended to be regarded as second-class citizens and the genial atmosphere was not there. I found myself surrounded by people with a driving right-wing agenda. Young Gary Bauer, who later was to run for president as a "family values" archconservative, as well as Martin and Anneliese Anderson and others made me wonder what I was doing there. Relatively early on,

I met Ed Meese, the future attorney general. A good friend of mine from my Army Reserve unit, Colonel Phil Coleman, had asked me to extend his regards should I see Meese. Coleman and Meese had served together in the same civil affairs unit in California. I remember Meese's asking me how I had managed to attend the Army War College. I had no idea at the time what a formidable force in the future Reagan administration he would be.

The real marvel in the shift to the Reagan camp was Jim Baker's performance. That he as Bush's campaign manager in such a bitter primary contest could now so readily occupy a position of influence and become Reagan's chief of staff was a phenomenon.

Time moved quickly without the stages that primaries had delineated during the nomination race. Before I knew it, we were in the final week of October ready for a key debate in Cleveland, Ohio, between Carter and Reagan. The latter's sunny disposition and acting ability on that occasion gave him a distinct advantage over Carter, who appeared sallow and ill at ease. As Carter attacked him on various issues, Reagan repeatedly responded with the phrase, "There you go again." which amused the audience and became an awaited rejoinder. With great effect Reagan asked a series of questions directed at the audience couched in terms of "Are you better off today than you were four years ago?" He tied the query each time to rampant inflation, unemployment, crime, and America's world situation. He struck a nerve, touching directly on Carter's statement months earlier about America's being in a state of national malaise.[6]

A week later, Reagan was elected president of the United States. His victory presaged a shift in the American electorate. He won in forty-four of the states with a popular majority of 51 percent, a figure that would have been higher had John Anderson not drawn off a total of 7 percent from the other candidates. Reagan cut into the working-class vote, as well as the former "solid South," both of which had been Democratic preserves.

Once the election was over, our campaign status changed. We were now part of the Office of the President-Elect. Our headquarters moved from Arlington, Virginia, to M Street NW, in downtown Washington, D.C., and the focus of the staff became one of "Where will I fit into the new administration?" and "Will I get a job?" A form was passed out on which one provided a résumé and information for a transition personnel officer. There was a great deal of jockeying for position and concern. I recall meeting Gary Bauer one morning by the copying machine. His anxiety was palpable. Was he going to be given a job? As I look back on it now, he need not have feared. The way the office finally shut down, however, could have been improved. I recall going to work at our M Street office prior to the inauguration simply to find the doors locked.

Unceremoniously, things had been shifted over to the White House and the Executive Office Building without so much as a word to most of the people who had worked at M Street. Campaign workers arrived only to find themselves on the street. There was some frantic telephoning to persons on the transition staff inquiring about job openings.

A number of the volunteers with very modest backgrounds and qualifications were, within a relatively short time, to occupy Schedule C (political appointment) positions over far more highly qualified government employees. Bauer was to become under secretary of education. Our teammate Connie Horner, a former schoolteacher, subsequently became head of the Office of Personnel Management, the successor to the Civil Service Commission. A West Coast automobile dealer on the staff became the secretary of the Air Force, and so on. I contrasted this with the career progression in the Foreign Service, where a few years earlier one of our officers who had been a Rhodes Scholar with a fine record, but not competitive enough to pull him through a tight promotion and selection-out process, committed suicide.

In a democracy the spoils system seems to be a necessary part of the process. However, there should be a better way. I also remember how ridiculous it all seemed to me back in the days when I was on the UNESCO staff. Then a younger former assistant professor, who had been in the Kennedy campaign, was brought in under Schedule C to head our organization, which had senior officers with PhDs who could well have been presidents of universities. Indeed, some of our FSOs did retire to such positions. Back in 1968 our economic counselor in Tripoli left to become president of a university in Florida.[7]

When asked what sort of position I might be interested in after filling out my form, I indicated that if something suitable came up in the Department of Defense where I might be of service, I wished to be considered. However, I did not pursue the matter. As it was, I was secure financially. I had been in some form of government harness for thirty-eight years and it was time I looked to new horizons and my family. I could now do the things I had not been able to do over the decades and looked forward to the opportunity.

As January 20, 1981, neared, my wife and I received a large white envelope with an equally impressive, large gold-embossed invitation to attend the Inauguration of President-Elect Ronald Reagan and Vice President-Elect George Herbert Walker Bush, as well as another large one to attend the Inauguration Ball. Members of the National Campaign Staff received small gifts as mementos from the candidates.[8] When male members received a set of blazer buttons with the Vice Presidential Seal from

Bush, I was appreciative but amused, as they seemed in keeping with the "preppy" image critics had ascribed to us.

On Inauguration Day, Elsa and I went down to the Capitol to see the new president and vice president of the United States sworn in. That evening, accompanied by a host of others, we went to the Inaugural Ball, and with that my year in the cauldron of domestic politics came to an end. All in all, I had a memorable time in one of America's great political pastimes. Eight years later, when Vice President Bush was running for president again, I received a telephone call from one of his aides at National Campaign Headquarters urging me to rejoin the crusade. I politely declined. A little bit of learning goes a long way!

18
Epilogue

My year of education in campaign politics over, I took stock of what I wanted to do next. I had always intended to focus on my earlier vocation as an artist. Consequently, I took steps to familiarize myself with developments in that field. I enrolled in a short specialized course entitled "The Business of Art" at the University of Maryland. I also registered with the Corcoran School of Art for a semester of evening sessions in oil painting. My fellow students ranged widely from young college level aspirants to elderly retirees pursuing art as a hobby.

My earlier training put me at a stage beyond my classmates. I did, however, come away with an exposure to some of the newer materials and techniques for mixing oil paints and preparing canvases. The fact that I painted on expensive linen stretched over hardwood frames and used high-quality sable brushes and Rembrandt oils tended to set me apart. I also made my own heavy wooden frames, or miter-cut four-inch-wide, six-foot-long Florentine "sticks," for my pictures. The "sticks" were beautiful, gilded, ornately carved pieces of wood imported from Italy, which could be cut and then assembled into "museum" frames.[1]

I soon became aware that being able to set my own pace creating artwork was a disadvantage. There always seemed to be other demands on my time. Former Army Reserve colleagues called upon me to act as a consultant in matters dealing with civil affairs. The Army was reorganizing its civil affairs structure and I was asked to participate in the deliberations. I became involved in a program related to providing prosthetics for wounded and handicapped persons in several foreign countries.

I also found that my evenings were taken up in a variety of meetings. Our Chevy Chase United Methodist church was having problems with its minister. At the time he was being replaced I was approached by one of the leading parishioners to take over the position of chairman of the Administrative Board. Evidently word had been circulated that when a similar crisis had arisen in the American Community Church in Bonn,

Germany, I had been called upon to handle that situation diplomatical-ly.[2] Other church-related activities included my becoming a certified lay speaker (minister) of the Methodist Church.

Elsa and I intended to remain in the Washington area, with its focus on national and international affairs. We enjoyed attending functions at the State Department, foreign embassies, and Meridian House Interna-tional Center. Then, too, Washington has many cultural attractions, not the least of which is the National Opera, for which we had season tickets. As a member of DACOR, Diplomatic and Consular Officers, Retired, I take pleasure participating in its numerous activities. DACOR Bacon House, the club's residence near the White House, is a gracious setting for its member luncheons and programs. Many of its programs feature prominent speak-ers on aspects of foreign affairs. The opportunity to meet regularly on an informal basis with perceptive retired diplomats in the club's library to discuss current events provides insights not readily gained elsewhere.

An encompassing activity in retirement I had not anticipated grew out of responding to an item I saw in a newspaper in 1993 indicating that a reunion of veterans from the World War II 17th Airborne Division As-sociation was to be held later that year. I had spent so much time out of the country, I had no knowledge such a group existed. I was astounded to learn that the association consisted of 3,000 members and had been in existence since 1953.[3] Wartime comrades, I was told, had been searching for me for years.

Shortly thereafter, I attended a gathering of my old company in Bur-lington, Vermont, and then an annual association reunion in Pinehurst, North Carolina. It was a homecoming. Some of my old cohorts were more than surprised that the "college boy, wise-guy private" had meta-morphosed into a "responsible bird colonel." I soon became caught up in veterans affairs, was pressed into becoming a member of the association's board of directors, then historian, vice president, and subsequently presi-dent.

As historian of the 17th Airborne Division Association, a position I have now held for many years, I am charged with a vast amount of cor-respondence with veterans, their families, and others. The historian re-sponds to requests for information about wartime activities and maintains files, documents, unit histories, after-action reports, casualty lists, and nu-merous other items. In addition, the historian chairs a committee respon-sible for the disposition of numerous valuable artifacts in the association's War Room museum, which contains everything from weapons and uni-forms to paintings, medals, books, and more. The value of many of these items, individually, runs into the hundreds, if not thousands of dollars. It is now the committee's responsibility to ensure that much of this collection is placed in military museums in the United States and abroad, many of which have already expectantly approached the association.

My efforts as association historian led to the preparation of articles for military publications, especially the association's own journal, *Thunder from Heaven*.[4] To date, I have written more than two dozen articles on subjects related to airborne operations carried out by England, Germany, the Soviet Union, France, Japan, Italy, and the United States. Other authors have used accounts of my World War II activities in their books. Television's "History Channel" has presented a program on my wartime experiences on several occasions.

A New York TV producer at the time of this writing is creating a series of programs he expects to be shown in Germany and on public television in the United States entitled "Germans and Democracy." He has interviewed me extensively about my experiences spanning six decades.

Perhaps one of my strangest encounters came in 2000. With other members of the 17th Airborne Division, I met with veterans of the *Bund Deutscher Fallshirmjaeger* (German paratrooper association) at the site of our fateful airborne drop during World War II near Wesel, Germany. We assembled in a lovely little hotel in a forest but a stone's throw from where I landed on March 24, 1945. It was a convivial, yet poignant gathering of German and American World War II paratroopers, brave men sharing memories. "Politicians declare war and soldiers have to fight them," a handicapped German veteran told us. At one point, Erich Heiken, the vice president of the German association, a fine, warm-hearted man, who had suffered terrible head wounds, laughed, clapped me on the back, and joked, "John, you know I had you in my gun-sight while you were coming down that day. I'm glad I missed!"

The following day, the anniversary date of "Operation Varsity," we were joined by comrades from the British 6th Airborne Division at Diesfort German Military Cemetery for a memorial service. German, American, and British veterans, as well as family members, Wesel city officials, and townspeople gathered there to remember and honor the fallen.[5] I was asked to address the gathering, which I did first in English and then in German.

My veterans' affairs activities include serving as the Washington area representative for the 17th Airborne Division Association at ceremonies at Arlington Cemetery. For the past half-dozen years, I have been a speaker there on Airborne Veterans Day. In 1999, I gave a memorial address at the funeral of one of our division's paratroopers, a highly decorated sergeant, whose body was discovered in a shallow grave in the thick underbrush of Belgium's Ardennes Forest fifty-four years after he was killed.[6] The holder of the Silver Star, two Bronze Stars, and two Purple Heart medals, he was laid to rest with full military honors.

The 82nd and the 101st Airborne Divisions lived on after World War II, while the 17th over the years tended to be forgotten by the public at large. Not so for those who had fought in the snows of the Ardennes or lived through the hell that was "Operation Varsity." In 2002, the 17th Airborne Association moved to erect a magnificent bronze monument to honor its fallen and all those who had served in the Division. Two years later, the monument was completed on the "Field of Sacrifice" at Fort Benning, Georgia, the home of the U.S. Army's Airborne School. When I reflect on my days as a paratrooper private during World War II, never in my wildest dreams did I ever envisage that sixty years later I would be the person to give the dedication address. When I expressed surprise upon being asked to do so, I was told that "the Association wanted the speaker to be one of the Division's own." I have never received a finer or more humbling tribute.

Over the years, my wife and I have watched our children mature, marry, and provide us with eight grandchildren. My older son, Brad, after West Point, spent six years in the Army, left the service, obtained an MBA from Duke University's School of Business, and then worked for a decade with the Naval Air Systems Command as the deputy program manager for the F-14 fighter plane. He left that position to become the chief engineer of the National Administration for the Blind and the Handicapped, a branch of the Library of Congress with offices in forty-nine states. The family likes to quip, he went from "bombs to beneficence!" Our daughter, Andrea, after Dartmouth, earned an MBA from Stanford, worked as vice president for GT International, an investment management firm, first in San Francisco and then in London, where she married a British financier. She now heads her own international marketing firm. Our younger son, Matthew, after graduating from McDaniel College, served as an Army intelligence officer. He subsequently worked for Naval Intelligence and the Transportation Security Administration. He has become one of our government's leading experts on counterterrorism and the Middle East.

At the height of the Cold War in 1983, my long-standing concern about the possibility of some form of catastrophic attack on Washington led to action. My wife and I had been thinking of purchasing a vacation home at the shore. However, after considerable thought we chose instead to buy a house and a speedboat on a large lake in the mountains of western Maryland, which could also serve as a retreat. "Eagle's Tarn" can accommodate the entire family. It has become a source of togetherness and enjoyment for us throughout the year, with swimming, boating, and fishing from our dock in the summer and skiing on the nearby slopes in the winter.[7] At an altitude of 2,600 feet, the deck at Eagle's Tarn looks out above Deep Creek Lake. In spring and autumn, with gatherings of family and friends often numbering fifteen people, we host "dock parties" to put in and haul out the dock's heavy sections from the lake. Afterwards at sunset, an outdoor meal on the deck often elicits the comment, "It doesn't get any better than this!"

Over several decades our family has survived the vicissitudes of Foreign Service life on four continents and remains close-knit. My concern today is for the existence my four grandsons and four granddaughters, all bright and healthy children, will have in a world that increasingly shows signs of continual turmoil. Scientific advancement and technology, while a boon in many respects, carry with them inherent debilitation at best and destructive forces at worst. It pains me to watch children playing mindless video games for hours on end.

On the world scene, I am alarmed seeing weapons becoming ever more lethal. After the carnage of World War II, it seems that the promises of world cooperation at the founding of the United Nations have evaporated. While the scourge of communism and the Cold War have blessedly passed on, we are now confronted with what may be a "clash of civilizations," of Islam against the West. Then, too, the specters of the proliferation of weapons of mass destruction and international terrorism cast a pall over everything.

Reflecting on my years with the State Department, I would be remiss if I did not comment on those I worked with in the Foreign Service. They were a superb lot, dedicated and hard working. For those who came from a privileged background, there was a sense of *noblesse oblige*. When it came to hazardous assignments, the State Department never lacked for volunteers. The Foreign Service was often criticized for being "elitist" and full of "striped pants cookie pushers," but many staffed dangerous hardship posts in Africa, Asia, and Latin America without complaint.

I will never forget a conversation I had with an Army officer in Libya right after the 1967 Arab-Israeli War. He was complaining about an interruption in the commissary supplies flown in for his people by American military aircraft. When I mentioned that my Foreign Service staff had to live off the economy, he responded, "Your families are used to hardship." Four FSOs I worked with over the years were assassinated. Three had become ambassadors and the fourth a deputy chief of mission. Many of our FSOs had also fought in the military in our nation's wars and were highly decorated veterans.

My years with the Army—first as an enlisted man, then as an active and Reserve officer—did much to shape my views toward war and its aftermath. I believe it gave me a sense of the military's role in national and world affairs, what it could accomplish and what it should not be called upon to do. As fewer members of Congress and the Executive Branch and their family members serve in the armed forces, there seems to be an inherent lack of appreciation for the social, political, and economic consequences of our military becoming overcommitted around the world.

America has been and should be the nation of the citizen-soldier. Our armed forces should be representative of all sectors of society. The current all-volunteer concept, while fielding an effective fighting force, has as a consequence enabled the more affluent and influential in our nation to avoid service, which is not in keeping with the concept of democracy as envisaged by our founding fathers. George Washington wrote in 1783:

> It may be laid down as a primary position, and the basis of our system, that every Citizen who enjoys the protection of a free Government, owes not only of his property, but even of his personal service to the defence of it.

As I look back, I believe I was fortunate to have lived at the time I did. I grew up when Lindbergh flew across the Atlantic alone and horse-drawn wagons were used to deliver milk to New York City apartment dwellers. With World War II, I made my first flight in an early airplane, only to jump out as a would-be paratrooper. I witnessed the collapse of Nazi Germany and had a role in punishing members of that criminal regime. In Berlin, 1945–1947, I was among those who early warned about and fought in the Cold War.[8] As a diplomat I had a bit role in fostering the rise of democracy in Germany.

On the other hand, I was a political officer in our Embassy in Manila when dictator Ferdinand Marcos came to power and in Libya as the scene was set for the takeover by Muhumar al-Quadhafi. I was in Egypt after the 1973 "Yom Kippur War" and watched as our Middle East diplomacy did little to set the United States on a proper course for relations with the Muslim world. Throughout the years, for reasons I have yet to fathom, I always seemed to have been where things were happening. For that I am grateful, but also sad that events at times turned out as they did, for they meant hardship and suffering for many. Throughout it all, however, it was a wonderful course I was permitted to run over these many years. Now as I close, I render a final salute to all of the talented and courageous colleagues in the Foreign Service and the military with whom I was privileged to serve.

Notes

1. Boyhood Years

1.   Dr. Leff's Hospital, which no longer exists, was located on 111th Street between Fifth and Madison Avenues in New York City.

2.   The entire area north of 110th Street and Fifth Avenue was demolished and is now a vast housing development.

3.   The part of Hermann Behr's property that is now a cloverleaf on New York Interstate 287 was at State Route 59 in Nanuet, New York.

4.   P.S. 170 was located at 111th and 112th Streets between Fifth and Lenox Avenues.

5.   The High School of Music and Art, 135th Street and Convent Avenue.

6.   A two-building apartment house complex, 521–523 West 112th Street.

7.   Three of Berton Braley's poems may be found in Hazel Felleman, *Best Loved Poems of the American People* (New York: Doubleday, 1936).

8.   First German Baptist Church of Harlem, located in the 1930s at 118th Street between Second and Third Avenues, no longer exists.

2. Young Manhood

1.   The ship's policy in this regard was very strict. Only ship's officers and seamen having specific duties were allowed on the passenger decks.

2.   Reflecting on the matter now, sitting with feet dangling over the bow, at times in heavy waves and swells, was not a very sensible thing to do, but I was young and fearless.

3.   In later years, it was impossible to detect where that stand had been located, for the city has expanded far beyond the jungle area described.

4.   Bernhard Kranke's jeweler's establishment was located on 41st Street between Fifth and Madison Avenues.

5.   In later years, my wife damaged a ring I had given her in Berlin in 1947 by accidentally cracking the green chrysoprase stone into which an intricate family crest had been carved. All efforts to restore the ring had been fruitless until taken to an old world jeweler in New York City's Maiden Lane district.

6.   Each brokerage house and stock exchange had areas with boxes, similar to those in a post office, where stock certificates would be placed for transmittal.

Today, of course, dispatching stock certificates to and from buyers and sellers is a thing of the past. Brokerage houses now hold the customers' stocks in "street name."

7.   It is interesting to note that the "selectivity/desirability" of Ivy League colleges changes over the years. When my daughter Andrea went to college in the 1970s, she chose Dartmouth as the "in school," although she had her choice of any of the others. Currently, it seems that Brown University enjoys a similar reputation.

8.   The test I took for entrance to Columbia College, as I recall, was called the Thorndike Examination.

9.   Dr. Brown expresses these thoughts in an article on page 17 of Edward R. Morrow's book *This I Believe* (New York: Simon & Schuster, 1952). However, my mother expressed them in much the same words twenty years earlier.

10.   The intervention of my mother in my life at times had far-reaching consequences. The plea to "be merciful" in combat is described later on in the book.

11.   Had there been an Army ROTC at Columbia, I probably would have enrolled in it, since I sought air cadet training. The Air Force did not come into being until after World War II. Not wishing to enter the U.S. Navy, which at the time had V-5 and V-12 programs at Columbia, I did nothing. Although the local draft board assured me that I would be able to opt for air cadet training upon being drafted, it did not work out that way. Once receiving the "greetings" letter, one simply became a victim of the vagaries of the Army system.

3. "You're in the Army Now!"

1.   In hindsight, considering the importance of the AGCTs, for a variety of reasons there should have been some provision for retesting. For example, I noted that some draftees were ill from inoculations.

2.   Although there was no allotment of monthly pay to dependents in my case, there was still a deduction from my $21 for the mandatory $10,000 insurance policy.

3.   Had the Army processing been more efficient, it would have focused on my college training and fluent German language ability. Eventually I arrived in a position where I was able to be of maximum use to the Army, but only after much wasted time, and then largely by chance.

4.   The Army Specialized Training Program (ASTP) was of benefit to participants, particularly since in many cases college credit was later given. However, for the government it was largely a bureaucratic waste, because the training was not put to use, nor were any commissions awarded.

5.   Despite some efforts to imitate West Point, ASTP at Rhode Island State College was a far cry from that institution.

6.   I have no record of the action. However, I believe my name was submitted for paratrooper training at that juncture.

7.   Many ASTP students at Rhode Island State College were sent to the 78th (Lightning) and the 26th (Yankee) Infantry Divisions. A few, including the author, went to the 17th Airborne Division. ASTP, with the exception of the medical program, was stopped abruptly in early 1944. Many students, who were the upper

strata of Army enlisted personnel, simply became infantry division replacements. One of my roommates was killed in combat in that process.

8.   The CG-4A Glider was produced by four companies in the United States at a cost of about $40,000 each. It was the basic glider used by the U.S. airborne and, to some extent, the British airborne forces. A total of 19,900 were produced. For further information see *Silent Wings* by Gerard M. Devlin, (New York: St. Martin's Press, 1985).

9.   My son volunteered for parachute training at Ft. Benning, Georgia while at the U.S. Military Academy in 1974.

10.   That jumper was Private Cecil Cruttenden, a friend and later fellow motorcycle courier, now deceased.

11.   The British "Hamilcar," a large glider capable of carrying a small tank, was used in "Operation Varsity."

12.   "Operation Dragoon, " the airborne invasion of southern France, was launched on August 15, 1944, by the First Allied Airborne Task Force, which included among others, the U.S. 517th Parachute Infantry Regiment, the British 2nd Independent Brigade Group, the U.S. 509th and 551st Parachute Infantry battalions, and the 550th Glider Infantry Battalion.

13.   "Operation Market Garden," the airborne invasion of Holland on September 17, 1944, included the U.S. 82nd and 101st Airborne Divisions, the British 1st Airborne Division, and a Polish Brigade. The 17th Airborne Division, originally scheduled to go, did not participate for lack of air transport.

14.   In 1942, over 700 Allied merchant vessels fell prey in the Atlantic to U-boats. Although the situation had improved by 1944, U-boats posed a constant danger.

15.   Mickey Rooney was reported in so many places in World War II that I wondered whether he actually was aboard the U.S.S. *Wakefield*.

4. Under a Wartime Sky

1.   I was amazed when returning to the Chiseldon Barracks area in the year 2000 with a group of 17th Airborne Division veterans to find no trace of the buildings, including the large mess hall and the field hospital. We found only open fields and a narrow tree-lined road, likely the main street of the camp.

2.   The First Allied Airborne Army (FAAA) was commanded by U.S. Air Corps Lt. Gen. Lewis Brereton. His deputy was British Lt. Gen. Frederick (Boy) Browning. FAAA included the 82nd, 101st, and 17th U.S. Airborne Divisions; the 1st and 6th British Airborne Divisions; the Polish Airborne Brigade; various small foreign Allied airborne units; and American and British tactical air carrier groups.

3.   The 17th Airborne was attached to Lt. Gen. Troy Middleton's VIII Corps for ground fighting in the Battle of the Bulge by General Orders, 3rd Army (Patton), effective January 1, 1945.

4.   Accounts of the 101st Airborne Division's action at Bastogne may be found in Clay Blair, *Ridgway's Paratroopers* (Garden City, N.Y.: Dial Press, 1956), and Gerard M. Devlin, *Paratrooper* (New York: St. Martin's Press, 1979).

5.   This unusual glider action is recounted in Gerard M. Devlin, *Silent Wings* (New York: St. Martin's Press, 1985), pages 294–97.

6.   The NCO was Master Sergeant Severin Wallach, who later saw to it that I was attached to the 17th CIC Detachment in the aftermath of "Operation Varsity."

7.   I often regretted not keeping that unusual weapon. Had I acquired it more toward the end of the war, when I was in CIC, I might have done so.

8.   There were several airborne operations under consideration, among them "Operation Eclipse," a drop of two American airborne divisions (82nd and 101st) on Berlin and the much larger scheme, "Operation Arena," which contemplated landing six Airborne divisions (U.S. 13th, 17th, 82nd, and 101st and British 1st and 6th) 200 miles into Germany near Kassel.

9.   I was so angered by my mother's letter that I almost wrote to her about it before departing on the flight to Germany. That would have been a most unfortunate mistake.

10.   The new C-46 "Air Commando" had a grievous weakness, its exposed fuel lines, which made it vulnerable. The planes were dubbed "Flaming Coffins." Ironically, the two parachute regiments (507th and 513th) in the 17th Airborne initially vied with one another as to which would have the honor of flying in the C-46 in "Varsity." The 513th as the more senior in time with the division won out, with the result that many of its paratroopers were killed.

11.   I have recounted to audiences on several occasions the "be merciful" incident, which could have been a major tragedy. In story form, it was featured in the *Washington Post*'s special section of May 28, 2004, at the time of the dedication of the World War II Memorial in Washington, D.C.

12.   It was a foolish macho decision. The knee wound, which took a long while to heal, had serious consequences for me in later life requiring surgery. As a result, I received neither the Purple Heart nor the Bronze Star.

13.   *Ridgeway's Paratroopers*, pages 459–61, gives an informative account of the losses in planes and gliders.

14.   Lt. Gen James M. Gavin *On to Berlin: Battles of an Airborne Commander, 1943–1946* (New York: Viking Press, 1978), 309. The figures given by Gavin as to losses in personnel, however, are low and do not appear to match with official casualty lists. He uses the figure of 23,680 participating in the drop. That was larger than the total complement of the two airborne divisions, normally. However, a significant portion of both airborne divisions crossed the Rhine along with the ground attack. The Allied airborne figure for participants in the "Varsity" drop is 17,200.

15.   The Allied losses generally attributed to "Operation Varsity" were 1,070 killed and over 3,000 wounded. However, the time frame for those figures is not clear. In a study done by Professor William C. Mitchell for the 17th Airborne Association, he compares "Varsity" to the losses of the 2nd Marine Division's (18,000-man) attack on Tarawa, generally considered one of the most intense of World War II. In three days, 894 Marines were killed.

16.   The 17th Airborne Division had four recipients of the Congressional Medal of Honor, the most of any airborne division in World War II. It also had almost double the average daily casualties of any of the airborne divisions in the war, although it was not as long in combat.

5. Assigned to Intelligence

1.   Given its expanded mission, there was an immediate need for additional CIC personnel. The loss of agents killed and wounded in "Varsity" compounded the problem.

2.   Field Marshal Walther Model was asked to surrender his 300,000 German troops. He refused and committed suicide instead.

3.   *Arrest Categories Handbook*, SHAEF, April 1945.

4.   Numerous sources touch on Nazi organizations: Franz Neumann, *Behemoth* (New York: Oxford University Press, 1942); John G. Kormann, *U.S. Denazification Policy in Germany, 1944-50* (U.S. High Commission for Germany Historical Division, 1952). The most definitive, however, is the party's own publication: *Organisationsbuch der Nationalsozialistischen Deutschen Arbeiterpartei* (Munich: NSDAP, 1943).

5.   A graphic description of the final days in Berlin may be found in Antony Beevor, *Berlin, the Downfall, 1945* (London: Viking Press, 2002).

6.   The Franklin D. Roosevelt Library/Museum at Hyde Park, New York, was pleased to receive the plaque and a piece of the red marble from Hitler's office for its new wing, which was soon to be constructed.

7.   The alias most used was Special Agent Robert King, or Mr. King.

8.   The 970th CIC Detachment subsequently in the 1950s became the 66th CIC Group.

9.   The portrait in its massive gold frame was almost 7 feet high and 5 ½ feet wide and weighed almost 50 lbs.

10.   In 2003, Marguerite (Maggie) Higgins was honored posthumously as the subject of a U.S. postage stamp in the "Women in Journalism" series.

11.   I never did find out what became of the scientist.

12.   Another forerunner of organization names prior to the CIA was the SSU (Special Service Unit).

13.   Kormann, *U.S. Denazification Policy in Germany, 1944–1950*, provides an extensive bibliography of books, articles, and government documents that touch on this subject.

6. Berlin's Treasure Trove

1.   To my knowledge, no CIC special agent was kidnapped during those years, but this was certainly as close a case as one could imagine.

2.   In actuality, I was in the final stages of completing the processing for civilian employment when I learned I would have to give up commanding the Neukoelln Subregion. My negative reaction and failure to complete the process irritated the Army personnel section.

3.   Elsa Wells, my future wife, at age seventeen taught English at Dueppel Center, a refugee camp for victims of the concentration camps. One of her instructions was never to discuss her students' experiences with them because it was too traumatic and painful.

4.   To use up the liquor, a "birthday party" was even celebrated for my dog Socrates. The invitees were sent printed invitations. Berlin was a party town!

5.   It made sense to have the prisoner escorted by a CIC officer escort who had a special ID and badge, as well as the authorization to carry a weapon.

6.   Fort Holabird, Baltimore, Maryland, was the CIC training center.

7.   In those days, without air-conditioning to take the moisture out of the air, life must have been miserable for those stationed on that damp air base in the Atlantic Ocean.

7. The Return to Civilian Life

1.   My father-in-law, Roger Wells, an officer in World War I, was a founding member of the American Legion. Nevertheless, for most of my life I had little to do with veterans' organizations, until at age seventy I became actively engaged with the 17th Airborne Division Association, subsequently becoming its president and historian.

2.   Cavanaugh's Restaurant no longer exists in that location.

3.   The incident described has subsequently been the subject of a sermon and numerous talks to church groups and service clubs.

4.   Eisenhower was not a popular figure at Columbia University, which had been used to having presidents who were leading scholars, such as Nobel Peace Prize laureate Nicholas Murray Butler. Eisenhower's draconian actions did not help. Had he not been induced to run for President of the United States, one wonders whether he would have remained at Columbia.

5.   In retrospect, my challenging Eisler in a meeting filled with leftists and Communists was risky. I might have been taken for an FBI plant.

6.   The process was a typical example of bureaucratic myopia. I did not again encounter the personnel officer who turned me away at the JPA level.

7.   The Drano story is one of the better teaching illustrations. I have used it often.

8.   While many of the diplomatic niceties are still employed, card-bending is largely an outmoded practice.

9.   Ship voyages had a great many advantages over today's jet plane travel. The officer not only could take a great deal of clothing, but crated household effects, months of food supplies, and a vehicle. These were all in the ship's hold ready to be off-loaded and available upon arrival. Today one might wait months until those things arrived.

8. Governing Occupied Germany

1.   *Field Organization of the Office of the High Commissioner for Germany* (HICOG, Historical Division, 1952).

2.   I returned to the Hohenfels Training Area in 2001, fifty years after it was requisitioned by the U.S. Army. By that time, it was a major facility with office buildings, a housing complex, PX, and the rest. It had become NATO's prime tank-training area, used by the various countries in that multinational organization.

3.   There are a number of works on military government; see, for example, Harold Zink, *American Military Government in Germany* (New York: Macmillan,1947), and Hajo Holborn, *American Military Government: Its Organization and Policies* (Washington: Infantry Journal Press, 1947).

4.   This was a tragic aspect of the closing down of the occupation. Many loyal German employees were stigmatized by their countrymen for having worked for the Americans.

5.   The Germans watched the presidential race between Dwight Eisenhower and Adlai Stevenson in 1952 with great interest.

6.   The Queen's birthday was always celebrated in June, so as to take advantage of better weather.

7.   In 2003, the centennial of Kennan's birthday, there was a major celebration and symposium at Princeton University, where he had spent his later years as a professor. Kennan was alive and active. I was present on that occasion and recalled the SS *America* homecoming incident to the organizers.

8.   The Cohn and Shine escapades in West Germany, taking "Communist" and so-called "leftist" books off the shelves of American information centers, was an embarrassment and defaming in the eyes of the Germans.

9.   Robert (Bob) Lochner was the son of famed journalist and foreign correspondent Louis Lochner.

10.   Kay Boyle, the noted American novelist, was under investigation for having "leftist" views and alleged links to the Communist party. Franckenstein as a young man in the 1930s apparently was a member of a Communist youth group.

9. Washington: Challenges and Opportunities

1.   The Francis Scott Key Hotel on 20th Street NW between E and F Streets in Foggy Bottom was a favorite place to stay for FSOs returning from overseas. It no longer exists. The property is now part of the George Washington University.

2.   For an interesting and intimate account of the Operations Coordinating Board see Roy M. Melbourne, *Conflict and Crises* (Lanham, Md.: University Press of America, 1993). Melbourne is a former FSO and was deputy staff director of the OCB.

3.   I raised the point in one of the meetings that the procedure might be considered a form of censorship. However, it had then already been in effect for some time. The overall national concern with communism and its readily assumed subversive nature simply ran roughshod over any rational objections.

4.   Kennedy's record in the Senate was less than impressive.

5.   It was fortunate for the Kormanns that one of the neighbors was a builder who taught me a few things about home maintenance.

6.   In those days, the concern the FBI and the Department of State had when one met with a Russian official in the United States was ludicrous. Overseas in the course of contact at social and other functions it was more relaxed. Even then, however, any substantive discussion had to be reported in a memorandum of conversation.

7.   In a first meeting after Sputnik went up, American scientists who were members of the U.S. National Commission for UNESCO correctly indicated that within a short period of time we would surpass the Russians in space, simply because we could outstrip them in basic research and had the industrial might to support projects the Soviets could not match. Even at that early juncture, they were absolutely correct.

8.   While I was a resident officer in Germany in the early 1950s, I received several visits from HICOG education officials who derided the two-track system and urged me to laud the American system as being in keeping with a democracy.

9.   In hindsight, there was an element of risk in having a former intelligence officer accompanying the delegation. I should have raised the matter at the time.

10.   The Special Warfare Center in its infancy was in an old wooden building on "Smoke Bomb Hill." It was a far cry from the elaborate structures now in existence. With the focus now on battling terrorism and strengthening Special Forces, even more resources should be available.

11.   Milton Barall was a colonel in the Army Reserve. In the State Department, he was the chairman of the Caribbean Study Group, with the personal rank of ambassador.

12.   Henry Wriston was a distinguished educator and president of Brown University who served in a number of government positions. He was chairman of a commission to reorganize the State Department.

13.   With requirements in 2005 growing out of the war in Iraq, the number of persons taken into the Foreign Service has expanded considerably.

14.   Controversy developed after my departure regarding P/PG's relationship with the National Student Association, especially in terms of the latter's participation in communist-sponsored World Youth Festivals.

15.   I never did learn what transpired when the Finnish embassy was informed of the mistake.

16.   That InfoGuide became the definitive statement of U.S. policy on the Sino-Soviet split.

17.   It was later reported that Secretary Herter had been in the Oval Office when the U-2 flight was discussed and urged against its being undertaken.

10. The Philippines: From Macapagal to Marcos

1.   The American community in Manila alone at that time numbered about 10,000 persons. Vestiges of an American colony were everywhere.

2.   Paul Kattenburg became a distinguished professor at the University of South Carolina after leaving the Foreign Service.

3.   As the most powerful nation in SEATO, the United States had great influence and used it to press for Vargas's appointment.

4.   Visitors to the Philippines were always anxious about the state of "the Communist uprisings," associating them with links to the Soviet Union or Communist China. In reality, they had more to do with the state of poverty in the country or, in the southern Philippines, with Muslim irredentism.

5.   The fact that Indonesia, a Muslim country, would also present a problem regarding Ramadan was never mentioned at the time.

6.   I undertook many control officer assignments and secretly wished I had been given the Nixon visit and the opportunity to become more closely acquainted with him. A control officer occasionally may spend extended periods of time alone with the visitor.

7.   Raymond Bonner, *Waltzing with a Dictator* (New York: Times Books, 1987).

8.   Stanley Karnow, *In Our Image: America's Empire in the Philippines* (New York: Random House, 1990).

11. The Libyan Adventures

1.   Normally when one was assigned to an Arabic-speaking country, particularly to a more isolated post, one would be given Arabic language training beforehand. In my case there was a need to man the position promptly, and arrangements were made for me to study at post.

2.   Personal friendship was highly regarded among the Bedouins. Arab members of my household staff remained loyal even after the Arab-Israeli War of 1967 broke out and America became the subject of much criticism for supporting Israel.

3.   The aged USS *McCard* was the flagship of the commodore's destroyer squadron.

4.   The British frigate was the HMS *Lowestoft*.

5.   Mario Martinez, *The Lady's Men* (Annapolis, Md.: Naval Institute Press, 1995), provides a detailed account of the *Lady Be Good* tragedy.

6.   Weeks before my trip into the desert there had been a fatal accident involving an oil exploration team encountering a slip-faced dune.

7.   In the early 1990s, my son Matthew borrowed photographs of the Kufra expedition to lend to a colleague who worked with him in Naval Intelligence. That person was Jonathan Pollard, who was later imprisoned for espionage. The photographs were never recovered and were possibly sent to Israel.

8.   The British had been reducing its overseas commitments. While it still maintained a position in Hong Kong at the time, its departure from Libya in February 1968 seemed to many as the end of an era, the sun setting on the British Empire.

9.   The decision not to provide two of the five gas masks to the women was a difficult one, but necessary if the destruction of highly classified material was to be accomplished.

10.   The photograph and message signed by the staff is now in the President Johnson Library and Museum in Austin, Texas.

11.   Years later persons who have seen the log book in the National Archives have commented with surprise about the attack on Embassy Office Benghazi.

12.   The attack was not made public until 1999, when an account appeared in *Life in the Foreign Service*, a collection of stories on the DACOR website.

13.   Mayor Bin Younis visited the United States at U.S. government expense in 1970. He did not have an opportunity to meet with any high-level officials and was offended by his treatment. I learned about the matter too late or I would have tried to assist.

14.   Benghazi's hardship allowance at the time was 15 percent. Some posts elsewhere received allowances as high as 25 percent.

12. The State Department and African Affairs

1.   Unlike the military, where families can be moved from one military post to another that has housing, schools, hospitals, etc., the Foreign Service generally is expected to ensconce themselves within the local community overseas. This usually places a burden on the household, particularly on the spouse.

2.   I was sorely tempted to report the major. The loss of the classified documents, which contained comments about Liberian military programs, might well have caused problems between our governments. By then I had been promoted to lieutenant colonel in the Army Reserve.

3.   The 354th Civil Affairs Area (B) was responsible for the Middle East and Africa. It also served as the unit assigned to train with, and subsequently support, the 82nd Airborne Division (the Rapid Deployment Force) in the event of activation.

4.   There have been numerous articles written about the plight of the displaced inhabitants of Diego Garcia who have not been assimilated into their new environments. After all these years, they still seek to return to their former island.

5.   *U.S. Military Assistance to Africa: Problems and Prospects*, a monograph by John G. Kormann, U.S. Army War College, 1973, provides data and analysis of the program at that period.

6.   Ibid.

7.   The author recently came across a Web site dedicated to individuals who had formerly worked at the Kagnew communications facility.

8.   See further references to Lieutenant Colonel Fritz Kraemer in Chapter 9, "Washington: Challenges and Opportunities."

13. A Year at the Army War College

1.   *Officer Biographic Sketches, 1973*, U.S. Army War College, Carlisle Barracks, Pa., is a large bound volume containing bios of faculty, students, and administrative personnel.

2.   Several of the war college students had PhDs. Some were authors and established military historians.

3.   The TV program *It's Academic* continues at this writing and is considered one of the better instruments for promoting excellence in education.

4.   I learned that Brigadier General Edward T. Meyer, the college's deputy commandant at the time, also had a hand in informing the Pentagon about my qualifications. General Meyer, a superb officer, rose to become a four-star general and army chief of staff.

5.   At the time of this writing the Reserves are suffering numerous casualties in Iraq and are subject to repetitive tours. The highest-ranking military casualty to date, for example, was a lieutenant colonel from the author's 352nd Civil Affairs Command.

6.   President Nixon's harsh pronouncement was a death sentence for Curt Moore, a fact which has not been forgotten by his friends.

7.   The author's status as a diplomat lent itself to a number of hilarious cartoons in the publication. The military loved to poke fun at the State Department.

14. Munich, An Interrupted Tour

1.   Enlisted personnel below the rank of sergeant were not permitted to bring dependents overseas. Some wives followed their husbands, nevertheless, and lived on the economy, a number seeking employment in German households. This world "turned upside down" was noted by the Germans.

2.   It was the time of the Cold War when the United States had over 200,000 troops stationed in Germany.

3.   The tendency of the more affluent Germans to look down on the American military irritated me. In the United States, the average citizen regarded our military as "patriotic citizens," but in Germany ironically they were seen as a symbol of that nation's weakness.

4.   Franz-Josef Strauss was a mercurial figure in German politics who had been the Federal Republic's minister of defense. From time to time there were reports he might become chancellor of Germany. See President Jimmy Carter's comments about him in his memoir, *Keeping Faith* (New York: Bantam Books, 1982), 500–501.

5.   Later during the Reagan administration, my cousin Franz told of an encounter he had had with American ambassador to Austria Helene Von Damm (President Reagan's former secretary), when he served as a Catholic Church *Konsistialrat.* Using her influence, she wished to purchase property for a personal vacation house in a restricted nature preserve controlled by the Church. As the American ambassador, she thought an exception would be made and was furious when Franz put his foot down and said "No."

15. Cairo and Shuttle Diplomacy

1.   Hermann Eilts had extensive experience in the Middle East. An Arabist trained in the language, he had served as ambassador to Saudi Arabia and in numerous posts in Iran, Iraq, Yemen, and Libya, as well as in London as the political officer monitoring the Middle East.

2.   It was my view that the Maadi DCM house would have made a better ambassadorial residence than the one used by Eilts in the city center. However, it was ten miles out of town and less convenient to the Embassy and Egyptian offices.

3.   Gromyko's visit proved embarrassing for the Soviets, since it was overshadowed by the Kissinger shuttle diplomacy. The Egyptians also did not go out of their way to herald Gromyko's stopover.

4.   Richard W. Smith was replaced by Bryce Gerlach as administrative officer not long after my arrival.

5.   *State Department Bulletin,* May 1974.

6.   At times locating documents in the middle of the night with the Embassy closed was quite a problem. Often they were in safes with combination locks that proved vexing.

7.   At one point there was an effort to start up a Protestant church service in Maadi, which did not materialize while the author was in Cairo.

8.   There are interesting accounts on the subject of wives' duties in Jewel Fenzi and Carl L. Nelson, *Married to the Foreign Service: An Oral History of the American*

Diplomatic Spouse (New York: Twayne Publishers, 1994). My wife is quoted in the book.

9.	General George Guay and the author were good friends. His wife helped greatly in urging the military wives to assist in embassy entertaining.

10.	For an informative account of Kissinger's early life and relations with Fritz Kraemer, see Walter Isaacson, *Kissinger: A Biography* (New York: Simon and Schuster, 1992).

16. Coordinating National Intelligence Operations

1.	See John Ranelagh, *The Agency: The Rise and Decline of CIA* (New York: Simon & Schuster,1986). Ranelagh states that the Church Committee's attacks were unrelenting.

2.	Henry Kissinger, *Years of Renewal* (New York: Simon and Schuster, 1999), 113. Isaacson, *Kissinger,* 612, quotes Kissinger as calling Perle "ruthless," a "little bastard," and a "son of Mensheviks who think all Bolsheviks are evil."

3.	While Admiral Turner did press for greater technological intelligence gathering, I noted no effort to cut back on HUMINT. However, it should have been increased.

4.	For an account of the attempted kidnapping by the Soviet NKVD of the American CIC agent in question, see chapter 6.

5.	I returned to other areas such as Tempelhof Airport and the Columbia House Hotel, finding them much the same. Traveling on the U-Bahn (subway), I seemed to pick up the death smell of all those poor souls who lost their lives down there when the SS flooded the tunnels to prevent the Russians from coming through them into the city.

6.	Some of Carter's appointees were involved in scandals that diminished his administration in the eyes of public servants.

7.	For an account of the Benghazi airlift during the 1967 Arab-Israeli War, see chapter 11.

8.	As of this writing, personnel from the 352nd Civil Affairs Command have been called up repeatedly for extended periods of duty in Iraq and other places in the Middle East.

9.	See David Corn, *Blond Ghost: Ted Shackley and the CIA's Crusades* (New York: Simon & Schuster, 1994).

17. An Education in Politics: The 1980 Bush/ Reagan Campaigns

1.	For an account of Bush's run for the nomination see Herbert S. Parmet, *George Bush: The Life of a Lone Star Yankee* (New York: Scribner, 1997).

2.	Fitzhugh Greene, *George Bush: An Intimate Portrait* (New York: Hippocrene Books, 1989), 176–77. Also Parmet, *George Bush.*

3.	Parmet, ibid.

4.	At the time the media commented about possible U.S. government efforts to provide the Iranians with spare parts for their military equipment.

5.	The question of legality arises when private individuals deal with a foreign government in such circumstances.

6.   Carter's statement about America's being in a state of "malaise" was a disastrous mistake that cost him dearly. Reagan, by contrast, was a sunny "optimist."

7.   Paul Francis Geren, PhD, the economic counselor in Tripoli, Libya, in 1966–68, retired to become president of Stetson University, Deland, Florida.

8.   At the conclusion of a successful campaign, mementos (medallions, pins, etc.) are generally presented to the staff as gifts. Reagan's gift was a large presidential coin on a stand suitable for display on one's desk.

18. Epilogue

1.   The purchase of ready-made "museum" frames, if they can be acquired in the required size, can be inordinately expensive.

2.   For an account of the church crisis in Bonn, Germany, see chapter 8.

3.   The 17th Airborne Division Association, P.O. Box 4793, Dowling Park, FL 32064-1508. Not all 3,000 members of the Association are veterans. That figure includes widows and honorary members.

4.   *Thunder From Heaven,* 4 Cain Court, Montville, NJ 07045-9151, Joe Quade, editor.

5.   The Allied airborne casualties in "Operation Varsity" were the highest single-day airborne losses in World War II.

6.   The soldier found was Technical Sergeant John W. Early, 507th Parachute Infantry Regiment, whose body was discovered by relic hunters in September 1998. It evidently had been covered by snow when he was killed by enemy fire in February 1945 and subsequently buried in a shallow grave by some well-meaning person.

7.   The fishing from "Eagle's Tarn's" dock is considered by many to be the best on the lake.

8.   The author was amused belatedly to receive a "Certificate of Appreciation" in 1999 from the Department of Defense for his role in "winning the Cold War."

Selective Bibliography

Andrew, Christopher. *For the President's Eyes Only*. New York: Harper Collins, 1995.

Ball, George W. *The Past Has Another Pattern: Memoirs*. New York: W. W. Norton, 1982.

Ball, Harry P. *Of Responsible Command: A History of the U.S. Army War College*. Carlisle, PA: Alumni Association of the U.S. Army War College, 1994.

Beam, Jacob D. *Multiple Exposure: An American Ambassador's Unique Perspective on East-West Issues*. New York: W. W. Norton, 1978.

Beevor, Antony. *Berlin: The Downfall 1945*. London: Penguin Books, London, 2002.

Blair, Clay. *Ridgway's Paratroopers*. Garden City, NY: Dial Press, 1956.

Bonner, Raymond. *Waltzing with a Dictator*. New York: Times Books, 1982.

Carter, Jimmy. *Keeping Faith*. New York: Bantam Books, 1982.

Corn, David. *Blond Ghost, Ted Shackley and the CIA's Crusades*. New York: Simon & Schuster, 1994.

Devlin, Gerard M. *Paratrooper!* New York: St. Martin's Press, 1979.

_____. *Silent Wings: The Saga of the U.S. Army and Marine Combat Glider Pilots During World War II*. New York: St. Martin's Press, 1985.

Felleman, Hazel, ed. *Best Loved Poems of the American People*. Garden City, NY: Doubleday, 1936.

Fenzi, Jewel, with Carl L. Nelson. *Married to the Foreign Service: An Oral History of the American Diplomatic Spouse*. New York: Twayne, 1994.

Gabel, Kurt, with William C. Mitchell. *The Making of a Paratrooper*. Lawrence, KS: University Press of Kansas, 1990.

Gavin, James M. *On to Berlin*. New York: Bantam Books, 1978.

Green, Fitzhugh. *George Bush: An Intimate Portrait*. New York: Hippocrene, 1989.

Holborn, Hajo. *American Military Government: Its Organization and Policies*. Washington: Infantry Journal Press, 1947.

Hoyt, Edwin P. *Airborne: The History of American Parachute Forces*. New York: Stein, 1979.

Isaacson, Walter. *Kissenger: A Biography*. New York: Simon & Schuster, 1992.

Karnow, Stanley. *In Our Image: America's Empire in the Philippines*. New York: Random House, 1989.

Keith, Agnes Newton. *Children of Allah: Between the Sea and the Sahara*. Boston: Little Brown, 1965.

Kessler, Ronald. *Inside the CIA*. New York: Pocket Books, 1992.

Kissenger, Henry. *Years of Renewal*. New York: Simon & Schuster, 1999.

_____. *Years of Upheaval*. Boston: Little Brown, 1982.

Kormann, John. *U.S. Denazification Policy in Germany, 1944-50*. Bonn, Germany: HICOG, Historical Division, 1952.

_____. *U.S. Military Assistance to Africa: Problems and Prospects*. Carlisle, PA: U.S. Army War College, 1973.

Kormann, John, and Elsa Kormann. *Freedom of Information in the United States: Report to the United Nations*. Washington: Department of State, 1961.

Lee, Guy. *Field Organization of the Office of the High Commissioner for Germany*. Bonn, Germany: HICOG, Historical Division, 1952.

Lefever, Ernest. *Spear and Scepter: Army, Police and Politics in Tropical Africa*. Washington: Brookings Institute, 1970.

Martinez, Mario. *Lady's Men: The Story of World War II's Mystery Bomber and Her Crew*. Annapolis, MD: Naval Institute Press, 1995.

Melbourne, Roy M. *Conflict and Crises: A Foreign Service Story*. Lanham, MD: University Press of America, 1993.

Mitchell, George C. *Matthew B. Ridgway: Soldier, Statesman, Scholar, Citizen*. Pittsburgh, PA: Cathedral Publishing, 1999.

Murphy, Robert. *Diplomat Among Warriors*. Garden City, NY: Doubleday, 1964.

Murrow, Edward R. *This I Believe*. New York: Simon & Schuster, 1952.

Neumann, Franz. *Behemoth: The Structure and Practice of National Socialism*. New York: Oxford University Press, 1942.

Parmet, Herbert S. *George Bush: The Life of a Lone Star Yankee*. New York: Scribner, 1997.

Ranelagh, John. *The Agency: The Rise and Decline of the CIA*. New York: Simon & Schuster, 1986.

Ridgway, Matthew B. *Soldier: The Memoirs of General Ridgway*. New York: Harper, 1956.

Supreme Headquarters, Allied Expeditionary Force. *Arrest Categories Handbook: Germany*. 1945.

Smith, Jean Edward. *Lucius D. Clay: An American Life*. New York: Henry Holt, 1990.

Speer, Albert. *Inside the Third Reich: Memoirs*. New York: Macmillan, 1970.

Taylor, John M. *General Maxwell Taylor: The Sword and the Pen*. New York: Doubleday, 1989.

Thwaite, Anthony. *The Deserts of the Hesperides: An Experience of Libya*. London: Secker & Warburg, 1969.

Trevor-Roper, Hugh, ed. *Final Entries, 1945: The Diaries of Joseph Goebbels*. New York: G. P. Putnam & Sons, 1978.

Turner, Barry. *Countdown to Victory*. London: Hodder and Stoughton, 2004.

Turner, Stansfield. *Secrecy and Democracy: The CIA in Transition*. Boston: Houghton Miflin, 1985.

U.S. Department of State. *State Department Bulletin*. Washington, D.C., May 1974.

Zink, Harold. *American Military Government in Germany*. New York: Macmillan, 1947.

Index

www.ingramcontent.com/pod-product-compliance
Lightning Source LLC
Chambersburg PA
CBHW020329270326
41926CB00007B/112